FUNDAMENTALS OF CULINARY ART

(Theory & Practice of Cooking)

[For the Students of Hotel Management]

Dr. Jagmohan Negi
Gaurav M.J., Ritushka and Suniti
With the Assistance of
The International Culinary Foundation & Himalayan Tourism and Recreation in Mountains, India

S. CHAND
PUBLISHING

S Chand And Company Limited
(ISO 9001 Certified Company)

S Chand And Company Limited
(ISO 9001 Certified Company)

Head Office: Block B-1, House No. D-1, Ground Floor, Mohan Co-operative Industrial Estate, New Delhi – 110 044 | Phone: 011-66672000

Registered Office: A-27, 2nd Floor, Mohan Co-operative Industrial Estate, New Delhi – 110 044 Phone: 011-49731800

www.**schandpublishing.com**; e-mail: **info@schandpublishing.com**

Branches

Chennai : Ph: 23632120; chennai@schandpublishing.com
Guwahati : Ph: 2738811, 2735640; guwahati@schandpublishing.com
Hyderabad : Ph: 40186018; hyderabad@schandpublishing.com
Jalandhar : Ph: 4645630; jalandhar@schandpublishing.com
Kolkata : Ph: 23357458, 23353914; kolkata@schandpublishing.com
Lucknow : Ph: 4003633; lucknow@schandpublishing.com
Mumbai : Ph: 25000297; mumbai@schandpublishing.com
Patna : Ph: 2260011; patna@schandpublishing.com

First Edition 2013

ISBN : 978-81-219-4029-0 **Product Code** : H8CUA60HTRM10ENAA13O

PRINTED IN INDIA

By Vikas Publishing House Private Limited, Plot 20/4, Site-IV, Industrial Area Sahibabad, Ghaziabad – 201 010 and Published by S Chand And Company Limited, A-27, 2nd Floor, Mohan Co-operative Industrial Estate, New Delhi – 110 044.

This project was supported by The International Culinary Foundation

and

Himalayan Tourism and Recreation in Mountains

Project Coordinator and Executive Editor

Dr. Jagmohan Negi

This Page has been intentionally left blank

PREFACE

Fundamentals of Culinary Arts, is a practical hand book for students and trainees of the IHMs, Culinary Schools, Hotel Management Departments, Food Craft students and trainees in hotel management and restaurant who are undergoing training to become Chefs/Food Production and Beverage Managers/service employees. The textbook serves two purposes:

1. Upgrades general knowledge and skills of kitchen and food production of students and trainees.
2. Develops professional language skills by means of close-to-life, authentic texts, practical exercise role lay , group exercises and observations.
3. Preparing students/trainees to face the professional examinations and placement tests.

The hand book consists of basic terns and techniques of \food production and cuisine. The text contains exercises, objective type problems, dialogues, role lay and group and number of practical tasks and assignments. Level of language used in the textbook is very simple. Fundamentals of Culinary Arts, was piloted and finalised with the assistance of the International Culinary Foundation and Himalayan Tourism and in Himalayan Tourism and Recreation in Mountains in summer months of June - August 2011. We welcome any kind of recommendations or suggestions which might arise during the study and teaching process. We welcome any kind of recommendations or suggestions which might arise during the learning and teaching process.

Food is eaten and typically enjoyed through the sense of taste, the perception of flavour from eating and drinking. Certain tastes are more enjoyable for evolutionary purposes while others are not. The term "cooking" encompasses a vast range of methods, tools and combinations of ingredients to improve the flavour or digestibility of food. Cooking technique, known as culinary art, generally requires the selection, measurement and combining of ingredients in an ordered procedure and effort to achieve the desired result. Constraints on success include the variability of ingredients, ambient conditions, tools, and the skill of the individual cook. The diversity of cooking worldwide is a reflection of the myriad nutritional, aesthetic, agricultural, economic, cultural and religious considerations that affect it.

Cooking requires applying heat to a food, which usually, though not always, chemically changes the molecules, thus changing its flavour, texture, appearance, and nutritional properties. Cooking certain proteins, such as egg whites, meats and fish denature the protein causing it to be firm.

While many foods can be eaten raw, many foods undergo some form of preparation for reasons of safety, palatability, texture or flavour. At the simplest level this may involve washing, cutting, trimming or adding other foods or ingredients, such as spices. It may also involve mixing, heating or cooling, pressure-cooking, fermentation, or combination with other foods. In a home, most food preparation takes place in a kitchen. Some preparation is done to enhance the taste or aesthetic appeal; other preparation may help to preserve the food; and others may be involved in cultural identity. A meal is made up of food, which is prepared to be eaten at a specific time and place.

There are so many methods of cooking, most of which have been known since antiquity. These include baking, roasting, frying, grilling, barbecuing, smoking, boiling, steaming and braising. A more recent innovation is microwaving. Various methods use differing levels of heat and moisture and vary in cooking time. The method chosen greatly affects the end result. Some foods are more appropriate to some methods than others. Some major hot cooking techniques include:

1. **Roasting** : Roasting - Barbecuing - Grilling - Rotisserie - Searing
2. **Baking** : Baking - Baking Blind - Broiling - Flash baking
3. **Boiling** : Boiling - Blanching - Braising - Coddling - Double steaming - Infusion - Poaching - Pressure cooking - Simmering - Steaming - Steeping - Stewing - Vacuum flask cooking
4. **Frying** : Frying - Deep frying - Hot salt frying - Hot sandfrying - Pan frying - Pressure frying - Sautéing - Stir frying
5. **Smoking** : Food smoking

Although cooking has traditionally been a process carried out informally at home or around a communal fire, cooking is often, and increasingly, carried out outside the home. Bakeries were an early form of cooking outside the home, and bakeries in the past often offered the cooking of foods provided by their customers as an additional service. In the present day, factory food preparation is rapidly becoming the norm, with many "ready-to-eat" foods being prepared and cooked in factories.

"Home-cooking" may be associated with comfort food, and some commercially produced foods are presented as having been "home-cooked", regardless of their actual origin.

India is a diverse country with many regional cultures; each region has its own food specialties, primarily at regional level, but also at provincial level. The differences can come from a local culture and geographical location whether a region is close to the sea, desert or the mountains. Indian cuisine is also seasonal with priority placed on the use of fresh produce.

Indian cuisine is the general name for the foods of the Indian sub-continent, characterised by the use of various spices, herbs and other vegetables, and sometimes fruits grown in India and also for the widespread practice of vegetarianism in Indian society. Each family of Indian cuisine includes a wide assortment of dishes and cooking techniques. As a consequence, it varies from region to region, reflecting the varied demographics of the ethnically diverse sub-continent.

Diversified Indian beliefs and culture have played an influential role in the evolution of Indian cuisine. However, cuisine across India also evolved as a result of the subcontinent's large-scale cultural interactions with Mongols and Britain making it a unique blend of various cuisines. The spice trade between India and Europe is often cited as the main catalyst for Europe's Age of Discovery. The colonial period introduced European cooking styles to India, adding to the flexibility and diversity of Indian cuisine. Indian cuisine has influenced cuisines across the world, especially those from South-east Asia and the Caribbean.

Indian cooking derives from a 5000-year-old timeline, during which culture has changed, geographical boundaries have changed significantly leading to confusing terms such as sub-continental cuisine while other parts of a region want a separate culinary identity. Indian Cooking has however evolved significantly over time and the varying influences brought into the country by the various rulers and travelers, it has not lost its original identity, rather become richer with the assimilation of the myriad influences. This is very apparent in some of the unique regional cuisines.

The staples of Indian cuisine are *chawal* (rice), *atta* (whole wheat flour), and a variety of pulses, the most important of which are *masoor* (most often red lentil), *channa (bengal* gram), *toor* (pigeon pea or yellow gram), urad (black gram), and *moong* (green gram). Pulses may be used whole, dehusked – for example, *dhuli moong* or *dhuli urad* – or split. Split pulses, or *daal*, are used extensively. Some pulses like *channa* and *moong,* are also processed into flour *(besan)*.

Most Indian curries are cooked in vegetable oil. In northern and western India, peanut oil is most popular for cooking, while in eastern India, mustard oil is more commonly used. Coconut oil is used widely along the western coast and in southern India; *gingelly* oil is common in the south as well. In recent decades, sunflower oil and soybean oil have gained popularity all over India. Hydrogenated vegetable oil, known as *Vanaspati ghee,* is another popular cooking medium. Butter-based *ghee,* or *desi ghee*, is less used than formerly.

The most important or frequently used spices in Indian cuisine are *mirchee* (chilli pepper), black mustard seed *(rai),* cumin (jeera), turmeric (*haldi, manjal),* fenugreek *(methi),* asafoetida *(hing, perungayam),* ginger (*adrak, inji*), coriander *(dhania),* and garlic (*lehsun, poondu).* Popular spice mixes are *garam masala,* a powder that typically includes five or more dried spices, especially cardamom, cinnamon, and clove. Each region, and sometimes each individual chef, has a distinctive blend of *garam masala. Goda masala* is a similar sweet spice mix, popular in Maharashtra. Some leaves are commonly used, including *tejpat (*cinnamon leaf), coriander leaf, fenugreek leaf, and mint leaf. The common use of curry leaves and curry roots is typical of all South Indian cuisine. Sweet dishes are seasoned with cardamom, saffron, nutmeg, and rose petal essences.

This Culinary Art textbook focuses on styles of cooking. It provides introduction to a variety of styles of cooking and the mouth-watering recipes. Additionally, the book details healthy cooking ideas or discuss the business end of running a successful restaurant.

Beginners can use this textbook, however, the level of experience required to complete some of the recipes may be higher than required for the recipes listed in an introductory level culinary textbook.

Authors

FOREWORD

A revolution is underway in the art of cooking. Modern cuisine has in recent ears blown through the boundaries of the culinary arts, borrowing techniques room the kitchens; chefs have incorporated a deeper understanding of science and advances in cooking technology into their culinary art. A fundamental of culinary arts is a landmark contribution o the craft of cooking and understanding of its underlying principles. Its detail and experimental recipes are unmatched by any other book on the subject. It will be an invaluable resource for any one with serious interest in cooking techniques, whether the professional innovations of the last few decades or eh long-traditions on which they build.

Culinary Art is the subject of this beautifully conceived book. Whether you go to food or food comes to you, the nature of the encounter is what defines a food experience. Making experiences memorable is a way the travel industry adds value—and profit—to an essential service like food. Indeed, the tourism and hospitality industries design experiences, including culinary ones, within the constraints of the tourist's time, space, and means. Culinary art creates opportunities to find, test, and push thresholds of the unfamiliar. Newness arises from unpredictability and culinary art, to the degree that it constitutes a break with one's daily routine and even with the predictability of the tourism industry, affords innumerable occasions for new experiences.

It gives me great leisure to commend this book for you. Not only does it gives you the basics of culinary art but also supports you in your professional examination and tests. There are enumerable books on Cookery on the market, each with its own peculiar zeal, however this book offers an opportunity to understand the fundamental of international cuisine. I hope you will enjoy using this book and would ask you to recommend it to your fellow trainees and students.

This book has a place in the library for all who want to understand and build their basic cooking skills. The book is for hundreds of thousands of trainee chefs to master the basics of their craft. Packed with experimental recipes and more information this book is the cornerstone resource offers complete, step-by-step instruction in the cooking theory and techniques necessary to succeed at the professional level. Special features include: recipes - including new recipes for meats, poultry, vegetables, and grains, as well as a chapter on cooking for vegetarian diets. Superb photography- illustrations and photos highlighting ingredients, step-by-step techniques, and plated dishes.

Easily the most comprehensive and exhaustive look at art of cuisine available, this groundbreaking classic marks presence in the academic field. This highly acclaimed collection offers a wealth of insight for amateurs and experts alike. Every technique associated with food is described step by step in great detail, along with illustrations to guide the reader through everything from filleting fish to rolling omelets. Sections on the meal preparations, ingredients and selecting and cutting fish, chicken and vegetables offer great insight into the culture as well as the food. The topics of the book are divided by cooking method rather than food type, including grilled and pan-fried, steamed, simmered and deep-fried. Dishes range from the simple to the more complex, and many dishes are vegetarian. Cutting processes are covered in depth, as are knives, the proper way to slice the fish, and decorative presentations. A complete guide to art of cooking, this collection is must-have for anyone interested in culinary food or culture.

Once you learn how to handle these fundamental techniques, you will be able to handle most recipes. Cooking is not just about recipes, it is about how to take ingredients and make them taste as good as possible. Recipes are great road maps to show us how someone else got there, but one of the joys of cooking is to find your own paths.

The basic cooking techniques are very important to gain knowledge of as possessing this knowledge not only increases the ease in which cooking projects are completed other than also increases the overall enjoyment of cooking. Very often basic cooking techniques have specific names that are universal among cookbook authors, cooking schools and chefs. Learning these basic cooking methods and techniques are essential to successfully learning how to cook.

The book breaks down these cooking techniques into different groups. The basic fundamental cooking techniques that is most important to learn like baking and braising. More specific cooking techniques like cooking pasta and deglazing are thoroughly explain. How to cut an onion and how to grill corn are some of the basic incorporated in the text. Basic knife skills are one of the most important skills a chef must learn. From preparing fruits and vegetables to cutting correct fillets knife skills are a must. Making the transition from prep cook to line cook to chef won't happen without knowing which knife to use when and how to use it.

If you plan to become a professional chef, these techniques—among others—are required learning. If cooking is not your thing, but you love to bake there are many skills worth learning too. The basis for any education is proper technique. It's only after the fundamentals have been grasped that mastery can be obtained. Each new skill serves as the building block for the skills that follow. As each brick is placed, the foundation of knowledge grows and a fully rounded education emerges. Each new culinary skill prepares students that aspire to someday be professional chefs for a lifetime of continued learning in the culinary arts.

To become aspiring professional chefs in this competitive world, students will prepare and learn all about different aspects of culinary cooking. The correct technique of cooking different types of food, learn what food ingredients complement each other, and more. One of the most important parts of cooking is food safety and food safe courses to be taken to cooking food safe. Learn how to prepare food safely, learn proper cooking temperatures for various foods and nutritional benefits, health aspects of different types of food. Students need to know while you're cooking, what's in food and what it will affect certain types of people with different health risks.

Before you jump in full force, dedicate some time to learning the French cooking terms that you need to know before getting started.

The French codified the language of the kitchen. The four mother sauces of French cuisine are béchamel, espagnole, veloute, and allemande. Know them and you can create nearly all of the remaining sauces of classical cuisine. Then, choose the foods that you enjoy and create the French cooking recipes that you will enjoy. Here are some French cooking tips to help you to get those French cooking recipes into your everyday life:

Firstly, start with one French cooking recipe. Don't attempt to change your entire menu all at one time with French cooking recipes. You will want to take the time to look for French cooking recipes that work for you and your family. This means picking foods that you are all comfortable with eating and just preparing them in a unique way. Don't add too many new meals to your menu or you will be burned out, too.

Secondly, ingredients, ingredients. Getting the right French cooking ingredients will be crucial. Don't substitute fresh herbs for dried ones. Don't assume that you can change up the French cooking ingredients in sauces or other meals. You want to look for high quality French cooking ingredients and you can do this today easier than ever. More and more supermarkets are carrying higher quality foods as well as the more in demand international cuisine, which is where French cooking recipes will fall under.

Thirdly, take your time to learn the French cooking methods. Probably the most important part of learning to prepare French cooking recipes is to learn the French cooking methods first. You can learn French cooking on your own or through French cooking home study programs, or dedicate some time to taking local French cooking courses. Each of these will provide you with an opportunity for success.

French cooking recipes are easily found throughout the Internet and in many French cooking cookbooks. Start with something simple and build up until you find French cooking recipes that are going to impress anyone around you. Add a few of these French cooking recipes to your everyday meals and you will quickly improve the quality and health of the meals that your family consumes.

What do these chefs have in common with you? These chefs have something in common with you. Is it the interest for cooking? But there's something else you and them have in common. And that is the basic skill and techniques for cooking. Everyone has to start at the basic. The basics are considered the first steps to anything you want to learn. The basics are the most important part of the culinary arts curriculum. Yes, it's true. Some people might find it boring, especially when they don't have the patience or are too eager to learn the art, but they have to understand the importance of learning the basics first.

You have to learn how to properly cut up the ingredients, especially livestock. It doesn't matter much if you're cooking for your home, but if you're planning to embark on a career as a professional chef, you need to make sure that not only are your dishes delicious, they should also look organized and well prepared. That is only possible if you learn the basics first.

No skill in this world is acquired instantly. You have to persevere and practice hard in order to learn what you are trying to learn. There's no way you can fast forward through lessons and acquire instant learning, not unless you're super special and of extreme intelligence and aptitude.

India is located to the southwest of China and is bordered by China, Nepal, and Pakistan. The Bay of Bengal, the Laccadive Sea, and the Arabian Sea surround it on two sides. Many people travel to India to see the Taj Mahal or retreat to ashrams or visit temples in India. Part of Indian culture is to treat guests as if they were part of the family. History, elders, and traditions make up an important part of India's culture, which makes sense as India is home to some of the world's oldest civilization. India is the second largest country in the world with a population of more than one billion people.

With so many people, it's not surprising the India is richly diverse. Across India, hundreds of dialects are spoken and thousands of gods are worshipped. Each state has its own unique culture, including bits that are popular in the Western world such as Bollywood films, *bhangra* dancing, henna "*tattoos*", and colorful clothing. Religion is an integral part of Indian culture and some of the more popular religions include Hinduism, Buddhism, Jainism, Sikhism, Islam, and Christianity. These religions determine the many festivals that are held throughout India, including the Hindu festival of Diwali, known as the Festival of Lights. Muslims celebrate Ramzan Id, and Christian celebrates Christmas. Culinary programs in India can teach you about the role religion and traditions have played in shaping Indian cuisine, especially as many Hindus practice vegetarianism. Indian food is largely known for its use of spices, herbs, colors, and vegetables. Each spice is chosen for the healing and nutritional properties it provides for the body. Some spices common to Indian cuisine include turmeric, red chili, mustard seed, clove, fennel, cumin, and coriander. Indian cuisine strives to appeal to all the senses and blend various spices and herbs in different proportions and combinations to create unique flavors.

In addition to spices, common ingredients in Indian cooking include vegetables, grains, and potatoes. Famous dishes in India are curry, a traditional spicy stew-like dish, and daal, a dish made of lentils. But there is a lot more to Indian cuisine than curry, different regions disagree on what makes a good curry, as there are a wide range of curry recipes. There is no one national dish to India.

India has a diverse geography with cuisine that varies throughout the different regions. In northern India, home to what's known as Punjab cuisine, ghee (clarified butter) is used in a lot of the cooking and you'll find kebabs and meats cooked in tandoors (clay ovens). Southern Indian food, including Goan cuisine, is known for its use of fish and shellfish.

Dr. Sunil Gulati
Chairman
Ellbee Hospitality Worldwide (P) Ltd.
Tourism & Hospitality Consultancy and
Academic Advisor & Formerly Hony. Secretary,
Federation of Hotel & Restaurant Associations of India

This Page has been intentionally left blank

CONTENTS

PART – I : INTRODUCTION

PART – II : FOOD PREPARATION

PART – III : TECHNIQUES OF COOKING FOOD

PART – IV : FOOD PRODUCTION

PART - I

INTRODUCTION

1.1

Food and Beverage: An Introduction

CHAPTER OBJECTIVES

After studying this lesson you should be able :

- To explain the growth of the hospitality industry;
- To list different food service establishments;
- To describe the relationships between international and Indian cuisine; and
- To identify the ranks of cooks in food establishments.

The food and beverage service industry is growing rapidly. Operators have learned to stay solvent and independent. They know how to manage themselves. The techniques and styles of cuisine as applicable to this industry are uniform and closely related. Regional differences exist, and are mainly caused by climate, supply, and other factors. Now cookery is part of the international cuisine of world civilization. Continuous needs for more skilled manpower are projected in the future. The skill levels required are not as high as the ones demanded from the trained continental chef.

Food and service establishments are commercial concerns which serve freshly cooked food directly to consumers. These businesses produce and also retail the product. Therefore, a food service establishments may be divided into different parts :

1. The service part, called the front of the house
2. The food-producing kitchen part, called the back of the house, and
3. The office or business administration.

The growth and development of the food and beverage service industry and the increase in the number of its customers have evidence that more skilled cooks are needed. Eating away from home is an increasing trend. Statistics from many sources show a constant growth in the manpower needs of the food service industry.

When pre-cooked convenience food was introduced, it was forecasted that the use of this type of food would revolutionize the restaurant industry. People were expected to cook at home instead of eating in restaurants. This forecast has yet to come true.

For the last few years customers have indicated a need for fresh cooked food, gourmet food, or luxury food in appropriate settings. Therefore, the young cook must take his professional learning seriously. He must acquire manual skill, theoretical knowledge, work experience, and the personality characteristics needed to get along with co-workers. As soon as he succeeds, his future will be a bright one.

Employees in each one of these groups have had a different training background and perhaps have some class consciousness. This class consciousness may be a source of friction among the staff members. Such friction must be avoided in order to have a successful business.

Today's food craft centres, hospitality schools and training centres try to unify these groups. Groups are being trained together, and each person is aware of the difficulty of the others' work. All have a great responsibility. It is stressed that working together has more advantages than competing against each other.

In India most of the food and beverage units are known as *dhaabas* or in ordinary language term as 'hotels'. Food and beverage service has a long and colorful history. Cookshops and taverns in England were mentioned in literature as early as the twelfth century. In time, cookshops became restaurants, and taverns became hotels. These two concepts dominated the hospitality field until recently. Then the concepts of hotels appeared with 'no service no food approach'. This was designed to make traveling cheaper for the customer. The new concept seemed very competitive to hotels at first, but the no service policy did not last. The hospitality industry is still based on the same principles as every development in traveling and transportation modes brought the city hotel concept to the forefront again. Motels became more hotel-like and a newer concept, that on the drive-in motor-hotels, is now widely accepted.

Restaurants at international level have been given through changes during the last half century. At first, they were full-service restaurants and served breakfast, lunch, and dinner. Then they were divided into special groups serving different foods to different customers at different meal times.

The new trend of the restaurant field is an economically necessary measure for the success of the business. Full-service restaurants are many in operation. It is a hard task for the chef to supervise them. One working shift of seven and a half hours does not cover the service time open to the public. Second and third shifts have to be set up. This causes wasteful overlaps of working hours. For this reason, the full-service restaurants have no future and as such are gradually disappearing.

Mostly large city hotels maintain dining rooms, luncheon rooms, grillrooms, coffeeshops, bistros, banquet facilities, and room service. A hotel remains the most interesting working place for the young cook. The new branches of the hospitality industry are found in the many types of specialized food serving places. Speciality houses include linners, steak, fish, and spaghetti houses; Indian, Chinese, Mexican their French, Italian, German, and other ethnic restaurants; luncheonettes, sandwich counters, fibrous, and delicatessens. All have a limited food selection and short service hours. In addition, there are summer and winter resorts, camps, ships, air-lines trains, hospitals, institutions, canteens, catering companies, and industrial cafeterias. Different types of food services establishments usually found on international scale are given in Figure. 1.1A.

Food and Beverage Establishments

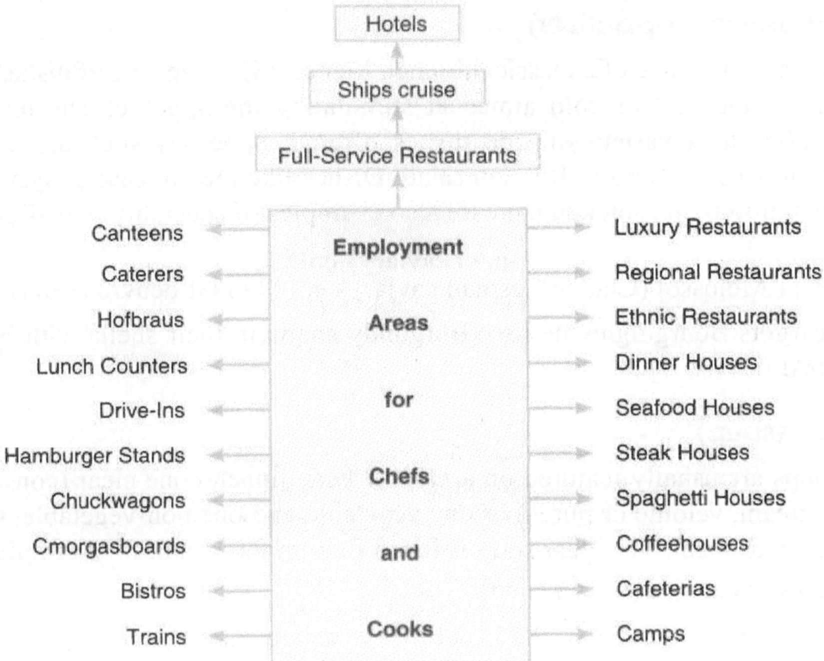

Fig. 1.1A. A Food and Beverage Service Establishments

INTERNATIONAL AND REGIONAL CUISINE

A regional style of cooking emphasizes the best native food products of a region. Regional cuisine also developes a special style of cooking suitable to climate and consumers. Lobsters, oysters, and seafood are famous. England is well known for heavy dishes, such as baked beans and chowder, which are preferred in the colder climates. Florida and California abound in fruits and vegetables, then sea food is served mostly in salad mixture. In countries, such as India, Pakistan, Bangladesh having humid climate, seafood preparations place great emphasis on the use of more spices, many of them hot. In addition local labour laws, union locals, and socio-economic levels are responsible for other differences. When moving to another country it is wise to accept a position where local working habits and cooking differences can be learned.

The style of cooking practiced in most modern and deluxe kitchen is called the International Cuisine. Asians and Africans regions have their own styles of cooking and eating. The style of cooking of continental Europe is strongly influenced by the Italians and the French. The immigrants from Europe brought along them customs and achieved a mixing of the various cuisines by selecting the best that each group had to offer. However the increases in travel and in the export and import of foods has made the restaurant cuisine basically the same all over the world. Because of this newly developed structure, the cooks and chefs of to-day are able to and rather choose many areas and foreign countries in which to practice their craft.

FRENCH CLASSICAL MENU

1. Hors d'oeuvre (appetizer)

This is the first course of a classical French Menu. It is composed of dishes of a tangy, salty nature, either hot or cold aimed at stimulating the appetite. The term 'oeuvre' usually applies to a variety of side dishes offered, appetizer such as, potato salad, anchovies, prawns, olives and Russian salad. Dishes like melon, caviar, oysters, smoked salmon, salami sausage, smoked ham are also examples of speciality hors d'oeuvrem, for example,

(a) Caviar Molossol (Choice Caspian caviar) - cold hors d'oeuvre (froid).

(b) Escargots Bourguignonne (Six Burgundy snails in their shells with butter) - hot hors d'oeuvre.

2. Potage (soup)

Two soups are usually featured on a *table d'hote* dinner - one clear (consomme) and one thick (cream, veloute or puree) or one vegetable and one non-vegetable. Only one is served with each meal. The clear soup is listed first on the menu, for example,

(a) Gratin Lyonnaise (Onion soup).

(b) Cream Dubary Givre (Chilled cauliflower cream soup with beetroot julienne).

3. Poisson (fish)

Two kinds of fish are frequently offered. Baked or steamed fish in one style. Plainly steamed or boiled potatoes are usually offered with this type of fish. Fried fish could be other kind. Lobsters and prawn could also form a part of this course, for example,

(a) Langoustine a la creme (small rock lobsters, lightly seasoned and simmered in fresh cream).

(b) Filet et quenelles de bekti (Calcutta Bekti fillet and quenelles on a mango mousseline with prawns).

4. Entreé

This is the first of main courses. At dinner usually it is complete in itself that it is accompanied by its own appropriate vegetables or other garnishes. Pasta or egg could also feature in this course, for example,

Ragout de Volaille Maxicainne (Chicken liver Mexican style) - chicken liver cooked in its own juice and red wine, garnished with pimentos, capsicum, diced mushroom and chopped onions.

5. Remove/Releve (Main Course)

Remove is a larger joint or "piece de resistance" and may consist of a sadlle of lamb, braised ham or venison. Potatoes and two other vegetables are served with this course. This course also referred to as "Plats Principaux"—literally means main course, for example :

(a) Tournedos Aux Trois Poivres (A brace of small fillet steak with a black, green and white peppercorn sauce).

(b) Poisson a la citron (Boneless squab chicken with a lemon sauce with vegetables and semolina gnocchi).

6. Sorbet

This course is intended to be a pause during a long meal. A sorbet helps "settle" dishes already served and stimulates the appetite. It is ice water usually flavoured with champagne or other delicate wine or a fruit juice. Russian or Egyptian cigarettes or cigars are also passed around. for example,

(a) Lemon Sorbet - Made of egg white and milk blended in lemon juice and iced.

(b) Cigar like Havana, Tiamo, etc. are passed around at this stage of the meal.

7. Roti (Roast)

This course consists of poultry or game such as chicken, duck, turkey, pheasant, grouse or partridge served with sauces or gravy. A dressed salad is served separately. for example,

(a) Canard roti a la Mangue (roasted farm raised duckling with mango).

(b) Salade de saison (avec assaisonement au choix) - Seasonal salads from the display with a dressing of your choice.

8. Legumes (Vegetables)

The French customarily serve a finely dressed vegetables as a separate course e.g. asparagus served with sauce hollandaise, for example,

(a) Brochette de legume et fromage blanc (Skewered vegetables and cottage cheese served with rice and tomato concasse).

(b) Rotatouille des champignons sur asperage (A mushroom medley with herbs and tomato on a puff paste).

9. Entrement (Sweet)

This may consist of a pudding such as souffle or an ice such as a coupe glace, for example, Mousse au chocolat (Chocolate Mousse).

10. Savoures (Savouries)

A savoury usually consists of tit-bits on a hot canape of toast or fried bread. Alternatively, the cheese platter (particular at luncheon) may be presented with biscuits, butter celery stalks as probable accompaniments. for examples—Champignons, Edam Ball, Cheddar, etc.

11. Dessert

This finale consists of basket of fresh fruit (possible dried fruits and nuts). They are sometimes placed on the table as part of the decorations, for example,

(a) Fresh fruits (b) Nuts

12. Tea/Coffee

Finally tea or coffee is served to end the meal. Tea / coffee can be of various types, for example,

(a) Irish Coffee- with Irish whiskey and cream.

(b) Cappuccino - black coffee with cinnamon and chocolate powder.

(c) Green Tea, etc.

SKILL LEVELS AND RANKS

Culinary art is a part of India's historical gastronomic culture. Knowledge about gastronomy is not an immediate necessity for the young cook. It is important for the student to be aware of its existence and to plans to learn about it during his work experience. Tomorrows needs imply that the cook's future is secure, and food service will not be a field where automation can take over, as it has done with other vocations.

Trainees preparing food

The higher the skill levels attained, the more secure a chef's future will be. Master chefs are not apt to be replaced. As long as customers clamour for good food, skilled cooks will be promoted to higher ranks with higher salaries and better fringe benefits.

In this industry, elevation in rank comes as a reward for service. Skill levels and ranks go hand in hand. Skill alone, even when matched with professional knowledge, is not enough to be promoted. Personality, reliability, and honesty are qualities just as important. A good business sense, a capability for public relations, and a cool head are as important in a chef as his top culinary performance. The shortage of good chefs is so great that many establishments are satisfied with a chef whose business sense is greater than his culinary know-how. **Table 1.1A and 1.1B** indicates some of the ranks in kitchen and the corresponding levels as per American and French system.

Chef working in a kitchen

The student, ready for a cooks job, becomes integrated into the working process. He decides which way to go. He may become a skilled master chef or he may be satisfied with a job that offers money and social comfort with less demands on knowledge and skill.

French and American ranks for a kitchen brigade are given in Table 1.1A, 1.1B and 1.1C.

Table 1.1A. French Ranks of a Cook Brigade

Chef de Cuisine	Executive Chef
↓	↓
Sous Chef	Sous Chef
↓	↓
Chef de Partie	Station Chef
↓	↓
Premier Commis	Station Cook
↓	↓
Deuxieme Commis	Cooking Helper
↓	↓
Troisieme Commis	Cooking Helper-Assistant

Table 1.1B. American Ranks of Cooking Brigade

In a Large Hotel or Passenger Liner	*In a Medium Restaurant*	*In a Small Restaurant*
Executive Chef	Head Chef	Chef
↓	↓	↓
Day Chef (Sous Chef)	Night Chef	Broilerman
↓	↓	↓
Night Chef (Sous Chef)	Second Chef	Pantryman
↓	↓	
Banquet Chef (Sous Chef)	Broiler – Short Orderman	
↓	↓	
Second Cook	Pantryman	
↓	↓	
Chef Garde-manger	Steamtman	
↓	↓	
Station Cook	Foreman	
↓		
Broilerman – Short Orderman		
↓		
Cooking Helper – Fryman		
↓		
Steamtable Man – Carver		
↓		
Pantry man		
↓		
Pastry Chef		

Note: These rank tables will be exactly the same in different regions/areas. They are influenced by classifications and management preferences.

Executive Chef requires a Chef garde-manger, Second Cook, Banquet Chef, or Sous Chef. For a Head Chef"s job in the average restaurant, experience as Pantry or Broiler Man, Station Cook or Second Cook is enough. For a working chef in a special type of restaurant, partial knowledge of cookery could well meet the requirements.

Table 1.1C. Skill Levels : American French and Indian Style Levels

American Style	
Executive Chef	(Master Chef and Administrator)
Day Chef – Night Garde-manger	(Skilled Chef, Department Head)
Banquet Chef – Chef Garde-manger	(Master Chef)
Second Cook	(Skilled Cook)
Station Cook	(Skilled Cook)
Broiler–Short Orderman	(Semi-skilled Cook)
Pantryman	(Semi-skilled Cook)
Cook's Helper–Fryman	(Unskilled workers)
Steamtable–Carver	(Unskilled workers)
French Style	
Chef de Cuisine	(Master Chef and Administrator)
Sous Chef	(Master Chef)
Chef de partie	(Master Chef or Skilled Cook)
Premier Commis	(Skilled Cook (5 years minimum experience))
Deuxieme Commis	(Skilled Cook Cook (1-5 years experience))
Troisieme Commis	(Skilled Cook (first year after apprenticeship))
Indian Style	
Master Chef/Head Cook	
Departmental Head Cook	
Senior Cook	
Cook	
Masalchis	
Helper	

SECTIONS OF A KITCHEN IN A HOTEL

Kitchens may be divided into sections or work stations. This way of organizing speeds up production and improves the quality of cooking. In vocational cooking, all kitchens use either the French style work station division or an American adaptation of it. The crew of chefs, cooks, bakers, butchers, and helpers who work under the Executive Chef (Chef de Cuisine) is called a *brigade.* Some cooks like specialized work and rarely change from one station to the other; others prefer more variety and experience and make it a point to change stations often. Stations seldom have more than three cooks under one Station Cook (Chef de partie). If there is more work than they can handle, the station is sub-divided. For example, one section of the Sauce Cooks work may be given to one or two new cooks called Saute Men. The new sub-divided Saute Station pan fries (sautes) all dishes made to order. Other Sauce cooks perform certain duties. All Sauce cooks help with the preparatory work. Preparation for orders served later is very important for the efficient functioning of a kitchen. In chefs terms, the phrase, *mis en place* is used to describe this preparatory action. Cooks with the title chef de partie, chef saucier, chef rotisseur, chef intermitter, and others are department heads and rank next under the Sous Chef. The divisions of a kitchen in French English and American style are given in Table. 1.1D.

Most of the large city hotels and cruise liners use the French type division. The American adaptations is for smaller establishments or those on a cheaper level. Two or three stations are combined and the work is supervised by one chef. This approach creates the Second Cook who is often a combination of Sous Chef, Saucier Entremetier, and Potager. The American adaptation is also responsible for the Short Order Cook, a rather unique position for the coffeeshop type establishment. A Short Order Cook, as the name implies, cooks only fast foods in portion sizes. He does not produce cooked foods such as soups, stews, and roasts. In contrast Skilled Cook implies that a cook has been trained to work every stations of a large kitchen. He knows all working procedures and skills. After enough years of experience, he will become Executive Chef or Head Chef.

Table 1.1D. Divisions/Stations of a Kitchen

French Style	*English style rank*	*American Station*		*Indian Equivalent*
Saucier	Sauce Station	Sauce Cook	Second Cook Station	
Poissonier	Fish Station			Master Cooks
Potager	Soup Station	Vegetable Cook		Regional Cooks
Entremetier	Vegetable and Egg Station			Tandoor
				North Indian
Rotisseur	Roast and Broiler Station	Broiler–Short Order		South Indian
		Breakfast		Avadi
Garde-manger	Cold Pantry	Salad and Sandwich		Hyderabadi
Buffetier	Buffet Carver	Pantry		Rajasthani
Patissier	Pastry Station	Pastry and Dessert Pantry		
Tournant	Relief	Swing Shift		

QUESTIONS AND DISCUSSIONS

Multiple Choice

Q.1. Read each question carefully and select the best answer :

(i) Which one of these chefs is likely to supervise the largest brigade?

(a) Head Chef (b) Executive Chef

(c) Banquet Chef (d) Day Chef.

(ii) Which one of these cooks is likely to have the least skill?
(a) Broiler Man (b) Pantry Man
(c) Steamtable Man (d) Troisieme Commis.

(iii) Which one of the following is a full service restaurant?
(a) Ship's dining room (b) Dinnerhouse
(c) Nationality restaurant (d) Luxury restaurant.

(iv) Which of the following would be likely to need a French type cooking brigade?
(a) Luxury restaurant (b) Hospital
(c) Steakhouse (d) Passenger ship.

(v) Which one of these establishments is likely to serve breakfast, lunch, and dinner every day?
(a) Coffeeshop (b) Resort hotel
(c) Caterer (d) Bistro.

(vi) Which one of these needs the highest skill level?
(a) Broiler – Short Order (b) Night Chef
(c) Garde-manger (d) Second Cook.

[**Ans.:** (i) (b); (ii) (c); (iii) (c);
(iv) (a); (v) (b); (vi) (b)]

Q.2. List the following in order, from most to least skilled:

(a) (i) Deuxieme Commis (ii) Station Cook
(iii) Troisieme Commis (iv) Sous Chef.
(v) Chef de Cuisine

(b) (i) Executive Chef (ii) Station Cook
(iii) Station Chef (iv) Sous Chef.
(v) Cook's Helper

[**Ans.:** (a) (v), (iv), (ii), (i), (iii);
(b) (i), (iv), (iii), (ii), (v)]

Matching Type

Q 3. Match the English terminology in the Table 'A' with the terminology in the Table 'B'.

Table 'A'	*Table 'B'*
(a) Soup Cook	(i) Garde-manger
(b) Pastry Cook	(ii) Buffetier
(c) Relief Cook	(iii) Saucier
(d) Cold Pantry Cook	(iv) Poissonier
(e) Fish Cook	(v) Rotisseur
(f) Buffet Cook	(vi) Potager
(g) Roast Cooks	(vii) Entremetier
(h) Sauce Cook	(viii) Patissier
(i) Vegetable and Egg Cook	(ix) Tournant.

[**Ans.:** (a) (vi); (b) (viii); (c) (ix); (d) (I); (e) (iv);
(f) (ii); (g) (v); (h) (iii); (i) (vii)]

Short Answer Type

Q.4. 'There is a trend toward specialty restaurants.' Explain.

Q.5. What are the differences in skill levels of American French cooks and Indian cooks?

Q.6. Explain the gastronomic culture.

Q.7. What is advertising influence on the food buying of a restaurant ?

Q.8. Define a master chef.

Q.9. Explain the strengths and the future of service industries.

Descriptive Answer Type

Q.10. Describe the continuous growth of Indian hospitality industry.

Q.11. Name twelve different food and wantage service establishments in your locality.

Q.12. Why are more skilled cooks needed ?

Q.13. Explain the bonds between international and Indian restaurant cuisine.

Q.14. Explain the followings :

(a) Bistro
(b) Brigade
(c) Caterer
(d) Cuisine
(e) Gastronomy
(f) Gastronomic culture
(g) Mis en place
(h) Short order cook.

Q.15. Highlight regional influences on cuisine in your area.

Assignments/Activity Type

Q.16. Arrange a dinner-field trip (if possible) to a luxury restaurant or hotel, banquet style.

Q.17. Invite a chef from a five star hotel for lecture for a question and answer session in regard to his responsibilities.

Q.18. Arrange field trips to various food service establishments, such as

(a) International hotels
(b) Large luxury restaurant
(c) Hospital or institution
(d) Air catering or residential college mess.

1.2

The Art and Science of Cooking

CHAPTER OBJECTIVES

After studying this lesson you should be able :

- To describe the origins and growth of Indian style of cooking;
- To identify the sciences which contribute in the developments of food technology;
- To observe the areas where artistic talents in cookery can be applied; and
- To explain the role of apprenticeship in modern cooking.

The need for food is one of the few things early man and modern man have in common. Some forms of cooking started with man's earlier history. Therefore, the roots of cookery reach back to the dawn of mankind and the history of food goes back only several thousand years. We can assumed that cooking meat over an open fire was the first form of cookery.

Cooking is subject to the availability of supplies and develops accordingly. Early in its past it became an art, later a craft. It was taught for hundreds of years through the system of apprenticeship, and only recently through trade schools. Later on the new food technology was conceived by the close bond of food knowledge, organic chemistry, microbiology, and cookery. In turn, the research done by food technologists involves more knowledge pertaining to Culinary Art, and in this way helped to change it to cooking technology. (**Ref.** Figure : 1.2A)

Although a part of cookery has changed to technology some of the art parts will always remain. It is basically a difference of talents which causes cooks to become great chefs. Even today, disregarding progress and a better understanding of nutrition, man still eats what he likes and the popularity of the steakhouse indicates that meat cooked over an open fire, as the oldest from of cooking is also the most popular one.

The origin of the art of cookery and storing of food greatly influenced the growth of civilization all over the world. Man's first cooked food may have been meat burned in a forest fire. After he was freed from searching day by day, he had time to think, experiment, and progress.

Trainees at work

Let us take an example of man who is hungry. A hungy man eats everything that is available and edible and then gets to like it by habit. When supplies become plentiful, his appetite gets changed. He searches for new taste sensations, and eats more selectively. As soon as he gets used to these foods, they become everyday fare. In his search for the new, he is finding the old again. There is very little really new in the world of food. Cooking has made the least number of contributions to the technology of man. Today's preference of consumers has gone back to meat broiled over an open fire as it was done thousands of years ago. The only change that we observer is the hand which in turned the spit has been replaced by an electric motor.

First records of cooking go back many thousand years, but contemporary cookery emerged about two hundred years ago. The style cooking depended on the supply of food and the amount of technical knowledge. In certain geographic regions, special dishes were prepared because the raw materials for them existed there in abundance, other foods were unknown or unavailable because of the lack of facilities of fast transportation.

Like any other art and science cookery has developed through trial and error. As some people showed talent while working with food, cookery evolved into an art which was handed down from mothers to daughters and from masters to apprentices.

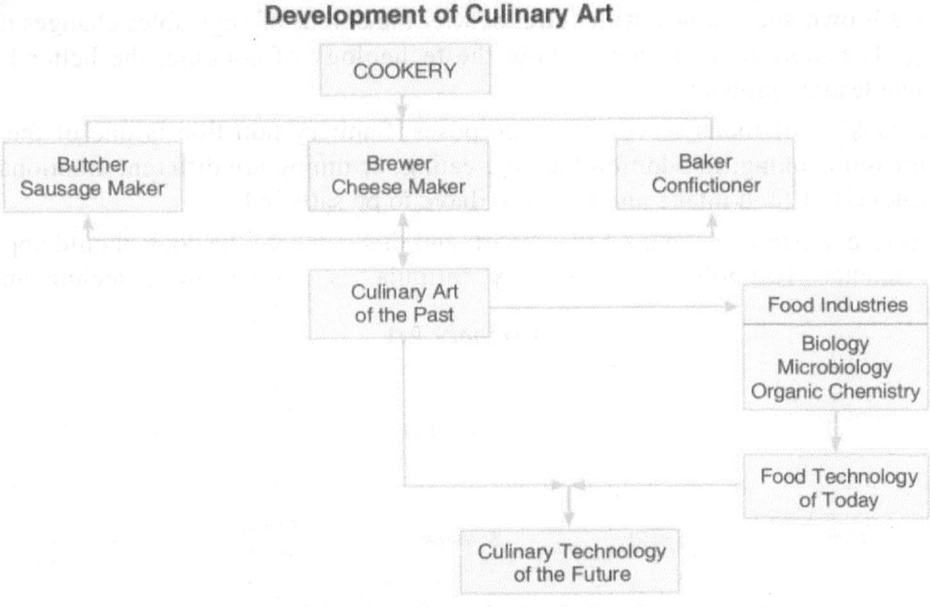

Fig. 1.2A. A Development and Progress of Culinary Art

Culinary art gradually changed from art to craft and from craft to science. Now most chefs, scientists, and other members of the food service industry have became research-minded. They have gained better opportunities to experiment and to communicate. Research results became stepping stones to more research and there is a discovery of new knowledge and skills. Food preservation grew into food processing and food processing became food technology. Culinary Art, influenced by food technology, developed into culinary technology, medical art prodded by Gastronomic art developed the sciences of dietetics and nutrition (Ref. Fig. 1.2A).

Louis Pasteur (1822–95), the famous French microbiologist, known to the world as the healer of rabies and inventor of inoculation, is the father of modern food technology. His research into fermentation, pasteurization (a sterilization process named after him), and bacteriology paved the way for modern food preservation. His discoveries initiated the change from culinary art and craft to the culinary art and science of today.

FOOD PRESERVATION AND CULINARY TECHNOLOGY

Sun-drying (dehydration), salting and smoking have been known as means of food preservation for thousands of years. It was not until 1809 that Francis Appert discovered by chance that food, sealed in airtight containers and boiled in water for a considerable time, became immune against spoilage. Thus, the canning process was created. Later on Louis Pasteur found them. From then on food preservation became an industry and grew to a powerful force. During these early times, cooks and master chefs, chemists and biologists banded together and the discoveries of these groups became food technology. The new industry continued to employ scientists and chefs in the search of better methods and new products. All this in different ways, was beneficial to culinary art, and thus, to culinary technology.

Cooking technology is the part of culinary art. It explains why meat roasted in the oven gets brown and changes its texture, or why the colour of vegetables changes during cooking. The more a cook knows about the technology of cooking, the better he can create wholesome products.

The cooking of foods serves many purposes. Sanitary nutrition is one of the most basic aims in cooking. In addition feeding, eating, or dining are different emotional and cultural levels of food intake and they, too, have to be satisfied.

Therefore, a part of culinary will stay art, and this is where the cook should apply his artistic talents. Technology, cooking by formula, is applied by a technician, but

Culinary Art

Skill	Empirical Learning	**Science Knowledge**	Artistic Talent	Culinary art of Yesterday Past

Skill	Knowledge	**Science**	Artistic Talent	Culinary art of Today Present

Fig. 1.2B. Culinary Art in Past and Present

craftsmanship includes the artistic vein. It is the talent to please people by creating food that is nutritionally sound and appetizing. The final criterion is that the food must be exciting and tasty to the palate. (Ref. Figure 1.2B)

All these above factors create different levels of craftsmanship. Art, culinary or otherwise, is a value judgment; so is taste. They are formed by environment and habit. Craftsmanship is recognized universally as being functional. Craftsmanship without artistic talent is acceptable, but food prepared by artistic talent alone with out the functionality of craftsmanship is barely tolerable. Craftsmanship includes all that a good chef should stand for. It is a reflection of his work.

The chef as a creative artist is an unique position. Like the commercial artist, he has to arouse the buying impulse of the consumer, satisfy it, and make him want to come back again soon. Many creative chefs have established their own little restaurants with a personal tough. Their food is mostly of ethnic origins. Their restaurants are styled in a unique way. They express themselves gastronomically. A few of these restaurants are famous all over the world.

The Head Cook of a large establishment may be feeding hundreds of customers per day. He works for an institution where the audience is captive. This chef must evaluate his customers, it must find out what they consider attractive, valuable, and tasty. The chef must adjust his artistic presentation to the level of his customers.

All chefs must understand that primarily they are to prepare edible food. They are not in competition with artists who create permanent but inedible works of art. Most customers who consistently return to the same restaurant do so for the food. "The proof for the pudding is in the tasting" goes an old saying.

Apprenticeship was one of the first forms of organized learning, and it retains some usefulness until today. It grew and changed whenever the conditions of the working men changed.

In modern times art turned towards a food craft and hotel school education. With the full-service restaurant fading away and the emergence of the specialty restaurant, apprenticeship could not teach all phases of cookery. Trade schools not only teach everything that pertains to cookery, but they also offer supplementary education in many fields such as chemistry, microbiology, and business management.

Let us divide this work into "thinking units" and "doing units". The thinking unit develops through academic learning. The doing unit develops better by practical learning. Learning by doing is an established fact. Apprenticeship cook which is closer to learning by looking and copying than by practice does not give the wide scope of theory, background, and understanding that a good school does. Even the best establishments are output-centered. Quantity and speed to them are more important than quality and understanding. For the brights young student cooks of today, a good food craft school offers the best vocational education.

REGIONAL DISHES OF INDIA

The cuisines of India differ from the State to State as is in the case of the foods of European continent, which differ from one country to another. However, there are

A stack of Naan, a flatbread that is an Indian staple food

Indian Chicken Tikka with Basmati Rice

features that link all states of India—the whole country has in common i.e. the vast variety of spices and seasonings. Although Indian restaurant food is excellent, India hides much of its real treasure of food in the millions of private homes scattered across the country.

From the temperate northern state of Kashmir, where food is eaten to keep body warm, to the tropical southern state of Tamil Nadu and Kerala, where the food are of necessity cooling, the food variety in India is incredible. It is unfortunate that many traditional hotels and restaurants do not experiment much with Indian cookery rather they keep the old tried and tested methods, which although good, are becoming rather boring.

All Indian foods are served with either rice or bread or both. In the north, it is whole wheat breads, such as *Chappatis* and *Paraunthas*, that are commonly eaten, and in the south; there are the rice dishes. The traditional Indian bread is flat, baked on castiron griddles. The Muslims introduced oven where sour dough and plain breads, such as *Naan* and *Shirmal*, could be baked. (Ref. Table 1.2A)

Table 1.2A. Central Indian Style—A Typical Menu

Menu-I	*Menu-II*
Rice-Poori	Matar Pulao
Arhar Daal	Poori
Rasadar Aloo	Sabut Bhindi
Kaddu ki Sabzi	Shami Kebab
Boondi Raita	Sukha Aloo
Sounth	Raita
Jelabi	Beasn Laddu

According to *Ayurveda*, the ancient science of Indian medicine, all spices and herbs have medicinal properties. Turmeric for example is an *antiseptic* (often put on fish before frying). Asafoetida is a *digestive* (hence it is often put in pulses). Garlic is good for *circulatory* aliments; coriander and tamarind for *constipation*; cloves for toning up the heart and black pepper for giving *energy*.

NORTH INDIAN REGION

Delhi

Delhi, India's capital since the early part of 20th century, has been invaded, pillaged and conquered by *Scythians, Partians, Turks, Afghans, Moghuls and British.* As years passed many of their food stuffs were absorbed into the city's life style - some others changed. *Pulao* and *Samosas* are both derivations of Middle-eastern cuisine - spilt peas cooked with ginger and cumin *(Daal)*; meat cooked with fried onions *(Do pyaza)*; chicken and almonds braised in yoghourt *(Dumpukht)* - all these and more have been added over the years to the northern Indian and particularly Delhi cuisine.

Paani poori, a popular snack in India

Mostly middle-eastern dishes were just added to the Hindu dishes already in existence and this made the repertoire more extensive. *Pakhoras* of every type, mint and coriander *chutneys, aloo ki tikiyas* (potato cakes) eaten with sour *imli chutney. Chapatis* eaten with potato, peas and cauliflower combined with turmeric ginger and chillies.

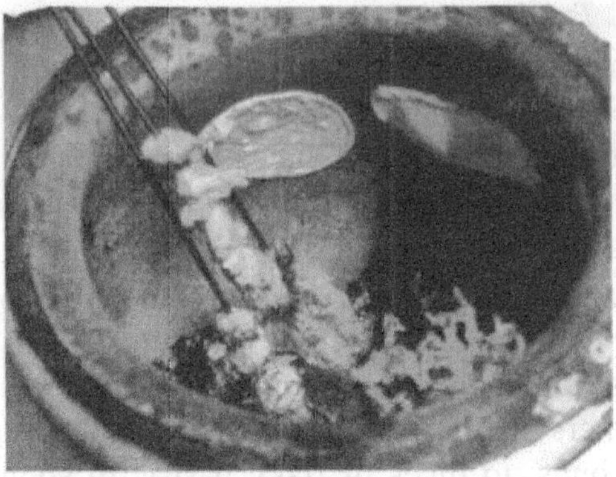

Tandoor

Tandoori Chicken

Tandoori food was brought to Delhi after partition in 1947 and this style of cooking not only caught on in Delhi, now, most of the world's Indian restaurants are specialized in *Tandoori* cuisine (chicken specially).

Punjab

Many Punjabis are farmers and consequently some of Punjab's best food is hearty country food, based on buttermilk, *ghee* and freshly harvested produce. Layered *paraunthas* (griddle bread) stuffed with grated radish or pomegranate seeds; butterly-mustard green (*sarson da sag*), to be eaten with fresh corn bread; black-eyed beans and red kidney beans; *channa bhatura* (spicy chick peas eaten with deep fried breads).

Table 1.2B. Northern Indian Style—A Typical Menu

Menu-I	*Menu-II*
Naan	Chappti
Tandoori Murgh	Mahan ki Daal
Matar Pillau	Jeera Chawal
Sudh Aloo	Baigan Bharta
Shahi Korma	Paneer Makhani
Raita	Saag Gosht
Kheer	Sooji Halwa

Jammu & Kashmir

The beauty of Kashmir is awesome. One of the most beautiful sights is acre of mauve crocuses flowers that provide an ancient crop, saffron. Local people use the saffron, sparingly of course, as it is very expensive, to flavour rice and leaf dishes.

For their cuisine, the Hindu and later on the Muslim inhabitants of the land drew on what they could find, raise or grow, acknowledging the culinary whims of their changing overlords—Afghans, Mohguls, Sikhs and Britons. The upland forest of Kishtwar is carpeted with juicy morels. Mushrooms grow everywhere and can be harvested at no cost. There is rhubarb, and plenty of wild asparagus. There are enough pastures to raise sheep and goats, raised for milk and wool. Growing food is more of a problem. Terraces are reserved for the staple-rice. Wheat, too, is grown to make superb breads such as the bun-shaped *Kulcha,* and the sesame encrusted *Tsachvaru.*

With the abundance of mountain lakes, Kashmiris harvest the water, especially in the case of lotus roots, which taste of artichoke hearts. Called *Nedr,* they are cooked with fish, *Wastahaak* (tender spring greens) and with lamp; best of all they are fried in mustard oil to make crunchy chips. The lake water also produces *edible lotus seeds, water chestnuts, and many fish.*

Day begins in Kashmir with tea called *Kahva*—China like tea-mixed with cardamoms and crushed almonds. The bread of Kashmir is unique. Related more to the breads of Afghanistan, Central Asia and the middle east rather then the traditional Hindu breads, they are generally baked by traditional bakers in clay or brick ovens and bought everyday. They range from short-bread like buns, to dices of flaky pastry, to spongy, chewy creations something like doughnut. They can be sweet or salty—some are encrusted with sesame seeds, others with poppy seeds.

Vegetables, mostly seasonable greens, are staple and invariably cooked in mustard oil and water with the addition of chillies. Hindus use asafetida also as flavouring while the Muslims use garlic.

Lamb is the main meat, cooked with yoghourt or milk—again the flavouring depends on the religion. Hindus use the *asafetida* and ginger or fennel; Muslims use the garlic and onions. The Kashmiri onion is different to another onions—it is a cross between a shallots and a spring onion called *Praan.* While summer and autumn in Kashmir produce an abundance of vegetables there is a constant awareness of the dearth of winter. Every vegetable that can be cut and dried is grown and these include, turnips, green leaves, tomatoes, chillies and of course the fishermen do likewise. Their dried fish, *hogaad*, has to last until spring.

Kashmiris make exquisite Chutneys using walnuts or sour cherries, or yellow pumpkin, or white radishes. Other specialties include *Heddar* (mushrooms cooked with tomatoes, ginger and fennel). *Shinkar* (lightly vinegared duck cooked with garlic and chilies), and *gurd muj* (fish cooked with white radish). The ultimate Kashmir meat dish is rib chops braised in broth then fried until crisp.

Uttar Pradesh

Benares dates back at least 600 years - pilgrims visit from all over India - it is typically traditional city in spite of its large moving population. One of the larger communities are Marwaris - originally from Rajasthan, who have settled all over the north but particularly in Benares. Marwari kitchens may be entered only by a professional cook called a 'Maharaj'. For religious reasons the food is served directly from cooking pots on to *thalis*. A *thali* might contain for a meal - a salad of shredded fresh ginger with radish and chillies and aubergine *kalonj*, potatoes and cauliflower; a *daal*, a chickpea and yoghourt *karhi*; *Rasgullas; Kachoris, Roti* and *Pappads*.

Lucknow has a strong Muslim influence. *Kakori kebabs* are a Lucknow speciality. This is meat pounded with poppy seeds and cloves. Breakfast in Lucknow could consists of *Kulchas* (flat sour-dough bread) eaten with *Nahari* - a stew or *Roghni Roti*, rich whole wheat bread eaten with spicy fried liver.

More formal meals have a taste of the Middle East. Whole marinated legs of lamb, *naan* cooked with almonds and poppy seeds; whole chicken stuffed with quail, elaborate pilafs and *shirmals* (flaky oven bread flavoured with saffron).

Uttarakhand

There are ennumerable varity of dishes to taste. The most delecious dishes prepared from the organic foods and species.

Chicken Masala

Rajasthan

To the west of U.P. stretches the desert of Rajasthan. The ancient Rajputs hunted and ate wild animal *(Shikars)*. The fat and skin of the animal may be cooked with fried onions, coriander, cumin, ginger and garlic - it can also be used to flavour *Moong Daal*. In Rajasthan, meats including poultry, game and fish are marinated, skewed and grilled over fires to make *Soola Kebab. Laal Maas* is a famous mutton dish cooked with onion, garlic, ginger and lots of spicy red chillies.

Madhya Pradesh

South of U.P. lies the central Indian state of Madhya Pradesh with its capital Bhopal - where the food is traditionally Muslim in character. Spicy and aromatic *Korma* is served with an equally aromatic *Baghare Chawal (*rice) which is flavoured with ginger and garlic and *Baigan Ki Boorani,* an Afghan dish (fried slices of aubergine topped with garlic flavoured yoghourt). Fish from Bhopal's lake are also very popular. White fleshed fish such as *Sanwal* is cut, dipped in seasoned yoghourt and then in coriander, chilli and garlic paste and fried. Yoghurt, coriander, chillies and ginger are a large part of cooking in Bhopal.

CENTRAL-WESTERN REGION

Gujarat

The modern state of Gujarat was formed only in 1960. Gujarati food belongs Gujarati-speaking people, whether they happen to be in Ahmedabad, the state capital, in Saurashtra, the western portion of the state, in cosmopolitan Mumbai (not in the state at all although it was formerly) or in one of the thousands of villages throughout the area. For many of Gujarati vegetarians much of the food is based on grains, beans roots and vegetables grown on family farms. Millet, a grain that has more protein, Vitamin E, and iron than wheat is staple here. It is grounded, mixed with spinach and green chilli to make a dough and then formed into breads - *Dherbras* - on a cast iron griddle. These breads can be eaten with *Chundo,* a sweet chutney made with green mangoes, cardamom, cloves and yoghurt. *Batata Shaak* are diced potatoes sauted with mustard and cumin seeds; and *Dhoklas,* savoury steamed cake made from split pea batter.

Dhokla

Much of the states sugar cane production goes to make jaggery, which is raw unprocessed lump sugar. Most of the jaggery is made into loaf like lumps. Gujarati, often like to sweeten their split peas and vegetables with jaggery. Red chillies are also cropped in great profusion here. They are used to make one of Saurashtra'a all important spice mixture; *Lehson Masala* or garlic spice mixture; this adds up to a lot of their foods.

One of the special bread is *Batloo,* a flat griddle bread of millet flour, packed with tiny depression looks like the cracked earth of the surrounding country.

Ahmedabad has one distinction that sets it apart from other provincial capitals. It is the only city where the best of regional flavoure may be sampled in a fine restaurant. The vegeterian restaurant, Vishala, is set up like a village with banquet style dining.

Pandavas were served here, savoury spilt pea cakes, encrusted with sesame seeds; rice steamed with tiny stuffed aubergines; corn cooked with drumsticks; and *khandvi* - tiny rolled crepes.

One of the oldest Muslim communities in Gujarat is that of the Bohris, disciples of the 11th century missionary, Abdullah, and converted from Hinduism. They are among the very few communities in the country with the passion for serving soups; hot soup, cold soup, breakfast soup and soup made with all manner of foods. A favourite is *Sarki, a* cold summer soup that uses *Toovar Dual* for the basic stock and then adds diced cucumber, tomatoes and spring onions, before garnishing with yoghurt. Parsis are another Gujarati-speaking minority. They are Zoroashtrians who fled Iran in the 8th century and landed just north of Bombay. Parsi food is a delicious blend of western influences, a Gujaratis love of sweet and sour mixes, and the Persian genius for combining meat with dried fruit.

One of their delicious chutney is *Meva-Nu-Achar* made with carrots, and dried fruit; *Soli Jardaloo Murgi* is a sweet and sour dish of chicken and dried apricots. One of their well-known meat dishes is *Dhansak,* usually mutton cooked with *daal.*

Maharashtra

Starting around Maharashtra, one can almost begin to draw a line that divides basically wheat-eating north from the rice eating south. Maharashtrians eat both wheat and rice, but the later is given a place of prominence. It is used in every form imaginable from steamed rice flour sweet dumplings (*modaks*), to delicate rice form biscuits called *Anarsa.* Anarsa typifies the best of Maharashtrian food. This cuisine from India's heartland aims to satisfy and delight. It depends, for its final taste, not so much on rare ingredients as on the expert blending of sweet, salty, hot and sour flavours.

While the food of certain communities around Pune may be restrained and vegetarian, one has only to look at the extravagance and richness of the diet of the Marathas' headquarter at Kolhapur or title spicy exuberance of that of the coastal fisher-folks to realize that, even within the state of Maharashtra, there are several different cuisines.

The Marathas, belonging to a caste of working-class agriculturists, are the best warriors of India. They have traditionally eaten and enjoyed whatever came their way. On hunts they marinate quail in yoghourt, cloves and black peper, wrap them in wet clay and bake them. Marathis eat their food hot and unsweetened.

Ratnagiri on the Konkan coast has the distinction of producing one of the most sought after Mangos. It is called Alphonsu-pulp with a clear yellow skin touched with red, it is juicy, and sweet. One of the most delicious products of these mangoes is *Amba Barfi. Srikhand* is the famous dessert of Maharashtra and is basically sweetened whipped hung curd flavoured with cardamom and even mangoes.

Mumbai, the state capital and western India's principal seaport, is a vibrant blend of Gujarati Hindu merchants, Parsi industrialists, Maharashtrian intellectuals, Baghdadi jews, Muslim movie stars, Goan lawyers and the original Koli fisher-folk. But there is one equalizer in Mumbai to which everyone succumbs and that is *Bhel-Poori.* The place to eat *bhel-poori* is Chowpatty beach. Some puffed rice is put in a bowl, wheat flour crisps are crumbled over, generous, sprinklings of chopped onion and potato-two chutneys are spooned in, a sharp, hot green one made from tamarind and dates. Some *sev,* vermicelli made from chickpea flour finishes of the snack. Another famous dish is *Pav Bhaji* (A spicy dry preparation of mashed vegetables cooked in butter and served with savory square *buns*). (Ref. Table 1.2 C)

Table 1.2C. Western Indian Style—A Typical Menu

Menu-I	*Menu-II*
Rice	Masale Bhat
Bharaleli Wangi	Bhakri
Jhinge Batana	Aloo Bhaji
Aloo Shak	Mirchi Salan
Puran Poori	Srikhand/Amrakhand

EASTERN REGION

Bengal and North East

No meal in Bengal is considered complete without fish. However, salt-water fish is disdained and the freshwater variety is much priced. Bengalis not only eat fish, they are exceedingly particular about it when they shop. They examine the eyes of fish for clearness and the inside of gills for redness; they know that *Leta* fish is good for invalids and must be brought live, as should *Koi* or climbing perch, as well as carp-like *Rui* and female crabs rich with roe. Hilsa is the supreme Bengali fish and is brought whenever the availability of fish coincides with the availability of extra cash needed to buy it. Hilsa may be cooked in many ways - it can be boned (not an easy task as Hilsa is full of tiny bones) and smoked, and it can be prepared as *Elish Bhapa.* Pieces of Hilsa are also mixed with the paste of ground mustard seeds, mustard oil, red and green chillies, turmeric and salt. This is then cooked either wrapped in banana leaves or steamed. This dish is famously known as *Ilish Machcher Paturi*

Mustard oil and mustard seeds are very much part of Bengal cuisine. Many Bengali dishes require mustard seeds to do a triple duty - as an (i) oil, (ii) popped, nutty seed, and (iii) fiery seed paste as well.

Kolkata, Bengal's capital city lived the longest under continuous and very direct foreign rule, and has therefore a mixed culinary history - Portuguese, Moghul and British. But the Bengali, however westernized- never gave up his language neither he did give up his passion for fish, rice and sweets. Date jaggery is one of the sweet delicacies made by tapping the date palm.

However, India's premier sweet is *Rosogollas,* which is crudled milk, yoghurt squeezed out, rolled into balls and dropped into boiling syrup where they puff up. *Sandesh* is the same dough mixed with syrup and cooked over a low flame until all moisture evaporates. In the spring, jaggery is used instead of the traditional sugar syrup giving a *Nutan Gurer Sandesh* or *Nolen Gurer Sandesh which* has a caramel flavour and colour.

A lunch time favourite is *Shukto.* It starts the meal and is a mixture of diced and fried vegetables like bitter gourd, white radish potato, *Seem* (a hard skinned flat bean) plus leaves and stems peculiar to Bengalis; split peas are added and then the whole mixture is cooled with milk and water flavoured with giger, mustard seeds, cumin and turmeric. *Panchphoran* is a spice mixture used in Bengal, and consists of whole cumin seeds, whole fennel seeds, whole fenugreek seeds and whole *Radhuni* (like parsley seeds). This *panchphoran* is added to the *sukto*. Another famous Bengali sweet dish is *Mishti doi*, a thick, sweetened yoghourt set in earthen cups. (Ref. Table 1.2D)

Table 1.2D. Eastern Indian Style—A Typical Menu

Menu-I	*Menu-II*
Rice	Ghee Bhaat
Masoor daal	Mooger Dal
Choch Chori	Begun Bhaja
Sarshee Mach	Panchphoron ChorChori
Mangsho Jol	Bhapa Rui / Ilish
Rassgolla	Kosha Mangsho
Mishti Doi	

SOUTHERN REGION

Andhra Pradesh

The cuisine of Hyderabad, nurtured by what was once a wealthy Muslim court in the heart of Hindu south India, combines the very best of Muslim foods. *kebabs, pilafs, kormas,* and yoghourt dishes - with the aromatic, tart, pungent and creamy flavourings of the south. Mustard seeds, *kebab cheeni*, cinnamon, curry leaves, not chillies, peas nuts, tamarind and coconut milk. A sauce of roasted and ground sesame seeds is mixed with green chillies and tamarind paste to become a *Til Ki Chutny.* Dried beans and lamb, which are often stewed together in Persian cookery, are served up here with delectable *Dalcha* of Hyderabad.

Some of Hyderabad's best dishes includes - *lukmi*, ravioli-like squares pastry filled in the center with spiced meat and deep fried; *Chippe Ka Gosht,* chunks of meat marinated in a paste of onion. Green chillies and coconut, garlic, *garam masala* and yoghourt and then cooked very slowly in a clay pot; *Ambaday Ki Bhaji,* a dish of sorrel-like greens; *Baghare Baigan,* small, whole aubergines, slit, browned and cooked in nutty sauce of sesame and peanuts; *Tomato Kut,* an aromatic tomato puree with tamarind, curry leaves and garlic; *Murgh Methi,* chicken cooked with freshly sprouted fenugreek greens; *Kacchi Biryani,* a rice and meat mixture and finally *Kacche Dahi Ke Koftay,* minced meat spiced with coriander, mint, garlic and *garam masala* is ground to a fine paste, formed into balls and fried, put into yoghourt beaten with garlic, mustard seeds, curry leaves and chillies.

Karnataka

Karnataka is renowned for its *Bisi Beta Huli Anna,* a hot, tart porridge of rice, split peas and vegetables; garlic flavoured *Idlis* as well as *Anay Pad Wade,* large *wadas*; *Soppu Pallya,* a dish of steamed spinach, enriched with thick milk and flavoured with mustard and cumin.

Rice is the king of grains in both Karnataka and Andhra. No meal is possible without it making an appearance in one or another. Many peoples are vegetarians. Grains and split peas are the core of the diet. These basic grains and humble split peas can be transformed into *Sevai* (fresh noodles) and sweet jellies such as the *Hulbai* of Mysore.

Tamil Nadu

South Indians are serious coffee drinkers. In Madras they make strong filtered coffee, but mixed it with lots of hot milk and flavoured with Chicory beans. Served with morning coffee are *Dosas,* which are thin, round, golden crisp savory pancake which is smooth on one side and white slightly yielding batter on the other. Made out the same batter, both *Dosas* and *Idlis* are the bread of south, nourishing and digestible. They may be eaten with butter and honey, or with *chutneys*, or stuffed with a spicy blend of the potatoes and onions called *Masala. Sambar* which is staple of the area, is, cooked with *toovar daal* which is boiled with turmeric.

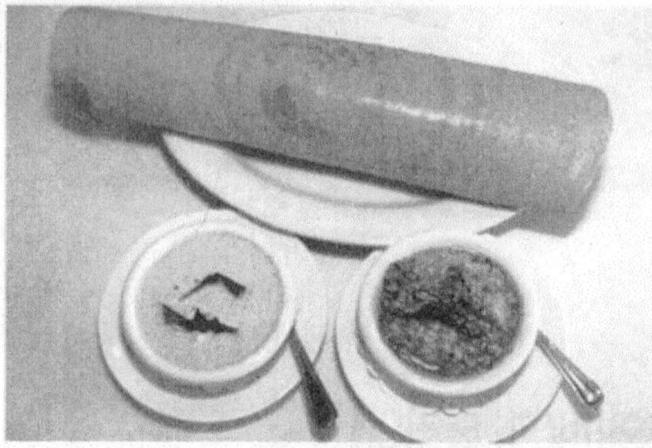

Dosa – A favourite food in Southwest Asia. It is a crepe made from rice and black lentils and it is eaten for breakfast or dinner, and is rich in carbohydrates and protein.

When soft, the solids settle at the bottom. The thin broth at the top, is ladled off to make *Rasam.* Some pieces of pumpkin are poached in tamarind water and added to the thick *daal. Sambar* powder, a ground spices mixture including chillies, *channa daal*, coriander and fenugreek are mixed in along with curry leaves popped in hot oil. The *sambar* is ready. For the soupy *rasam*, the *daal* broth is mixed with tamarind water, ground black pepper, red chillies and cumin with coriander leaves sprinkled over. (Ref. Table 1.2 E)

Table 1.2E. Southern Indian Style—A Typical Menu

Menu-I	*Menu-II*
Masala Dosa	Hyderabadi Biryani
Sambar	Baghare Baigan
Thankal Chutney	
Payasam	

Kerala

Kerala is the spice area of India. Peppercorns, nutmeg (and with it mace), cinnamon clove and tamarind, cardamom, ginger and turmeric, along with special curry leaves and Coconut - a fruit that makes the food of Kerala most unique.

Stews made of meat or chicken simmered in coconut water is eaten with *Uppams. Uppmns* or *Appams* are rice flour pancakes designed to have thick, soft, spongy centers and thin, golden crisp edges. Today, the coconut plant is used as a fermenting agent for the batter of these *Appams,* and after leaving all night to ferment is thinned down in the morning with coconut milk.

Fish is often prepared in fiercy chilli pastes and left for several days to mature in terra cotta pots.

Vegetables are cooked simply. Green papaya and jackfrutt are prepared as vegetables and cooked with variety of seasonings plus the inevitable coconut milk. Kerala is also very famous for its jackfruit and banana chips fried in coconut oil.

A specialty dessert is *Prathaman; moong daal* boiled with coconut and flavoured with raw palm sugar, cardamom and ginger.

Use of Herbs and Spices

Herbs and spice play an important role in the preperation and cooking of food. Each herb and spice has its own properties and as such used extensively in the cooking of food. Some important point regarding spices are:

1. Aids digestion by stimulating gastric juices
2. Enhances flavour of dishes
3. Medicinal value e.g. trumeric has antiseptic qualities
4. Used as a preservative for pickling and canning
5. Enhance seasoning and improve palatability
6. Improve appearance by providing colour contrast.

QUESTIONS AND DISCUSSIONS

Fill in the Blanks

Q.1. Read and complete the following statements:

(a) The inventor of the canning process was French confectioner by the name of ....

(b) The two branches of science that contributed to food technology are .... and ....

(c) Culinary Art became more science-oriented due to tremendous progress in...........

(d) One of the oldest forms of organized learning is the ....

(e) One of the earliest forms of cookery was the exposure of meat to the open.........

(f) Chefs must restrict their artistic endeavors to materials which are...............

(g) The beginning of food storage and cookery spawned the beginning of.............

(h) A special sterilization process of food called pasteurization was invented by...............

[**Ans.:** (a) Francis Abbert; (b) mirco-biology and food processing; (c) food technology; (d) Apprenticeship; (e) fire; (f) to the level of customers (g) civilization (h) Louis Pasteur.]

Multiple Choice Type

Q.2. Read each question carefully and select the best answer :

(i) Which influence has changed the Culinary Art of yesterday to the Culinary Technology of today?

(a) Empirical learning (b) Equipment improvement
(c) Food technology (d) Food and drug administration.

(ii) The development of Culinary Art was dependent on the availability of

(a) Microwave ovens (b) Raw food supplies
(c) Refrigeration (d) Food technologists.

(iii) Which one of these sciences has not contributed to food technology?

(a) Organic chemistry (b) Inorganic chemistry
(c) Biology (d) Microbiology.

[**Ans.:** (i) (c); (ii) (d); (iii) (b)]

Descriptive Type

Q.3. Briefly describe the stages in the development of culinary technology from its assumed beginning (early man finding some burnt meat) up to today.

Q.4. Name the areas where artistic talents in cookery can be applied.

Q.5. Give a description of the origins of Indian cooking.

Q.6. Compare the relationship between apprenticeship and school.

Q.7. Predict the future of cooking technology, and justify your prediction by giving examples of food craft and hotel.

Q.8. State the type of cooking was done by early man.

Q.9. As a Chef how-could you show artistic expression?

Q.10. What is a cook's status in the food processing industry?

Q.11. Explain the influences which created cooking technology.

Short Answer Type

Q.12. Explain each of the following 'Herbs and Spices' in three/four sentences .

(a) Herbs (b) Fine Herbs (in French)
(c) Common Herbs (d) Spices
(e) Fine Spices (f) Mixed Spices
(g) Bouquet Garni (h) Common Spices

[**Ans.:**

(a) Leaves of aromatic plants used dried/ fresh for flavouring or garnishing dishes. 1/2 tsp dried herbs = 2 tsp freshly minced herbs. Fresh herbs are highly perishable and must be cut, chopped or minced to bring out the flavour.

(b) Chopped parsley. In olden style cookery, chopped mushrooms and truffles were mixed with herbs.

(c) Basil, bayleaf, coriander, leaves, marjoram, mint, parsley, rosemary, sage, tarragon & thyme.

(d) Parts of aromatic plants such as roots, bark seeds, etc. suitable for processing - drying and grinding, before use.

(e) According to Larousse - comprise of white pepper- 700 g; mace- 100g; red pepper- 300g; cloves, cerramon, sage, bayleaf, marjoram, nutmeg-50g; each.

(f) Dried, pounded mixture of 2/3rd thyme, bayleaf, basil, sage, coriander seeds and mace with 1/3rd white pepper powder.

(g) Assortment of herbs and/ or spices added while cooking and discarded before service includes parsley, thyme, bayleaf and celery.

(h) Doves, cinnamon, mace, ginger, saffron, turmeric, paprika, pepper, asfoetida, etc.]

Q.13. Define the following terms:

(a) Apprentice

(b) Craftsmanship

(c) Technology

Assignments & Activity Type

Q.14. Arrange a field trip to a :

(a) Cannery

(b) Food production plant

(c) A microbiology lab

(d) Kitchen of a luxury establishment.

Q.15. Arrange for demonstration of simple food chemistry text.

Q.16. Show a film or photos from Culinary Art Show.

Q.17. Make a list of school library books which refer to history and origin of Indian cooking.

1.3

Manual Skills and Modern Technology

CHAPTER OBJECTIVES

After studying this lesson you should be able :

- To explain the importance and reasons for cutting food;
- To identify food cuts of different shapes and their corresponding names.;
- To draw sketch of knife blade;
- To identify mean basic knife groups;
- To explain the need for and are speed tools; and
- To list common machinery used in modern kitchens.

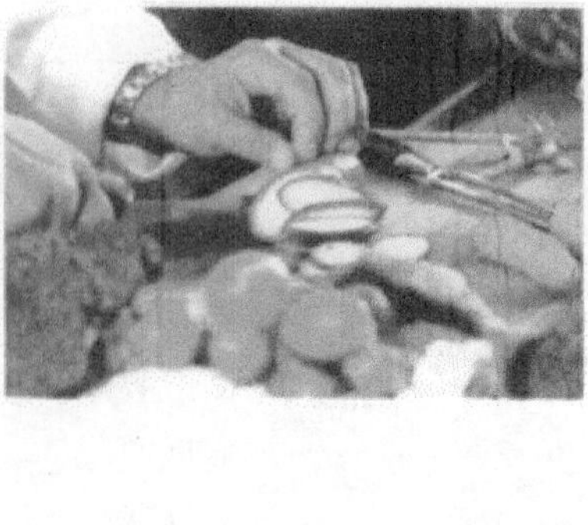

Previously, cooks had to be physically strong for all the lifting, pouring, straining, and cutting. Today, most of this work is done with mechanical help. Culinary procedures have been changed since the machinery has been improved. Some machinery has brought semi-trained people into the kitchens. As a result, the number of female cooks has increased.

Now a days, a cook by choosing certain foods and using modern machinery, can easily cook food for thousands persons in a few hours. To do this work only ten times as many man-hours were needed only a few years ago. It is unlikely that food service will be affected by automation as much as many other vocations. Emphasis must remain on the service part of the food industry. People are travelling and eating away from home in larger numbers. Eating establishments which give good service and good food for a proper price are the ones that have more customers each year.

A cook needs only a few manual skills and all of them are simple. Doing techniques are divided into block, such as flipping a pan, stirring in a pan, mixing in a bowl, and pouring liquids from one container to another, the lifting of pots and pans, moving them, using knives, forks, spatulas, whips, larding needle, or vegetable peelers. Turning over hot objects with the help of simple tools is another example of a doing technique. The trainee needs time and practice to master these skills safely and efficiently.

We have mechanical progress, but manual skills are still needed. It takes more time to use a machine and clean it again, than to cut certain foods by hand.

Knives remain the most important hand tools in kitchen and the cook must learn to master them effectively. Proper food cutting before cooking is of importance to the total preparation.

For faster communication at work skilled cooks and chefs use their own kitchen terms based on the French language. Although models have improved, the basic designs of kitchen machinery have remained the same for many years. Automation will not affect the cook's job security, if he has acquired skill, knowledge, and a service-minded attitude.

CUTTING TECHNIQUES

French Knife

There are different ways of cutting. Four styles of cutting are very famous, based on which, there are four basic knife groups. The tip of the chef's knife slides backward and forward on the board. During the forward movement, the knife is pressed down on the food to be cut. The other hand holds the food. The palm of the hand rests on the board, fingernails are in line with the knife blade, the fingers act likeavise to keep the stood in place.

French style

The first and most common method of cutting is with the chef's knife, also called a French knife. For this, the food is placed on a cutting board, held with one hand, and the knife is used with the other. The slicing motion of the knife and the correlated holding down and moving motion of the second hand need extensive practicing.

Paring knife

The second way of cutting is with the paring knife. The trimming (paring) is done in the air. The object to be trimmed is held in one hand, the knife used with the other. Peeling an apple is a good example.

Slicing

The third way of cutting is carving, which is visualized as cutting with a slicing motion. For cooked food, you may use variously shaped slicers either in a horizontal or a vertical way.

Seaming

The fourth way of cutting is the seaming of row meat. This is done with the same motions, except with steak knives or scimitar-shaped butcher knives. The boning knife is used to bone, separate, disjoint, and skin meat of fish ready for cooking.

The best way to learn these cutting skills is to watch several cutting demonstrations. Such demonstration are most important, and, with enough practice, learn to master this necessary skill.

When a new skill is to be learned, the trainee must basically concentrate on mastering the proper techniques and disregard speed completely. Many trainees, in their eagerness for speed, sacrifice quality for quantity. The employee is then never able to produce quality because be only learned fast, sloppy habits. If quality is stressed from the beginning, speed will come later.

OBJECTIVES

There are many important reasons for the cutting of food, such as

1. Raw meat is cut up for the separation of edibles from inedible, and for faster, better, and easier cooking.
2. Cooked food is cut for easier serving and eating.
3. Raw food is cut uniformly, so that in each lot each piece has the same shape and same size. This allows food, cooked in one batch, to be done at the same time.
4. The smaller raw food is cut, the shorter will be the cooking time.
5. Another reason for cutting food is that it can be placed in help to containers and molds for serving and storing.

Professional cooks use many names for cutting foods into various shapes. Exact cutting by hand of mechanical means is important and serves the following purposes:

(a) Mixed sizes of food to reduce to the same size and shape resulting in a shorter cooking time.
(b) Various shapes add to eye appeal and give the impression of variety.
(c) Eating and chewing is made easier by precutting.
(d) Cutting shortens cooking time.
(e) Less cooking time save vitamins, nutrients, flavour and working time.
(f) Cutting vegetables neatly and fast is the trademark of a good culinary craftsman.

Special terms help to identify the various shapes into which food is cut. Some terms vary with geographic locations. In general, one group includes :

(a) Slicing and shredding
(b) Cutting-slicing,
(c) Mincing, and
(d) Chopping.

Luxury cuisine uses mostly French terms of identification. It can be visualized best by a slice of bread, a slice of cheese, a slice of meat, or a sliced tomatoes.

(a) Shredding means the cutting of leaf vegetables into strips, such as shredded lettucc, cabbage, and so on. It is here that the French term of julienne is applied. Shredded cabbage would be translated as a julienne of cabbage. Culinary terminology in America refers to as julienne of ham, cheese, or vegatables, whenever a stick shape ranging from one inch to three inches in length and 1/6 to 1/8 inch in thickness is required.
(b) The words cubing and dicing are inter-changeable and used by personal preference. The size is referred to as 1/8. 1/4, or 1/2 inch cube or dice.
(c) Mincing or chopping are the terms used for a very small cube-like shape. Cooks also mince with a meat grinder or with a knife. It is similar to chopping.

(d) Chopping may also imply the use of a cleaver. Only bones are chopped with a cleaver. Edible foods are chopped with a knife. (Ref. Figure : 3.1A)

The science of culinary art uses many terminology. Many French terms describe certain shaped cuts. Some of these shapes and names are used for vegetables as in "mirepoix", "Fermer" and "Paysanne". Names like "Julienne" and "Brunoise" are applied to all foods cut into the particular shape.

Table 3.1A. Various Type of Cuts and Shape of Food

S.No.	*Term*		*Explanation*
1.	Julienne	:	A common way of cutting, but the sizes vary. Strips may range form 3/4 inch to 2 inches in length and form 1/16 to 1/8 inch in width. Julienne is a noodle shape.
2.	Brunoise (fine dice)	:	A fine cut, resembles mincing, consisting of tiny cubes of about 1/8 inch side length.
3.	Medium Cube (med. dice)	:	A cube, approx. 1/4 inch side length.
4.	Large Cube (large dice)	:	Same as above, but approx. 1/2 inch side length.
5.	Mirepoix	:	A larger, inexactly cubed cut of about one inch in length, applied as name to root vegetables.
6.	Fermier (farmers)	:	A slice, approx, 1/2 inch square and 1/16 to 1/8 inch thick.
7.	Paysanne (peasant)	:	*A triangular slice, 3/4 inch base and 1/16 to 1/8 inch thick.*

Cutting Turkey Breast Tenderloins

Turkey tenderloins may be cut from each breast half. They are located on the inside of each breast half next to the keel bone. The tenderloin is a long cylindrically shaped muscle that is easily removed from the rest of the breast meat. The tendon in the middle of the tenderloin should be removed before cooking. Pull on the end of the tendon while making swiping cuts along the meat attached to the length of the tendon.

(a)

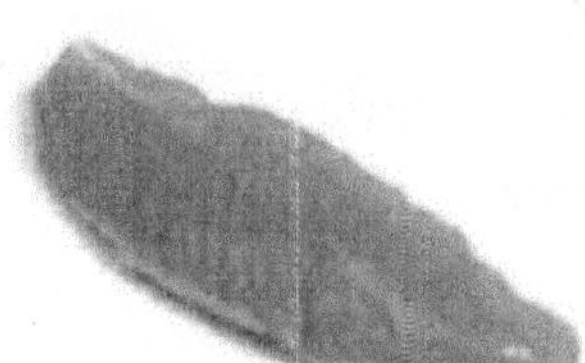

(b)

Back Meat

After removing the wings, legs, and breast, the remaining portion of the turkey carcass is the back. There is some meat and skin that can be removed, which can be ground or used in soups and casseroles.

(c)

After the choice bits have been removed, the bones and any remaining meat can be used for stock.

Cutting Up Vegetables

Cutting up food into uniform pieces is one of the most important skills to master in cooking. Once you learn to use an all-purpose chef's knife, it's easier than you think.

The chef's knife may be called as the original food processor. It can slice, mince, chop, crush, tenderize, and scoop up food. You can even use the end of the handle to grind spices. Complement it with a smaller paring knife for finer cutting and making garnishes, and you'll be ready for just about anything.

Chinese Chef's Knife

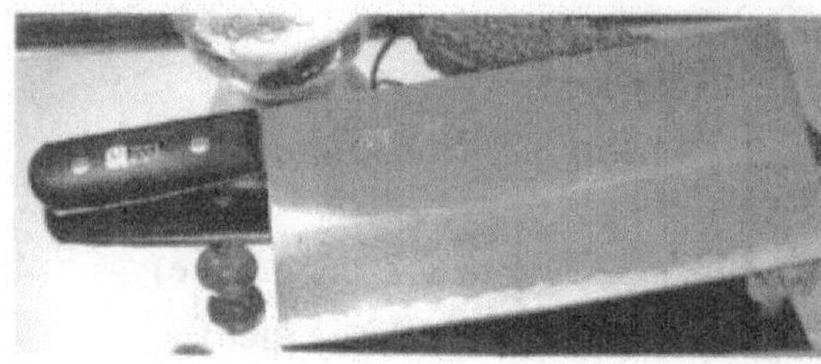
Chef's Knife

The lightweight, all-purpose chef's knife is sometimes called a cleaver and looks like a Western meat cleaver. It's a different tool altogether (and thus should never be used for hacking bones - for that you'll need a heavier one). A good Chinese chef's knife is well balanced, well constructed, and has a fine blade that holds an edge. Always remember that a sharp knife is a safer knife.

Traditional carbon steel Chinese chef's knives are available in Asian hardware stores. They are easy to sharpen, but they rust and will discolor acidic foods like onions and lemons. Ordinary inexpensive stainless steel, on the other hand, can dull quickly and is hard to sharpen. For years, I couldn't find a good, functional all-purpose Chinese kitchen knife. High-carbon stainless steel won't discolor food and keeps a fine, sharp edge.

In some high-quality chef's knifes, the end of the blade, extends all the way to the end of the handle and is held in place by three rivets. You can also find traditional knives with cylindrical wooden handles (which tend to loosen and crack over time). Test the balance of the knife and the comfort of the handle as you hold it. It should feel substantial, yet not so heavy that you have to be a bodybuilder to lift it.

Things you need for cutting vegetable are:

1. Vegetables
2. Sharp Chef's Knife, and
3. Cutting Bord.

Getting a Grip of a Knife

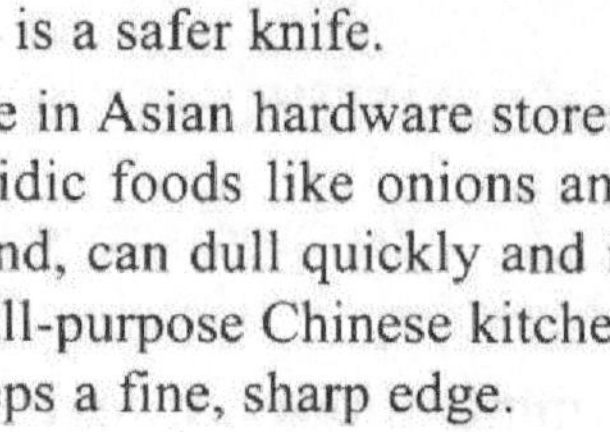
Getting a Grip of a Knife

You should hold the knife in your writing hand (the Chinese call this the "chopstick hand").

Move your hand all the way up the handle so that your thumb is on one side of the blade and your index finger on the other side. Curling your index finger slightly, grasp the blade firmly between your thumb and index finger.

This may feel a bit strange at first, but once you get used to it, you'll find that grasping the blade in this way gives you much more control than simply wrapping all your fingers around the handle.

Use your free hand to hold the food in place, curling your fingertips under.

Use the flat side of the blade alongside the first knuckles of your free hand, and as you slice or chop, slide your free hand along to guide the blade and keep it vertical.

To avoid cutting yourself, never uncurl the fingers of your free hand, and never raise the blade higher than the first knuckle.

The idea is to move your fingers, not remove them

Try not to wiggle the blade while cutting.

Use a firm downward and slightly forward motion.

Slicing

Holding the food and the chef knife firmly, cut straight down, using the knuckles of your free hand as a guide.

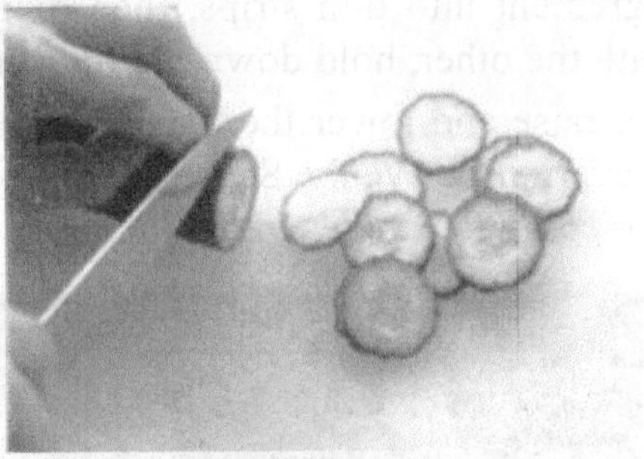

Slicing

Julienne and shredding

Stack a few slices.

Use the slicing technique, cutting straight down through the stack to create sticks.

For matchstick julienne, start with 1/8-inch slices, and cut them into 1/8-inch sticks.

To shred food into fine slivers, begin by cutting paper-thin slices, then cut across them in the same way to create thin strip.

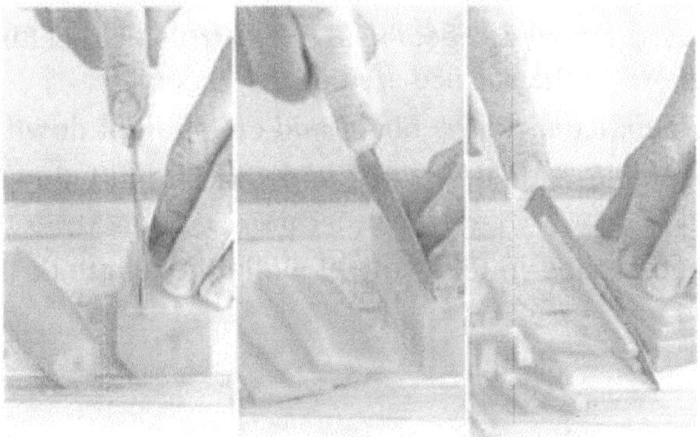

Julienne and shredding

Dicing

Line sticks up perpendicular to the blade, and slice straight down across them, creating cubes.

Dicing

Mincing

Start by cutting the ingredient into thin strips, then dice the strips. Hold the knife handle in one hand and, with the other, hold down the tip of the blunt edge of the blade.

Using the tip as a pivot, raise and lower the blade in a chopping motion, moving it from side to side to mince everything evenly. Scoop up minced ingredients occasionally, flip them over, and keep chopping to ensure even mincing.

Mincing

Roll-Cutting

This technique is used for long vegetables, like carrots or zucchini. It makes attractive chunks and exposes more of the surface area of the vegetable.

Hold the blade perpendicular to the board and cut straight down on the diagonal.

Then roll the vegetable a quarter-turn, and cut straight down again at the same diagonal angle.

Continue rolling and cutting in this way all along the length of the vegetable.

Roll-Cutting

Parallel Cutting

Used to cut broad, thin slices of meat or vegetables.

Lay the food close to the edge of the board with the fingers of your free hand flat on top of it.

Angle the chef's knife so that it's almost parallel to the board, slanting slightly downward.

Move it slowly and carefully back and forth to slice the food, paying close attention to avoid cutting your fingers.

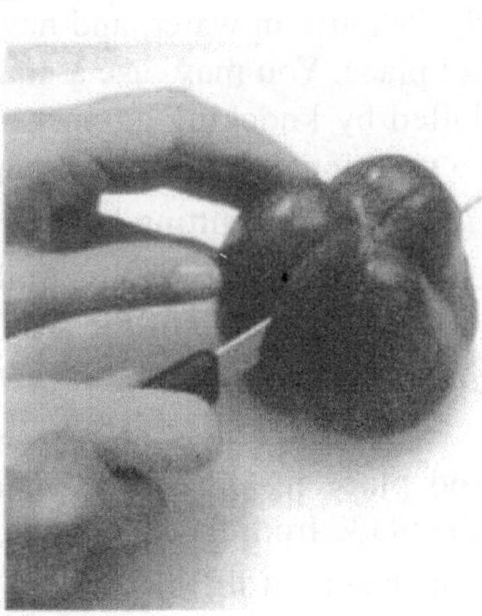

Parallel Cutting

Crushing

To crush ginger or garlic, place it near the edge of the cutting board, lay the knife blade flat over it with the blade facing away from you, and with the heel of your free hand, give the side of the blade a good whack, being careful to avoid the edge of the blade.

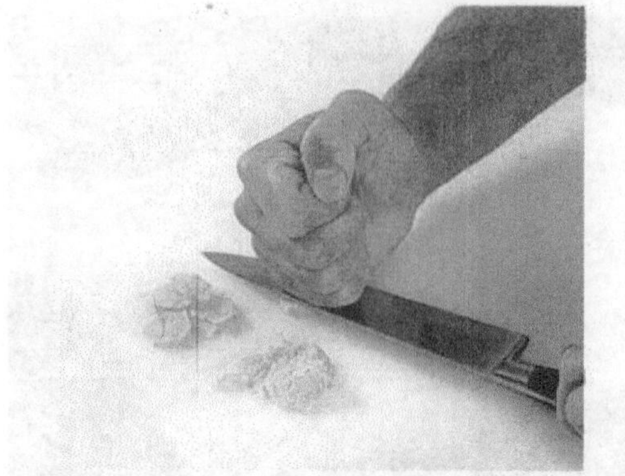

Crushing

Tenderizing

Use the blunt edge of the chef's knife to tenderize meat by pounding it in a crisscross pattern.

It's even more fun to get out your aggressions by turning the blade on its side and slapping the surface of the meat.

Care and Cleaning

Wash your chef's knife after each use in warm, soapy water and dry it well. To preserve its handle, never soak a chef's knife in water, and never put it in the dishwater. Store your knife in its own protected place. You may use a magnetic knife rack, not in a drawer where its edge might be dulled by knocking against other tools. To maintain a sharp edge, it is recommend using a traditional knife sharpening steel.

1. Hold the steel firmly, placing its tip on a cutting board.
2. Position the knife at a 20-degree angle to the steel with the blade facing down and the handle of the knife just below the handle of the steel.
3. Push the blade downward along the steel, pulling it toward you as you go, until you reach the steel's tip.
4. Move the blade back up and place its other side against the steel: repeat the sharpening action, moving the blade from the steel handle to its tip.
5. Repeat six to eight times on each side of the blade.

The Cutting Board

The cutting is your knife's partner and best friend. Whether you prefer one made of wood or plastic, the key is to use a board that's big enough to hold what you're chopping so things don't go flying all over the place.

To keep the board from sliding around, fold a damp kitchen towel in half and lay it under the board.

Avoid cutting on hard surfaces such as marble - this is bad for your knife.

There are a built-in butcher block surface could be used but I still like to place a smaller wood or plastic board over it to preserve its surface. These smaller boards are also easier to store and clean. That's especially important when you've been cutting meat, poultry, or fish. Some people like to reserve a separate board just for that purpose to avoid cross-contamination of other foods.

No matter what you're chopping, it's a good idea to scrub your cutting board with soap and hot water after each use and to clean it occasionally with a mild solution of bleach or baking soda and water. Vinegar or lemon juice can also be used to clean and deodorize a cutting board.

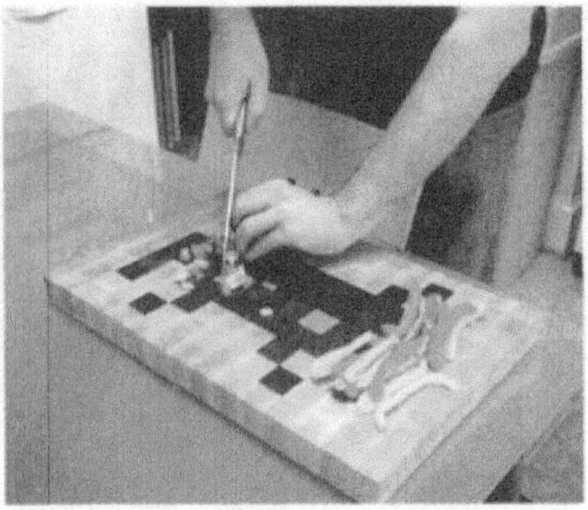

The Cutting Board

Dicing of vegetables

A diced vegetable is cut into small cubes. It's easy to dice quickly and evenly once you have the knack. Just think "slices, sticks, and cubes."

Vegetables

Diced vegetables

Step 1. Clean your cutting board and knife.

Step 2. Peel the skin from the vegetable, if necessary, and discard it.

Step 3. For round vegetables like carrots and potatoes, cut in half lengthwise and lay cut-side down on the cutting board. This will keep the vegetable from rolling.

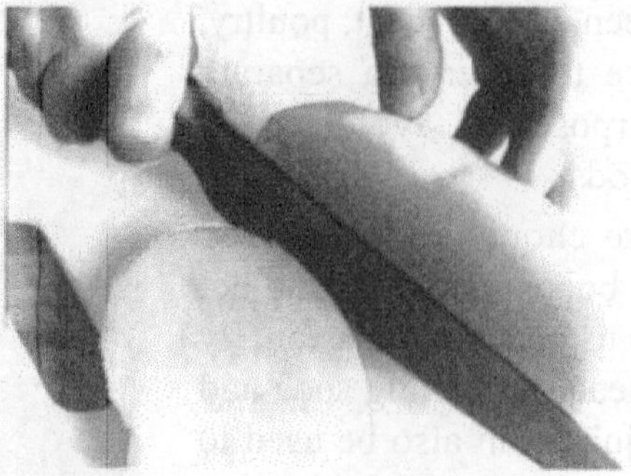

Step 4. Cut the vegetable lengthwise into even slices, then stack the slices and cut them into long sticks. (Long vegetables like celery and leeks need only be sliced into sticks.)

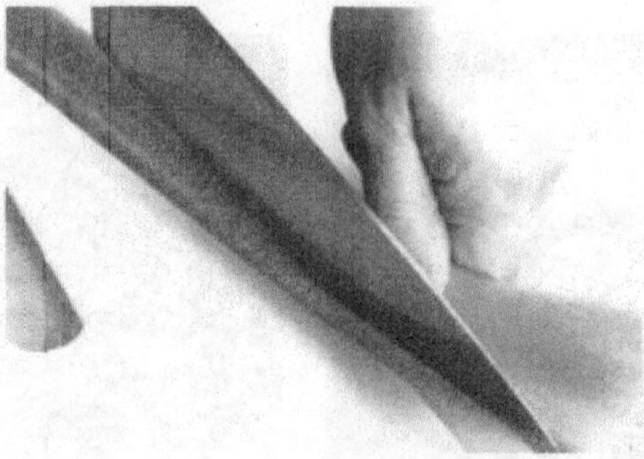

Step 5. Gather the sticks and cut them crosswise into cubes. Make sure to get the cubes as even as you can.

Step 6. To dice a tomato, cut it in quarters vertically, through the stem. It is not necessary to cut the stem out just yet.

Step 7. Cut away the inner pulpy part of each tomato quarter, cutting away the stem with it. Discard it or save for another use.

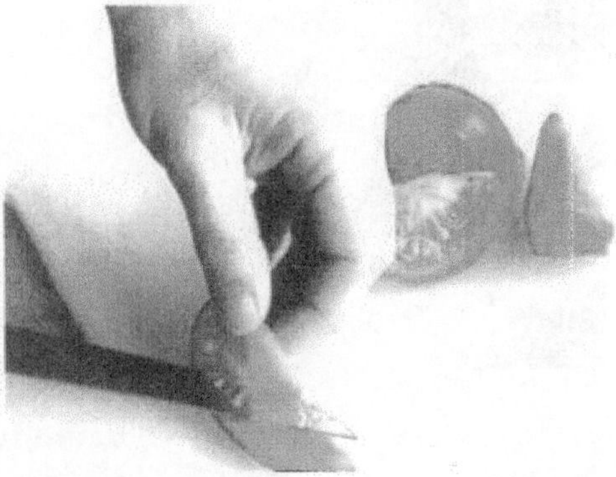

Step 8. Slice the remaining outer flesh into thin strips, then cut the strips crosswise into a dice.

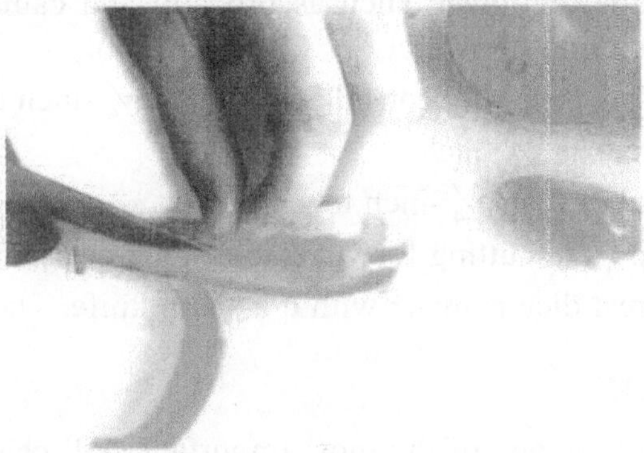

Step 9. To dice cucumber, peel the skin with a vegetable peeler and slice the cucumber in half lengthwise.

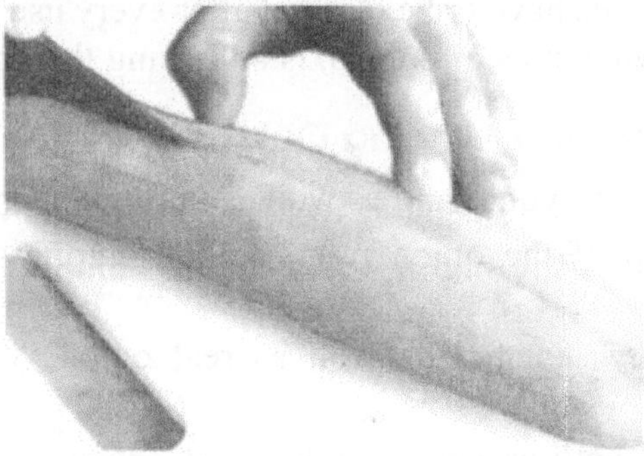

Step 10. Using a teaspoon, scrape the seeds and pulpy interior from each half.

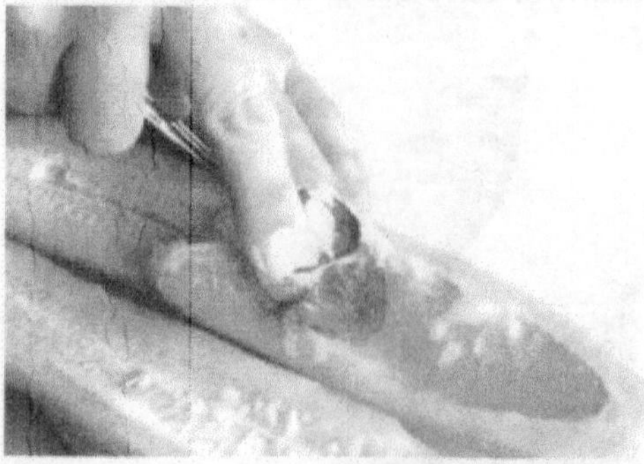

Tips for Dicing

1. The dicing technique will vary for specific vegetables.
2. You must always be aiming to get the vegetables, which you can easily cut, into cubes.
3. Vegetables made of flower, such as broccoli and cauliflower, are not typically dice, but broken into "flowerets".
4. A "small dice" is generally considered to be a $\frac{1}{4}$-inch cube.
5. A "medium dice" is $\frac{1}{2}$-inch.
6. A large dice is between $\frac{3}{4}$-inch to 1 inch.
7. Save any scrap from cutting for vegetable stock or use n other recipes.
8. The best, clearest dice is made with q a sharp knife. The sharer the better.

CUTTING OF ONIONS

1. Handling a knife is one of the most important skill characteristics a cook has to acquire.
2. Workmen are judged by the way they handle their tools and show their manual skill.
3. All mechanical aids have to be cleaned after every use therefore the fastest way of mincing small quantities of onions, is still using the knife.

Guideline for Cutting and Mincing Onions

1. Safety First : Cheek your hand as well as knife blade position constantly.
2. Realize that top of the onion refers to the onion's position while still in the ground.
3. Watch and study sketches as well as real onion. Visualize your steps before starting to cut.
4. Cut very slowly until process is understood, speed will come later.

Experimental Recipe 1.

Techniques of Cutting and Mincing of Onions

Equipment

1. Stainless steel cooking knife : 8 or 10 inch
2. Chopping board or chopping surface : One

Ingredient

3. Unpeeled onions.

Method

1. Prepare all required material.
2. Peel the onion.
3. Clean and Wash.
4. Cut the onion in half from top to bottom.
5. Align onion half on the board. Onion's bottom side to your left.
6. Use left hand to press onion to the board.
7. Apply first vertical cuts about one sixteenth of an inch apart a cross 2/3 of onion but leave the left end of the onion uncut.
8. Apply two parallel horizontal cuts of the same direction and depth as before. (If step-7 seems too complicated omit it until later)
9. Apply second vertical cuts above one sixteenth inch apart at zero degree angle to the first cut onions will fall apart by itself after this final cut has been applied.

Slice and Chop Onions

Step 1. To slice onions, cut off the root end, then peel away the skin. Slice in whole round slices and separate into rings, or else cut the onion in half first and then slice into half-moon shapes.

(a)

Step 2. To chop small (without a processor), leave the root intact, then peel away the skin from the top end. Now cut the onion in half and place each half on a flat surface, round side up. Next, make cuts vertically from the root end but leaving the root intact to hold it together.

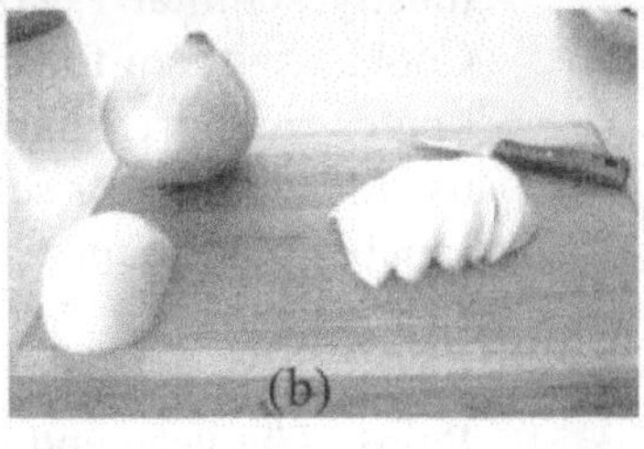

(b)

Step 3. Then make horizontal cuts across the vertical cuts whilst you hold on to the root end firmly. The last cut will be the little root bit, and this can be discarded.

Step 4. Rough chopping is as above, making about three cuts vertically across each onion and then three horizontally.

(c)

CHEF'S PERSONAL TOOLS

Kitchen knives are the most important hand wide of the cook. Every craftman's work performance depends greatly on the quantity of his tools. Cooks buy and use only high quality knives. Quality has its price, and good knives are expensive. Modern cooks use stainless steel knives. Carbon, steel knives oxidize when in contact with acid fruits or vegetables. Then they discolour, smell, and look unappetizing. Stainless steel knives last longer and are sharper than carbon steel knives of you part the edge of knife baled under a microscope you find that it will resemble a saw with irregular teeth. Therefore all cutting, regardless of the type of knife used, is done in a sawing-slicing motion; pressing a knife straight down will not cut properly at all.

Basic Knives

Basic knives for a kitchen fall into the following four groups:

1. **French Knife**

   The Chef or French Knife has a blade length from 6 to 14 inches. It is sharply pointed, and the height of the blade near the handle should be at least 1 1/2 inches. It is used in a swinging motion, with the point of the knife seldom leaving the board while cutting. The material to be cut lies on a smooth, flat, straight board or table top.

2. **Paring Knife :**

   The Paring Knife is a small knife with a blade length from 3 1/2 inches. It is also called a vegetable or fruit knife. The food cut with this knife is hand held.

3. **Slicing Knife :**

   The slicer is a straight and long knife with a blade from 10 to 16 inches. It can only be used in a sawing motion. The food which is cut has to be held in a secured position. Slicers are now available with serrated or fluted (Granton type) blades. They are selected by personal preference.

4. **Butcher Knife :**

   Butcher and boning knives come in various sizes for different uses. They are mostly scimitar (sword) shaped and are handled differently from other knives. Cooks use them for the cutting of raw meat or fish. They are also known as steak knives. A short, sharp, thin bladed, pointed knife from 5 to 6 1/2 inches long is used for boning or seaming of meat. They are called boning knives and may have flexible blades and safety handles.

A Kitchen Knife

1. **Point:** The very end of the knife, which is used for piercing.
2. **Tip:** The first third of the blade (approximately), which is used for small or delicate work. Also known as belly or curve when curved, as on a chief's knife.
3. **Edge:** The entire cutting surface of the knife, which extends from the point to the heel. The edge may be beveled or symmetric.
4. **Heel:** The rear part oft he blade, used for cutting activities that require more force.

5. **Spine:** The top, thicker portion of the blade, which adds weight and strength.
6. **Bolster:** The thick metal portion joining the handle and the blade, which adds weight and balance.
7. **Finger Guard:** The portion of the bolster that keeps the cook's hand from slipping onto the blade.
8. **Return:** The point where the heel meets the bolster.
9. **Tang:** The portion of the metal blade that extends into the handle, giving the knife stability and extra weight.
10. **Scales:** The two portions of handle material (wood, plastic, composite, etc.) that are attached to either side of the tang.
11. **Rivets:** The metal pins (usually 3) that hold the scales to the tang.
12. **Handle Guard:** The tip below the butt of the handle, which gives the knife a better grip and prevents slipping.
13. **Butt:** The terminal end of the handle. (Ref. Fig. 1.3A)

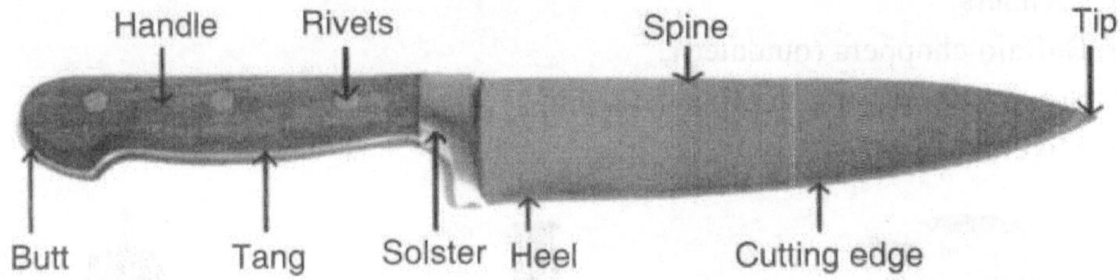

Fig. 1.3A Kitchen knife

Tools

The higher salaries of today are earned by a higher work output. This increased output is made possible by speeding up preparations (mostly cutting) and reducing cooking time.

There has been demand for speed tools which restated into better, faster meat slicers and vegetable cutters. Blenders are used for salad dressing and sauces, and the created work saver is the (Hobart) horizontal speed cutter, For example, the making of mayonnaise (homemade in many quality-conscious establishments) in a regular mixer

Trainees preparing Food

Trainees in the kitchen

would take half an hour of work. The same quantity of may analyze made in a speed cutter takes five minutes.

You may reduce the cooking time by the use of pressure steam equipment, new fryer models, and a new approach to cooking in general. Vegetable cooking times are cut in half, and tender meats of today make long stewing obsolete.

Use of Machines

There has been a technical progress all around. However, the machines used in food service, in spite of the general technical progress, have not changed as much as one might expect. The mechanical equipment of a kitchen consists of :

(a) Meat grinders (choppers)
(b) Meat chasers.
(c) Meat saws
(d) Meat tenderizers
(e) Meat patty molders
(f) Blenders
(g) Buffalo choppers (outdated),
(h) Speed or horizontal food cutters, and
(i) Mixers.

Food Mixer

Food Blender

Commercial Blender

More modern ovens include convection ovens, rotation ovens, and smoke ovens. Relatively new are automatic deep fryers, pressure deep fryers, pressure steamers, speedy steam kettles, and microwave ovens. In culinary art the automated equipment is only as good as the person being the machine.

The basic principles of food machinery have remained simple, with just the models changing from time to time. The machines are designed for the average worker and can be handled easily by reading the instruction manual. No special training is needed to use them. Keeping the machines clean after every use is the important thing for a Chef to keep in mind.

QUESTIONS AND DISCUSSIONS

Fill in the blanks

Q.1. Complete the following statements:

(a) The most common type of knife used for cutting vegetables is called a ....

(b) Thin, uniformly cut ham strips for a chef's salad are identified in French kitchen terminology as a ham................

(c) All knives should be used in a slicing type motion, because a magnified knife edge resembles a.............

(d) A trainee in the beginning, while cutting, should disregard speed and emphasize that he is able to produce..............

(e) Chances are good that well-trained cooks will not be affected by the progress of automation, provided the emphasis of their work is on...........

(f) Speed tools reduce general preparation time and increase worker's..........

[**Ans.:** (a) chef's knife and kitchen knife; (b) Juliene; (c) Saw with irregular teeth; (d) quality; (e) skilled knowledge and service minded attitude; (f) out put]

Multiple Choice Type

Q.2. Read each question carefully and select the best answer :

(i) The most suitable tool to peel oranges would be

(a) A potato peeler (b) A decorative pealer

(c) A paring knife (d) A short boning knife.

(ii) Shreddering cabbage for cole slaw means

(a) To quarter and wash a head of cabbage

(b) To cut cabbage into a julienne of cabbage

(c) To cut cabbage with a buffalo chopper

(d) To cut cabbage in to medium chunks.

(iii) The cutting of vegetables before cooking serves many purposes, but does not

(a) Reduce cooking time (b) Make them cook uniformly

(c) Preserve more vitamins (d) Make them easier to serve.

(iv) While cleaning a meat slicer one must make certain that

(a) Only cold water and a clean towel is used

(b) Stainless steel is unbreakable

(c) The electronic current is unplugged or disconnected

(d) Only a weak detergent solution is applied on the rotary blade.

(v) A Brunoise of celery for a chicken salad means

(a) To mince celery finely

(b) To cut celery into cubes approximately 1/8 of an inch long

(c) To cut root celery into 1/4 inch cubes

(d) To mince celery with the meat grinder.

(vi) The best expensive chef knives are made from stainless steel because
(a). Stainless steel can be sharpened fast
(b) Stainless steel is unbreakable
(c) Stainless steel is not-oxidant and rustproof
(d) Stainless steel outlasts carbon steel three times.

[**Ans** : (i) (c); (ii) (b); (iii) (c);
(iv) (c); (v) (b); (vi) (c)]

Matching Type

Q.3. On left the Table 'A' are listed food items to be cut or prepared. Match them with tools or machinery from given in the right Table 'B'

Table 'A'	*Table 'B'*
(a) French bread	(i) Straight regular slicer
(b) Oranges	(ii) Electric slicer
(c) Italian Salami	(iii) Serrated slicer
(d) Asparagus	(iv) Steak knife
(e) Shredded lettuce	(v) Boning knife
(f) Minced meat	(vi) Paring knife
(g) Disjointed chicken	(vii) Meat grinder
(h) Hot Roast Beef	(viii) Speed cutter
(i) Mayonnaise	(ix) Potato peeler
(j) Beef stew	(x) Chef's knife

[**Ans :** (a) (i); (b) (vi); (c) (ii); (d) (ix);
(e) (x); (f) (vii); (g) (v); (h) (iii);
(i) (viii); (j) (iv)]

Short Answer Type

Q.4. Explain various safety aspects in the use of hand tools and machinery.

Q.5. Explain the uses and benefits of tools and machinery.

Q.6. State the reasons for selecting, buying, and maintaining personal tools.

Q.7. Why is there a need for manual skills of terminology in the field of occupational work important ?

Q.8. Inspite the progress in shopphisticated kitchen machinery there is a need for manual skills in the kitchen. Explain by giving suitable example.

Q.9. Why should food be cut into comparatively uniform shapes ?

Q.10. 'Quality is more important than quantity in production by manual skill.' Explain this statement by giving suitable examples.

Q.11. Write notes on :

(a) Brunoise	(f) Julienne
(b) Fermier	(g) Paring
(c) Mirepoix	(h) Seaming
(d) Paysanne	(i) Zester
(e) Carving	

Descriptive Answer Type

Q.12. Name and briefly describe the various basic knife groups.

Q.13. List the main reasons for cutting food.

Q.14. Explain the need for speed tools.

Q.15. List and explain the use of ten common machines used in a modern kitchens.

Assignments/Activity Type

Q.16. Demonstrate safe knife handling.

Q.17. Demonstrate and practice :

(a) Shredding using chef's knife.

(b) Peeling and carving fruits using paring knife.

(c) Peeling (potatoes, squash, asparagus, etc.) with vegetable peeler.

(d) Slicing (French bread with serrated slicer, cold cuts with straight blade, etc.).

(e) Parsley chopping with chef's knife.

(f) The cutting of various vegetable shapes: julienne, fine slice, small dice, medium dice, large dice.

(g) The seaming and cutting of meat for stew with the butcher knife.

(h) Practice the doing and disjointing of a chicken with the doing knife.

(i) Onion mincing the professional way.

1.4

Sanitation and Safety

CHAPTER OBJECTIVES

After studying this lesson you should be able :

- To explain the importance of sanitation to food and beverages service;
- To identify causes of bacterial contamination;
- To name the processes used to keep food safe;
- To explain uses and importance of food warmers and hazards;
- To point out the dangers of a commercial kitchen; and
- To list rules for preventing accidents in food and beverages establishments.

Sanitation and safety awareness are importants part of a trainees's daily routine. Cleanliness and personal hygiene help to safeguard the health of customers and coworkers. Since kitchen conditions are conducive to bacterial growth, there is a need for constant preventive cleaning. The awareness of sanitation and safety must start at the moment the cook arrives at this station and continues until the end of the work shift. Sanitation and safety are related and must be integrated into the work of every day.

One of the main objectives of sanitation practice is to prevent health hazards to customers. Safety is practiced to avoid injuries, not only to oneself but also to workers and customers as well. Accidents can be definitely minimized, when workers act and behave in a mature manner. Accident proneness is a state of mind.

The observation of rules, the learning of regulations, and the use of common sense are the best ways to avoid accidents. A food service tranee has to accept sanitation and safety. Sanitation is a safeguard to health. Safety is the awareness of avoiding all mechanical-physical perils to which food service employees are constantly exposed.

Sanitation is applied cleanliness to all the chores of a kitchen. Sanitizing raw food, cooked food, utensils, dishes, areas, and humans also means cleaning, washing, cooking, pasteurizing, sterilizing, and refrigerating. Sanitary, originally a Latin word, is used to assert that everything related to the health of a living being is handled in a safe way. A sanitarian is an officer of a local of municipal health department who is charged with supervising all health rules and regulations. For example, the rule of no smoking in kitchens should be supervised by the local health department.

The practice of sanitation together with common sense will make a food and beverage service establishment safe for its customers. Dirty dishes, rest rooms, work stations, pantries, hand tools, doorknobs, and human beings are the transmitters of micro-organisms, also called bacteria.

The importance of the dish washing operation is stressed. The pasteurization at 140°F. and sterilization at 212°F. of food are some of the safeguards.

The use of refregeration prevents short time spoilage, but may allow food contamination, if storage is extended. A knowledge of the kitchen temperature tables is essential for every cook.

Bacteria, or micro-organisms, are found everywhere except in a medically sterile environment. They are not visible to the naked eye, but you can be seen them through a microscope. Some bacteria are harmless. Some are helpful (yeast), and some are dangerous. Food areas are ideal places for bacteria to multiply. Bacteria need food, warmth, and moisture. If conditions are right, these microbes grow at a very taste rate and can reach the point of danger quickly. In a public food establishments, there are many people who may have come into combine with possible contaminations. Then by becoming infected themselves, they could continue this dangerous circle endlessly.

PERSONAL HYGIENE

The first area of concern in cooking is personal hygiene. Generally a good service worker coming from home can be carrying harmful bacteria to his work. This could lead a vicious circle of infections. Therefore some important personal hygiene habits have to be observed. A bath and clean garments especially under-garments, are a must for every day. A clean shave for men, with short cut and clean hair, or a hairnet for long haired persons are also very important. Trimmed, clean finger nails and clean hands are another must. Washing of one's hands every time after switching from one working process to the next or when the rest room is used is a habit to be formed by you. Strictly observing, no smoking rule on the job is one rule which is also helpful to the worker. The wearing of a clean uniform goes without saying, and in some instances, aprons have to be changed twice per shift. More specific rules of the place of employment can be added to this.

Following personal grooming guidelines be observed :-

1. Wear clean clothes going to shift and clean uniform on shift.
2. Never appear unkept or unshaven at work.
3. Cover long hair with hairnet, apply only a little make-up.
4. Keep fingernails short and clean.
5. Avoid body odours, bad breath, and too much perfume.
6. Do not overdress, especially when a uniform is not required.
7. Change under-garments frequently.
8. See doctor immediately at signs of illness.

Preventive Cleaning Process

You will understand there exist different standards of cleanliness. Two persons cleaning identical objects may not achieve the same level of cleanliness. Food service workers must accept guidance and supervision by their superiors and follow exactly all rules and regulations. Mostly dirt might not be visible. It does not imply that looking clean means to be clean all the way. Preventive sanitation includes the systematic scheduled cleaning of all facilities, tools, and equipment in operation.

Dishwashing is one of the important cleaning processes. In this process water, chemicals, and heat are combined to sanitize table wares before they are used again. If this is not done properly, cross contamination from one customer to another could occur. The actual cleaning comes from the dishwashing compound combined with the mechanical action of pressure spraying the warm water. The tableware is clean, but the detergent may have left a harmful residue. To wash this residue off, a final waterspray of not less than 180° F. is required. Cooler water might bring new bacteria from the outside to the clean dishes. The dishwashing room is an important part of all food service establishments.

The pot-washing area is essential, too. If an improperly cleaned container is used to store cooked food, contamination could ultimately occur. Cooks do not usually wash pots, but sometimes they have to clean a needed utensil. This is one example of why it is necessary for trainee to understand every work level of a food service establishment.

Sterilization Process

Sterilization means making ineffective or killing most micro-organisms. Exposure to sufficient heat helps to kill bacteria. The length of time and amount of heat necessary vary for different organisms. The heating of liquids, like milk, juices, beer, wine, etc. to 140° F. for thirty minutes is called pasteurization; it is effectively used in food manufacturing plants. Most food establishments lack the time to use this process. Many of them sterilize by using boiling water. When boiling starts, it is certain that water has reached a temperature of 212°F. A few minutes of exposure to this heat will make everything safe and sterile. This explains the reason for reaching the boiling points whenever cooked food is prepared or reheated.

SERVICE-READY FOOD

Food warmers are pieces of equipment called bain-maries (French for steam table). Some examples are thermometes, quartz, lamps, heated compartments, and dry heat servers. The purpose of these equipment is to keep pre-cooked food service-ready at a minimum temperature of 140°F. At the same time, food must be prevented from drying out and shrinking, or from becoming watery, overcooked, and mushy.

The guidelines to this service-readiness help you in understanding of minimum acceptable food quality. Then, you may establish maximum time spans for keeping food hot. An important guideline to observe is that food warmers must not be used to warm up any precooked food, refrigerated from a previous day. All foods have to be cooked or reheated to the sterilization point before they can be placed in the food warmer. (Ref. Table 1.4A)

Table 1.4A. Temperatures in The Kitchen (in degree Fahrenheit

S.No.	*Activity*	*Required Temperature*
1.	Water boils at sea level, sterilization of bacteria after short exposure	212°F
2.	Starches coagulate (cook)	205°F
3.	Simmering of water.	195°–185° F.
4.	Sterilizing rinse spray of dishwasher	180°F.
5.	Egg and meat proteins coagulate (cook).	170°–150° F.
6.	Keeping food "service-ready" in food warmer	150°–140°F.
7.	Pasteurization begins, time span of exposure thirty minutes	140° F
8.	Danger zones for fast bacteria multiplication.	140°–70°F.
9.	Normal kitchen temperature range in which becterise will slowly multiply under right conditions	70°–50°F.
10.	Vegetable and fruit refrigeration.	45°–40°F.
11.	Meat, dairy and cooked food refrigeration.	40°–34°F.
12.	Melting of ice.	33°F.
13.	Freezing of water.	32°F
14.	Deep freezer storage.	+ 10°F, –0°F–10°F.

The heat span from 70°F - 140°F is a dangerous one for foods in a kitchen. Bacteria multiply fast in this temperature range. Pasteurization uses 140°F. of heat for thirty consecutive minutes to sterilize food without destroying too many vitamins and nutrients. At 130°F., many bacteria, such as salmonella, still multiply. If food from the refrigerator (average temperature 45°f.) is put into a 140°F. warmer, it will take long hours before it becomes pasteurized. During this slow warm-up, food could spoil and cause food poisoning when served.

REFRIGERATION

You may store cooked or perishable raw foods in temperatures ranging from 34°F-45°F. They are then called refrigerated. Walk-in refrigerators are room-like areas of various sizes with shelves. Reach-in refrigerators resemble boxes with doors or drawers. The air in these refrigerated units is circulated (moved by fan); cooled, and also humidity controlled. Moisture encourages bacterial growth, but in dry air this growth is retarded. On the other hand, dry air will dehydrate stored food faster. To prevent this, different humidity ranges are kept. Fruits and vegetables need more moisture than meat. Dairy products need the least moisture.

Sanitary refrigeration is essential to food service. You must always cover containers. All stored goods must be at least six inches from the floor. Special meat units may have additional antibacterial blue light. Thermometers to check the temperature range may be installed so that they can be read from the outside. Thermostats may be used to maintain an even temperature.

Most walk-in units are powerful enough to hold even hot foods and refrigerate them quickly. Older units may break—down when they are overloaded with too much hot food.

Walk-in refrigerators must have safeguards to prevent a person's being locked in them by accident.

Deep freezers are also common in used. They are similar to refrigerators except that their cooling temperature ranges from -20° F. to + 20°F to keep food forezen solid.

All the rules and quickness valid for refrigerators also apply to deep frezers. For refrigeration 'Do's' and Dont's, are given below :

Do's and Don'ts for use of Refrigeration

1. Check and be familiar with all safety devices of the cooler
2. Keep door closed at all times
3. Do *not* impair flow of cool air through stored objects
4. Do not store food directly on the floor
5. Change open canned food to a different container before it is refrigerated
6. Use clear plastic wrap to cover container
7. Do *not* store liquids in containers above eye level
8. Clean up any spilled food or water immediately.

Food service workers carry great responsibilities. Carelessness results in the food poisoning of people. The public has a right to be protected. Food service workers should take pride that they are competent.

Precautions

Kitchens, have mechanical and physical perils to which workers are exposed. The most common areas of danger are as under :

1. Hazards such as colliding with other persons or objects, and slipping over spilled liquids, vegetable peels, oil spots
2. Electric-mechanical equipment with the danger of shocks caused by short circuits.
3. Personal hand tools, such as knives, cleavers, forks, and needles.
4. The handling of boiling liquids, such as sauces, stocks, or hot fat. This demands know-how, a sure grip, and often physical strength.
5. Heat sources such as ovens, ranges, griddles, steamers, deep-fries, and broilers which may cause painful burns. In many cases, carelessness with one of these is the reason for the burning down of a whole establishment.
6. Walk-in refrigerators and walk-in deep freezers. Frequent exposure to low temperature may cause damage to a worker's health. Accidental locking into a deep freezer could become fatal.

Nobody wants accidents, but they do happen. Statistics show that the majority of all accidents are caused by carelessness. An employee, either ignorant or thoughtless, may fail in observing his responsibilities. The accident-prone employee is easily found. He is a person not interested in his job. He might despise work, have a chip on his shoulder, or might lead a troubled life. For whatever reasons an employee is not attentive on the job, no excuses exist. Work is an exchange action. A person does his job in order to get paid.

In exchange, he earns money. Decent pay can only be expected for work done to a given standard. If standards of responsibility are achieved, accidents will be reduced. By realizing that accidents are caused by carelessness, workers can avoid them.

USE OF COMMON SENSE PREVENTS ACCIDENTS

Common sense means the making of intelligent decision in situation not expected or foreseen. It means to relate a previous experience to a new situation. Some causes of accidents which could be avoided by using common sense are given below :

1. Playfulness, horseplay, and practical jokes.
2. Using defective, unsafe equipment which is not reported immediately and not repaired.
3. Handling hot cooking utensils without proper protection for hands.
4. Using a meat grinder without a stomper.
5. Cleaning electrical equipment which is not disconnected.
6. Failing to replace safeguards after cleaning of food machinery.
7. Knives carried incorrectly with their blades pointing up.
8. Trying to catch knives falling down from a table.
9. Lifting heavy objects without a good footing.
10. Spilled liquids which are not wiped up immediately.
11. Trying to extinguish grease fires without a CO_2 fire extinguisher.
12. Tasting food in the mixer while the machine is still in use.
13. Lighting a gas oven and forgetting to keep the door half open until all burners are on.
14. Leaving utensils on floors.
15. Handling new equipment without learning instructions first.

QUESTIONS AND DISCUSSIONS

Fill in the Blanks

Q.1. Complete the following statements :

(a) An integrated part of personal grooming is personal ....

(b) Most accidents are the result of someone's ....

(c) The final rinse of a dishwasher must have a minimum temperature of ....

(d) Preventive sanitation calls for cleaning and sterilizing in a method that is called...............

(e) Strict obeservation of rules is the best accident prevention method next to the use of................

(f) A chef's daily work must always include safety awareness and ....

(g) Preventive cleanliness is imperative to food sanitation, because kitchens are conducive to bacterial ....

(h) In kitchens serving the public, it is not legal to ....

(i) Bacteria multiply fastest when they have food, warmth, and ....

(j) Bacteria which are everywhere, except in a sterile environment, can only be seen with a ....

[**Ans.** : (a) hygiene; (b) carelessness; (c) 18°F;
(d) sanitizer; (e) common sense; (f) safety;
(g) growth; (h) avoid rules and regulation of sanitation
(i) moisture; (j) microscope.]

Multiple Choice Type

Q. 2. Read each question carefully and select the *best* answer:

(i) Cooks sterilize most food they prepare through
(a) Refrigeration (b) Pasteurization
(c) Salting (d) Boiling.

(ii) Food warmers are needed because
(a) Serving time exceeds the period in which food stays warm by itself
(b) They are a good way to warm up leftover food
(c) Restaurant patrons like to be served hot food
(d) They reduce labour costs.

(iii) Good refrigeration retards food spoilage, because
(a) Bacteria cannot multiply fast without warmth
(b) It deprives bacteria of food
(c) It kills bacteria completely
(d) It prevents contamination of food.

(iv) Pasteurization is a sterilization process at a temperature of
(a) 100° Fahrenheit (b) 120° Fahrenheit
(c) 140° Fahrenheit (d) 160° Fahrenheit.

(v) A falling knife should not be
(a) Used without researching it first
(b) Picked up, unless one knows the owner
(c) Caught in the air while falling
(d) Used without pasteurizing it first.

(vi) When water starts to boil, it has reached a temperature of
(a) 208° Fahrenheit
(b) 212° Fahrenheit
(c) 216° Fahrenheit

[**Ans.**: (i) (d); (ii) (c); (iii) (a);
(iv) (c); (v) (c); (vi) (b)]

Matching Type

Q.3. Match the degrees of temperature in the Table 'B' into the corresponding areas in Table 'A'.

Table 'A'	*Table 'B'*
(a) Freezing point of water	(i) 205°F.
(b) Boiling point of water	(ii) 185°F. – 195°F.
(c) Pasteurization for 30 minutes	(iii) 180°F.
(d) Meat, dairy storage	(iv) 212°F.
(e) Vegetable and fruit storage	(v) 140°F. – 150°F.
(f) Final spray of dishwashing machine	(vi) 140°F.
(g) Cooking (Coagulation) of starches	(vii) 70°F. – 140°F.
(h) Safe food warmer range	(viii) 40°F – 45°F.
(i) Fast bacteria multiplication range	(ix) 34°F. – 40°F.
(j) Simmering range of water	(x) 32°F.

[**Ans.:** (a) (x); (b) (iv); (c) (vi); (d) (ix);
(e) (viii); (f) (iii); (g) (i); (h) (v);
(i) (vii); (j) (ii)]

Short Answer Type

Q.4. Explain the importance personal grooming and hygiene in cooking.

Q.5. State and enlist 10 rules to be observed for preventing accidents.

Q.6. Name and describe 5 dangers in a commercial kitchen.

Q.7. Explain the uses and importances of food warmers and the hazards of their use. Name some instance where a food warmer should not be used.

Q.8. Name and describe the processes used to keep food safe.

Q.9. Explain the important sanitation in every working level.

Q.10. How will you avoid bacterial growth? What process will you adopt for to avoid bacteria growth?

Q.11. Explain the importance of personal grooming.

Q.12. Should a preventive cleaning schedule be supervised ?

Q.13. Do cooks practice sterilization of food ?

Q.14. Are food warmers an asset or a liability ?

Q.15. Are kitchens more danger as today than yesterday ?

Q.16. Are there really accident-prone person ?

Q.17. What is commonsens ?

Q.18. How can accidents be prevented ?

Q.19. Write notes on:

(a) Hygiene

(b) Safety

(c) Sanitation
(d) Sterilization.

Assignments/Activity Type

Q.20. Keep a table of statistics indicating daily how many days have passed without accidents in your establishment.

Q.21. Draw the following:

(a) A plan (blueprint) of a residential school's walk-in refrigeration unit and try to improve the layout.

(b) Design of a posters and invent slogans in regard to dangers in the kitchen.

Q.22. Observe a set-up food plate in a food warmer for different time spans. Then discuss the observations.

Q.23. Use yeast in an experiment as an example of how fast food bacteria multiply.

Q.24. Inspect kitchen machinery for cleanliness.

PART - II

FOOD PREPARATION

This Page has been intentionally left blank

2.1

Vegetables and Fruits

CHAPTER OBJECTIVES

After studying this lesson you should be able :

- To describe the different varieties of vegetables, and fruits;
- To explain the importance and process of cleaning of vegetables before storage; and
- To explain produce storage procedures of a commercial kitchen.

Mostly a meat or fish dish is made at least with some vegetables as part of the preparation. The common vegetables used in cooking are seldom marked on the menus or seen on the plates of food served. These vegetables require handling, storage, cleaning, and often more care than meat or fish.

You must also be fully aware of the looks of good and fresh produce. It is the chef's duty to receive and check the ordered supplies. Received deliveries be placed under refrigeration as soon as possible to prevent unnecessary loss of quality. Some vegetables need to be pre-cleaned before storage to save space in the refrigerator and help keep it clean. Proper storage retains food value, which is the ultimate reason for cooking. Fruits, which are handled like vegetables generally come from the same supplier. Frozen vegetable and fruits are gaining more popularity, not for its better taste, but for the convenience of needing less labour. Management must make the decision between cooking for their own convenience or for producing a variety of quality food for the public.

Vegetable suppliers to commercial kitchens are called vegetable and fruits dealers. Their stock consists of fresh or frozen vegetables and fruits, eggs, and sometimes synthetic non-dairy cream products. Like meat suppliers, they are semi -whole salers and use special terms for the ordering of their goods. This packaging information is essential to the chef for meeting his food costs. (Ref. Table 2.1A)

Tomatoes

In most of the countries price for tomatoes is quoted per *lug* (box). A lug is a flat wooden crate

Table 2.1A. Fresh Vegetables

S.No.	Name	Packing Size	Quantity
1.	Artichokes	Carton	Count #18 to #36
2.	Asparagus	Crate	30 ib.½ 15 lb., gross, medium, large, jumbo
3.	Avocados	Flat	Count #12 to #18
4.	Beans, green	Carton	Loose, 30 lb.
5.	Brussels Sprouts	Carton	Loose, 30 lb.
6.	Broccoli	Carton	24/1 lb. Bunches
7.	Cabbage, red	Carton	Loose, 40 lb.
8.	Cabbage, white	Carton or sack	40 lb.
9.	Carrots	Sack	25 lb., 50 lb., 100 lb.
10.	Cauliflower	Crate	Count 12, 16, 18, 24
11.	Celery	Crate	24 stalks, (bunches)
12.	Chard	Carton	24 bunches, of about 1 ib. each
13.	Chives	Bunch	12 bunches =1 bundle
14.	Eggplants	Crate	30 lb. loose
15.	Garlic	Bag	5 lb. - lb. loose
16.	Leeks	Bunch	24 bunches in 1 carton
17.	Lettuce	Carton	24 heads
18.	Mint	Bunch	12 bunches = 1 bundle
19.	Mushrooms	Basket	2½ lb. per basket; 12 baskets = 1 carton 30 lb.
20.	Okra	Loose	....
21.	Onions	Sacks	50 lb., 100 lb., med., large, jumbo
22.	Parsley	Bunch	12 bunches = 1 bundle
23.	Parsnips	Sacks	25 lb., 50 lb.
24.	Pearl onions	Bag	5 lb.
25.	Potatoes, Russet	Sack	100 lb. graded 8 to 10 ounces
26.	Potatoes, Russet	Carton	50 lb. graded - 4/6, 6/8, 8/10, 10/12 oz.,
27.	Potatoes, Field	Sack	100 lb. ....
28.	Potatoes, Salad	Carton	50 lb. ....
29.	Radishes	Bunch	12 bunches = 1 bundle
30.	Romaine	Crate	24 heads
31.	Scallions	Bunch	12 bunches = 1 bundle
32.	Shallots	Bag	5 lb., 10 lb.
33.	Spinach	Bunch	24 bunches to 1 carton
34.	Squash, summer	Carton	30 lb. loose
35.	Squash, yellow	Per lb.	Loose
36.	Squash, zucchini	Lug	30 lb., loose
37.	Tomatoes	Lug	Sized, layers, 5/4 largest – 6/8
38.	Turnips	Per Ib.	Loose
39.	Watercress	Buck	12 bunches = 1 bundle.

holding a standard weight quantity of tomatoes. A lug, market "5/5", contains 5 rows of tomatoes each way, a total of 25 tomatoes in one layer. Tomatoes of this size need two layers to fill a lug, or a total of 50 tomatoes. The label "6/7" means 42 tomatoes per layer. Since they are smaller, 3 layers are needed to fill one lug. This makes a total of 126 tomatoes per layer. Since they are smaller, 3 layers are needed to fill one lug. This makes a total of 126 tomatoes, as compared to 50 tomatoes of the same weight, for the same price. Obviously, there is a big difference in portion size and cost. The largest tomatoes available are "5/4", and the smallest are "7/8". A few other produce items, such as peaches and pears, are packed in the same way.

Packaging is standard because vegetable and fruits are from the same commercial growing areas and are sent nationwide. At the height of the season these may be packed loose, especially for immediate local use. This means it will be uncounted, of different sizes, and all in the same box. The box has the same weight as the standard lug. Loose packed items are cheaper in price, but not always cheaper in yield. Odd sizes do not allow portion control and loose packaging damages the content.

A number marked on the packed box shows the individual size of the content. The lower number indicates the larger size of the fruit or vegetable inside, while the upper number stands for the smaller size.

Onions

Onions are available in various colours such as yellow, white, or red. Basically these are the same, with just a minor taste difference in sweetness or sharpness. They are packed in 50– or 100- pound sacks, graded as medium, large, and jumbo sizes. Green onions, are sold in benches (12 bunches equals 1 bundle). Shallots and pearl onions, which are small boiling onions, are supplied in 5-pound bags. Storage should be in a cool, dry place to prevent sprouting. Only leeks and green onions need washing. All others are peeled dry, often in advance and kept in clear plastic wrap, under refrigeration, until needed.

Garlic

A special flavour- giving vegetable garlic has a heavy smell much like onions or shallots. It is sold loose the pound by but otherwise handled like onions.

Potatoes

Potatoes are supposed to be of American origin, and were introduced to the rest of the world by Sir Walter Raleigh. These are now the staple starch of the world. Baking potatoes are of a late crop, large and oval in shape. Their skin is rough and in USA they are called "russets" or "American 1". They are of the Idaho type and considered the best potato in the world. They are size-graded from 6 to 12 ounces and are available in 50-pound boxes or 100-pound sacks. They are also available at a cheaper price as irregular #1 or #2 "fieldgrade" (bruised).

Boiling or salad potatoes are new of first crop potatoes and have a smooth skin and irregular shape. They are mostly of the "White Rose" or "Red Rose" variety and are packed in 50-pound boxes.

Root Vegetables

The most common root vegetables are carrots, parsnips, celery roots, turnips, radishes, and beets. They all need cool, humidity-controlled storage. They are packed in sacks or boxes from 25 to 100 pounds. Radishes and beets, with the greens still on, come in bunches.

Mushrooms

The cultured fresh mushrooms sold in the USA are called "Champignon" and are considered essential by most chefs. Mushrooms are quite expensive. They are grown on mushroom farms and are often distributed by them directly. The smallest packed unit is a 2½-pound open cardboard basket. Fresh mushrooms are moist, heavy, and snow white, with a typical raw mushroom smell. When they are only a few days old they lose the good appearance and flavour. Their storage is difficult because the right humidity range is so important. Many Chefs precook mushrooms as soon as they are delivered because they keep better when cooked.

Artichokes

Artichokes are packed in cardboard boxes, with the number showing their size. Number 18 is one of the largest, and 36 is one of the smallest graded artichokes. The very small artichoke hearts are sold by the pound, loose or in boxes.

Asparagus

Asparagus is packed in special conical crates to protect the tips. They weigh 30 pounds. The asparagus thickness is shown on the crate by the imprint of "grass" (the thinnest), medium, large, or jumbo. A cheaper second grade with crooked stems is called *crooks*.

White asparagus

Warm green asparagus Hollandaise sauce and Maltese sauce

Cauliflower

Cauliflower comes in crates by head count. The lowest number is the largest size.

Broccoli

Broccoli is tied into bunches of about 1 pound each. Usually 2 dozen are in a crate. All vegetable packing falls into the same pattern. As soon as you understand how the most commonly used products are handled, you will become familiar with the rest in a short time. The basic packing information given in table will help the young cook to understand vegetable ordering.

Lettuce

Generally, Romaine lettuce should be packed with 24 heads in one large wooden crate. This lettuce has many soiled unusable outer leaves. For better storage and space-

EXPERIENTIAL RECIPE 2.

Cleaning and Washing Romance Lettuce

Equipment

1. Double vegetable sink
2. Garbage disposal unit
3. Running water
4. Paring knife
5. Colanders
6. Storage containers.

Ingredients : Romance Lettuce

Romance Lettuce

Method

1. Prepare-all required ingredients.
2. Stop up sink without disposal. Fill with cool water.
3. Open wooden crate carefully (watch for sticking out nails).
4. Remove heads of lettuce from crate, one by one, and cut of the end of the stem.
5. Remove loose, bruised or bad looking outer leaves and throw them into disposal.
6. Put trimmed head into first sink, now filled with water.
7. Repeat this with other heads of lettuce until all are soaked.
8. Clean up other sink, run all the refuse through garbage disposal.
9. While lettuce is still in deep water, take each head into one hand, holding stems with three or four fingers.
10. Move lettuce rapidly up and down in the water for quite a few seconds (10-15 times) to loosen dirt.
11. Check each head by inspection. If clean, lift it cut of the water, shake out and put into cleaned other ship for drainage.
12. Drain water of first sink and clean it. Notice residue of sand and dirt accumulated at bottom of sink.
13. Fill first sink with clean cool water again.
14. Repeat steps 6, 8, 9, 10
15. Check heads again, lift out of water, shake out and put on colanders for better drainage.
16. Transfer to nonoxidizing container, cover with plastic wrap or wet towel, place cooler.

use, lettuce is prewashed and stored in nonoxidizing (non-rusting) containers, under refregitation. Iceberg, Boston, Butter, Limestone, Endive, and other types of lettuce are packed in cardboard boxes and should be handled the same way.

Precleaning of bulky leaf vegetables saves space and helps to keep the *reefer* (short for refrigerator) clean and sanitary. Precleaning and orderly storage allow for better checking of stock on hand. It also makes the shelf-life of the produce longer. Spinach, chard, turnip greens, celery, and many others belong to the leaf vegetable group and should be proclaimed, except for cabbage. Parsley, watercress, and mint have to be washed, soaked for a while, and then stored with the leaves up cut-flower style in a pail with water, so they will not become limp. The standard procedure for Romaine lettuce cleaning should be used in cleaning of all leaf vegetables. (Ref. Experiment Recipe 2)

Receiving

Vegetables are just as perishable as meat, fish, or dairy products. Some vegetables are expensive and easily damaged. Deliveries are checked against the order sheet and the invoice. Each item is checked for weight, count, specifications, damage, and visible freshness. As soon as the delivery is accepted, storage begins.

Storage of Vegetables

Most of the clean vegetables such as tomatoes, mushrooms, artichokes, asparagus, broccoli, cauliflower, carrots, and parsnips are stored in their original containers. These must be opened, and the covers and nails must be removed. Containers must be easy to reach in order to prevent damage to the contents by impatient helpers. All goods have to be stored in the same areas on shelves at all times. This avoids the confusion of not finding what is needed. Stock must be roated after each one is inspected for freshness, not just by its arrival date.

Retention of Food Value

Vegetables and fruits produce should not be kept in water needlessly. Cold water leaches out all the vitamins and nutrients which are valuable to the diet. The habit of storing peeled or cleaned vegetables in cold water to prevent a change in colour should never be allowed.

Fruits

All commercial kitchens use at least some fruits in their daily operations. Oranges are often used for decorations. Lemons or apples are used for cooking in most cuisine. Where breakfasts are served, grapefruits, melons, berries, and bananas should be in stock. Fresh fruits in restaurants are used for pastry baking and desserts, to add to other dishes, and to be served as either plain fruits or in salads. Fruit

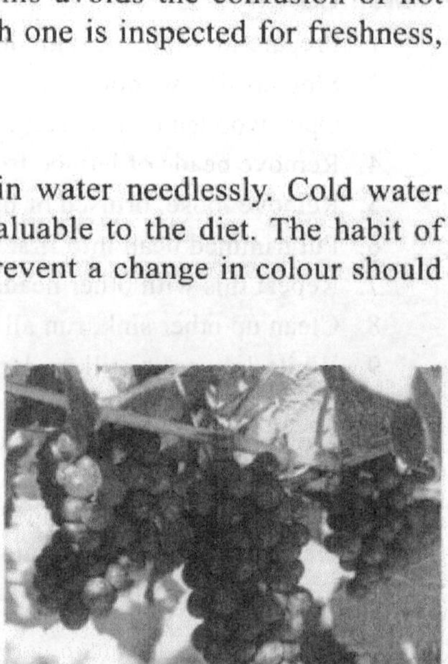

Grapes

popularity depends on the supply and geographic region. In fruit-growing states buffet tables at breakfast, brunch, lunch, and dinner are full of fresh, nicely presented fruits. In areas where fruits are expensive, the displays are much smaller. Fruits, supplied by the produce dealer, are handled in the same way and by the same people as the vegetables. Soft fruits without a protective peel, like berries, do not keep as well in storage as those with a peel that protects them. Green fruits keep much better than ripe fruits, but have to be ripened in a warm place for one or two days before they can be used. Fruit terminology, is used to avoid misunderstandings and speed up ordering. (Ref. Table 2.2B)

Table 2.2B. Fruit Packaging Information

S.No.	*Name*	*Packing Size*	*Quantity*
1.	Apples (a) Delicious (b) Yellow (c) red; (d) Pippin, (e) McIntosh, (f) Jonathan's etc.	carton	Count #72 (large) - #96 (small)
2.	Apricots	Lug	30 lb., loose packed, medium & large
3.	Bananas	Carton	40 lb., ½ 20 lb. & single "hand"
4.	Berries	Flat	12 baskets, about 1 lb. each
5.	Cantaloupes	Crate	Count #45 (smallest)
6.	Carnshaws	Crate	Count #4-5 biggest, (seasonal)
7.	Cherries	Lug	30 lb, loose packed, medium, large
8.	Grapefruits	Carton	Count, #36 (largest) – 64
9.	Grapes	Lug	30 lb. specify: Musket, Thompson, etc.
10.	Honeydews	Crate	Count #36 (smallest)
11.	Lemons	Carton	Select, read.
12.	Mangos.	Box	Count, 8 to 12 (large)
13.	Mangos, Mexico	Flat	Count, 18, 24, 36
14.	Nectarines	Lug	Sized; 6/7, 6/7
15.	Oranges	Carton	Count, #42 (largest) – 64, 72, 88, 96
16.	Papayas	Box	Count, 6 - 10 large
17.	Peaches	Lug	Sized, 6/8, 6/7
18.	Pears	Lug	Medium to large
19.	Pineapples	Flat	Count 4, 5, or 6
20.	Plums	Lug	30 lb. loose
21.	Watermelons	Per lb.	Individual pieces.

(a)

(b)

Slicing of Citrus

Frozen Vegetables and Fruits

Every vegetable and nearly all fruits are available frozen. Frozen vagetables and fruits has the advantage of being fully cleaned, cut up, and pre-blanched. It is a great time saver for the cook. Fresh frozen green peas are a real convenience and give very good quality to the consumer. They are accepted by nearly all chefs. For other varities, vegetables, and especially for fruits, the ratio of acceptance varies and depends on the quality level of the establishment. The decision to use frozen vegetables for the sake of convenience, rests with the management. Some of the chain-type restaurants have designed their facilities in such a way that no space for fresh vegetable handling and storing is included.

The institutional trade handles frozen vegetables in 2½ or 3- pound packages, with 30 pounds to one box. Frozen peas, corns, beans and some others are also supplied loose in 20-pound boxes and are cheaper. Frozen fruits are packed by different companies with little standardized packing. The frozen food distributors will gladly inform the new cook what is available.

QUESTIONS AND DISCUSSIONS

Fill in the Blanks

Q.1. Read and complete the following statements :

(a) Rarely is a meat or fish dish made without ....

(b) Vegetables and fruit suppliers call themselves ....

(c) Packaging should prevent fruits and vegetables from ....

(d) Tomatoes are packed in lugs and their "count" is based on ....

(e) Like purveyors,vegetable and fruit dealers use a special ordering ....

(f) Size specifications of fruits and vegetables are needed for ....

(g) Some vegetables are expensive and also easily ....

(h) Most produce, like, meat, fish, and dairy goods are ....

(i) Pre-cleaning before storage saves valuable refrigerated ....

(j) Food freezing has grown to such a scope that nearly all different varieties of vegetables are ....

[**Ans.:** (a) vegetable; (b) dealers; (c) spoilage;
(d) standard weight quantity; (e) terms;
(f) avoiding misunderstanding and speeding up order.
(g) get damaged; (h) perishable;
(i) space and helps to keep the refer clean and sanitary;
(j) forzen].

Multiple Choice

Q.2. Read each question carefully and select the best answer :–

(i) A produce dealer sells food to institutions on a
 (a) Come-and-get-it basis (b) Delivery, but retail price basis
 (c) Semi whole sale basis (d) Portion-controlled basis.

(ii) A modern refrigerator where unwrapped food is stored should have shelves and containers which are:
 (a) Non-oxidizing material (b) Aluminum for best conduction
 (c) Easily reached and handled (d) Moveable and easy to clean.

(iii) Without efficient vegetable cleaning facilities, a large restaurant cannot serve with their diners :
 (a) French fried potatoes (b) Fresh fruit salads
 (c) Buttered spinach (d) Tossed salad greens.

(iv) On incoming produce deliveries, purchase orders and goods must correspond to assure the :
 (a) Quality of the produce ordered (b) Pricing of the produce ordered
 (c) Freshness of the produce ordered (d) Specifications of the produce ordered.

(v) Potatoes for baking are bought graded to assure that :
 (a) They have a shorter baking time
 (b) They provide automatic portion control
 (c) They are of the best quality
 (d) They can also be used for salads.

(vi) The containers which hold commercially packed tomatoes are called :
 (a) Cartons (b) Lugs
 (c) Crates (d) bags

(vii) Onions to be cleaned do not need washing except :
 (a) The small boiling ones (b) Scallions
 (c) Shallots (d) The large yellow ones.

(viii) The use of frozen vegetables is on the increase because :
 (a) They are better tasting (b) They retain more vitamins
 (c) They need less preparation (d) They provide greater variety.

(ix) Asparagus are packed in a conical shaped crate because :
 (a) They are easier to handle (b) They protect the tip
 (c) They proctect the stem (d) This is the cheapest way of doing it.

(x) Prepealed onions are best kept in the refrigerator by :
  (a) Soaking them in cold water
  (b) Wrapping them in clear plastic
  (c) Covering them with a damp towel
  (d) Moveable and easy to clean.

[**Ans.:** (i) (c); (ii) (c); (iii) (b); (iv) (d);
(v) (c); (vi) (b); (vii) (b); (viii) (c);
(ix) (b); (x) (b)]

Matching Type

Q.3. From the terms in Table 'A' choose the one that is used for each produce item in Table 'B'. Each letter may be used more than once.

Table 'A'	*Tables 'B'*
(a) Sacks	(i) Apples
(b) Crates	(ii) Avocados
(c) Bunches	(iii) Artichokes
(d) Cartons	(iv) Apricots
(e) Flats	(v) Berries
(f) Lugs	(vi) Carrots
	(vii) Cabbage
	(viii) Cauliflower
	(ix) Cherries
	(x) Chives
	(xi) Eggplants
	(xii) Grapes
	(xiii) Leeks
	(xiv) Melons
	(xv) Mangos
	(xvi) Onions
	(xvii) Parsnipsz
	(xviii) Pineapples
	(xix) Plums
	(xx) Potatoes, fieldgrade
	(xxi) Radishes
	(xxii) Romaine
	(xxiii) Salad Potatoes
	(xxiv) Scallions
	(xxv) Watercress.

[**Ans.:** (a) (vi), (xx); (b) (viii), (x), (ix), (xi), (xxii);
(c) (x), (xiii), (xxi), (xxiv), (xxv);
(d) (i), (iii), (vii), (xiv), (xviii); (e) (ii), (v), (xviii);
(f) (iv), (xii), (xv), (xvi), (xix)]

Short Answer Type

Q.4. Explain common types of potatoes in a sentence.

[**Ans.:**

- (a) Alluminatte : Matchstick potatoes, fried in deep fat.
- (b) Allemande : Saute potatoes cut in thick round and coated with butter.
- (c) Anna : Round shaped, cooked in a pan with butter by arranging in layers.
- (d) Boulangere : Sliced potatoes cooked in butter with sliced onions and moistened with consomme.
- (e) Chateau : Shape like, olive, blanched, roasted nice brown colour in butter.
- (f) Croquettes : Puree potatoes, egg and bread crumb fried in deep fat.
- (g) Duchesse : Puree potatoes thickened with egg yolk.
- (h) Four : Jacket potatoes baked in the oven.
- (i) Gratinees : Mashed potatoes mixed with butter sprinkled with cheese and baked.
- (j) Lyonnaise : Saute potatoes mixed with onions.
- (k) Mignonette : Double the size of Alluminatte, fried in deep fat.
- (l) Noisette : Potatoes cut with a round scoop, roasted with butter.
- (m) Pannentier : Half-inch cubes cooked in butter.
- (n) Persilles : Potatoes cooked with butter and chopped parsley.]

Q.5. Explain different types of 'Lettuce' in one/two sentences.

[**Ans.:**

- (a) Endive : Broad leaves, outer edge curling inside, center firm and white.
- (b) Escarole : Broad leaves lettuce, curly and crisp.
- (c) Bibb Lettuce : Open and cup like.
- (d) Boston Lettuce : Soft head, oily to touch and very tender.
- (e) Iceberg Lettuce : Green in colour, leaves are curled like a ball.
- (f) Leaf Lettuce : Pale green in colour and main stem is slightly creamish and firm.
- (g) Romaine (COS) : Cylindrical head with coarse leaves.
- (h) Belgium Lettuce : Solid, small and tightly packed spear like head.
- (i) Racicchio : Cross of cabbage and endive pinkish green in colour, big leaves, firm stem.
- (j) Cabbage
  - (i) Savoy cabbage-smaller in size, mild in flavour.
  - (ii) Red/violet cabbage- violet coloured leaves,
  - (iii) Chinese cabbage- elongated leaves, firm and crisp pale green in colour.]

Descriptive Answer Type

Q.6. Define the follwing terms:

(a) Crate	(b) Grass	(c) Lug
(d) Champignon	(e) Cotton	(f) Cook
(g) Fat	(h) Nannoxidising.	(i) Box

Q.7. Describe the cleaning and washing of lettuce.

Q.8. Compare the storage of vegetables with the storage of fruits.

Q.9. Why do produce dealers and purveyors prefer to use their own terminology?

Q.10. Is a produce container chosen at random or for reasons ?

Q.11. Are food costs and packing information related ?

Q.12. Explain the benefits of the organized storage of perishable foods.

Q.13. Explain the pros and cons for using frozen vegetables.

Assignments/Activity Type

Q.14. Visit a hotel and check invoices and deliveries.

Q.15. Make a visit to a supermarket produce section, for the purpose of identifying fresh vegetables.

Q.16. Take a field trip to a produce market.

Q.17. Inspect a vegetable walk-in refregerator.

Q.18. Practices washing romaine lettuce.

Q.19. Write out a produce order.

2.2

Eggs and Dairy Produce

CHAPTER OBJECTIVES

After studying this lesson you should be able :

- To explain the importance of a need for extra storage care of dairy and egg of products.
- To explain the quality grading of eggs at international level
- To list the graded sizes and weights of eggs;
- To understand and classify and classify cheese of the world; and
- To establish the reasons why chefs need quality in dairy products.

This group of perishable foods consists of eggs and dairy goods, both of them supplied by the dairy truck or what is commonly called the milkman. Milk, milk products and eggs have to be continuously refrigerated. They are easily infected with bacteria. Eggs, as chicken products, may be potential salmonella carriers. Salmonella, the feared bacteria of kitchens, are responsible for most of human's food-borne illnesses. Fortunately, they are seldom fatal but still bothersome. The local authority checks and supervises egg distribution and grading, as well as milk distribution facilities, and frequent checks on milk handling equipment are common. The local muncipal authority is completely independent of the local health inspector. In fresh milk products, as compared to cheese, freshness is a part of quality. The other part is butter-fat content. Cream sauces or cheese dishes can never be better than the quality of the dairy products used. Butter, the most important milk product, is important in cookery. There are substitutes for butter's nutritional values, but not for its characteristic flavour. Unsalted butter is superior to salted butter. Cheese, made from the best part of milk, has been known to making for several thousand years. It is not accepted by all the people of the world as food. In China it is considered 'spoiled milk' and is not eaten. About 400 to 500 different cheeses exist. Cheese making, like cooking, can be classified and reduced to a few simple processes. In high class resultants, cheeses are not only used for cooking but also for table service as a final course. Cheese has an important place in the cuisines of the world. All cautions should be used in the promotion of cheese combination dishes if they have doubtful culinary value.

Eggs and dairy produce are one more group of perishable foods used in cooking. Eggs have no relations to dairy food. They are perishable and often used with dairy goods. The milkman who delivers to institutional kitchens supplies eggs on request.

Eggs

Eggs have been best protein source for human beings. Today they are needed in all styles of cookery. Their price is reasonable in all the countries. Other countries have much higher prices. Eggs are fragile, very perishable and possible salmonella carriers. *Salmonella* is a bacteria that causes most of the common food borne illnesses, such as upset stomach and food poisoning. Salmonella can be found every where, but they are nearly always on poultry products. Continuous refrigeration of the produce is a necessity. Careless, or not cold enough, storage will create dangers to health. This applies to raw eggs, with or without shells, and dishes with raw or partially raw yolks in them.

Grading of eggs is done for wholesomeness, quality, and size. The difference lies in their freshness. All eggs which are sold commercially come from the same type of chicken (leghorns). The freshest eggs are graded AA, the rest A, and all those with blemishes or cracks on the outside, but still wholesome, are graded B. Grade B eggs, because of the cracks, should only be used in baking, where full sterilization through heat can take place. Only the best and freshest AA should be used if the eggs are to be used raw, or only partly cooked. Fried eggs. "Sunny-side up", are only partly cooked. The yield stays raw. Mayonnaises or butterecreams contain raw egg. youlds. Warm egg sauces like "Hollandaise" or "Soyabean" are raw since they are heated to 125°F. or 130°F. This prevents curdling.

Egg size are graded by certain standards. The largest size is called Jumbo, then Extra Large, Large Medium, Small, and Peewee. Bigger eggs give a better yield. Peewees are used in pantry and buffet work for decorative looks rather than nutritional value. Breakfast restaurants have become famous for serving fresh jumbo eggs on fried, poached, and boiled egg orders. For scrambled eggs or omelettes, smaller ones may be used without changing the portion size.

Table 2.2A. Grade of Eggs, Weight & Quality

S.No.	*Grade*	*Weight per dozen*
(1)	Jumbo	30 ounces
(2)	Extra large	27 ounces
(3)	Large	24 ounces
(4)	Medium	21 ounces
(5)	Small	18 ounces
(6)	Peewee	15 ounces

Quality grading Standards

AA = Fresh Fancy

A = Grade A

B = Grade B

The three quality grades are based on the storage potential and actual freshness on the day of inspection. When grading for AA Fancy and Grade A, all cracked eggs at the time of inspection are removed and added to the Grade B.

Eggs for institutional supply are packed 15 dozens to one box. Each box contains 7 corrugated eggtrays for protecting eggs. In between are 6 layers of 30 eggs each. Eggs are graded into 6 sizes as given in Table 2.2A.

DAIRY PRODUCTS

Milk

Generally, fresh milk is pasteurized and homogenized, then distributed in a great variety of containers for many different purposes. Milk in food establishments can be resold as a table beverage or used for cooking. The chef handles the milk. In cooking, milk is used for preparation of soups, sauces, and desserts. Sauces made from milk often become part of other dishes. When real milk is used (instead of the lately popular non-dairy milk substitutes), the freshest and richest milk is best. Rich milk has high butterfat content. Fresh milk sours easily and has to be stored as close as possible to a 34°F. temperature. Milk is heated or scalded in a double boiler, with controlled temperature to prevent boiling over. When milk boils over, some of the milk is lost. Milk will often scorch when heated. In milk that *curdles,* the milk separates into water and milk solids. Many chefs have changed to milk substitutes because curdling of milk happens more often now than it used to do. It may take a long time to transport milk from home to consumer. The local municipal authority checks food service establishments to be sure milk is of good quality. Coffee shops and fast food services, where milk is made into milk shakes and soft ice cream, are checked most often.

Cream

Luxury cuisine uses much cream in its cooking. In milk that is not homogenized, the lighter butter fat rises in the container. It is taken off and called *cream*. After the cream is taken off the milk, the rest is called *skim milk*. Cream is classified by its butter-fat content.

1. Whipping cream, also called heavy cream, has between 30 and 40 percent butterfat.

2. Manufacturing cream, which is whipping cream in three-gallon cans, can be handled at a cheaper price.

3. Commercial, *or coffee cream*: It has a 20 percent butter-fat content. *Half and half* has 14 percent and in mostly used for coffee. Sour cream with 18 percent is a favorite with baked potatoes and in salad dressings.

Milk products are not graded for quality, like meat and eggs. They are classified by butterfat content. The wholesomeness of milk products is assured by local municipal authority's supervision during processing. The standard for milk products are regulated by state laws. Products of some dairies have a butterfat content which is higher than the state laws require. For quality cookery, dairy products should have a high fat content and be absolutely fresh. The quality of a cream sauce is directly related to the quality of butter, milk, and cream used for it (Ref. Table 2.2B).

Table 2.2.B. Use of Milk & Cream in Cooking

	Milk	*Cream Sour*	*Half & Half*	*Cream, Coffee*	*Cream, Manufac–uring*	*Cream, Heavy Fresh*	*Cream, Heavy whipping*
1. Uses	Cream sauce	Salads	Cream sauce	Supreme sauce	Supreme sauce	Supreme sauce	Pastry
	Custard	Dressing	Cream soups	Sauce refinement	Sauce refinement	Sauce refinement	Fruit salads
	Chowders	Vegetables	Chawder	Cream soups	Cream soups	Beverage soups	Bevarage Topping
	Baking	Special Sauces	Oyster Stew				
2. Container sizes	(a) 1/2 pint (b) 1/3 pint (c) pint (d) quart, (e) gallon	(a) 1/2 pint (b) pint (c) quart (d) gallon	(a) pint (b) quart (c) gallon	(a) pint (b) quart (c) gallon	(a) 3-gallon	(a) 1/2 pint (b) pint (c) quart	(a) 1/2 pint (b) pint (c) quart

Butter

In famous French-continental cuisine butter is used for its ability to give flavour. In areas where vegetable oils are not common, butter is ranked first among animal fats for easiest digestibility. There is no substitute for true butter flavour. There are substitutes for the nutritional values of butter. But they are only substitutes. European place more value on milk products (butter, cream and cheese) than on milk itself. Butter and cream cannot be replaced in French-Continental a like cuisine, without losing the quality this cuisine demands. A certain superiority of the best French cooking in France can be related to the superiority of the dairy products available there.

Butter, when not fresh, develops an off taste and becomes rancid. Butter marked and sold as "sweet" is misapplied and meaningless. Salt is added to butter to increase the storage time. Unsalted butter is better than salted butter. Salted butter absorbs more water. This light rancid taste caused by overstorage is not easily found with the salt flavour. Unsalted butter is available in many western countries for a much higher price than regular butter. The milkman who delivers dairy goods supplies butter. It is packed in ¼-pound cubes, in 1-pound bricks, and in 50-pound blocks. He also supplies unsalted butter if it is ordered.

Cheese

Cheeses are fermented milk solids and have been a food source for several thousand years. They are now accepted in most parts of the world. Some large population groups, such as the Chinese and those influenced by their culture, refuse to eat what they call "*spoiled milk*" Natural cheese is made under 400-500 different names. Like cooking, cheese making is classified into a few basic groups. Beginning procedures of cheese making are alike. Only the finishing processes are slightly different. All cheese making has three factors that vary: (a) the kind of milk, (b) the micro–organism used for coagulation, and (c) the aging-curing factor.

Most cheeses are made of cow's milk, but a few are made of sheep or goat's milk. Some strange cheeses, are made of milk from buffaloes, llamas, mares (female horses), reindeer, yaks, and zebras.

About 18 varieties of cheeses can include all the others. The more general classifications are hard cheeses, smeared cheeses, and soft cheeses. Nutritional values of cheese are high. Caloric value varies with the butter-fat content, which can be from 5 to 75 percent. Natural cheeses for table and cooking use have a range from 30 to 50 percent butter-fat. Some of the excellent French triple cream cheeses may have 80 percent. Most hard cheeses are used only for cooking. They can be grated before use or kept pregrated in a cool, dry area for quite some time. Soft and semi-hard cheese must be retrograded from storage. When it is to be used at the table, cheese is taken out of refrigerator and warmed up at room temperature for a few hourse before serving. Temperatures for cheeses and red wines, which often go well together, should be about 68°F. The cheese groups listed on Figure 2.2A are classified under the best known names of their types.

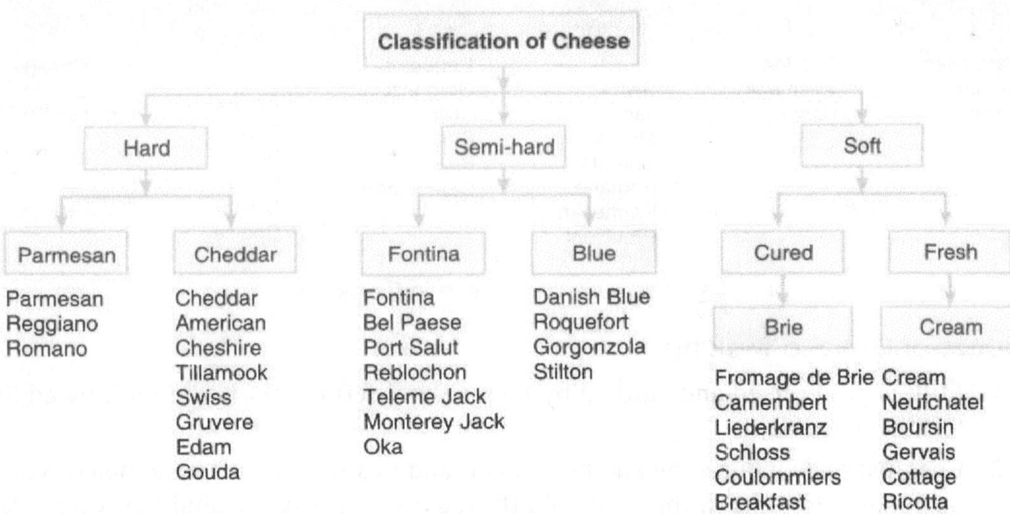

Fig. 2.2A. Classification of Cheese and their most popular names

Classification of Cheese

Cheese is a product of curds, drained and more often than not fermented. The milk of cows, ewes and even asses can be used to make cheese. Depending on the kind of milk used, cheese may be classified into: (Ref. Fig. 2.2A and 2.2B)

1. *Soft or "cream cheese"* : Whole milk or enriched milk (cream added) is used.
2. *Semi-hard* : Part whole milk and part skimmed milk (fat removed).
3. *Hard* : Skimmed milk
4. *Blue* : Skewered with copper wires with a kind of penicillin (penicillin glucose) introduced.
5. *Processed* : May be grinding the cheese and then cooking in vacuum cookers, pouring into moulds and wrapping in tin foil.

Dietically speaking, cheese is rich in proteins, fats, vitamins A, Bl, 2, C and mineral salts.

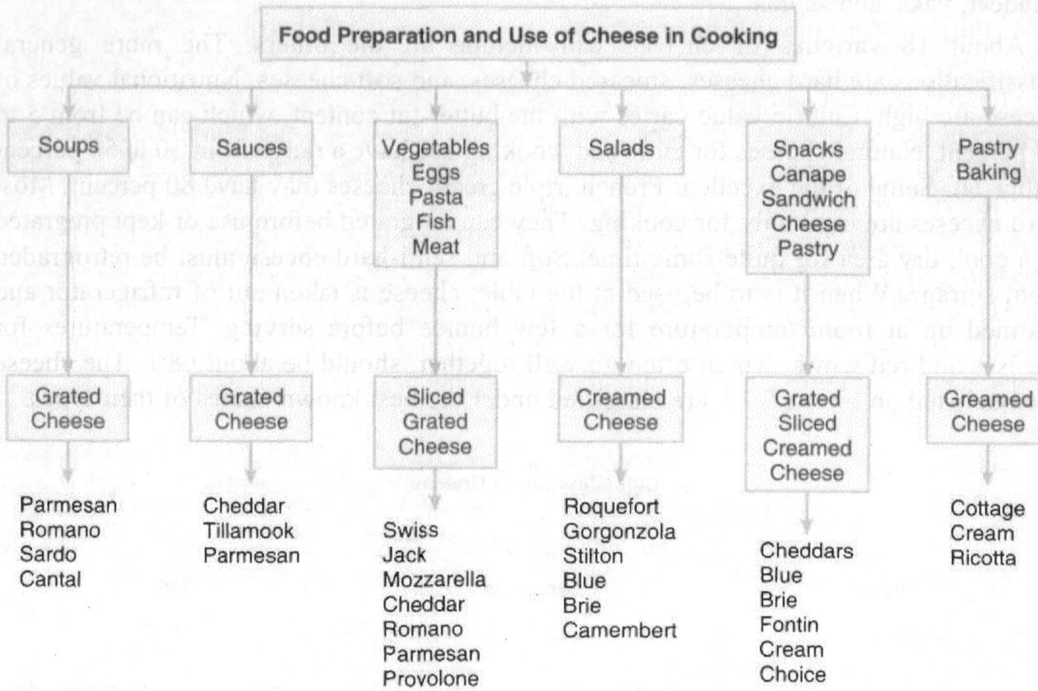

Fig. 2.2B. Use of Cheese in Cooking

Process of Cheese Making

1. Milk is pasteurized and curdled by then natural fermenters in the milk by adding 'starter' bacteria.
2. Coagulation is induced by adding 'rennet' and extract from the abdomen of young mammals. Proteins in the curd solidify readily and leave behind the watery part called 'whey'.
3. Drainage is the stage when all moisture is allowed to escape by pressing between boards, soft cheese is gently pressed whereas great pressure is applied in case of hard cheese.
4. Moulding is when the curds are put into moulds and allowed to mature; fermentation occurs and the rind flavour and taste develop.

FAMOUS BRANDS OF EUROPEAN CHEESE

French (France) Cheese

1. *Camembert* : Soft cheese from cow's milk, pale yellow, smooth (no holes) firm. Served with Tournedo Steaks. ..
2. *Roquefort* : Blue cheese made from ewes milk. The curds are mixed with a special type of bread crumb and a

greenish mould is allowed to develop. Has a grey rind and is yellowish in colour. Comes in a polythene pack and is famous as a dressing for salads.

3. *Brie* : Soft cheese made from cow's milk. Pale yellow in colour.

4. *Fromage a la pie* : French equivalent for fresh, and unfermented cheese also known as cottage cheese. Eaten with salt and cream.

Italian (Italy) Cheese

1. *Bel Paese* : Semi hard cheese, creamy coloured, mild flavoured cheese. Resembles a cake in shape.

2. *Gorgonzola Parmesan* : Blue cheese, semi-hard, has blue veins on its rind. Used mostly for cooking. It is grainy cheese.

Swiss (Switzerland)Cheese

1. *Emmgntal* : Hard cheese, yellow in colour, has 'eyes' or holes larger than that of gruyere, flavoured for cooking.

2. *Gruyere* : Pale yellow, with a golden rind. Hard cheese with smaller 'eyes' than emmentaler, pungent flavoured and preserved ideally in a cloth soaked in salt water. Favourite kitchen cheese.

   (Both the above cheeses come in rectangular loaves).

Dutch (Holland) Cheese

1. *Edam or Edam Ball* : Partly skimmed milk is used to make this cheese a semi-hard one, has a red rind due to the addition of 'Annato' dye. Shaped like a sphere.

2. *Gouda* : Pate yellow, waxy, semi hard cheese.

Danish (Denmark) Cheese

1. Danish blue : Blue cheese made from cow's milk.

English Cheese

1. *Cheddar* : Yellow coloured, semi-hard cheese with a 'nutty' flavour, widely used in cooking.

2. *Stilton* : Blue veined cheese made of whole milk in tall cylindrical moulds.

3. *Cheshire* : Semi-hard cheese, strong flavoured cheese made from cow's milk. Cylindrical shape.

Other brands available in our hotel are 'Kraft' a processed cheese from Australia, and ' Amul' and Indian processed cheese.

Service of Cheese

The cheese course 'savoures' precedes a dessert course (fresh or dry fruits) but follows an entrement or a sweet items. A B/B knife and fish fork, with a B/B plate are used as 'cover.' Accompaniments are placed on the table after paying the cover. They are:

1. Salt and pepper
2. Butter
3. Celery, radish (if in season), fennel bulbs (belonging to the radish family) are put on a bed of crushed ice in a Roly Poly glass or a Champagne Saucer on an underliner.
4. Biscuits, cream crackers, brown bread are placed in a bread boat.
5. If served in a buffet, pickled vegetables and olives are placed in a supreme bowl in a glass insert.

Assorted Cheese

The cheese board or trolley is presented to the guest, the selected variety is cut with a cheese knife and the cheese is picked up in the teeth of the knife. Never remove the rind of a cheese while cutting it. An assorted platter of cheese is served on a dessert plate with a brass plate as an underliner. The rind is cut in this case.

The best wines with cheese are red wine such as 'Beaujolais and Chateau Neuf de Pape'.

Cooked Cheese Dishes

In cooking of dishes cheese is mixed into a preparation or can be sprinkled on as a topping. It can be used in slices to cover a surface. Then it melts and browns under heat. The browned cheese crust, with a appetizing smell, is called "*au gratin*" or sometimes "gratinate". Cheese is usually made into a cheese sauce first (Sauce Bechamel + Cheese = Sauce Mornay) then used to cover the food in a dish. Cheese can be mixed into food as a binder for baking, or stirred into a finished risotto. Whenever cheese is used, the cheese flavour is expected to be noticed. Smoother and tastier sauces, as well as lighter and fluffier browned crusts are made from cheese with higher butterfat content. The selection of cheeses to use is a value judgement of the chef or the consumer. A grilled cheese sandwich, a cheeseburger, a cheese souffle and custard cheese combinations are classified as cheese dishes. Food preparations and corresponding cheeses to be used are listed in Table 2.2B and Table 2.3C.

Table 2.3C. Cheeses for Cheese Board (after Dinner): Buffet or Table Service

Cheese Dishes Sliceable ↓	*Semi-hard Cheeses* ↓	*Blue Veined Cheeses* ↓	*Fermented Soft Cheeses* ↓	*Fresh Soft Double Creamed* ↓
Tillamook	Bel Paese	Stilton	Fromage de Brie	Boursin
Swiss	Fontina	Roquefort	Camembert	Gervais
Gouda	Port Salut		Coulommiers	
	Reblochon			

For a display, cheeses are served in their original packaging, so that brands are visible. Only cheeses with the best reputation should be presented.

Uncooked Cheese Dishes

These are food combinations in which cheese is neither heated nor melted. The plain cheese sandwich can be changed into a "Gourmet" treat by using different breads, a variety of cheeses, and some better ways of presentation. The American luncheon dishes of Cottage Cheese and Fruits, or Fresh Fruit Salad with Cottage Cheese and dressing are standard on most lunch menus. There are cocktail cheese canapes and appetizers, celery sticks with cheese fillings, fruits with cheese filling, cheese cream deserts, and the famous blue cheese or roquefort salad dressings.

Some of the leading cheese names for table use are listed in **Table 2.3C**. Countries which export cheese often sponsor cheese recipe contests to find new ways of using cheese. Cheese has a place in many regional and other food preparations, and at the end of a fine dinner. A preparation named "All Italian" is not necessarily covered with parmeasan cheese.

QUESTIONS AND DISCUSSIONS

Fill in the Blanks

Q.1. Read and complete the following statements :

(i) Egg grading as A A, A, B is essentially a grading for.............

(ii) Milk is not only easily soured by bacteria, but reacts unfavorable when incorrectly heated. When this happens, it is said that the milk is ....

(iii) A fried egg "sunny-side up" is technically.................

(iv) Today's milk is pasteurized and ....

(v) Salmonella, good-borne bacteria, is responsible for many food-borne ....

(vi) Coagulated milk solids, molded and cured, are sold under the name of.............

(vii) Mayonnaise contains egg yolks that are ....

(viii) Eggs are an excellent and inexpensive source of ....

(ix) Continuous refrigeration of dairy goods is a ....

(x) In French-Continental cuisine, butter is used for its easy digestibility and.............

(xi) Butter substitutes can only replace the value butter has to ....

[**Ans.:** (i) wholesomeness, quality and size; (ii) curdles;
(iii) partly cooked; (iv) homogenized;
(v) illness such as upset stomach and food poisoning;
(vi) cheese; (vii) raw;
(viii) protein; (ix) necessity;
(x) ability to give it flavour (xi) for nutrional values]

Multiple Choice

Q.2 Read each question carefully and select the best answer :–

(i) Eggs graded for size are *not* given one of the following names :
(a) Peewee (b) Country
(c) Jumbo (d) Medium.

(ii) Eggs graded for freshness and wholesomeness are *not* stamped :
(a) AAA (b) AA
(c) A (d) B.

(iii) The egg size called Jumbo should weigh, by the dozen, :
(a) 36 ounces (b) 33 ounces
(c) 30 ounces (d) 27 ounces.

(iv) Manufacturing cream, which is cheaper in price than whipping cream, has a butterfat content of about :
(a) 42% (b) 34%
(c) 26% (d) 18%.

(v) Skim milk is milk without a normal content of :
(a) Calcium (b) Milk solids
(c) Butterfat (d) Vitamins.

(vi) The minimum butterfat content of whipping cream is regulated by :
(a) Local Municipal Authority (b) Public Health Department
(c) Dairy industry (d) State law.

(vii) Cheese is sold under close to 500 names. The number of basic groups in only about :
(a) 22 (b) 20
(c) 18 (d) 16.

(viii) In the general classification of cheese one group *not* included is :
(a) Fermented (b) Soft
(c) Semi-hard (d) Hard.

(ix) The law requires that all milk products sold commercially are :
(a) Homogenized (b) Pasteurized
(c) Sterilized (d) Osterized.

(x) One of the best known hard cheeses is :
(a) Mozarella (b) Parmesan
(c) Fontina (d) Port Salut.

[**Ans.:** (i) (b); (ii) (a); (iii) (a); (iv) (b); (v) (b);
(vi) (a); (vii) (c); (viii) (a); (ix) (b); (x) (b)]

Matching Type

Q.3. Match the egg grades in Table 'A' with the weight listed in Table 'B' :

Table 'A'		*Table 'B'*	
(a)	Large	(i)	15 ounces
(b)	Peewee	(ii)	18 ounces
(c)	Jumbo	(iii)	21 ounces
(d)	Medium	(iv)	24 ounces
(e)	Extra Large	(vi)	27 ounces
(f)	Small	(vii)	30 ounces

[**Ans.:** (a) (iv); (b) (i); (c) (vi); (d) (iii);
(e) (v); (f) (ii)]

Q.4. Match each cheese in Table 'A' with its closest relative in Table 'B':

Table 'A'		*Table 'B'*	
(a)	Cheddar	(i)	Gervais
(b)	Parmesan	(ii)	Liederkranz
(c)	Edam	(iii)	Gorgonzola
(d)	Port Salut	(iv)	Reggiano
(e)	Stilton	(v)	Tillamook
(f)	Camembert	(vi)	Oka
(g)	Neufehatel	(vii)	Gouda.

[**Ans.:** (a) (v); (b) (iv); (c) (vii); (d) (vi);
(e) (iii); (f) (ii); (g) (i)].

Short Answer Type

Q.5. Does butter really have an irreplaceable characteristic ?

Q.6. To which section of cooking could cheese making be compared ?

Q.7. Why is unsalted butter not generally preferred ?

Q.8. Was it necessary for chefs to switch to nondairy cream products ?

Q.9. Why is milk pasteurized and homogenized ?

Q.10. Do cooks have to be concerned as much about salmonella as chefs and managers?

Q.11. Will it be economical to use smaller eggs, when shelled eggs by the cup are required ?

Q.12. Is egg grading a valid indication of freshness ?

Assignments/Activity Type

Q.13. Define the following:

(a) Curdle

(b) Skim milk

(c) Homogenize
(d) Pasteurize
(e) Ricotta.

Q.14. Film presentation on:
(a) Dairy farming
(b) A dairy plant
(c) Cheese making.

Q.15. Make a field trip to :
(a) A dairy plant
(b) A cheese factory.

Q.16. Participate in cheese tasting, with a follow-up essay discussing the differences.

2.3

Breeding and Coating

CHAPTER OBJECTIVES

After studying this lesson you should be able :

- To state the reasons for and purpose of breading;
- To identify the various breading ingredients;
- To explain the breading process;
- To list the steps of the breading sequence;
- To define various batters; and
- To explain the deep frying of batter-covered foods as compared to breaded foods.

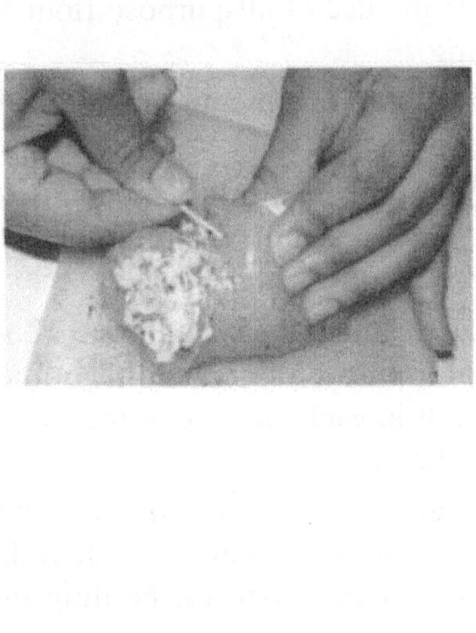

The most important and most widely used coating is breading. The term breading may be describe as the coating of portion-sized or smaller pieces of raw or cooked food with flour, egg, and bread crumbs. Bread crumbs are an economical leftover use of stale bread, which should never be wasted. The purpose of breading are many: better appearance, better acceptance, and improved nutritional value. Luxury cuisine uses ground coconuts and almonds instead of the more common crumbs. Cracker crumbs, which are cheaper, may be substituted for real bread crumbs. Every kitchen should have enough leftover bread to make crumbs. Understanding the correct sequence and lineup of the breading process saves time and produces better food. Breading is very convenient for the fast food operator, since it can be done in advance and the deep frying is not complicated.

Breading means coating portion-sized or smaller pieces of raw or precooked food with flour, eggs, and bread crumbs before frying them in hot fat. The term 'breading' originally meant that bread in the form of crumbs was used as coating. Chefs liked the better looks, taste, and handling of breaded foods, so they experimented and replaced bread crumbs with similar or fancier products. Frying is a fast cooking process which does not tenderize tough food. Some foods must to propelled and cooled, then breaded and refried to the order, when needed.

For frying, fat is heated to a minimum temperature of 325°F. Starch, which is in all coatings, cooks near 200°F. Thus, food covered with starch can be exposed to frying heat for only a short time, without getting too brown. This is why tender foods can be cooked from the raw stage, but tough foods are tenderized first by boiling.

Food has always been considered precious, and bread is symbolic for food. It is never wasted or thrown away. Leftover stale bread was made into crumbs and its best use became the breading of today.

PURPOSES OF BREADING

1. Breading keeps food juicier, therefore, better tasting.
2. Breading adds nutritional values to food.
3. Breading gives a better look to fried foods.
4. Breading uses up leftover bread.
5. Breading preserves the original food taste by acting as a shield against the frying fat.
6. Breading permits the refrying of leftover cooked foods.
7. Breading changes many foods into finger food, as snacks and appetizers.

Breading can be done in advance. Breaded raw or cooked food can be kept under refrigeration or frozen. These are two important advantages as compared to plain flour or batter coating. Breading is used on all meats, fish shellfish, vegetables, and even a piece of Swiss cheese or a hard boiled egg can be breaded, fried, and served as a specialty.

Today a variety of crumbs are used. Cheapest and most common, but not best, are cracker crumbs. French bread crumbs, at a high price, are available from French bread bakeries. Most chefs make their own crumbs from all leftover and dried white bread. For special quality breading they use French bread without crust. For unusual effects and taste, cornmeal (gritty) can be used. Luxury cuisine uses ground, unsweetened coconut and grated white or brown almonds. Raw, well-beaten eggs, sometimes diluted with water, milk, or oil may be used to keep the crumbs stuck to the food. There is a trick of the trade, but unknown to many food service employes is the use of all-purpose flour to prevent the egg from peeling off the food while it is frying.

Breading not done in the proper sequence becomes a waste of time and material. It also results in messy, unsatisfactory food.

The sequence of breading described is a manual process for one right-handed cook. Food processing plant use different types of conveyor belts, machines, and automatic sifters, but the principle of breading and its flow of work remains unchanged.

The most practical utensils are two large flat standard steamtable pans and one 12 to 18 inch stainless steel bowl. One pan is filled with sifted all-purpose flour, and the other pan is filled with sifted bread crumbs. A few grains are put in each pan according to the quantity of food to be breaded. Well beaten eggs go into the bowl.

On a large enough working table, the items to be breaded are placed at the left end. Next to them are the pan with the flour, the bowl with the well-beaten eggs, and then the pan with the bread crumbs. On the right end of this line is a sheet pan for holding the breaded food.

Experimental Recipe 3.

Shrimp Cutlet

Ingredients

1. Potatoes	:	2 big
2. Slice of bread	:	1 No.
3. Pepper powder	:	1/2 tsp
4. Salt	:	To taste.

For the coating

1. Breadcrumb	:	1/2 cup

For the filling

1. Shrimp peeled and deveined	:	1 cup
2. Fresh coconut grated	:	1/2 cup.
3. Onions finely chopped	:	1 cup
4. Red chilli powder	:	1 tsp
5. Turmeric powder	:	1/2 tsp
6. *Dhania-jeera* powder	:	1 tsp
7. Coriander leaves chopped	:	1/2 cup
8. Salt	:	To taste.

Method

1. Prepare all required ingrediants.
2. Boil potatoes and mash while still hot.
3. Soak a slice of bread in water.
4. Drain all water from the bread and add it to the potatoes.
5. Add pepper powder and salt. Knead well and keep aside
6. Wash and clean shrimps. Add salt, turmeric powder and chilli powder to it.
7. Fry chopped onions in little oil for a minute.
8. Add shrimps and *dhana-jeera* powder and fry a little more.
9. Add approx a cup of water to it.
10. Cover the pot and let shrimps cook for 10 minutes or so.
11. Once shrimps are cooked increase the heat and dry the mixture.
12. Add coconut and chopped coriander to it. Keep it aside.
13. Make balls of mashed potatoes and flatten on your palm.
14. Add a spoonful of shrimp mixture to it and close the balls.
15. Flatten gently on your palm.
16. Roll it in bread crumb and deep fry.
17. Serve with tomato ketchup or mint *chutney*.

Pork chops

Certain steps be followed for breading process. If the items to be breaded are pork chops, the guideliness for actual breading are as follows :

1. Pick up one single pork chop (*without* the help of the right hand) with left hand and dips both sides into the flour.
2. Extra flour is shaken off the chop, still with the left hand only to remove extra flour, and the chop is dropped into the egg, to be covered fully with egg. The *left hand* picks the chop out of the egg, drips off the extra egg and drops the chop into the bread crumbs. At this time it must be emphasized that the hand which touches flour and egg must never touch the bread crumbs. If it does, big lumps of gluey breading mass will stick to the fingers of the left hands and make proper and clean breading impossible.
3. Repeat the whole process by putting the left hand going immediately back to the raw pork chops.
4. At the same time as the left hand goes back the right hand (which must be dry and clean) covers the chop with crumbs and pats them on, making sure that all parts of the meat are properly covered.
5. The right hand lifts out the chop, shakes off any extra bread crumbs, and places the breaded chop flat on the sheet pan.

Breaded foods are ready for immediate deep or pan frying, they have to be stored at least for the length of the service period. If the foods are not sold, they are kept however until the next day. To prevent them from sticking together, breaded items must be laid out neatly, in rows, on a flat pan that has been dusted with bread crumbs and is completely dry. The sheet should be covered with paper towels or butcher paper. Breaded foods must never be stacked, unless frozen. For short periods during service, two layers with paper in between would be acceptable. There should be enough air circulation through the breaded items to prevent a loss of quality and any sticking together of the food. Too long a storage time is not advised. If breaded food has to be frozen for later use, then the freezing should be done with food in single layers on sheets of waxed paper. When frozen solid the food can be stacked in a box, with paper between. After it is wrapped in plastic, it can be kept frozen for only a few weeks.

BATTER FOR FRYING

Plain or fancy batters can be used to cover various deep fried foods. Batters are more time consuming to handle and not as convenient as regular breaded food. The plainest methods of using a batter is similar to breading. Eggwash, diluted well-beaten egg with an equal quantity of milk, is used instead of pure egg, and no bread crumbs are used. The food is merely dipped into the flour, thereby creating a batter. For a crisper batter, food can be dipped once more into eggwash before it is deep fried. True batters are pre-made and consist of water, milk, wine or beer, flour, eggs, and baking powder or yeast. All-purpose flour is used most often. In special recipes, rice, corn or potato starch can be added to the batter. Most fruits and vegetables fried in batter are called fritters. The most widely known dish made with batter is the English "Fish and Chips".

Flour mixed with liquids is called batter as long as it stays in a liquid or semi-liquid state. Usually batter has the consistency of a sauce. Most batters are improved with egg yolks, egg whites, or whole eggs, and contain baking powder or yeast. Batter-fried foods

Experimental Recipe 4.

Fillet of Sole or Similar Food stems

Portion 20

Ingredlants

1. Fresh fillet of sole	:	4 kg
2. All-purpose flour	:	2 kg
3. Bread or cracker crumbs	:	2 kg
4. Well-blended eggs	:	2½ cups
5. Oil or water	:	1 ounce.

Method

1. Prepare all required ingredients.
2. Wash and clean the fish.
3. Trimmed fish for 200 portions, salted moderately on both sides.
4. One standard steam table size pan with flour.
5. Another pan of the same size with the crumbs.
6. A dry, 18" × 24" bake sheet, covered with butcher paper.

The Breading

1. Pick up only one piece of fish with the left hand, dip both sides of fish into flour. Shake off surplus flour.
2. Drop fish completely into egg bowl. Pick up fish with *left hand* and strip off surplus egg by using the side wall of the bowl.
3. Drop fish, flat and straight, into the middle of the bread crumbs, but do not touch crumbs with the left hand.
4. With the *right hand* cover fish with crumbs. Pat them on.
5. Lift the crumb-covered fish carefully. Do *not* tear the breading. Shake off extra crumbs. Place fish flat on the baking sheet.
6. Repeat these phases until all pieces of fish are breaded.

   There must be no overlap of hands. If the hand used for flour and eggs gets into the crumbs, the fingers will get "breaded" instead of the food. Each hand has its own function. As soon as these movements are coordinated and controlled, the speed of working should increase. With practice, the breading of 20 food orders should take about 10 minutes.

Cleanup

1. Wash and dry your hands thoroughly.
2. Move the breaded food to a refrigerator.
3. Refrigerate the leftover eggs for further use, or discards them.
4. Sift the flour and puts it into a clean container for storage.
5. Sift the bread crumbs and puts them in a clean container.
6. Shake out sifter and returns it to the storage.
7. Return all utensil and materials to proper storage.
8. Wipe the working table clean with a wet towel.
9. Wash your hands again and reports to the chef that he is ready for the next assignment.

have a completely different appearance, texture, and taste than the same foods breaded. To use batter is a culinary variation, not an economic one.

Handling Precautions

Food which has been dipped into batter need be fried immediately to prevent the batter from running off the food. This makes batter less practical to handle than breading. Another pitfall to batter frying in a commercial deep fryer is the fact that deep fryers use baskets to hold food. Batter-dipped food which is dropped into the frying basket sinks to the bottom while the batter is still raw. Then it sticks to the wire of the basket. When the cooked food is moved, the crust breaks open. The food gets greasy and soggy and the purpose of the batter frying is lost. To prevent this food must not be dropped directly into the hot fat. It must be held by hand with half of the food covered with hot fat for several seconds until the outer crust forms. Thus, the deep frying of batter-coated food takes too much time and is often wasteful.

Use of Batter

Many fruits fried in batter are called fritters, such as apple fritters and banana ftrtters in french terminology, little rolls of cooked, chopped food, bound together with some sauce are called "*Cromesquis*" These are similar to "Croquettes" because both are made the same way and deep fried. But croquettes are breaded and cromesquis are batter covered. The most well-known of the foods fried in batter are the English "Fish and Chips" and the Japanese "Tempera". Both are a combination of fish and vegetable, dipped in batter, and fried to order. All foods fried in batters must be served immediately or they will lose appearance and texture. Guidelines for batters are:

1. Dry ingredients are sifted and mixed well.
2. Wet ingredients are blended together.
3. Combine dry ingredients with 2/3 of the wet mixture to a smooth paste with out lumps.
4. When smooth, add the remaining liquid slowly.
5. Whip until sauce-like thickness is reached.
6. Put all batters, except those with yeast, under refrigeration from 3 hours to overnight.
7. Stir before use, and test with a small amount of food first.

Following points may also be observed:

1. Reread "Batter Handling" before frying.
2. Batter will only stick to food while frying if the food is completely dry.
3. The best method is to dip all food into flour, as for breading, before dipping it into the batter.

Experimental Recipe 5.

Simple Batter (Common for fish and chips)

Portions : 20

Ingredients

1. All-purpose flour	:	3 cups
2. Cornstarch	:	½ cup
3. Salt	:	2 teaspoons
4. Banking powder	:	2 teaspoons
5. Half whipped	:	3 egg whites
6. Cold water	:	1 cup
7. Additional cold water	:	¾ cup to 1 cup.

Procedure

See general rules for all batters.

Experemental Recipe 6

Wine Batter for Fruits and Desserts

Portion : 20

Ingredients

1. All purpose flour	:	3½ cups
2. Baking powder	:	2 teaspoons
3. Sugar	:	2 teaspoons
4. Salt	:	1 treaspoon
5. Well-beaten eggs	:	4 whole
6. Dry white wine	:	¾ cup
7. *Additional:*		
White wine	:	1 cup.

Procedure

See general rules for all batters.

Types of Batters

The simplest batter consists of a pan of flour and a bowl of eggwash. *Eggwash* is the term for beaten eggs diluted with liquid and used for various coatings. A good mixture is made of one part beaten whole egg and one part rich milk. The procedure is similar to breading except that bread crumbs are not used. The sequence for this simple dip is flour, eggwash, flour, and then into the hot fat to fry. A better crust-producing dip is flour, eggwash, flour and eggwash once more. Then it goes into the hot fat for frying. Many chefs have developed their own special variations.

Expermental Recepe 7.

Beer and Yeast Batter (for meat and fish specialties)

Portion : 20

Ingredients

1. All purpose flour	:	3½ cup
2. Sugar	:	½ teaspoon
3. Instant dry yeast	:	1 teaspoon
4. Yolks	:	4 egg
5. Stale warm beer	:	12 ounces.

Procedure

1. When combined as usual, put batter in a warm place (85°F. to 90°F.) for about one hour, or until batter has doubled.
2. Punch down and dilute with 3/4 to a cup of additional beer to desired thickness.
3. Add 1 teaspoon of salt.
4. Batter is ready for use, or may be kept under refrigeration to slow yeast growth.
5. Additional Procedure :
   See general rules for all batters.

True Batters

True batters may be prepared in many variations. The liquid can be different: such as, water, milk, buttermilk, sour cream, wine, beer, or a combination of these. The flour is mostly all-purpose. Rice, corn, or even potato starch is often added. The ratio of flour to liquid has a wide span and by adding whole eggs or parts of them, many different batters can be created. In addition, to control the crispness and desired outcome of the food, *leavening* agents (baking powder and yeast) are used in addition to or instead of the eggs. The contents of a batter depend on the intentions of the chef. Wine and egg batters are often used for fruit fritters. Beer and yeast batters are more often used for the heavier meat and fish preparations. Batters can be changed as the cook wishes.

QUESTIONS AND DISCUSSIONS

Fill in the Blanks

Q.1. Read and complete the following statements:

(a) Breading keeps food juicier, therefore ....

(b) Fruits fried in batter are called ....

(c) A piece of Swish cheese, as a special dessert, can be ....

(d) Food coated with batter just dropped into the deep fryer basket has the tendency to get ....

(e) For fancy breading, luxury cuisine uses sometimes brown ....

(f) Batter frying is not as convenient as breading. It consumes more ....

(g) The best known English dish made with a batter and is called ....

(h) The cheapest bread crumb substitutes are ....

(i) Breading means coating food with flour, egg, and ....

(j) The breading process can be applied to all tender ....

[**Ans.:** (a) better tasting; (b) fritter; (c) breaded; (d) sunk to the bottom while the batter is still raw; (e) almonds; (f) time; (g) fish and chips; (h) cracker crubs; (i) bread crumbs; (j) raw or cooked food].

Multiple Choice Type

Q.2. Read each question carefully and select the *best* answer:

(i) Which of the following cannot be substituted for bread crumbs in breading?

(a) Cracker crumbs (b) Cracked wheat

(c) Ground almonds (d) Ground coconuts.

(ii) The finest bread crumbs are chef-made in the kitchen from:

(a) Leftover dried toasts (b) Leftover dried bread

(c) Leftover dried french bread (d) No-crust dried french bread.

(iii) The correct lineup for breading meat is:

(a) Meat, flour, crumbs, eggs (b) Meat, crumbs, eggs, flour

(c) Meat, flour, eggs, crumbs (d) meat, eggs, flour, crumbs.

(iv) Only small pieces of food can be coated for frying because:

(a) The deep fryer has a size limitation

(b) Deep fried food should be used for finger food

(c) Big pieces would use too much fat

(d) Too long frying time would burn the coating.

(v) Which of the following could not be used as the liquid for batter ?

(a) Oil (b) Wine

(c) Milk (d) Water.

(vi) Which one of these foods is most likely to be fried in a wine batter ?

(a) Corn fritters (b) Banana fritters

(c) Chicken croquettes (d) Fish and chips.

[**Ans.:** (i) (b); (ii) (b); (iii) (c); (iv) (b); (v) (a); (vi) (b)]

Short Answer Type

Q.3. Does breading have quality differences ?

Q.4. Why are there different batters for different uses ?

Q.5. Explain the reason for introducing breading as a cooking method.

Descriptive Ansnwer Type

Q.6. List the ingredients for beer batter.

Q.7. Compare the use of batter to the use of breading. (ingredients, procedure, usage).

Q.8. Briefly describe the breading process by giving statable example.

Q.9. List as many reasons as you can for breading food.

Assignments/Activity Type

Q.10. Define the following leavening agent:

(a) Butcher paper

(b) Eggwash

(c) Tempura.

Q.11. Examine samples of different crumbs. Distinguish cracker from bread crumbs.

Q.12. Watch the demonstration of breading by one cook.

Q.13. Practice breading and its proper lineup.

2.4

Meat and Poultry

CHAPTER OBJECTIVES

After studying this lesson you should be able :

- To explain the need for butcher knowledge;
- To describe the change of quality control;
- To identify the reason for and importance of meat inspection;
- To list the different meat grades;
- To explain the need and importance of portion control;
- To compare meat cuts to cooking methods; and
- To discuss different phases of portion control.

All over the world, meat and poultry are the most important and expensive food products. They can be purchased at different levels of preparation and for different prices. The food service management should decide what to buy. Whatever foods are bought, chefs must know about the total preparation process in order to make correct judgements. Quality levels be well defined, measured, established and maintained. Meat cuts be selected according to menu and preparation needs. Ordering or specifying selection and quantity is another of the chef's responsibilities. Chef must establish and maintain food costs. Therefore, the total handling of food from purchase selection to receiving to storage to rotation and use must be the chef's concern. The Chef must establish portion size policy together with the management. The enforcing of portion control, checking yields and costs, and keeping customer satisfaction are the reasons for the chef's position.

Portion-controlled fresh or frozen supplies are new to the market. A food service establishment is in an unusual position: to its supplier, it is a consumer; but to its guests, who are the true consumers, it is the producer. The use of frozen meat and poultry raw products is a convenience to the producer and a quality loss to the consumer. The chef and the management of the food service establishment must make many joint decisions.

Meat and poultry are the most expensive food materials used in food and beverage operations. These are supplied by *purveyors*. They are specialists in the semi whole sale jobbing of meat and poultry to hotels, restaurants, and institutions. Purveyors handle everything from meat on the carcass to frozen steaks and from smoked meats to pre-cooked hamburgers. Most meat and poultry items today are available in convenient forms, such as portion-controlled, processed, semi cooked, or frozen. Food service operators can choose to handle fresh meats or to buy all their needs processed and frozen or precooked.

Chefs butcher must have enough knowledge of meat and poultry handling to be efficient. The selection of fresh food is a decisive factor to the finished product. Many chefs feel that personal handling of these supplies is of the greatest importance. They are proud of their special ways of trimming, cutting, and boning meat before it is cooked. Some food and beverages service establishments do all their own meat cutting and portioning on the premises. They do not use frozen supplies even in emergencies. Other places prefer a minimum of fresh meat handling and depend entirely on portion-controlled supplies. Whatever the choice, chefs must have enough meat know-how to supervise both of these operations.

Traditionally, chefs used to go to the markets at the break of dawn and select the meats which they considered to be the best available. This judgment was the only grading available, and it was perfected over many years of personal experience. Now a days there is compulsory municipal meat inspection and voluntary meat quality grading. Meat inspection approves the wholesomeness of the meat, whereas meat grading standardizes the quality of meat. Municipal officials stamps a round mark with a number on all carcasses. The number identifies the slaughterhouse and the inspectors. (Ref. Fig. 2.4A and 2.4B) A shield-like stamp is used to indicate the grade range of the meat. These grades in most foreign countries are Prime, Choice, Good, Standard, Commercial, Utility, Cutter, and Canner. Purveyors and retail meat markets handle most of the first five grades. The last three are reserved for the manufacture of meat products. Without municipal inspection and grading, meat purchasing would still be very difficult and time consuming for the average chef.

All part of a slaughtered animal, especially of the moving family (ox, cow), do not have the same characteristics. Tenderness, juiciness, and flavour of meat vary. These depend on which muscles have been exercised and the amount of fat (marble) deposited between the meat fibers. Although the whole animal is graded "Prime", the difference in usability of various parts is considerable. Experienced chefs and butchers do not always agree with regard to a selection of meat cuts.

The ordinary coffee shop or restaurant uses a wide variety of steaks, roasts, pot roasts, stews, hamburgers and cold meats. The meat purveyor and the chef use a standard meat terminology, without reference to the intended use of the meat. Hotel Management Schools encourages the nationwide use of this terminology, since grading could be done also on a national basis. Standard terms avoid misunderstandings.

AGMARK

AGMARK 'seal' provided by AGMARK standard set up by the Directorate of Marketing and Inspection of the Government of India in 1937 ensures quality and purity of a product. The main objective is to promote Grading and Standardization of Agricultural and allied commodities under agricultural Produce (Grading & Marketing) Act, 1937. (Ref. Fig. 2.4A)

Quality standards for agricultural commodities are framed based on their intrinsic quality. Food safety factors are being incorporated in the standards to complete in World Trade. Standards are being harmonized with international standards keeping in view the WTO requirements. Certification of agricultural commodities is carried out for the benefit of producer/manufacturer and consumer. Certification of adulteration prone commodities viz. Butter, Ghee, Vegetable oil, Ground-Spices, Honey, wheat Atta etc. is very popular. Blended Edible Vegetable Oils Fat Spreads are compulsorily required to be certified under Agmark.

Fig. 2.4A. Specimen Agmark Seal

A stamp of the local municipality is a must for wholesomeness only. The number marked indicates the slaughter house plant where the meat was inspected and passed. These are the assigned grades appearing in the form of a rolled-on ribbon over the entire carcass. If grades are in a numerical order, they would appear as given in Fig 2.4B.

1. Prime
2. Choice
3. Good
4. Standard
5. Commercial
6. Utility
7. Cutter
8. Canner.

Inspection and Grading Stamp

Fig. 2.4 B. Inspection and Grading Stamps

For true quality steaks and roast only the primal cuts of meat graded prime or choice should be used.

Various raw meats

Grain products are often baked, and are rich sources of complex and simple carbohydrates

SELECTION OF MEAT

The establishment of a quality standard of tenderness and flavour for the individual preparations of a kitchen is the duty of management and the chef. For this purpose, the chef must know which cuts of meat to use for a specific preparation. There is no choice for a New York Fillet, T-Bone or Top Sirloin Steak. The names on the menu clearly establish the meat cuts to be used. For brochetters, sautes, stews, roasts, and cutlets, a choice of suitable meat cuts must be made.

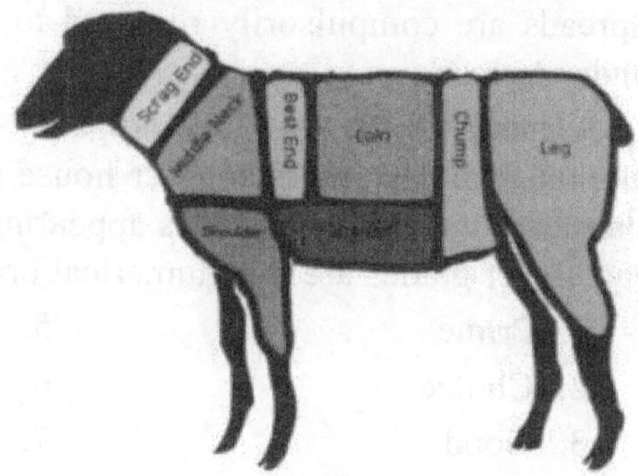

Lamb cuts

Meat Identification

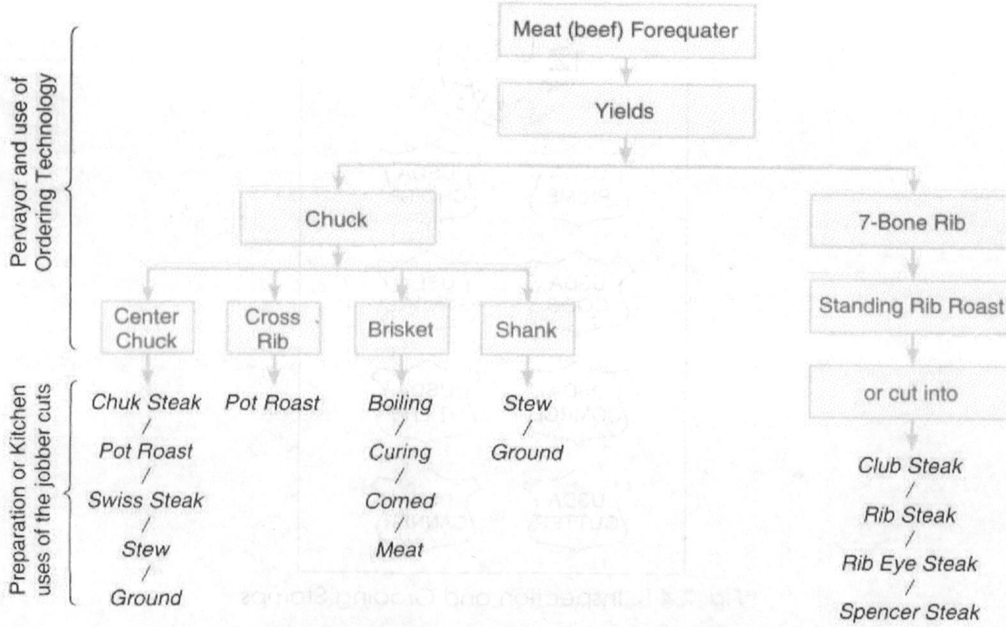

Fig. 2.4C. Meat (Beef) Forequarter Identifications Meat Hindquarter

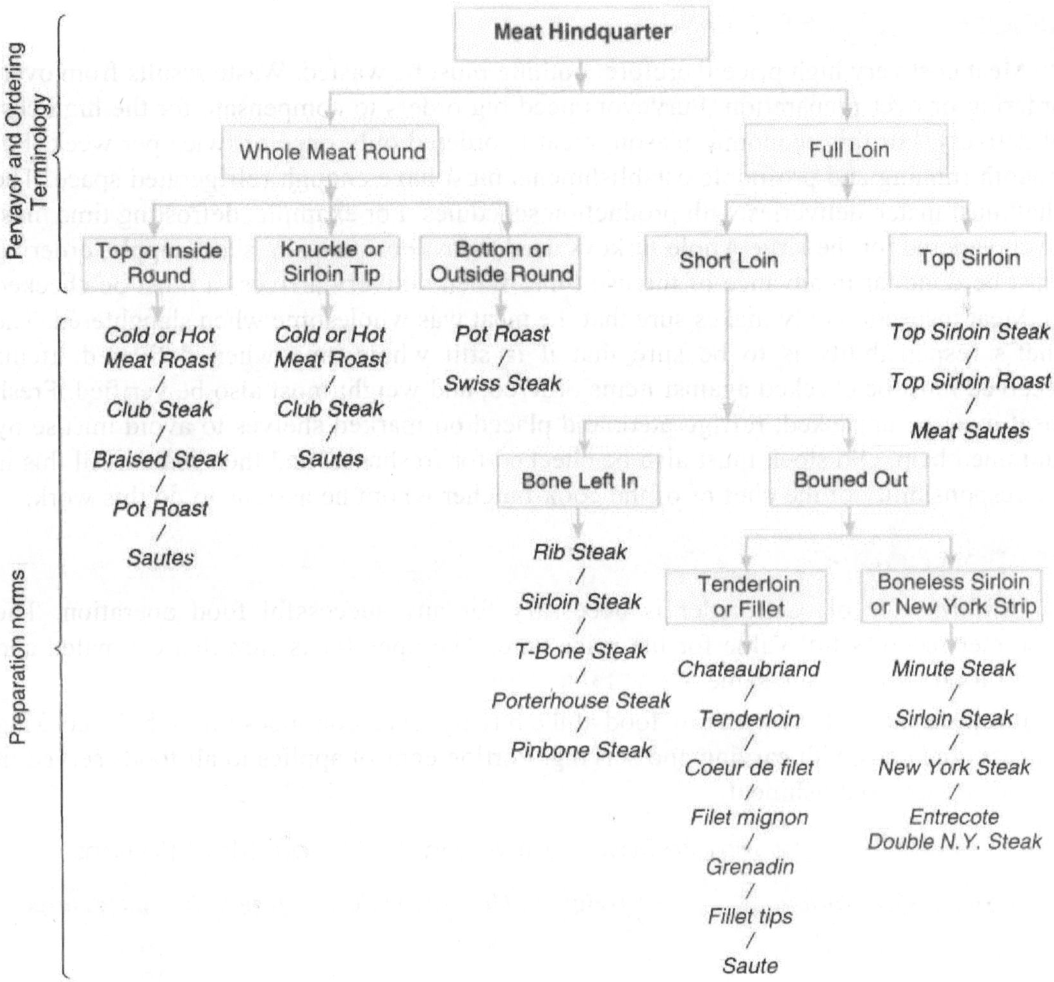

Fig. 2.4D. Meat Hindquarter Identification

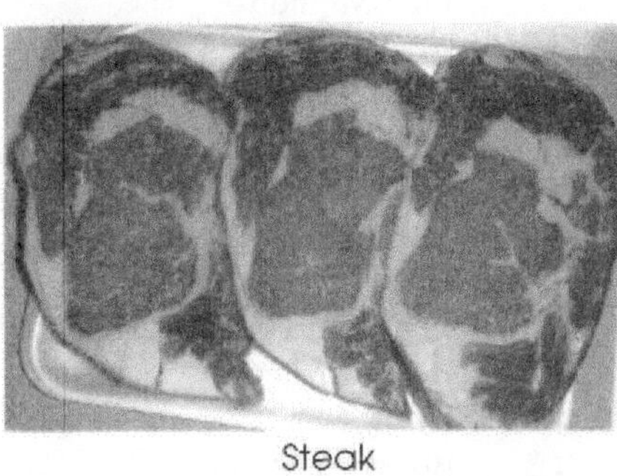

Steak

This choice is based on price, clientele, and the reputation to be maintained by the establishment. First cuts differ from secondary cuts in cost and characteristics. Secondary cuts should be used instead of a first cut only if the quality is adequate. Chefs have different opinions of what is a better or a good enough cut for a certain preparation. Chuck (the squared-off forequarter) is generally used for braised steaks, pot roasts, cold roast meats and club steaks. Meat beef loin and meat beef rib both first cuts, are used for steaks, prime roasts, brochettes, and quality sautes like meat "Beef Stroganoff" However, prime chuck meat, when properly *seamed* (cut along the natural divisions), can be used for many speciality dishes with great advantages. (Ref Fig. 2.4C and 2.4D)

REFRIGERATION AND STORAGE

Meat cost very high price therefore, nothing must be wasted. Waste results from over-ordering or over preparation. Purveyors need big orders to compensate for the high cost of delivery. For this economic reason, meat is ordered only once or twice per week. For smooth running and profitable establishments must have enough refrigerated space. The chef must match deliveries with production schedules. For example, defrosting time must be considered for the large whole turkeys used today. For items in short supply, ordering must be done far in advance of the use time. When delivery arrives; it must be checked in. Meat inspection only makes sure that the meat was wholesome when slaughtered. The chef's responsibility is to be sure that it is still wholesome when delivered. Items received must be checked against items ordered, and weight must also be verified. Fresh meat must be unpacked, refrigerated, and placed on marked shelves to avoid misuse by untrained help. Old stock must also be checked for freshness, and then roated. All this is the responsibility of the chef or of the cook-butcher whom he assigns to do this work.

PORTION CONTROL

Uniform size of each order is necessary for any successful food operation. The customer receives full value for the price paid. The operator is sure that estimated and actual food costs are the same. (Ref. Table 2.4A)

Portion control starts with raw food at the buying level, continues through the cooking process, and ends with carving and serving. Portion control applies to all foods served in a food service establishment.

Table 2.4A. Approximate Raw meat Weight for Various Meat Portions

S.No.	*Meat Portion*	*Weight in Ounces Small*	*Weight in Ounces large*
1.	Minute Steak	8	10
2.	Fillet Steak	6	10
3.	Tornadoes	6	10
4.	Coeur de Filet	6	10
5.	Filet Mignon	6	10
6.	New York Steak	12	16
7.	Sirloin Steak	12	16
8.	Entrecote	12	16
9.	Loin Strip Steak	12	16
10.	T-Bone Steak	14	18
11.	Porterhouse Steak for 2	22	28
12.	Chateaubriand for 2	16	20
13.	Beef brochette	5	7
14.	Beef Saute	4	7
15.	Boneless Cutlet	4	6
16.	Porkchop, breaded	4	7
17.	Porkchop, broiled, single	7	9
18.	Porkchops (2), broiled, each	5	6
19.	Lambchops (3), frenched, each	2.50	3.25
20.	Scallopine (3), each	2	2.75
	Meats are reasonably defatted and trimmed.		

Portion size is influenced by many factors. One is the caloric value of food, or the need of the average customer to satisfy his hunger. There are sales prices and customs of the region. Some customers are used to larger steak and potato order than others. In addition, other factors are the image which the establishment wants to create, the sex and age of average customers, and the actual preparation method.

When you serve a 4-ounce boneless and breaded fried pork chop, with tomato sauce, it will look larger and have more calories than a 6-ounce bone-in broiled pork chop, served with applesauce. Orders served *a la carte* should be larger than orders served on the dinner. The meat appears larger if a 14-ounce untrimmed New York Steak is served, compared to the potato and the vegetable. The same steak, trimmed of fat and gristle to about 11 ounces, looks daintier when compared the same way. After eating the untrimmed steak, if the customer realizes that 30% of his steak could not be eaten there is a definite psychological effect. From the trimmed steak, he leaves only 10% fat, or even nothing at all. The trimmed steak is not only more satisfying, but also less of a fire hazard while it is cooking. Young cooks should be prepared to accept counsel before deciding on portion sizes.

Hamburger patties are the ideal food for potion control. Ground meat is used. There are no left-over trimmings. The patty is machine molded. It has exact weight to the quarter ounce. One patty is just like the next. This accounts for the popularity of hamburger chains and franchises. From a food control point of view, there is no difference between selling meat patties or selling ice cream bars.

It is quiet difficult to portion control a regular steak. The weight, shape and fat content of one piece of meat is never exactly the same as the next. If a 12-pound trimmed New York strip is bought, in theory, it means that 16 trimmed 12-ounce New York steaks could be cut from it. The average yield will actually be 15 or more likely 14, or even only 13. If the 12-pound strip were machine cut into 16 equal-sized steaks, some of the steaks would be better than acceptable (very well trimmed), but others would be totally unacceptable (too much fat and skin) for customer satisfaction. Portion-cut steaks supplied by the meat purveyor are about 90 to 95% acceptable.

The price per pound for portion-cut meat is so much higher than the price for uncut meat that portion-controlled buying of steaks does not result in real savings.

Grading by size of chickens is a real advantage. Poultry is purchased *eviscerated* (completely cleaned) within a range of 2 ounces. This means that a chicken graded as a 1½ pound size may weight from 23 ounces to 25 ounces. A 1¾ pound chicken may weigh from 27 ounces to 29 ounces. Breast or leg quarters of chickens can also be purchased. These may even be stuffed all are within one ounce of specification.

Portion-controlled raw supplies are available for chickens, steaks, chops, cutlets, scaloppine, brochettes, chopped steaks, and meat patties. True portion control begins after the cooking of roasts, stew, and others.

FROZEN FOOD PRODUCES : MEAT AND POULTRY

The freezing of food began for the purpose of mass feeding in times of war and emergencies. Development was continued for the purpose of being helpful to the consumer. Soon it was found that the freezing of meat and poultry never became a convenience to the consumer. It was a convenience only for the producer. The freezing and necessary extra handling of food reduces its quality. This can be proved with a large fresh steak which has been cut in half. Wrap and freeze one half. Cello wrap and refrigerate the other half. After three or four days you may cook both halves at the same time in exactly the same way and compare. The results speak for themselves. Now a days housewives who are interested in good food have found the difference between a frozen and a fresh chicken. Frozen raw supplies of meat and poultry are a convenience to the producer and a quality loss to the consumer.

HOW TO CUT A WHOLE CHICKEN ?

Step 1. Use a cutting board and be sure to sanitize it and your knife after use.

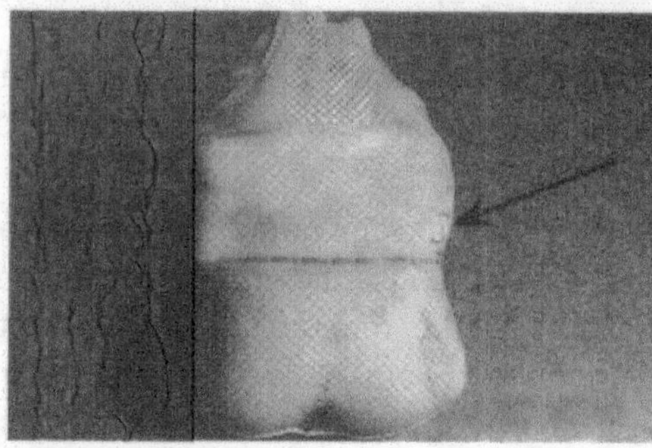

Step 2. Remove the packaging, rinse the bird and remove the giblets and neck from the cavity.

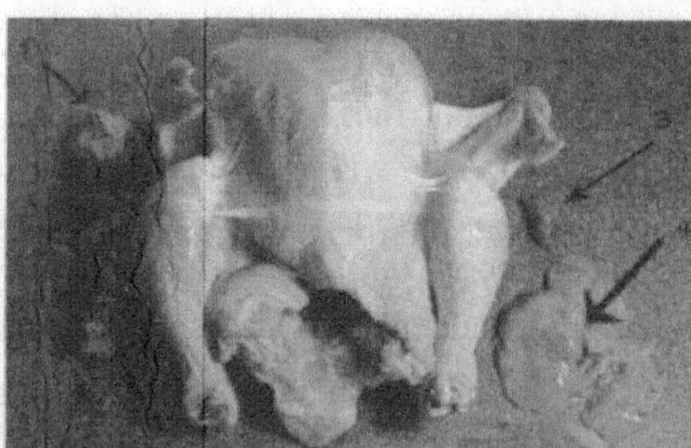

Checken Parts

1. Gizzard 2. Neck 3. Heart 4. Liver

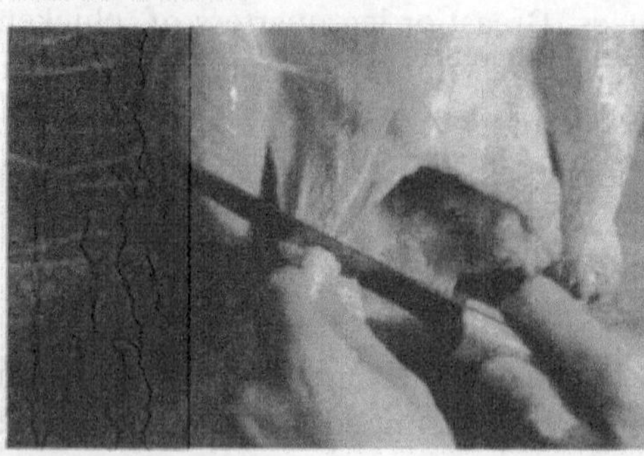

Step 3. Cut away the fat at the opening of the cavity, it just gets in the way later.

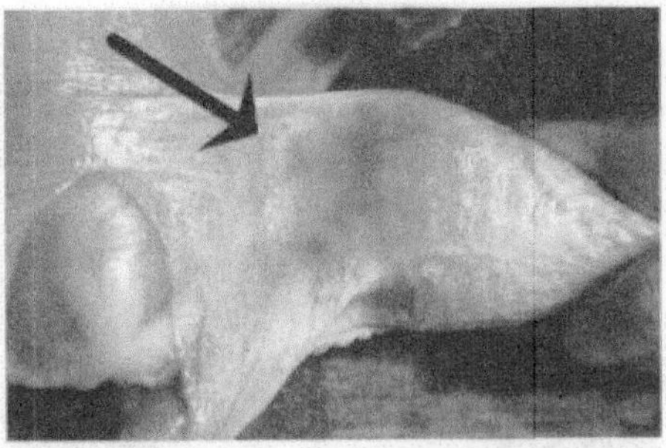

Step 4. Cut through the skin connecting the leg to the body, this makes the thigh joint easier to locate.

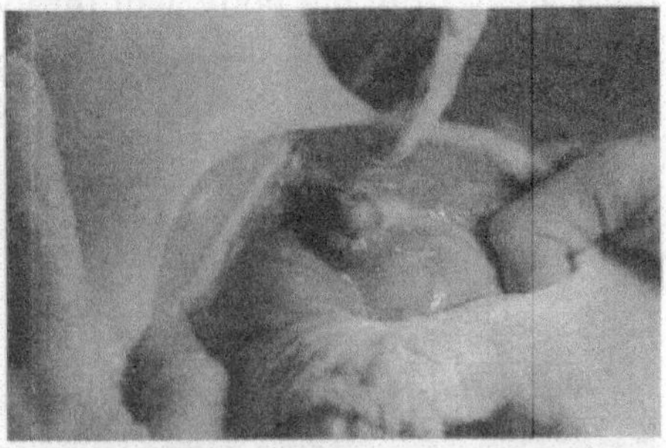

Step 5. Hold the body of the chicken in place with one hand and grasp the leg in the other. Twist the leg up and out of the joint, dislocating the hip. This gives you a place to cut the leg and thigh away from the chicken.

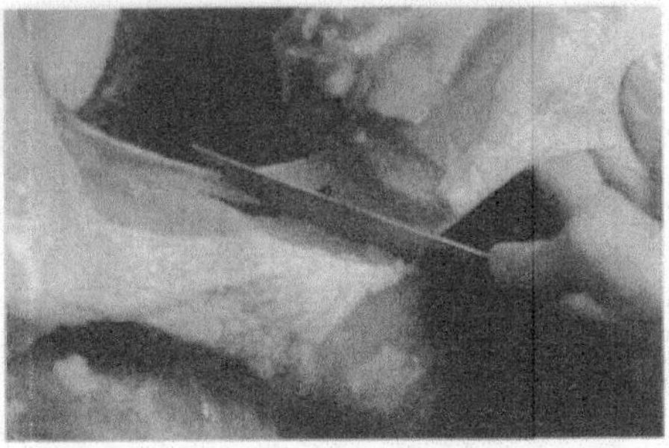

Step 6. To separate the thigh from the leg, grasp the thigh in one hand and the leg in the other and dislocate the knee.

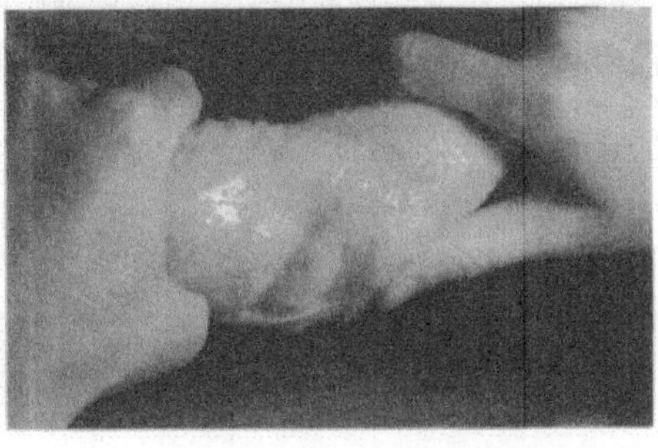

Step 7. Then cut through the joint.

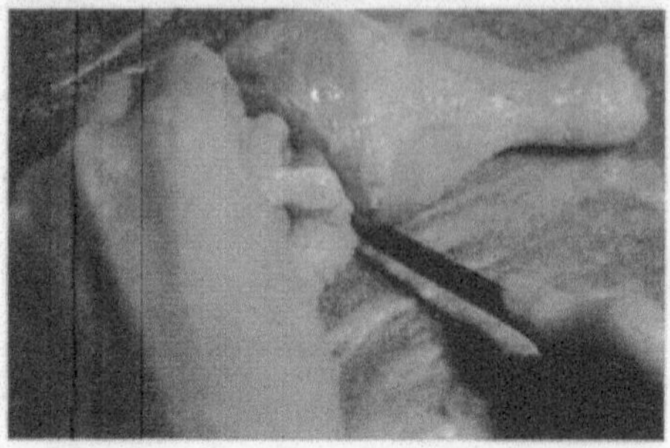

Step 8. Then repeat these steps on the other side before moving on to the wings. Grab the body of the chicken in one hand and the upper part of the wing in the other and twist away from the body. Cut through the shoulder joint.

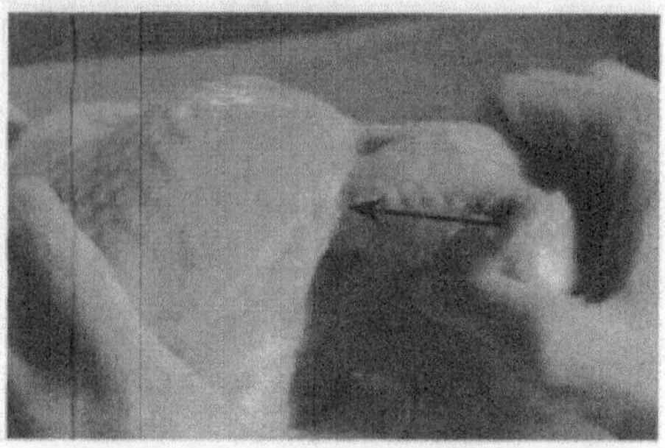

Step 9. Then separate the drumette from the rest of the wing, by dislocating the elbow and cutting through that joint.

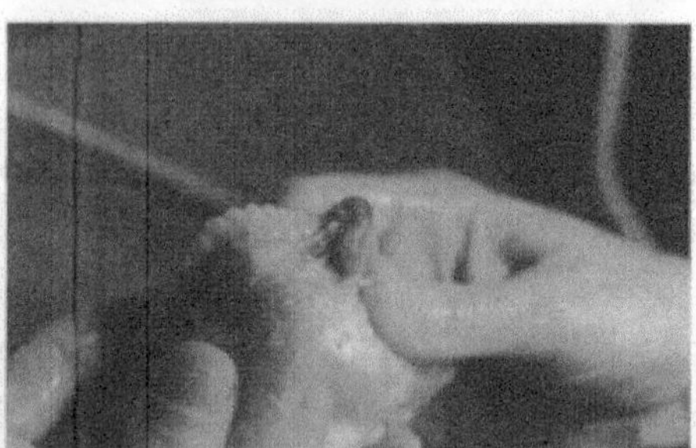

Step 10. If you'd like, separate the wing tip from the wing, in the same manner. I use the wingtips for chicken stock.

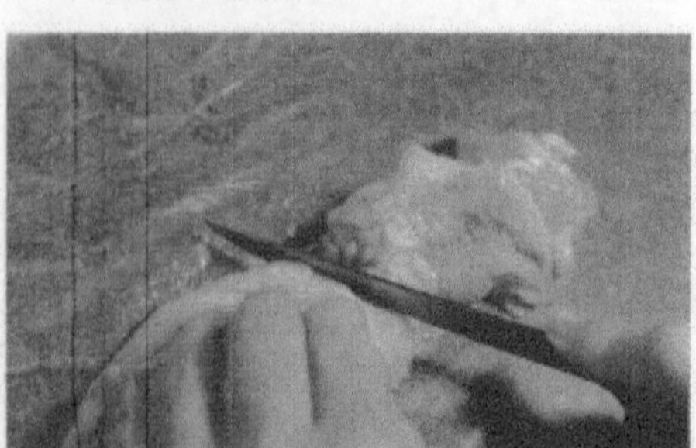

Step 11. Repeat on the other side. (Sense a theme there?)

Grasp the back of the chicken firmly below the tail (the chicken should be upside down). Cut straight down through the ribs to mostly separate the back from the breast of the chicken. This will have to be done on both sides.

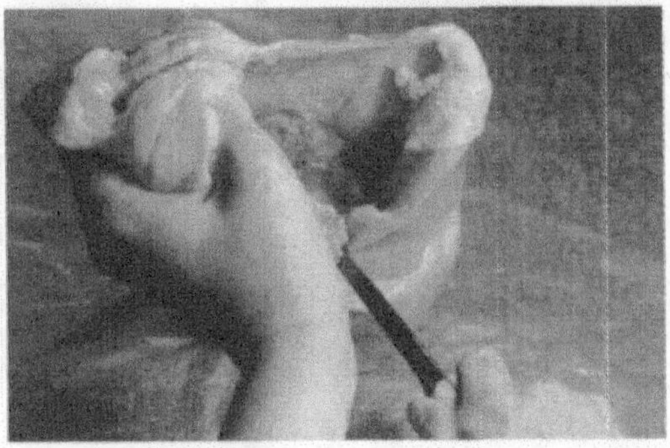

Step 12. Cut through both shoulders.

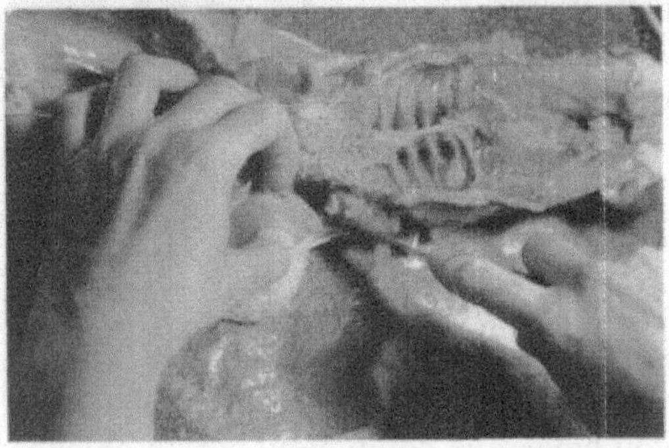

Step 13. The back and breast are now separate. Save the back for stock. There is some meat on it and the the portion just under the shoulder blades are referred to as the oysters of the chicken and are a prized cut. However, they are small and one chicken only has two. Just don't miss these when you roast a whole chicken.

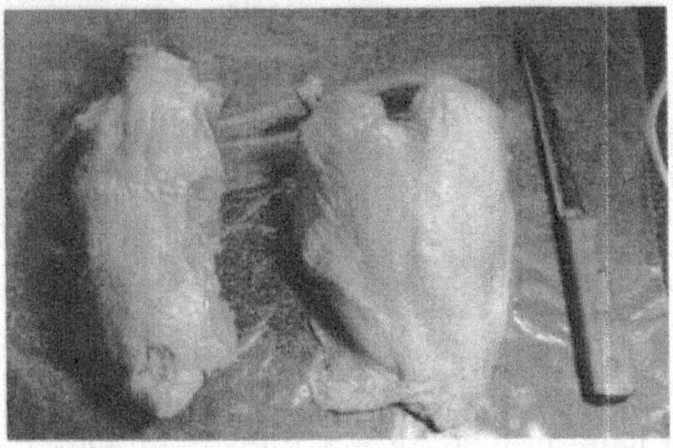

Step 14. Use a utility knife during almost the whole process, but for these last two cuts, switch to large chef knife as it takes a little bit of strength to accomplish it.

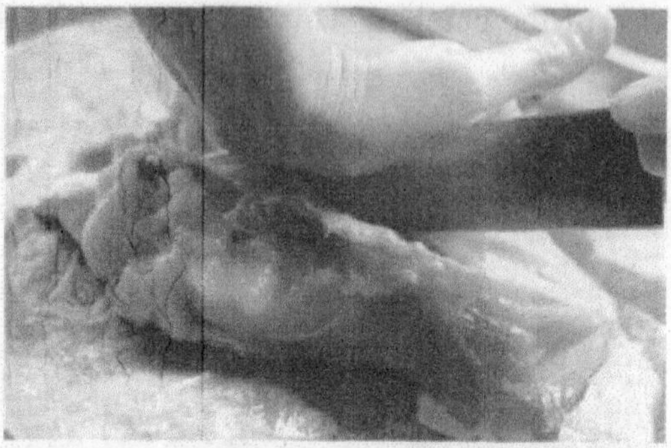

Step 15. Cut through the sternum to split the chicken breasts. You may need to flip the bird over and finish cutting through the skin.

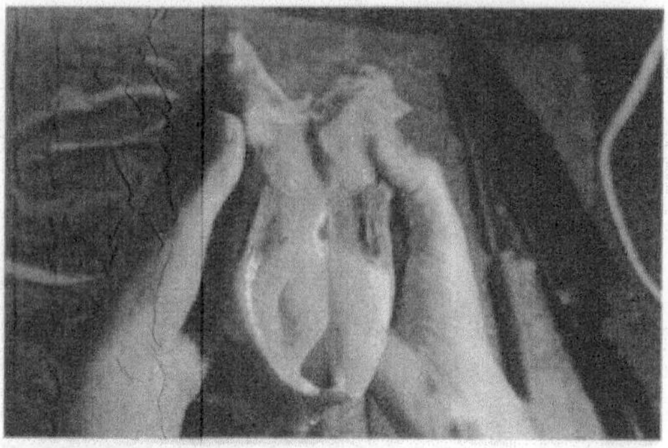

Step 16. And there you have, one completely cut up chicken. Due to space, only put one leg and one wing in the picture. Unless your chicken is mutant (and why would you eat that) you'll have more parts.

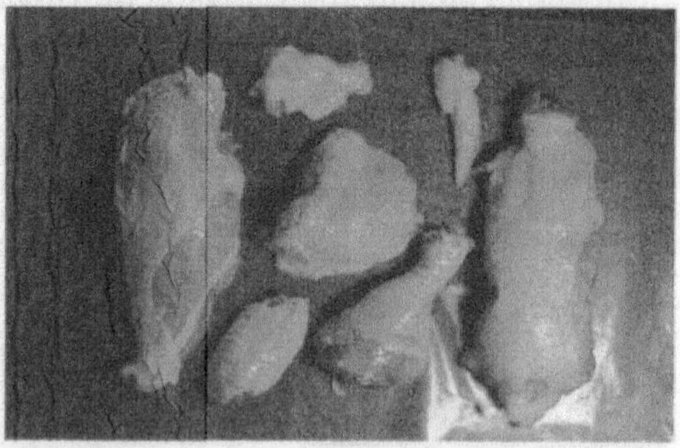

It will take a little practice to feel confident in this skill, but once you have the knack it will get much faster. Your first experience will be messy and clumsy, but hang in there; a few dinners down the line and you'll tear that chicken up in no time.

CUT UP A WHOLE CHICKEN: Indian Style

This is a basic method for cutting up and disjointing a whole chicken with the least amount of waste.

Step 1. Remove the legs: Place the chicken breast side up on a solid cutting board. Pull one leg away from the body and cut through the skin between the body and both sides of the thigh.

Bend the whole leg firmly away from the body until the ball of the thighbone pops from the hip socket. Cut between the ball and the socket to separate the leg. Repeat with the other leg.

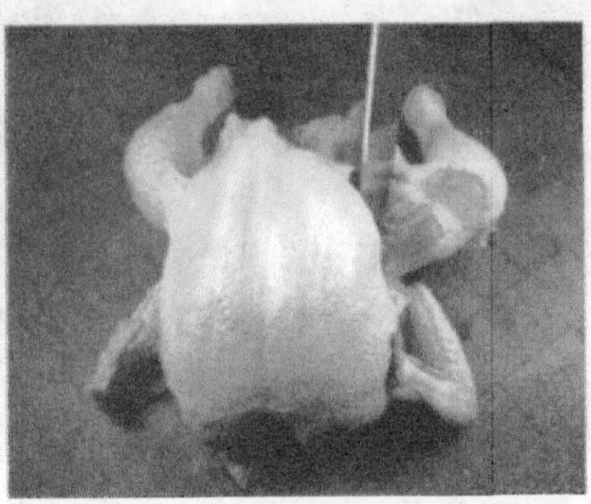

Step 2. Divide The Legs: Place the chicken leg skin side down on the cutting board. Cut down firmly through the joint between the drumstick and the thigh.

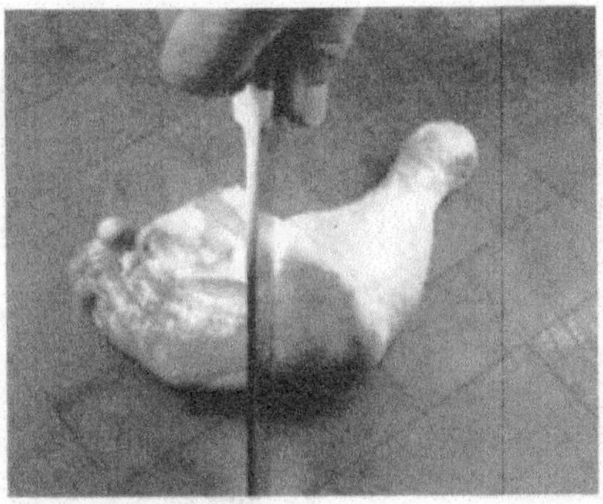

Step 3. Remove The Wings: With chicken on it's back, remove wing by cutting inside of wing just over joint. Pull wing away from body and cut from down through the skin and the joint. Repeat with the other wing.

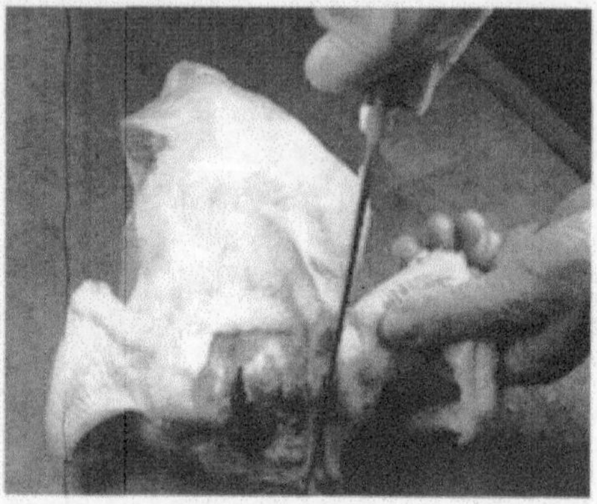

Step 4. Cut Carcass in Half: Cut through the cavity of the bird from the tail end and slice through the thin area around the shoulder joint Cut parallel to the backbone and slice the bones of the rib cage. Repeat on the opposite side of the backbone.

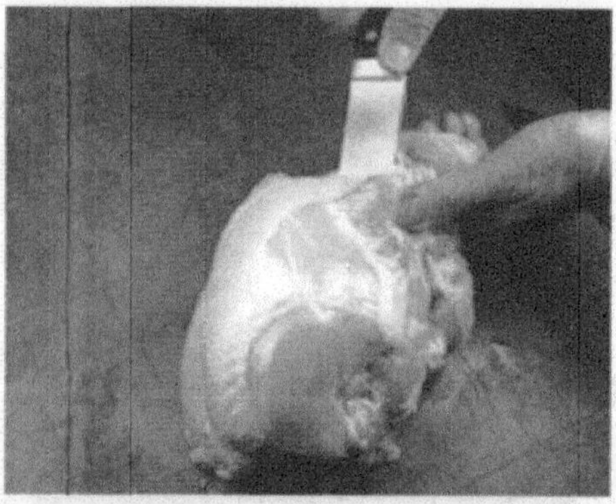

Step 5. Remove The Breast: Pull apart the breast and the back. Cut down trough the shoulder bones to detach the breast from the back.

Cut the back into two pieces by cutting across the backbone where the ribs end.

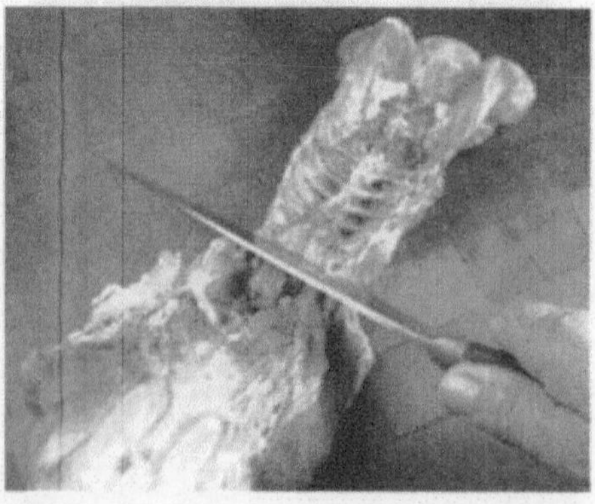

Step 6. Cut Breast In Half: You may leave the breast whole if your recipe requires. To cut in half, use a strong, steady pressure and cut downward along the length of the breastbone to separate the breast into two pieces.

CUTTING UP CHICKEN: 10 Pieces

A whole chicken can be cooked whole but if you want to fry it or use it for a recipe calling for pieces, the whole chicken will have to be cut up first. You will need to make sure you have a sharp knife to work with and a work surface that is washable. A poultry shears or kitchen shears will also be very beneficial when cutting some of the sections where you have to cut through the bones. Cutting up a whole chicken can be difficult if you do not have the proper tools and do not use proper methods.

Experience using different techniques will help you determine which methods work best for you and will eventually make this task easier. There are several methods that can be used and different methods can produce different number of pieces when completed.

Removing Leg-Thigh Portion

Step 1. With breast side up, place the chicken on the cutting board. Pull the leg away from the body and cut through the skin connecting the body and leg. Then cut down between the body and the thigh to the thigh joint.

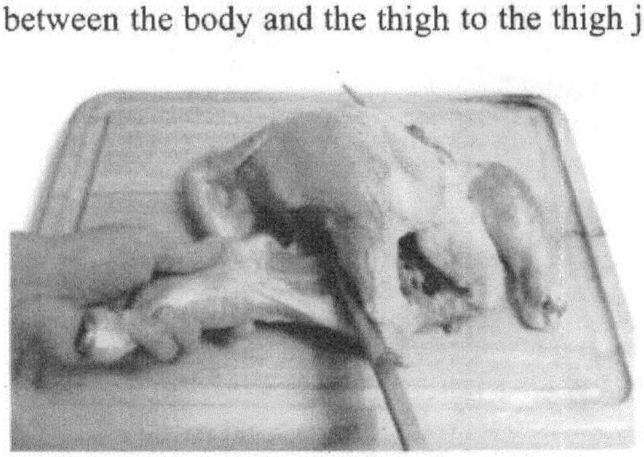

Step 2. Bend the leg-thigh portion back until the thighbone pops from the joint. Use the tip of the knife to cut through the joint area and then cut close to the

backbone to detach the leg-thigh portion from the body. Repeat the same steps on the opposite side to detach the other thigh-leg portion.

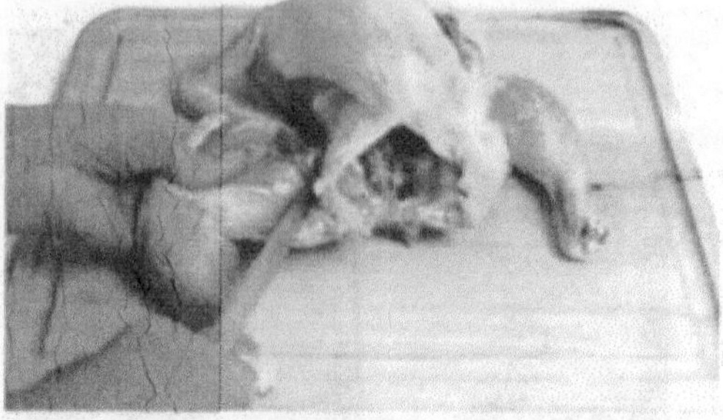

Step 3. Separate the leg and thigh by place the leg-thigh portion skin side down on the cutting board. Following the yellow line of fat, locate the joint connecting the two and use a sharp knife to cut completely through the joint to separating the leg from the thigh. Repeat this process to separate the other leg-thigh portion.

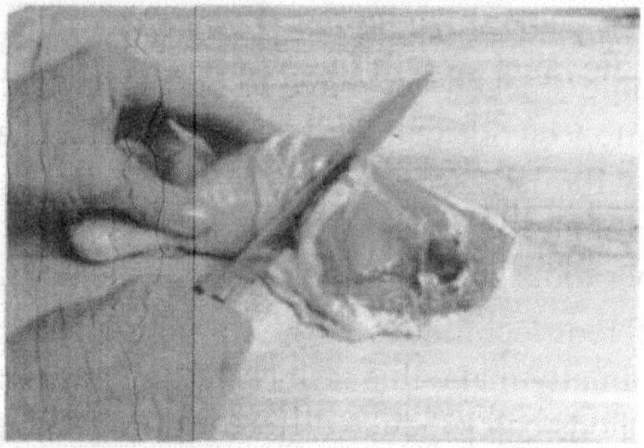

Step 4. *Removing the Wings:* Place the chicken on the cutting board breast side down. Pull the wing portion out away from the body and cut the joint between the wing and the breast to detach it from the body. A little of the breast meat can be cut off with the wing to produce a meatier wing, if desired. Repeat this process on the opposite side.

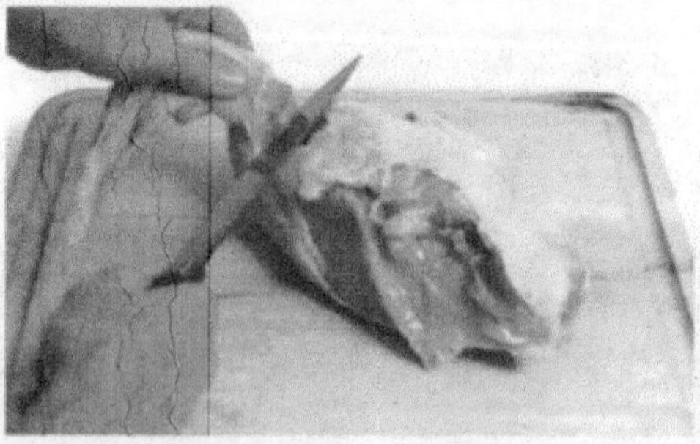

Step 5. *Removing the Backbone:* Starting at the tail end, cut along one side of the backbone and continue cutting to the neck. Then cut along the other side of the backbone.

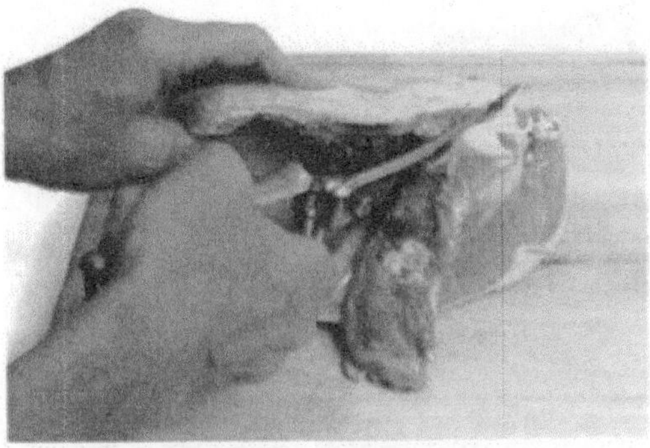

Step 6. Cut through the collarbone to remove the backbone: A poultry shears or kitchen shears may be helpful in making the cuts to remove the backbone. Discard the backbone or save to make stock.

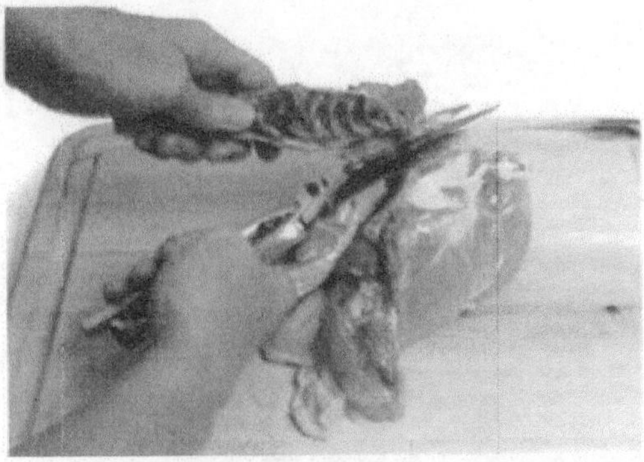

Step 7. *Cutting Breast in Half:* Before cutting breasts in half remove the excess piece that is locate on each side of the lower breast. Cut along the side of the breast, starting at the bottom and cut up along the bottom of the rib cage, leaving the ribs attached.

Step 8. Begin by Making a half inch slit at the top center of the keel bone (the bone separating the two halves).

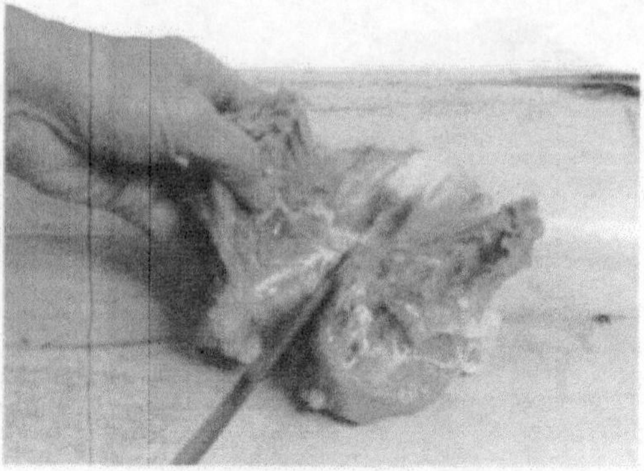

Step 9. Hold the breast in both hands, skin side down with the top of the breast towards you. Bend both sides back until the keel bone pops out where the incision was made. Bend the sides back to expose as much of the keel as possible.

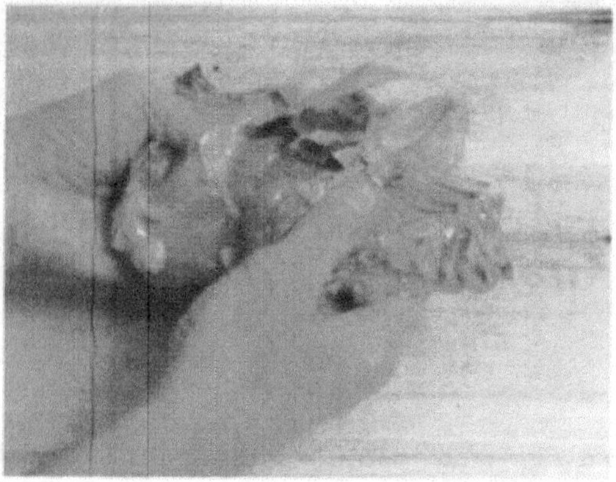

Step 10. Place the breast back on the cutting board and loosen the keel bone by running at thumb or finger along each side of the bone.

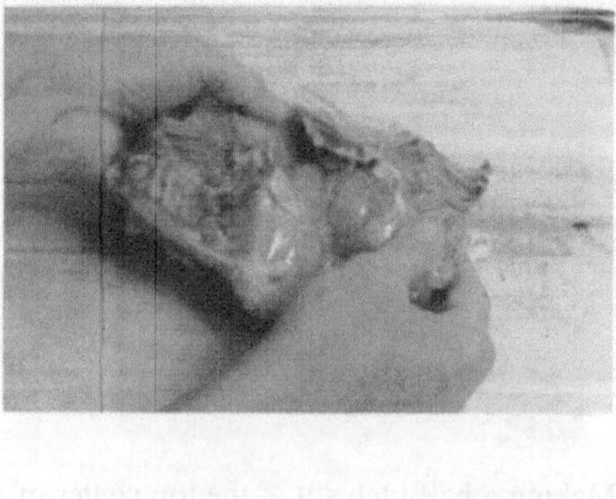

Step 11. Take hold of the top of the keel bone and pull it off the breast.

Step 12. Using a sharp knife or kitchen shears, cut down through the center of the breast to produce two halves.

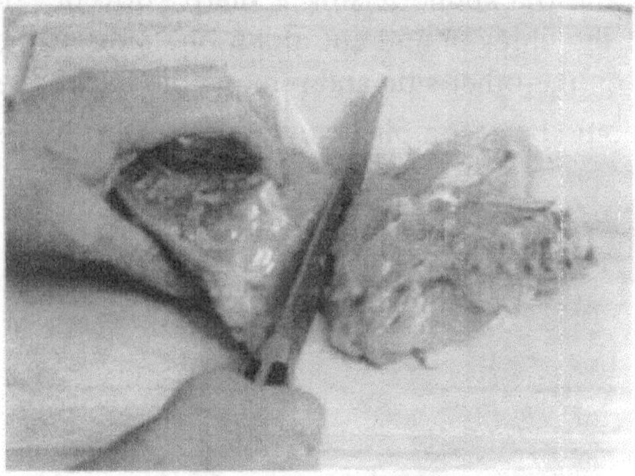

Step 13. Cut the halves into quarters by cutting across the breast halves at an angle just below the rib bones.

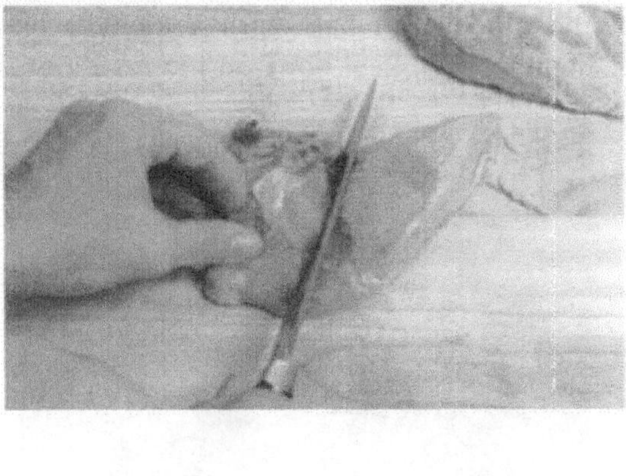

Step 14. Cutting up a whole chicken following the instructions shown above will produce the ten pieces shown here.

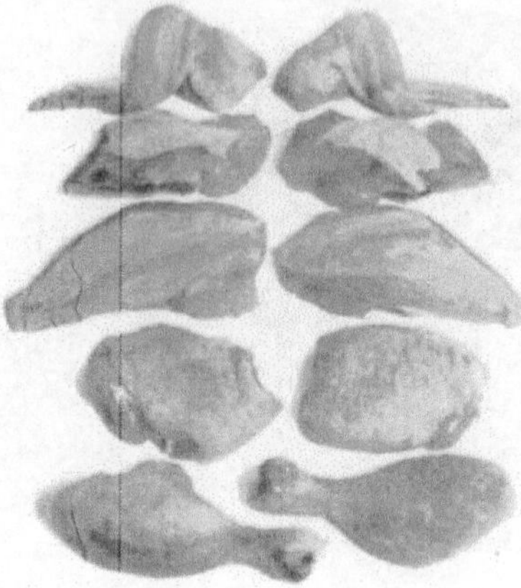

CUTTING UP CHICKEN: 12 Pieces

Step 1. Removing the Backbone: Using a sharp knife or poultry shears start at the tail end of the chicken and cut along one side of the backbone. Repeat the procedure on the other side and remove the backbone.

This task could be accomplished with less effort when using a poultry shears.

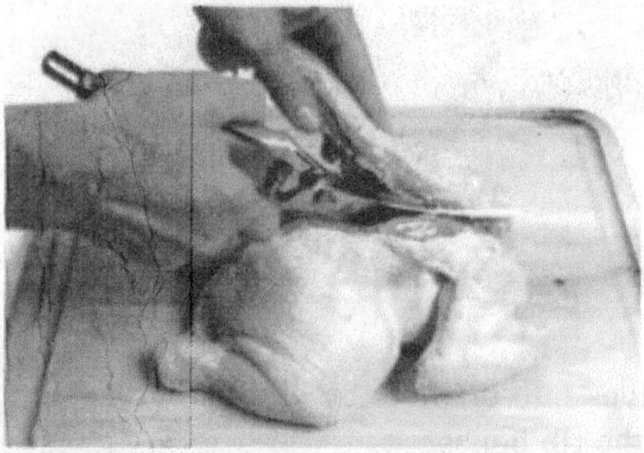

Step 2. Cut Chicken in Half: Place the chicken breast side down on the cutting board. Cut the chicken in half with a cleaver or sharp knife by cutting through the center of the keel bone on the inside of the breast.

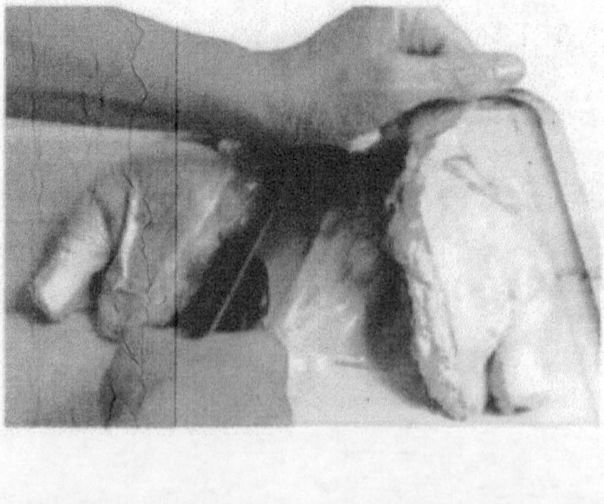

Step 3. After this cut is made you should have two equal halves.

Step 4. Separating the Breast Quarter from the Leg Quarter.

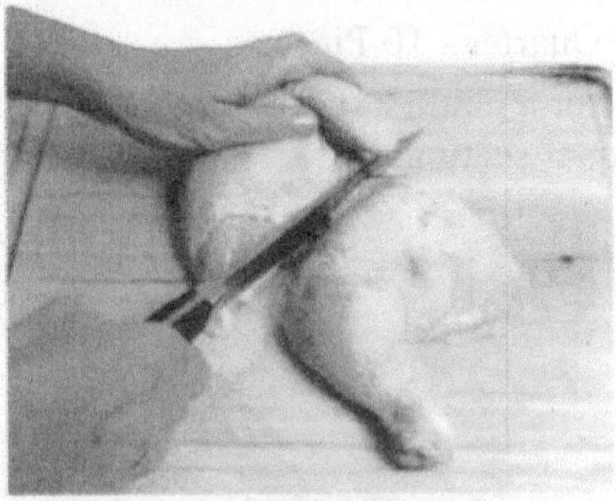

Step 5. Once the cut is made you will have a breast quarter and a leg quarter from each half of the chicken.

Step 6. Separating the Leg Quarter

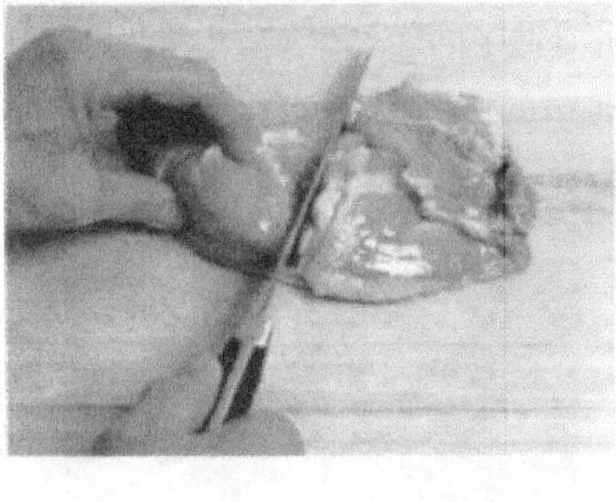

Step 7. Using a knife or a poultry shears, cut the thigh from the back section of the leg quarter to produce two pieces.

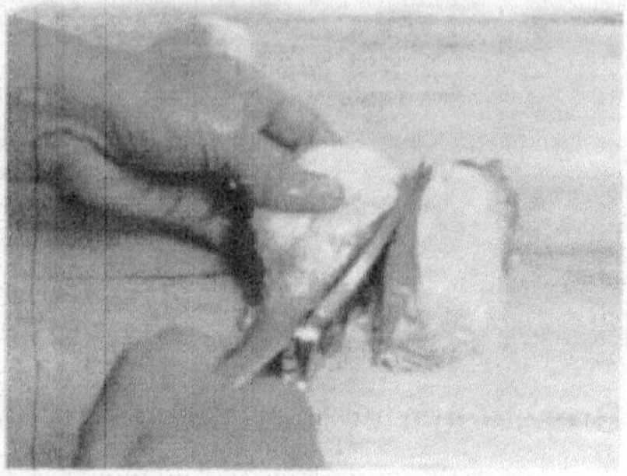

Step 8. Cutting Breast Quarter - 10 Pieces

Step 9. Using a cleaver or a poultry shears, cut the breast quarter crosswise in half to produce two equal sections.

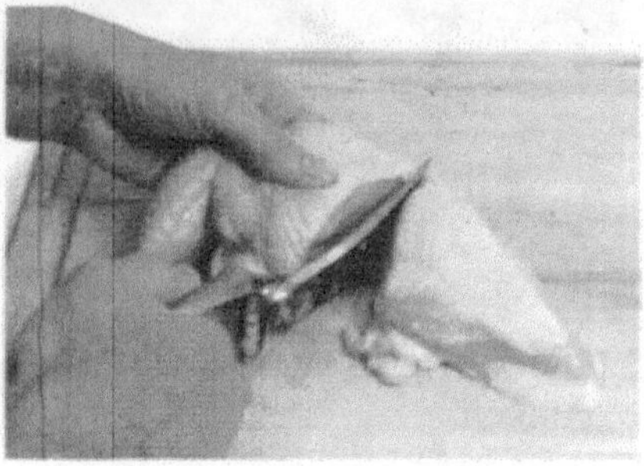

Step 10. Cutting the breast quarter in half will produce 10 pieces of chicken when both halves have been cut.

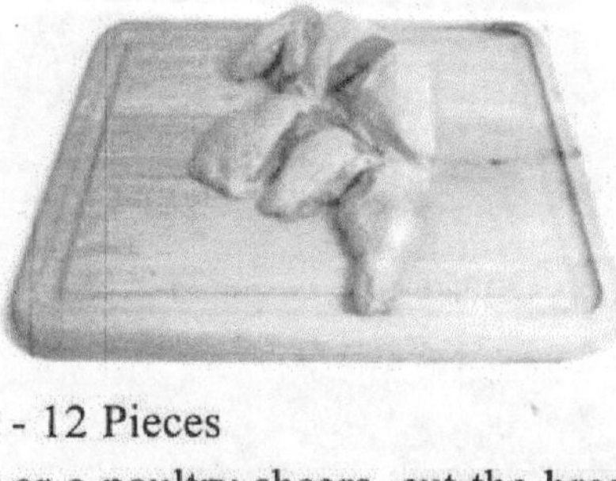

Step 11. Cutting Quarter - 12 Pieces

Step 12. Using a cleaver or a poultry shears, cut the breast quarter crosswise in three equal sections.

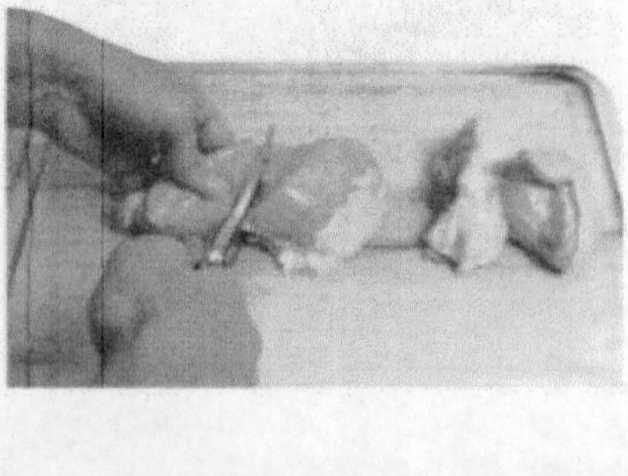

Step 13. Cutting the breast quarter in three equal sections will produce 12 pieces of chicken when both halves have been cut.

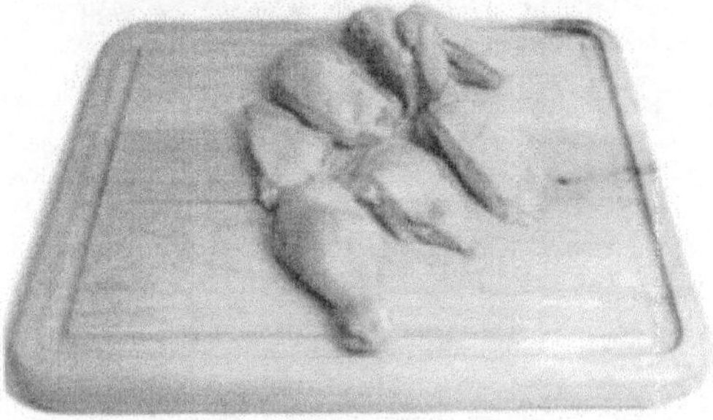

Whether the breast quarter is cut in half or in three equal sections will be your own personal preference. Factors that may affect your decision are the size of the chicken and the number of servings you would like to produce. If the chicken is smaller, cutting the breast quarter in thirds may make the pieces too small. If the chicken is larger, cutting the breast quarter in half may make the servings too large, especially if serving children. Before cutting, consider number of servings needed, appetites of those being served, and the amount of other food being served with the chicken.

CUTTING WHOLE CHICKEN INTO HALVES & QUARTERS

Chicken halves and quarters are popular cuts for many roasted chicken recipes and they make an elegant presentation on the plate.

While you can find the chicken halves and quarters in the grocery store, you have more freedom with a recipe if you cut a whole chicken into halves and quarters yourself.

Step 1. Place the chicken , breast side down, on a cutting board with the neck end pointing away from you.

Step 2. To make the first cut to the chicken, insert the knife into the front of the chicken. Work the knife from the neck to the tail of the chicken, and cut along one side of the backbone. It is important to cut as close to the bone as possible.

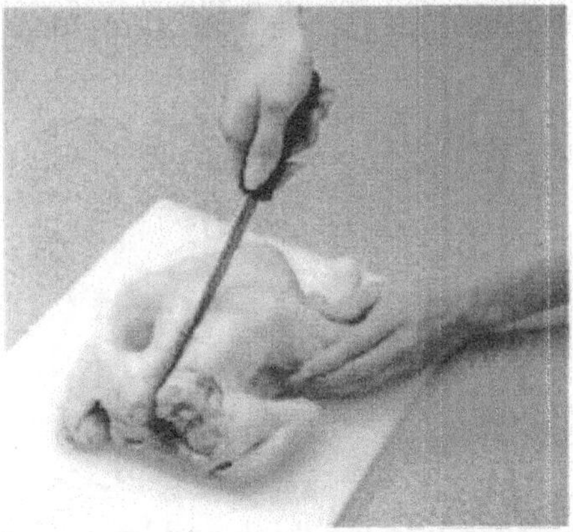

Cut from neck to tail along one side of the backbone.

Step 3. Cut down the other side of the backbone and remove it.

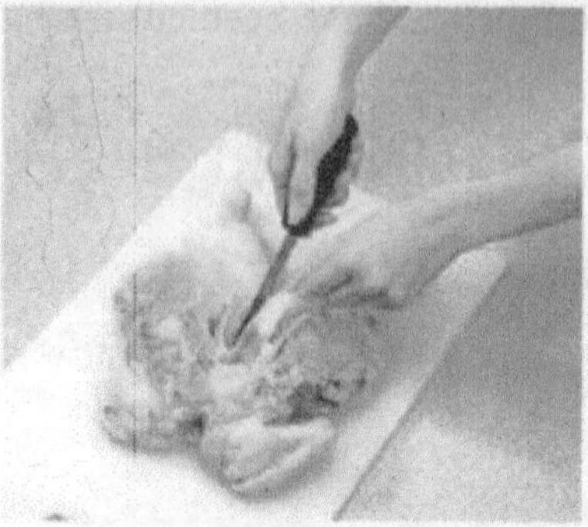

Remove both the breastbone and the cartilage.

Step 4. With the breast of the chicken still meaty side down, cut a small slit through the membrane and cartilage at the "V" of the neck end.

Step 5. Grasp the breast with both hands and gently bend both sides backward to snap the breastbone. With fingers, work along both sides of the breastbone to loosen the triangular keel bone; pull out the bone.

Step 6. With the tip of a sharp knife, cut along both sides of the cartilage at the end of the breastbone, remove cartilage.

Step 7. Turn the chicken, skin side up. Cut lengthwise down the center of the chicken to split it into halves.

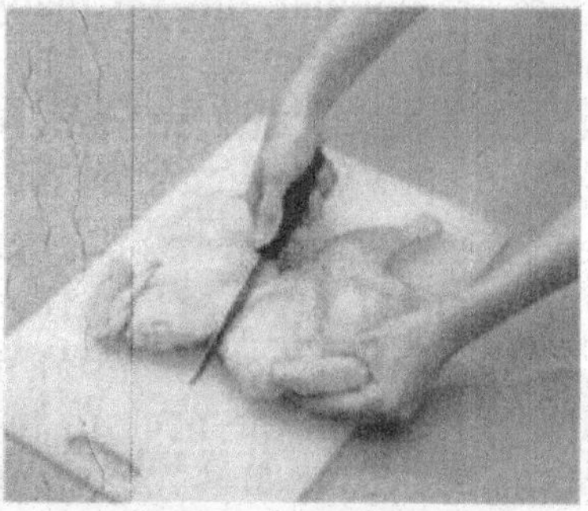

Split the chicken lengthwise down the center tomake halves

Step 8. To cut into quarters, cut through the skin separarting the thighs from the breast.

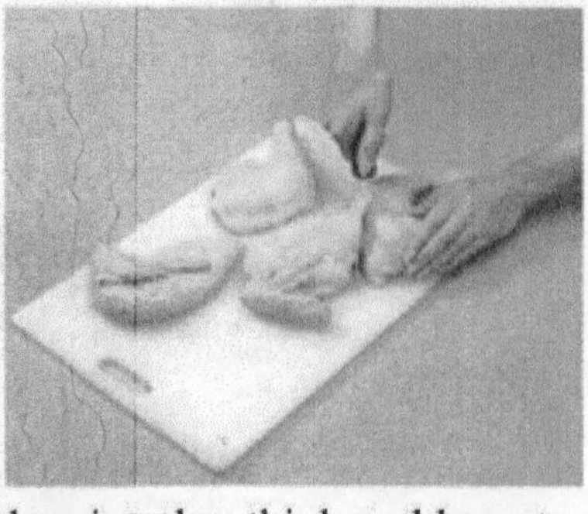

Step 9. Separate the chicken into leg-thigh and breast-wing sections for quarters.

Cutting Whole Chicken into Pieces

Most familiar and easy chicken recipes — like baked chicken, fried chicken, or chicken cacciatore — call for "chicken pieces." But stores charge extra for doing the knife work. You can save money by cutting up a whole chicken at home rather than buying chicken pieces pre-cut and packaged at the supermarket. The steps are quite simple.

Step 1. Place the chicken, breast side up, on a cutting board.

Step 2. Cut between the thigh and body to the hip joint.

Step 3. Bend the leg back slightly to free the hip joint from the socket. Cut through the hip joint and remove the leg. Repeat to remove the other leg.

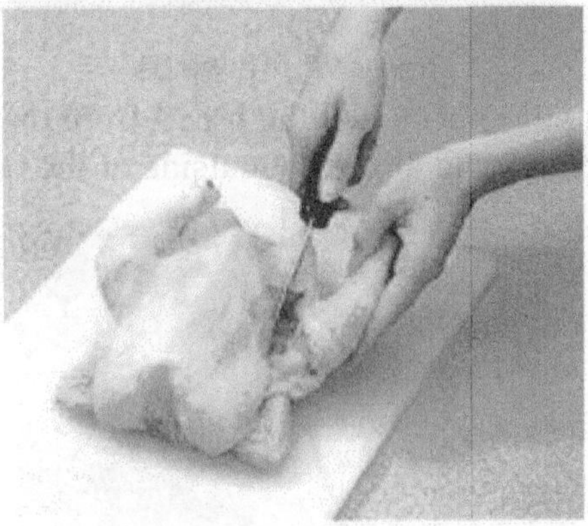

First remove the legs and thighs by cutting through the hip joint

Step 4. Place the leg, skin side down, on a cutting board. Locate the joint by moving the thigh back and forth with one hand while holding the drumstick with the other hand. Cut completely through the joint. Repeat with the other leg.

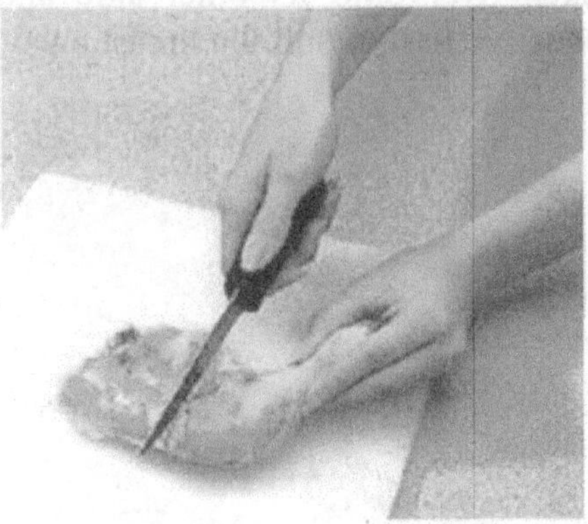

Bend the leg back slightly in order to free the hip joint from the socket.

Step 5. Place the chicken on its side. Pull one wing out from the body; cut through the shoulder joint. Turn the chicken over and repeat to remove the other wing.

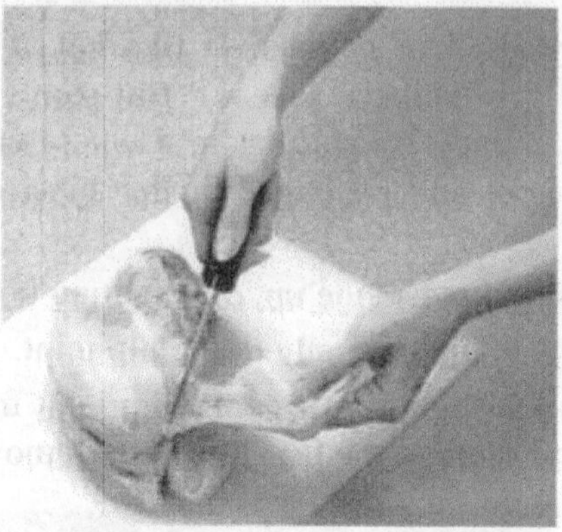

Remove the wings

Step 6. Working from tail to neck, cut the breast from the backbone, cutting through the small rib bones and along the outside of the collarbone.

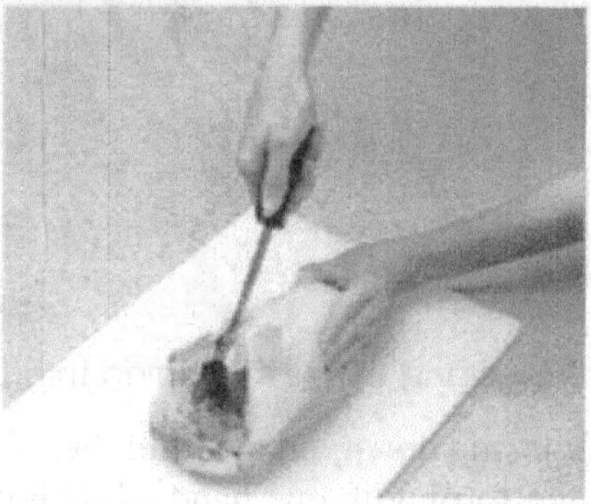

The rib bones are easy to cut right through

Step 7. Turn the chicken over onto its other side and repeat. Cut through any remaining connective tissue; pull the breast away from the backbone.

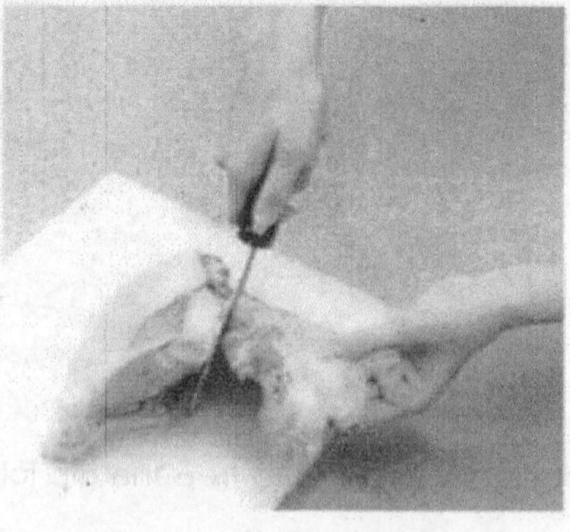

Fig.

Step 8. Place the breast, breast, skin side up, on a cutting board. Split the breast into halves by cutting along one side of the breastbone.

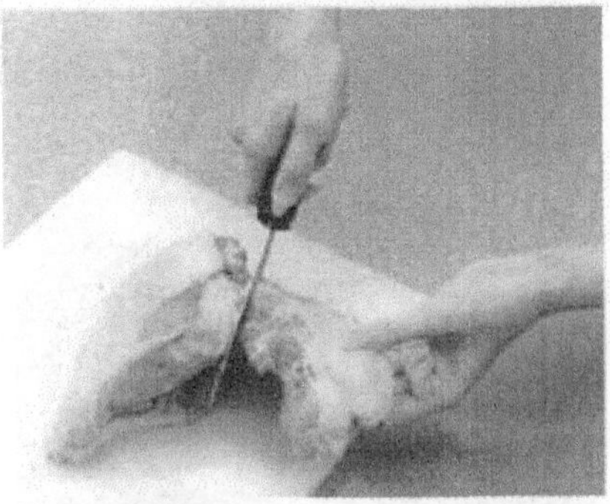

Once the breast has been split into halves, each portion should be between 4 and 10 ounces

CHOPPING UP A CHICKEN: Chinese-Style

Chinese-style cutting is an older definition for cutting a whole chicken into smaller, serving-size pieces of bone-in chicken. You can use this style of cutting for any Asian dish or other recipe that calls for chicken cut into serving-size pieces.

These pieces should be smaller than chicken pieces generally are cut. A cleaver is the best utensil for the job, although poultry shears or a sharp knife also may be used.

Step 1. Place the chicken, breast-side up, on a heavy cutting board. Cut the chicken in half lengthwise, cutting slightly to one side of the breastbone and backbone.

Cut completely through the chicken to make two pieces.

Step 2. Remove and discard the backbone entirely

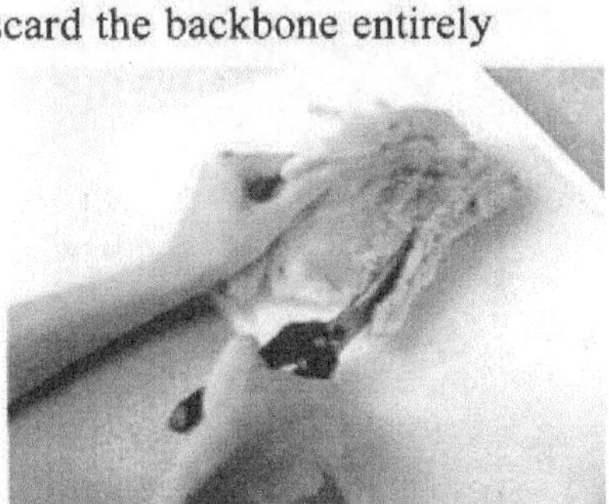

Remove the backbone quickly with kitchen shears

Step 3. Pull each leg up slightly from the breast section; cut through the ball and socket joint to remove each leg. Cut through the knee joint of each leg to separate it into a drumstick and a thigh.

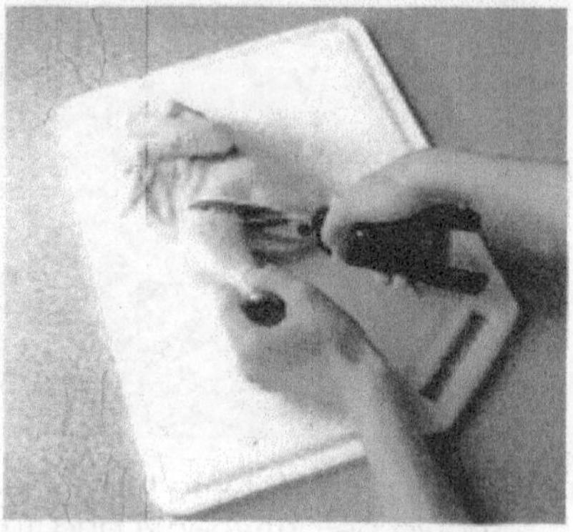

Cut wing off cleanly at the breast

Step 4. Pull each wing away from the breast section; cut through the joint next to the breast. Pull wing away from the breast to make an even cut through the joint of the chicken. Sharp kitchen shears also can cut through the joints of the chicken easily.

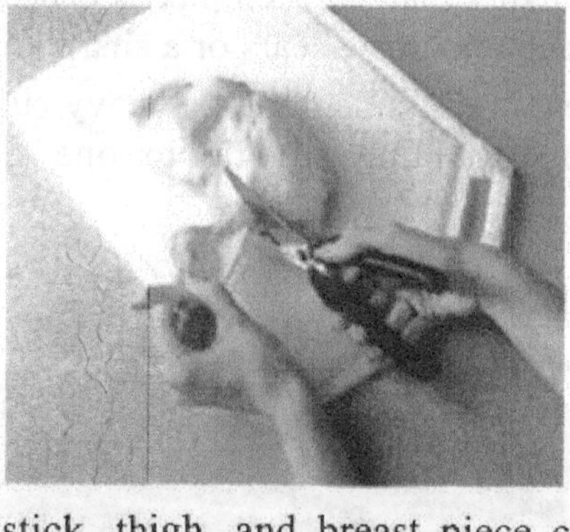

Step 5. Cut each drumstick, thigh, and breast piece crosswise into three pieces, cutting completely through the bones.

Step 6. Cut each wing into two pieces. This technique will result in 22 small, serving size pieces.

This technique results in 22 small, serving-size pieces

Whether you're cooking with smaller, serving-size chicken pieces or the standard size, skinning the pieces before cooking can reduce fat. There's a simple trick for easily skinning uncooked chicken pieces. We'll show it to you in the next section.

CHOPPING UP A CHICKEN, Chinese-Style

Chinese and south-east Asian recipes often require bone-in chicken cut into serving sized pieces. This is different from the selection of thighs, breast, and drumsticks that we find in UK supermarkets. Chinese-style pieces are cut through the bone adding richness to the stock or sauce they are simmering in.

It's also a thrifty way of making use of a whole chicken. Buy the best, organic free-range chicken you can afford, it often ends up cheaper than buying pre-packed joints separately. You will need a good chopping board and a heavy cleaver bought from a Chinese supermarket. Don't try and use a chef's knife as it just won't stand up to the job. A pair of heavy duty kitchen scissors or shears will come in handy though.

The Chinese chefs chop through barbecued meats with a heavy cleaver and incredibly good aim. That said it's not so much about technique but arm strength, proper tools and experience. If you use a strong, clean motion, it should split the bone and let you follow through and cut the meat. For the inexperienced, the cleaver will pierce and stick into the bone. At this point use your other hand to pound the cleaver into the meat. Kitchen shears can tackle smaller bones and joints.

Half a chicken will give you seven serving sized pierces. Freeze the other half of chicken, cut up for future use. Before cutting, wash the chicken under running water and pat dry with kitchen towels.

SKINNING CHICKEN

Using skinless chicken pieces in recipes has gained in popularity. Skinning the chicken before cooking can reduce fat and make a dish easier to eat and enjoy.

Removing the skin also can help the chicken meat more readily absorb the flavors of marinades and cooking sauces.

If you want to skin chicken, it's best to use cold chicken. Cold chicken is easier to skin, so plan ahead.

1. Freeze the chicken pieces just until firm, but not hard. For safety reasons, make sure that you do not refreeze thawed chicken.
2. Grasp the skin with a clean cotton kitchen towel to improve your grip.
3. You can also use a clean piece of paper towel, if you want an easy throw-away method.
4. Take the towel and pull the skin away from the meat. Be sure to discard the skin A kitchen towel or sheet of paper towel improves your grip.
5. When finished skinning the chicken, launder the towel before using it again.

DEBONING A CHICKEN

While skinless chicken pieces have become more popular, there is another kind of chicken that has eclipsed everything else when it comes to easy, fast, low-fat cooking: boneless, skinless chicken breasts. Here are some guidelines on removing the bones from a skinless chicken breast and making it ready for a variety of cooking methods:

Step 1. Place the skinless whole chicken breast, meaty side down, on a cutting board. Cut a small slit through the membrane and cartilage at the V of the neck end.

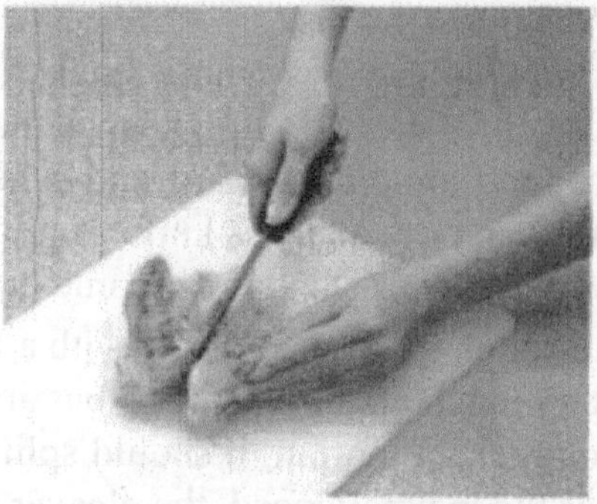

Use a sharp knife or kitchen shears to cut through the cartilage.

Step 2. Grasp the breast with both hands and gently bend both sides backward to snap the breastbone.

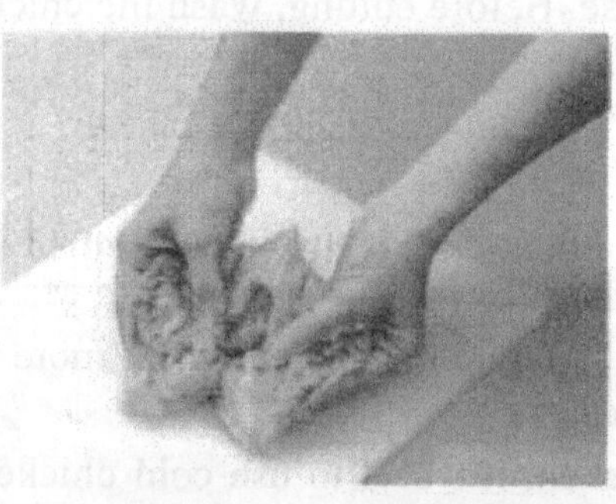

Place your thumbs on either side of the breastbone for leverage

Step 3. With fingers, work along both sides of the breastbone to loosen the triangular keel bone; pull out the bone.

Be sure to remove all of the keel bone. Check for any splinters or shards that might have broken off.

Step 6. With the tip of a sharp knife, cut along both sides of the cartilage at the end of the breastbone; remove cartilage.

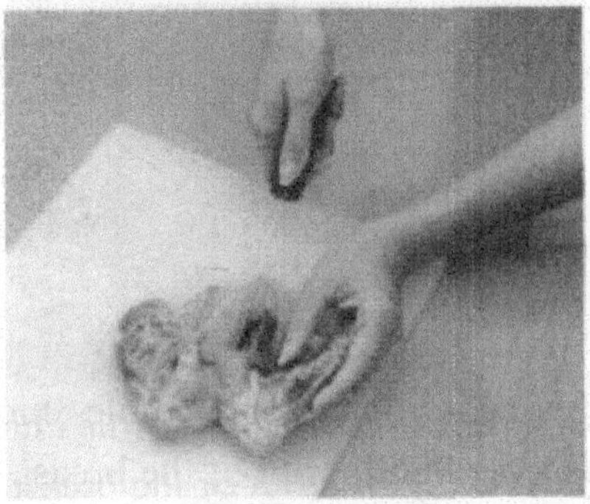

Make short, light chops with the tip of the knife to separate the cartilage.

Step 7. Slip the point of the knife under the long rib bone on one side of the breast. Cut and scrape the meat from the rib bones, pulling the bones away from the meat.

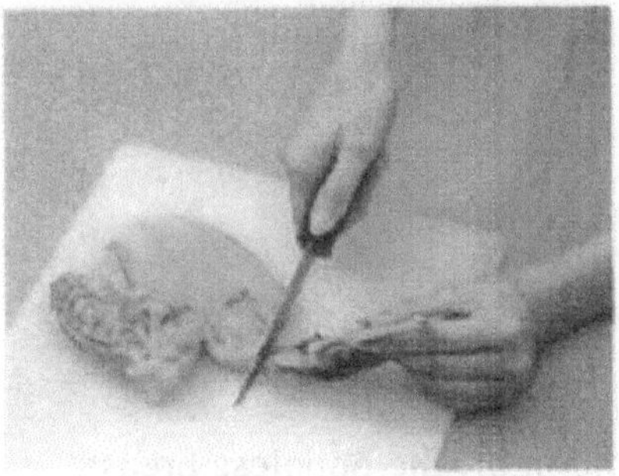

The rib bones are connected by a membrane.

Step 8. Cut the meat away from the collarbone; remove the bone. Repeat the procedure to debone the other side of the breast.

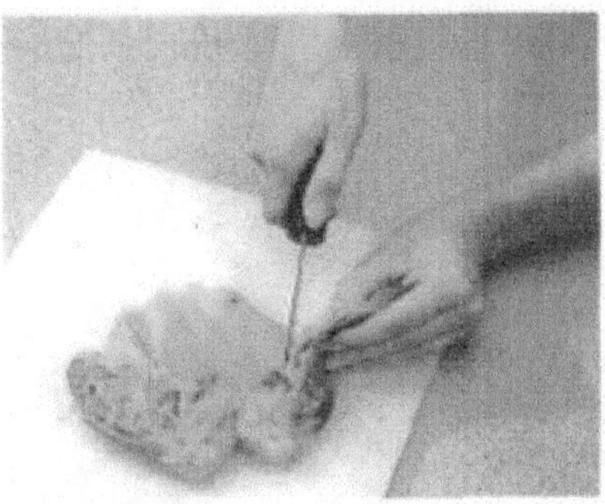

Remove the collarbone from the breast.

Step 9. Packaged whole, bone-in breasts already have the wishbone removed. If you cut up a whole chicken at home, you will need to remove the wishbone. Cut the meat away from the bone with the tip of the knife.

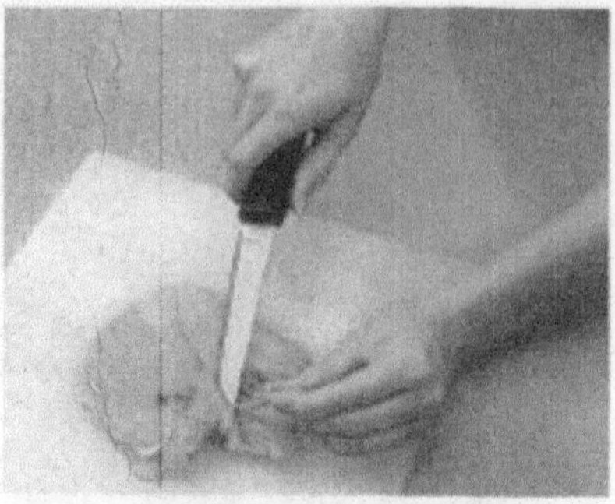

Remove the wishbone if you cut up a whole chicken.

Step 10. Grasp the wishbone and pull it out of the breast.

To remove the white tendon from each side of the breast, cut enough meat away from each tendon so you can grasp it. (Use a paper towel for a firmer grasp.) Pull out the tendon.

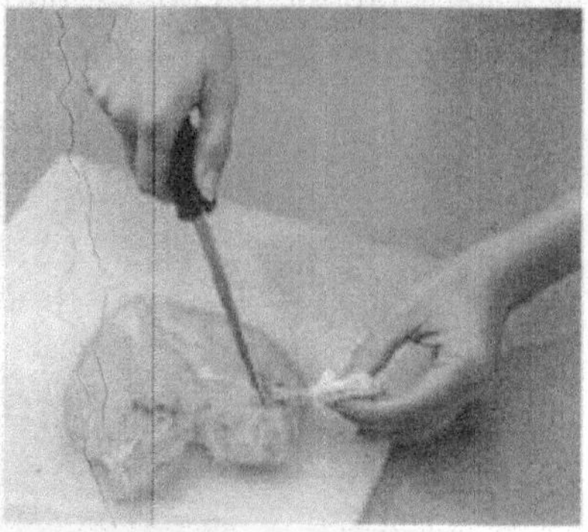

Cut the white tendon off the boneless breast.

Step 11. Turn the breast meaty side up. If desired, remove the chicken tenders from the thickest edge of each breast half and reserve for another use, such as a fast sweet and sour chicken or stir-fried chicken and vegetables. Trim any loosened connective tissue that remains.

Step 12. Cut the whole chicken breast into halves lengthwise to make two, perfect single-serving pieces.

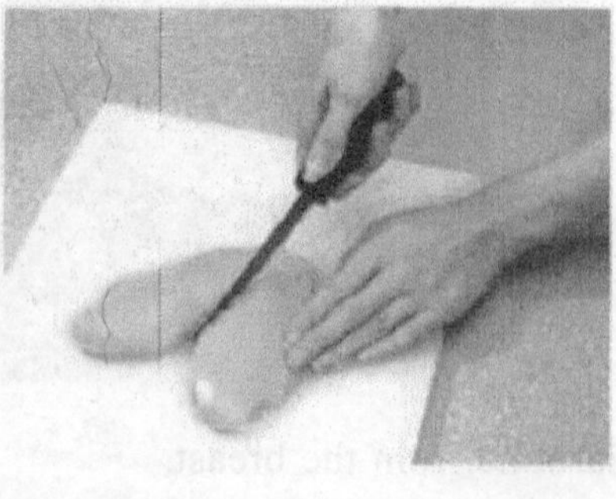

Cut in half to make two perfect servings.

Sometimes a recipe calls for sliced, diced, or shredded chicken.

SKINNING AND BONNING CHICKEN

Follow these helpful hints to prepare your chicken properly.

Preparing Chicken Breasts

Step 1. To skin chicken breasts, place the whole breast, skin-side-up, on a cutting board. Starting on one side of the breast, use your hand to pull the skin away from the meat. Discard the skin.

Step 2. To bone chicken breasts, cut the meat away from one side of the breastbone, using a thin, sharp knife. Then move the knife over the rib bones, pulling away the meat. Repeat on the other side.

Step 3. To remove the long, white tendon from each breast half, hold one end of the tendon with your fingers. Use the tip of the knife to scrape the meat away from the tendon as you pull it out.

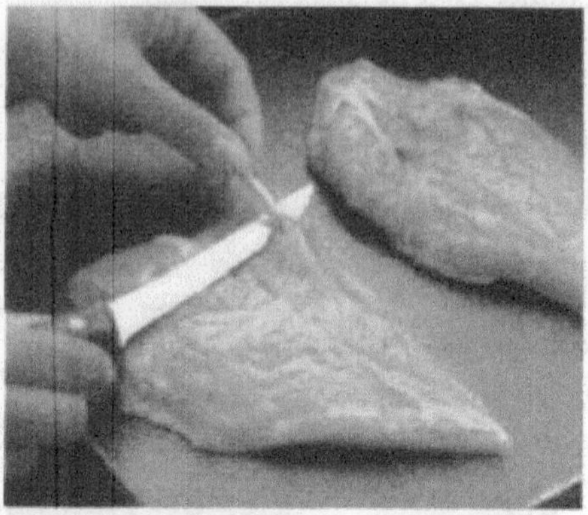

BONING CHICKEN

Preparing a Whole Chicken

Step 1. Starting from the inside of the neck opening, use your fingers to find the joints where the wings attach to the back. With a small sharp knife, make a cut just inside the neck opening on each side of the bird to expose the bones that from the joints. Cut through the joints and ligaments, as shown.

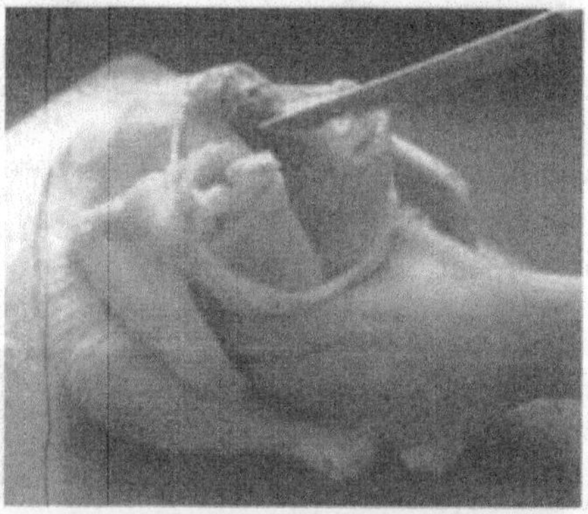

Step 2. Loosen the meat from the wishbone with your fingers. Use a knife or kitchen shears to cut the ligaments as necessary. Remove the wishbone. It may be necessary to cut the wishbone away from the breastbone.

Step 3. Work your index finger down along each side of the breastbone, freeing the meat from the bone as you go. Use a knife to loosen the white cartilage from the skin, if necessary, to release the breastbone.

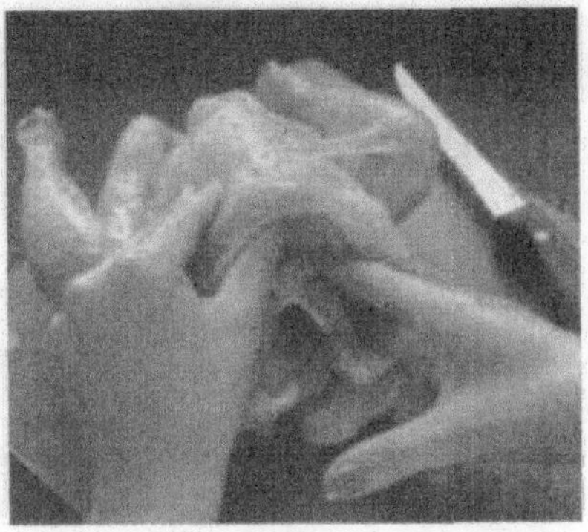

Step 4. Work your fingers around the rib cage to the back and as far down the backbone as you can. Loosen the meat and cut the cartilage, if necessary. Turn the bird over to make detaching the meat from the backbone easier.

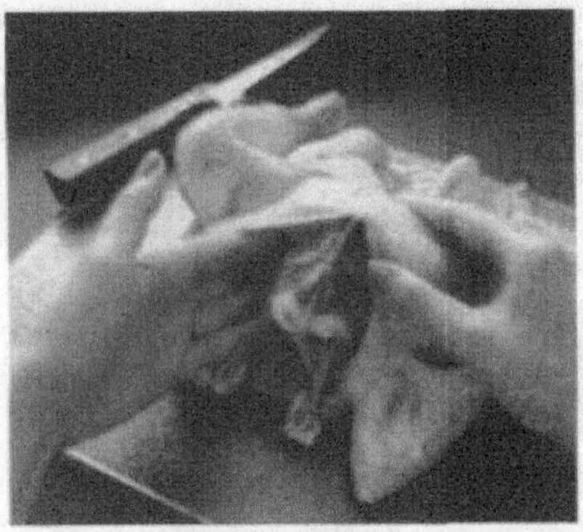

Step 5. With your fingers, break the portion of the ribs and backbone that have been freed of meat. Remove them through the opening, along with the attached breastbone, as shown.

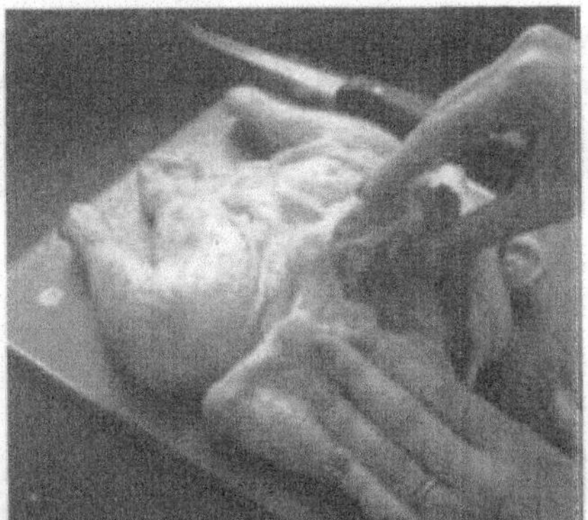

Step 6. Break the joints that connect the lower backbone to the thighbones. Pull the meat away from the joints and cut through the ligaments at the joints.

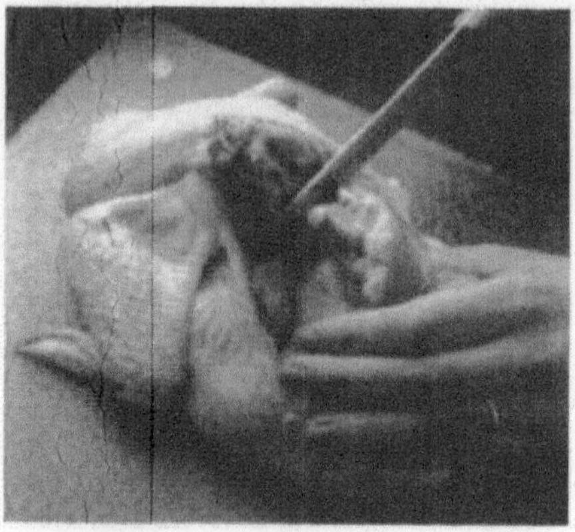

Step 7. Remove the remaining portion of the rib cage and backbone. For larger birds, such as turkeys, it is easier to remove the rib cage-backbone portions through the larger bottom opening of the bird.

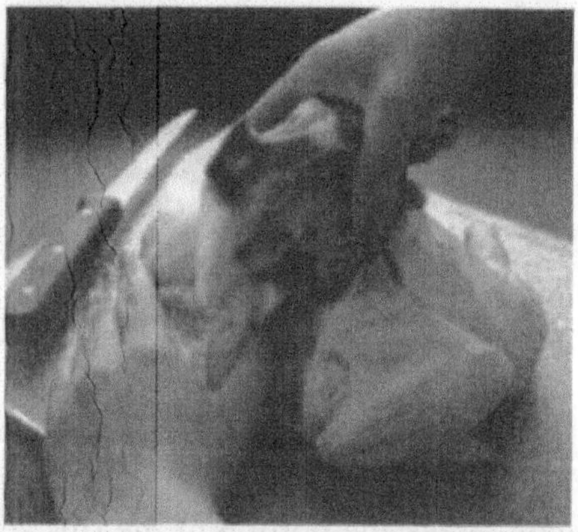

Step 8. Break the joints between the legs and thighs. From the inside of the bird, loosen or scrape the meat from the thighbones, cutting the ligaments as necessary. Remove the thighbones, as shown.

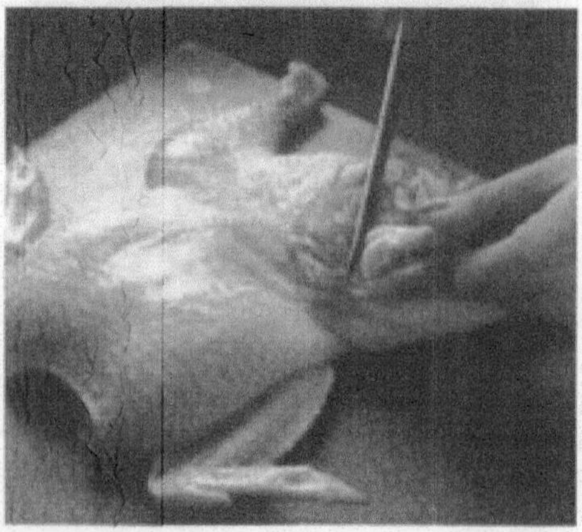

HOW TO DE-BONE AND BUTTERFLY A CHICKEN ?

Once the chicken is de-boned, opened butterfly, and flattened, it can be rolled and stuffed in a variety of ways.

Use a free range, naturally fed chicken for the best result, about 5-6 lb (4-5 lb after bones are removed).

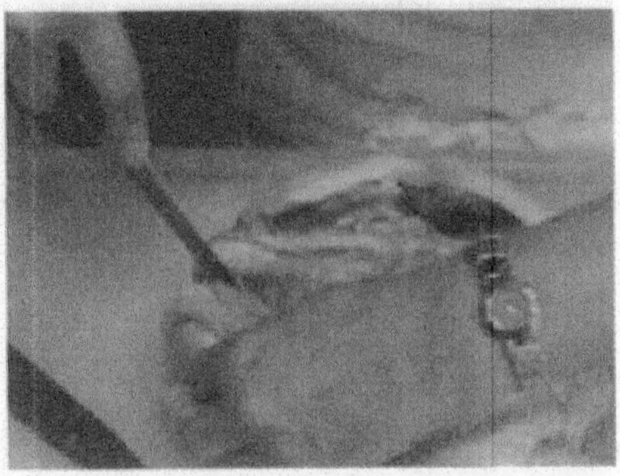

Step 1. Lift the skin of the neck. Using a small knife, separate the wishbone from the flesh by cutting around it.

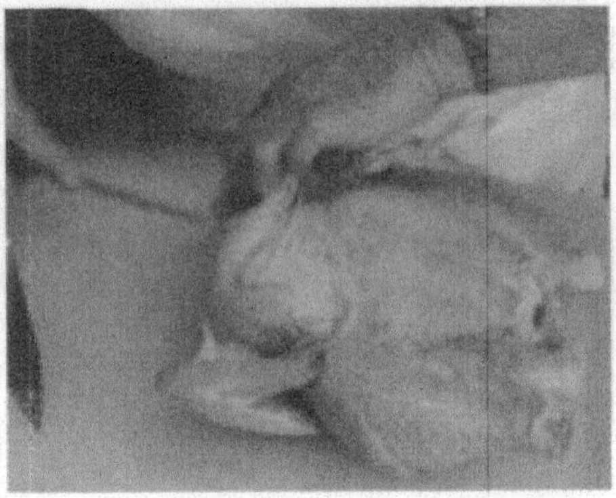

Step 2. Pull the wishbone out.

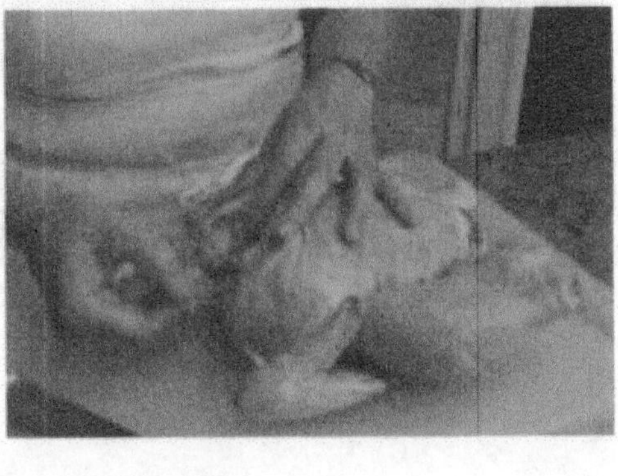

Step 3. Place the chicken upside down on its breasts, and cut longitudinally along the backbone.

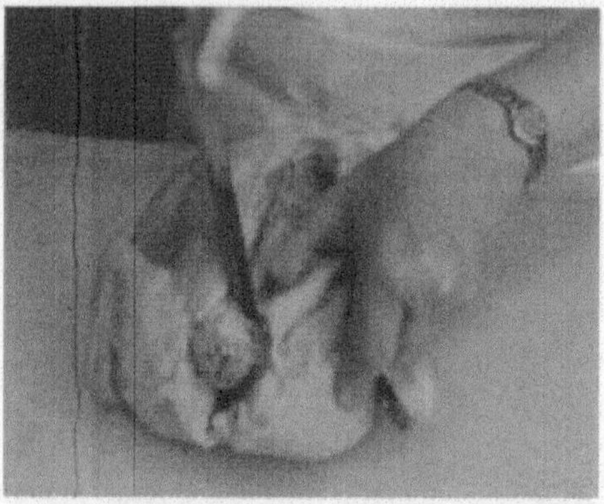

Step 4. With the tip of the knife, cut evenly all around to separate the bones from the meat. Also cut the connections of the legs and wings to the carcass.

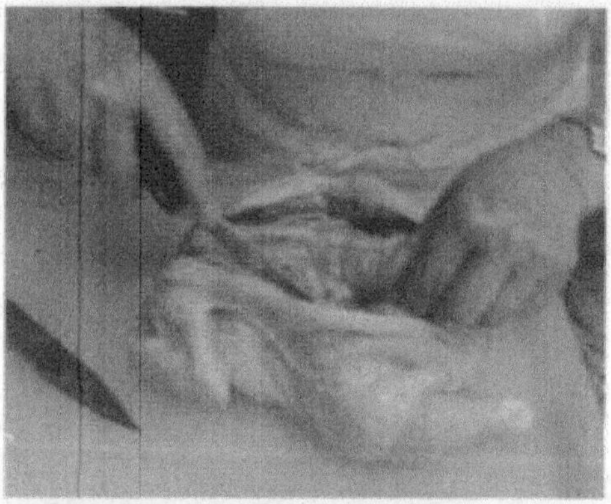

Step 5. Pull away the carcass in one piece.

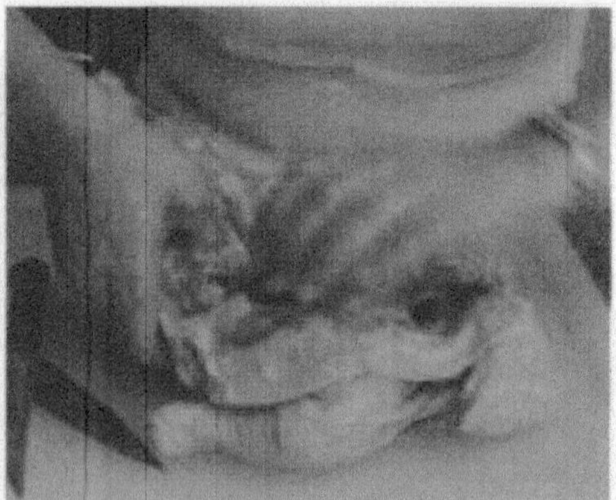

Step 6. Cut the skin at the end of the drumstick. Lift the thigh and cut to separate the meat from the bone all around, pushing the meat back.

Step 7. The fillets will come out loose. Use them to patch the areas under the breasts where there is no meat on the skin in order to have the whole surface covered with meat.

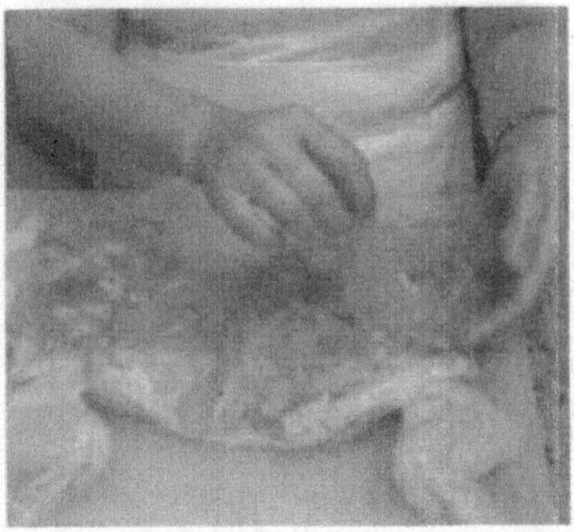

Step 8. Remove the end of the wings. Cut all around the wing bones to separate the meat from the bone.

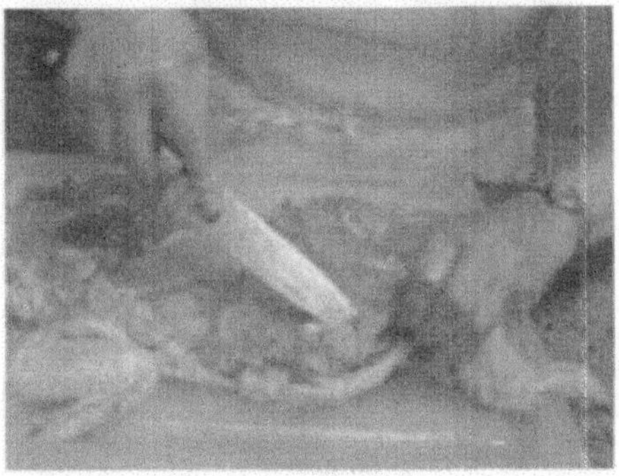

Step 9. Now that the chicken is completely de-bond, place a plastic sheet on the chicken and pound it with a meat pounder to flatten it.

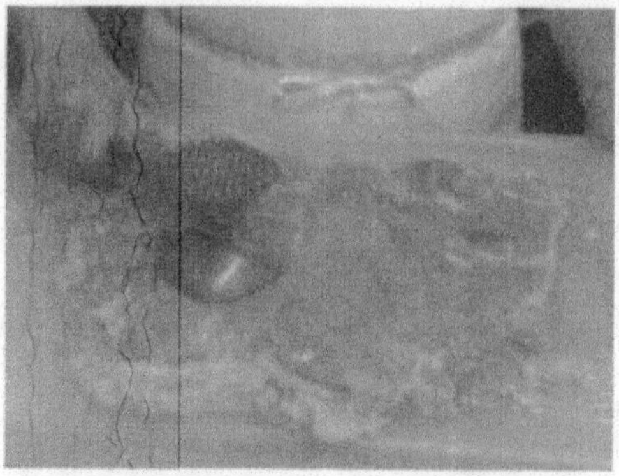

Step 10. The bones and trimmings of the chicken can be used to make an excellent chicken broth.

HOW TO DEBONE A CHICKEN BREAST ?

It is frequently easier to debone chicken breasts yourself than to buy them deboned. They are fresher, since they've been handled less, and you can leave the skin on when you want the fat to baste the roasting breast.

Step 1. Using a sharp knife, cuf the ribs away from the breast meat.

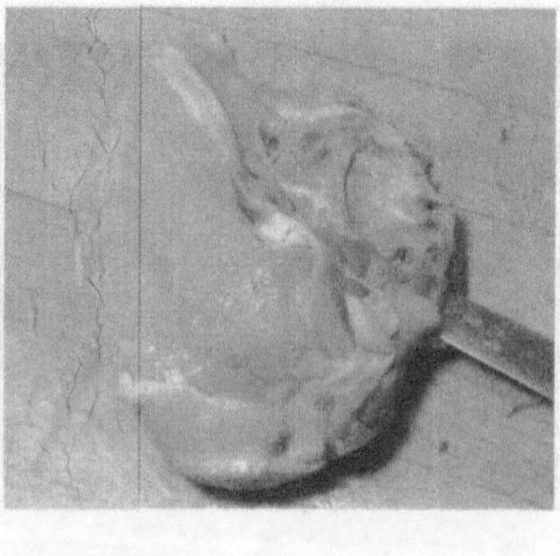

Step 2. Trim off the ribs with a pair of scissors or kitchen shears.

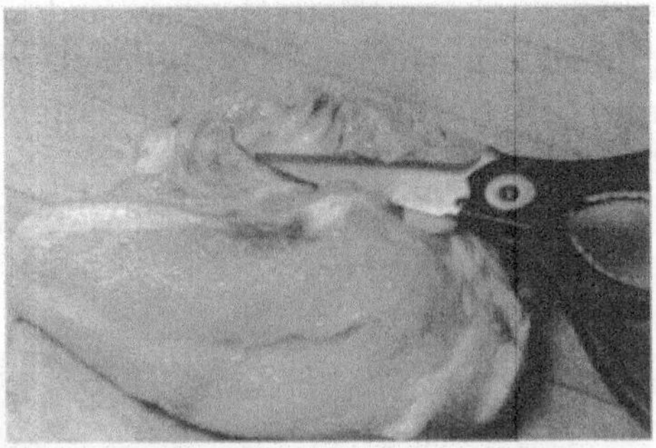

Step 3. Cut the breastbone away from the breast meat.

Step 4. Cut around the wishbone and remove it.

Step 5. Cut around the wishbone and remove it.

Be sure to wash the knife in hot, soapy water before using for any other purpose. Be sure to wash the cutting thoroughly.

DEBONNING CHICKEN THIGHS

Boning/deboning chicken thighs is relatively easy and a reasonable trade off with regard to frugality. With practice it becomes a fairly quick process. The cost difference per pound can be staggering between chicken breasts and thighs. Many people prefer the moistness and flavor of the dark meat.

Step 1. Use a sharp knife to cut the membrane that attaches the skin to the muscle and peel the skin off of the thigh.

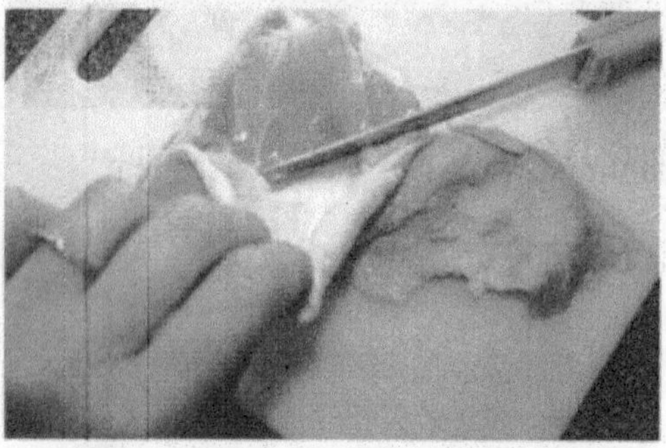

Step 2. Trim off any excess fat.

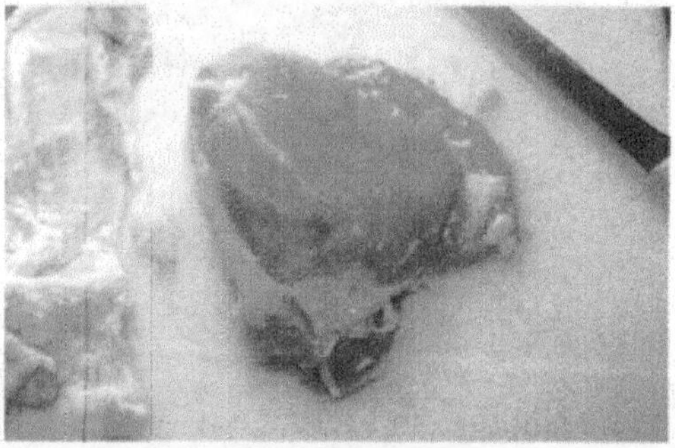

Step 3. Make a deep cut as cose to the bone as possible, but be careful not to slice all the way through the thigh.

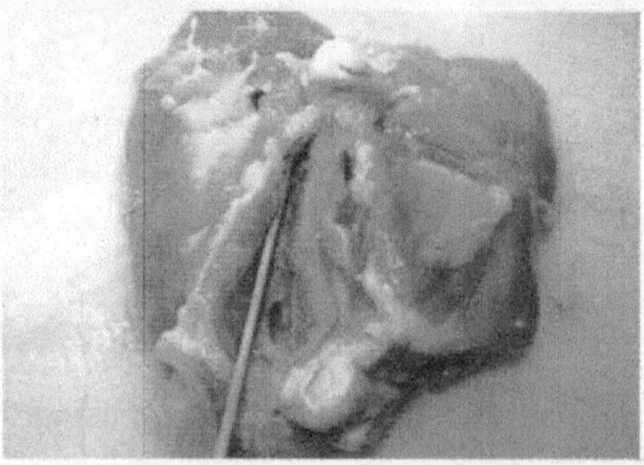

Step 4. Slice the knife behind the bone and again cut as close as possible. After this point one end should be free.

Step 5. Grasp the free end and continue cutting the muscle away from the bone.

Step 6. Always check the meat for gristle or bone fragments.

Step 7. Cut it away and you are done. Boneless skinless thighs can be used in any recipe calling for boneless skinless chicken breasts, feel free to experiment.

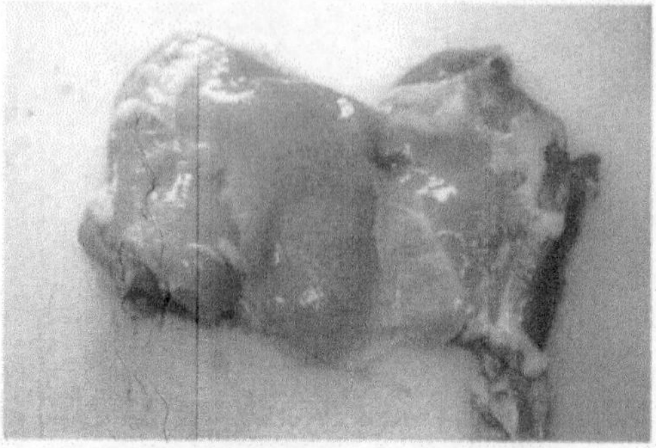

CUTTING UP A TURKEY

There are many ways to enjoy turkey other than roasting the whole bird. Many people have discovered quick, easy, and delicious meals can be prepared from turkey pieces and parts such as turkey boneless breasts, breast steaks or cutlets, drumsticks, thighs, and wings. These can be prepared in countless ways.

The least expensive way to enjoy turkey pieces and parts is to cut the whole turkey up yourself. It is surprisingly easy.

Turkey parts such as wings, legs, and breasts can be purchased at most food stores already cut and packaged, but it is usually more economical to purchase a whole turkey and cut it up at home. The turkey should be well chilled, which will allow it to be cut up more easily. A sharp knife is essential and a heavy-duty kitchen shears is helpful to ensure proper results.

Pictured below are the pieces that can obtained when cutting up a whole turkey.

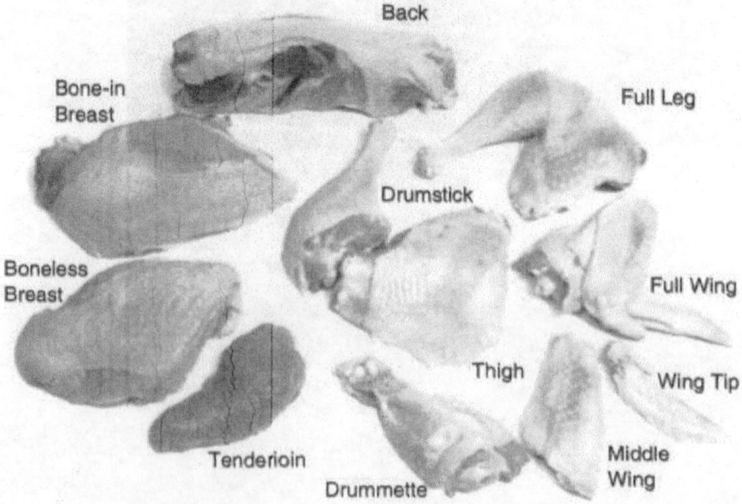

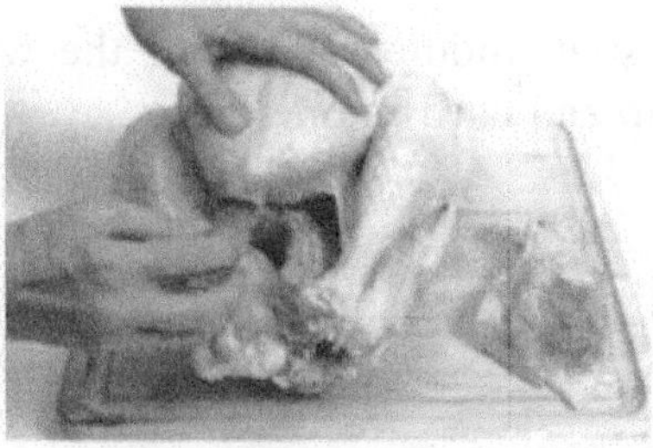

(a)

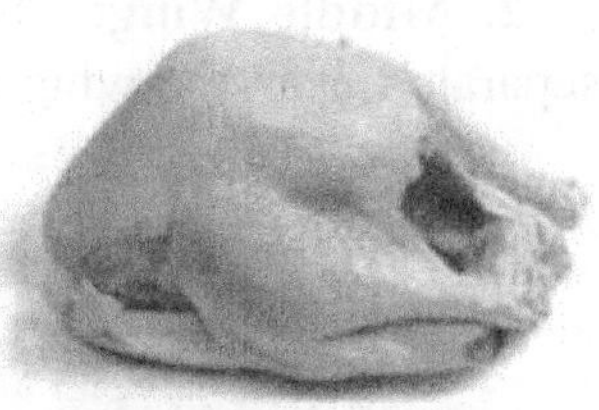

(b)

Remove the giblets and neck, which are usually found in a package in the body cavity.

Before you can begin cutting the turkey into individual parts, remove the leg clamp.

CUTTING THE WINGS

Cutting the Wings from the BodyA turkey wing can be removed by pulling it away from the body and cutting into the hollow area between the wing and the breast. When the wing joint (shoulder joint) has been exposed, cut through it while continuing to pull on the wing in order to release it from the body. The process can be repeated for the other wing.

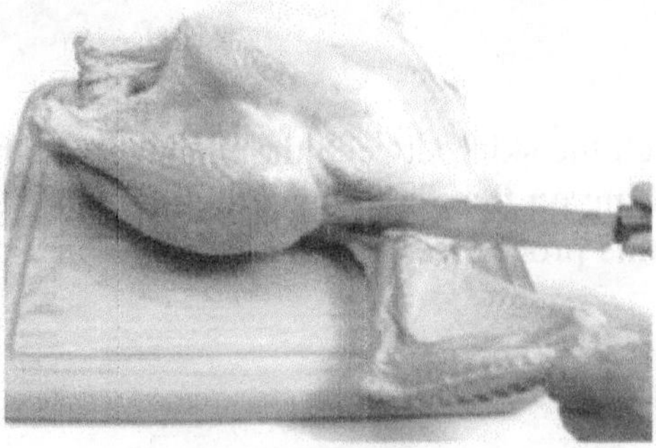

(a)

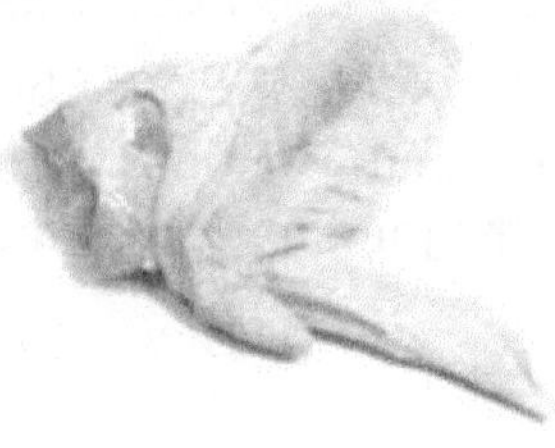

(b)

Cutting the Wings into Pieces

The wing can be cut into three sections:

1. Drummette: The upper portion can be cut at the elbow joint. This section is known as the drummette. (It is worth noting that a turkey drummette from a bird weighing 12 pounds or more is larger than a drumstick from a chicken.)

(a)

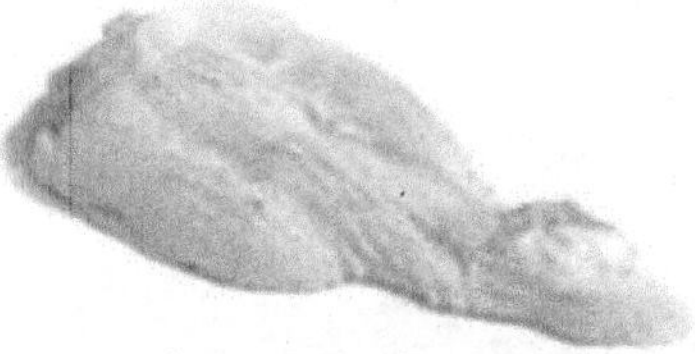

(b)

2. Middle Wing: The flat middle section of the wing beyond the elbow may be separated from the wing tip and used as one piece.

(a)

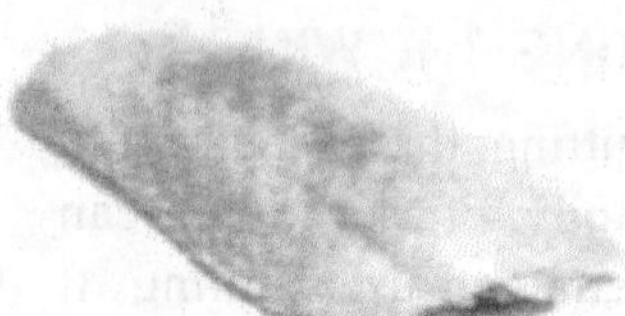

(b)

3. Wing: TipThere is not much meat on the wing tip, but it may be saved and added to soup or stock to provide flavoring.

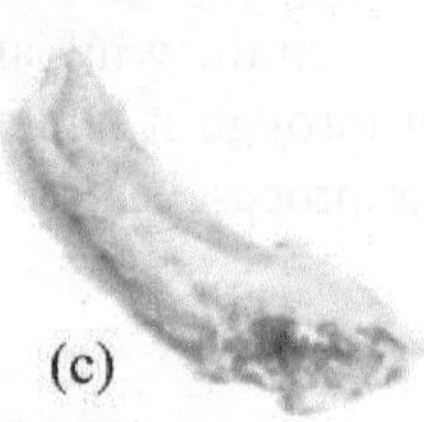

(c)

CUTTING THE LEGS

Cutting the Legs from the Body

A turkey leg is removed by cutting through the skin between the thigh and the body to reveal the joint. Continue cutting while pushing on the leg to open the joint and then cut through the joint to release the leg. Repeat this procedure for the other leg.

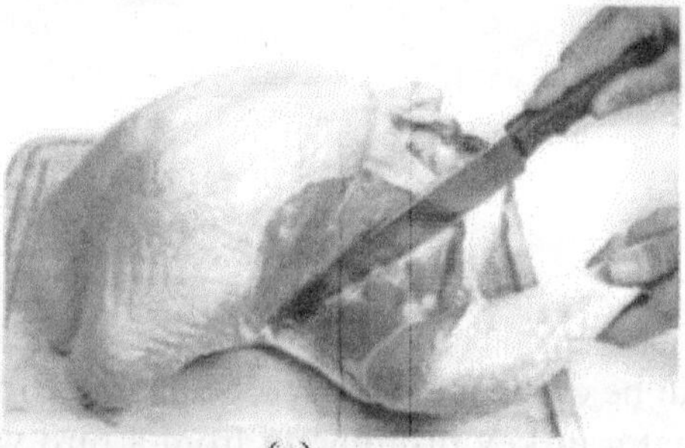

(a)

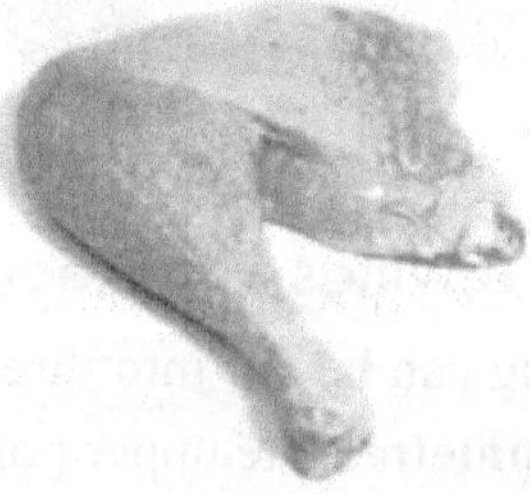

(b)

Cutting the Legs into Pieces

The leg can be left as is or it may be cut at the middle joint to form two pieces known as the thigh and the drumstick. Thigh meat is often sold with the bone removed.

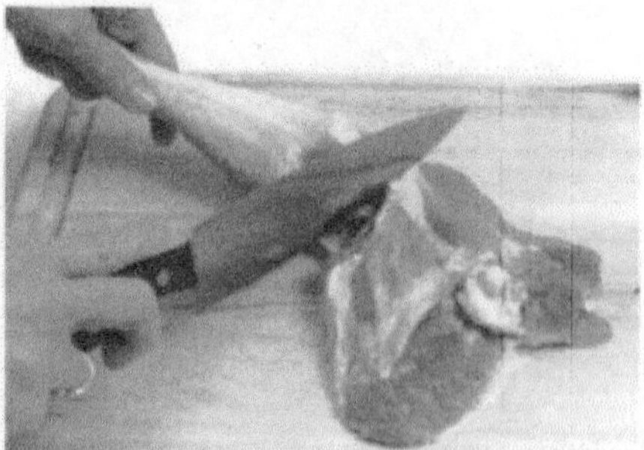

(a)

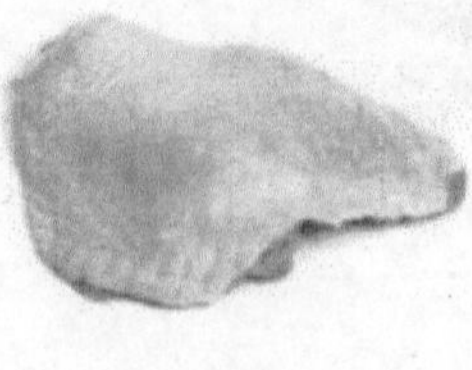

(b)

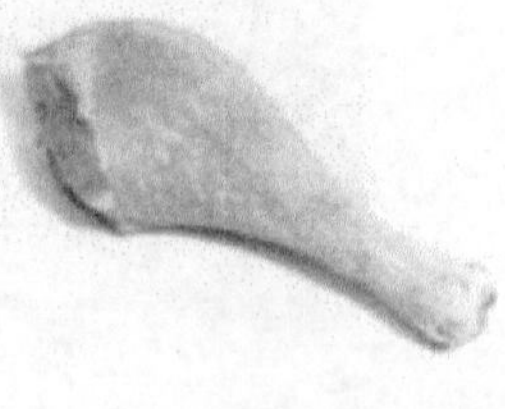

(c)

CUTTING THE BREAST

Cutting the Breast from the Body

The breast can be removed whole or in halves. The bones can be left or they can be removed to make preparation and serving easier.

In order to remove the breast from the body cavity, cut along the rib cage from the the tail end to the neck on both sides of the bird.

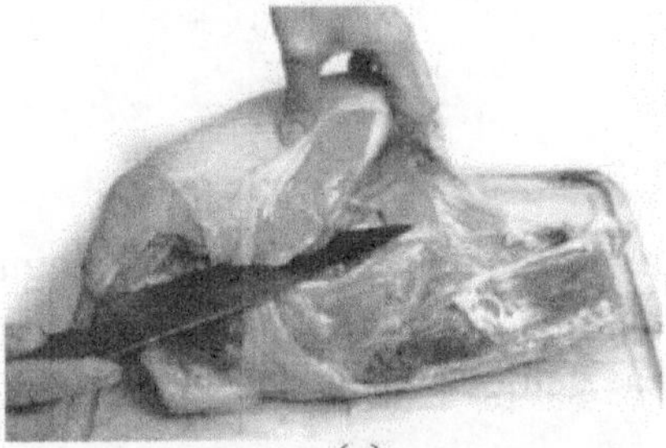

(a)

(b)

Place the breast upside down (skin side down) and cut along the breastbone through the bone and the meat, which will split the breast into halves.

Removing the Bones from the Breast Meat

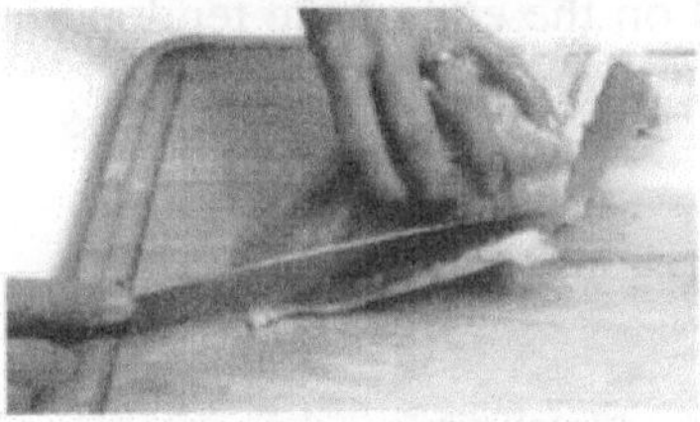

Cut the meat along the breastbone

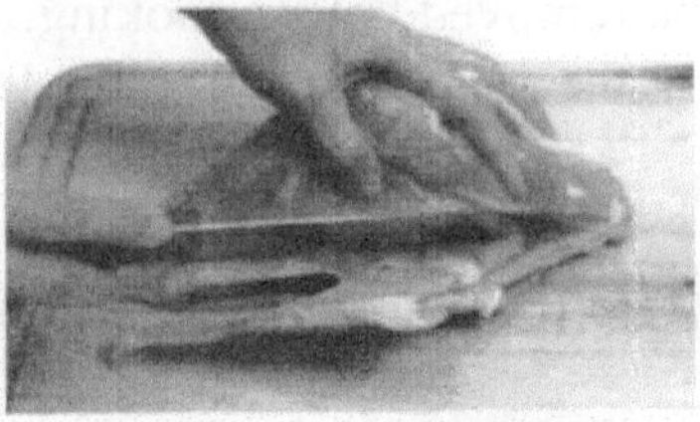

Cut along the edge of the wishbone and the keel bone.

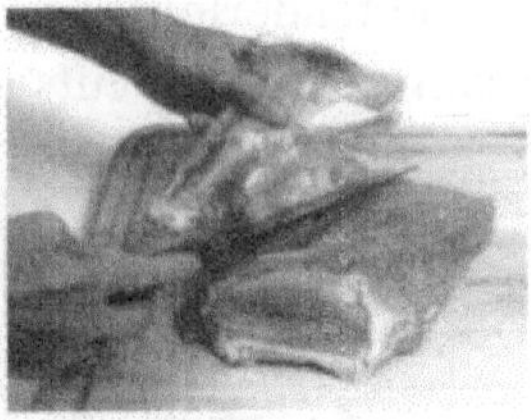

Cut along the ribs on one side of the breastbone using short, swipping cuts.

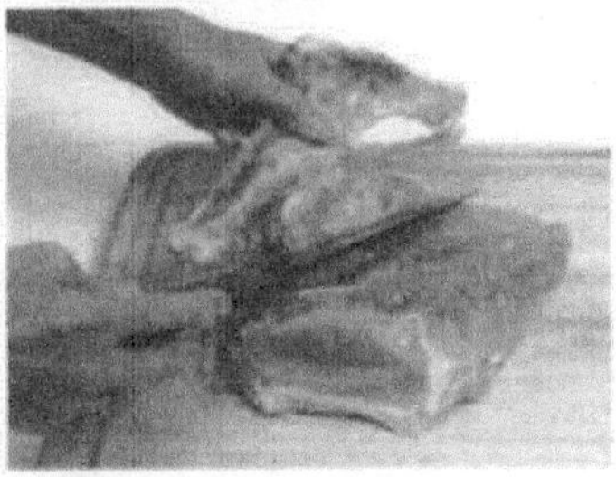

Remove the ribs from the breast half and save them for use in the soup or stock pot.

The boneless breast turned skin side up.

Cutting Turkey Breast Steaks and Cutlets

A boneless turkey breast can be cut across the grain to yield steaks that are ½ to 1 inch thick. Two of the steaks make an ample serving for one person.

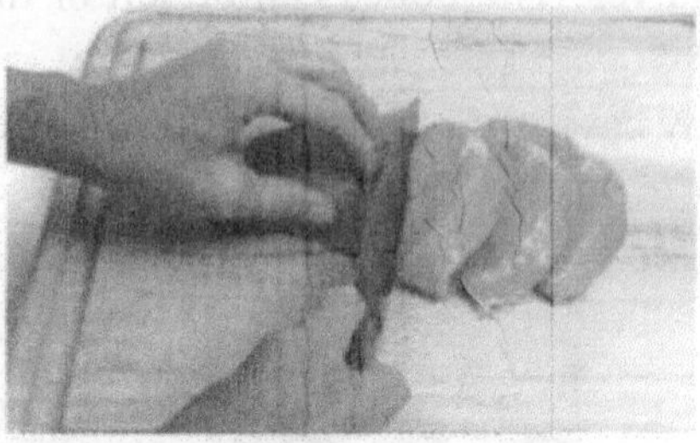

(a)

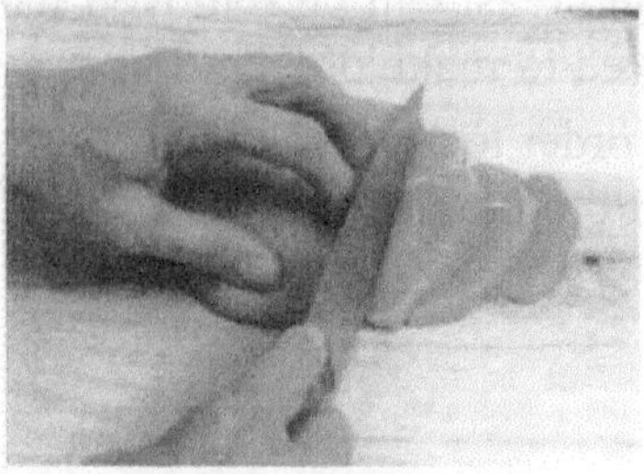

(b)

The breast can also be cut across the grain to produce cutlets, which are thinner than steaks and cook much more quickly. The cutlets can be pounded to make them even thinner and to tenderize them. The pounded cutlets can be sautéed and used for a number of recipes.

Cutting Turkey Breast Tenderloins

Turkey tenderloins may be cut from each breast half. They are located on the inside of each breast half next to the keel bone. The tenderloin is a long cylindrically shaped muscle that is easily removed from the rest of the breast meat. The tendon in the middle of the tenderloin should be removed before cooking. Pull on the end of the tendon while making swiping cuts along the meat attached to the length of the tendon.

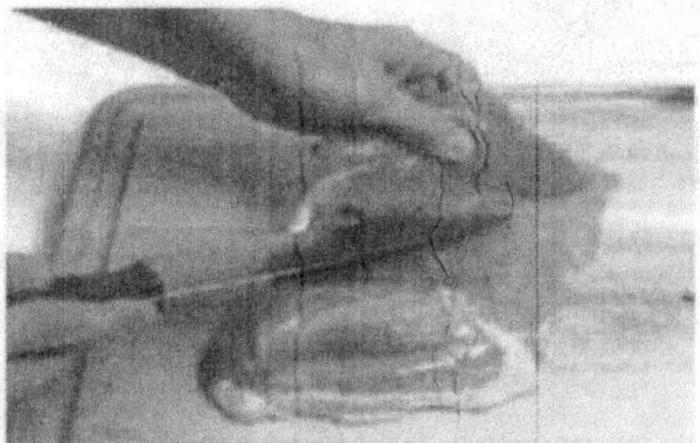

(a)

(b)

Back Meat

After removing the wings, legs, and breast, the remaining portion of the turkey carcass is the back. There is some meat and skin that can be removed, which can be ground or used in soups and casseroles. After the choice bits have been removed, the bones and any remaining meat can be used for stock.

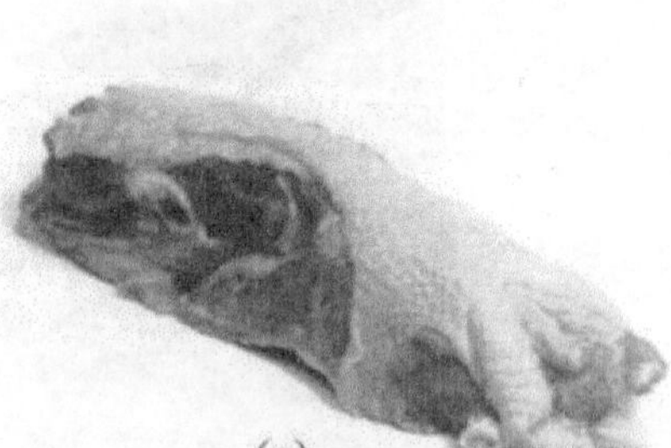

(c)

QUESTIONS AND DISCUSSIONS

Fill in the Blanks

Q.1. Read and complete the following statements :

(a) Since meat has a high food cost, its ordering must be strictly according to ....

(b) Not all parts of a beef animal have the same ....

(c) Portion size policy is established by the Chef and ....

(d) Meat inspection before and after slaughter for wholesomeness is ....

(e) Food service operators today can use supplies which are pre-cooked or ....

(f) For a first class steak, the meat is not only on primal cut, it is also graded ....

(g) Portion control assures that the same value is given to each ....

(h) Portion size is related to total caloric value of the food served. Therefore, of importance is the food's ....

(i) The checking in a delivered meat is the responsibility of the ....

(j) Chefs have special ways of boning meat before it is ....

(k) Portion control benefits the customer as well as the ....

(l) The freezing of poultry and meat must be considered as a convenience to the ....

(m) All beef meat can be sub-divided into prime cuts and ....

[**Ans.:** (a) production schedule; (b) characteristics; (c) the management; (d) compulsory; (e) pre-protioned; (f) prime; (g) portion size; (h) preparation method; (i) chef; (j) cooked; (k) operator; (l) customer; (m) Choicecuts]

Multiple Choice

Q.2. Read each question carefully. Select the *best* answer :—

(i) Although a chef must have butcher skills to a certain degree, he need not be able to :

(a) Cut up a whole beef round (b) Bone a chicken
(c) Skin a calf (d) Make veal meat balls.

(ii) For most dishes portion control begins after the cooking process, but not for :

(a) Roast beef (b) Pot roast
(c) Beef stew (d) Swiss steak.

(iii) An untrimmed steak may look 30% larger than same steak trimmed. Still, customers prefer the trimmed one because :

(a) It fits better on the plate (b) It is easier to chew and digest
(c) It is all meat, no trimming left (d) It has a better taste.

(iv) To select meat quality in the past, the chef had to depend on his experience. Today he is greatly assisted by :

(a) Fair Trade Laws (b) The Central Health Department
(c) The Department of Agriculture (d) The Department of Health and Welfare.

(v) Meat that is graded prime has :

(a) More nutritional value (b) Tenderness and flavour

(c) Less fat per pound (d) Better digestibility.

(vi) Portion control is an important tool to a profitable operation and means:

(a) Reducing the size of steaks when meat is high priced

(b) Adjusting selling price of cooked food to purchase price of raw food

(c) Keeping each portion of food constantly to the same size

(d) Watching that all customers are getting serving before food runs out.

(vii) The grading of whole chickens to size has become so exact that fluctuations are not more than :

(a) One ounce per chicken (b) Two ounces per chicken

(c) Three ounces per chicken (d) Four ounces per chicken.

(viii) Meat ordering is the chef's responsibility but does not include :

(a) Placing orders in time for delivery

(b) Specifying quality standards

(c) Estimating his need

(d) Selecting meat at the market.

(ix) Which one of these meat grades does not belong to the first four ?

(a) Prime (b) Good

(c) Standard (d) Commercial.

(x) Primal cuts of prime meats are expensive and are not used for the preparations of :

(a) Roast top sirloin (b) Roast rib of beef

(c) German Sauerbraten (d) Porterhouse Steak.

[**Ans.:** (i) (c); (ii) (d); (iii) (c); (iv) (b); (v) (b);
(vi) (c); (vii) (b); (viii) (b); (ix) (d); (x) (c)]

Matching Type

Q.3. Match the Beef Grades of Table 'A' with the numbers of Table 'B'

Table A	*Table B*
(a) Choice	(i) First
(b) Good	(ii) Second
(c) Prime	(iii) Third
(d) Canner	(iv) Fourth
(e) Commercial	(v) Fifth
(f) Standard	(vi) Sixth
(g) Cutter	(vii) Seventh
(h) Utility	(viii) Eighth

[**Ans.:** (a) (ii); (b) (iii); (c) (i); (d) (viii);
(e) (v); (f) (iv); (g) (vii); (h) (vi)]

Q.4. Match the preparations of Table 'A' with the average portion weight of Table 'B'

Table 'A'	*Table 'B'*
(a) Filet Mignon	(i) 5 Ounces
(b) Sirloin Steak	(ii) 6 Ounces
(c) Minute Steak	(iii) 8 Ounces
(d) T-Bone Steak	(iv) 9 Ounces
(e) Chateaubriand	(v) 14 Ounces
(f) Porterhouse Steak	(vi) 16 Ounces
(g) Boneless Cutlet	(vii) 18 Ounces
(h) Beef Brochette	(viii) 25 Ounces

[**Ans.:** (a) (iii); (b) (v); (c) (iv); (d) (vi);
(e) (vii); (f) (viii); (g) (i); (h) (vi)]

Short Answer Type

Q.5. Is frozen meat a blessing?

Q.6. Describe the benefits of frozen meat in cooking.

Q.7. Ellaborate the benefits of portion control.

Q.8. What is the importance and why is there nationwide meat grading?

Q.9. Explain the need for meat inspection.

Q.10. Define quality of meat.

Q.11. Why do chefs need butchering skills ?

Q.12. Describe the advantages of open market buying.

Assignments / Activity Type

Q.13. View demonstration of "Meat Identification" using wall charts.

Q.14. Arranged a field trip to

(a) A slaughter house

(b) A wholesale butcher (purveyor)

(c) A meat freezing plant

(d) A supermarket meat counter

(e) To a wholesale poultry house.

Q.15. View films of lamb beef etc available from hotels and similar other establishments

Q.16. Discuss the different phases of portion control.

Q.17. Identify the main reasons for meat inspection.

Q.18. Describe the change of quality control.

Q.19. Explain the importance for the chef's need for butcher knowledge.

2.5

Sea Food: Fish and Shellfish

CHAPTER OBJECTIVES

After studying this lesson you should be able :

- To identify the different kinds of edible seafood;
- To name the area of origin of some of the important seafood;
- To explain the fish cooking methods;
- To name the important principle in the handling of shellfish;
- To explain the need for fish butchering; and
- To describe some hazards of frozen fish products.

Seafood is a term used for live edible food taken from the waters. It is high in nutritional value and low in fat. Seafood must be used absolutely fresh. It has a much shorter storage time than meat. For this reason, most seafood available today is frozen. The same species of fish taken from different regions show a considerable difference in taste and texture. Processed fish and seafood specialties originating in various countries are known and appreciated all over the world.

Food from the sea i.e. sea food is the term used for all edible fish and shellfish. There are saltwater, freshwater, and migratory fish. Shellfish can be divided into crustaceans and mollusks. Some of the crustaceans are lobsters, prawns, shrimps, crabs, and crayfish. Some of the mollusks are edible clams, oysters, scallops, and squid.

Fish cookery is the same as general cooking procedures, except that long cooking times are not needed. All shellfish must be kept alive until it is cooked. Oysters and some clams are eaten alive from the shell. Crustaceans are well accepted by the public and considered a specialty. The king of the crustacean is the American lobster, with langustes, crabs, and shrimps being close in popularity.

Fish butchering means doing the same thing to fresh fish that a regular butcher does to meat. It is an important job, very necessary for any food establishment interested in providing the best seafood for its customers.

A large variety of fish and fish products are available in the form of convenience foods. Most of them are ready to be deep fried but some are precooked to such an extent that only reheating is needed. In many areas, fish and shellfish are only available in a frozen form. Transporting and distributing fresh unfrozen salt water fish to some faraway inland area is too expensive and difficult.

Fish is easy to digest, but shellfish is not. Seafood must always be absolutely fresh. It has a very short storage time. Because of the improvement in freezing techniques, frozen seafood is shipped to all areas of the country. Most seafoods eaten are not raised on fish farms. They are game fish which have developed certain characteristics of the place where they live. Therefore, seafood from one region is often thought to be superior to seafood from another region.

No grading standards exist for frozen seafood, which means that fish buyers have to check carefully before committing themselves to large quantities. For fresh fish, no standards of grading are needed. Fish quality is self-evident by looks, touch, and smell. In general, raw shellfish freezes better than raw fish. A great quality margin exists for frozen salt water fish, depending on the origin of the raw fish and the applied freezing and handling procedures.

The best and true lobster, with claws, lives only in the cold waters of the North Atlantic. This eastern areas feature lobster restaurants where this crustacean is king.

Spiny lobsters, also called *languste* or rock lobsters, have no claws, look like giant shrimps and are caught in the warmer waters (off California and Mexico.) There is a great difference in meat texture and flavour between the spiny and Atlanta lobsters. The "Maine Lobsters" from New England and the Canadian waters are considered to be the best.

There are regional differences in crabs, prawns, shrimps, oysters, and the various kinds of fish. There are many seafood restaurants in and near coastal areas. They promote the best native seafood of their regions. Some of these seafood areas have developed special preserving processes, such as marinating or smoking. The native catch, combined with the special processing, has often become famous all around the world. These products are listed under appetizers on restaurant menus. They should be well known to both chefs and gourmets.

Blue Crab

Oyster

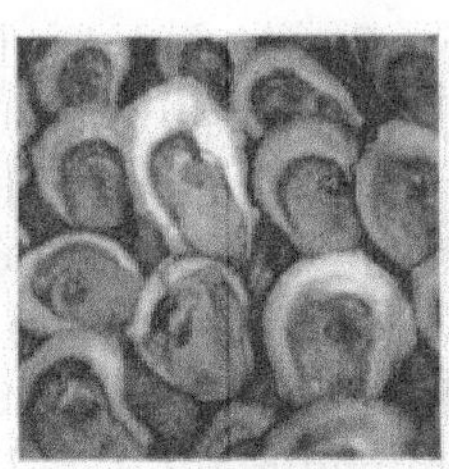
Oyster Beds

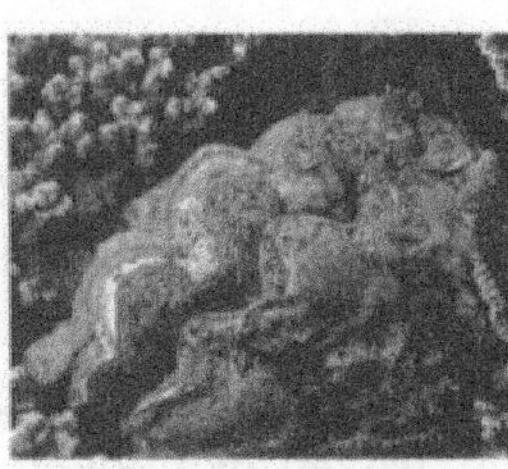
Giant Clam

Silver pomfret

Stone Clams

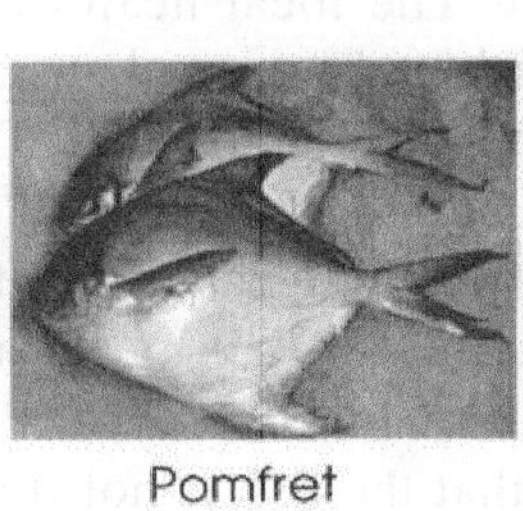
Pomfret

Cherry Stone Clams

FISH SPECIALITIES

Smoked salmon, a delicacy, can be made from any fresh salmon. The best quality ones come from Scotland, Germany, and Nova Scotia. The best sardines in olive oil come from Portugal and southern France. Herring, pickled or marinated, are special to Sweden and Germany. The best smoked herring, also known as kippers, are from Scotland and Germany. Smoked haddock, or Fanning haddie, comes from Scotland and Nova Scotia. Pickled eel is a specialty of Commachio, Italy. The most expensive of all the preserved fish delicacies is *Caviar,* or the slightly salted roe of a sturgeon. The best ones are of Iranian or Russian origin. Russia, Scandinavian, and some of the other colder countries produce a large variety of cured, brined, pickled and smoked fish for their own local use. These are only few delicacies mentioned. Here are only a few of those that are available from all over the world.

Many of the cooking methods used for meat are also used in preparing seafood. Because seafood is very tender, prolonged cooking methods are not needed. Since it is a brittle food, it should be handled in portion sizes. Seafoods, because they are very lean, are most popular if deep fried or sauteed. They can also be broiled or poached. Fish stews, or whole braised fish, in the sense of the combination methods, are rarely made.

A well-accepted, original French saute method for fish is called a la meunier. Flour-dusted fish pieces are sauteed in butter until done and then sprinkled with chopped parsley and a row drops of lemon juice. Freshly browned butter is poured over this dish before serving. Fish broiling is well accepted for salmon steak, halibut steak, swordfish steak, seabass, red snapper, and cod. All fish with coarse-textured flesh allow for rougher handling, such as in broiling. Fish with fine-textured flash, such as sole, sandbag, and trout are better pan fried or poached.

Cooking a whole fish by baking or roasting is never done commercially. It is messy and has no advantage to taste or handling. A whole fish for display at a buffet, is boiled (simmered) or poached. Fish cooking has no different rules. Prevention of overcooking is very important since fish is a pure *albumin* (protein such as in egg white) a food which only toughens and dried out when exposed to too much heat.

Fish must always be fresh, and no fish odour should be present. There is much difference between fresh and freshly defrosted fish. Shellfish, if unfrozen, must be alive until seconds before cooking. Oysters and clams, clams, eaten on the half shell (raw), are still alive when they are eaten. For additional assurance of freshness, they are served on crushed ice. Due to the chemical makeup of seafood, toxic changes could take place if the shellfish were not frozen or cooked immediately. Grading for fish quality does not exist. The local health department inspectors check the fish processing plants for general cleanliness and freshness of the product. The quality of fresh fish as easily found by looking at the colour and firmness of the flesh and the absence of any fishy smell. Some fish buyers also look at the redness of the gills and the shine of the fish eyes. Pale colour and dullness indicate that the fish is not fresh.

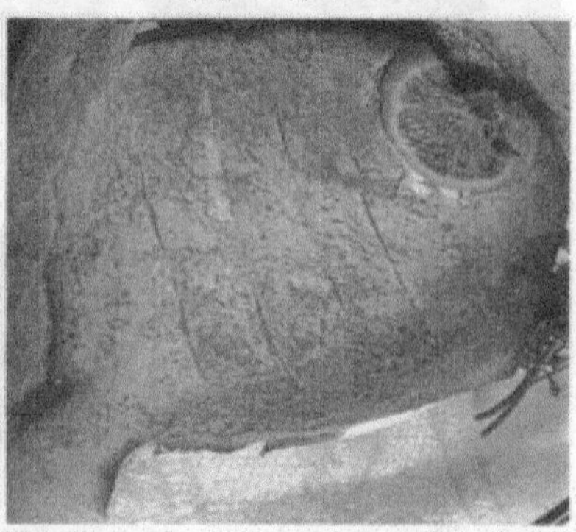

Fish Roast – Microwave Method

EDIBLE CRUSTACEANS

Crustaceans enjoy a great popularity in the Western countries. The giant frozen Alaskan King Crab is distributed on a nationwide basis. This delighful crab meat is now available cooked and frozen in a variety of packaging sizes.

Crab

The east coast of America has "Blue Shell Crabs" and "Soft Shell Crabs" which are blue crabs after they have shed their shells. "Dungeness Crabs" are found on the West coast America. They are larger than blue crabs but smaller than king crabs. Crabs are available live or cooked and frozen. When cooled and frozen, they are sold as crab meat. Crab meat in cans is overcooked and inferior to the frozen food. Soft shell crabs are not boiled, they are only pan fried or sauteed to order.

American obsters, with claws, are a specialty from New England to North Eastern Gaspe in Canada. Lobsters are boiled alive and may be eaten either hot or cold. An excellent preparation is live broiled lobster, an American speciality. "Lobster American" on the other hand is a true French speciality. For Lobster American or "American" as it is properly spelled, a live lobster is chopped in about 8 or 10 pieces. It is sauteed immediately in butter with some fine chopped onions, shallots, parsley and tomatoes, then deglazed with brandy and white wine and finished, with a cover, for a few minutes more.

Live, Pacific spiny lobsters, or langoustes without claws, are handled like "Maine Lobsters" but usually they can be bought cooked and frozen.

Shrimps and prawns may be distinguished by size. The very small ones, called shrimps, are available cleaned and cooked, either canned or frozen. The various larger sizes are called *prawns,* although they belong to the shrimp family. They are available semi-cleaned and raw frozen (shell on) of fully cleaned, peeled, divined, and raw frozen. The most common preparation for prawns is deep frying. They are also boiled for "Shrimp Cocktail" and "Shrimp Louis". In better restaurants, they are sauteed or broiled on skewers.

EDIBLE MOLLUSKS

The most popular edible mollusks, are oysters, scallops, various clams, mussels, and squid. Oysters, are eaten raw on the half shell, but they can also be fried, sauteed or poached. Clams are eaten the same way, or they may be used in soups (Clam chowder), sauces, or as a garnish in fish dishes. Scallops are prefered fried; the most popular French preparation is poached with white wine and cheese, known under the name of "Coquille St. Jacques". Scallops are known in Europe as "St. Jacques mussel" or the "Pilgrim's Shell" because pilgrims returning from the Holy Land pinned the shells on their robes, as a proof that they were there.

Abalones, from the Pacific, are large mollusks with scallop-like meat. They are popular in the Far East and with Americans from the West Coast. Americans eat abalones fried, sauteed, and broiled; but in the Far East, they are parboiled in water, sliced when cold, and then used in various ways.

Squid, also known as Calamari, are fried, sauteed, and sometimes even boiled, stuffed and finished in the oven.

BUTCHERING OF FISH

Fish butchering means the art of cleaning, filleting, skinning, and cutting a raw fresh fish into portions or cookable pieces. Some years ago, larger food establishments in coastal areas had their own fish cooks and fish butchers. In smaller America establishments, fish is handled by the meat butcher or the cook designated to do this type of work. Today only seafood specialty restaurants do their own fish butchering. Many people are never forced for economic reasons to live on fish as their main protein source. They are unwilling to even taste fish. The main reason is the fear of choking on a fish bone. Every chef who handles fish must see to it that fish portions are as boneless as they can be. The butchering of fish on the job and the serving of fish without bones will help the customer to overcome his fears. Commercial fish boning places emphasis on speed and the least amount of trimmings. This is not as good as having the fish butcher fillet and portion fish according to his needs and the standards of the establishment.

The fish butcher's job is to make fish ready for cooking. Like the meat butcher, he is also responsible for the ordering and storage of his supplies. The fish refrigerator should be set for about 34°F. and should have good air circulation. He should only use stainless tools and utensils to handle and store raw fish.

Cuts of Fish

The fish is highly evolved and its body regulates many important functions on a daily basis. Even though the body structures of each fish depends on the environment of the fish, here are a few common parts. (Ref. Fig. 2.5A)

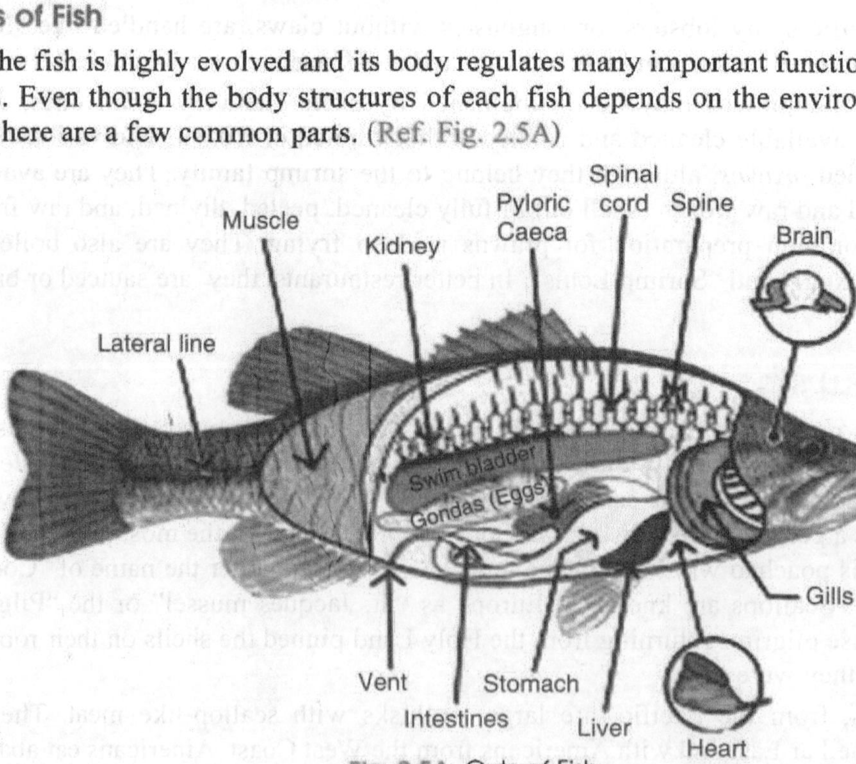

Fig. 2.5A. Cuts of Fish

Fins

There are many varieties of fin shapes and sizes. The most well known is the ray fin, which is fan-like in structure. Fins propel fish through their aquatic environments.

Gills

Gills allow fish to breathe. Fish take oxygen-filled bubbles in through their mouths. The gills are full of carbon dioxide bubble-rich blood. Since the gills are so thin, the oxygen passes into the gills, displacing the carbon dioxide bubbles and supplying the fish with fresh oxygen.

Operculum

The operculum is a boney flap that covers and protects the gills from damage. It forms most of the side of the head behind the eye. The back edge of the operculum defines the area between the head and body in most fish.

Swim Bladder

The swim bladder is located in the body cavity. It contains gas, usually oxygen, which helps the fish keep its buoyancy. It allows the fish to maintain its depth in water without floating upward or sinking.

Cooking of Fish

Wash and clean the fish and then scour it on both sides. Next rub in the tapioca flour. Heat up some deep oil in the pan and when hot enough, fry the fish on both sides unitl golden brown. Serve with fresh vegetables and a dip made from hot chillies, shallots and an equal amount of lime juice and fish sauce.

Cleaning of pomfret

How to Fillet a Fish ?

Here are a series of 15 pictures describing the simple techniques of filleting reasonable sized fish like coral trout, barramundi, mangrove jack, salmon etc.

This method can be adapted to suit most fish species with scaled skin, and the end result will give you beautiful clean fillets, little bones and virtually no wastage.

1. What is required is a simple cutting board or flat surface, a thin flexible blade for cutting along the backbone, and a borad flat blade for removing the had skin.
2. Holding the fish flat on the cutting board, and while using the thin knife, pierce the skin behind the front dorsal fin.
3. Slice the knife diagonally across the fish, cutting to, but not through, the backbone.

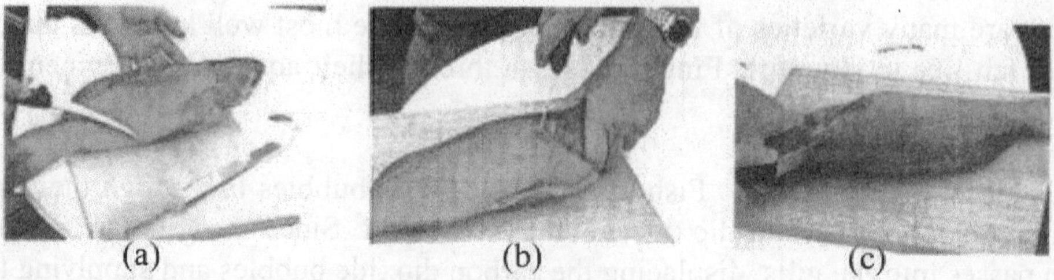

(a) (b) (c)

4. Hold the fish by the head and run the blade down the backbone towards the tial with a sawing motion. Do not try to cut too much of the fillet off the backbone at this stage, this will come later.
5. When near the tial region, hold the knife flat against the backbone and push the point right through the side of the fillet. With the knife protruding out the other side, cut right through the remaining fillet towards the tail. 6 & 7 Peel the fillet back with one hand while cutting the fillet away from the backbone using small slicing motions. Don't try to cut too much away in one stroke. It is better to use many small cuts, guiding the knife along any bony structures and removing all that beautiful flesh.

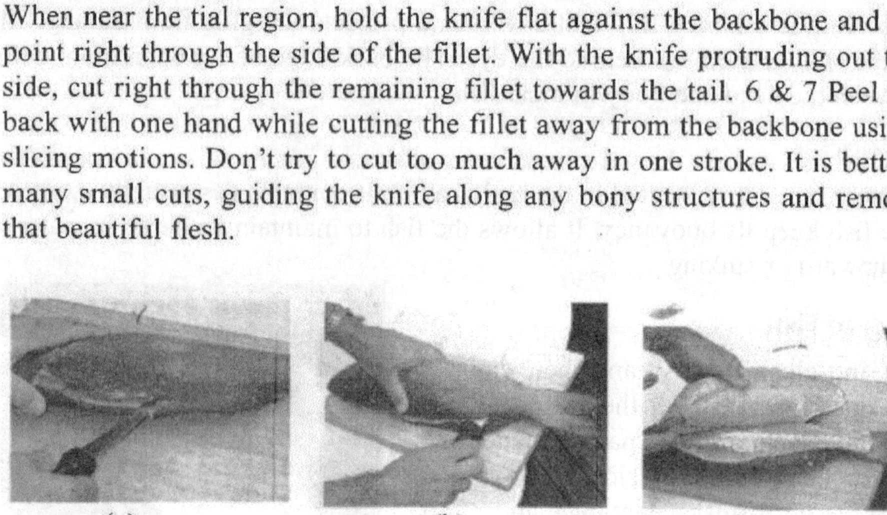

(a) (b) (c)

8. The most difficult task is to remove the fillet from the rib cage area. A very sharp knife is essential here. Using small strokes again, just feel your way around the bones, eventually completely removing one side of the flesh.
9. Turn the fish over making sure to hold the fish fairly flat on the cutting surface, and repeat the procedure to remove the other fillet. Some fisherman will keep the first fillet loosely attached to the backbone to improve the "shape" of the fish and making it easier to work for removing the second fillet.

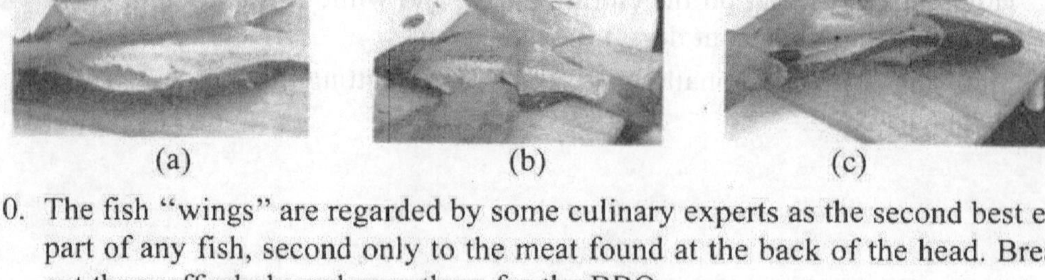

(a) (b) (c)

10. The fish "wings" are regarded by some culinary experts as the second best eating part of any fish, second only to the meat found at the back of the head. Break or cut them off whole and save them for the BBQ.

11. And there you have it, two superb fillets, the wings and the carcass.
12. Next comes the removal of the skin, note that the fish has not been scaled and this is not necessary. Hold the tough skin in one hand and using the flat bladed knife, slice a small portion of the flesh away from the skin.

(a)

(b)

13. Cut a "finger hole" into the skin.
14. Hold the skin by the finger hole, and using the broad bladed knife, gently remove the skin from the remaining fillet. It is important to hold the knife at the correct angle and to pull on the skin, not push or cut with the knife. Holding the blade too flat will result in a jagged cutting action and probably leave some skin on, hold it too upright and you will slice through the skin and make it difficult to re-start the procedure. There is no substitute for practice, so go catch a few and give it some trial and error until you work the right angle to suite your blade.
15. The completed job.

(a)

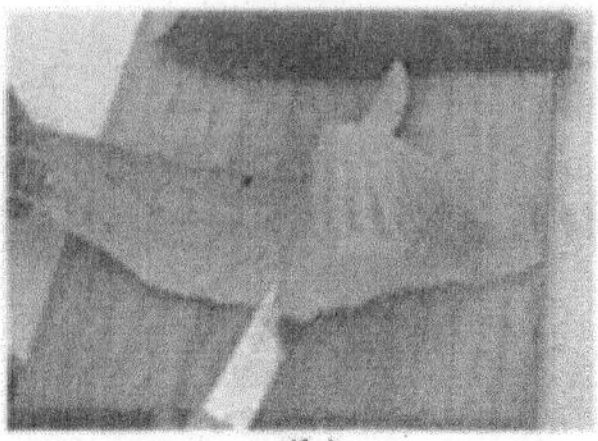
(b)

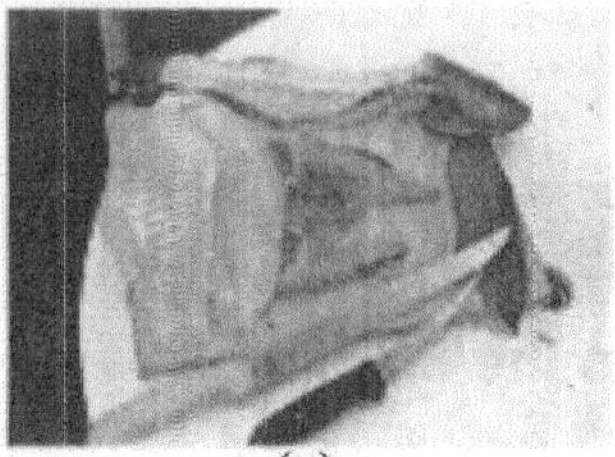
(c)

FROZEN FISH

Fish is available frozen in many different ways. Stuffed, processed and precooked fish cutlets fish sticks, fish balls, paupiettes and many other items are on the market, ready to be deep fried when needed. Customers of seafood are the fast food operators, some institutions, and all those places which do not have qualified help available. In general, most fish today must be purchased frozen. Only big port cities, with their seafood reputation of the past, are still able to get some supplies of fresh fish. Frozen fish comes in many packages: large 50-pound blocks of imported halibut and cod, 5-and 10-pound packages of domestic fish fillet, individual frozen (I.Q.F.) whole fish fillets, and portion-cut fish steaks graded to size.

Shellfish comes in all sizes from all parts of the world. Most common are raw South African and Australian rock lobster tails in the shell or as meat. Also raw are the frozen prawns, which come mostly from mexico and Louisiana. Prawns come from India, Thailand, Japan, Hong Kong, Chile, Denmark, and many other place, too. Some of these supplies are of a quality which is below any standard of acceptance. Some look good while still frozen but have off-tastes and poor textures when they are cooked.

One should not depend on the supplier for a quality judgement. It is risky. First, there is no government grading standard for frozen seafood. Second, in a frozen product the final quality can only be checked after the food is cooked and eaten. To test quality, there is no substitute for eating.

One of the most common problems with frozen fish is that the move from one cold storage to the next may not be fast enough. Foods get partially thawed, and then are refrozen automatically when properly stored again. The government agency, such as USDA or AGMARK are very aware that a transit problem of frozen food exists. A pamphlet of the goverment department will help buyers to check deliveries before acceptance.

A large amount of water expands during freezing and breaks the cell walls of fish. When it is defrosted, the water oozes out, and the portion size shrinks. Frozen fish dealers suggest that fish should be cooked while it is still frozen. This does not really change anything, except that cooking takes longer and the water oozing out is not seen. A cook should handle frozen fish the way management wants him to handle it. Whatever he may do the results, in most cases are inferior to fresh fish. Raw shellfish freezes better than regular fish. Processed or precooked fish handles better than raw frozen fish. A huge difference in quality is found among the many available kinds of fresh and salt water fish. This is because of the origin of the raw fish, as well as its processing, storing, and handling in transit.

QUESTIONS AND DISCUSSIONS

Fill in the Blanks

Q.1. Read and complete the following statements:

(a) When eaten, iced oysters on the half shell are still ....

(b) The true lobster exists only in the waters of the ....

(c) Abalones are native to the ....

(d) Fish is high in nutritional value and very low in ....

(e) Lobsters, crabs, and prawns are classified as ....

(f) Most fish eaten is classified as ....

(g) Kippers, a breakfast food, are smoked ....

(h) The quality of fresh fish is judged by looks, touch, and ....

(i) Dungeness crabs are native to the ....

(j) Fish is easy to digest; shellfish is ....

(k) Finnan Haddie, originally from Scotland, is a fish that has been ....

(l) Fish that can be broiled are only those with flesh that is ....

(m) Clams, oysters, and squid are classified as ....

(n) King crabs are native to ....

(o) For tender seafood, the cooking time must be ....

(p) Sturgeon roe, slightly salted, is called ....

(q) A method to process fish specialties is ....

(r) Spiny lobsters, or languishes, come from waters off ....

(s) For health reasons, shellfish before cooking must be ....

(t) Blue shell crabs are native to the ....

[**Ans.:** (a) alive; (b) Attantic; (c) Pecific; (d) fat; (e) crustaccans; (f) edible; (g) herring; (h) smell; (i) West coast; (j) not; (k) smoked; (l) lean; (m) mollusk; (n) Alaskan; (o) very short; (p) caviar; (q) marinating; (r) California and Mexico; (s) alive; (t) East Coast.]

Multiple Choice Type

Q.2. Read each queston carefully and select the best answer:

(i) Smoked salmon is produced best in

(a) Sweden (b) Italy

(c) Scotland (d) France.

(ii) Crabs from different regions are of different sizes and have flesh of different textures. Which crabs are the biggest ?

(a) Soft-shell crabs (b) East coast crabs

(c) West coast crabs (d) Alaskan crabs.

(iii) Which of these mollusks are often eatern raw ?

(a) Abalones (b) Squid

(c) Oysters (d) Scallops.

(iv) Tender and brittle fish is handled better when :—

(a) Frozen (b) Portion cut

(c) Processed whole (d) Pre-blanched.

(v) Which one of the cooking methods is *not* common for lobster ?

(a) a l' Amoricane (b) a l' meuniere.

(c) Broiled (d) Boilled.

(vi) Which of the following is *not* a crustacean ?

(a) Languste (b) Scallop

(c) Prawn (d) Crab.

(vii) Which of these cooking methods is rarely used on fish ?

(a) Pot-roasting (b) Broiling

(c) Boiling (d) Frying.

(viii) Quality of fresh fish is judged by :—

(a) A grading stamp (b) Packaging label

(c) Its origin (d) Looks and smell.

(ix) Which of the following is *not* a shellfish ?
(a) Shrimp (b) Scallop
(c) Haddock (d) Prawn.

(x) Which of the following is *not* a fish preservation method ?
(a) Curing (b) Smoking
(c) Barbecuing (d) Pickling.

(xi) Many people who do not eat fish are afraid of
(a) Fish poisoning (b) Fish bones
(c) Fish indigestibility (d) Fish preparations..

(xii) Which of these fish steaks does not belong to the group ?
(a) Halibut steak (b) Salmon steak
(c) Trout steak (d) Seabass steak.

[Ans.: (i) (c); (ii) (d); (iii) (c); (iv) (b);
(v) (b); (vi) (b); (vii) (a); (viii) (d);
(ix) (c); (x) (c); (xi) (b); (xii) (c)]

Matching Type

Q.3. Match the seafood dishes in Table 'A' with the geographic and area of their origin in Tables 'B'

Table 'A'	*Table 'B'*
(i) Lobster Americane	(a) Far East
(ii) Broiled Lobster	(b) West Coast of USA
(iii) Pickled Eel	(c) USA
(iv) Sardines in olive oil	(d) East Coast of USA
(v) Raw oysters	(e) France
(vi) Fried Scallops	(f) Scotland-Nova Scotia
(vii) Abalone sauteed	(g) Portugal
(viii) Abalone boiled	(h) Italy
(ix) Fanning Haddie	(i) Russia
(x) Pickled Herring.	(j) Sweden.
(xi) Caviar	
(xii) Coquille St. Jecques.	

[Ans.: (i) e;. (ii) c; (iii) h; (iv) g;
(v) d; (vi) c; (vii) b; (viii) a;
(ix) f; (x) j; (xi) i; (xii) e.]

Short Answer Type

Q.4. Define the following terms :
(a) Caviar (b) Languste
(c) Mollusk (d) Paupiette
(e) Pickling (f) Seafood
(g) Smoking.

Q.5. Describe the tradition of sea food restaurants.

Q.6. Will fish be the future protein source of the world ?

Q.7. Explain the reasons for regional quality differences an national and international.

Q.8. Has frozen fish more merit than frozen meat ?

Q.9. Why must shellfish be cooked alive ?

Q.10. It is good business practice to eliminate the fish butcher ?

Q.11. Are live oysters really a delicacy ?

Q.12. Why are fish cooking methods the same as most cooking methods ?

Descriptive Types

Q.13. Describe some hazards of frozen fish products.

Q.14. Explain the need for fish butchering.

Q.15. Name the important principle in the handling of shellfish.

Q.16. Explain the different kinds of edible seafoods.

Assignments/Activity Type

Q.17. Demonstrate :

(a) The handling of live lobster and crab

(b) Handling of frozen whole lobster.

Q.18. Visits :

(a) A gourmet section of a food store to look for processed and imported food specialties

(b) A fish counter of a supermarket to view fresh and defrosted fish.

Q.19. Take a field trip to a fish processing plant or fish dealer.

PART - III

TECHNIQUES OF COOKING FOOD

3.1

Methods of Cooking

CHAPTER OBJECTIVES

After studying this lesson you should be able :

- To explain the importantance of heat and how heat changes food;
- To list the various substances which prevent food from burning;
- To name the basic modern categories of cookery; and
- To describe the cook's obligations to his/her occupation and to the consumers.

In cooking technology *'gastronomy* may be defined as an art and science of good eating. In its wider meaning, it adds the art of serving and the art of cooking to the art of dining. Gastronomic culture develops best in affluence, but it also requires respect for the preciousness of food. Gastronomic culture is a part of general culture. Several important factors of a medical, nutrional, or religious nature influence this culture. Publicity from pressure groups selling their own products results in the formation of eating and food buying habits of people thus creating a gastronomy culture. The study of gastronomic culture reveals why specific dishes can or cannot be found on public menus in certain areas. It explains why an upsurge in vegetarian dining, milk consumption, or a new food trend comes into existence. For the cook, the chef, and the restaurant operator, it is absolutely necessary to have some understanding of gastronomic art and culture. The cooking technology is based upon the definition of cooking as the heating of food to a certain temperature to make the food edible (eatable). The cooking means the preparation of food.

The most significant action of all cooking is the carrying of heat into food. The cooking processes are based on the several ways in which heat enters food. Cookery uses three shields to protect foods from being charred or burned before they are cooked. These shields are *air, liquid, and fat.*

We may divide cookery into some basic categories which are used for all foods to be cooked. In addition, the similarity of the chemical makeup of food results in a similarity of cooking methods. The immediate objectives of cooking or heat induction are to produce a change of flavour (caramelization), to improve digestibility (tenderization), and to prevent bacterial infection (sterilization).

Understanding and recognizing the approach of basic categories, makes all cooking easier to understand and accomplishes the cook's obligation to nutrition and to the public he serves. Applying this approach makes the one to realize that the many existing food dishes from all over the world are based on only five cooking methods, several main ingredients, and a variety of flavour-given additions.

OBJECTIVES

The objectives of cooking could be based on the principles of nutrition and an obligation to the public. If foods in service to the public neglect these objectives, then they have failed in the responsibilities. The objectives are :

(1) To satisfy the nutritional needs of the people served
(2) To preserve food quality and natural taste
(3) To consider the aesthetic needs of the public
(4) To utilize the variety of all foods available
(5) To uphold sanitary requirements of the food service industry.

Heating of food breaks-down the *cellulose* (fibers) of plant food and partly dissolves connective tissues in meat in order to increase tenderness. Heating evaporates water. In some cases, it also fluffs starches, as in baked potatoes. Heat melts sugar; *caramelizes* it (changes its colour to brown), and finally, *carbonizes* (burns) it completely. Heat breaks down, browns, and melts fats. As a result, heat changes the flavour and appearance of food. When enough heat is applied to food, it sterilizes the food by killing the bacteria. These physical and chemical changes tenderize food for easier chewing and digestion and sterilize the food to guard against bacterial infections.

Food could be divided into groups based on the menu sequence. Some of these groups are appetizers, soups, fish, meat, poultry and game, vegetables, salads, egg dishes, and desserts. For each of these categories, different cooking methods are listed. Sauces are sub-divided by flavour and colour. For example in his book *Culinary Guide* August Escoffier (1847-1955), authority in cooking, listed two different tomato sauces. The sauce is made from tomatoes, meat stock, and bacon. The other sauce, intended for Lenten use (Sauce Tomato Meigre), is made without any meat or meat stock at all.

Cooking deals, mainly with five techniques based on the actual cooking procedure rather than on the menu sequences. These categories involve putting heat into food through a *conductor,* or carrier of heat. All cooking pots are heat conductors, e.g. frying pans and some other utensils. In addition to conduction, convection and radiation also transfer heat. Convection means that heat is carried by warmed air. *Radiation* means exposure to direct rays from an open flame. (Ref. Fig. 3.1A).

Unprotected or unshielded food placed in fire burns or *chars* (carbonizes) instead of being cooked. A shield must exist between the heat source and the food to be cooked. Regardless of the type of heat transfer, i.e. conduction, convection, or radiation, the shields for foods are air, liquid, and fat.

Cooking Process for Meat, Fish, Dairy, Vegetable and Fruits

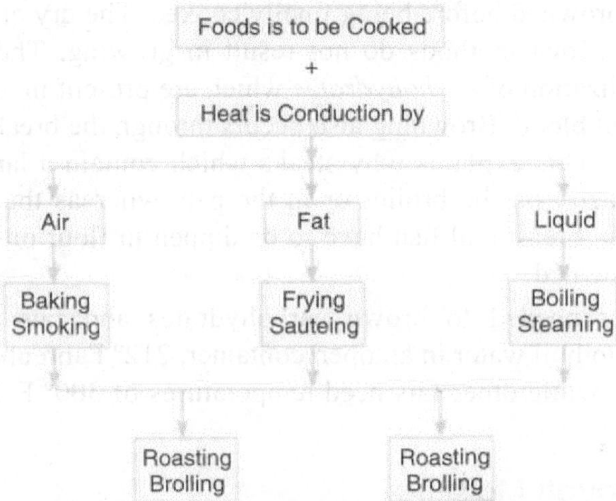

Fig. 3.1A. Basic Cooking Processes for Meat, Fish, Dairy, Vegetable and Fruits.

The five categories of cooking based on actual cooking procedures are :

1. **Dry Hot Air**

   In this method cooking hot air is done in and as called convection cooking or baking. When small quantities of fat are added, the process is called *roasting*. When the heat radiates from an open fire, the process is called spit roasting or broiling.

2. **Liquid or Water**

   In this methods the cooking foods is placed in liquids. It is known as *boiling* (*simmering*) or steaming. Other liquid methods are *poaching and pressure cooking.*

3. **Browning in Hot Fat**

   This type of cooking may be divided into groups depending on the amount of fat used. The process may be called *flip frying, pan frying, griddle frying, deep frying* or *pressure deep frying.*

4. **The Combination**

   In this methods, food is exposed to all three previous categories in a sequence of even together in the same pot. This process in commonly known as *stewing, braising, pot roasting* or *fricasseeing.*

5. **Extraction of Liquefiable Foods**

   This method uses the by-products of foods which have been simmered in liquids. When the foods so cooked are the main result, such as boiled chicken or boiled beef, the liquid is called *broth*. When the food and flavour value of otherwise unusable meat, fish and vegetable leftovers is extracted by a slow simmering or steeping method, the liquid is called *stock.* When a starch ingredient is added to these liquids, the results are soups, sauces, and gravies.

Caramelizing Starches

Many foods are browned before being finally cooked. The dry or fat cooking methods result in browning. Moist methods do not result in growing. The desirable browning results from caramelization of *carbohydrates* which are present in various amounts in all plant food and animal blood. Browning also occurs through the break-down of fats, a first step toward burning. This explains why steaks which contain a large percentage of fat and blood, brown easily on the broiler or in the pan, whereas the lean white meats of veal, skinless chicken breast and fish have to be dippen in flour or other starches before frying to become browned.

The temperatures needed to brown carbohydrates and fats are higher than the temperature needed to boil water in an open container, 212° Fahrenheit (F.) Beef fat starts browning at 225° F., while other fats need temperatures of 300° F. Sugar caramelizes at about 300°F.

Tenderization Through Moisture

The moist cooking methods is used in the preparation of dry plant foods and old tough meat with little fat content to avoid over browning and the resulting burnt taste. The connective tissues in meat are unrefined *gelatine*. The older the animal, the tougher the tissue. To tenderize this tissue, hot water is needed to dissolve the gelatine.

Moisture in a food is often used as a measure of whether or not a food is edible. Food which is to dry or dehydrates must be reconstituted by the addition of water or other liquid to make it edible. The moisture content of food is used as an indication of its juiciness. In general, the juicier a food, the better it tastes.

Caramelizing Cum Tenderizing

This *combination* category of cooking first caramelizes food by frying or roasting to obtain a more acceptable taste, then it is tenderized by adding liquid (water) to complete the cooking.

Liquid Food Extracts

A broth is the by-product of simmering food in water to which flavour ingredients, such as vegetables, herbs, and spices, have been added. The *leaching* (extraction) process of the water causes some flavour and many nutrients to be transferred from the food in to the broth. The broth is simmered until the food it covers is tenderized, then it is strained and used primarily in the making of soups.

Stock is the result of simmering surplus bones, *sinews, and gristle* trimmed from raw meat. Various root vegetables, herbs, and spices are added to the stock to improve the flavour. Stock must simmer for many hours until all nutrients and flavours have leached out into the liquid. Stock is used for sauces, in gravies, and for the braising or combination method.

QUESTIONS AND DISCUSSIONS

Fill in the Blanks

Q.1. Complete the following statements:

(a) Many chefs consider the final authority of cooking to be ....

(b) Baking or dry heat cookery can also be called cooking by.......

(c) Cooking by moist heat is used mainly to tenderize food and to prevent it from

(d) Shields used to prevent burning of foods are fat, air, and...........

(e) Cooking changes the flavour of food through the process of browning known as..........

(f) In the combination method of cooking, food is tenderized by the moist method after the frying or roasting has achieved a certain.........

(g) Cookery books usually divide food into groups based on the ....sequence.

(h) Cooking pots and frying pans are heat..........

(i) The connective tissues of meat are unrefined.........

(j) The by-product of boiled food is called........

[**Ans.:** (a) the heat; (b) convection cooking;
(c) over browning; (d) water;
(e) caramelization; (f) acceptable taste;
(g) menu; (h) conductors;
(i) gelatine; (j) broth]

Multiple Choice Type

Q.2. Read each of the following question carefully and select the best answer.

(i) At what approximate temperature does sugar begin to caramelize?
(a) 212°F (b) 225°F
(c) 300°F (d) 400°F.

(ii) Most people of Western countries prefer meat which is
(a) Baked (b) Browned
(c) Steamed (d) Unsalted.

(iii) Of the following, the one which does not occur when food is exposed to heat for a sufficient time is
(a) Sterilization of bacteria (b) Tenderization of muscles
(c) Changes of flavor. (d) Increase of vitamin value

(iv) When food is put into an open fire it will
(a) Overcook (b) Burn or char
(c) Toughen (d) Redden.

(v) To get a brown crust on a fried chicken the meat has to be dipped first in
(a) Butter (b) Flour
(c) Milk (d) Egg whites.

(vi) The following name which is not used to describe the combination method of caramelizing and tenderizing is
(a) Poaching (b) Braising
(c) Fricasseeing (d) Stewing.

(vii) Beefsteaks are brown very well because they contain

(a) Protein and water (b) Unrefined gelatine

(c) Blood sugar and far (d) Vitamins and minerals.

[**Ans.:** (i) (c); (ii) (b); (iii) (d); (iv) (b);
(v) (a); (vi) (a); (vii) (c)]

Short Answer Type

Q.3. Write short notes on:—

(a) Aesthetics
(b) Roasting
(c) Conduction
(d) Dehydrated
(e) Nutrition
(f) Sterilization
(g) Stock
(h) Broth
(i) Carbohydrates
(j) Convection
(k) Leaching
(l) Radiation
(m) Caramelization.

Q.4. Answer the following methods of cooking in one or two sentences:-

(a) Boiling
(b) Poaching
(c) Steaming
(d) Stewing
(e) Braising
(f) Roasting
(g) Baking
(h) Grilling
(i) Frying - deep fry & shallow fry
(j) Tandoor.

[**Ans.:**

(a) Boiling : Cooking in water or stock.

(b) Poaching : Coking slowly with little liquid which should not be allowed to boil.

(c) Steaming : Cooking in moist heat e.g. place the item in a perforated container over a saucepan of water.

(d) Stewing : Simmer gently with little quantity of water or stock.

(e) Braising : Cooking-in a pan covered with a lid to prevent evaporation so that the food retains its own juice.

(f) Roasting : Cooking in oven with fat.

(g) Baking : Cooking in oven by dry heat e.g. cakes, pastries.

(h) Grilling : Cooking in grill covered with fat.

(i) Frying : With oil.

(i) Deep fry in a deep fry fryer. (ii) Shallow fry in a pan.

(j) Tandoor : Cooking in clay oven with charcoal.]

Descriptive Answer Type

Q.5. Explain the nature of caramelizing or browning .

Q.6. Does the cook's vocation have a greater obligation to the public than most other occupations ?

Q.7. What are some reasons for food to be inedible ?

Q.8. What is the differenceiate between broth and stock ?

Q.9. Does Indian cuisine use the same basic categories as the ones introduced in this lesson ?

Q.10. Explain the modern approach to cooking mean.

Q.11. Why are food preparation workers called Sauce Cooks, Roast Cooks, Pastry Cooks, etc.,?

Q.12. What happens when foods are exposed to heat ?

Assignments/Activity Type

Q.13. Look at three books with a traditional Indian menu sequence, and compare them to each other.

Q.14. Interview a food preparation worker and ask his opinion of the five techniques as a basis for categories of cooking procedures.

3.2

The Extraction of Flavour

CHAPTER OBJECTIVES

After studying this lesson you should be able :

- To define flavour extraction;
- To define and explain broth and stock;
- To identify and explain different stocks;
- To explain the need for and importance of roux in cooking;
- To list four various groups of soups; and
- To explain and practice the making of cream soups.

The extraction of liquefiable foods is the most demanding cooking process. This is commonly known as the making of stocks, soups, gravies, and sauces. Sauce and soup cookery demands more skill than some of the other cooking techniques. The base of all sauces, gravies, and soups is stock and broth. Stock is an extraction from meat bones and trimmings. Broth is the by-product of simmering food for consumption. Cold liquid has more dissolving ability than hot liquid. When several foods simmer together in broth, osmosis and water equalization properties interchange flavours from one food to the other. Lamb bones which have a strong flavour must be kept separate when stock or broth is made.

The most used basic white sauce is called veloute and the most used brown sauce is called espagnole. French Continental cuisine uses roux, an equal weight mixture of fat and flour fried over low heat, to thicken cooking liquids. The making or roux and sauce demands exactness of work and same artistic touch, since the quality of sauce is a value judgement.

Popular soups from all over the world have been interchanged from country to country. Speciality soups have colorful names and remind patrons of far away places. Cooking techniques for extracting liquid foods have been analyzed and improved by culinary technology to such an extent that soup, sauce, and liquid food cookery is no longer really difficult.

EXTRACTION METHOD

Cold water poured over food and brought slowly to simmering extracts more nutrients and flavours than does boiling water when poured over food. When one is cooking for flavour extraction, food is started with cold water, but for the retaining of flavour in boiled foods, hot boiling water is used to start the simmering.

Tea leaves brewed with boiling water become an infusion. When the liquid tea is extracted, the leached out leaves became valueless. Soluble solids can be taken from most foods in a similar way.

Expermental Recipe 8.

Tamarind Chutney

Ingredients

(1) Tamarind : 100 gm
(2) Sugar : 150 gm
(3) Ginger powder : Pinch
(4) Water : 150 ml

Method

(1) Prepare all required ingradients.
(2) Soak and boiled tamarind in water.
(3) Strain and extract the pulp.
(4) Add sugar and colour.
(5) Serve with snacks item.

THE BROTH

If you want to boil a chicken, covered with boiling water, salt, herbs, spices and vegetables are added and it is kept simmering until tender. By osmosis (equalization properties of the water), flavour from vegetables, herbs, and spices is transferred to the chicken and vice versa. At the end of the cooking, all flavours are mixed together. Some flavours stay in the chicken, some are in the vegetables and the rest are in the liquid. Nutrients, such as proteins, vitamins, and minerals are also present in the chicken, vegetables, and liquid. The chicken has lost some of its food value, but the cooking water has gained much food value. It has become a broth. After the tender chicken is removed from this broth, then the broth is strained, defatted and used for the intended purpose. Depending on the ratio of water to chicken and vegetables used, the broth could be weak, normal or very strong. Other broths such as beef, fish, or vegetable, are made in exactly the same way. (Ref. Fig. 3.2A)

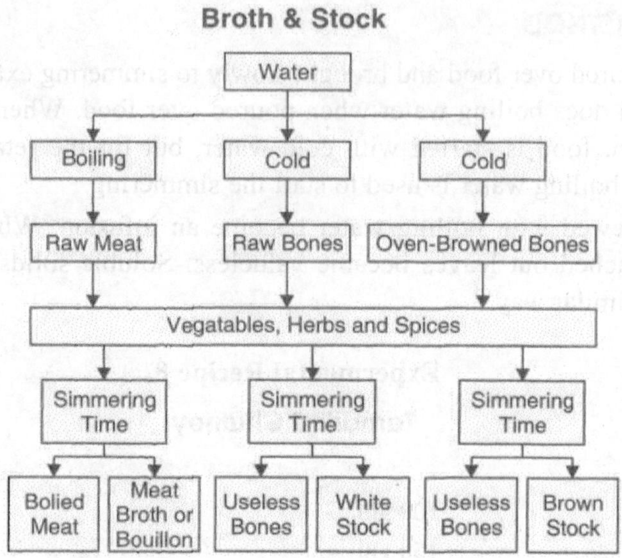

Fig. 3.2A. Broth and Stock-Flow Chart

THE STOCK

Stock is an extraction similar to broth. Instead of using valuable raw chicken, the leftover raw chicken, the leftover raw chicken bones, skin and giblets are used. The same process, with the same vegetables, spices, and herbs is used. After starting in cold water, the bones and trimmings are simmered from 2 to 8 hours, depending on the bones used. When it seems that all the flavour has been extracted from the bones, the liquid is called stock. The stock is handled like broth. The names of the bones used give the name of the stock yielded. For example chicken bones yield chicken stock, beef bones yield beef stock, fish bones fish stock (also called couribouillon) and so on. The ratio of bones and trimming to the water, the additional vegetables, herbs and spices, and the length of simmering are the factors responsible for taste and strength of the stock.

Varieties of Stocks

The bigger a kitchen, the greater is the variety of stocks which could be made. Depending on the needs of the menu, chicken stock, white meat stock (mixed), brown meat stock, and sometimes even fish stock are available. All stocks except brown stock, are simmered from raw bones. Brown stock gets its colour from the pre-roasting of bones which are then simmered. Tomatoes may also be added. General meat socks are usually mixed. Beef, veal, pork, and poultry bones are used together. Lamb has too strong a flavour to be used in this way. Fish stock is made mostly in fish restaurants, but many general food establishments, make it.

Usage of Stock

Escofficer, the famous classical chef, insisted that the quality of all cooking depended on the quality of the stocks made. This is only partially true because today's cooking trends are toward a sauceless cookery. Freshly cooked vegetables and tender fast-cooked meats need less of the flavour addition which a good sauce gives to many dishes. Brown meat stock is used to make basic brown sauce which is called Espagnol. It is also used to make pan gravy, which is called "jus de viande" and the meat glaze called glace de viande.

White stock is used for most soups and for the ivory coloured basic white sauce, called veloute. When meat and poultry bones are not mixed, chicken veloute, and others can be made and used for special purposes. Fish stock is white and is used for a basic fish sauce called fish veloute, as well as for the making of seafood dishes and soups.

(a) **Stock Pot** (b)

CHANGING STOCK TO SAUCE

Making a perfect sauce is considered by many people as the most difficult of all the cooking procedures. Today, culinary technology has analyzed what makes a sauce and most difficulties disappeared. Sauces based on starch are made from water with a floater (called stock), a thickener made of starch (flour), and fat. The quality of a sauce is judged by flavour, texture, and colour. These are value judgment. Flavour depends on the quality of the stock, flour, and fat used. Texture depends on the ratio of starch to fat and liquid. Colour depends on the ingredients and their handling.

Stock to Sauces

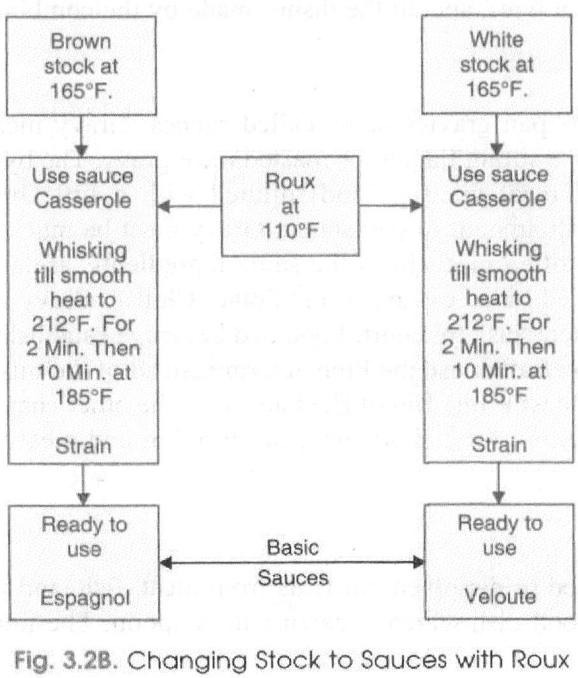

Fig. 3.2B. Changing Stock to Sauces with Roux

Starches most often used are all-purpose flour and cornstarch. Some chefs use potato, rice, or arrowroot flour as the starch. For quality cookery, all-purpose flour is mixed with fat, heated, and fried lightly. This mixture, called *roux,* is added to the stock and simmered for a short while. This procedure changes stock to a sauce.

Other cooking styles do not mix fat and flour into a roux. Starch, which had been stirred into some cold water, is added to the simmering stock. In this procedure the sauce has a different texture and taste.

Preparation and Use of Roux

Roux is an essential ingredient to French continental cookery. It is used directly and indirectly for nearly every thing that French Continental Cuisine produces. (Ref. Table 3.2A)

Table 3.2A. Formula for Roux-Preparation.

$$\frac{\text{I cup fat}}{\text{heat}} + \frac{\text{I}\frac{1}{2}\text{ cups flour}}{\text{heat}} + \frac{\text{whisking stir}}{\text{heat}} \times \frac{\text{5 min}}{\text{heat}} + \frac{\text{off}}{\text{heat}} = \frac{\text{roux}}{110°\text{F}}$$

160°F.	160°F.	195°F.	120°F.	75°F.

Roux is made from any good fat (as in sauteing), and the approximate equal weight of flour. Frying over low heat or in the oven is done in three stages. These are white, golden, or brown, depending on the colour of the sauce wanted. Roux can be made once a day or once a week. It keeps for a long time if kept under proper refrigeration and if the correct fat is used. The ratio of roux to liquid governs the texture of the sauce. Roux is also used for soups, gravies, and all the dishes made by the combination method.

PAN GRAVIES OR "JUS"

Gravies should be pan gravies or be called sauces. Gravy means a thinly textured liquid substance with a strong flavour or roasted meat gravy. The by-product of a roast, is made of coagulated meat juices (blood) diluted with a little brown stock and then thickened with a small amount of cornstarch. Gravy must be much thinner than a sauce. Gravies and sauces, often made from the same ingredients, are as different from each other as "Cottage Fried Potatoes" are from "Potato Chips". Gravy is equal to the French "Jus de Viande", called "jus" for short. Food and beverage establishments specializing in roast prime ribs of beef often use the French term instead of the misused word gravy and make their menus "Roast Prime Rib of Beef au Jus". The other characteristic of good pan gravy is that after setting for a short time, fat dripping and meat juices separate like a salad dressing.

SOUPS

Soups are extracted or dissolved nutrients from meat, fish, and vegetables. These are made into a liquid food dish which is eaten with a spoon. The liquid for making them may be water, stock or milk. There are clear soups, thickened soups, puree soups and speciality soups.

Clear Soups is Made From Broth

Strained chicken or beef broth is called bouillon. When served in a bouillon cup without any garnish it is called "Bouillon en taste". When cooked rice and chopped chicken meat are added, it becomes "Old-fashioned chicken broth". Bouillon served with fine noodles is called vermicelli soup. With wider noodles it is called beef or chicken noodle soup. A tasty bouillon is appetizing when served at the beginning of a meal and it can be varied with a great number of garnishes. In the past, bouillon and consomme were considered important because they brought important meat proteins to old people who had lost their teeth. (Ref. Fig. 3.2C)

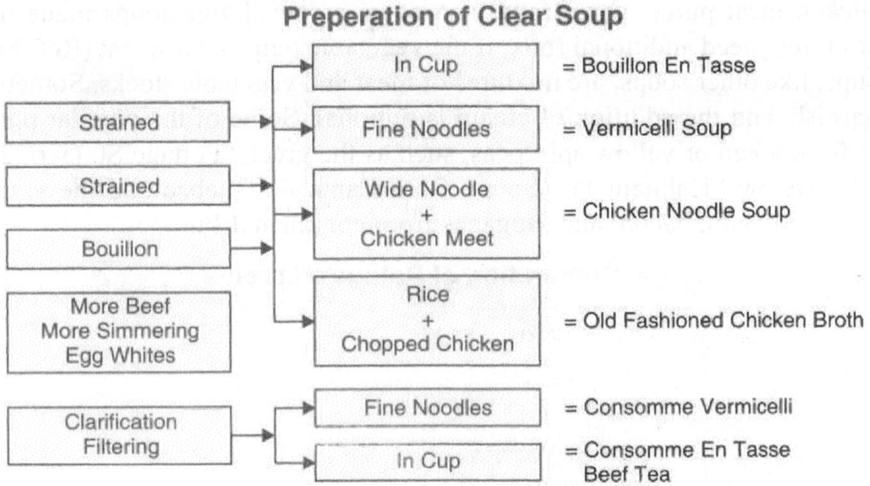

Fig. 3.2C. Flow Chart for Preparation of Clear Soups

Consomme

Consomme has tasty soup essence. It is made by simmering lean beef meat and vegetables with herbs and spices in already made bouillon. The bouillon thus becomes doubly strong. In England, this soup is called Beef Tea. While a consomme simmers, it clarifies itself. Raw egg whites are added to the still cold bouillon to aid in clarification. When heated to the simmering point, the egg whites coagulate (gather together) and attract additional protein impurities from the bouillon. The egg white and the impurities float as foam to the top of the consomme and are removed after simmering. Consomme is served in the same manner as bouillon.

Soups Made With Roux

Soups thickened with roux are made of meat, fish, and vegetable stock, with an optional garnish. For texture improvement, rich cream can be added. A thickened chicken soup which has been improved with cream is called "Cream of Chicken Soup". It is made in the same way as chicken veloute sauce is made, and the cream is added just before serving. The difference between chicken sauce and chicken soup is in the texture. The soup should be thinner than the sauce.

Soups thickened with roux are made from protein food and vegetables combined. Roux is added to soup in the same manner as it is to a sauce. Garnish and cream are optional.

Pureed Soups

Purees can be made from most food substances. Meat puree and vegetable puree are very common. Fish puree is sometimes made for special preparations. Puree·soups contain a high percentage of food pulp which is used to bring out the flavour and provide texture in place of the roux. Some starchy vegetables change to puree easily. These include potatoes, split peas, lentils beans, and some fresh vegetables such as cauliflower, spinach, and tomatoes. Chicken puree soup, called "Pottage a la Reine" is made with white chicken meat puree, some roux, and some cream. Puree soups made of starchy vegetables rarely need additional roux, if the vegetable pulp is sufficient (Ref. Fig. 3.3D). Puree soups, like other soups, are mixtures of meat and vegetable stocks. Sometimes they have a garnish, and the addition of cream is optional. Some of the popular puree soups are made from green or yellow split peas, such as the green "Pottage St. Germane" from France, the yellow "Habitant Pea Soup" from Canada's Quebec and the various peas soups made with ham, bacon, and saugages from continental Europe.

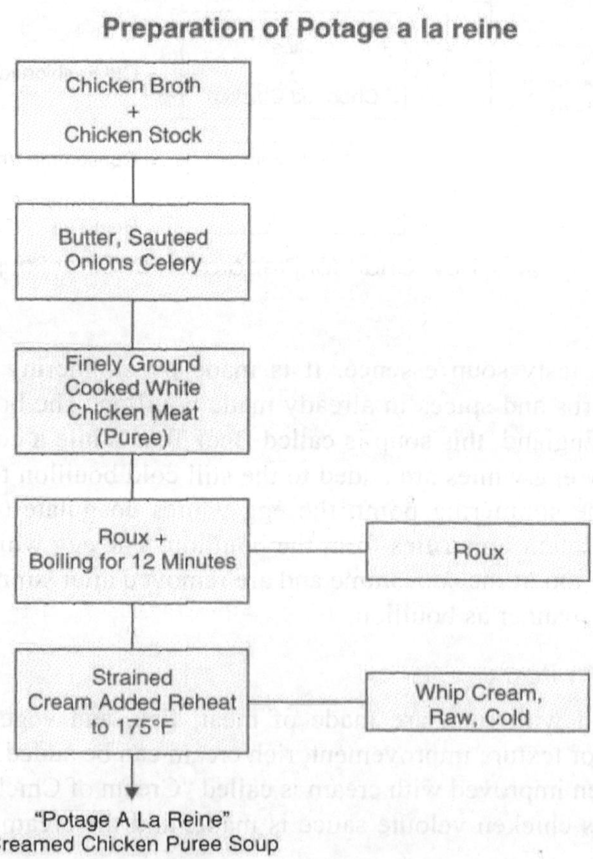

Fig. 3.3D. Flow Chart for Preparation of Potage a la reine, a Deluxe Soup

Speciality Soups

These are substantial soups which originated from soupy kettle stews. Today they are used as lunch dishes, and in the cold reading special soup restaurants sell them over the counter at lunch time. These soups are full of calories and a bowl is a meal in itself. Now speciality soups come from many parts of the world.

Speciality soups may be made from a semi-clear liquid, or from one thickened with puree or roux. They have a rich starch or protein garnish to provide the necessary filling. Although they come from different cultures, their preparation procedures are as simple as any other soup.

Soups such as Boston Clam Chowder, the Philadelphia Pepperpot, and the Louisiana Chicken Gumbo are produced in USA. Some European speciality soups are Marmite (France), Minestrone (Italy), Tax-paid (Spain), and Barest (Russia). When speciality soups representing different regions are prepared, you as an young cook should be sure that the soup retains as much of its national or regional character as possible.

Cooking Techniques for Liquids

According to Escoffier' the quality of cooking depends on the quality of the stock made, is very important for the soup and sauce cook; The second cook, or the saucier's job it is to prepare liquid food. Culinary technology has found ways to simplify many procedures. Some of the guidelines are given below which help the student trainee to make excellent soups and sauces in a short time.

Guidelines for Working with Stock

1. Trimmings, bones and vegetables must be fresh and clean.
2. Use enough bones, meat, and vegetables to have the correct water-food ratio.
3. Cold water extracts better than hot water.
4. The slower and longer the simmering, the better the broth.
5. Liquids must be kept refrigerated in non-oxidizing containers.
6. Stored liquids must be rotated.

Guidelines for Working with Roux

1. Roux should be added to liquid for better texture control.
2. For mixing, the roux should be luckewarm and the liquid should be a about 170°F.
3. A whisk should be used to work roux into liquid.
4. The sauce casserole used is very important; it must be low, wide, made of a heavy gauge material and not warped.
5. The approximate ratio of roux to liquid for sauces is 1½ to 2 cups of well fried roux to one gallon of liquid.
6. Sauce must come to a rolling full boil and then continue to bubble for 10-15 minutes.
7. When sauces become too thick, they should be diluted with stock.
8. For keeping sauces hot, uncovered, a buttered paper on the sauce's surface will avoid a dried out skim.

9. There is no substitute for fresh whipping cream.
10. Garnishes for soups and sauces are better when sauteed in butter first.

QUESTIONS AND DISCUSSIONS

Fill in the Blanks

Q.1. Read and complete the following:

(a) The important part of making pan gravy is the inclusion of ....

(b) For brown stock and sauce, meat bones have to be ....

(c) Meat stock, which is extracted food from bones into water, should be started with water that is ....

(d) Broth, as the by-product of food simmered for eating, should be started with water that is ....

(e) It is believed that speciality soups have originated from soupy ....

(f) A tasty strained chicken broth when garnished with fine noodles is called ....

(g) The quality of a sauce is judged by its flavour, colour and ....

(h) The additional ingredient which helps to clarify consomme is ....

(i) Making sauces with roux is the style of the .... cuisine

(j) A chicken simmered in water loses more food values than a chicken roasted in the oven. The missing nutrients are found in the ....

(k) Soups are a form of liquid food, because nutrients from meat, fish, and vegetables have been ....

(l) Consomme, which is a strong, deeply coloured clear meat broth, is appropriately called ....

(m) To make a mixed meat stock, all conventionally used bones are used with the exception of ....

(n) Stocks or other liquids are changed to sauces through the addition of ....

(o) Properly made roux is heated and fried ....

[**Ans.:** (a) roasted meat; (b) pre-roasted; (c) cold; (d) boiling; (e) kettles stews; (f) Vermiccelli soup; (g) texture; (h) raw egg white; (i) quality; (j) stock; (k) extracted; (l) bullion entasse; (m) raw chicken white; (n) roux; (o) over low heat]

Multiple Choice Type

Q.2. Read each question carefully and select the *best* answer:

(i) Stock or broth, regardless of how it was started, should continuously

(a) Boil for several hours (b) Steep for several hours

(c) Simmer for several hours (d) Steam for several hours.

(ii) Speciality, puree, and thickened soups have substantial food value and by comparison to sauces should be

(a) Heavier (b) Richer
(c) Spicier (d) Thinner.

(iii) The clear meat soup with the greatest amount of meat extract in it is called
(a) Beef Tea (b) Beef Bouillon
(c) Beef Broth (d) Vermicide Soup.

(iv) Chicken cream soup is made of chicken stock, roux and
(a) Whipping cream (b) Chicken meat puree
(c) Chicken giblets (d) Rice or Noodles.

(v) Roux is a mixture of measured fat and flour in the following proportions:
(a) 1 cup fat + 1 cup flour (volume) (b) 1 cup fat + 2 cups floor (volume)
(c) 8 oz. fat + 12 oz. flour (weight) (d) 8 oz. fat + 8 oz. flour (weight).

(vi) Not all raw foods can be used to extract flavour. From the ones listed, which is the most *unlikely* to be used?
(a) Ham (b) Eggs
(c) Bacon (d) Potatoes.

(vii) All of the listed regional speciality soups are American except
(a) Clam Chowder (b) Minestrone
(c) Pepperpot (d) Chicken Gumbo.

(viii) The clean meat soup with the greatest amount of meat extract in it is called
(a) Beef Tea (b) Beef Bouillon
(c) Beef Broth (d) Vermicelli Soup.

(ix) Puree soups made from starchy vegetables like split peas or dried legumes are not made with
(a) Strong meat stock (b) Vegetable and meat garnish
(c) Roux or cornstarch (d) Herbs and spices.

(x) To make consomme, bouillon is not only clarified by egg whites but also flavour improved with
(a) More vegetables (b) Additional meat
(c) Tomato puree (d) More spices.

(xi) Roux is used to thicken many food preparations, but not
(a) Tomato sauce (b) Beef stew
(c) Cream soup (d) Liver saute.

(xii) Common sense should indicate that bones used for stock making should be
(a) Cut as small as possible (b) Cut as large as possible
(c) Split lengthwise only (d) Left as they are.

[**Ans.:** (i) (c); (ii) (b); (iii) (a); (iv) (a); (v) (d);
(vi) (d); (vii) (b); (viii) (b); (ix) (a); (x) (a);
(xi) (a); (xii) (c)].

Matching Type

Q.3. Match the speciality soups of Table 'A' with the geographic areas of Tables 'B'

Table A	*Table B*
(a) Minestrone	(i) Boston
(b) Pepperpot	(ii) Canada
(c) Burst	(iii) Spain
(d) Plottage St. Germain	(iv) Louisiana
(e) Clam Chowder	(v) Philadelphia
(f) Gazette	(vi) Italy
(g) Chicken Gumbo	(vii) Russia
(h) Habitant Pea Soup	(viii) France

[**Ans.:** (a) (vi); (b) (v); (c) (vii); (d) (viii);
(e) (i); (f) (iii); (g) (iv); (h) (ii)]

Q.4. Match the food terminology of Table 'A' with the English name of Table 'B'.

Table 'A'	*Table 'B'*
(a) Espagnol	(i) Meat extract
(b) Bouillon	(ii) Fine noodle soup
(c) Jus de Viande	(iii) Chicken essence
(d) Veloute	(iv) Fish stock
(e) Court Bouillon	(v) Brown sauce
(f) Beef Tea	(vi) Strained broth
(g) Pottage a la Reine	(vii) Pan gravy
(h) Glace de Viande	(viii) White meat sauce
(i) Chicken Consomme	(ix) Chicken pure soup
(j) Vermicelli Soup	(x) Beef essence.

[**Ans.:** (a) (v); (b) (vi); (c) (vii); (d) (viii);
(e) (iv); (f) (ii); (g) (ix); (h) (x);
(i) (iii); (j) (ii)].

Short Answer Type

Q.5. Explain the importance of pan gravy.

Q.6. Differentiate between:

(a) Sauces made with roux and sauces made with the starch water mixture

(b) Kitchen-made stock and convenience stock base.

Q.7. According to Escoffier, "the quality of cooking depends on the quality of the stocks made." Explain this statement in the present day context.

Q.8. What is the importance of soups and what is their historical role?

Discriptive Type

Q.9. Describe how cream soups are made.

Q.10. Name and explain the four groups of soups.

Q.11. Describe roux and its use.

Assignments/Activity Type

Q.12. Perform the following: (Infusion - Extraction comparison.)

(a) Soak two teaspoon of tea leaves in one cup of cold water overnight.

(b) Brew one cup of tea with one teaspoon of leaves, cool it off. Compare the results.

Q.13. Perform the following:

Step 1 Make a roux of two tablespoons of oil and three tablespoon of flour and fry on lowest heat until roux bubbles.

Step 2 Take it off the heat and cool for 5 to 10 minutes.

Step 3 Add 2¼ cups of hot water, approx. 165°F., whisk it smooth and bring mixture to a boil.

Step 4 Wait for a rolling boil, keep whisking, reduce heat to bubbling and continue for 10 more minutes.

Step 5 Take mixture of the burner, strain through a tea sieve, check for lumps. Examine this tasteless water sauce for texture smoothness flow, and looks.

3.3

Baking Roasting & Broiling: Dry Heat Methods

CHAPTER OBJECTIVES

After studying this lesson you should be able :

- To explain importance and the reasons for roasting and broiling food;
- To identify the main meat cuts for broiling and roasting;
- To describe the principles and theories of roasting;
- To explain the importance of recirculation of juices;
- To list common food holding times for the warmer;
- To identify different types of ovens and broilers used in modern kitchen; and
- To list the safety hazards of a broiler.

The techniques of cooking with dry heat is one of the oldest but still one of the most desirable ways to cook. According to dieticians and nutritionists, baking, roasting and broiling are better than other forms of cooking. The baking in cooking is mostly called roasting, which implies the presence of fat.

Baking-Croissants Proofing on plastic try

Only tender meat cuts can be dry heat cooked. Meat roasting as well as other forms of cookery can be analyzed in relation to thermodynamic laws which explain what actually happens. Large roasts should cook at low heat for a longer time, but smaller roasts need higher heat for a shorter cooking time. Broiling has advantages to the customer as well as to the restaurateur and is similar to roasting. The terms grilling, broiling, and griddling are sometimes mixed up. There are a variety of different broiler models used for different heat sources available.

Cooking with dry heat is one of the five basic cooking methods. Dry heat is mostly used in baking, roasting, and broiling. The methods of baking and roasting sequence the of use convection heat with additional conduction. Broiling uses radiation and less conduction. Since the general tenderness of meat improves constantly, dry cooking methods are becoming acceptable for a wider range of meat cuts.

BAKING TECHNIQUE

The term baking should be used for the cooking of vegetable substance, such as cakes, pies, breads, or baked beans. For meat wrapped in dough, (as in Beef filet Wellington or dough filled with meat, as in a "Beefsteak and Kidney" Pie,) the term baking is correct.

Croissants

A Trainee holding tray of assotted pastries in bakery

Bread Rolls

Hamburger and French Fries

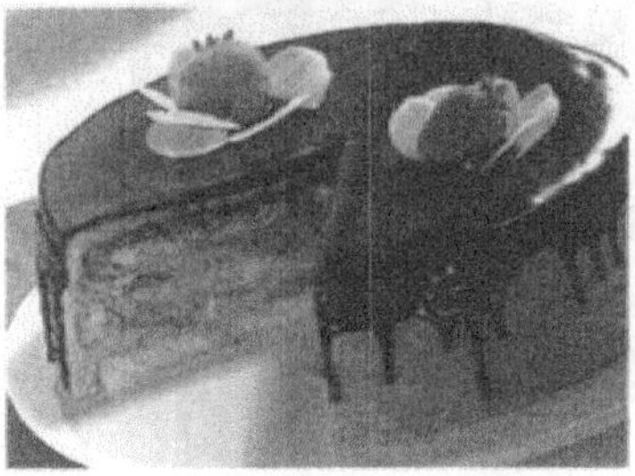

Torte: Torte is the German word for cake, though it is typically used to describe a moistcake made with many eggs, and often made with ground nuts or bread crumbs. Tortes may be either a multi-layered cake or a single layer. Examples: Chocolate pecan Torte, Walnut Raspberry Torte

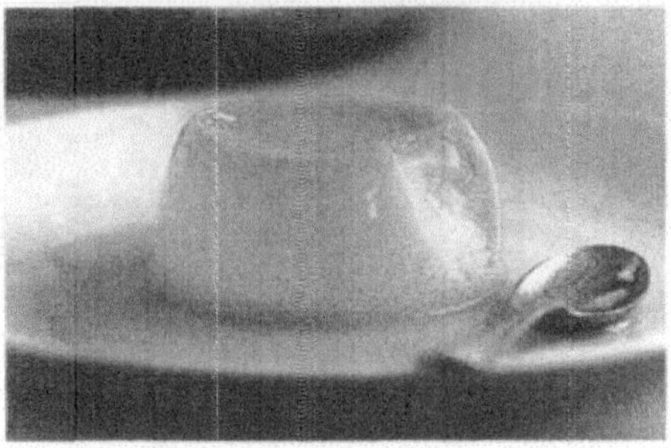

Creme Caramel

Experimental Recipe 9.
Nan Khatai

Ingredients

(1) Flour	:	1¼Cup
(2) Besan	:	¼ Cup
(3) Sugar	:	¾ Cup
(4) Oil	:	¾ Cup
(5) Baking Powder	:	1 tsp.

Method

(1) Prepare all required ingredients.
(2) Sieve flour, baking powder, besan and castor sugar twice.
(3) Melt fat and mix sieved dry ingredients to make soft dough
(4) Divide the dough into parts.
(5) Make balls and flatten them in the shape of biscuits
(6) Place them in a greased baking tray.
(7) Bake for 20-30 minutes.

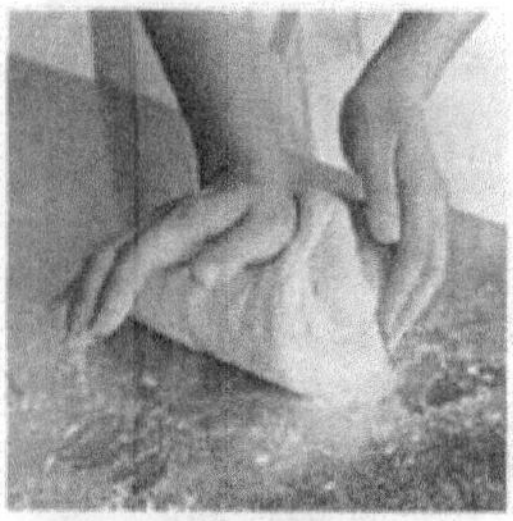
Hands on Dough

Bakery Bread

Chocolate Marble Cake

Chocolate Marble Cake

Baked Fish

ROASTING

The term roasting applies to large pieces of meat (more than three portions) cooked by dry heat with only the addition of fat, salt, and spices. The roasting process results in browing. Browning occurs through the caramelization of carbohydrates and fats present. A turkey cooked by dry heat should be called a roast turkey, not a baked turkey.

'Caramelization' is the term used to describe the change of sugar to caramel under the influence of heat, Caramelization is also suger's last stage before burning. Sugar and starch are carbohydrates. Meat, mostly protein, has only a few carbohydrates in it. These are called glucose or blood sugar. Fat also browns and melts at the same time. With enough heat, both sugar and fat will burn completely.

Carbohydrates and fats, when browned, change flavour. This different flavour of browned food are preferred by a majority of people. The minimum degree of heat needed for browning is 225° F. for beef fat and 300° F. for carbohydrates. Water in an open container boils at 212°F., changes into steam, and evaporates into the air. In other words so long as water is present in a cooking process, the temperature can never be higher than 212°F. This explains why dry cooking processes, which are different from moist cooking processes, are used whenever the characteristic (tenderness, fat, and moisture content) of the food allow it.

All cuts of meat cannot be roasted. All cuts which can be roasted are also excellent when broiled. Dry cooking methods do not dissolve, but only tenderize, most of the gelatinous (called collagen) that hold muscle fibers together. When this collagen comes from animals of old age, the tenderization through roasting is not sufficient and the meat remains tough. For cooking meat of all young animals, dry cooking methods are very satisfying. Young animals are those raised for a not longer than six months before they are processed.

Meat mostly one or two years old, is divided into first and second cuts. Fist, or prime cuts come from the full loin and part of the rib. These are all areas where the animal muscles are used the least. Prime cuts are used for roasts, steaks, chops, chops, and cutlet. All the meat a butcher calls roast or steak can not be cooked by dry heat. True beef roasts and steaks must come from prime cuts to be tender and juicy. Veal, pork, and lamb, as a rule, are young enough so that any part of the carcass may be roasted. In poultry class, hens or fowl are too old, and only those marked roasters and fryers can be dry heat cooked.

MEAT ROASTING

In roasting large meat pieces are exposed to such a degree of dry heat that the center of the roast becomes just done and stays juice. At the same time, the surface of the roast browns without being charred or dried out.

In order to roast meat efficiently, one must understand some theories of thermodynamics. Radiated heat rays are electromagnetic waves. Once strike a surface, the molecular action is increased and this moving action within the substance produced heat. Fast moving molecules cause high heat, slower ones cause less heat. Till the time these rays continue, more heat is created. Heat has a unique characteristic. Unless completely insulated, it will always equalize itself with all the other substances with which it comes in contact.

HEAT TRANSFER EXPERIMENT

In the cooking, process heat is transmitted by direct radiation (open fire), conduction (candle experiment), or convection (air currents). Try experiment shown in Experimental Recipe 10.

This experiment will help you to visualize heat equalization by methods of conduction, convection, and radiation.

Experimental Recipe 10.

Heat Transfer Experiment Candle Experiment

Materials needed

1. One household candle.
2. Six inches of straight copper wire, not insulated.

Procedure/method

1. Light the candle.
2. Hold flat, outstretched palm of hand horizontally six inches away from flame. Wait one minute and see how much heat can be felt, if any at all.
3. Hold wire on end between thumb and forefinger. Stick other end into flame. Hold same position as before. Wait one minute or stop any time the wire gets too hot
4. Hold that palm of hand over the top of the candle flame, about six inches Check the time it takes to make it too hot.

Conclusion

1. The cable flame has radiated heat into a 360° sphare, but radiation over a distance of six inches could not be felt.
2. Since copper is one of the best heat conductors the heat of the flame is transmitted to the fingers.
3. The radiant flame is heating air all around the candle but the heated air becoming lighter than the cold air rises up high and dissipates into the surrounding air. This shows the principle of convection.

When meat is exposed to heat, conduction transports the heat from the surface of the roast to the center of the roast. Heat creates its own equalization as long as new heat waves are directed against its surface.

If heat, directed against the surface of a roast, is more than 300°F., the caramelizaton of the surface takes place quickly. The meat is not able to conduct most of this heat toward, the center. The heat will be concentrated on the surface. In other words, a roast exposed to more heat than its size can absorb, will burn on the surface while the center remains cold.

ROASTING TIME

According to Brillat-Savarin, the great French food philosopher (0755-1826), "Making the best sauce can be learned, but cooking the perfect roast is a talent" These words are still as true as ever. Many factors are involved. Everyone can learn to roast close to the "point", but cooks have to work out roasting techniques of their own. Different ovens, different roasting pans, different meats with a different *marble* (visible fat veins), and different desired results need different individual approaches.

The following guidelines for roasting could be useful:

1. Roasting time depends on the size, type and geometric shape of the roast, as well as the heat degrees of the oven.
2. Large roasts need lower heat for a longer time.
3. Small roasts need higher heat for a shorter time.

Fish Preparation

You will find that low heat for large roasts will reduce shrinkage, prevent burning and produce an evenly cooked good roast. Low heat for small roasts results in overcooking before browning has been achieved. This is also true for roasts with a geometrical shape which allows fast heat penetration.

Management and some executive are often too concerned with *yield.* Yield means that the less shrinkage there is in a roast, the more portions there are to be sold. Shrinkage describes food weight loss during any cooking process. Enough heat melts fats and evaporates water. For example, while frying bacon, the liquid fat burns away, or is at least separated from the lean. As a result, there is shrinkage in cooked bacon. For the sake of good cooking, it is more important to serve tasty food, than to gain a few more portions. Preparations must come up to expectations. If the browning has not occurred, the roast is not a roast, because it does not taste like a roast.

RECIRCULATION OF JUICES

When you find a roast appears to be cooked, carry-over heat must be considered. The heat from the original source is stopped by removing the roast form the oven and from the pan. The heat of this mass still needs to equalize within itself. Some heat will flow into the surrounding air and some will pass deeper to the center. The meat juices will recirculate. This carry-over action of heat has to be considered while the roast is still in the oven. If meat roast or a steak is cooked to medium, then removed from the heat source, carry-over heat will make it nearly well done.

A recirculation, also known as setting time, is absolutely necessary. Warm meat juices and heat must equalize themselves within the roast, before you attempt carving. A medium-rare beef roast, which is cooled to a 145°F. inside temperature and then cut in half without setting, will show a dry overcooked ring of meat beneath the surface and a nearly raw center. When the same roast is allowed to set for the juices to recirculate, a uniform pinkish red will cover the whole slice. The larger the roast, the more setting time must be allowed.

WARMKEEPING

Setting time and warmkeeping are the two important phases in roosting. Setting time is a must for a better roast., but warmkeeping after setting is a necessary evil to make the serving of roasts easier in a restaurant. (Ref. Table 3.3A)

You may use various types of food warmers to keep cooked food "service ready". The larger the roast, the longer it can be kept warm without too much drying out. It is important to time the cooking so that only the shortest warmkeeping time is needed.

Table 3.3.A. Recirculation and maximum Warmkeeping Times for Various Roasts

	Type of Roast	*Weight*	*Setting Time*	*Holding Time*
(1)	Rib of Beef	25-30 lbs	35-45 minutes	2-3 hours
(2)	Boneless Rib Eye	12-16 lbs	20-25 minutes	1-1½ hours
(3)	Baron of Beef	55-75 lbs	55-75 minutes	4-5 hours
(4)	Striploin	10-14 lbs	15-20 minutes	¾-1 hours
(5)	Fillet of Beef	6-8 lbs	10-15 minutes	¾-1 hours
(6)	Rack of Lamb	2-3 lbs	5-10 minutes	¾ hours
(7)	Leg of Lamb	6-8 lbs	20-25 minutes	1½-2 hours
(8)	Loin of Pork	7-10 lbs	15-20 minutes	1-1½ hours
(9)	Let of Pork	12-18 lbs	20-30 minutes	1½-2 hours
(10)	Roast Turkey	25-30 lbs	25-30 minutes	2-2½ hours
(11)	Roasted Capon	4½ - 6 lbs	10-15 minutes	¼-½ hours

While handling roast, from the oven to the warmer, following order may be observed:

(1) Take roast and pan out of the oven.

(2) Remove the roast from the pan to a holding container.

(3) Reserve the hot roasting pan, with all dripping, for gravy.

(4) Cool off the roast at room temperature, for the time needed according to its size.

(5) Place the roast in the warmer (Bain-Marie) until it is to be carved.

Carving

Different type of food and beverage establishments use different serving techniques, which depend on their price levels. The best way is to cut each order, when needed. This is expensive and requires one more cook. Such expense would be reflected in the price on the menu.

Carving is not difficult. The cook needs sharp knives, a blueprint for the carving of specific roasts, and practice. He should understand that guests must be served appetizing and reasonable warm orders.

Roasts should be cut so that the slice has a short *grain.* Grain is the visible structure of the meat fibers. The short grain is accomplished by holding the knife at a 90° angle against the fibers. Lamb or pork legs, ribs, loins, poultry, and fish are carved in distinct ways, either for the sake of appearance or for efficiency.

BROILING AND ROASTING

Broiling is a good example of why culinary art is unlikely to change totally to culinary technology. Some parts of art will always remain. A variety of factors difies attempts to establish a formula for the broiling the many existing dishes. Every cut of meat, even from the same animal, has a different distribution of fat with in its fibres density of mussels and a deterrent geometric shape. All of these are factors in heat conduction. More variables exist from tone animal to the next. These are breed age, feeding and the method of slaughtering. Such variables change the fat percentage and its distribution, the conformation (shape) and the water (blood) content of each piece of meat. The size of the steak and the customer's own concept of doneness also vary. For instance, it has been concluded by meat researchers that some consumers accept broiled or roasted meat about one step higher than other category customers. A steak, considered rare in the Midwest, is considered medium rare in the West. There is also the recirculation and holding time. Broiler cooks often have to allow for the time it takes the diner to eat.

Experimental Recipe 11

Tawa Chapatti

Ingredients

(1) Whole Wheat Flour : 200 gm
(2) Water : To need
(3) Salt : Pinch.

Method

(1) Prepare all required ingredients.
(2) Sieve the flour along with salt.
(3) Add water and knead to smooth dough.
(4) Prepare bolls of 50 - 70 gm each.
(5) Know pin and cook on hot plate.
(6) Serve with vegetables and *daal*.

Broiling does to one portion of meat what roasting does to one piece (several portions in one) of meat. The same meat cuts and the same additions of salt, spices, and fat are used. The dry heat process of cooking is applied, but the convection heat (hot air) is replaced by radiated heat for a stronger impact. Regular roasting ovens maintain their highest temperature at about 500°F., but a good broiler may have up to 1200°F. heat output with some going as high as 1600°F.

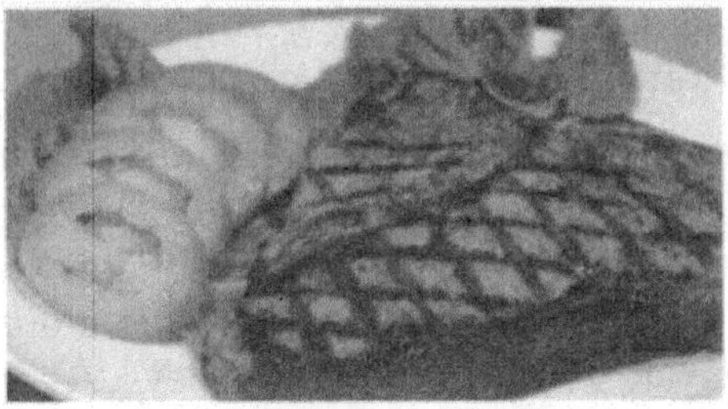

Char-Broiled T-Bone

A single steak is too small to be roasted in an oven. If it were placed in 500°F. oven, the steak would be well done inside before getting a crust on the surface.

For double or triple portions steaks, experienced cooks always used the broiler first and then the oven. The high broiler heat browns and marks the steak, then the oven finishes cooking it without burning the surface.

A trainee who wants to become a good broiler cook, needs to understand these theories, have a cool head, and a strong sense of responsibility. Then, with a few demonstrations of how it should be done and a lot of experience, he attains this goal in due time.

The good broiler cook had knowledge and experience. The perfect broiler cook, like the perfect roast cook, has some added inborn talent.

All broiled food need to be cooked when ordered. Cooking time for the largest steak is seldom more than twenty minutes. No precooking is needed and no cooked food is left over to spoil. A steak house keeps a refrigerator full of pre-cut raw steaks and the cook "fire" them when ordered. The command *fire a steak* means to cook pre-ordered food at this very moment

Refrigerated meat could be kept for long day. Steaks can be counted and checked easily, and no elaborate cooking process is needed in their preparation. A steakhouse is an ideal setup for the restaurateur.

All customers, like fresh-made orders. A stock, ordered rare, assures the customer that he will not get any leftover warmed-up meat or some reconstituted convenience food.

According to dieticians broiled food is healthier than pan-fried or even sauteed food. Most of the fat drips off the meat, and even some of the juices are lost. Therefore, the caloric count for a broiled steak is lower than for the same steak sauteed.

A broiled meat dish, when done to perfection, is one of the finest dishes, even to sophisticated diners. Perfection means quality meat cooked as ordered,. with only basic salt added, and the meat not burned. Food quality is much more visible in plain dishes than in fancy food combinations where everything is covered with sauces and garnishes.

An experienced broiler cook can prepare almost any dish on the broiler. Obviously, some dishes are easier to handle than others. Since production is the watchword of the modern food service establishment, menus often contain those dishes which are easiest to handle.

A steak is the most popular meal among foreign tourists. Most steak loving region offer rib, spencer, and Delmonico steaks in addition to the full loin cats which are used in all their variations. A boneless sirloin strip steak is called a New York cut steak. Regional differences in names are common, but the specific cuts used are the same all over.

Lamb chops in a variety of cuts and shish kebabs are next in popularity. Then pork, often as Satays from (spiced skewers of meat), chicken, and turkey steaks follow. Form the waters come salmon, halibut, swordfish, fresh tuna, bass, lobsters, langustes, prawns, scallops, and abalones. Another group of foods to be broiled includes the off-als, such as liver, sweetbreads, and kidneys. As a basic rule of what to broil, it can be said :

1. Fat meats and firm seafood are generally preferred for taste and ease in handling.
2. Vegetables are very rarely cooked on the broiler.

Lean pieces of meat can be larded. Small pieces, such as chicken livers, prawns, or scallops can be lined up on skewers for easier handling. There are few limitations for the creative and interested broiler cook.

In western cooking broiling is the accepted term for dry heat cooking by radiation. In English speaking areas, the word grilling is used. The "grillroom" is a restaurant serving food only from the grill, "Mixgrill" is the internationally accepted name for a combination of lamb meats and offal cooked on the broiler. A grill (or grille) is an open grating similar to the type used for grilling meat. Many cooks use the term grilling, whenever they mean griddling, which is a commercial form of pan frying. To avoid misunderstanding, it is important to check out the local usage of the term.

USE OF BROILERS

Broilers are available in may shapes, forms, and models. Most of them are gas fired, and are lined with special fire bricks to reflect and concentrate the heat. Electrical broilers for commercial use are not very popular. Gas or electric broilers are easier to handle and to keep clean than the charcoal broilers. They have fewer fire hazards, since their heat can be regulated faster. For overall customer appeal and flavour, nothing can beat the old fashioned charcoal broiler. It is basically the oldest unchanged piece of equipment still in use. The charcoal broiler, used properly, produced beautiful food and is highly regarded by the eating public.

CHARCOAL BROILERS

Charcoal broilers have great emotional appeal with the public. They look simple, giving the impression of something natural. They produce pleasant, appetizing smells. Their fire looks romantic, and they do produce a more flavourful meal, especially if hickory or maple coal is used. Real charcoal broilers are mostly used to day in specially houses. Sometimes, the business is even centered around this broiler.

A platter of Indian Tandoori Chicken thighs with herbs and condiments

These facets make the steakhouse a very popular type of eating establishment. Many franchises and food service chains, which specialize in only broiled food have come into existence. They are trying to take the fullest advantage of the broiler's emotional appeal.

The burning of organic substance results in a residue of carbon or coal good and beverage operation coal is neither healthy nor food. However, there are many guests who believe that a steak charred on the surface and raw on the inside is a sophisticated way to eat. Guests who order their food charred are only hurting themselves. It is more dangerous to the public that many untrained or uneducated broiler cooks take extreme delight in broiling with flames burning high. Some even pour grease on the coals to get this fiery effect. This practice is a health hazard to the unsuspecting diner. The guest trusts the chefs who cook for them. They are not aware that a cook even unknowingly would do something harmful to the diner's well-being. It has been proved that burned organic matter is *carcinogenous* (cancer induction) to mice and humans. Common sense alone should stop such disgusting and unprofessional broiler handling.

Broilers have a provision for container to collect the fat drippings of the broiled meat. Hot fat, even in small quantities, is a fire hazard. This is especially true if the fat is close to an open fire. Drip pans of broilers must be checked and emptied rountinely. Most fires in food and beverage establishments have started at a carelessly handled broiler. Most danger factors on broilers are overheating, sloppy working habits, and too much fat left on the raw meat. A cook, if he is working nervously, can easily burn himself. First aid kits and CO_2 fire extinguishers must be within the reach of any broiler cook. Broiler cooks, chefs, and managers should post rules of what to do in emergencies. Fire drills at regular intervals should be held.

Charcoal broilers need more care and attention than gas or electronic broilers, but the greatest danger to any broiler is a careless and irresponsible cook.

QUESTIONS AND DISCUSSIONS

Fill in the Blanks

Q.1. Read the following and complete the sentence :–

(a) A charcoal broiler appeals to the customer's ....

(b) A baked ham is cooked by the method of ....

(c) Dry heat cooking processes are also called baking, roasting, and ....

(d) A San Franciscan might order a steak rare in Omaha and find it cooked to ....

(e) Burned organic substances are unhealthy and have lately been referred to as ....

(f) When a turkey is cooked by the dry heat method, it should be called ....

(g) The most practical heat source for a broiler is ....

(h) A distinct roast flavour can only be achieved after the roast has been ....

(i) A cook's concept of a rare steak and a customer's concept of a rare steak may not be the ....

(j) The term grilling is used in many English speaking countries to imply ....

(k) Variable meat factors are some of the reasons why broiling is likely to remain an ....

[**Ans.:** (a) emotional appeal; (b) baking; (c) broiling; (d) medium rare (e) cancer inducing; (f) roasting; (g) charcoal; (h) browned; (i) same; (j) dry heat cooking by radiation (broiling); (k) art.]

Multiple Choice Types

Q.2. Read each question carefully and completely before answering it. Select the best answer :

(i) Cooking with dry heat is also called

(a) Radiation (b) Conduction

(c) Dehydration (d) Pasteurization.

(ii) All of these conventional ways of cooking are dry heat methods with the exception of

(a) Broiling (b) Frying

(c) Roasting (d) Baking.

(iii) Broiled food is preferred on many a diet, because it

(a) Tastes better (b) Maintains more calories

(c) Is comparatively fatless (d) Is easier to digest.

(iv) A beef rib roast of about 28 pounds weight has a recirculation of

(a) 10 minutes (b) 20 minutes

(c) 30 minutes (d) 40 minutes.

(v) To achieve the purpose of roasting,

(a) A small roast needs high heat, short cooking time

(b) A small roast needs high heat, long cooking time

(c) A large roast needs high heat, long cooking time

(d) A large roast needs heat, short cooking time.

(vi) Placing a "service-ready" roast into a food warmer, means to

(a) Transfer it immediately from oven to warmer

(b) Let it set at kitchen temperature for some time

(c) Chill it off in the refrigerator to reduce carry-over heat

(d) Keep the roast under the desired degree of doneness.

(vii) The browning or caramelization of sugar needs a minimum temperature of

(a) 250° Fahrenheit (b) 275° Fahrenheit

(c) 300° Fahrenheit (d) 325° Fahrenheit.

(viii) Lean white meats contain less blood than dark meats and have therefore

(a) Less protein (b) Less flavour

(c) Less glucose (d) Less eye appeal.

(ix) The decisive factor for the cooking time of a roast is

(a) Untrimmed weight (b) Fat content of meat

(c) Geometric shape (d) Percentage of bones.

(x) In broiling, the heat transfer method used is called

(a) Forced air circulation (b) Intensified conduction

(c) Contact heating (d) Direct radiation.

(xi) The boneless Sirloin steak is also called

(a) Delmonico Steak (b) New York cut Steak

(c) Boston Steak (d) Spencer Steak.

(xii) The probability of starting a fire through a broiler is not reduced by :—

(a) Trimming the excess fat off meat

(b) Emptying the drip pan routinely

(c) Having a CO_2 extinguisher within reach

(d) Guarding against overheating

(xiii) Broiling is not suitable for cooking tough meat, because dry heat

(a) Does not soften collagens sufficiently

(b) Tenderizes the fat (marble) of meat only

(c) Burns the increased glucose of tougher meat

(d) Dehydrates meat completely.

[**Ans.**: (i) (a); (ii) (b); (iii) (a); (iv) (d); (v) (a);
(vi) (b); (vii) (c); (viii) (a); (ix) (c); (x) (d);
(xi) (b); (xii) (c); (xiii) (a).]

Matching Type

Q.3. Match the words of Table 'A' with their most fitting counterparts of Table 'B'

Table 'A'	*Table 'B'*
(a) Grilling	(i) Visible fat veins
(b) Baked Ham	(ii) Touch heat transfer
(c) Recirculation	(iii) Unrefined gelating
(d) Radiation	(iv) Broiled lamb meats
(e) Convection	(v) Boneless Sirloin steak
(f) Bain-Marie	(vi) Steakhouse
(g) Carbonizing	(vii) Food warmer
(h) Conduction	(viii) Heat from open fire
(i) Carcinogenous	(ix) Broiling
(j) Mix Grill	(x) Setting time
(k) New York Steak	(xi) Airheat equalization
(l) Glucose	(xii) Charring
(m) Collagen	(xiii) Slicer
(n) Grillroom	(xiv) Cancer-inducting
(o) Carving knife	(xv) Blood sugar
(p) Marble	(xvi) Roasted smoked pork leg.

[**Ans.:** (a) (vi); (b) (xvi); (c) (x); (d) (viii); (e) (xi);
(f) (vii); (g) (xii); (h) (ii); (i) (xiv); (j) (iv);
(k) (v); (l) (xv); (m) (iii); (n) (ix); (o) (xiii);
(p) (i)]

Short Answer Type

Q.4. Should flavour and looks of a roast be sacrificed to proved yield ?

Q.5. Explain the advantages of the shortorder restaurant to customer and operator.

Q.6. Describe the types of broilers and how are they used for different purposes.

Q.7. How for do emotions influence the food selections of customers?

Q.8. Does barbecuing or broiling have to be a health hazard ?

Q.9. Why did Brillat-Savarin consider roasting and reboiling a real talent ?

Q.10. The broiler cook with all these responsibilities is not considered a skilled master chef . By what means should the broiler cook develop his concepts of medium, medium rare, and rare meats ?

Q.11. A good meat thermometer be used to establish the exact degree of doneness of every steak or roast.

Q.12. Explain some possible causes of fire in a kitchen and how can fire be prevented.

Q.13. Write notes on:

(a) Carcinogenous
(b) Conformation
(c) Mix grill
(d) Recirculation
(e) Collagen
(f) To fire a steak
(g) Offal.

Descriptive Answer types

Q.14. (a) State possible sources of fire in the kitchen and ways to prevent a fire from starting.

(b) Describe the theories of roasting by giving suitable examples.

Q.15. Explain the importance of recirulation.

Q.16. Name the meat cuts that are generally broiled and those are generally roasted.

Assignments/Activity Type

Q.17. Demonstrate:

(a) The handling of various oven type.

(b) The handling of all three broiler types: gas, electric, and charcoal.

(c) Make a recirculation test. Broil two equal steaks cut in sequence. Cut one immediately, and the other one after setting.

(d) Steak cooking on a broiler, and emphasize grillmarks.

(e) The handling of CO_2 extinguisher. Have a fire drill.

(f) Fish cooking on the broiler.

(g) The cleaning and maintenance of the broiler.

(h) The handling of a meat thermometer on differently shaped roasts.

Q.18. Measure the actual heat in various parts of an ordinary commercial roasting oven and compare it to the thermostat.

Q.19. Perform experiment in heat transmission.

3.4

Moist Heat Method

CHAPTER OBJECTIVES

After studying this lesson you should be able :

- To state and explain the plain moist heat cooking method;
- To explain the need and importance for of food boiling;
- To describe the sight recognition of boiling temperatures of water;
- To differentiated between steaming, boiling, and simmering; and
- To explain the reasons for shrinkage.

Cooking with moist heat is one of the basic cooking methods, it also known as simmering, boiling, or steaming. Cooking with moist heat is known best as boiling, but for best results, with the exception of boiling pasta, the cooking liquid should only simmer.The term poaching, which is sometimes used, comes from the French verb "pocher". It is applied only to fish or eggs simmered in water or liquid.

Poaching is similar to simmering, but this term is applied only to eggs and fish. Moist cooking methods are used to dissolve collagen in the meat from older animals. Other reasons for moist cooking are the desalting and rehydration of dried, cured, or smoked foods. Fine bubbles on the surface of heating water is a sign that a simmering temperature between 185°F. and 195°F. has been reached. The rolling boil shows that the water is a 212°F., boiling water changes to steam and, if not collected for further use, disappears into the air.

The use of live steam is preferable to a rolling boil. The more gentle steam does not break up vegetables or tender foods as much as the rolling boil.

Pressure steaming produces higher temperatures than 212°F. and cooks foods faster, saving nearly 50% of the cooking time.

Shrinkage is the loss of weight through cooking. The hotter the cooking temperatures, the greater the loss of fats and juices (blood, water). Meat boiled at the minimum temperatures needed for the coagulation of proteins have little shrinkage, but develops a different taste, which is liked by many people through habit, especially by those who live in a cold climate.

All foods can be cooked in water, if it is so desired. In the past, most foods had to be cooked with moist heat in order to become edible. Now, fewer meats need tenderization through moisture. Boiling of meats is not popular anymore.

The boiling of meat provided a by-product called broth. True chicken soup cannot be made without first boiling a chicken to produced the broth.

Chicken poaching in a pan

Foods preserved by salting, dehydration, or a combination of both, need water to become edible. Water helps to desalt and reconstitute these foods. Corned beef, pastrami, smoked meats, and Smithfield ham are good examples of meat which need water. Some cereals and legumes, such as dried beans and peas also need water to become edible. Moisture is added whenever the preparation of a dish needs a soupy or liquid consistency.

CONTROL OF HEAT

Water is an excellent and uniform heat conductor. You can easily see approximate temperature of the water. Before the invention of the thermometer, this was helpful in the control of heat. Today heat is measured by more craft methods and "simmering" means water heated to 185°F. – 195°F. Little bubbles of air rise from the bottom of the cooking pot and burst on the surface of the water.

When you raise the temperature of simmering water, splashing bubbles are created and this is called a rolling boil. This action indicates that the highest temperature of 212°F. has been reached.

When a temperature of 212°F. is maintained, the rolling boil continues, water transforms to steam and disappears into the air. The temperature of steam is slightly higher than that of the boiling water. The escaping steam can be channelled through baskets filled with food, thereby creating the steam cooking process. All this applies to sea level only. At higher altitudes, the pressure is lower and less heat is needed for a rolling boil or steam. Cooking times, then must be adjusted accordingly; that is, slightly longer.

Of these three different visible heat levels, simmering is the slowest and steaming is the fastest. The rolling boil is harmful to the cooking of vegetables and tender proteins. The strong movements break up or cook apart all but the toughest foods.

The rolling boil is useful only for the cooking of "pasta", or paste. Paste is the generic name for starchy food made of flour, water, salt, and sometimes eggs, which is shaped into types of noodles, spaghetti, macaroni, shells vermicelli, and others. Paste items are dried and have to be re-hydrated or reconstituted in water in order to become edible. Flour, a starch, needs 200°F. to be thickened. Simmering does not have enough heat.

Steaming does not provide enough liquid to swell up dried starch and make it edible. Here the rolling boil is useful.

The process of cooking food in water is known as boiling. The action of osmosis must be considered when food is boiled. Osmosis is the tendency of fluids to equalize their saturation level with other fluids whenever possible.

Blood contains salts (taste). Therefore, a salt level exists in meats. If raw meat is covered with unsalted water, osmosis will equalize the salt of the meat, leaving it without flavour. Therefore all foods which are to be boiled must be simmered in pre-salted water.

Vegetables contain up to 80% water in which their taste-providing substances (salts) are dissolved. Hence, vegetables cooked in saluted water lose their taste through osmosis in the same way. Therefore, it may be concluded that all boiled foods must have a given salt content in their cooking liquids in order to prevent the complete leaching of flavours and taste.

The more a student trainee knows about boiling, the easier it will be for him, as a cook to prepare good food. The more a traince understands about the nature of heat, the composition of foods, and their interactions, the better his cooking will become.

As a cook you should know that good boiling techniques make certain that the pre-salted cooking liquid is never above the simmering temperature. Temperature control is necessary. Cooks can watch the fine bubbles coming to the surface. A thermostatic control set at 195°F. is even better. The extra minutes of cooking time will be well spent in return for a superior quality.

Food and beverage service establishments today have less need for boiling than in the past. The American customer does not favour boiled meat. In colder climates, boiled meat is liked better than in warmer climates. Europeans still like boiled meats, but they too, prefer steaks and roasts if the quality of the meat is improved.

Table 3.4A. Comparison of Moist Heat Methods of Cooking

Moist Heat Method of Cooking	*Time*	*Sogginess*	*Firmness*	*Kept Shape*	*Taste*
Pressure Steam		1.			
		2.			
		3.			
Live Steam		1.			
		2.			
		3.			
Rolling Boil		1.			
		2.			
		3.			
Simmering		1.			
		2.			
		3.			

Live crabs must be boiled for the sake of efficiency, but lobsters need not be boiled. Many people prefer broiled lobster to the boiled lobster. Prawns, shrimps, and mussels come frozen or even cooked. Meat tenderness has increased so much that broiling and roasting have become the preferred ways of preparation. Corned, smoked, and cold meats– used mostly as sandwich fillings – are supplied precooked.

Food processing plants using thermostatic controls are very efficient in controlling shrinkage food and beverage operators feel that it is better to but pree-cooked foods even though they are higher priced to buy.

Boiling of Potatoes

Cook the same type of potatoes by four different boiling methods and find the difference of handling, yield, and quality. Conclude which methods seems to the best.

Experimental Recipe 12.

Potatoes Boiling

Utensil

1. A pressure steam cooker;
2. A potato steamer (both either commercial or household types);
3. Two identical pots;
4. Large enough to hold potatoes in a layer;
5. A paring knife;
6. Four time clocks.

Ingredients

1. Four batches of four potatoes each, of the same kind, size, and weight;
2. salt.

Method

1. Prepare all required ingredients.
2. Wash all potatoes, place one batch into each of the two pots.
3. Add salt, cover them with boiling water and bring to reboil immediately.
4. Keep one pot on simmering, the other on a rolling boil; set timers for estimated cooking time.
5. Handle remaining batches the same way but in the two steam cookers.
6. Cook by estimated time or manual inspection until done. Record cooking time of each batch.
7. Drain each batch when ready. Cool, peel, and taste.
8. Compare for the following: time, sogginess, firmness, remaining shape, weight loss, test. Record on Table 3.4A.
9. Compare data, weight advantages against disadvantages. Make a conclusion to which method seems to be the best.

SIMMERING

The simmering method of cooking creates a light movement of the water only and its degree of heat is best for cooking most foods, except starches. In the past, simmering was used only for eggs without shells and fish. This was called poaching. Hence, the terms still in use are poached eggs and poached fish. Simmering is also best for meats because it cooks proteins without toughening them. Simmering is best for vegetables because the water does not evaporate much and the flavour and nutrients are retained. The vegetable water should also be used.

STEAMING

Steaming methods is hotter and therefore, cooks faster than simmering or boiling. It does not have the forceful action of the rolling boil and it does not break foods appart. In addition, less water is used than in submerged simmering. Therefore, less vitamins, nutrients, and flavours are leached (washed) out. Since live steam disappears into the air, little condensation occurs, and there is no broth. Steaming is advisable for cooking potatoes and other root vegetables which do not discolour. Steamed vegetables do not have to be drained after cooking. This saves time and accidental mishandling. For the cooking of meats or fowl, steaming is not too advantageous, since it makes no broth. Heat over 190°F. makes proteins and albumins (egg whites) tough and chewy.

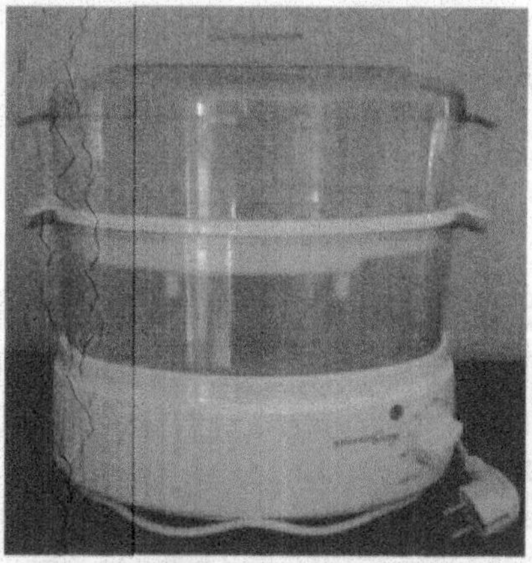

Steam Cooker

Most steam cookers also feature a juice catchment, which allows all nutrients (otherwise lost as steam) to also really be consumed. When other cooking techniques are used (eg frying with butter or oil), these nutrients are also generally lost as most is discarded after banking.

Due to their health aspect (cooking without any oil), food steamers are used extensively in health-diets as cuisine minceur, the rawfood diet, okinawa diet, macrobiotic-diet and CRON-diet.

Food steamers release less heat to the kitchen environment, therefore helping keep the kitchen cool during hot summers.

A microwave oven, or simply a microwave, is a kitchen appliance that cooks or heats food by dielectric heating. This is accomplished by using microwave radiation to heat polarized molecules within the food. This excitation is fairly uniform, leading to food being more evenly heated throughout (except in dense objects) than generally occurs in other cooking techniques.

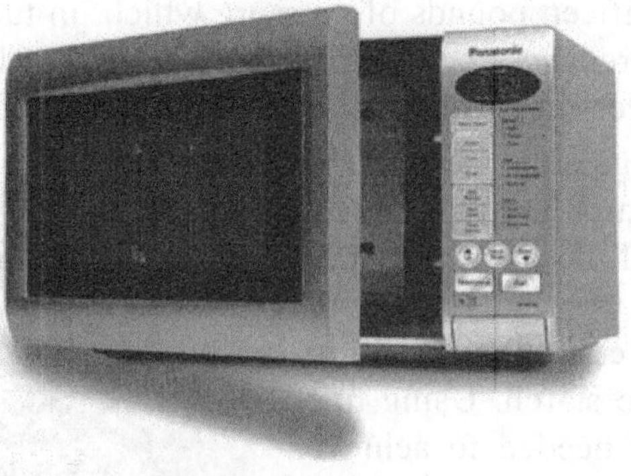

Microwave Oven

Basic microwave ovens heat foods quickly and efficiently, but do not brown or bake food in the way conventional ovens do. This makes them unsuitable for cooking certain foods, or to achieve certain culinary effects. Additional kinds of heat sources can be added to microwave packaging, or into combination microwave ovens, to add these additional effe.

Experimental Recipe 13.

Idly

Ingredients

1. Idly rice : 2 cups
2. *Urad daal* : 1 cup
3. Cooked rice : 1/2 cup
4. Fenugreek seeds (*Methi*) : 1/4 tsp
5. Salt : As per taste.

Method

1. Prepare all required ingredients.
2. Soak Idly rice and Methi together in water for about 5-6 hours.
3. Soak *urud daal* in water for 3 1/2 hours.
4. Drain the water from *urad daal* and grind it in blender with little water.
5. Fine grind it until the mixture is frothy. Keep aside
6. Now drain water from soaked rice and *methi.*
7. Grind these along with cooked rice and little water in blender.
8. Now mix the ground items and add salt.
9. Allow it to ferment for 16-18 hours.
10. Then make idlys in the idly steamer.
11. Steam the idlys on high for 10 minutes.

STEAM COOKING UNDER PRESSURE

A pressure steam cooker consists of pressure proof compartments where live steam builds up. The temperature increases with every pound of pressure. Most pressure cookers generate up to fifteen pounds of pressure which, in turn, produces 250°F. moist heat. The increased heat reduces cooking time from 40-50%. Therefore, overcooking is a greater possibility and pressure steam cookers must be watched very closely.

Potatoes, a starchy vegetable, need 200°F. to coagulate the 20% starch content. When the inside temperature of the potato reaches 200°F., the water in the cell structure simmers and breaks the cell open which, at the same time, cooks the starch. Using live steam (212°F), the time needed to achieve this might be thirty minutes. A pressure cooker generating 250°F. cooks the same potato in fifteen minutes. Heat of 212°F. needs thirty minutes to transfer 200°F. to the center of the potato. But heat of 250°F. needs only fifteen minutes to do the same.

Momos served in a tomato-based broth

Accidental overcooking by only 15% of the time needed may completely ruin some foods. Many foods cooked in pressure cookers keep their qualities only if they are timed correctly. The real advantage of the pressure cooker lies in its ability to cook most green vegetables and even small cut potatoes (Parisian potatoes) in a few minutes, assuring freshly cooked vegetables and the time.

SHRINKAGE

Shrinkage of food is the loss of weight occurring to all foods during any cooking process. This loss could be considerable, up to 30% of the trimmed weight. The fattier the meat, the more fat melts during cooking even before browning. Meat contains an average of 60% water and some of this water will merge with the cooking liquid. If meat is cooked to an inside temperature of 200°F., the bold (water) in its cells will flow out. It is the same reaction that happens during the dry cooking process, but there, the juices (water) evaporate. The hotter the cooking temperature, the greater is the shrinkage.

Overcooked meat loses fat, most of its juices and, as a result, also loses its flavour and texture. Overcooking is the greatest destroyer of taste and nutritional value. It also causes considerable shrinkage of the portion size.

QUESTIONS AND DISCUSSIONS

Fill in the Blanks

Q.1. Read and complete the following statements and fill in the blanks :—

(a) Foods, preserved by salting, need to be cooked in water, to become ....

(b) Steam under pressure generates more heat, therefore cooks ....

(c) Poached fish or eggs on the menu implies that these foods were ....

(d) In meat cookery, one reason for shrinkage is the melting ....

(e) Water, used for the boiling of foods, has to be salted in order to prevent the loss of flavour by ....

(f) The gentle action of steaming has a temperature high enough to coagulate search; it is the best way of boiling ....

(g) When the temperature of simmering water is increased, it will change to.....

(h) The rolling boil is a good method for the cooking of ....

[**Ans.:** (a) edible; (b) must watch presure cooker very closely;
(c) sinmered; (d) fat;
(e) boiling; (f) potatoes;
(g) rolling boil; (h) paste or paste.]

Multiplies Choice Type

Q.2. Read each question carefully. Select the best answer :

(i) Small potatoes which need 30-35 minutes of cooking time in a live steamer, are cooked in a pressure cooker under 15 pounds of steam pressure in

(a) 7-10 minutes (b) 11-14 minutes
(c) 15-18 minutes (d) 19-22 minutes.

(ii) Without a thermometer, the simmering of water can be recognized by

(a) Fine air bubbles coming to the surface
(b) Big air bubbles coming to the surface
(c) The splashing and steaming of the pot
(d) The gradual disappearing of the water.

(iii) Potatoes are cooked best in the pressure steam cooker, because

(a) The rolling boil may cook them apart
(b) Simmering needs too long a cooking time
(c) The pressure steam cooker does not break them up
(d) The live steam cooker changes their taste.

(iv) The rolling boil can reach a maximum temperature of

(a) 208°Fahrenheit (b) 212° Fahrenheit
(c) 216° Fahrenheit (d) 220° Fahrenheit.

(v) Shrinkage reduces the weight of food while it cooks. To prevent unnecessary shrinkage, meat is boiled best

(a) Without salt (b) At 15 pounds of pressure
(c) In live steam (d) By simmering at 190°F.

(vi) Simmering generates heat from 185°F. - 195°F. which is enough to cook these foods except

(a) Chicken (b) Fish
(c) Eggs (d) Spaghetti.

(vii) A Virginia Ham, soaked in cold water overnight, will lose some of its salt through the process of

(a) Rehydration
(d) Coagulation
(c) Osmosis
(d) Moisturizing.

[**Ans.:** (i) (c); (ii) (a); (iii) (b); (iv) (b);
(v) (d); (vi) (a); (vii) (a)]

Short Answer Type

Q.3. Define the following terms :

(a) Albumins
(b) Osmosis
(c) Saturation
(d) Simmering
(e) Leaching
(f) Pasta
(g) Shrinkage.

Descriptive Types

Q.4. State the reasons for boiling food and explain by giving examples.

Q.5. Explain in brief and list the four moist heat cooking methods.

Q.6. Explain the reasons for shrinkage.

Q.7. Boiled meat is liked better in some areas than in other's. Explain this statement.

Q.8. Explain that the pressure steam cookers are helpful for a continuous supply of freshly cooked vegetables.

Q.9. Giving examples explain whether a chef be more concerned about taste, quality, or yields.

Assignments/Activity Type

Q.10. Perform and demonstrate a potato boiling experiment.

Q.11. Demonstrate:

(a) Pasta cooking (film, if available).
(b) The handling a pressure steam cooker.
(c) The handling of a live steam cooker.
(d) Estimate, as well as measure, temperatures of water from shimmering to boiling.

3.5

Cooking in Fat or Frying

CHAPTER OBJECTIVES

After studying this lesson you should be able :

- To differentiate between pan frying and sauteing;
- To differentiate between pay frying and deep frying;
- To identify and explain three different coating for food;
- To demonstrate and practice the flipping of food in a skillet; and
- To explain why a "Beef Stroganoff" is called a saute dish.

Cooking in fat, or frying, is one of the five basic cooking methods. It includes sauteing and deep fat frying. In sauteing, a small quantity of good fat is mixed into the dish. In deep fat frying, the food is separared from the larger amount of fat after cooking.

The techniques of frying can be grouped into two, pan or deep frying and sauteing or flip frying. In deep frying, the cooked food is separated from the cooking fat. Deep frying today is mostly done in commercial deep fryers. Deep fried food must be at least half submerged in the frying fat. Nutritionists consider deep frying undesirable, but fast food operators enjoy the profit-making characteristics of the process. Not all deep fried food is bad. The commercial deep fry allows for considerable abuse, and too few conscientious chefs are trying to avoid these abuses. The frying and sauteing processes can be applied to all foods that are tender and need only a short cooking time. Deep fried foods have to be coated first. One of the more popular methods of coating is called breading. Sauteing (flip frying) is one of the finest cooking methods the skilled cook has at his disposal. Sauteing preserves the taste and texture quality of freshly browned meat (like steak) and adds the quality of a separately made sauce. Saute cooking is done mostly for "gourmet cooking" and in Chinese cuisine and accounts for the freshness, taste, and nutritional values these cuisines have to offer. In sauteing, fat is absorbed as part of the preparation. Trainees must learn to be aware of this great distinction between frying and sauteing. Originally all frying was done in skillets on the top of the stove. The modern deep-fryer and the griddle were developed as a result of the increase in restaurant business. On dry heat cooking, the griddle is sometimes called a grill.

Fats when overheated burn and become combustible. An electric deep-fryer will explode into flames if it is overheated. Obviously, fat fires are dangerous and difficult to bring under control even with a CO_2 fire extinguisher. Pan frying on the open range has dangers, too. Overflowing fat is apt to catchs fire and the confusion following such an incident multiplies the dangers. The only true prevention of an accidental and serious fire is common sense and maturity on the part of the cook.

Any food to be cooked in fat, either deep-fried or sauteed, must be tender before it is fried. The size of the food is of importance, also. Saute dishes should be cut evenly in small pieces. One portion at a time is the largest piece of food cooked by the deep frying methods. Examples are one pork chop, one veal cutlet, one quarter of chicken, and one portion of fish. Fish and seafood can be either deep or flip fried. All tender or prime cuts of meat and poultry may also be cooked by either methods. The food selection is similar to that for broiling.

Vegetables may be cooked by deep frying or sauteing, but cooks prefer to blanch or pre-cook some vegetables for a different appearance and flavour. An example is the difference between home fried potatoes and cottage. Slices of browned potato pieces are served under both names.

The home fried potatoes and boiled "in the jacket" (unpeeled) first, peeled, cooled, sliced, and then re-fried in a skillet with a *good fat* such as butter. In this case, the sauteing process is used, and in some areas home fried potatoes are called "saute potatoes".

For cottage fried potatoes, raw potatoes are peeled, slide and sauteed in a skillet with a *good fat* such as butter, until they are done. This may need up to 20 minutes of sauteing time, with the skillet covered in the beginning, in order to prevent the drying out of the potatoes.

The emphasis for such preparations is on *good fat*, since the fat becomes a part of the dish and is not separated from the potatoes after the cooking.

An example of another way of cooking potato slices is shown by potato chips. They are made by slicing raw peeled potatoes uniformly, then deep frying them in very hot shortening or deep frying fat until they are done, brown and crisp. The potato is separated from the frying fat after cooking. The result is startling since the same raw materials were used. The difference is caused simply by surrounding the potatoes with more intense heat through the same conductor.

DEEP FAT FRYING

Pan fried food and deep fried food preparations are similar in theory. Pan fried food is only half submerged in fat, while deep fried food is fully submerged in fat. Frying fats which are heated to 350°F. add the browned taste to the cooked food.

The deep fryer uses a large quantity of fat, and reheats and uses this fat over and over again. The steam and flavour of the food escape into the fat of the fryer, changing the original composition of the frying fat. Generally the first batches of food in a kettle of fresh frying fat comes out tasty and golden brown, the next batches are not of the same high quality. The food accepts the flavours of previously cooked food from the fat. This results in the loss of appetizing, browning ability and adds an undesirable taste.

The old-fashioned pat frying process, where food is half submerged in fat, lets steam and volatile oils escape into the air, thus keeping the fat cleaner than in the deep frying process. Since a much smaller amount of fat is used per batch of food, the fat can be strained immediately after each use and saved for other purposes. In better food and beverage establishments the fat is used only once, and then discarded.

Pan frying uses more fat and is less economical, but gives better quality food. The deep fryer fries faster, reuses the same fat over and over again and reduces food costs. From a quality point of view, pan frying is preferred.

Coatings for Foods

All deep fried foods have a coating except for all types of french fried potatoes. The coating is usually a mixture of starch, eggs, and liquid. Depending on how these three ingredients are used, the coating is referred to as a batter, an eggwash, or a breading. Fish and chips are a good example of deep frying in a batter. Some fried chicken represents fried food which is coated only. A veal cutlet is usually breaded. Food need to the coated before deep frying for the safeguarding of the frying fat, the protection of natural food flavours, a better golden browned appearance, and additional caloric value. The coating also acts as a shield between the fat and food. It absorbs some of the food flavour and juices on the inside and prevents the intrusion of frying fat into the food from the outside.

Deep Frying

The use of the modern deep fryer has become a mixed blessing to culinary art. Nutrition Scientists know that proper diet is the key to the well-being of all human. They are opposed to the concept of modern deep frying. Commercial deep frying is based on the principles of fast cooking and reuse of the frying fat. This combination causes the break-down of the fats used. The break-down of fats is the same as the burning of fats. Deep fried food absorbs more of the burned fat than there should be in anyone's diet. Young people can eat large quantities of french fries and other fried foods without feeling ill effects at the time. Boned fat causes ulcers and other medical problems. Any burned matter is carcinogenous (cancercausing). Persons who eat too much deep fried food sooner or later have medical bills. Nutritionists see the dangers, but their voices are not heard.

Deep fried foods can be handled easily by unskilled workers. Modern deep fryers have timer controlled pop-up devices. Precut, prebreaded and precooked frozen food is available everywhere. Skilled chefs are not needed to fry whatever is ordered.

Fast Food

Most of the modern fast food service establishments of today work mostly with griddle and deep fryer. They feature breaded fried items rather than batter fried items. Breading can be done in advance. Pre-breaded food can be stored under refrigeration until it is used. Dipping into batter must be done at the very moment before frying. It takes additional time and this food is much more difficult to handle than breaded or even coated food.

Flip Frying or Sauteing

The term sauteing comes from the French word *saute.* It implies that the food in a skillet is not turned with a spatula while the skillet is on the stove. The pan is flipped in such a way that its contents fly through the air, turn over and fall back into the pan. This is fast and efficient work for small quantities, and it keeps food in an attractive shape. Sauteing food is considered as one of the best ways of cooking by connoisseurs (people knowledgeable about food). Chinese cuisine, which has a great reputation for taste and nutrition, is based almost entirely on sauteing. The Chinese call it stir-fry cooking in a wok. Saute cooking applied to all foods, if they are tender from the start. All foods that can be broiled or deep fried can also be sauteed.

Difference between a Saute and a Stew

A saute made of meat, poultry, or fish and vegetable might look like a stew and even taste like a stew, but it is not made like a stew. Sautes are made when ordered, and they are made from choice raw materials. Stews are cooked in advance to use up secondary cuts and tough foods. Sautes have names like "Beef Stroganoff", "Emincée de eau a la Suisse" "Gypsy liver" or veal kidneys saute. They are made by the sauteing technique. The food which gives the dish its name and the appropriate garnish are sauted freshly, then finished with a previously made sauce.

A saute made to order should be compared to the cocktail made by a bartender. For Beef Stronganoff, a julienne of raw fillet meat is sauteed quickly, then pre-sauteed sliced mushrooms and shallots are added. The combination is finished by the addition of some brown sauce and sour cream. Emincee de Veau a la Suisse consists of sliced veal leg, onions, brown sauce, fresh cream, and white wine. The Gypsy Liver is equal to a Beef Stroganoff with liver replacing the beef fillet. The preparation for all meat sautes is the same. A saute dish retains the flavour of fresh cooking (like a steak) and the quality of a previously made sauce. Cookery that is called French Luxury or Gourmet cuisine is actually saute cooking at its finest.

The Griddle Cooking

A griddle can be considered a large stationary skillet, used for frying foods in a small quantity of fat similar to broiling. To the quality-concerned chef, griddling of food is not as good as broiling or sauteing. As a fast all around method griddling is useful to the breakfast and short order cooks. Cooking in fat has many safety hazards. All trainees students and cooks must be completely familiar with the handling of equipment and precautions which have to be observed.

Griddle or grill cooking is a form of commercial saute cooking. The disadvantage is that all meat juices are lost. It also resembles broiling and many restaurants with insufficient facilities substitute a griddled steak for a broiled one. Griddles are efficient and fast for short order work. This makes them very popular in coffeeshops and restaurants with breakfast service. Hotcakes, pancakes, griddle cakes, eggs, bacon, ham, steaks, hamburgers, and grilled sandwiches can be made on it all at the same time.

The griddle, like the deep-fryer, is not equipment for quality work. It has its place when quantity and speed production are important. Griddle cookery, like deep frying, has been abused by unskilled and untrained workers. The quality conscious cook can easily use a griddle with satisfying results if he keeps it clean.

PAN FRYING

Safety Rules

Use a skillet or pan on the top of the range with enough fat to float the foods to be cooked.

(1) Do not fill skillet more than half with fat. Keep skillet in a safe position on the range. Do not leave skillet on fire unattended.

Experimental Recipe 14.

Fish Amritsari

Ingredients

1. Boneless sole fish or king fish pieces clearned : 600 grams
2. Lemon juice : 1 tablespoon
3. Gram flour : 1 cup
4. Yoghurt : 2 yoghurt
5. Egg lightly beaten : 1 No.
6. Red chilli powder : 1 tablespoons
7. Garlic paste : 2 tablespoons
8. Ginger paste : 2 tablespoons
9. Thymol seeds (*ajwain*) : ½ teaspoon
10. *Garam masala* (hot spice mix) : 1 tablespoon
11. Lemon juice : 1 tablespoon
12. Salt : To taste
13. Oil : To deep fry
14. Lemon wedges : To garnish.

Method

1. Prepared all required ingredients.
2. Sprinkle a little gram flour, salt and some lemon juice on the fish pieces and rub well. Keep aside for 5 minutes and then wash well.
3. Rub in the rest lemon juice and keep aside for 15 minutes.
4. Remove from the vinegar and pat dry well. It is important that the vinegar is removed from the fish pieces by gently wiping them repeatedly with an absorbent kitchen towel.
5. In a bowl, mix the rest of the ingredients and rub well on the fish pieces. Marinate for about half an hour.
6. Heat the oil till it is very hot. Slide in the fish pieces and deep-fry in batches till they are crisp and golden brown in colour.
7. Granish with lemon wedges.

(2) Do not put wet foods into hot fats. Fat will foam, spill and catch fire. Do not overheat fat.

(3) Do not start frying until all necessary utensils like skimmer, carrier for finished food, etc. are on hand.

(4) Overheated fat can be cooled off by adding more cold fat.

DEEP FRYING SAFETY RULES

(1) Use a piece of equipment consisting of a kettle with drain valve, heating elements, fry basket, and control panel.

(2) Most fryers have electric elements, but a few are still gas fired.

(3) Do not leave control knobs over 325°F. when fryer is unattended.

(4) Do not depend on automatic features alone; they may misfunction.

(5) Do not put too much food into basket at one time.

(6) Do not put wet food into basket at any time.

(7) Danger moments at the fryer are not while frying, but when filtering or changing fat.

(8) Before draining kettle, make certain all controls are off. Do not turn heat on unless elements are completely covered with fat.

(9) Automatic deep fryers are set to work with a full kettle of frying fat. Make certain fat is filled to the proper level to prevent overheating.

Guidelines in the case of Spilled fat Burning of the Range Top

(1) Shut off exhaust fan to prevent exhaust catching fire.

(2) Shut off all gas burners which still feed the flames.

(3) Suffocate flames with salt, baking soda, old rags or sand when available. Do not use water as it will spread the flames more. Do not use sugar or flour. Carbohydrates burn.

Familiarize yourself with the emergency regulations of the establishment. Keep calm. Do not panic. Never start your working shift without checking to see that the CO_2 extinguisher of your station is in reach and usable. Have a tight fitting heavy cover for the skillet; in case fat catches fire, cover the burning skillet tightly. This methods will shut off the oxygen supply to the fire and suffocate it immediately. It is the best way to extinguish small grease fires in a skillet. This methods is also used when a saute pan catches fire during flip frying over the open flames.

QUESTIONS AND DISCUSSIONS

Fill in the blanks

Q.1. A read and complete the following: statements:

(a) In a commercial deep fryer, fat is reheated and reused many...........

(b) An electric deep fryer with fault controls could overheat and burst into ....

(c) Modern deep fryers have pop-up devices which are controlled by ....

(d) In deep frying, the food is separated from the frying fat after the cooking, but in sauteing the fat is ....

(e) Foods usable for one of the cooking in fat method variations must be ....

(f) Nutritionists believe that the best diet is not ....

(g) Sauteing, unlike deep frying, falls into the working performance of the skilled ....

(h) Originally deep frying was done in pans on top of the ....

(i) "Beef Stroganoff" made correctly belongs to the group of preparations made by the method of ....

(j) Fast food service establishments work mostly with griddle and ....

(k) Increased coffee shop business developed the use of the griddle instead of the ....

(l) Coating improves the deep frying of foods with the exception of various types of ....

[**Ans.:** (a) times; (b) flames; (c) unskilled worker; (d) not separated; (e) tender before they are fried; (f) deep fried; (g) worker; (h) fat; (i) satueing; (j) deep fryer; (k) deeping; (l) frenchfried pototoes.]

Multiple Choice Type

Q.2. Read each question carefully and select the best answer :—

(i) Saute coking is the most used method in
- (a) Italian cookery
- (b) American cookery
- (c) Southern type cookery
- (d) Chinese cookery.

(ii) Deep fried foods are coated for all the listed reasons except one:
- (a) For a better browned crust
- (b) For retaining more meat flavour and juices
- (c) For protecting the frying fat
- (d) For quicker frying.

(iii) Nutritionists say that deep fried foods are not as healthy as broiled foods because
- (a) Deep fried food is not cooked long enough
- (b) Deep frying destroys more vitamins
- (c) Deep fried food absorbs too much burned fat
- (d) Deep fried food does not provide enough calories.

(iv) Restaurants using commercial deep fryers almost exclusively are called:
- (a) Commercial kitchens
- (b) Fast food operations
- (c) Coffee shops
- (d) Seafood restaurants.

(v) How safe an electric deep fryer is, depends on
- (a) The thermostatic controls
- (b) The presence of a CO_2 fire extinguisher
- (c) The maturity and common sense of the attendant
- (d) The quantity of fat used.

(vi) The term pan frying implies that food is
- (a) Cooked in a commercial deep fryer
- (b) Floating in fat while frying
- (c) Coated with a batter before being fried
- (d) Sauteed in butter or olive oil.

(vii) Foods to be sauteed should be first
(a) Cut into a uniform size (b) Washed well before cooking
(c) Dipped into a batter (d) Breaded like a veal cutlet.

(viii) The making of cottage fried potatoes can be analyzed as follows:
(a) Raw potatoes peeled, sliced, deep fried
(b) Raw potatoes peeled, sliced, sauteed, half the time covered
(c) Boiled potatoes peeled, sliced and sauteed
(d) Boiled potatoes, peeled, sliced and deep fried.

(ix) Fat, in a deep fryer controlled by a thermostat, which has been heated over and over again
(a) Stays constantly fresh (b) Keeps fried foods especially crisp
(c) Develops an off flavour (d) Will never taste burned.

(x) A griddle in a coffee shop is ideal for the making of
(a) Home fried potatoes (b) Hotcakes
(c) Breakfast steaks (d) Beef Strognoff.

[Ans.: (i) (d); (ii) (c); (iii) (b); (iv) (a); (v) (a);
(vi) (c); (vii) (a); (viii) (b); (ix) (c); (x) (b)]

Short Answer Type

Q.3. How do the safety aspects of a grill compare to that of a broiler?
Q.4. Differential between in griddle, grill, and broiler.
Q.5. Describe characteristics of a saute.
Q.6. Define a fast food operations.
Q.7. Nutritionally explain the advantages of deep fried food.
Q.8. Explain the advantages of pan frying.

Descriptive Type

Q.9. Differentials between :
(a) Pan frying and sauteing
(b) Pan frying and deep frying.

Q10. Identify the three different coatings for frying food.
Q.11. Explain why a "Beef Stroganoff" is called a saute dish.

Assignments/Activities Type

Q.12. Demonstrate:
(a) Flipping and pan frying on suitable pans and skillets.
(b) The handling of the deep fryer including filtering and changing of fat.
(c) The safety features of the modern deep fryer.
(d) Flipping of food in a skillet, using the proper skillet and raw beans or other suitable materials.

Q.13. The use of the griddle and its cleaning procedure by using the grill stone.
Q.14. Have a fire drill.

3.6

Caramelizing and Tenderizing Combination Method

CHAPTER OBJECTIVES

After studying this lesson you should be able :

- To explain the importance of reasons for using the combination method of cooking;
- To define the terms and differentiale between the terms stewing, braising and pot-roasting;
- To explain and practice the basic procedures of the combination method;
- To identify the most practical meat cuts used for the combination method; and
- To describe the similarity of cooking for all terms in use.

Caramelizing and tenderizing combined is the combination method. Other methods such as stewing, braising and pot-roasting are well known terms in cooking methods. Presently each of these terms implies a limited application, referring to the size of the meat pieces and the looks of the dish instead of the preparation method. Caramelizing and tenderizing is one of the basic cooking methods of cooking. This method makes tough meats digestible and tasty. The moist heat method is applied for tenderization. At the same time caramelization is added to give the meat a more acceptable taste. Students and young cooks should remember that all these terms describe the same working procedure. All these various names have developed through time and the mixing different cultures. All basic cooking procedures of the combination method are the same, regardless of names and ingredients used. The trainees who have learned to master the basic technique of making a good stew, can apply the same techniques to all the preparations.

The combination methods pre-browns food, preserves the drippings and adds vegetables, spices, and liquid. This mixture is simmered slowly together until tender, creating its own sauce while cooking. Only tough foods have to be braised for tenderization. Tender foods are sometimes braised by habit and taste preference. Dinner houses with large menus are economically better off if they prepare chicken saute instead of a chicken stew.

Combination cooking developed as an improvement of boiling which had been necessary to make tough meats edible. Its use today and for the future becomes less and less necessary. Overall meat quality has improved and continues to do so. The combination process is used for tender meats by habit and preference only. For example, it is more economical and tastier to saute chickens and finish them with a garnish and a premade sauce than to make chicken stew in advance. The stew may have to be kept warm for hours (thereby reducing its quality) and there may be a large quantity of wasted leftovers. With food prices constantly on the rise, food costs are more important than ever.

Since few cuts in each meat carcass are suitable for roasting, true roasts are highly priced. Carcasses contain more pounds of the cheaper cuts, such as beef roast, chuck roast, cross rib roast, and rump roast. The combination method is the only way to prepare tough but tasty and nourishing beef cuts. On many menus, pot roast is called beef roast. This distinguishes it from "roast beet", in which the emphasis is on roasting, the dry heat cooking method. "Beef roast" implies that a quantity of beef meat has been cooked in one piece before being carved and served.

The terminology used at present differentiates between sizes of various meat cuts, colours of the sauce and ways of serving. A stew, served in the same container in which it was cooked, becomes a casserole. A braised steak cooked and served in a fireproof china casserole with a cover, is called a potted steak. Americans are more steak and roast conscious than most other nationals. Stewed meat does not have great appeal to the majority of food and beverage establishes patrons, and fancy terminology is used to avoid any thought of a stew.

DEFINITION OF TERMS

Different terms are used in order to distinguish between the sizes of meat pieces used in this combination method. A beef carcass does not consist of fillet and sirloin exclusively. Secondary meat cuts are offered to the customers in a variety of forms. Different terms are used to avoid the word stew. Potted steak, Casserole of Beef, Swiss Steak, sauerbraten, and Burgundy Beer, are some of the terms better accepted. They are in addition to stew, pot roast, and braised meat.

Stewing

The slow cooking together of foods in a closed pot is called stewing. A little juice and fat are used, which creates a sauce. For stews, pieces of meat are cut so small that several pieces together are needed to make one portion. The term "stew" always implies cut-up pieces of mixed food like meat or poultry as well as some fish and vegetables.

Braising

It is exactly the same cooking process as stewing. For braising, food is cut in a single portion size. There are braised steaks, park chops, or short ribs, but not stewed ones. Braising comes from the French word "bruiser" meaning the same as stewing. It is used on English language menus to avoid the implied meaning of the word 'stew'. In some food and bevevage establishments "Braised Beef" could mean any piece of beef cooked by the combination method.

Pot-Roasting

Pot-roasting itself describes the stewing process. A large piece of meat with many portions in it is cooked the same way. By saying 'roasted in the pot' it is implied that large pieces of meat have been stewed.

Fricasseeing

Fricasseeing is a French term which implies that the same combination method has been used on cup-up portion-size white meat. Only a veal fricassee, a chicken fricassee or a turkey breast fricassee exist. This term is never used with beef, lamb, or venison. In food and beverage establishments with French influences, a chicken stew is likely to be called a chicken fricassee.

Basic Procedures

The combination method of cooking uses three other methods of cooking. For example, a pot roast is started by the dry heat cooking method. When the meat is browned, stock or water, herbs, spices, and browned, flavour-giving vegetables are added. The container is then covered and simmered slowly on top of the range (i.e. roasted in the pot) or remains in the oven at a low temperature, covered or uncovered, until done.

Braised steaks are pan-browned or griddle-browned, transferred to a suitable container and then finished the same way as the pot roast. Meat stews are started like sautes but after the liquid has been added, they are simmered continuously until the meat is tender. A 'stew; made of white meat and vegetables, without tomatoes, in a white sauce, is called fricassee.

Meat Cuts

The modern progress in meat breading has resulted in more tender meats. Pork, veal, lamb, poultry, and fish do not need the combination method to become tender. If a lamb, chicken or veal stew is made, it is done by preference or ignorance. Moisture is needed to tenderize many cuts of beef. These come from the chuck or shoulder and the rump. Chuck meat, which has to be well trimmed in order to make it free of gristle and sinews, is commonly used for stews. Rump meat from the outside or bottom round and the knuckle are used for Swiss steaks and pot roasts. When selecting meat cuts, you remember that all meat cuts could be used for the combination method. Choice becomes a matter of price, labour needed to trim, habit, and personal preference.

The main difference is the size of the pieces into which meat is cut up. A bottom round can be cut as a stew, a stack, or be left whole as a pot roast. The cooking is done by the same method, the same garnish of green peas, carrots, cauliflower, brussels sprouts, and mushrooms is added to the sauce. The same spices and herbs are used. Another difference is the cooking time. Stew and steak will cook faster (smaller cut faster heat penetration) than the roast. When served, the three dishes will be named Beef Stew Jardinier, Braised Steak Jardinier, and Potroast Jadinier. In the last instance the dish might be called Beef Jardinier. Jardinier is the French word for gardener and the reference is to the added garnish of fresh vegetables, supplied by the gardener. For lamb stew jardinier, lamb replace the beef, and for Chicken Fricassee Jardinier tomatoes are avoided in order to keep the ivory colour of the sauce.

QUESTIONS AND DISCUSSIONS

Fill in the Blanks

Q.1. Read and complete the following:

(a) Combination cooking or braising has emerged as an improvement of ....

(b) The difference between Burgundy Beef stew and Burgundy Pot Roast is in the ....

(c) Many people like stews at home, but in restaurants they prefer steaks and ....

(d) The combination method uses moist heat to tenderize and adds flavour by ....

(e) Meat stews are started like sautes, but finished by ....

(f) The combination method is not only used by economic necessity but also by habit and ....

(g) True roast cuts from beef are used for steaks and roasts, secondary beef cuts are sued for ....

(h) Chicken fricassee is a stew where tomatoes have been ....

(i) Pot roasts must simmer a long time to become tender but first they have to be ....

(j) Most people believe stew is meat that has been ....

[**Ans.:** (a) boiling method; (b) Size of pieces;
(c) cesorale; (d) caramalization;
(e) adding garnish of fresh vegetables; (f) proferences;
(g) stew; (h) avoided;
(i) stewed; (j) pot roasted.]

Multiple Choice Type

Q.2. Read each question carefully and completely before answering it. Select the best answer :–

(i) Pot-roasting implies a large piece of meat, browned first and finished by
(a) Roasting in the oven (b) Boiling in the soup pot
(c) Gridling until tender (d) Simmering in a little juice.

(ii) Meat for a lamb stew has to be cut to such a size that one order consists of
(a) One slice (b) Two slices
(c) Two pieces (d) Four to six pieces.

(iii) Which of the following preparations is not a pot roast?
(a) Sauerbraten (b) Beef Jardinier
(c) Beef Stroganoff (d) Burgundy Beef Roast.

(iv) The cooking time for Swiss Steak is
(a) Shorter than for beef stew (b) The same as for pot roast
(c) The same as for beef stew (d) Longer than for pot roast.

(v) Which one of these steaks is served without sauce?
   (a) Potted Steak   (b) Broiled Steak
   (c) Braised Steak   (d) Swiss Steak.

(vi) For a Chicken Fricassee Hard-liner which of the following ingredients has to be omitted?
   (a) Green peas   (b) Carrots
   (c) Tomatoes   (d) Mushrooms.

(vii) Which of the following types of meat is suitable for fricasseeing?
   (a) Veal   (b) Venison
   (c) Lamb   (d) Beef.

(viii) To be used in a beef stew, chuck meat has to be
   (a) Well trimmed   (b) Cooked
   (c) Spiced   (d) Tenderized

[**Ans.:** (i) (d); (ii) (d); (iii) (c); (iv) (a);
(v) (a); (vi) (c); (vii) (c); (viii) (a)]

Matching Type

Q.3. Match the terms listed in Table 'A' with the best corresponding terms of Table 'B'

Table 'A'	*Table 'B'*
(a) Braising	(i) Trimmed Chuck
(b) Swiss Steak	(ii) True Roast
(c) Pot Roast	(iii) Veal stew with no tomatoes
(d) Beef Casserole	(iv) Veal stew with tomatoes & vegetables
(e) Beef Roast	(v) Stewing
(f) Red Wine Beef Stew	(vi) Sauerbraten
(g) Veal Fricassee	(vii) Potted Steak
(h) Stew Meat	(viii) Bottom Round
(i) Veal Stew Jardinier	(ix) Pot Roast
(j) Raw Pot Roast	(x) Secondary cut
(k) Beef Fillet	(xi) Burgundy Beef Stew
(l) Chuck Roast	(xii) Beef stew.

Short Answer Type

Q.4. Are there economic differences between broiled steaks and Swiss steaks? If so, what are they?

Q.5. Why are stews not preferred in restaurants?

Q.6. What are the differentials between roast Beef and Beef Roast?

Q.7. What are the similarites and advantages of stews and sautes?

Q.8. What is the other name for stew?

Discriptive Type

Q.9. Identify the most practical meat cuts for the combination method of cooking.

Q.10. Define the differential between stewing, braising, and pot-roasting.

Q.11. Explain the basic procedures of the combination method of cooking.

3.7

Salads, Fruit Salad, Salad Dressing and Sandwiches

CHAPTER OBJECTIVES

After studying this lesson you should be able :

- To understand how to prepare potato salad in a professional manner;
- To explain prepare and arrange plain Waldorf Salad;
- To demonstrate how to cut and set up a melon ball cocktail;
- To make and demonstrate how to prepare a three-decker club sandwhich;
- To prepare how to a garnished steak sandwich;
- To explain the popuarity of the Hofbrau Sandwich;
- To know the procedure of mixing of basic Frech dressing;
- To practice and make mayonnaise with the eletric mixer;
- To demonstrate,prepare and toss Romaine with Roquefort dressing;
- To make a commercial onion dressing;
- To set up a Green Goddess salad; and
- To explain in details the mixing of a Caesar Salad.to explain in details the mixing of a Caesar Salad.

Salads came into being as a use for left-overs. The Grade-manger of the French kitchen brigade is an important person for his ability to recycle left-overs without any loss. Pantry cooks are not truly grade-mangers. The preparation of cooked salad is the work of the pantry cook. Those who work luncheon shifts fix only sandwiches, salads, and dressings. Those in a dinnerhouse, where sandwiches are seldom served, handle all salads, appetizers, and hors d'oeuvres.

Cooked salads were first made to use up left-over cooked foods. Professional chefs, know the pantry man's importance to the guarding of food. He has the name Grade-manger, in the French kitchen brigade. The Garde-manger has the skill level of a master chef. The job description for pantry cooks in American restaurants does not include all of the Garde-manger's work.

Some pantry cooks cook their own meats, fish and vegetables. Others will get them from the chef or second cook. Grade-mangers will do their own cooking if they feel that special preparation of raw food is the only way to get the desired results for buffet work.

Pantry cook working lunch shifts are in charge of salad, dressing, and sandwiches. Some hot sandwiches are made by short order cooks, but the garnish cames from the pantry. The pantry cooks in dinner houses set up and prepare all salads for a la carte and dinner service. They also prepare the dressing, appetizers, and hors d'oeuvres.

COOKED SALADS

Salad can be grouped losely into tossed greens and mixed cooked salad. These are, in principle, quite alike. The dressings are the same. Salad dressing must be seen as cold sauces holding salads together, much like warm sauces holding stew together. Although dresing are creamy and thick, their texture is not based on the starch of hot sauces, but on the mixing of oil and liquid. Pantry work and serving need more artistic expression than plain cooking. A trainee chef will do well to learn as much as possible about the guiding principles of pictorial and graphic art.

Cooked salads are prepared from cooked foods, whereas "Toosed Green Salad" are made from raw vegetables with the occasional addition of cooked food. Cooked salad are prepared from vegetables, seafood or meat. Sometimes they are mixtures of several main ingredients, several flavour additions, and the dressing. Salad combinations are endless and exact group classificastion is impossible. nearly all foods which can be eaten warm can be eaten as cold salad.

The protein and starch foods used for salads are boiled, steamed, baked, or roasted. Rarely are they sauteed, deep fried, or stewed. The pantry cook uses his own cold sauce in the form of a manyonnaise or a dressing.

Cooked salads are divided by their ingredients, the way these ingredients are cut or shaped, and their table presentation. Vegetables are cooked whole, so as not to lose their flavour. They must be cooked fresh, then cooled off, cut, and blended with the dressing. Potato salad, if made from potatotoes in the refregerator for a day, will .taste like old potato salad. Protien foods are not as sensitive as starch foods. They can be used as long as they are still wholesome. Fresh prepared and mixed salads can be stored under refrigeration for a few days.

Salad Dishes and Their Garnishes

The way salad are presented depends on the style of the establishment. In most of the western countries lettuce leaves are used to underline nearly every salad or cocktail. Parsley, watercress, lemon wedges for seafood, hard boiled eggs, olives, tomatoes, cucumbers, pickles, and pimentos are some of the other garnishes used. For an elegant looking salad, it is important to have the right service dish. Absolutely clean work, a sence of spacing or symmetry, and a sense for colour is neeeded. The more articstic telents a cook has, the better his pantry creations will look. There are many wrong ideas about the use of additional colours. Only colours which appear natuarally on edible foods can be used. The exceptions are non-poisonous flowers without any smell. They are used as a food garnish in some unique specialty restaurants. Afrtificial colouring in culinary art is only used to bring out the natural colours of the food. Pale red, yellow, brown, and green are the only colours possible. Blue have no place in food except in blueberries and plums.

The public is well aware of the importance of salads as a part of thir diets. Many salad ingredient, the right climate and excellent promotion have made salads important in restaurants. They are often presented in elaborate settings.

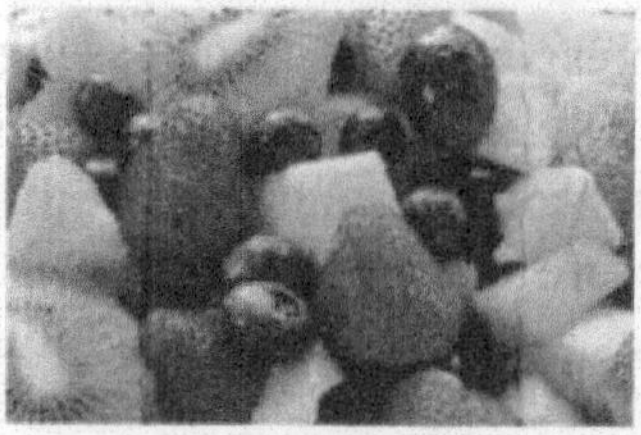

Fruit salad

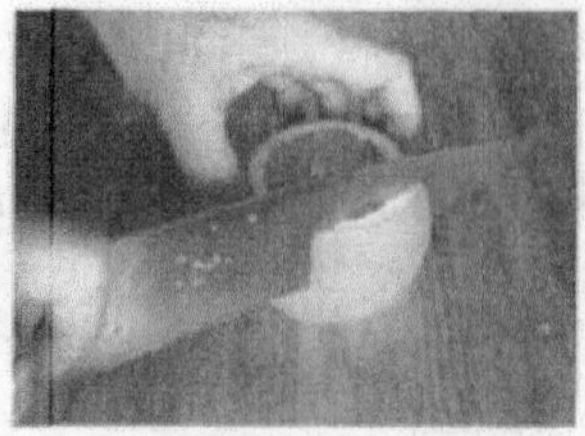

Citrus Fruits

Cutting of Citrus Fruit

Table 3.7A. Ingredients for Salad Compositions : Vegetables and Proteins

1. Lettuce

(i) Romaine
(ii) Endive (Belgian & domestic) Limestone
(iii) Chinese Cabbage,a and many regional varieties.
(iv) Iceberg
(v) Chicory
(vi) Boston
(vii) Escarole
(viii) Butter.
The choice depends on the season and growing area.

2. Vegetables, Raw

(i) Tomatoes	(ii) Cadishes
(iii) Chillis	(iv) Avocadoes
(v) Cabbage	(vi) Onions
(vii) Cucumbers	(viii) Mushrooms
(ix) Scallions	(x) Celery
(xi) Bell peppers	(xii) Zucchini.

3. Vegetables Cooked

(i) Artichokes	(ii) Water chestnuts.
(iii) Beets	(iv) Bamboo
(v) Palm hearts.	

4. Proteins

(i) Shirmp	(ii) Eggs
(iii) Cheese	(iv) Crab
(v) Ham	(vi) Lobster
(vii) Beef	(viii) Seafood
(ix) Chicken.	

5. Herbs

(i) Parsley	(ii) Watercress
(iii) Rosemary	(iv) Chive
(v) Sorrel	(vi) Garlic
(vii) Dill	(viii) Tarragon
(ix) Shallots and others.	(x) Cilantro
(xi) Basil.	

SALAD DRESSINGS

One of the most important part of the salad, for flavour, is the dressing. Most lettuce is eaten for its textures crunchiness, and vitamin content. A salad dressing is a cold sauce which helps to digest the raw vegetables, and adds taste to the salad. Human beings can live on raw meat, but not on raw unprocessed vegetables or grains. Raw salads without oil are hard to digest. Oil by itself is not too tasty, because of its richness.

A mixture of oil, acid (to make the oil more platable), and spices was created to be used as a salad dressing.

Basic Salad Dressings

Dressing are a blended mixture of fat, acid, liquid, herbs, and spices. Thery are divided into three basic groups:

1. Oil and vinegar emulsion
2. Mayonnaise, and
3. Sour cream.

These bases, as in sauce cookery, reflect the culinary taste of the chef. Catsup, mastard, avocado or any other vegetable pulp, hardboiled eggs, cheeses, anchovies, capers, onions, garlic, peppers, olives, pickles, and pimentos are some of the ingredients the chef may add.

Two chefs rarely make the same dressing, even when using the same names. For instance, Roquefort, or Blue Cheese dressing, is accepted in many different variations. The true French Roquefort dressing has four parts : Roquefort, one part fresh cream and six to eight parts plain French dressing. It should be mixed fresh on the table whenver it is ordered. Other variations use blue cheese for the roquefort, with sour cream as a base. This allows greater dilution of the cheese. The name Roquefort or Roquefort Dressing is a trademark. It can be used only if true French imported Roquefort cheese is served or used.

Some dressings with a specific name, like Roqufort, Russian or Tousand Islands. can be served over any salad. Others, such as Green Goddess Caesar dressing, should be served over a specific kind or lettuce only. Garlic is optional but if used in a subtle way, enhances the flavour and digestibility of every salad.

Due to dressing, salad combinations are endless. They truly show the cook's sense of beaty and taste.

French Dressing

The oil and vinegar emulsion is called French dressing. It is made by mixing two or three parts oil with one part venegar. Salt, pepper, and sometimes mustard are added. The mixing is done in a salad bowl or a bar shaker. The use of a blender gives a better result. French dressing will separate after some time. It has to be made fresh, or at least reblended, whenever it is needed. If more spices or other ingredients are added, the basic French dressing is changed to a a dressing of another name.

Mayonnaise ·

Mayonnaise is a creamy mixtue of egg yolks, oil, acid, liquid and spice. The egg yolk acts as emulsifier to the process of whiping with a wire whisk. The yolks, while whipped vigorously, absorbs the oil in very small amount at a time. All the ingredients used must be in a temperature range of 65°F. to 75°F. If they are colder than that, emulsion will not take place and the mixture will curdle. The same will happen if the oil is added too rapidly. Mayonnaise may also be made in the blender. For real commercial amounts a centrifuge is used.

Table 3.7B. Combination Dressing

S.No.	*Dressing*		*Explanation*
1.	Sauce Verte	:	Cooked ppinach, parsley, anchoves are osterized with lemon juice and worcester sauce, and mixed with mayonnaise
2.	Sauce Remoulade	:	Parsley, chives, capers, pickles, achovies, and mayonnaise
3.	Sauce Tyrolienne	:	Remoulade sauce, mixed with catsup
4.	Sauce Andalouse	:	Catsup, chpped bell peppers, and mayonnaise
5.	Sauce Verdi	:	Sour cream, pickles, chives, and mayonnaise
6.	Sauce Mousseline	:	Whipped cream and mayonnaise, in equal parts
7.	Sauce Suedoise	:	Reduced apple sauce, horseradish, lemon juice, and mayonnaise
8.	Sauce Ravigotte	:	Cooked egg whites, anchovies, shallots, parsley, and mayonnaise
9.	Sauce Aurore	:	Reduce tomato chutney, lemon jice, and mayonnaise
10.	Sauce Indienne	:	Apple sauce, sour cream, curry, and mayonnaise
11.	Thousand Island Dressing	:	Pimento, bell pepper, chilli, castup, French dressing, and mayonnaise
12.	Indienn Dressinhg	:	Mayonnaise, sour cream, curry, mango, chutney, sugar, and lemon
13.	Chiffonade Dressing	:	French dressing, chopped herbs, and beets
14.	Russian Drssing	:	Tartar sauce with catsup and caviar
15.	Roquefort Dressing	:	Roquefort cheese, cream, and French dressing
16.	Ble Cheese Drssing	:	Blue cheese, sour cream, and mayonnaise
17.	Avocado Dressing	:	French dressing, avocado pulp, and lemon
18.	Onion Dressing	:	French dressing, raw onion pulp, parsley, sugar, and pepper
19.	Mustard Dressing	:	French mustard, mayonnaise, sour cream, dry mustard, and prek.

Cold Sauces or Dressings Based on Mayonnaise

Mayonnaise, the base for salad dressings and cold sauces, is also a sandwich spread. It has been known since the beginning of the 18th century in Boyonne, France. Like hot sauces, cold sauces start from a base. Fruit purees are one base, and mayonnaise is the other. The only difference between a mayonnaise sauce and a mayonaise dressing is the consistency. The sauce or spread is kept at a stiffer or heavier consistency. Sauces can be used as dressing. Dressings can be used as sauces.

Combinations based on mayonnaise are endless and it is left to the cook to blend what he consdiders best. Measurements are not given, since neither the consistency of the mayonnaise nor the strength and taste of the condiments are standardized. In all, the grainish must either be chopped, osterized, or cut very small. The basic mayonnaise is used. As a guide to amount, it is suggested that for Tartar Sauce, 2 cups of freshly made mayonnaise are diluted with 2 tablespoons of mustard, 1 tablespoon of chopped capers, and 3 tablspoon of finely chopped dill pickles, raw onions, and parsley. Salt, additional lemon juice, or vinegar are added to taste.

MAKING MAYONNAISE

1. Mayonnaise, like the Hollandaise, is sensitive to metal oxidation. Only stainless, non-oxidizing utensils must be used.

Experimetal Recipe 15.

Basic Mayonnaise

Equipment

1. Stailess bowl, and
2. utensils.

Ingredients

1. Yolks : 5 egg
2. Prepared mustard : 1 tablespoon
3. Sald oil : 3 cups
4. Vinegar : 3-4 tablespoons.
5. Salt, White papper

Method

1. Prepare all required ingredients
2. Clean bowl with a towel.
3. Separate yolks into the bowl.
4. Add the mustard.
5. Start mixer on low, then switch to high speed.
6. Add very thin flow of oil. Watch emulsion occuring. Stop a after one cup of oil is used.
7. Reduce to slow speed. Add half the vinegar.
8. Continue on high speed. Add the remaining oil.
9. Slow mixer again. Add salt, pepper, and remaining vinegar.
10. Mix all and taste. Remove mayonnaise to storage container and store in 45°F. to 60°F. area.

2. Be sure that all ingredients are at room temperature (65°F. to 75°F) before mayonnaise is started.
3. Keep mixer in clean condition.
4. Stop mixer before tasting.
5. Separate yolk and egg white neatly. Too much egg white will change three consistency of the finished mayonnasie.

These dressing are commonly used for dinner salad, included on the dinner, and served from the pantry instead of the salad cart. These dressings are also available from commercial sources. The skilled cook will always find that he is able to make dressing not only with a personal touch but also of a better quality at a cheaper price.

SPECIALLTY SALADES TOSSED AT THE TABLE

Specialty salads tossed at the table are served for two, and are *a la carte* dishes. They are comparatively expensive. Sometimes the emphasis is on the quality of the clettuce, at other times the emphasis is on the preparation of the dressing. Begian Endive or Limestone Lettuce are very delicate and expensive salad greens which are themselves the attractions. These should be served with a mild plain dressing, based on quality ingredients only. The dressing must be mixed at the table. The olive oil, vinegar, mustard, etc. should be in the original containers so that there is no doubt about quality.

Comparatively less expensive combinations on the menu are Romaine, Boston, or Butter Lettuce, and Tossed Greens. A soft salad like butter lettuce must have a light dressing. If it were to be mixed with mayonnaise, the dish would become a gluey, unappetizing dish. Many times a restaurant lists two or three lettuce combinations and then offers a choice of dressing.

Green Goddess

A California salad speciality, this was first made at the Place Hotel in San Francisco. Many years ago, a famous actor stayed at this well-known hotel while playing the title role in *Green Goddess,* Which was a hit play. He loved salads, so the chef created this one for him and culinary history was made. This salad, although one of the finest and true California creations, is relatively unknown. Many similar or slightly varied salads are served under different names all over California. It may be cured as a dinner appetizer or a summer lunch with french bread.

Green goddess is a favourite for ladies launcheons and it can be made with different seafoods or cooked chicken.

Green Goddess Salad

Green Goddes is a favourite for ladies' luncheons and it can be made with different seafoods or cooked chicken.

Green Salad

Most luxury restaurants promote the serving of green salads through elaborate and elegnt salad carts, salad bars, or other serving setups. They also employ trained persoNnel to serve the salads in style.

Some of the finest, most luscious and sophisticated salads are very popular in the warmer regions, and in the large, metropolitan areas. Salads are served as first course, side dishes to meat, full meals, or snacks. The reasons for this popularity are the right climate, the right ingredients, and promotions.

In gredients of salads and the serving plates and implements should be ice cold when prsented. Salads must be served immediately after the greens have been toosed. All salad mixing should be done in front of the patrons. Salad must look fresh, fluffy, clean, appetizing, tempting, and dainty. The tossing must be made into a perfromance of skill and showmanship. The salad server (tosser) should know that good salads are never too oily, too sour, or over-spiced. He also knows that a full platter filled over the rim is never served. Salad ingredients must match in flavour. The next course of the meal must also be considered. In France and other wine-drinking countries, salads are served after the main course. This does not interfere with the wines served at the meal. Salads and wines do not match and, in general, are not served together.

(a) (b) (c) (d)

Colanders

PREPARATION GREEN GODDESS SALAD

1. All rules for salad in general have to be observed.
2. Watercress should be used to garnish the table-ready plate.
3. Two tomato wedges can be used to add colour to the plate.
4. Freshly ground pepper is added last.

Salad Maxmimilian

This is a combination of bay shrimps, or cream-avocado dressing, and artichokes. For banquet service a salad like this could be set up in advance by filling the bay shrimps into artichokes, with the dressing as a cover.

This salad, although one of the finest and true California creations, is relatively unknown. Many similar or slightly varied salads are served under different names all over California. It may be used as a dinner appetizer or a summer lunch with French bread.

Experential Recipe 16.

Green Goddess Salad with shellfish

Ingredients

1. Head of Romaine, cleaned, washed drained cut to 2-3 inch lengths : 1
2. Ripe, peeled, and sliced : 1 avocado
3. Alaska King Crab, shrimp, lobster or similar cooked, cold shellfish : 6 ounces
4. Finely chopped anchovies in oil : 1 tablespoon
5. Lemon, Juiced : ½
6. Sour cream : 5-6 tablespoons
7. Mayonnaise : 5-6 tablespoons
8. Additional olive oil and wine vinegar : if needed
9. Salt, Pepper : To taste.

Method

1. Prepare all required ingredients.
2. Have all dressing ingredients arranged in large bowl. Mix well.
3. Add all romaine, avocado, and shellfish.
4. Salt and toss lightly.
5. Taste. if necessary, add more of the ingredients to achieve desired taste, and toss again.
6. Serve.

Experiential Recipe 17.

Salad Maximilian

Ingredients

1. Head Romaine : 1
2. Sliced, cooked artichoke bottoms : 1
3. Watercress : ½ bunch
4. Cooked, tiny Bay shrimps : 6 ounces
5. Buttermilk : 2 ounces
6. Sour cream : 2 ounces
7. Dash of dill, Salt, Pepper : To taste
8. Chopped onion : 1 teaspoon.

Dressing

Avocado : ¼

Lemon : 1.

Method

1. Prepare all required ingredients.
2. Blend avocado with buttermilk, onion, and half the lemon juice.
3. Put in sour cream, and season to taste with the remaining ingredients.
4. Adjust consistency by adding or diluting.
5. Have all salad ingredients except watercress properly cut up in a large salad bowl.
6. Pour enough dressing on, but not too much. Toss slightly.
7. Taste, and add what is necessary.
8. Put on dinner plate or large salad plate.
9. Garnish with watercress, sprinkle a little dill on top. Use pepper mill.
10. Serve immediately.

Ceasar Salad

This very popular salad has to be made very mild so that the anchovies, garlic, and parmesan do not destroy the taste sensitivity of the palate for the rest of the meal.

This salad comes from Southern California and was created by a headwaiter named Caesar. It may be served as a luncheon to some people or a dinner appetizer to others.

Experimental Recipe 18.

Caesar Salad

Ingredients

1. Measured portions of clean, cut-up Romaine : 2
2. Grated parmensan cheese : 4 tablespoons
3. Juice of lemon : 1/2
4. Large coddled egg (blanched in boiling water for one minute) : 1
5. Garlic croutons : 1/3 cup
6. Mashedup anchovies : 2-3
7. Watercress and two tomato wedges for decoration
8. Red wine vinegar : 1 tablespoons
9. Olive oil : 1 tablespoons
10. Salt, Freshly ground pepper : To taste.

Method

1. Prepare all required ingredients
2. Observe all rules in regard to salad preparation.
3. Place salad in mixing bowl.
4. Add remaining ingredients except pepper, tomato, and watercress in any order.
5. Finish. Put on plate. Add garnish and pepper.
6. Serve immediately.

Tomato and Watercress

This salad is made without lettuce. For an appetizer, this is not unusual. Other preparations can aslo be made this way.

No matter where salads are set up, if in the pantry or tossed at the table and finished by the headwaiter, the chef bears the responsibility for the initial and partial preparation. If the chef fails to keep the salad pantry on a high quality level, the best headwaiter will not be able to make a worthy salad.

This salad is made and served without any kind of lettuce, but is still considered a salad. It is eaten as an appetizer before dinner and can be served like old artichokes, hearts of palms, or asparagus. Tossing is not absolutely essential. The tomatoes should be sliced and arranged with the watercress on a plate, and the marinade or dressing spooned or basted over this layout. This is very convenient for party service on individial plates. This is not a bulky salad or appetizer and can be served on a small plate or glass dish.

Experimental Recipe 19.

Tomato and Watercress Salad

Ingredients

1. Tomatoes	:	2 medium
2. Watercress	:	1/2 bunch
3. Red wine Vinegar	:	As required
4. Olive oil	:	As needed
5. Tarragon	:	As needed
6. Garlic	:	As needed
7. Salt	:	To Taste.
8. Pepper	:	

Method

1. Prepare all required ingredients
2. Peel and wedge tomatoes. Clean watercress. Place into salad bowl.
3. Add salt and pepper, a dash of tarragon, garlic about one tablespoon vinegar, and 2-3 tablespoons oil.
4. Toss quickly, taste, and serve.

Some of the finest, most luscious and sophisticated salads are very popular in the warmer regions, and in the large metropolitan areas. Salads are served as first courses, side dishes to meat, full meals, or snackes. The reasons for this popularity are the right climate, the right ingredients, and promotion.

Comparatively salads have low food cost, but need skilled labour for their presentation. The variety of salad combinations make them acceptance to serve at every occasion. Lettuce and vegetable used in preparations are important, but more so is the dressing. Salad dressings are cold sauces based on oil or fat as the thickener. The oil is needed to make salads easier to digest. The acid and seasoning of the dressing enchances the blandness of the greens and the richness of the oil. A plain oil and vinegar emulsion is called French dressing. It serves as a base for many dresing variations. Mayonaise and sour cream are the other two bases for cold and sald sauces.

Salads for dinner are generally prepared in the pantry, by speciality salads are a la carte orders tossed at the table, the salad cart, or the salad bar. Although manyonnaise and mayonnaise dressing are available on a commerical basis , every skilled cook must know how to make them. Making his own dressing provides the chef's personal touch to his cookery. It also has a better food cost. The public sometimes. expects the chef to toss a salad at the table for his favourite guests. The young cook will do well to practice salad making in the dining room.

Potato Salad

Some people think it is easy to make a good potato salad. There are tricks of the trade which make the difference between a good salad and an excellent one. *Experiment*

Recipe 20 gives a detailed description of making potato salads and it is suggested that every step be followed.

POTATO MAYONNAISE SALAD

Many varieties of potato salad and methods of making exist. The best potato salad is made by one basic method. Trainee should try and taste different method, then taste, judge, and select what they considered best.

Experimental Recipe 20.

Potato Mayannnalse Salad

Key Points

1. Potatoes are boiled in the jacket, peeled, and cooled about two hours before mixing.
2. All flavours and spcies have to be mixed with the potatoes first. After potatoes are coated with mayonnaise, or any oil, they will not absorb the flavouring.
3. For salad making, white or red rose potatoes are preferred.
4. Since natural grown foods are seldom uniform, and processed foods vary from maker to maker, a recipe can never be handled like a chemical formula. The cook must make allowance for these differences and mix the ingredients with personal judgement.

Ingredients

1.	Approximately white or red rose potatoes	:	5 pounds
2.	Chopped dill pickles	:	1/4 cup
3.	Onions	:	1/2 cup
4.	Prepared mustard	:	2-3 tablespoons
5.	Salt , pepper, vinegar or pickle juice	:	To taste
6.	Mayonnaise of heavy texture	:	1 - 1½ cups

Method

1. Prepare all required ingredients.
2. Slice potatoes thin. Put them into bowl. Add the pickles.
3. Osterized onions with 1/4 to 1/2 cup of vinegar or pickle juice.
4. Mix mustard into the osterized onions.
5. Salt, pepper the sliced potatoes. Add parsley and onion pulp.
6. Mix all together carefully and check for the taste.
7. Add mayonnaise in just a sufficient amount gradually. Taste again, and add what may be needed.

Macaroni Salad

It is an inexpensive, filling salad for Smorgasbords and coffee shop mass production. It is made like potato mayonnaise salad, with short, cooked macaroni or other pasta in place of potatoes.

French Vegetable Salad

This salad is often used for buffet work. It differs from potato salad by the cut and variety of the vgegetables used. The main ingredients are diced, about green pea-size. The vegetable ratio is 3 parts green peas, 3 parts cooked celeriac (root celery), 3 parts carrots, 6 parts potatoes, 2 parts pickles, and 1/2 part finely chopped onions. Mustard, mayonnaise, and extra vinegar are used for the dressing.

Italian Frascatti Salad

All of the meat in this mixed salad are cut short julienne : 2 parts ham, 2parts veal, chicken or turkey, 2 parts well-done beef, 2 parts green peas, 2 parts carrots, 2 parts pickles, and 6 parts potatoes. Mayonnaise, catsup, mustard and some basil-vinegar are used for the dressing.

Tuna Fish Salad

The tuna fish could be replacfed by cooked salmon or any other coarse, flaked fish. Experiment Recipe 21 gives detaled instructions for making tuna fish salad. The tuna fish could be replaced by cooled salmon or any other coarse, flaked fish.

TUNA FISH SALAD

Tuna fish salad can be used as a sandwich filling or a lucheon meat. It is one of the most popular fish salad dishes. In many areas it is the number one Friday lunch special.

1. For salad bowls, the tuna can be chopped coarsely
2. For sandwich filling it should be chopped fine or run through the meat grider using a fine or medium plate.

Experimental Recipe 21.

20 Tuna Fish Salad

Equipment

1. Salad bowl
2. Osterizer
3. Rubber spatual.

Ingredients

1. One chunk tuna fish in light oil	:	60 -ounce
2. Finely diced celery	:	2 cups
3. Hard boild eggs	:	3
4. Chopped onions		
5. Pickle chips	:	1/2 cup
6. Salt		
7. Pepper		
8. Juice of lemon	:	To taste
9. Mayonnaise	:	1-2 cups.

Method

1. Prepare all required ingredients
2. Drain tuna. Save the oil.
3. Chop drained tuna fish, place in salad bowl, mix with celery.
4. Take 1/2 cup liquid from tuna, picles, onions, eggs, lemon juuice, and osterize.
5. Pour osterized pulp over tuna. Add salt and pepper.
6. Add myonnaise gradually. Mix well. Taste and finish accordingly.

Shellfish Salad

Prawns, shrimps, lobster, crabs, crayfish, abalones, or even squid can be used in a shellfish salad. The principles of general salad mixing are applied.

Egg Salad

The salad from hard boiled eggs is common as a sandwich filling or garnish.

The prodcedure of how to make egg salad is given in Experimental Recipe 22.

Egg salad is best known as a sandwich filling. It is a basic salad which can be used as part of a salad plate or to stuff tomatoes or other vegetables.

Hard cooked cold eggs can be chopped by hand, with the egg slicer, shredded with a coarse grater, or the meat grinder.

Experimental Recipe 22.

Egg Salad

Equipment :

1. Salad bowl,
2. Large rubber spatual

Ingridients

1. Hard boiled, shelled eggs, chopped or grated : 2 dozen
2. Finely chopped celery : 2 cups
3. Mayonnaise : 1/4 - 1 cup
4. Pepper
5. Tabasco sauce
6. Dry mustard.

Method

1. Prepare all required ingredients
2. Place all dry ingredients into salad bowl and mix together.
3. Add mayonnaise gradually.
4. Taste, and finish accordingly.

Combination with Fruits

Peaches, apples, raw or cooked pineapples, and other hard fruits are mixed into combination salads.

Chicken Waldorf Salad

This is a mild-tasting luncheon salad of cubed chicken meat, celery, green apples. walnuts and mayonnaise, with only salt used for seasoning. Plain Waldorf Salad is the same mixture without the chicken.

FRUIT SALADS

Fruits can be mixed into many combinations, using raw fruits, compote fruits (canned), or a mixture of both. All of them are served as salad. Different cuts or shapes are used. A melon ball salad (cut with the melon ball cutter) made of different coloured melons can be very attractive. These salads are also served as cocktails, such as fruit cocktail, melon ball cocktail, avocado and citrus cocktail, and others. Dry sherry can be usedd to macerate (marinate) them.

Experimental Recipe 23.

Fruit Salad

Ingredients

1. Whipped cream or beàten fresh cream : 350 gm
2. Banana sliced into small pieces : 1½ cup
3. Apples (cut into small cubes) : 1 cup
4. Sweet Black Grapes (remove the seeds) : ¼ cup
5. Peaches (cut into small cubes) : ¼ cup
6. Mangoes (cut into small cubes) : ¼ cup
7. Cantaloupe or Musk Melon (cut into small cubes) : ¼ cup
8. Sugar : ½ cup.

Method

1. Parapre all required ingredients.
2. Add sugar to the fruit mixture and mix well.
3. Finally add cool whip or whipped cream or beaten fresh cream to the mixture and fold it well so that the fruits are well blended with the cream.
4. Refrigerate it for at least 1 hour before serving as dessert.

For dressing

1. Lemon juice : 04 Tsp
2. Chat masala : ½ tsp
3. Chopped mint : ¼ tsp
4. Chopped fresh coriander : ¼ tsp
5. Black salt : To taste.

All mixed together and used as dressing for salad.

Fruit salad may be served with dressing on the side. It could be whipped cream, Mousseline Sauce, mayonnaise with lemon juice, a Honey-Olive oil-Lemon dressing or others. Fruits with cottage cheese are an speerial creation. They can be served with a good dressing, such as sour cream or shipped cream, or just plain. Fruit salads, like other combination salads, are appetizers, luncheon dishes, or in-between snacks. In the fruit-growing regions they are made especially attractive.

SALAD DISHES AND THEIR GARNISHES

The way salads are presented depends on the style of the establishment. In the USA lettuce leaves are used to underline nearly every salad or cocktail. This practice is not used all over the world.

Parsley, watercress, lemon wedges for seafood, hard boiled eggs, olives, tomatoes, cucumbers, pickles, and pimentos are some of the other garnishes used. For an elegant looking salad, it is important to have the right service dish. Absolutely clean work, a sense of spacing or symmetry and a sense for color is needed. The more artistic talents a cook has, the better his pantry creations will look. There are many wrong ideas about the use of additional colors. Only colours which appear naturally on edible foods can be used. The exceptions are non-poisonous flowers without any smell. They are used as a food garnish in some unique specialty restaurants. Artificial coloring in culinary art is only used to bring out the natural colors of the food. Pale reds, yellows, browns and greens are the only colors possible. Blues have no place in food except in blueberries and plums.

SANDWICHES

Sandwich-making becomes a more important skill as the pupularity of sandwiches increases. They are served most often as light luncheon dishes. Any food served in a roll or two slices of bread can be called a sandwich. Three deckers are work combination sandwiches fashioned after the worldwide well known club sandwich (in some areas called clubhouse sandwich). Its popularity is making it known to the rest of the world. Delicatesen sandwiches overwhelm by sheer quantity and quality of their filling. They can be considered the sandwich man's sandwich. Hofbrau sandwiches are simple, but solid and fresh in content. They are made before the watchful eyes of the customer.

The Earl of Sandwich, a well-known horse racing fan and gambler, asked his butler to place a steak between two slices of bread and wrap it up. He took it along to the races to eat for lunch, thus, not missing any action. This, as the story goes, was the birth of the sandwich, named after its inventor.

Tuna Nicoise Reciple : This lovely entree salad originated in Nice, France

Plain or Toasted Sandwiches

Sandwiches serve many purposes, from a snack to a filling meal. They are eaten at any time of the day. They are available in many price ranges. The sandwich is made of

Experimental Recipe 24.

Plain or Tossted Sandwiches

Equipment

1. Sandwich station setup
2. Cutting board
3. 10-inch cook's knife
4. Spatula.

Ingredients

1. Sandwich bread
2. Spread
3. Filling.

Method

1. Prepare all required ingredients.
2. Spread one slice of bread with mayonnaise.
3. Put on it from 1½ - 3 ounces of cooked ham and a trimmed lettuce leaf.
4. Spread second slice of bread as the first one.
5. Put on sandwich, spread side down.
6. Trim all four sides carefully to remove crust, or leave crust as it is.
7. Cut either diagonally or straight into 2 or 4 equal sections.
8. Arrange pleasantly on a plate.
9. arnish with parsley (minimum).

Procedure for a Plain Cheese Sandwich

1. Prepare all required ingredients.
2. Spread sliced bread with butter or marrgarine.
3. Place slices of cheese (1 - 2½ ounces) on it.
4. Spread second slice of bread as first one.
5. Put on sandwich, buttered side down. Trim crust if desire.
6. Cut diagonally into two equal triangles.
7. Arrange neatly on a platter.
8. Add the garnish.
9. Serve.

A plain ham and cheese sandwich is made with two slices bread as above, but ham and cheese (one slice each) are used for a filling. A ham and cheese on rye is the same sandwich as the one described here, but on rye bread.

As soon as a student is able to make one sandwich, he is able to make any sandwich, if the customer specifies what he wants in it.

A toasted sandwich is made like the plain one, but the bread (2-3 days old) is toasted first. Toasted sandwiches are better when spread with soft butter instead of mayonnaise.

two slice of bread with a filling between them. It is cut in halves or quarters, to be eaten with bare fingers. A sandwich was never intended to be eaten with knife and fork and therefore, should not be served that way. (Ref Exeparimental Recipee 24)

The composition, the work process and the presentation of the plain sandwich is explained here for all of these plain or toasted sandwiches.

The making of a plain sandwich is as simple as it looks. However, both knowledge and skill are required to own a sandwich shop.

Breads: The bread may be shaped regular, square, round, oval, stub, or as rolls. White, wheat, rye, french, black, and sweet spreads are used.

Spreads: Butter margarine, fat cream, cheese special butter, peanet butter, mustard, mayannaise, and all varities of spread are used.

Filling: Cooked meats, cold cuts, cheeses, salad vegetables, meat, fish or combination salads, jams or marmalades, cured, smoked, marinated or canned food specialities, or any suitable combination may be used.

Working Process: The four crust *may* be trimmed off. The sandwich *may* be cut into special forms, such as triangles, squares, rectangles, or strips, but should be small enough to be eaten with one hand.

Presentation and Garnish

Sandwiches served on plates are usually garnished. The garnish may be lettuce, raw or cooked vegetables, fruits, vegetable combination salads, fresh whole parsley, watercress or mint. Fancy toothpicks, sword-picks, paper frills and other small niceties are often used with colorful and decorative foods to create an appetizing and eye-appealing appearance. Garnishes must be a taste compliment to the sandwich and their eye appeal should improve its sales.

Toasted Club Sandwiches

The sandwich called Club or Clubhouse is a generous luncheon dish. When served at its best, it has three slices of buttered toast filled with sliced chicken breast, lettuce and mayonnaise on one layer, and crisp, fried bacon, with tomatoes, on the other. A club

Double layered Sandwich

Club Sandwich

sandwich is cut into four triangles which are held together individually by a toothpick through the middle. To keep it warm, it is half wrapped in a prewarmed linen napkin and served on a warmed plate. The food cost of a real club sandwich has gone so high that many average-priced establishments cannot afford to keep them on their menus.

Just like any sandwich, a toasted Three Decker can be made with a variety of fillings on different breads. Fried ham, eggs, onions, avocados, and many meats can be used. The

Experimental Recipe 25

Club Sandwich

Equipment & Ingredients

1.	Sandwich station setup		
2.	White sandwich stub bread, stale	:	3 slices
3.	Lettuce leaf	:	1
4.	Center slices of tomatoes	:	4
5.	Cooked, warm, bacon strips, cut in half	:	4
6.	Sliced chicken or turkey breast	:	2 ounces
7.	Mayonnaise	:	2 tablespoons
8.	Butter for toast		
9.	Salt, Pepper	:	To taste
10.	Toothpicks and olives: 4 or frilly canape picks	:	4
11.	Boston lettuce, Watercress, Gherkins, Coleslaw or chips	:	As a garnish.

Procedure

1. Prepare all required ingredients
2. Toast three slices of break.
3. Butter toast. Lay it on sandwich board.
4. Place sliced chicken on bread.
5. Spread half the mayonnaise on the chicken.
6. Place flattened lettuce leaf on chicken.
7. Put second buttered toast on. Butter toast on second side.
8. Put bacon on top of toast.
9. Put sliced tomatoes on bacon, salt and pepper.
10. Spread remaining mayonnaise on buttered side of third toast.
11. Cover tomatoes, buttered side down.
12. Square sandwich. Press together lightly.
13. Stick picks into sandwich, straight down in the middle of each of the four rims about one and a half fingers away from the outside.
14. Cut diagonally twice, into four traingles.
15. Transfer with the cutting knife used as a lifter or pallet to the serving dish lined with an opened napkin.
16. Finish platter with garnish and
17. Serve immediately.

garnishes are often french fries, potato chips, or coleslaw. A garnish should not repeat any ingredient already in the filling.

A CLUB SANDWICH

For many years the club (or clubhouse) sandwich has been a speciality preparation of coffe shops or luncheon rooms. Most important for a sandwich man is his preparation or mis-en-place. If he also knows his menu, keeps calm when the orders are piling in, and pays attention instead of talking, he will be a valuable employee.

Steak Sandwiches

According to culinary history, steak sandwiches are the original sandwiches, and are still very popular. It is logical that the American hamburger started as the poor man's

Experimental Recipe 26.

Steak Sandwich

Ingredients

1. Flattened, renderized steaks : 4 pieces, 4-5 ounces each
2. French rolls, sour dough : 4
3. Cherry tomatoes : 16 medium
4. Sweet sour gherkins : 16 small
5. Watercress : 1 bunch cleaned
6. Lettuce leaves : 4 buttern
7. Mixture of French mustard : 1 ounces
8. Soy a sauce : 1 ounce
9. Catsup : 2 ounces
10. Dry English mustered salt : ½ ounce
11. Pepper : To taste.

Procedure

1. Prapare all required ingredients.
2. Salt and pepper steak.
3. Cook medium rare on broiler or grill.
4. At the same time, split roll.
5. Toast on the inside only (salamander, broiler, etc.)
6. Butter roll.
7. Dip both sides of the medium rare steak into sauce mixture.
8. Place between roll.
9. Cut in half.
10. Transfer to warm dinner plate.
11. Serve with garnish of 4 tomatoes, 4 gherkins and watercress in butter lettuce cup. French fries are usually added.

    This is a different steak sandwich. Basically it is made as any other steak sandwich.

steak sandwich. Steak sandwiches can be made at every quality and price level, depending on the size and cut of meat used. Least expensive is the ground meat patty or hamburger. Next in order are the tenderized rump steak, the cubed steak, the club steak, top sirloin, sirloin, and tenderloin steak. A steak larger than 6 ounces would be difficult to eat in a sandwich. Steaks, like burger, should be cooked to the order, rare, medium or well. The finishing of a steak sandwich is the same as any other sandwich.

The steak or bookmaker sandwich is made in various price ranges, depending on the meat cut and portion size. As a late evening snack it is ideal. It is also a lunch favourite of men who prefer to eat at the bar.

Experimental Recipe 27.

Tandoori Chicken Sandwich

Ingredients

1.	White bread	:	8 slices
2.	Cooked *tandoori* chicken boneless	:	1 cup
3.	Onion, slice	:	1 No.
4.	Coriander leaves	:	1/2 cup
5.	Green chillies, chopped finely	:	3 No.
6.	Salt	:	As per taste
7.	Mayonnaise	:	1/4 cup
8.	Tomato ketchup	:	1/4 cup
9.	Butter	:	As required.

Method

1. Prepare all required ingredient
2. Mix all the ingredients except bread and butter well
3. Spread the mixture evenly on top of one bread slice
4. Cover it with one bread slice
5. Repeat the same with all breads.
6. Serve with Cole slaw.

THE DELICATESSEN SANDWICH

The word 'delicatessen' is from the German language. It means something fine to eat. A delicatessen shop is a gourmet shop and sandwich restaurant in one. It has gourmet food items for sale. Counter-assembled fine foods may also be eaten here. Some of the delicatessen items used as sandwich fillings, appetizers, or horse d'oeuvres are :

1. Cold cuts

(a) Italian salami
(b) Danish salami
(c) Liverwurst
(d) Galantina
(e) Westphalian ham
(f) Corned Beef
(g) Cooked salami
(h) Kosher salami

Experimental Recipe 28.

The Saratoga

Ingredients

1. Sesame seed hamburger buns : 6
2. Cubed steak : 6 (4 ounces)
3. Diced onions : 2 cups
4. French type prepared mustard
5. Butter or oil : ½ cup
6. Tomato halves, seed removed : 6
7. Dill pickle sticks : 12
8. Canned or fresh sauerkraut : ¾ cup
9. Watercress : ½ bunch
10. Ripe olives : 3 pitted

Method

1. Prepare all required Ingredients
2. Arrange sauerkraut on top of salted and peppered tomato halves; decorate with ½ ripe olive.
3. Divide cleaned watercress into 6 bouquets and place on 6 plates large enough to hold the sandwich and garnish.
4. Place stuffed tomato halves over the watercress stems on plate. Garnish with pickle stick and keep refrigerated until needed.
5. Saute onions to brown. Keep them warm.
6. Dip inside of sesame bun into butter. Place it on hot griddle and toast it.
7. At the same time, salt and pepper steaks. Fry them to desired doneness.
8. Spread mustard on the toasted buns. Pace one steak each on bottom part.
9. Divide fried onions on top of steaks.
10. Cover with mustard-spread top bun. Cut sandwich in half.
11. Serve on garnished plate immediately.

(i) Met wurst
(j) Head cheese
(k) Virginia ham
(l) Smoked congue
(m) German salami
(n) Beef salami
(o) Mortedella
(p) Parma ham
(q) Bundnerfleish
(r) Ham
(s) Hungarian salami
(t) Summer sausage
(u) Bologna
(v) Prosciutto
(w) Pastrami
(x) Bacon
(y) Pork.

2. **Cheeses, vegetable preserves**
   - (a) All pickled cucumber varieties
   - (b) Artichokes
   - (c) Sauerkraut
   - (d) Asparagus
   - (e) Melon
   - (f) Chilis
   - (g) mixed pickles
   - (j) olives
   - (h) Kumquats
   - (k) Beans
   - (i) Peppers
   - (l) Tomatoes
3. **Caviar and canned fish**
   - (a) Tuna
   - (b) Kippers
   - (c) Salmon
   - (d) Matjes
   - (e) Oysters
   - (f) Mackerels
   - (g) Sardines
   - (h) Anchovies.

All marinated fish in barrels or jars, herrings (all varieties : bismarck, rollmops, cream, tomato), eels, smoked fish : salmon, sturgeon, eel, herring, mackerel, cod, oysters, tuna, carp, white fish and many more.

A large assortment of breads, condiments, and spreads are also found in a delicatessen shop.

Delicatessen sandwiches are made in a delicatessen shop. They may also be sandwiches filled with the food, the delicatessen shop specializes in. Delicatessen sandwiches are a little more expensive than those from a coffe shop. They have a better amount and quality of filling than the average sandwich. Delicatessen shops are most often ethnic oriented, serving German, Italian, Jewish, Hungarian, Armenian, Greek or other specialities.

THE HOFBRAU SANDWICH

Hafbraus are types of restaurants serving limited food in a distinct way. Basically they are a type of cafeteria with a selected menu. Hofbraus feature huge cuts of meat, such as steamship rounds of beef, baked hams, roast turkeys and corned beef. All these meats are kept warm during the time the hofbrau stays open. The hofbrau carvers stand behind the food on steam table counters. They are ready to make sandwiches as ordered. The customers in front of them choose the meats they like, select the bread and pick up the orders just as in a regular cafeteria.

This service is popular because the customer can see what sandwich he will get. If the ham looks too fat or the beef too rare, he does not need to order it. The fresh cut from the big roast is psychologically appealing, since the quality appeals to the eye and there is no dealing with a middle man or server. The customer can tell the cook directly what he wants to eat.

The hofbrau sandwich in itself is rather simple. It has the fresh cut meat on a split roll of bread of choice, with self-service condiments. Most hofbraus serve their few main dishes with as many side dishes as they can produce. They try to present as large a variety as possible. To cook the food, cooks and a chef work in a kitchen in the back. The carver deals with the customer.

QUESTIONS AND DISCUSSIONS

Fill in the Blanks

Q.1. Read and complete the following statements:

(a) A salad of apples, celery, walnuts and myonnaise is called ....

(b) Cooked, peeled potatoes left refrigerated to long make potato salad taste....................

(c) Preparing cooked salad is the work of the ....

(d) American fruit salds are often served with ....

(e) French vegetable salad is commonly used for ....

(f) Cooked salads are held together with ....

(g) Salad vegetables are cooked whole, in order not to lose ....

(h) Grade-mangers have the skill of a ....

(i) Club Sandwiches are filled with bacon, tamaotes, lettuce, may on naise and ....

[**Ans.**: (a) chiken waldorf salad; (b) old potato salad; (c) Pantry cook/gardmager; (d) cottage cheese; (e) buffet work; (f) salad dressing; (g) flavour; (h) Master Chef; (i) Chicken.]

Q.2. Read and complete the following statements:

(a) Homemade French dressings, after standing a while, have to be ....

(b) Salads are tossed just before serving in order to assure ....

(c) Specialty salad portions are usually for ....

(d) Salads and salad utensils must be visible ....

(e) Without dressing, lettuce is not ....

(f) Mayonnaise is not only a sauce-dressing, but also a ....

(g) Belgian Endive is a salad which is very ....

(h) Good salad dressings should always be ....

(i) For Boston or Butter Lettuce the dressing must be ....

[**Ans.**: (a) reblended; (b) quality; (c) a la carte dishes; (d) to guests; (e) tasty; (f) sandwich spread; (g) dedicate and expensive; (h) Cold sauces based on oil or fat as the thickner; (i) light.]

Multiple Choice Type

Q.3. Read each questions carefully and select the best answer:

(i) Fruit salads served as a luncheon dish are popular with:

(a) Sugar and lemon juice (b) French dressing and whipped cream

(c) Cottage cheese and sour cream (d) Bourbon and Mousseline dressing.

(ii) Italian Frascatti Salad has the ingredients cut into:

(a) Small dice (b) Large cubes

(c) Short julienne (d) Thine slices.

(iii) When cooked potatoes are mixed into the salad, it is important to add the mayonnaise:

(a) In one lot. (b) Mixed with the seasoning.

(c) Before the seasoning. (d) After the seasoning.

(iv) Tuna fish, for large quantities of salad, should be chopped with the

(a) Meat grinder (b) Chef's knife

(c) Osterizer (d) Fish knife.

(v) Sandwiches, when ordered toasted, should be spread with

(a) Butter (b) Mayonnaise

(c) Peanut butter (d) Cream cheese.

(vi) Delicatessen stores are likely to make more interesting sandwiches than coffee shops because they:

(a) Employ grade-mangers to make sandwiches.

(b) Have a larger assortment of fillings

(c) Use a special spread on the bread.

(d) Take more time to make them.

(vii) Potato salad will be at its best when the potatoes are cooked:

(a) The day before (b) Without peel

(c) About 3 hours before mixing (d) After having been peeled and cut.

(viii) According to culinary history, the first sandwich made was:

(a) The Club Sandwich (b) The Hofbrau Sandwich

(c) The Steak sandwich (d) Hamburger.

(ix) A Chiken Waldorf Salad is dressed with:

(a) French dressing (b) Sour cream.

(c) Waldorf dressing (d) Mayonnaise.

(x) Salad and sandwich garnishes are intended to:

(a) Make the order appear larger. (b) Supplement taste and boost sales

(c) Repeat and show the filling (d) Justify a higher price.

[**Ans.:** (i) (c); (ii) (c); (iii) (d); (iv) (a); (v) (b);
(vi) (a); (vii) (c); (viii) (c); (ix) (d); (x) (b)]

Q.4. Read each question carefully and select the *best* answer :-

(i) The dressing of the Salad Maximilian has a base of

(a) Sour cream (b) Mayonnaise

(c) Olive oil (d) Salad oil.

(ii) Salad dressing may be composed of many different ingredients, but must always contain

(a) Fats (b) Proteins

(c) Starch (d) Sugar.

(iii) The French people, like the Americans, are great salad eaters. The French serve salad:

(a) As an appetizer (b) After the soup

(c) With the main course (d) After the main course.

(iv) A good Roquefort cheese dressing can be made with
(a) Roquefort and buttermilk. (b) Roquefort and French dressing
(c) Blue cheese and sour cream (d) Blue Cheese and mayonnaise.

(v) A maynnaise is an emulsion where the egg yolks absorb oil
(a) Unlimited (b) Gradually
(c) Rapidly (d) Not at all.

(vi) For plain French dressing, the oil to vinegar ratio is :—
(a) 1 part oil to 3 parts vinegar (b) 2 parts oil to 2 parts vinegar
(c) 3 parts oil to 1 part vinegar (d) 8 parts oil to 1 part vinegar.

(vii) Mayonnaise, a cold, basic sauce contains mostly
(a) Vinegar (b) Cornstarch
(c) Oil (d) Egg yolk.

(viii) For making mayonnaise by hand, it is essential to have a
(a) Hand beater (b) Stainless whip
(c) Wooden fork (d) Rubber spatual.

(ix) For the Tomato Watercress Salad, a la carte, the tomatoes should be
(a) Large (b) Soft
(c) Peeled (d) Marinated.

(x) The lettuce base of the Green Goddess Salad is
(a) Iceberg (b) Butter Lettuce
(c) Endive (d) Romaine.

[**Ans.:** (i) (a); (ii) (a); (iii) (d); (iv) (b); (v) (b);
(vi) (c); (vii) (d); (viii) (a); (ix) (c); (x) (d)]

Matching Type

Q.5. Match the name of the preparation in Table 'A' with the ingredients listed in Table 'B'

Table 'A'	*Table 'B'*
(a) Sauce Tartare	(i) Mayonnaise, catsup, bell pepper, pimentos, chillis
(b) Sauce Remoulade	(ii) Oil, vinegar, cream requefort
(c) Sauce Suedoise	(iii) Oil vinegar, herbs, beets
(d) Sauce Aurore	(iv) Mayonnaise, capers pickles, mustard, onions,
(e) Sauce Ravigotte	(v) Parsley
(f) Chiffonade Dressing	(vi) Mayonnaise, tomato chutney, lemon
(g) Russian Dressing	(vii) Mayonnaise, apple sauce, horseradish, lemon
(h) Roquefort Dressing	(viii) Mayonnasie, sour cream, dry and prepared mustards, papper
(i) Thousand Island Dressing	(ix) Mayonnaise, egg whites, anchovies, shallots, parsley
(j) Mustard Dressing	(x) Mayonnaise, capers, mustard, pickles, onions parsley, catsup, caviar

[Ans.: (a) (iv); (b) (v); (c) (vii); (d) (vi); (e) (ix);
(f) (iii); (g) (x); (h) (ii); (i) (i); (j) (viii)]

Short Answer Type

Q.6. 'Salads reflect a restaurant's "Gourmet" image. Explain.
Q.7. How do food cost and quality of dressings compare with convenience?
Q.8. Is there a difference between Roquefort and Blue Cheese?
Q.9. Analyze buffet work. How difficult is it?
Q.10. Match foods for salad combinations.
Q.11. Why do fruit salads have such wide acceptance?
Q.12. Is there a place for an inexpensive, good sandwich varietion?
Q.13. What are some of the new steak sandwich variations?
Q.14. How can the coffee shop sandwich image be improved?
Q.15. Define the following:
(a) Appetizing (b) Emulsion
(c) Oxidation (d) Wedge
(e) Mousseline.
Q.16. Define the following:
(a) Delicatessen (b) Hofbrau
(c) Sandwich (d) Garde-manger.

Assignments/Activity Type

Q.17. Review–Cleaning of Romaine Lettuce.
Q.18. Identify different kinds of lettuce.
Q.19. Make a plain French dressing with whip and bowl.
Q.20. Make onion dressing with the blender.
Q.21. Make mayonnaise with the mixer.
Q.22. Prepare romaine with Roquefort dressing.
Q.23. Set up for a Green Goddess Salad.
Q.24. Make about 2½ pounds of Potato Salad.
Q.25. Compute the food needed for 10 pounds of Italian Frascatti Salad.
Q.26. Prepare about 2 pounds of Frascatti Salad.
Q.27. Make, serve and garnish 2 orders of plain Waldorf Salad.
Q.28. Make and set up a melon ball cocktail.
Q.29. Make a three docker with fried eggs, bacon and tomatoes.
Q.30. Prepare the Saratoga Sandwich step-by-step from a recipe.
Q.31. Visit a hofbrau and watch a carver's performance.

3.8

Cooking of Vegetables

CHAPTER OBJECTIVES

After studying this lesson you should be able :

- To prepare and demonstrate the preparation procedure of Artichoke Antipasto;
- To cook and demonstrate the method of preparation of Asparagus princess;
- To practice and make Carrots Vichy;
- To demonstrate the procedure of Saute Cabbage a la Mode;
- To Prepare and demonstrate the preparation of Cauliflower a la Polonaise, and
- To make and demonstrate the method of preparation of a Mushroom Dexulles.

In the past it was thought that vegetables had to be cooked for a long time to become digestible. Newer studies have shown that this is not true. For cooking of vegetabls same principles are applied as in the cooking of all other foods. Any of the methods are chosen for the same reasons as in meat and fish cookery. Cooking has progressed with technology and medical knowledge. Now, old habits must be put aside of newer cooking methods. Since the objective of cookery is to provide tasty sustenance, the nutritional values of vegetables must be used as much as possible. Better taste is a welcome by-product of the progressive way of cooking. Most preparations are interchangeable, just as in meat cookery. Most vegetables have the same carbohydrate and water content. For example, the preparation of carrots vichy is excellent for parsnisps, celeriac, kohlrabi, and white radishes. Cabbage is very versatile and tasty good in any flavour combinations if no over-scooking occurs. Nearly all vegetables, except the watery ones like tomatoes and eggplant, can be creamed. Student trainees who understand these principles of the basic similarity of cookery will have no difficulty in creating the most interesting, nutritious, and tastey vegetable combinations.

For vegetables cookery like other cookery, vitamin retention must be the cook's main objective. If nutrients are saved, the taste of vegetables will be better, since minerals and flavour salts in vegetables are identical. Vegetables contain mostly Vitamin C and carotene, which helps the body to convert its own Vitamin. Vitamin C, being water soluble and

(a) Skillet (b)

affected by the heat, is destroyed easily during the cooking process. Time controlled pressure, steaming, sauteing, and baking are better vegetable preparation methods than boiling in water. All vegetables are tender enough to be prepared in one of the preferred ways.

In most of the countries, boiling vegetables in water is a popular preparation. Students should realize that vegetable cookery has a long way to go before the vegetables served to the public in most eating establishments have the standard of quality and nutritional value they should have.

The preservation of food values is a most important cooking objective. Long heat exposure destroys most of the vitamins, minerals, and other foods.

Progressive vegetable cookery means the preserving of the vegetable nutrients. For nutrietious, tasty vegetables, the cooking must be done just before serving. They must have the shortest possible cooking time in order to become just tender.

There are two methods which have been proved best for the cooking of vegetables. One is exact time-controlled pressure steaming with additional sauteing. The other is plain sauteing started from the raw stage.

The baking of vegetables is very good from the nutritional point, but most vegetables can not be baked very successfully. Deep frying, a fast process which is quite tasty when done right, adds too many calories to the restaurant diet. Boiling, in which the food is separated from the cooking water after it has been cooked, is the least suitable process. In this process, most nutrients are leached out of the vegetables, dissolve in the cooking water, and the boiled vegetables are left much less nutritious.

Vegetable cookery must be seen and practiced in the same way as meat cookery. For example, cut-up cauliflower can be covered with a minimum of boiling, salted water, and simmered to near doneness. Then by adding a little butter roux to the cooking liquid (the cauliflower water), it will become a white sauce. The dish is then served, just like a veal blanquette. But the same amount of raw cauliflower should *not* be boiled in a large pot of water until tender, then drained, with the vegetables being rinsed in cold water to prevent overcooking. The vegetable would then have to be heated when needed, and finished for serving. It is much better to pressure steam cook fresh cauliflower (2-3 minutes) and serve immediately with brown butter sauce Hollandaise, or in some other conventional way. For keeping the most taste and food value at the same time, the freshly washed and cut-up vegetable should be sauteed with butter in a covered skillet. A little stock or water is added for about five minutes. This changes the sauteing into stewing. Other vegetables, such as mushrooms, contain so much water of their own that strict sauteing without any additional liquid is enough to produce a tasty and nutritious dish.

Vitamins

Vitamins are chemical compounds which are necessary to nutirtion. They occur in the normal diet in very small amounts, and are most neccessay for good health. Theye also help in the use of other healthful food factors.

Table 3.8A. Vitamins in Vegetables

Vitamin 'A'
Vitamin A is needed for growth, fucntioning of the body's internal and external surfaces, and for vision in dim light. It also aids the body in resisting. infection. Carotene, a yellow pigment substance formed in green plants, can be changed into Vitamin A within the body. The green colouring matter of plants covers it to make it invisible, but it is found in leafy vegetables. Because of this carotene content, many green leafy and yellow vegetables are known as sources of Vitamin A. Some of the best sources of Vitamin A are kale, chard, collards, broccoli, spinch, green lettuce, turnip tops, green peas, green beans, yellow squash, carrots, sweet potatoes, and tomatoes.
Vitamin 'B'
Vitamins, B_1, B_2, and B_3 are also found in vgegetables, but not in large enough amounts.
Vitamin 'C'
The greatest concern of chefs is ascorbic acid of Vitamin C. It is found in most fresh vegetabls and fruits. Members of the cabbage family have a very high C content. It oxidizes easily, is destroyed through cooking, and is water soluble. Even raw vegetables, soaked in cold water, will lose their Vitamin C value. The more water that is used for processing, the more vitamins are lost. Humans need Vitamin C in large quantities and constantly. Therefore, cooks must preserve it in cooked vegetables by using progressive cooking methods. They should try to add as many fresh raw fruits and vegetables as possible to regular menus.

Boiling

Boiling, or steaming, is the simplest and most widely used vegetable cooking method. To much unsalted, luckewarm water for cooking, followed by draining and cold rinsing causes loss of value. The use of soda bicarbonate to keep the green colour is another poor practice. Pressure steaming often results in overcooking since the chef is not able to look at the food while it is cooking. However, strict time-contolled pressure steam-cooking of vegetables, as they are needed, is the answer to quality vegetable cookery for hostpital tray lines and other institutions. *Time-controlled* means to use a timer and to remove the vegetables from the heat immediately after cooking. Shutting off the pressure automatically is not enough. The carry-over heat will do the damage. It also means that the same load and kind of vegetable must be cooked for the same time with same amount of heat each time, after, the cooking norms have been established by tests. It must be ralized that a pressuere steamer is a powerful heat source in which one or two minutes of overcooking or exposure to carry-over heat will completely destroy whatever food values were left in the vegetable.

Boiled Vegetables

Blanching

Ravioli in steam basket

Restaurant chefs do not like to use pressure steamers for green vegetables, since it is difficult to keep the fresh colour which is eye appealing. Cooks too often think only about the eye appeal of their vegetables. The loss of taste and nutrients through faulty cooking methods is covered up by adding herbs, spices, and sauces. On the other hand,

Experimental Recipe 29.

Aloo Jeera (Potato and Cumin)

Ingredients

1.	Potatoes	:	200 gm
2.	Oil	:	50 ml
3.	Cumin seeds	:	10 gm
4.	Ginger	:	20 gm
5.	Garlic	:	30 gm
6.	Turmeric	:	10 gm
7.	Red chilli power	:	20 gm
8.	Tomatoes	:	100 gm
9.	*Garam masala*	:	05 gm
10.	Coriander powder	:	20 gm
11.	Coriander leaves	:	10 gm
12.	Salt	:	To taste.

Method

1. Prepare all required ingredients
2. Boil potatoes and dice them.
3. Chop onions, garlic, ginger, coriander and the tomatoes.
4. Heat oil and saute cumin seeds until they crackle.
5. Add garlic and ginger and saute until golden.
6. Stir in chopped ginger and add the potatoes.
7. Sprinkle turmeric and chilli powder and stir.
8. Add tomatoes and simmer for about 5 minutes.

institutional cooks under the supervsion of dieticians are often concerned only about keeping vitamin values, but care very little for eye appeal and taste. In this unsatisfying vacuum of vegetable cookery, the consumer is definitely shortchanged.

Boiling of vegetables in water

1. Clean, cut and wash vegetables thoroughly.
2. Bring as much salted water to a boild as needed to cover the vegetables.
3. Make sure water is salted enough to prevent the leaching out, or washing away, of the vegetable's natural minerals.
4. When water boils vigourously, put vegetables in, then bring water to boiling point again, fast, then turn down heat and let simmer until vegetables are crunchy.

Experimental Recipe 30.
Aloo Sabji

Ingredients

1.	Chopped ginger	:	1/2 tsp
2.	Cumin	:	1/2 tsp
3.	Turmeric powder	:	1/2 tsp
4.	Red chilli powder	:	1/4 tsp
5.	Pepper powder	:	1/4 tsp
6.	Potatoes	:	450 gm.
7.	Green chillies	:	2 Nos.
8.	Tomato puree	:	1 tsp
9.	Coriander leaves	:	1 tsp
10.	Oil	:	4-5 tsp
11.	Salt	:	To taste.

Method

1. Prepare all required ingredients
2. Peel and cube the potatoes.
3. Heat oil in a deep-bottomed pan over medium flame, fry cumin seeds and ginger for 4-5 minutes. Stir frequently.
4. Reduce the heat to low, add turmeric powder, cumin powder, chillie and pepper powder. Stir well and fry for a minute.
5. Add the potatoes and green chilies. Stir and cook until the spices are blended completely. Stir in the tomato puree and salt.
6. Add the water and bring to a boil. Cover the pan and cook over medium to low heat for about 30 minutes till the potatoes are tender.
7. Remove from heat.
8. Stir in half the chopped coriander and sprinkle the remaining half on top.
9. Served with hot pooris.

5. Cooking time will vary for different vegetables. Cooking time will also vary for the *same* vegetables at different times of the year.
6. Cooking times may range from one minute for young peas or flat Italian beans to twenty minutes for late season Kentucky Wonder beans, cauliflower, carrots, etc.
7. Never cook vegetables longer than necessary. They should be cruchy.
8. Butter, season, or finish vegetables according to chef's ideas or recipes, and serve.
9. *Never* rinse freshly cooked vegetables with cold water. This washes away flavour and important vitamins and minerals.

Steaming of Frozen Vegetables

Frozen vegetables are food products of great convenience to the chef. They have repalced canned vegetables in most places where there is a deep freezer.

Before they are frozen and packed, the vegetables are cleaned, cut, and blanced. They need less labour and less cooking time than fresh vegetables. In general, they may be boiled or steamed the same way as fresh vegetables. Dietitians recommend cooking them while still frozen in order to retain full vitamin and mineral content. This is not always possible. When a 2½-pound block of vegetables is frozen solid, it must be pre-thawed and separated. If it is not, the outside will overcook while the inside will stay raw.

New time tables for cooking each kind of vegetable have to be established whenever a different brand is bought. To be sure of exact timing, a timer must be used. Overcooked vegetables are bad, both for eating and for dietetic values.

Pressure or live steam cooker models vary from maker to maker. The manufacturer's guidelines should be a starting point for the establishment for cooking times. It is also important to consider carry-over heat and steam table holding times when making these guidelines. Vegetabls that are also sauteed in a skillet can be salted and mixed in the skillet, but vegatables which are only steamed, then served plain or with a cover sauce, should be salted before they are steamed.

A pressure steamer is a machine. The quality of the vegetables cooked in any machine depends entirely on the intelligence and effectiveness of the cook who is standing behind it.

For the trainee who wants to become an excellent vegetable cook and chef, these guidelines are of the greatest importance. Nutrients, eye appeal, and taste in vegetables are kept by strictly time-controlled pressure steaming to the order, then sauteing in the skillet with butter and seasoning. It is even better to cut or slice vegetables into certain shapes and saute or short-stew them in the skillet to the order. Coated deep frying may be used if the quality principles are observed. Reader must realize that taste and nutrients are both kept or both lost.

SPECIFIC PREPARATIONS

Boiling and steaming procedure of various vegetable preparations are give below:

Artichokes

American Globe Artichokes are thistle-like plants, grown mostly in California, near Castroville. They are fresh or frozen. For luzury cookery, the de-leafed artichoke bottom, or sometimes the whole small artichoke (also called heart) is used.

Cleaning artichokes is the difficult part of the cooking. The leaves are tough and have thorns. Artichokes discolour easily when cut; non-oxidizing bowls or casseroles are a must.

After the inedible leaves are removed, the stem is trimmed and peeled. Now the center or the hairy choke must be removed. A stainless melon ball cutter or a special artichoke scraper can be used. The artichokes are then washed in slightly acid (lemon, ascorbic acid or vinegar) water.

Boiling in the slightly acid and salted water is done by inspection. It may take from 5 to 20 minutes, depending on the size and cleaning of the artichokes. Whether lemon or vinegar is used will also affect the time.

Artichokes may be eaten hot, with brown butter or Hollandaise Sauce. They may be cooled and served in any form as a salad. Luxury cuisine uses bottoms because they can be eaten with knife and fork. These bottoms are sometimes filled with another vegetable, meat, or seafood.

Different region ofter as a hot or cold appetizer, and less often as a vegetable to go with a main dish.

Clean An Artichoke-Step by Step Photos

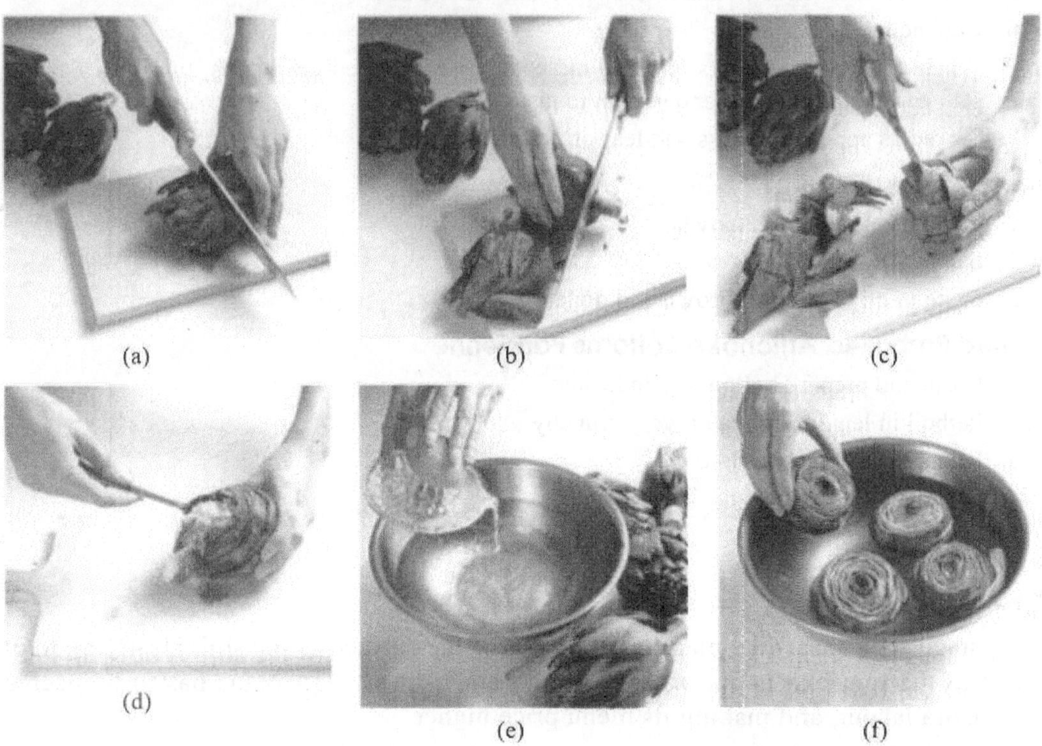

(a) (b) (c)

(d) (e) (f)

Artichoke Antipasto

Experiment Recepe 31.

Artichoke Antipasto

Ingredients

This is a cold Italian vegetable appetizer. It must be considered a regional dish. It can be made in many different varieties. It is a vegetable stew, coverd with only a little sauce, and well spiced to individual taste of the cook.

Small artichoke hearts are cleaned as usual, and weighed. Five vegetables are added. Each of these weighs 20 percent of the total artichoke weight. The vegetables used are pearl onions, mushrooms, celery, green peas, and cauliflower, in place of these could be asparagus, broccoli, zucchini, eggplant, carrots, or plain, cut-up onions. Also needed are olive oil, garlic oregano, and tomato catsup or tomato puree. All vegetables have to be cut to the same size.

Method

1. Prepare all required ingredients.
2. Heat olive oil, and braise all vegetables together. (start with onions and artichokes. Add softest ones last.)
3. Add salt and spices and garlic.
4. Add tomato puree or catsup and bring to a full boil.
5. If vegetable is tender, but still crunchy, take off the fire.
6. Cool completely.
7. When cold, stir in capers, pickled olives, coarse chopped anchovies, tuna fish flakes, etc., additional olive oil and season to taste.
8. Served as appetizer on a salad leaf on a small plate.

Fried Baby Artichokes

1. Clean as usual, cut in halves.
2. Salt and flour well.
3. Saute in olive oil until brown and done.

Refried Parboiled Artichoke Bottoms Parisienne

1. Clean and prepare bottoms as indicated.
2. Parboil in lemon salt water, very crunchy.
3. Drain, dust well with flour.
4. Dip into well beaten egg.
5. Deep fry in olive oil.

Asparagus

Asparagus is a spear-like plant growing below the surface of the soil. Nearly up to 30 percent of the root end is discarded as tough and stringy. Asparagus has to be peeled, adding extra labour, and making its menu price higher.

Peeling is done by laying each spear on a table and holding the strem with one hand while using a vegetable peeler in even,and uniform strokes. The peeling starts about one inch below the top and goes down the stem to the point where the spear is held. Then the unpeeled asparagus end is broken off and thrown away. The next step is to soak and wash the peeled spears thoroughly, taking care that all the sand which is often in some of the fine leaves on the asparagus tip is removed.

The asparagus is now ready to be boiled or sauteed. One of the fine ways of serving it is as plain boiled asparagus spears with brown butter, or a Sauce hollandase. It may also be served cold, with mayonnhaise, "Mousseline Sauce" or a good French dressing. These preparations are served as vegetable courses, not as side dishes.

After its cleaning and washing, asparagus can be cut into one-inch long sticks and sauteed in a pan for a few minutes until done. Asparagus must never be overcooked. Like spaghetti, it should always be cruchy "al dente", whether it is hot or cold, sauteed or boiled.

Asparagus tips may be used to garnish many sauces, meat precparations, or even other vegetables.

Beans

Fresh green beans can be boild, steamed, sauteed, or stewed. There are many bean varieties which each need a different cooking time to be tenderized.

Experiment Recipe 32.

Asparagurs Princess 55 for Four

Ingredients

1. Peeled, washed asparagus (fresh, raw)	:	2 pounds
2. Fronzen green peas	:	About 4 ounces
3. Butter	:	2 ounces
4. Ladle of veloute sauce	:	2 ounces
5. Salt	:	To taste
6. Sugar	:	As required.
7. Chicken stock	:	About 2 ounces.

Method

1. Prepare all required ingredients.
2. Wash and clean asparagus, and green peas.
3. Cut a sparagus oriental style (diagonally).
4. Melt butter in skillet, add asparagus, salt and a little sugar.
5. Saute on hot fire 1-2 minutes.
6. Moisten the bottom of the skillet with chicken stock, then cover.
7. Reduce heat and simmer one or two more minutes.
8. Add green peas, flip and mix, replace cover.
9. Wait one more minute, remove cover, add sauce, flip and mix.
10. If necessary, dilute with more chicken stock.
11. Serve.

Asparagurs Princess 55 for Four

A saute dish can be made within 5 minutes. This is an excellent preparation served as an a la carte vegetable in luxury resaurants. This vegetable should not be saucy, but barely held together with some thin, light sauce. (Ref. Experimental Recipe 32)

Flat Italian Beans

These beans need the least cooking time. If sauteed in ther skillet without preboiling, they may need only two to three minutes. In a pressure steamer at fifteen pounds of pressure (250°F.), thirty to forty seconds is enough. If boiled in water, bringing them up to the reboiling point usually cooks them. Flat Italian beans are never "French" or Julienne cut. They are left whole or in halves. They taste best with brown butter only.

Blue Lake Beans

These beans are round and fleshy, of excellent taste, but have a slightly longer cooking time than the flat Italians. They are prepared whole or only cut in half.

Kentucky Wonder Beans

These are most often used is the Kentucky Wonder bean. This is a large meaty bean, which must be destringed before cutting. It can be french or plain cut. It has a longer cooking time than the Blue Lakes.

Lima Beans

Fresh or frozen, lima beans are better pre-cooked in moisture, then sauteed in butter and seasoned by choice.

Experimental Recipe 33.

Preparation a la Polonaise

Method

"A la Polonaise" is the name of a preparation technique for various vegetables, first steamed or boiled, then served with the following covering:

1. One weight part of fine bread crumbs, sifted, fried in an equal weight part of butter, like a roux, to a golden brown.
2. This bread crumb-butter is kept hot and spooned over the freshly cooked vegetables before they are served.
3. The fried bread crumbs on the vegetable are topped with a mixture of chopped hard boiled eggs and parsley.
4. Egg yolk, egg white and parsley can be kept separate and used in a colour pattern for better eye appeal.
5. The vegetables most often served a la Polonaise are cauliflower, asparagus, broccoli, brussels sprouts, wax beans, and string beans.

This preparation can be served as a side dish or as a separate vegetable appetizer.

Red Beets

Red beets are boiled first, then sauteed plain, or served sweet-sour in a little cornstarch-thickened sauce of their own juice. To maintain the red colour they must be boiled, unpeeled and uncut. This process prevents the leaching out of the juice. The salted cooking water should also be made a little acid, especially in hard water areas.

Broccoli

Broccoli is handled like cauliflower, but may have to be peeled, like asparagus.

Brussels Sprouts

Brussels Sprouts look like small cabbage heads. Outer leaves and stems are removed before they are steamed or boiled, then sauteed in butter or served a la "Polonaise"in Exerpimental Recipe 33. The Polonaise preparation style is listed below :

CABBAGE

Curly Cabbage

Also called Savoy Cabbage it tastes best stewed with raw grated potatoes, garlic, pepper, and beef stock. It should be *short*, which means it should have only a little sauce to hold it together.

Experimental Recipe 34

Cabbage Sauteed a la Mode

Ingredients

1. Large, cubed, cleaned cabbage	:	1/3 pound
2. Suitable saute fat (olive oil, oil, butter, etc.)	:	1 ounce
3. Salt, pepper, sugar for seasoning	:	As required
4. Choice of herbs	:	thyme, basil, marjoram, dill, oregono
5. Other additional choices; onions, garlic, tomato paste, shallots, sour cream.		

Method

1. Prepare all required ingredients.
2. A large enough saute pan, with cover, is heated with the chosen fat.
3. If onion or garlic is used, it is sauteed first.
4. The cabbage is added to the pan, seasoned by choice, and the pan is covered.
5. On medium high heat, the cabbage is sauteed for 2-3 minutes, then flipped.
6. It is covered for another minute of sauteing.
7. All other ingredients are added, and heat is increased, especially when sour cream or tomato puree is used.
8. Without the cover, pan is flip-fried until the liquid is reduced. Now it is tossed and served.

White Cabbage

When boiled for 30-40 minutes, white cabbage losses its vitamins. It also causes a smelly kitchen. Released sulphur is the cause of indigestion for many people. Boiling the same cabbage for only 3 to 5 minutes does not release sulphur, nor does it destroy the many vitamins in cabbage. Under-cooking of cabbage for many preparations is the answer, but the best solution is the saute method.The fastest, tastiest and most nutritious preparations of cabbage are made by the saute method step-by-step process for sauteed Cabbage a la Mode, as given in Experimental Recipes 34, 35 and 36.

Experiment Recipe 35.
Cabbage Sauteed a la Russe

Ingredients

1. White, cleaned and cubed cabbage : 3 pound
2. Dill weed : 1 teaspoon
3. Sour cream : 1/3 pint
4. Finely chopped onions : 2 tablespoons
5. Salt, dash of sugar, lemon jice : When needed
6. Pork fat or oil for sauteing : 2 ounces.

Method

1. Prepare all required ingredients.
2. Heat fat. Add onions. Saute for a few seonds.
3. Add cabbage and salt. Cover.
4. Saute or 2 to 3 minutes.
5. Add sour cream and dill (sugar and lemon juice as needed).
6. Uncover, increase heat, flip-fry until dish becomes fully mixed
7. Serve.

Experimental Recipe 36
Cabbage Saute California

Ingredients

1. White, cleaned and cubed cabbage : 3 pounds
2. Thyme : 2 teaspoons
3. Tomato puree : 1 cup
4. Finely chooped onions : 2 tablespoon
5. Olive oil : 2 as per table
6. Salt, pepper and sugar : To taste.

Method

1. Prepare all required ingredients
2. Heat the oil add onions and saute for a few seconds.
3. Add red cabbage, salt, sugar, and thyme. Cover.
4. Saute for several minutes, then add the tomato puree.
5. Uncover, increase heat and flip-fry until dish becomes fully mixed.
6. Taste, add pepper, and serve.

Red Cabbage

This is often prepared as Wine Cabbage or Bavarian Cabbage. Any of these preparations is a basic stew. The raw shredded cabbage is mixed with salt and kept under weight pressure for at least 20 minutes,. Then the water is squeezed from the softened cabbage by hand and thrown away. Then drained immediately to prevent change in colour and crispness of cabbage. Spices, such as cloves, allspice, or cinnamon may be added.

Carrots

Carrots are usually cut, preboiled or steamed, then pan sauteed or mixed with a veloute or bechamel sauce. They can be glazed with butter and sugar only. They can be made like beets with extra liquid and cornstarch to produce a shiny coat. One of the best preparations is Carrots Vichy as shown in Experimental Recipe 37.

The same preparation can be used for the cooking of parsnips, broccoli, asparagus, and many other vegetables. The sugar may be omitted.

Experimental Recipe 37.

Carrot Vichy

Ingredients

1. Raw carrots : 2 pounds
2. Butter or margarine : 3 ounces
3. Sugar : 3-4 tablespoons
4. Salt : 1/4 teaspoon
5. Skillet : 1 ten-inch
6. Cover : 1 ten-inch.

Method

1. Prepare all required ingredients.
2. Peel and wash carrots.
3. Slice cross wise into uniform wheels, approximately 3/32 inch thick.
4. Heat butter in ten-inch skillet.
5. Add carrots, sugar, and salt.
6. Put a tight-fitting cover on the skillet.
7. Keep on a low-medium heat for about 4 minutes.
8. Remove cover and mix carrots well.
9. Continue to stew for 2 minutes more.
10. Check for doneness. and taste. If carrots are too soupy, remove cover and leave them on a hot fire for the remainder of the time.
11. If carrots are too crunchy, continue cooking 2-3 more minutes.
12. When done, remove from stove and serve.

Cauliflower

Cauliflower is usually preboilded in salt and lemon water, then either sauteed in butter or served with Hollandaise or Cheese Sauce. It can also be creamed, mixed with other vegetables, or refried, either breaded or dipped in batter, as cauliflower fritters. Excellent and unusual is sauteed cauliflower mixed with raw eggs and some cream. For each pound of cauliflower, two ounces of butter, two eggs, and one-third cup of half and half cream are used. It is sauteed and finished like scrambled eggs in the skillet.

Celery

Celery needs only sauteing, but it can also be braised. Sometimes it is gratinated with cheese (a la Milanaise). Usually it is creamed, or served as a filler with mixed vegetables.

Chestnuts

Chestnuts must be peeled raw first. A cut is made against the fibers across the top. Small amounts of the chestnuts are placed in a 55°F. overn for a few minutes, until the shells pop open. They must be shelled immediately, while still hot. They are parboiled for a few minutes, and drained. Then they are finished by stewing with butter, salt, sugar, some of the boiling juice and some dry sherry wine.

Eggplant

This is an internationally well-known vegetable, it is know as Aubergines in French, Melanzani in Italian, and Eieirfruechte in German. It can be sauteed, deep fried or baked, but never boiled in water. One basic preparation is to peel, cut then stew with onions, garlic, tomatoes, etc. They may be left unpleeled, cut in half, scored around the rim and across the cut surface. Then bake in a hot oven at 475°F. for about 50 minutes. If seasoned from the beginning they can be served just this way. The flesh may be scraped out, chopped, mixed with other pre-cooked meat or vegetables, and put back into the peel for serving. They can be gratinated by sprinkinjg parmesan cheese over the refilled tops and browning them.

Bringles

How to cut eggplant in the slices?

When choosing eggplants, reach for the smallest ones you can find. Their flesh is usually more tender and less fibrous than the older, larger ones.

Round slices are the most basic cut. They're great for grilling, broiling, and traditional dishes like eggplant parmesan. Remember that eggplant loses moisture and shrinks when cooked. To compensate, cut the raw eggplant inot pieces about twice as large as you want the cooked pieces to be.

Cutting Bringles

Cheesy stuffed Aubergines

Lengthwise slices are good for grilling and layered dishes where you want the eggplant to have the most surface area. First stand the eggplant upright on its end and slice away a section of the peel. It gives the end slices more fleshy surface area to take on color and flavor when cooked.

Slice down the length of the eggplant to make slices as thick or thin as you like. You can slice away a section of skin on the other side of the eggplant when you're finished slicing.

Green Peas

Green peas or pea pods are also called sugar peas. These should only be sauteed in butter with salt and sugar. Boiling is not necessary at all.

Lentils

A lentil is a dried legume. It is a starch like dried beans. Lentils have a much shorter cooking time than bean. As a vegetable served often with game meat. The clean lentils are boild in a little beef stock with theyme, bay leaf, and salt, until tender. The stock should be completely reduced. Diced smoked bacon is sauteed to a golden brown and added, with its fat, to the lentils. The dish is seasoned with a jigger of red wine vinegar and some white pepper. It should be creamy without any extra starch.

Mushrooms

Mushrooms in skillet

One of the edible mushrooms, called *Chapignon,* is a domestic cultured vegetable. It has a place in culinary art.

Many wild mushrooms are also edible. Near each wild edible one, there also grows a poisonous one. They look very much alike. This makes eating wild mushroom dangerous; people all over the world have died from msushroom poisoning. Wild mushrooms are thought to be better tasting than cultured ones. In most European countries, they are sold in the markets. They are government inspected. The people who gather them know the difference between good and bad ones.

Since just one poisonous mushroom can kill a person, only cultured, safe mushrooms should handled. Fresh mushrooms have a fine flavour, smell, appearance, and consistency, After a few days, they lose these qualities repidly. In general, mushrooms are pre-cooked. They are not often put into a stew or preparation while still raw.

Experimental Recipe 38.

How to make and use Duxelles

Ingredients

1. Mushrooms : 2½ pounds
2. Onions : 1 pound
3. Tomato paste : 1 cup
4. Chopped parsley : 1 cup
5. Salt, Pepper, Garilic : As required
6. Olive oil : 1 cup.

Method

1. Prepare all required ingredients
2. Chop onions fine. Saute in oil 5-8 minutes.
3. Add finely chopped, cleaned mushrooms. Saute 5 minutes more.
4. Add garlic, tomato paste, salt and pepper. Saute 5 minutes more.
5. Add chopped parsley. Cover casserole. Stew 5 minutes more.
6. Take from the fire,-stir well. Cool off and use.

Uses of Duxelles

Duxelles, the mushroom paste, could also be used as a sauce :

Sauce Duxelles

An optional amount of duxelles is mixed into brown sauce, veloute sauce, or tomato sauce.

For Stuffing Mixes

1. Chooped, sauteed eggplant: ½ Duxelles and ½ .
2. Chopped, cooked ham: ½ Duxelles and ½ .
3. Chopped or ground leftover roast or cooked meat: ½ Duxelles and ½

These stuffings are used to fill refried pancakes, turnovers, meat rolls, other vegetabls, other vegetables, or combinations of them.

The most common use of Duxelles in vegetable cookery is for the stuffing of tomato halves, zucchini, cucumbers, summer squash, artichokes, and others. Grated parmesan cheese is then sprinkled over the top, and the dish is fast browned uinder the broiler.

For fancy meat preparations such as "Filet de Boeuf Wellington", veal chops or pork links in puff paste or pork tenderloins colbert, Duxelles is used as a flavouring spread on the dough before the meat is wrapped in it.

Steps in precooking mushrooms, cut or uncut :

1. The mushroom is wahsed well, but quickly, in a deep container of cold water which has been soured slightly with lemon juice, ascorbic acid, or vinegar. Deep water is necessary since the mushrooms are lighter than water and float to the top. Sand, earth, and dirt will sink to the bottom.
2. The floating mushrooms are lifted out the water, drained, and put into a frying pan already on stove, containing hot butter.
3. The pan is covered to preserve as much of the natural mushroom juice as poosible, and simmered from 3-10 minutes, according to the size of mushrooms. When taken from the heat, they are left in their own juice until needed. If handdled and stored properly under refrigeration, they should keep for a few days.

Duxelles

A stew of chopped mushrooms called "Duxelles" is an important part of French luxury cuisine. Duxelles has been adopted by cooks all over the countries. Dexelles is a vegetable paste made mainly from mushrooms and used to add to the flavour of other preparation. Its applications are many, not only in vegetable cookery, but also for meat and seafood preparations.For the step-by-step procedure of making Duxelles, see Ref Experimental Recipe 38.

*All the procedures for the handling of mushrooms are to be observed.

Breaded Deep-fried Mushrooms

Whole, fresh, raw mushroom buttons (stem cut off) are washed and immediately breaded. Then they are deep fried like prawns or scallops for 5-6 minutes. They are served immediately, as an appetizer or vegetabgle. For appetizers, serve with tartar sauce or mayonnaise.

Onions

Onions may be the oldest known vegetable. The ancient Egyptians worshipped anions as a God symbol. It is believed that the origin of onions is Asia. Today, Oriental Cookery uses onions even more than Western cuisine.

Onions are bulbs of the lily family and grow well in all moderate climates. Their vitamin, mineral and caloric content is about the same as other vegetables. They contain an element irritating to the eyes. When the outer dry skin of the onion is removed, this gas is freed.

Onions are used as a flavouring ingredient, more like garlic, herbs, or spices, and less as a vegetable dish. Sometimes menus have baked onions or onion salad. They may be used raw, sauteed (half fried), crisp fried (Viennese Fried), stewed, baked or boiled. Medical research shows that onions in any form are hard to digest. For ucler patients and "soft hospital diets" onions must be avoided completely. Raw onions in salads are some of the offenders causing heartburn, gas and indigestion. The experienced cook knows when to use them and when not to use them. They should be used sparingly, just as any other flavour ingredient. If a dish contains a lot of onions, it should be named accordingly to warn those who have to avoid them.

Following are same of the ways to reduce the eye irritation (tearing) caused by peeling of onions.

1. Onions may be cooled to bear freezing, 32°F., before they are peeled. The gas will remain liquid and escape only later when the temperature has risen again.
2. Use a draft which blows onion gases away from the peeling person. Ventilatiors are very helpful.
3. Onions may be peeled 2-3 days before being used. The gases will evaporate slowly and no irrtation of the eye will be caused when they are chopped or cut later. The use of modern plastic wraps makes it possble to store chopped or peeled onions under refrigeration for days without affecting other food in the refrigerator with penetrating smell.

Onions must always be cut with stainless steel knives. Carbon steel / ordinary knives will oxidize immediately on contact with onion juice. This causes a gray colour of the onion later, as well as a bad iron taste. The carbon knife itself turns black, becomes very smelly, and has to be cleaned thoroughly before it can be used again. This oxidation factor is very important, if a mechanical tool is used.

Onions are often used to top meats or vegetables as a garnish. French fried or breaded onion rings are popular in steak houses.

Romaine

Romaine is also known as green salad. The outer leaves may also be cleaned and and steamed or blanched. When they are chopped, they can be sauteed with onions, butter some white sauce, and green peas.

Spinach

Spinach is a green leafy vegetabgle with a slight mouth-constricting taste. It used to be thought of as highly nutritious for its vitamin and iron content. Newer research shows that this tartness comes from oxalic acid, which is poisionous in pure form or strong concentrations.

Spinach, freshly washed and still wet, can be sauteed in the usual manner. More often it is blanched in larger amounts of water. This reduces the oxalic acid content, but also causes a loss of vitamins. Then it is buttered or creamed. When spinach is creamed with milk, some of the acid is neutralized and the mouth-constricting tartness disappears.

Squash

Several varieties of both large and small squashes are available. Most popular of the large are banana and spaghetti squash. They can be baked or stewed. They need strong seasoning since they are vey bland.

1. Summer Squash: Summer squash is attractively small and round. It can be sauteed or staffed with meat, duxelles or some other filling, and then baked.

2. Italian Squash: Small and young Italian squash is popular under the name of "Zucchini" or "Zuchetti". It is served as a sauteed vegetable. Saute preparations are made with garlic, onions, tomatoes, and bell peppers. The cdabbage a la mode preparations (a la Russe & California) are excellent, also, used for zucchini. Zucchini Souffle Custard is an aunusual and practical zucchini dish.

Zucchini Souffle custard

This Italian squash dish is a practical and presentable vegetable creations, well suited as a local speciallty, its true origin is unknown, but is is probably a regional Northern Californaia dish, since all its ingredients are very popular in the San Francisco Bay area. (Ref. Experimental Recipe 39)

Experimental Recipe 39.

Zucchini Souffle Castard

Ingredients

1. Zucchini, approximately : 5 pounds
2. Large eggs : 8
3. Grated parmesan cheese : 3/4 cup
4. Bread crumbs : 1/2 cup
5. Cloves garlic, finely chopped : 2
6. Dill weed : 2 tablespoons
7. Salt : 1 teaspoon
8. Butter (for the baking dish) : 1 ounce
9. Olive oil : 3 ounces
10. White pepper : if desired.

Method

1. Prepare all required ingredients.
2. Slice squash like potato chips, saute in oil unitl half done.
3. Spread on a cookie sheet and cool completely; Drain off surplus liquid.
4. Break eggs, add spices and whip them well.
5. When squash has cooled off, add it to the eggs.
6. Add cheese and bread crumbs. Mix well with rubber spatula.
7. Taste of proper seasoning.
8. Fill into buttered crumb-coated and dill-dusted 2-quart Pyrex or similar flat baking dish.
9. Bake at 325°F. for about one hour.
10. Let set another 20 minutes before serving.

    This dish can be dept warm for hours if neccessary, and if left over could be easily rewarmed without loss of quality.

Tomatoes

Tomatoes are a very solt fruit-vegetable, used for sauces or as a flavour addition to stews. Tomato halves, cur lengthwise and seeds removed, can be grilled, sauteed, baked, or stuffed with another vegetable. Because of their bright colour and piquant taste, they are commonly used in cooking. Tomatoes should be considered a garnish rather than a filling vegetable.

Tomato Concasse

This tomato stew is used to fill egg omelettes or garnish some dishes, for its colour and taste. The ripe tomatoes are dipped into boiling water for 30 seconds, then into ice water. Then they are peeled halved, de-seeded, and uniformly cubed. When needed, they are quickly sauteed in butter or olive oil on high heat. They should just get hot. If cooked too long, they will turn into sauce. Tomato concasse is seasoned by choice with finely chopped onions, shallots, garlic, or herbs, salt, and sugar.

QUESTIONS AND DISCUSSIONS

Fill in the Blanks

Q.1. Read and complete the following statements

(a) For a la carte cooking one of the best vegetable preparation methods is ....

(b) Vitamin C is water soluble and therefore affected by ....

(c) Asparagus is peeled with a ....

(d) Deep rying of coated raw vegetables is acceptable but it adds to the diet many ....

(e) Vegetable cookery and meat cookery are ....

(f) Time-controlled pressure steam-cooking of vegetables is most common in ....

(g) Baking is a good vegetable cooking method but it can not be used for all ....

(h) Retention of nutrients is vegetable cooke's first ....

(i) Colour retention in cooked vegetables is important but more important is the retention of ....

(j) Taste salts react to cooking in a manner that is just like the reaction of .....

[**Ans.:** (a) sauteing;
(b) heat and distroyed quickly during cooking process;
(c) patato peeter; (d) calories;
(e) practical in similar manner; (f) cooking of vegetables;
(g) vegetables; (h) objective;
(i) vitamins (j) cooking.]

Multiple Choice Type

Q.2. Read each question carefully and select the *best* answer:

(i) A la Polonaise is a popular preparation for

(a) Asparagus (b) Carrots
(c) Parsnips (d) Mushrooms.

(ii) Tender green peas, fresh or frozen, can be sauteed and need a cooking time of :

(a) 2-5 minutes (b) 5-8 minutes

(c) 8-11 minutes (d) 11-14 minutes.

(iii) When preparing fresh jumbo asparagus for cooking, it has to be first:
(a) Blanched (b) Peeled
(c) Trimmed (d) Split.

(iv) Sliced carrots, sauteed with butter, salt, and sugar are called:
(a) Buttered Carrots (b) Glazed Carrots
(c) Vichy Carrots (d) Carrots.

(v) For clean, table-readyn artichokes, it is important that the artichoke:
(a) Has all leaves removed (b) Is boiled in lemon water
(c) Has the hairy inside removed (d) Is cooked very soft.

(vi) Tomato Caoncasse is a:
(a) Tomato sauce (b) Tomato salad
(c) Tomato stew (d) Tomato dressing.

(vii) Bavarian Red cabbage uses all the following ingredients *except* :
(a) Red wine (b) White cabbage
(c) Green apples (d) Yellow onions.

(viii) Cabbage Saute a la Russe is distinguished by the following ingredients:
(a) Tomato paste and thyme (b) Sugar and vinegar
(c) Sour creame and dil (d) Garlic and shallots.

(ix) Onions can be peeled with little eye irritation when the onions are :
(a) Fresh (b) Old
(c) Cold (d) Wet.

(x) Duxelles has, in addition to mushrooms, the following ingredients *except*:
(a) Parsley (b) Onions
(c) Tomato paste (d) Red wine

[**Ans.**: (i) (a); (ii) (a); (iii) (b); (iv) (c); (v) (b);
(vi) (c); (vii) (b); (viii) (c); (ix) (c); (x) (d)]

Short Answer Type

Q.3. Define:
(a) Vitamin (b) Nutrition
(c) al dente (d) Carotene
(e) Ascorbic acid

Q.4. Since taste is an accepted habit, should cooks try to influence the taste judgement of the general public ?

Q.5. Explain the vegetable cooking methods of different cuisines.

Q.6. What should cook know about vitamins and how to keep them ?

Assignments/Activity Type

Q.7. Make Artichoke Antipasto.

Q.8. Cook Asparagus Princess.

Q.9. Prepare Cavrot Vichy.

Q.10. Saute Cabbage a la Russe.

Q.11. Prepare a mushroom duxelles.

3.9

Starches: Potatoes and Pastas

CHAPTER OBJECTIVES

After studying this lesson you should be able :

- To explain the need for and role of starches in diets;
- To do the baking potatoes a la pushkin;
- To identify the shapes and names of different "pasta" varieties;
- To make and demonstrate the preparation of a Spinach Lasagne
- To write a detailed recipe for a Connelloni preparation; and
- To cook and demonstrate the preparation of a Risotto a la Milanese.

Starches make diet less expensive and more filling. Potatoes, flour in the form of paste and bread, rice, beans, and cornmeal are other staples of some ethinic groups and cultures. Potatoes can be adapted to any cooking process. Baking is the healthiest one, but deep frying is the more popular. Potatoes are usually found in some form on a menu. Paste, or pasta as it is called by the Italians, has been adopted by the rest of the world. Paste is a processed, dehydrated food made from starch and water. It has to be boiled in water to become adible. This is also true for all the other cereals and beans. All dried grains are reconstituted by the addition of water. Great care has to be taken to use only as much water as the grain can absorb. This avoids mushiness. or, worse, loss of nutrients. Orientals eat plain rice, just cooked in water. Other groups have improved their rice cookery with rosottos and paellas. Today's choice of starch is a wide one. In the past people had to be satisfied with those starches they were able to cultivate, due to the climatic conditions of thier countries.

In nutritional science, starch is a tasteless, odourless, white substance, classified as a complex carbohydrate. In culinary terms, starch, is a collective name for all foods that contain a large amount of flour. They may be processed foods in the form of paste, noodles, spaghetti or bread, made from wheat starch (flour). They may be the original vegetable from which starches are extracted. These vegetables are corn, rice, potatoes, beans, cereals and others.

Man could live by meat and vegetables alone, as he did in early times. Today's man could not afford it. This is why every country of the world has its own starchy staples. Starches are used in every country, but in different amounts. Mexico is well known for use of beans, Italy for pasta, China for rice, Indian subcontinent for rice and bread, Ireland for potatoes, and Germany for bread. The western countries use more wheat and potatoes. The Oriental world use more rice and beans. Most of the starches are inexpensive, nourishing, and filling.

POTATOES : A STAPLE FOOD

Potatoes are fruits from a tuber-bearing plant which grows in the dry soil of a cool climate. There are several hundred varieties of potatoes which differ in shape, skin colour and taste. Their nutritional value is very high and contain about 70 percent water. The rest is mostly starch, some sugar, minerals and vitamins, including Vitamin C.

In most of their cusine potatoes are used from the beginning to the end of a menu. They are found in soups, salads, casseroles, vegetable dishes, desserts and snacks. In many poor areas, potatoes may be the main dish of the day. Deep-fried potatoes are the most popular. Healthiest, from a dietetic viewpoint, is the baked potatoes, since all the minerals are preserved. Other nations prefer potatoes fixed in other ways, the Germans, for example, like them boiled.

Potatoes can be cooked in many different ways. Some of them are simple, but others are fancy. For the croquette potato, much manual skill and experience is needed.

The same preparations often have different names because they come from different countries, perhaps even at different times. In every potato eating country, fried potatoes are known as home fried potatoes, saute potatoes, or German fried potatoes. There are almost identical preparations, such as home fried potatoes and hashed browned potatoes. When just one different ingredient is added, the name changes again. Fried potatoes with onions are called Lyonnaise Potatoes.

Potato Preparation

The preparation of potatoes may be classified as under two main heading:

1. Processed before peeling.
   (a) In dry heat
   (b) In moist heat.
2. Processed after peeling :
   (a) In fat
   (b) In moist heat
   (c) Combined.

Potato Cooking Methods

The common basic cooking principles are used for cooking potatoes. The boiling of potatoes, peelded or unpeeled, may be done best in a pressure steamer. All rules of vegetable cookery are applicable. When steamed 'in the jacket' (unpeeled,), it is easier to peel them while they are still hot. When they cool off with the skin on, the peeling takes much more time and is wasteful. Raw peeled potatoes must be kept in cold water until used so that they will not change colour. Potatoes which are going to be sauteed after boiling should be a little undercooked. Every cooking methods can be used on potatoes since they are very versatile and adaptable. Steamed and baked potatoes cannot be rewarmed without loss in quality. When left over, they can be pan-fried successfully.

Table 3.9A. Classification of Potato Preparations

I. Raw Unpeeled Potatoes

Dry Heat

1. Baked
   - (a) Baked plain Potatoes
   - (b) Baked Pushkin Potatoes
   - (c) Baked Stuffed Potatoes
   - (d) Baked Stuffed Potatoes
   - (e) Mashed Potatoes

Moist Heat

2. Steamed, Peeled and Cooled
   - (a) Potato Salad, Cold or Warm
   - (b) Refried in Pan (Sauteed)
   - (c) Home fried Potatoes
   - (d) American Fried Potatoes
   - (e) German Fried Potatoes
   - (f) Hashed Browned Potatoes
   - (g) Lyonnaise Potatoes
3. Mixed with Cream or Source
   - (a) Creamed Potatoes
   - (b) Creamed Hashed Potatoes.
   - (c) Creamed Hasheld Potatoes
   - (d) Gratinated Potatoes
   - (e) Potaot-cheese Casserole
   - (f) Potato-ham Casserole
   - (g) Potato-egg Casserole

II. Raw Peeled Potatoes

In Fat

1. Sauteed
   - (1) Cottage Fried Potatoes
   - (2) Ana Potatoes
   - (3) Parisisenne Potatoes
   - (4) Noisette Potatoes
   - (5) Olivette Potatoes
   - (6) Chateau Potatoes

In Moisture

2. Steamed
   (1) Plain Steamed Potatoes
   (2) Pommes Vapeur
   (3) Buttered Potatoes
   (4) Parsley Potatoes
   (5) Dill Potatoes
   (6) Mashed Potatoes

Combination

3. Stewed
   (1) New Potatoes

Deep Fried

(1) Sticks
(2) Fries
(3) Crinkle Cuts
(4) Long Branches
(5) Cubes
(6) Parmentiers
(7) O'Briens
(8) Discs
(9) Chips
(10) Pommes Souffle

III. Mashed Potatoes

a. with Milk & Butter

(1) Mashed Potatoes
(2) Pommes a la Neige
(3) Puree Potatoes

b. With Egg Yolk & Butter

1. Duchess Pototoes
2. Croquette Potatoes
3. Croquete Berny (Alomnd Coated)

c. With Cream Puff & Paste

1. Dauphine Potatoes

d. Deep-fried, uncoated

Croquettes

Baked Potatoes

These are more popular in many countries specially due to the quality of the American Russet potatoes. Washed and scrubbed potatoes are scored with a form, to prevent them from exploding in the oven, and baked at 475°F. for 45 to 55 minutes according to size. They will taste excellent for the first 25 minutes after baking. They slowly become soggy. A good baked patato has a dry, fluffy texture. Plain baked potatoes are cut and split open before serving, and are eaten with butter or sour cream. Baked Potatoes a la Pushkin as given in Experimental Recipe 40 is a basic preparation for stuffed baked potatoes. Various combinations are possible. All are made by the same principle.

Experimental Recipe 40.

Baked Potatoes a la pushkin

Ingredients Little

1. Baking potatoes : 5 single No. 1s
2. Little : 0-12 ounces
3. Fresh butter : 1 cube (4 ounces).

Method

1. Prepare all the required ingredients
2. Wash and brush potatoes.
3. Pierce a few holes with a two-prong fork into the top of the skin
4. Oil the potatoes.
5. Bake in a pre-heated owven at 475°F. for 45 minutes.
6. Select the 4 best looking ones. Cut upper one-third of, length-wise.
7. Hollow them out with a spoon or melon ball cutter but leave enough potatoe so shell won't collapse.
8. If step 5th one was not needed, peel it, and add it to the scooped-out potatoe of the four others.
9. Press all the potatoe through a potatoe nicer.
10. Brown butter and pour over the riced fluffy pototoes.
11. Mix together very well. Salt if needed and refill the potato shells. Replace cover.
12. Reheat in oven for a few minutes and serve.

Boiled or Steamed Potatoes

Raw potatoes may be peeled first, then boiled in a salt water or steamed. Water-boiled potatoes are more diffucult to handle, and steaming of potatoes is the better way of cooking them. Depending on their size, they will need from 5 to 60 minutes cooking time (6-8-ounce whole potatoes will steam in about 45 minutes). They can be served plain or with melted butter, chopped parsley and butter, chives, caraway seeds or in other combinations.

French Fried Potatoes

Raw potatoes may be cut into sticks and deep fried. They are available pre-fried and frozen. Most eastablishments today put them this way, for convenience. The names depend on the shape of the cut potatoes. Americans call them, in addition to french fries, crinkle cuts, long branch, shoe strings, and chips. French terms are Pommes Pont Neuf, Pommes Allumette, Pommes paille, Pommes chips, Pommes Geofrette, Pommes Parmantier, Pommes Parisienne, and others.

Home Fried Potatoes

These are steamed in the skin, peeled while still hot, then cooled and sliced into 1/4-inch discs. When needed, they are sauteed in butter to a golden brown, then served.

Hashed Browned Potatoes

The potato is chopped or grated instead of sliced, but made like home fries.

Hashed Creamed Potatoes

Potatoes are boiled, cold, peeled then grated. They are reboiled in half and half cream with some salt and spices (nutmeg, ginger, pepper), to a very heavy pulp. This is put in a gratinating dish, brushed with butter, and browned under the broiler. This is also the principle of a potato casserole and variation made by using potatoes in different shapes, mixed with sauces, eggs, cheese, meats, vegetables, and seasoning.

Mashed Potatoes

Mashed potatoes can be made from freshly peeled steamed potatoes or from baked and pleed potatoes. In both cases, the cooked dry potato is mashed or pressed through a potato ricer. It is then whipped up with hot milk, butter and salt. Duchess Potaotes is a variation of mashed potatoes. Potato croquettes are made like Duchess potatoes, but formed into rools or balls. They are cooled, breaded and deep fried to the order.

DUCHESS POTATOES

These potatoes are a sophisticated version of mashed potatoes but far more attractive to look at, with a much greater ability to "Stay warm". They are made in advance, and can be hanlded very easily in a short time when needed.

Experimental Recipe 41.

Duchess Potatoes

Ingredients

1. Baking potatoes : 3 pounds
2. Butter : 3 ounces
3. Yolks : 3 egg
4. Salt, nutmeg or ginger : To taste.

Method

1. Prepare all required ingredients
2. Clean and bake potatoes as usual (475°F. for 50 minutes).
3. While still hot, peel or scoop them out, then press through a potato ricer or wire mesh sieve.
4. Add butter, yolks, salt and spices, Mix well with wooden spoon or whip.
5. Put mixture into a pastry bag with a No. 5 star tube.
6. Pipe them onto a buttered cookie sheet with a spiral-circular motion into little pyramids. Usually they are about 1 1/2 inches across the bottom and about a 1 inch high.
7. They can be refrigerated or frozen unitl further use.
8. When needed, they are baked at 400°F. for not longer than 10 minutes, or until brown.
9. They taste best when baked fresh and served with sauce or gravy.

PASTA

Pasta, an Italian word, is the collective name for all kinds of noodles. The most often used ones are : spaghetti, macaroni, vermicelli, shells, and other Itailan names for different shapes. All pasta must be boiled in lots of salted first. After boiling, it may be buttered, mixed with sauces, fish, meats, vegetables, cheeses, cream or others, Italians eat plain pasta as their full meal without meat or meat sauce. They use just butter, olive oil, grated dry cheese, and perhaps a little fresh cream. (Ref. Fig. 3.9A)

The best pasta, made from durum wheat, needs longer cooking time than a cheaper pasta. It will fluff up considerably more, and will keep its cruchy texture for a much longer time, while in the warmer. Italian are not the only pasta eaters. Most of the cultures have adopted pasta with great delight.

Pasta eaters are very particular about the softness of their noodles. *Pasta has to be cruchy (al dente)* to be perfect. Overcooked pasta is of of the worst things to be served. In many of the better Italian restaurants, all pasta is cooked to the order. Customers gladly wait 15 to 20 minutes just to get their orders right.

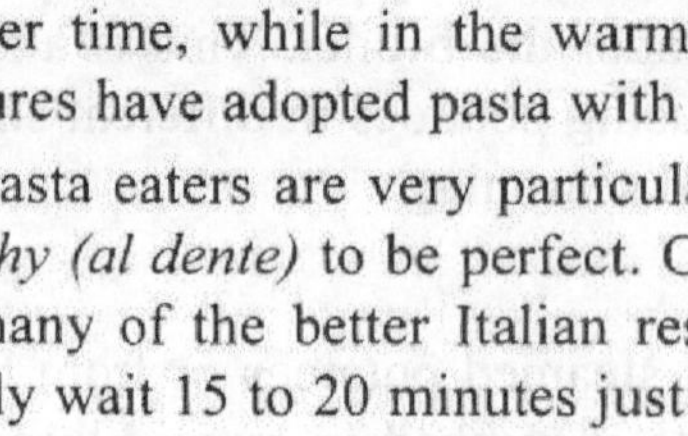

Spaghetti—round, long noodles

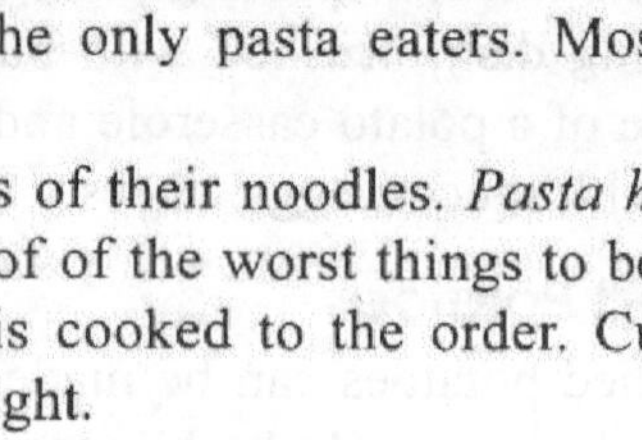

Spaghettini—thin, round, long noodles

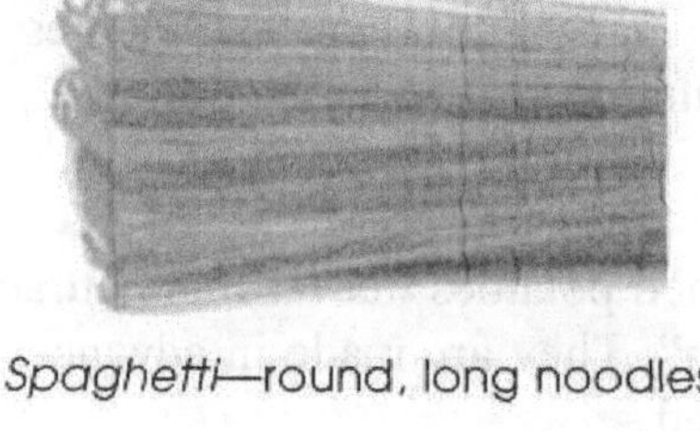

Macaroni—round, long, hollow noodles

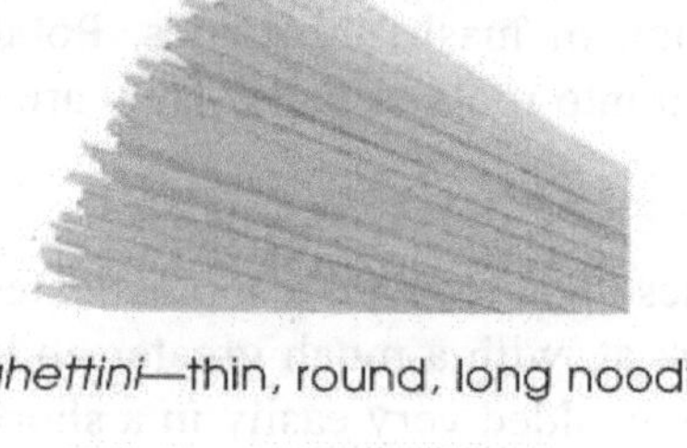

Elbow Macaroni—bent and cut macaroni

Salad Macaroni—very short cut macaroni

Vermicelli—extra thin, twisted, short, round, noodles

Contd..

Small Sea Shells—shell shaped pasta, machine moulded

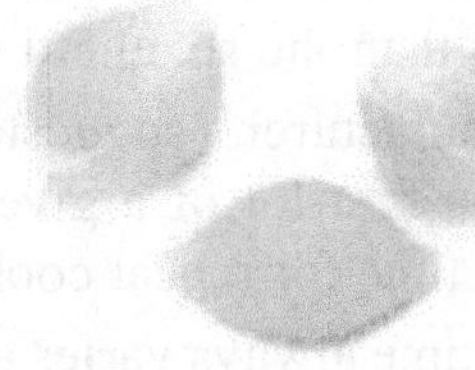

Large Sea Shells

Mostaccioli—diagonal cut macaroni machine moulded

Manicotti—giant stuffing macaroni. like cannelloni

Tagliatelle—long, flat noodles

Lasagne—extra wide noodles rippled at rim

Fettucine—wide, short, egg noodles

Fig. 3.9A. Shapes and Names of Pastas

SPAGHETTI OR SIMILAR PASTAS

Spaghetti or similar shaped pastas are supplied in the form of very long noodles. They are not shortened before, nor after boiling. When finally on the dinner plate, they are not cut, but are rolled onto a fork and eaten that way. Short shaped pasta can be cooked in a little less water than the spaghetti shapes. (Ref. Experimental Recipe 42)

1. The manufacturer's suggested cooking time on the pasta package is usually to long. Cook the first lot of a given pasta brand by inspection. Then establish the exact cooking time for repeat cooking.
2. Boiling time always varies according to the shape and wheat quality of the product.
3. Unbuttered cooked pasta, kept warm in the steamtable, will stick together.
4. For economy'ssake, it is better to keep pasta and pasta sauce separate in the steamtablė until serving.

Experimental Recipe 42.

The Cooking Spaghetti or Similar Pastas

Equipment

1. Stockepot : 1/2 gallon
2. Colander : Che's fork
3. Skillet : 12-inch.

Ingredients

1. Spaghetti : 2 pounds
2. Salt : 1½ tablespoons
3. Butter or olive oil : 6 ounces.

Method

1. Prepare all required ingredients.
2. Fill stockpot 3/4 full of water. Add salt and bring to a boil.
3. When water bubbles, push in spaghetti and bend them around the stockpot as oon as they soften.
4. Use the chef's fork to dip them moving while waiting for the reboiling of water.
5. When reboiling, reduce heat to prevent overflow, and keep stirring to prevent sticking together of pasta.
6. Check the tenderness of the pasta after about 5 minutes, then continue to cook by "inspection".
7. When considered done (al dente), drain through colander.
8. Rinse quickly with cold water to stop the carry-over heat and to wash off loose starch.
9. Shake off excess moisture.
10. Heat the skillet with the butter or olive oil.
11. Saute the drained spaghetti untill well mixed and hot.
12. Serve with any desired sauce.

Spinach Lasagne

Lasagne noodles, precooked and cooled, are laid in a buttered, square gratinating dish alternatively with buttered chopped spinach, grated parmesan cheese and melted butter. Between 3 layers of lasagne noodles, 2 layers of spinach are sandwiched in. The top layer of noodles is covered with slices of Mozarella cheese. This casserole is covered, and baked for 30 minutes at 350°F. Then it is uncovered and finished at 375°F. for 10 to 15 minutes more. When baked, the lasagne should set at least 15 minutes before it is portion cut and served. It is served with or without tomato sauce underneath.

Cannelloni

Cannelloni are made from noodle paste rolled paper thin and cut into 3" × 4" squares. These are prepared in true Italian style. For restaurant cannellonis, the paste square is often replaced with a large pancake (crepe).

Mixture for the noodle paste:

1. 3 cups of flour,
2. 4 whole eggs and one yolk,
3. 1/4 teasoopn salt.

Knead 10 to 15 minutes untill satin smooth, roll out and cut or shaped immediately. When dried they can be kept for a few days in a dry place.

The Cannelloni are boiled like pasta, carefully rained, cooled, fill, and rolled. The rolls are arranged in a buttered gratenating dish in which the bottom has been covered with about 1/2 inch of spicy tomato sauce. They are laid in rows, one next to the other. Then each Cannelloni roll is covered with a slice of mozarella cheese, and baked at 375°F. for 15 to 20 minutes.

The fillings are varied depending on the regional origin of the dish and the inventiveness of the chef. A good standard filling is :

1. Chopped, cooked, drained spinach : 1 lb.
2. Uncreamed cottage cheese (ricotta) : 1 lb.
3. Thick bechamel sauce : 1/2 cup
4. Egg yolks : 3
5. Parmesan cheese, salt, pepper, fried garlic, basil, etc. mixed together. : 1 cup
6. The spinach can be replaced with presauteed zucchini.
7. Various amounts of ground cooked meats can be added.
8. The ricotta cheese always remains in the mixture.

RICE AND OTHER CEREALS

Rice is the staple for the largest goup of people in the world. The orientals, eat rice three times a day. The rice used is unpolished (brown). Thus, it has not lost its vitamin value. American grown and processed rice has no vitamins, but does not need washing and has a shorter cooking time. All rice should be cooked by the original Chinese principle that all the cooking water should be obsorbed. Flavour or remaining nutrients are not lost. Average long grain rice needs two volume parts of water for each part of rice. Good rice cooking is done only in a casserole with a tight-fitting cover. The casserole should be flat and wide. Rice should not fill the casserole higher than 1½ inches. Never stirred rice during cooking. As soon as rice and water have come to a strong boil, the heat is reduced and the rice, according to type and quality, is simmered for a given time. When the rice is ready, it should be uncovered and loosened up to let the steam and extra heat escape. This will prevent overcooking.

PLAIN WHITE RICE

On the menu, it may be called buttered rice, steamed rice, or white rice. There are several ways of cooking, but the Chinese way is the best. No water is left over, and the rice is never too mush or still uncooked. (Ref. Experimental Recipe 43)

Experimental Recipe 43.

Cooking of Plain Rice

Equipments

Heavy 5-quart flat casserole with cover : One.

Ingredients

1. Long grain rice : 1 quart
2. Salt : 1 teaspoon
3. Boiling water : 2 quarts.

Method

1. Prepare all required ingredients
2. Put casserole with rice, salt, and the measured, boiling water on heat. Bring to a fast boil.
3. Stir with fork or ladle once, to mix thoroughlly. Reduce heat to simmering.
4. Cover casserole. Simmer for 30 minuts.
5. Turn heat off. Let rest for 10 more minutes.
6. When ready to serve, loosen rice with fork only, to fluff it up without smashing the grain. Keep it warm untill used.

Risotto

Europeans cookery have improved rice cookery by adding fat and sometimes vegetables. This mixture is called a *risotto.* For a risotto, a small amount of fat is put into the casserole first. Then finely cut onions or whatever vegetable is giving its name to the risotto are added and sauteed. The rice is added, sauteed a little, then covered with the measured hot liquid (water, soup, or stock). (Ref. Experimental Recipe 44). The Chinese process is then used.

Risottos can be made with meat, fish, or vegetables. Anything added to the raw rice must have the same cooking time as the rice.

Risttos can be made with zucchini, eggplants, green peas, celery, shrimps, prawns, fish fillets cubed, boneless chicken, chicken livers, tender lamb , veal, pork, and beef meat or in any combination of these. Saffron, chilli, paprika, turmeric, and cumin are some of the seasonings used.

Experimental Recipe 44.

Risotto Milanese

Ingredients

1. Long grain rice	:	2 cups
2. Chiken or meat bouillon	:	4¼ cups
3. Saffron stems (stigmas)	:	15-20
4. Pound one chopped onion	:	1 large
5. Butter	:	3 ounces
6. Parmeasn cheese	:	1 cup
7. Salt	:	1/4 teaspoon.

Method

1. Prepare all required ingredients.
2. Select a suitable casserole with lid and saute the onions in the butter.
3. At the same time bring chicken bouillon to a boil. Add the saffron stigmas and salt.
4. When onions are translucent, add the rice and heat thoroughly.
5. Pour simmering chicken bouillon over the rice. Bring to a boil. Stir or shake rice for even distribution.
6. Reduce heat to simmering. Place cover on casserole.
7. Move the casserole into an oven about 25°F. Leave it there for 30 minutes. Do not stir rice while in the oven.
8. When it is taken out of the oven, sprinkle parmesan over rice, and stir in with a kitchen fork.
9. Taste, checking for salt and softness.
10. Keep warm until serving.

Tomato Risotto

Tomato Risotto is prepared like a Risotto Milanese with the ingredients changed to :

1. Rice	:	4 cups
2. Chopped tomatoo pulp with juice	:	4 cups
3. Meat stock	:	4 cups
4. Butter or oil	:	4 ounces
5. Salt	:	1 teaspoon
6. Onion	:	1 small.

The use of parmesan is optional.

Mushroom Risotto

Mushroom Risotto is prepared like a Risotto Milanese with the ingredients change to:

1. Rice	:	4 cups
2. Beef stock	:	6 cups
3. Precooked Mushrooms in juice	:	2 cups diced

4. Butter or oil : 4 ounces
5. Salt : 1 teaspoon
6. Onion : 1 small.

The use of parmesan is optional.

Paella

This Spanish national risotto consists of a stew in which the liquid is measured and adapted to the rice quantity. Half an hour before the stew is tender, the raw rice is added. The dish is finished by the same general steps for risotto. Only the ingredients for the stew are unique. This is a mixture of chicken, pork, seafood, saffron, onions, tomatoes, peas and others.

Cereals

The term cereal comes from the Latin word "Ceres" which was the name of the Roman goddess of agriculture. Cereal includes all edible grains or grasses, but the name is applied mostly to breakfast foods. Cereals are not often served with main dishes. In the far west they are mostly breakfast foods such as oats, farina, cream of wheat, and cornmeal. Some are used as starch in the ethnic-regional cookery. These include bulgur (cracked wheat), barley, grits, cornmeal grits or mush (Polenta), and backwheat. The packer's instruction should be followed for cooking.

QUESTIONS AND DISCUSSIONS

Fill in the Blanks

Q.1. Read and complet the following statements:

(a) Potatoes are versatile and adapt to all ....
(b) Restaurant Cannelloni are made not from paste but from ....
(c) Paella is a meat-fish-vegetable risotto, native to ....
(d) In science, starch is seen as a complex ....
(e) Plain rice is cooked best by the methods of the ....
(f) Pasta is the collective name for same as ....
(g) Spaghetti are always cooked and served ....
(h) Europeans have improved rice cookery and call it ....
(i) Pasta is best when cooked to the stage of ....
(j) In Culinary Art, starchy is the same as ....

[**Ans.:** (a) cooking process; (b) the large pancake (crepe); (c) plain;
(d) carbohydrete; (e) chinese; (f) noodles;
(g) hot;
(h) collective name for all food that contain a large amount of flavour containing the largest amount of flour;
(i) risotto; (j) crunchy]

Multiple Choice Type

Q.2. Read each question carefull and select the best answer :—

(i) Cannelloni are rolls from thin pasta dough, filled with
- (a) Ground meat and tomatoes
- (b) Ground meat and spinach
- (c) Spinach and dry cottage cheese
- (d) Mashed potatoes and parmesan.

(ii) Baked potatoes can be transformed into all these listed preparations *except*
- (a) Chateau Potatoes
- (b) Duchess Potatoes
- (c) Pushkin Potatoes
- (d) Lyonnaise Potatoes.

(iii) Risotto, which is rice mixed with other foods, is always
- (a) Spiced with saffron
- (b) Baked for at least 2 hours
- (c) Sauteed in fat while still raw
- (d) Cooked by the Chinese method first, then mixed in with the meats.

(iv) A 10-ounce size baked potato will be fluffy and dry when baked for
- (a) 40 minutes at 475°F
- (b) 50 minutes at 475°F
- (c) 60 minutes at 400°F
- (d) 70 minutes at 325°F.

(v) One pound of raw pasta is cooked best with salt and
- (a) 1 quart of boiling water
- (b) 2 quarts of boiling water
- (c) 3 quarts of boiling water
- (d) 4 quarts of boiling water.

(vi) American grown and processed rice has a cooking time of
- (a) 20 minutes
- (b) 25 minutes
- (c) 30 minutes
- (d) 35 minutess.

(vii) When pasta has cooked to "al dente" stage, it is drained and
- (a) Rinsed with hot water
- (b) Rinsed with cold water
- (c) Cooled off in ice water
- (d) Not rinsed off at all.

[**Ans.:** (i) (c); (ii) (d); (iii) (d); (iv) (b); (v) (a); (vi) (c); (vii) (b)]

Matching Type

Q.3. Match the basic preparations of Table 'A' with the terminology used in Table 'B'

Table 'A'	*Table 'B'*
(a) Baked	(i) Duches
(b) Refried	(ii) Gratinated
(c) Creamed	(iii) Parsleyed
(d) Steamed	(iv) Lyonnaise
(e) Stewed	(v) Pushkin
(f) Sauteed	(vi) O'Brien
(g) Deep Fried	(vii) New Potatoes
(h) Mashed	(viii) Cottage.

[**Ans.:** (a) (v); (b) (iv); (c) (ii); (d) (iii); (e) (vii); (f) (viii); (g) (vi); (h) (i)]

Short Answer Type

Q.4. Why is starch known as the filler ?

Q.5. Trace the history of potatoes.

Q.6. Trace the origin and history of pasta. Where did it come from ?

Q.7. Why are starches the cheapest food source to man ?

Q.8. Define :

(a) Risotto
(b) Cannelloni
(c) Paella
(d) Paste.

Descriptive Type

Q.9. Compare the amounts of water used for pasta and for beans. Why are they so different ?

Q.10. Name and decrible different types of pasta.

Assignments/Activity Type

Q.11. Experiment with baking of potatoes : use two equal-sixed potatoes, bake one at 475°F. for 50 minutes, the other at 350°F. for one hour. Campare.

Q.12. Create a "mixed meat vegetable" risotto.

Q.13. Prepare

(a) Cannelloni
(b) Potatoes a la Pushin
(c) Zucchini Lasagne instead of Spinach Lasagne.

Q. 14. Prepare the following dishes:

(a) Duchess Potatoes from baked qotatoes
(b) Croquette Potatoes from Duchess Potatoes.

3.10

Eggs Preparations

CHAPTER OBJECTIVES

After studying this lesson you should be able :

- To explain the various egg preparations;
- To poach and serve plain poached eggs on toast;
- To explain the combination of Eggs Benedict;
- To prepare and make a Parmesan Cheese Omelette;
- To prepare and demonstrate the preparation of a Sabayon; and
- To prepare and demonstrate the preparation of plain French pancakes.

The egg is a most versatile popular food, and is one of the more important ingredients to cooking. All by itself, it can be prepared in seven different basic ways which do not resemble each other. Egg dishes can be served at every meal and are ideal as in-between snacks, due to their short cooking time.

You hardly find any other food as versatile and commonly used as the egg. Most of the cuisine use only chicken eggs, however there are other areas of the world who use some other kinds of bird eggs. Eggs have nourishing proteins. They probably were an important food source to early man.

Eggs are prepared by all the basic cooking methods : moist, dry, and in fat. Each of these methods give a different characteristic to the cooked egg. Cookery, as it is practiced today, depends largely on the use of eggs.

Omelettes and poached eggs are some of the more difficult egg preparations. The proper techniques for scrambling eggs just right also result from experience. The handling of hard boiled eggs is important. The quality of a boiled egg and the time used to handle it can be wasted if the proper procedures are not understood. Omelette-making is a skill performance which cooks should try to perfect.

Eggs are used in batters for custards and fast dessert such as Sabayon. French pancakes, crepes, have many uses in culinary art, either as a dessert in itself, or as a shell to hold different fillings (example: cannelloni). The making of omelettes, poached egg variations, crepes, custardsd and Sabayon are tasks of the skilled cook and future chef. It is important to do it well.

EGG DISHES

Ther are seven diffrent ways of cooking eggs by adding only fat. Hundreds of variations have come from these seven basic forms.

(1) Soft Boiled Eggs

The cooking time for egg is related to egg size or weight. An extra large egg is put in boiling water for 6-7 minutes. A meduim large egg will take 5 minutes. Some people like eggs very soft and ask for three-minute eggs. This applies to medium eggs, only large ones would still be too raw. Soft boiled eggs are served unpeedled in an egg cup or peeled in a glass. They are eaten plain.

(2) Poached Eggs

Raw eggs are dropped into simmering vinegar water for two to three minutes. This results in the egg white wrapping itself around the yolk, shaping the egg into a large raindrop. When done, these eggs are rinshed in boiling salt water, drained, and served in various ways.

(3) Scrambled Eggs

Raw eggs are cooked over a slow fire in butter and a little cream. They are stired with a whip until they have a creamy consistency. Then they are served plain, over toast, or other ways.

(4) Egg Omelette

The beaten eggs are cooked on a hot fire with constant stirring and shaking of the pan until they are nearly done. The eggs are folded into the shape of an omelette. Omelettes are served plain or with a filling.

(5) Plain Fried Eggs

The eggs are carefully cracked open, to keep the egg yolk whole. They are put into a hot skillet and cooked slowly until the egg white is completely set and stiff. The eggs are put on a plate and served. Shirred eggs are served in the same heat-proof dish in which they are cooked.

(6) Eggs in Casserole

One or two eggs poured into individual little buttered casseroles (pots). These are set in a skillet, filled with 1/4 inch of water and put into a moderate 350°F. oven. They are baked for a few (2-4) minutes until softly cooked. Do not overcook. Yolk has to stay soft.

(7) Deep Fried Eggs

Eggs are dropped individually into deep hot oil (similar to poaching) and the splattering frying egg white is wrapped around the yolk with the help of a spatula. One egg should be done in one minute. They are degreased on bloting paper, and served with ham, bacon, grilled tomatoes, toast, or tomato sauce.

In most countries eggs are considered breakfast dishes. Omelettes and poached eggs are excellent for lunches and light dinners. All egg dishes can be served for brunches and snacks.

POACHING

Poaching means to simmer. For example fish, half submered in liquid, the rest of the food cooks in its own steam. Poached eggs have to be simmered in lot of water, with white vinegar in it. A perfect poached egg has the shape of a large drop. It is a soft boiled egg, cooked without shell. The vinegar in the water prevents the egg from the dissolving. Poached eggs are served hot on meat, starch, or vegetable, bases, and covered with a sauce. There are also cold poached egg varieties, served in similar way and covered with a mayonnaise sauce.

Method

1. For poaching, a high sauce pan or pot of unsalted water is brought to a boil. For each quart or water, 1/2 cup of white vinegar is added.
2. A second pot with simmering salt water is kept nearby.
3. One egg at a time is cracked open and dropped into the simmering vinegar water. A fast cook can easily drop 6-8 eggs into one casserole within 30 second.
4. The eggs, depending on their size and desired softness, are steeped in the water for two to three minutes. They are tasted by light finger pressure. If done, they are moved from the vinegar water into the salted water. This washes off the sour taste and leaves a salty one. It must be done quickly, since too much time in the hot water will overcook the eggs.
5. Before serving, they are dried of any cooking water. A paper napkin is held in one hand, while the other hand skims the egg out of the water with a slotted spoon. The spoon is dipped onto the napkin and the egg is dried.
6. For breakfast, these poached eggs are often served on buttered tost. They may be finished in other ways.

For efficient restaurant service, the poached egg, after it is cooked in the vinegar poaching liquid, is completely cooled in salted ice water. It will stay soft and can be kept under refrigeration at least 36 hours for later use. When needed, they are warmed in simmering salt water for one or two minutes, then handled as if they were freshly made.

Eggs Benedict

Two halves of a toasted English muffin are buttered and covered with a slice of grilled Canadian bacon. A poached egg is placed on each muffin half. Each egg is covered with 2-3 tablespoon of Hollandaise. The top of the Hollandaise is decorated with a truffle slice. Watercess is used for garnish. This dish is ideal for being served under glass.

Poached Eggs Florentine

A buttered, shirred egg casserole is filled with a serving of buttered chopped spinach. Two hot poached eggs are set on top of it. Four to five tablespoons of Mornay sauce are poured over the eggs and spinach. One tablespoon of parmesan and a teaspoon of melted butter is sprinkled over the sauce, and the dish is browned under the broiler.

Poached Eggs Halevy

Arrange on a round service platter, a circle of six or eight small chicken hash patties. Top each one with a poached egg. Cover every second egg with heavy white chicken sauce. Cover the other eggs with tomato sauce. Serve one egg of each colour per person. Use watercress for garnish. (This dish is only attractive if three or four order are served together on one platter.)

Poached Egg Parmentier

A small, well formed baked potatoes hollowed out, then filled with ham hash. (Ham hash is chopped ham, onions, parsley, and the scooped-out potato meat.) A poached egg is set on top of it, covered with Sauce Mornay and browned under the broiler.

Many different foods can be used as a base. Fillings can be hashes, fine ragouts, or vegetables, and any cover sauce can be adapted to suit. Creative cooks may make as many different combinations as they have imagination.

FRENCH EGG OMELETTE

The plain omelette dish is simple in ingredients. It needs much skill and experience to be cooked right. Professional cooks and chefs use their omelette-making skill as a measure of achievement and gastronomic sophistication.

Experimental Recipe 45.

Omelette au Parmesan

Equipments

(1) 8-inch commerical restaurant skillet: One
(A regular skillet used for reheating sauce will make omelette stick)

(2) Wood or rubber spatula: 1

(3) Dinner plate: 1

Ingredients

(1) Eggs	:	3 Extra large
(2) Clear butter	:	1 tablespoon
(3) Grated parmesan cheese	:	3-4 tablespoons
(4) Parsley	:	for decoration.

Method

(1) Prepare all required ingredients.

(2) Break eggs into a non-oxidizing bowl and whip well
(for parmeasan cheese, salt can be omitted).

(3) Heat the dry omelette pan to approximately 325°F. Then pour in clear butter

(4) Pour in the whipped eggs.

(5) Let them set for a few second. Sprinkle cheese into eggs.

(6) Loosely shake pan over hot fire with one hand. Use the other hand with the spatula to control the egg movement inside the pan. Shake until omelette appears to set, then stop shaking and stirring.

(7) Tap ometlette pan on the handle until the eggs tilt into the omelette shape.

(8) Reverse hand grip on the handle, and turn omelette onto the pre-warmed dinner plate.

(9) Decorate with parsley and serve.

OMELETTE A PARMESAN

A parmesan cheese omelette can be made on the spur of the moment. All ingredients should be in any well organized kitchen as given in Experimental Recipe 45.

Omelette-making cannot be learned by only reading about it. You must see omelette demonstrations and practice it himself. The ingredients are whole, lightly beaten eggs, a dash of salt, and small bit of butter and omelette skillet of the right shape is important. Teflon, a modern convenience, can also help.

Key factors in omelette preparation are heat, timing, and the whipping of the raw eggs. The actual process is very much like the fast scrambling of eggs. The chef must know when to stop scrambling, and how to do the right flipping of the wrist for the perfect mold.

Omelettes can be served plain, with a variety of fillings, coverd with sauce, or with both a filling and a sauce. They are always made to order and must be eaten immediately. Omelettes can be served at any time of the day : breakfast, lunch, dinner, or supper. They may be a full meal and appetizer, or a snack.

Common Fillings

These are sometimes stired into the omelette while in the making. Sometimes they are filled into the nearly cooked one. Some times they are poured over the top of an omelette already cooked and turned out on a plate.

MUSHROOM OMLETTE

A fresh mushrrom omelette is carried on the menu of many restaurant and coffee shops. In a high class establishment, omelettes are not often listed on the menu, but is is uderstood that they can be served any time of the day. (Ref. Experimental Recipe 46)

Cheese, ham, bacon, fine herbs, tomatoes, mushrooms, Spanish sauce, spinach, chicken a la king, Shrimp Newburgh, and others can be used, Some of the fancy, luxury cusine fillings are asparagus, foie gras, chicken liver, veal or lamb kindeys, calf brains, seafood, and regouts.

HARD BOILED EGGS

The boiling of hard cooked eggs has to follow a simple procedure . The professional cook is concerned about certain facts in regard to hard boild eggs. First, there must not be any green or blue ring around the yolk. Second, the egg must peel easily, in a second. A cook with high hourly wages can but waste half an hour to peel two dozen hard boild eggs. The knowledge and skill of the cook must be used in the best possible way.

Following guideline are useful for boiling eggs:

1. Select large eggs with thin shells
2. Remove eggs from refriegrator 3-2 hours before cooking. It is important that they have room temperature.
3. Always use timer. Twenty percent overcooking will discolour yolk.
4. Starting in cold water cooks them faster.
5. Proper shocking with cold water makes it easy to peel the eggs.

Experimental Recipe 46.

Mushrooms Omelette

Equipments

(1) 8-inch commercial restaurant skillet: 1
(A regular skillet used for reheating sauces will make omelette stick)
(2) Wood or rubber spatula: 1
(3) Dinner plate: 1

Ingredients

(1) Eggs	:	3 Extra large
(2) Clear butter	:	1 tablespoon
(3) Chopped Fresh Parsley	:	1/4 teaspoon
(4) Salt	:	To taste
(5) Pepper	:	To taste.

Method

(1) Prepare all required ingredients.
(2) Break eggs into a non-oxidizing bowl add pinch of salt (white papper optional) and whip well.
(3) Heat the dry omelette to approximately 325°F. Then pour in clear butter.
(4) Add the pre-sauteed mushrooms (omit any liquid).
(5) Pour in the whipped eggs.
(6) Loosely shake pan over hot fire with one hand. Use the other hand with the spatula to control the egg movement inside the pan. Shake until omelette appears to set.
(7) Tap omelette pan on the handle untill the eggs tilt into the omelette shape.
(8) Reverse hand grip on the handle, and turn omelette onto the pre-warmed diner plate.
(9) Decorate with parsley and serve.

Method

1. Fill casserole half full with cold water.
2. Place eggs, carefully into water without cracking shells.
3. Be sure eggs are well covered with cold water.
4. Put lid on casserole. Bring to boil.
5. Turn heat low, to simmer.
6. Cook for 10 to 14 minutes, according to egg size.
7. Drain off all hot water.
8. Add ice cold water immediately, if possible with ice, to shock the hot eggs and cool them fast. This will avoid the green rings around the yolk.
9. Start peeling by hitting egg lightly and rolling it against hard surface to crack the shell.
10. Peel off shell and membrane.

11. Rinse under tap and remove shell particles.
12. Store eggs in salt water under refrigeration until used.
13. If used for chopping or salad, they can stored without water.

Hard boiled eggs are not served warm. They have their place in the sandwich and salad pantry.

EGG CUSTARD

It is a pudding-like dish made from eggs and milk. Some custards are used salty, as a garnish in consommes and clear soups. Custards are more often served as desserts. They may be plain or flavoured, such as caramel or a coffee custard.

Egg Sabayon

This must also be considered a custared-like preparation. It is a warm dessert made by cooks to the order.

Experimental Recipe 47.

Egg Sabayon

Equipments

(1) Copper or stainless steel bowl
(2) Stainless piano wire whisk
(3) Casserole, to improvise a double boiler for the bowl.

Ingredients

(1)	Whole eggs	: 2
(2)	Eggs yolk	: 4
(3)	Dry white wine	: 2/3 cup
(4)	Granulated sugar	: 3/4 cup
(5)	Lemon juice	: 1 teaspoon
(6)	Lemon zeste	
(7)	Brandy or liquor (optional for additional flavour)	: 1 ounce.

Procedure

(1) Prepare all required ingredients.
(2) Break eggs and yolks into bowl. Add wine and lemon juice and whip toghether.
(3) Add sugar, lemon zeste.
(4) Place on top of casserole half filled with simmering water, (improvised double boiler).
(5) Whip vigorously over heat until mixture becomes a thick, fourthy , custard. This may take from 5-10 minutes. (the custard temperature, if measured, would be about 130°F.)
(6) Take from heat and whip in brandy. Serve immediately if it is to be used as a hot custard or dessert sauce.
(7) If to be used as a cold or frozen custard sauce, put mixture into the bowl of the electric mixer.
(8) Whip on medium speed until completely cooled.

Sabayon, also known as Zabaione, or Zabaglione, is a frothy, custard-like cream. It is often served hot in a champagne glass. It can also be used as a sauce for a suitable dessert. It is made with wine as a base, but there are many regional varieties. The custard can be served chilled, even frozen. Experimental Recipe 47 gives step-by-step process.

PLAIN PANCAKES (CREPES)

The American breakfast pancakes are made from raised dough. The Contitnental pancake, or crepe (in French), resembles a Mexican tortilla. They have many applications, such as side dishes, garnishes, and snacks. The most popular used is as a dessert.

Guidelines

(1) Egg proteins are easily overcooked. At step 8, in Experimental Recipe 48 the test is not made in the center. If the center is cooked, the carry-over heat will overcook the custard.

Experimental Recipe 48.

Creme Renverse (unfolded caramel custard)

Ingredients

(1) Caramelized sugar : 1 pound
(2) Milk : 1 quart
(3) Whole eggs : 8
(4) Egg yolks : 8
(5) Sugar : 3/4 cup
(6) Dash of salt
(7) Vanilla flavour : optional
(8) Butter : for custard molds.

Method

(1) Prepare all required ingredients
(2) Butter the insides of the custard molds.
(3) Pour the caramelized hot sugar into each mold to cover the bottom with a thin layer of caramel.
(4) Break all the eggs and put the yolks into a non-oxidizing bowl. Whip together lightly.
(5) Mix in the salt, vanilla, sugar (3/4 cups) and milk.
(6) Fill the prepared molds about 4/5 full.
(7) Improvise a double boiler by setting molds into a cake pan and fill the pan with hot water.
(8) Bake at 350°F. until custard appears to be set. Test by inserting clean paring knife halfway between centre and rime of the mold. If dry, custard is done.
(9) Cool. Unmold by cutting edge of custard loose with paring knife, when needed. Pour caramel collected in the mold over the custard.
(10) This can be served with whipping cream or different sauces for a fancier appearance.

(2) The custard-making principle is used to make bread and butter pudding or diplomat pudding as well.

Guidelines for the proper pancake batter consistency

1. Use 1 ounces milk, 3 whole eggs, 1/4 teaspoon salt, and 6 ounces flour. Sometimes water is also adeed.
2. These ingredients are whipped or osterized together without lumps .
3. A suitable skillet is heated
4. Clear butter is poured in and poured out right away.
5. A small amount of batter, just enough to cover the bottom, is poured into the skillet.
6. The skillet is turned up and down in all directions to make the batter paper thin.
7. The skillet goes back on the heat to bake the first side golden brown. The crepe is turned and baked on the other side for only half the previous time.
8. Then the crepe is ready for further use.

Stuffed Italian Pancakes

1. Large, cold pancakes are filled with a mixture of 1/2 Duxelles and 1/2 chopped ham, then rolled like a jelly roll.
2. They are flattened a little to make them oblong when cut, and then put in the cooler for several hours.
3. When completely cold and firm, they are cut into diamond or other shapes, rebreaed in flour eggs, and bread, crumbs,
4. These are deep fried to the order and served with a creamed vegetable, or a hot or cold sauce.
5. They are used as an appetizer, side dish, or main dish.

Russian Piroshkis

Small pancakes are stuffed with meat hash or fried cabbage, folded like a package, dipped in batter, and deep-fried to a crisp brown. They are eaten as snacks or appetizers, without sauce.

QUESTIONS AND DISCUSSIONS

Fill in the Blanks

1. Read and complete the following statements:
   (a) Slow egg boiling procedures will result in ....
   (b) The principle of custard-making is used for many ....
   (c) The number of different basic egg dishes is ....
   (d) A sabayon is a different form of ....
   (e) The versatile egg can be prepared by all cooking ....

(f) No other dish is as simple in ingredients but as difficult to execute as the ....

(g) Egg dishes are not necessarily served for ....

(h) In culinary art, a crepe serves very often as a ....

[**Ans.:** (a) green rings around the yalk;
(b) bread and butter pudding or diplomat pudding;
(c) seven;
(d) dessert;
(e) methods;
(f) omellete and poached eggs;
(g) meals;
(h) side dishes garnishe and snacks]

Multiple Choice Type

Q.2. Read each question carefully and select the *best* answer:

(i) Egg cusard is baked best at
(a) 300°F (b) 350°F
(c) 400°F (d) 450°F.

(ii) Poached eggs are first simmered in water to which
(a) Salt has been added (b) Vinegar has been added
(c) Lemon juice has been added (d) Oil has been added.

(iii) Exta large hard boiled eggs should simmer for
(a) 8 minutes (b) 10 minutes
(c) 12 minutes (d) 14 minutes.

(iv) A parmesan omelette can stay true to its name when made with
(a) Fontina (b) Mozzarella
(c) Ricotta (d) Romano.

(v) Poaching of eggs needs speed and experience. A good cook can poach at once in one casserole
(a) 2-4 eggs (b) 4-6 eggs
(c) 6-8 eggs (d) 8-10 eggs.

(vi) Freshly made omelettes can be kept warm for
(a) 1-5 minutes (b) 5-10 minutes
(c) 10-15 minutes (d) 51-20 minutes.

(vii) Medium-sized eggs, to be soft boiled, need to simmer
(a) 3 minutes (b) 4 minutes
(c) 5 minutes (d) 6 minutes.

(viii) Eggs Benedict are topped with a
(a) Bechamel Sauce (b) Veloute Sauce
(c) Hollandaise Sauce (d) Supreme Sauce.

(ix) The doneness of a poached egg is checked by —
(a) Thermometer check (b) Finger touch
(c) Paring kinfe (d) Exact timing

(x) Sabayon is a whisked egg custurd with a base of

(a) Milk (b) Wine

(c) Water (d) Orange Juice

(xi) Poached eggs florentine are poached egg combinations with

(a) Bacon and tomatoes (b) Ham and hollandaise

(c) Spinach and cheese sauce (d) Ham hash and cheese

(xii) A visible sign of an overcooked hard egg is

(a) Gravy shell (b) Cracked shell

(c) Soft yolk (d) Greenin yolk

[Ans.: (i) (b); (ii) (b); (iii) (a); (iv) (d);
(v) (c); (vi) (a); (vii) (c); (viii) (c);
(ix) (b); (x) (b); (xi) (c); (xii) (d)]

Short Answer Type

Q.3. Why is Sabayon the speciality of Italian restaurants ?

Q.4. What are some of the dessert crepes which can be made easily ?

Q.5. Why are egg dishes so popular for Sunday brunch ?

Q.6. Explain the theory of omelette-making.

Q.7. Define:

(a) Crepe

(b) Sabayon

(c) Omelette

(d) Shirr

(e) Custard.

Assignments/Activity Type

Q. 8. Watch and practice all demonstrations of the following :

(a) Making of poached eggs

(b) At least three demonstrations of omelete-making

(c) Making creamy scrambled eggs

(d) Deep-fried eggs.

3.11

Stocks Sauces Soups and Gravies

CHAPTER OBJECTIVES

After studying this lesson you should be able :

- To prepare all mother sauces based on roux;
- To explain the procedure of extraction of brown stock from beef bones;
- To extract brown stock from beef bones;
- To prepare and demonstrate the procedure of making a sauce Hollandaise;
- To make sauce Hollandaise;
- To practice and prepare composition sauces by formula;
- To prepare and to make the clarification of consomme; and
- To prepare and make a de luxe vegetable cream soup.

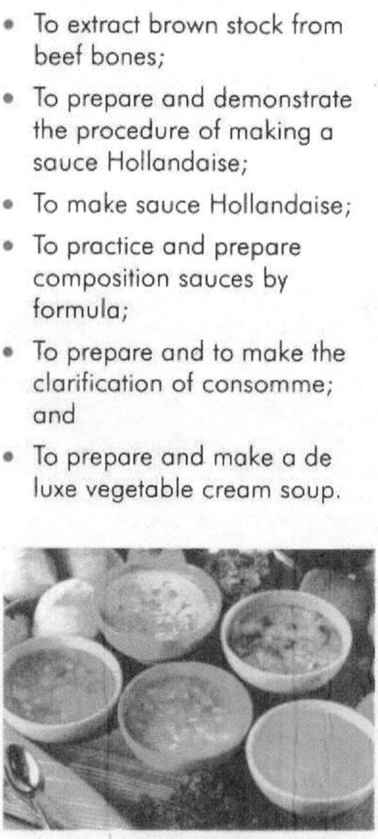

Stocks, sauces, and soups are foods made from nutrients dissolved in water. Milk is liquid food produced by an animal. Soup is liquid food prepared by the cook. The extraction of liquefiable foods is one of the method of cooking. For the cook, it is a very important skill which must be understood and mastered. Extracting liquefiable foods is the vary basis of stock sauce, and soup cookery. The main difference between a sauce or a soup very often lies in its texture only. The basic principles of making cream soups are like the ones of making sauces. Sauces have a more intense flavour than soups, if sauces and soups of the same raw ingredients are compared. The addition of starch changes a clear liquid to a thickened one. For the sake of quality in cuisine, western cuisine use a starch-fat combination, cooked for a little while, called roux. Sauces are classified into four basic roux sauces and one egg yolk-butter sauce called Hollandaise. Sauce cookery can be compared to bar mixing. The five basic sauces are changed with the addition of different wines, liquors, cream, cheese, herbs, spices, condiments, and special cut garnishes into a hundred different sauces. These are highly cherished by luxury cuisine. Sauce Hollandaise, the fifth of the basic or mother sauces, is the only one not based on starch. The texture of this sauce comes through the emulsification of fat and egg yolk, which enclose fine air bubbles, instead of the saturation of starch granules with liquid. Sauces based on eggs have a limited holding time and must be made fresh whenever needed.

Double stock pot

Soute Pan for Maing Rox

Stock pot

Sauce and soup cookery have a definite structure. Thus, they are easy to master and practice. Most important are the personal standard of understanding how a sauce should look and taste, the use of fresh quality ingredients, and careful, systematic work. Just as in all the other fields of cookery, the same principles are used over and over again.

Most liquid foods are known under the names of stocks, broths, soups, sauces, and gravies. All these have their food parts dissolved in water. They may be proteins, carbohydrates, or fats and are distinguished by taste, texture, or colour. Stocks and broths are clear liquids composed of proteins and fats. Soups, sauces, and gravies are made from stocks or broth by the addition of starch and more fat.

The boiling liquid for meat or fish is called broth. For preparing stock, the same procedure is used. Bones, sinews, and gristles are shimmered in cold water to make stock. Cold water is used to start the stockpiled, since cold water has a greater dissolving power. When all proteins and fats are dissolved and leached out, the water is called stock. The stock is drained off. The leached out sinews, bones and gristles which remain are discarded. Stock is either white or brown and have the flavour of the bones used. Stock is white when the bones and trimming are raw. Stock is brown if the bones and trimmings are roasted at high heat in the oven before they are boiled. Chicken and fish stock is kept white. Never mix fish with meat while cooking. Chicken bones are sometimes kept separate for pure chicken stock only, but they may be mixed in with the general meat stock, Beef, veal, and pork bones are used either for brown stock or for white stock. Lamb bones, because of their strong and unpopular flavour, are seldom used.

WHITE MEAT CHICKEN OR FISH STOCK

Brown stock

Always simmer slowly. Do not salt stock while simmering, because unsalted water will leach out better.

SAUCES

A sauce is normally a rich flavoured, thickened stock or liquid used to give moistness or flavour or otherwise to complement some food.

Following points be noted in sauces:

1. There should be no taste of uncooked starch.

Expremental Recipe 48.

Preparation of Fish Stock

Ingredients (needed for per gallon of water)

(1) Raw bones or trimmings of meat, chicken or fish : 2 to 3 pounds

(2) Mixed soup vegetables : 1 to 1½ pounds

(3) Parsley, parsnips, celery, carrots, onions, leeks, scallions.

Method

(1) Prepare all required ingredients.

(2) Wash and clean all ingredients.

(3) Cover bones, vegetables and spices with cold water.

(4) Bring to a slow boil, then simmer

— bones from young chickens, not more than 2 hours.

— bones from hens or turkeys, 3 to 4 hours.

— veal or pork bones 4 to 5 hours.

— beef bones, 5 to 7 hours.

— fish stock; cook vegetables 1 hour first, add fish trimmings and only cook for ½ hour more, then strain.

(5) Strain stock, cool off fast, use, or regrigerate

(6) Remove fat next morning before use.

2. The texture must be smooth and velvety.
3. Sauces should never be paste-like or excessively thick, though the consistency varies from sauce to sauce.
4. Sauces must be clear and have a nice seen.
5. No one flavour must predominate. It must be blend of several subtle flavours.

Importance of Sauces

Sauces are fundamental to continental cooking and play a big role in the final dish presented to a guest. Some important points to be known about sauces are:-

1. They are very nutritious, being rich in fats, starch and proteins.
2. Some sauces help in digestion, e.g. mint sauce.
3. They add flavour to the food.
4. They moisten the food, e.g. white sauce added to vegetables.
5. They give colour to food.
6. They can be the foundation for a dish, e.g. white sauce for cheese souffle.

Basic or Mother Sauces

There are six principal sauces from which other sauces are derived. These sauces are known as 'Basic or Mother Sauces'. They are :

1. Mayonnaise
2. Hollandaise

3. Bechamel or White Sauce
4. Espagnole or Brown Sauce
5. Veloute
6. Tomato sauce.

Types of Sauces

1. Made from roux	: Bechamel, Demiglace, Veloute
2. Made from egg or oil	: Mayonnaise, Hollandaise
3. Made from custard powder	: Corn flour, Sweet sauces, e.g. Custard sauce
4. Uncooked sauce	: Mint sauce
5. Puree sauces	: Tomato sauce, Apple sauce
6. Fruit syrups & jam sauces	: Strawberry Jam sauce
7. Sauce Foyot	: Bearnaise + meat glaze.
8. Sauce Capre	: Hollandaise + Caper.
9. Sauce Maltaise	: Hollandaise + orange + orange peel
10. Misc. sauces	: Gravy, Curry.

1. Derivatives of Veloute Sauce

(a) **Allemande Sauce**	:	Veloute + egg yolk.
(b) **Normande Sauce**	:	Fish veloute to which is added mushroom essence and oyster juice. It is bound with egg yolk and cream and finished with butter.
(c) **Supreme Sauce**	:	Reduced veloute finished with cream.
(d) **Ravigutte**	:	Tarragon leaves reduced in a mixture of white wine and vinegar, add veloute, beaten with shallot butter and garnished with chopped chervils and chives.
(e) **Sauce Aurore**	:	Tomato flavoured fish veloute finished with butter.
(f) **Sauce Bercy**	:	Fish veloute added to chopped shallots sauted in butter and moistened with fresh fumet and white wine. Chopped parsley is added and the sauce is finished with butter.
(g) **Nantua**	:	Fish veloute with tomato shrimp butter.
(h) **Sauce Dieppoise**	:	Sauce Normandy + mussel/oyster stock.
(i) **Duglere**	:	A fish veloute flavoured with crushed tomatoes.
(j) **Curry Sauce**	:	Chopped onions and apples sauted in butter, sprinkled with curry powder, moistened with coconut milk and veloute and finished with cream.
(k) **Tomato Sauce**	:	This is also a basic warm sauce. It is prepared by sauteing onions with garlic and carrots, adding bay leaf and pepper corns and lots of roughly chopped tomatoes. This mixture is moistened with chicken stock and thickened with brown roux.

2. Derivatives of Tomato Sauce

(a) **Bar-be-que Sauce** : Tomato sauce + paprika.

(b) **Sauce Bretonne** : Tomato sauce + fried chopped onions + white wine + chopped parsley + sugar + garlic.

(c) **Sauce Provecale** : Tomato sauce + tomato concasse + sliced mushroom + little sugar + garlic and chopped parsley.

(d) **Sauce Chaudfroid** : Tomato sauce + aspic jelly.

(e) **Hot Sauces** : The basic white sauce is sauce Bechamel. It is prepared by adding hot milk to cold white roux with bouquet garni and some onion studded with cloves. It is seasoned and strained and a little nutmeg may be added. It has several derivatives.

3. Derivatives of Bechamel Sauce

(a) **Cream Sauce** : Bechamel sauce finished with cream.

(b) **Sauce Mornay** : Bechamel sauce to which some butter and grated parmesan/gruyere cheese added, allowed to cool slightly and then egg yolks are whisked into the sauce e;g. fish mornay.

(c) **Sauce Soubise** : Onion sauce - sauted minced onions added to bechamel sauce and flavoured with some grated nutmeg.

(d) **Cardinal Sauce** : Bechamel + fish stock + truffle essence + lobster butter + cayenne pepper.

(e) **Egg Sauce** : Bechamel sauce to with butter is added, chopped hard-boiled egg then added and it is finished with cream.

(f) **Brown Sauce** : Brown sauce is also known as sauce Espagnole. It is the basic brown hot sauce. When it is reduced to half, it is known as demiglace.

To prepare this sauce, mire poix is sauted and then brown roux is added to which we add brown stock, and is cooked with some bouquet garni. It is cooked slowly for 10-12 hours, skimmed and strained.

(g) **Demiglace** : To derive demiglace, some tomato paste is added to the brown sauce along with some brown stock. The sauce is then reduced to half, skimmed and strained and the resultant product is demiglace.

Derivatives of demiglace are very important and widely used in continental cooking. Some important derivatives are:-

(a) **Bordelaise Sauce** : Chopped shallots and thyme and bayleaf are moistened with red wine and reduced. Demiglace is added, boiled and strained. The sauce is finished with butter. Marrow is served this sauce.

(b) **Madeira Sauce** : Demiglace + Madeira wine.

Basic Sauces

Almost all warm sauces common to luxury cuisine start from five "mother" or basic sauces. They are :

1. **Veloute** : Very coloured meat or fish sauce from white stock.
2. **Espagnole** : Brown, heavy meat sauce made from brown stock.
3. **Tomato** : Red vegetable sauce, made from tomato juice.
4. **Bechamel** : White cream sauce mode from milk.
5. **Hollandaise** : Yellow egg sauce made from yolks and butter.

Today, fewer basic sauces are recognized than in the past. All sauces except the Hollandaise are made the same way. They consist of one of the stocks and roux.

Experimental Recipe 49.

Brown Stock

Equipment

(1) Large roasting pan

(2) Steam kettle or stockpiled, about 96-quart size

Ingredients

(1) Beef and veal bones, trimmings, bacon rind, etc.	:	30-40 pounds
(2) Rough cut onions, celery, carrots parships	:	3 pounds each of
(3) Parsley	:	C-3 bunches
(4) Thyme, pickling spices, peppercorns	:	2 tablespoons each
(5) Garlic, bay leaves, cloves	:	Additional
(6) Tomato paste	:	2 pounds
(7) Cold water	:	15 gallons

Procedure

(1) Prepare all required ingredients

(2) Put chopped bones into a roasting pan.

(3) Put pan into pre-heated 475°F. oven.

(4) Stir bones about every ½ hour to brown them evenly.

(5) When brown, sprinkle the vegetables over the bones.

(6) Roast ½ hour more, then add the tomato paste.

(7) Continue roasting for ½ hour more.

(8) Take pan out of oven, transfer contents of pan to steam kettle, but reserve the fat.

(9) Fill kettle with 15 gallons of cold water.

(10) Add all spices and parsley.

(11) Bring to a slow boil, then simmer 5-6 hours.

(12) Strain stock, cool off, unless used immediately.

(13) Refrigerate overnight, skim fat off before use.

BROWN STOCK

Stock is similar to broth. It is made on by-products such as bones, sinews, and gristle, as well as meat and vegetable trimmings. These by-products are simmered in water and the result of this extraction is called stock. (Ref. Experimental Recipe 49)

1. Brawn stock can be made from beef, veal, or pone bones
2. Keep stock free of salt

ROUX

Roux is a French word used for a mixture of one weight part cooking fat and one weight part all-purpose flour. This mixture is fried for a short time on low heat. When added to a liquid and brought to a boil, it thickens the liquid immediately.

1. White meat stock with roux becomes veloute
2. Chicken stock with roux becomes chicken veloute sauce
3. Brown meat stock with roux is named espagnole sauce
4. Tomato juice with roux makes tomato sauce
5. Hot milk with roux is called bechamel sauce.

By adding to these four basic roux sauces various garnishes and refinements, nearly all type of cuisine are made. Only for a few special preparations is roux omitted and white wash (plain cornstarch dissolved in water) used. Roux consists of flour, lightly browned, in edible fat. Since starch burns easily under heat, it is best to use a heavy sauce pan of "sauteuse" which diffuses heat. Constant watching and stirring over a low fire is necessary. (Ref. Experimental Recipe 50)

Saute Pan Making Rox

Any good fat can be used. Chicken fat to make a chicken supreme sauce is acceptable, but neutral oils or butter are more common. All purpose flour is preferred. The finished roux can be kept warm close to the stove, and used all day or be kept under refrigeration for weeks without spoiling.

Roux cannot be eaten by itself. It must always be mixed into a liquid and be brought to a rolling boil to be sure that all starches have *gelatinized* (meaning the starch granules have absorbed liquid to their fullest capacity). For this reason, roux is called a thickening agent.

1. The best way of using roux is to add warm roux by eye measurement to nearly simmering liquid, stirring with whisk until smooth. Why by eye measurement? Because of the difference in liquids, sauce pans used, heat sources, ideas, habits, and desired textures. This is one of the instances where the cook becomes the artist. He

is the professional who uses his own standards, his own sophistication and understanding to determine how the expected product should be.

2. Do not use sizzling hot roux or cold water; in either case, it may cause a lumpy sauce.

Experimental Recipe 50.

Roux preparation and use

Serves: 30

Equipment

1/8-inch heavy aluminum "sauteuse" sauce pan.

Ingredients

(1) Clear fat	:	1 cup
(2) All purpose flour	:	1½ cups sifted,
(3) Wooden spatula or a whip	:	1.

Method

(1) Prepare all required ingredients.
(2) Put fat into casserole on low heat.
(3) When warm, stir flour in and keep stirring.
(4) Depending on the type of sauce needed, roux is taken off when
  (a) still white (4 to 5 minutes) or
  (b) light golden brown (6 to 10 minutes).
(5) Take from the heat and cool to about 175°F.
(6) Now, little by little, the roux is added to the liquid to be thickened, which should be about 185°F. to 195°F. Whisk liquid constantly while adding the roux. Stop adding it when the thickness has the desired look.
(7) Bring to a full boil. Beware of scorching, but keep boiling at least for 10 to 20 minutes.
(8) Check texture of the sauce. Change it if necessary by adding more roux or more liquid.
(9) Strain sauce into fresh container and keep uncovered in the steam table, or cool for storage under refrigeration.

HOLLANDAISE SAUCE

The most popular among sauces Hollandaise is a rich, warm, mayonnaise-like sauce made from egg yolk and butter, seasoned with lemon juice and salt. It is served with fish, vegetables, or eggs. Some of its more spicy variations; such as Sauce Bearnaise or Sauce Choron are served with meat. Hollandaise is also used to improve various sauces made with roux, especially when they are used for gratinated dishes. Egg sauces have a limited holding ability and should be made as close to serving time as possible. Egg sauces will curdle if kept too hot, and when cold, the butter will stiffen, making rewarming very difficult. Egg yolks contain sulfur, and lemon juice contains acid. Thus, only stainless steel, glass, or china can be used in the making of this sauce. A stainless steel whisk must also be used.

PREPARING HOLLANDISE SAUCE

1. The finished sauce should not be kept too long.
2. A suitable warm place must be found. The steam table is too hot. Storage must be in a temperature zone from 100°F. to 120°F.
3. All utensils used must be of nonoxidizing materials.

(Ref. Experimental Recipe 51)

Experimental Recipe 51.

Sauce Hollandaise

Serves: 30

Equipments

(1) Stainless steel bowl	:	One 12-inch
(2) Stainless steel whip	:	One 12-inch
(3) Tapered sauce pan (to improvise double boiler)	:	One 8-inch
(4) Rubber Spatula: One		

Ingredients

(1) Egg yolks	:	6 extra large
(2) Lemon juice	:	2 tablespoons
(3) Cold water	:	4 tablespoons
(4) Clarified warm butter, about 100°F	:	8 ounces

Method

(1) Prepare all required ingredients.
(2) The tapered sauce pan is half filled with hot water.
(3) Yolks, water, and lemon juice are mixed in the bowl.
(4) The bowl is set on top of the sauce pan with water.
(5) The improvised double boiler is put on the range.
(6) The yolk mixture is whipped over heat to a fluffy custard.
(7) Double boiler and bowl are taken off the heat.
(8) The clear butter is whipped into the custard in a thin.
(9) The sauce is tested for texture and tasted for salt, and lemon flavour. If it is too thin more heat is needed. If it is too thick, water or more lemon juice can be added.

MOTHER SAUCES AND SOME DERIVATIVES

Brown meat stock, made from veal and pork bones, can be reduced to a strong meat essence called Glace de Viande. This is done by slow simmering of the stock in a flat sauce pan. Most chefs today buy commercial meat bases or meat essences to save labour. Meat essence is used to give extra flavour to other sauces or dishes.

SAUCE COOKERY

Sauce texture in itself is a value judgement differing with cuisine and from chef to chef. It must be understood that two quarts of any sauce, simmering in a five-quart sauce pan for five minutes will have a different texture (thickness-thinness) than two quarts of the same sauce simmering for five minutes in a nine-inch tapered sauce pan.

1. The quality of a stock simmered slowly with proper ingredients.
2. The quality of the fat used for a roux.
3. The care extended to this roux.

Sauce cookery will be successful when the proper size of commercial casseroles of a heavy sauge material are used. Casseroles with thin bottoms which are made of material which does not diffuse heat uniformly will usually result in scorched or burned sauces.

Meat, Chicken or Fish Veloute

Take about one gallon of the desired stock and simmer with two cups of golden roux for about 30 minutes, then strained.

Sauce Supreme

1. Take 2 quarts of chicken veloute and 2 quarts of manufacturing cream and
2. Stammered to a desired texture.

Sauce Allemande

1. Take 3 quarts of meat veloute sauce are brought to a boil.
2. Add one pint of white wine.
3. Take a pint of heavy cream and 10 egg yolds are whipped together.
4. The simmering veloute is poured over this mixture, while it is still being whisked.
5. Season with nutmeg and salt.

Sauce Normande

1. 3 quarts of fish veloute,
2. 1 pint clam juice and the juice of half a lemon is brought to a boil.
3. Then it is finished with 10 egg yolks and one pint of heavy cream, as in Sauce Allemande.

Espagnole

Take about one gallon brown meat stock, one-half cup of caramelized tomato paste and one cup red wine and simmered with two cups of brown roux for at least 30 minutes, then strained.

Sauce Bordelaise

1. 1 cup of chopped shallots is sauteed in 2 ounces of olive oil, degalzed with 3 quarts of heavy claret type wine and reduced by one-third.
2. This is seasoned with type, nay leaf and black pepper.
3. Then it is blended with 2 quarts of espagnole and half a cup of meat essence. 4. It is then strained.
4. This sauce is often served with poached beef marrow as a garnish.

Sauce Poivrade

1. 2 cups vinegar, 2 cups burgundy, 1 cup onions, 1 cup parsley, several garlic cloves and 3 tablespoons of crushed pepper are simmered until reduced to half.

2. This is strained and then blended with 3 quarts of espagnole and one pint of tomato puree.

Sauce Robert

1. 2 cups chopped onions are sauteed in butter, deglazed with 1 cup of tarragon vinegar and 1 cup of stock.
2. It is simmered until reduced to half.
3. Then 1 cup of prepared french mustard is whisked in and blended with 1 ½ quarts of supreme sauce and 1 quart of espagnole.

Brown Mushroom Sauce

1. 2½ pounds (1 basket) of fresh mushrooms are sliced and sauteed, then blended with 3 quarts of espagnole and ½ cup of dry sherry wine.

Sauce Demi-glace

1. 4 quarts of brown stock are slowly reduced to half, then blended with 2 quarts of espangole and simmered for 30 minutes more.
2. To finish the sauce, 4 tablespoons of cornstarch are dissolved in ½ cup of dry port wine and added to the simmering sauce.

Bechamel

1. One gallon of fresh milk (or substitute) is heated in the steam table or a double boiler to about 140°F.
2. Two cups of chopped onions are sauteed in 2 ounces of bacon fat.
3. These are blended with the milk and 2 cups of roux made from clarified butter. 4. It is simmered for 20 minutes (scorches easily) and streamed.

Sauce Mornay (Cheese Sauce Plain)

1. 3 quarts of bechamel are brought to a boil. ½ pound of grated parmesan and ½ pound of grated Swiss cheese are whisked in.
2. It is then taken off the heat.
3. And ¼ pound of fresh butter is worked in.
4. Then it is seasoned with salt and cayenne.

Sauce Mornay (Cheese Sauce, for Gratinating)

1. For each quart of mornay, as described above, ½ to 1 cap of rich of rich Hollandaise is blended in when needed.

Tomato Sauce

1. Tomato sauces can be made in many varieties.
2. Every combination will have slightly different flavour. Spices, garlic, sugar, onions, bacon, or ham can be added at will. The tomato concentration of the sauce in itself allows for many variations.
3. Tomato juice, puree-paste or fresh tomatoes can be used with stock, fish stock, chicken stock, or water to dilute the tomato concentrates.

Creole Sauce

1. 2 cups each of the following are cut into a coarse julienne: onions, bell peppers, celery, mushrooms, and tomatoes.
2. They are lightly sauteed in 3 counces of olive oil, deglazed with 3 quarts of light tomato puree, spiced with sauteed garlic, salt, sugar, cayenne, and Oregonian.
3. This is simmered for 4-5 minutes (the vegetables must remain crunchy), then thickened with cornstarch dissolved in cold water.

Hungarian Lesco Sauce

1. 3 cups of onions, 2 cups of bell peppers and 3 cups of peeled, 2 cup of bell peppers and 3 cup of peeled, deseeded tomatoes are cut in a coarse julienne and sauteed in 3 ounces of bacon fat.
2. Then 2 tablespoons of finely chopped garlic and 2 tablespoons of fancy paprika are added.
3. Then 2 quarts of sour cream and 1 quart of tomato sauce are blended into it. It is brought to a full boil and reduced if necessary.

Guideline for use of Sauce

1. All sauces can be blended with other sauces, cream, sour cream, wine, juices, reductions, purees, eggs, cheese, butter, condiment and so on.
2. Sauces should be blended in small quantities at the time of serving.
3. Garnishes must be sauteed in butter or heated before they are added.
4. Garnishes must be edible and eye appealing.
5. Sauce are reduced (concentrated) by simmering, sometimes diluted with stock, or taken off the heat to prevent curdling.

The Table 3.11A lists the compositions and names of sauces, popular in luxury cuisine. No measurements or working methods are given. A chef who crates a sauce does it much the same way as an artist painting a picture. The ingredients are known but the rest is up to the individual. If quantities were standard it would not help too much, since the size, thickness, shape of the casserole, the heat source, and the food are different. Understanding comes through repeated practice.

The sauce named listed could be of regional origin, reflecting the specialty of a certain area. Other names indicate the flavour of the sauce. Some sauces have been dedicated to famous persons or historic events.

PAN GRAVY OR "JUS DE VIANDE"

Gravy is made from roast drippings, diluted with brown stock, then lightly thickened with roux and cornstarch. The word gravy is often misused to describe liquids which should be called a sauce. Gravy or pan juice must have a strong flavour. It should not be diluted unnecessarily. (Ref. Experimental Recipe 52)

Table 3.11A. Sauce Composition for Luxury Cusine

S.No.	Sauce Bearnaise			Composition
1.	Sauce Bearnaise	Hollandaise	:	Shallots, pepper, tarragon in vinegar reduction, chopped parsley.
2.	Sauce Bourguignonne	Espagnole	:	Burgundy wine, dash of sugar.
3.	Sauce Cardinale	Bachamel	:	Fish stock, mushroom essence, lobster puree, butter, cayenne pepper.
4.	Sauce Champignon	Espagnole	:	Sauteed mushrooms, Madeira wine.
5.	Sauce Chasseur	Espagnole	:	Mushrooms, tomatoes, with wine.
6.	Sauce Chorion	Hollandaise	:	Tomato paste concentrated.
7.	Sauce Bigarade	Espagnole	:	Orange zeste and juice in red wine reduced, lemon juice, sugar, currant jelly.
8.	Sauce Duxelles	Espagnole	:	Chopped onions, mushrooms, parsley sauteed, tomato paste.
9.	Sauce Estragon	Veloute	:	Tarragon reduced in white wine, fresh butter
10.	Sauce Godard	Espagnole	:	Mushrooms, white wine, chopped ham.
11.	Sauce Indine	Veloute	:	Fresh cream, curry paste, cooked potato cubes.
12.	Sauce Madder	Espagnole	:	Madeira wine reduced.
13.	Sauce Meyerbeer	Espagnole	:	Chicken livers, mushrooms, onions, sherry wine.
14.	Sauce Refract	Veloute	:	Horseradish, vinegar, dash sugar, fresh butter.
15.	Sauce Tortue	Espagnole	:	Tomato sauce, reduced clear turtle soup.
16.	Sauce Nantua	Bacchanal	:	Fish stock, cream, white sine, crayfish, paprika, cayenns, brandy.
17.	Sauce Newburg	Bachamel	:	Paprika, cream sherry.
18.	Sauce Perigueux	Espagnole	:	Demi-glace, mushrooms, truffles, red wine, madeira wine.

Soups

Food in a more liquid than solid state is called soup. It is eaten with a spoon. Soups are well liked by the public because they are easy to eat and digest. They are filling, nourishing, and not costly. Soups probably began as kettle stews. Many of today's regional specialty soups clearly indicate such a development.

For the cook, soups are easy to make when modern equipment is used with an understanding of the structure of soups. Soups can be grouped into clear soups or thickened soups. (Ref. Fig. 3.11A)

Thickened Soups

Thickened soups are grouped by :

1. The addition of plain starch or roux for better flavour and texture.
2. The addition of a vegetable, meat or fish pulp (puree) for thickening.

Experimental Recipe 52.

Gravy Preparation

Serves:30

Materials

(1) Roast drippings
(2) Mirepoix (roughty cubed equal parts of onions, celery, carrots)
(3) Brown stock
(4) Flour.

Method

(1) Prepare all required ingredients.
(2) Remove roast from pan; place pan with all the drippings on the top of the stove or range.
(3) If mirepoix was not added before, then it is added now.
(4) Reduce droppings over slow fire, until remaining fat is clear.
(5) Drain off most of the fat. Leave just enough to absorb flour for roux.
(6) If paprika is desired, it is added now. The flour, to absorb the fat, is stirred in and mixed well.
(7) Fill up with the minimum amount of hot stock needed, which matches the roasts.
(8) Bring back to simmering point, stir constantly, and simmer for at least 10 minutes or to desired consistency.
(9) Finish to taste and colour.
(10) Strain through China cap; keep warm in bainmarie.

3. The combing of puree, roux and, for absolute refinement, cream.

   Thickened soups, just as clear soups, may be served strained and plain, or they may have a garnish prepared in the same way as for the consomme.

SOUP MAKING

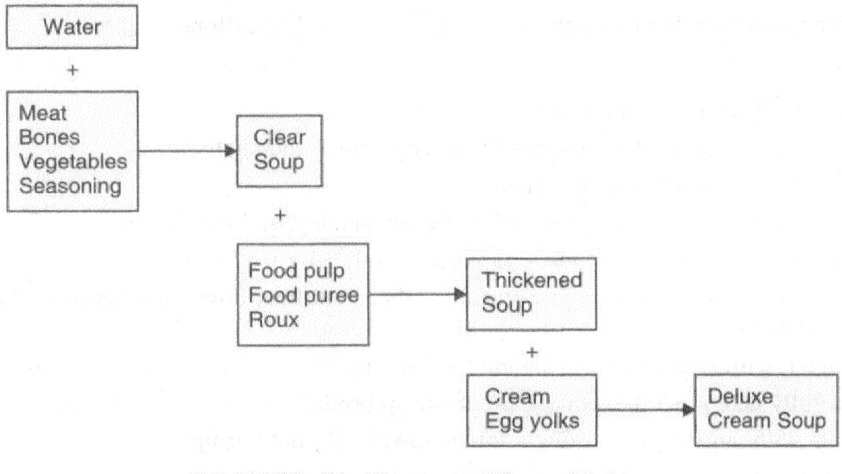

Fig. 3.11A. The Process of Soup Making

CONSOMME

1. Egg whites must be half-whipped and completely mixed with clairage and mirepoix.
2. If lukewarm stock is used, the two quarts stock of step 3 of Experimental Recipe 53 must be iced.
3. A few onion peels can be included for a darker colour.
4. The boiling point must be reached under constant supervision and stirring to prevent overbilling or scorching.
5. Shaking of pot will cloud clarification.

Exeperimental Recipe 53.

Preparation of Consomme

Serves : 30

Equipments

(1) 16 quart soup pot
(2) Claying cap
(3) 2 clean linen towels
(4) Large dipper
(5) Whip
(6) 1-2-gallon stainless steel soup inset.

Ingredients

(1) Coarse lean ground beef	:	5 lbs.
(2) Cloves	:	10
(3) Egg whites and shells	:	10
(4) Bay leaves	:	5
(5) Mixed onions, parsnips, leeks, celery, carrots	:	10 cups
(6) Salt	:	1 tablespoon
(7) Parsley	:	4 bunches
(8) Strong beef bouillon or stock	:	2 ½ gallons

Method

(1) Prepare all required ingredients.
(2) Ground raw lean beef is mixed with 10 egg withes and shells.
(3) Add 2 quarts cold stock, mix again.
(4) Add 10 cups chopped-up vegetables, cloves, parsley, and bay leaves.
(5) Add the remaining cold stock, 1 tablespoon salt. Mix well again.
(6) Bring to a very fast boil while starlings, then turn heat down and simmer. (Watch out, egg white might scorch)
(7) Simmer, without stirring or shaking for 2 hours.
(8) Carefully take it off the stove. Do not stir up broth.
(9) Strain with large dipper through double towels. Do not stir up.
(10) Season to finish, reheat to boiling point and serve.

6. Rinse linen towel with hot water and squeeze dry before using. (Emphasis: sanitation, better conduction)
7. The degreasing of strained consomme can be done with pieces of butcher paper. (Ref. Experimental Recipe 53)

CLEAR SOUPS

Clear soups may be unclarified plain broth or clarified consumme. Broth is leftover liquid from the nothing of protein foods. For a better flavour, vegetables are added to the broth. Vegetable broth is food too, but seldom as a single flavour. Other flavour-giving ingredients are even added to tomato soup. In home cookers vegetable soups are made without meat additives. Commercial cookery boasts even vegetable flavour with some kind of protein stock.

Consomme is clarified broth or stock. Its strength is improved with extra vegetables and proteins. It is served either clear or with a garnish. The garnish may be cooked with the soup, as in "Consomme Julienne" or prepared completely extra and added to the finished soup at the last minute, as in "Consomme Celestive". (Ref. Table 3.11B)

A large variety of clear soups exist. A soup without any mixed-in starch is called a clear soup. A meat broth is a clear soup. If it is served without garnish it is often called a bouillon, such as beef bouillon or chicken bouillon. The same broth served with cooked chopped chicken or beef meat and rice is called Chicken broth or Beef broth. Clarified and enriched (made stronger) broth is called consomme.

1. Clear soups are more appetizing than filling.
2. Adding the wrong garnish can cloud a consumme
3. Quality of a soup comes from the quality of the ingredients and slow simmering
4. Hot soups must be served as hot as possible, but cold soups should be surrounded with crushed ice.
5. Garnish cooked in separate broth, then added to consomme, will not cloud it.

Clear Soups includes:–

1. Bouillon	:	Strained meat or vegetable broth, no garnish.
2. Broth	:	Strained meat or vegetable broth, with garnish.
3. Consomme	:	Clarified, enriched meat and vegetable broth with or without garnish.

Lentil soup

Variations of this soup are made in all European countries. The sliced wienners can be replaced with different sausages, bacon, or ham pieces. Sometimes bread croutons are added, and spices for certain areas are used. (Ref. Experimental Recipe 54)

Table 3.11B. Clear Soups and their Compositions

S. No.	*Name*		*Composition*
1.	Consomme double	:	Strong consomme served hot in a cup.
2.	Jellied Consomme	:	Strong consomme with little gelatin added served chilled, in a cup.
3.	Beef Tea or Olio	:	Strong consomme in a cup.
4.	Tortue Clair	:	Clear turtle soup in a cup.
5.	Consomme Madrilene (cold)	:	Consomme and tomato juice in a cup.
6.	Consomme Madrilene (hot)	:	Consomme and tomato juice in a cup.
7.	Consomme au Sherry	:	Consomme and 10% dry sherry in a cup.
8.	Consomme au Madeira	:	Consomme and 10% Madeira in a cup.
9.	Consomme au Port	:	Consomme and 10% Port in a cup.
10.	Consomme Royal	:	Consomme and diced egg custard in a cup.
11.	Consomme Julienne	:	Consomme and sauteed vegetable julienne.
12.	Consomme Paysanne	:	Consomme and sauteed diced vegetable.
13.	Consomme Celestine	:	Consomme and pancake noodles.
14.	Consomme Vermicelli	:	Consomme and thin egg noodles.
15.	Consomme Maria Start	:	Consomme with tapioca and vegetable burnoise.
16.	Tortellini con Brodo	:	Consomme with Italian tortellinis.
17.	Ravioli con Brodo	:	Consomme with Italian raviolis.
18.	French Onion Soup	:	Beef broth, fried onions, croutons, parmesan cheese, gratinated.
19.	Chicken Giblet Soup	:	Chicken broth, gizzards and livers, cut vegetables and marrow dumplings.
20.	Chicken Noodle Soup	:	Chicken broth, vermicelli, mushroom and chicken meat julienne.

Experimental Recipe 54.

Australian Lentils Soup

Serves : 30

Ingredients

(1) Lentils : 5 cups

(2) Bay leaf, thyme, and 1 bunch parsley, tied together (bouquet grainy)

(3) Thinly sliced winners : 4 cups

(4) Onions : 2 whole

(5) Vinegar : 2 ounces

(6) Celery stalks : 2 whole

(7) Salt : To taste

(8) Parsnips : 2 whole

(9) Beef stock : 1½ gallons.

Method

(1) Prepare all required ingredients.
(2) Bring stock, vegetable, and bouquet grani to a boil.
(3) Add lentile, cook until completely tender or mashed.
(4) With a skimmer, fish out the uncut vegetables and discard them.
(5) Add thinly sliced winner and vinegar.
(6) Boil again.
(7) Finish to taste.
(8) Serve.

CALIFORNIA BEEF SOUP

It is a modern version of the Russian Cold Borscht. It is like a blender salad dressing with avocados as the emulsifying agent. Served ice cold it has become popular in warm areas during the summer time. (Ref. Experimental Recipe 55)

The colours, beet red, white, and green must be clearly visible for attractiveness.

Experimental Recipe 55.

Iced California Beet Soup

Serves : 30

Equipment

(1) Commercial blender or speed cutter
(2) One No. 10 can sliced, Pickled beets.

Ingredients

(1) Dill weed	:	4 tableshpoons.
(2) Tarragon	:	1 tablespoon.
(3) Avocados	:	4 ripe.
(4) Pickle julienne	:	2 cups
(5) Chopped parsley	:	1 cup
(6) Olive oil	:	½ cup
(7) Chopped celery hearts	:	1 cup
(8) Salt	:	To taste
(9) Chopped onions	:	½ cup
(10) Pepper	:	To taste
(11) Jellied consomme	:	One No. 51
(12) Tabasco sauce		
(13) Buttermilk	:	1 gallon
(14) Lemon juice		
(15) Sour cream	:	1 ping.

Method

(1) Prepare all required ingredients.

(2) Cut 2 cups of the beets into julienne and mix with the pickle julienne.
(3) Put all remaining ingredients except the sour cream into the blender and blend until completely smooth. Include the beet root liquid from the can. Season to taste.
(4) Check thickness. If too thick, add consomme. If too thin, add avocado.
(5) When it is right, transfer to container for chilling.
(6) When ready to serve, place about 2 tablespoons of the pickle-beets julienne into each preiced cup.
(7) Fill cup with cold soup. Put one tablespoon of sour cream on top and sprinkle additional dill weed into the middle of the sour cream dab.
(8) Serve immediately.

BEEF AND BARLEY SOUP

This is a variation of the well-known Scotch Broth made from lamb stock. When it is made from lamb stock, the soup is also a French specialty named Consomme Eccossaise. (Ref. Experimental Recipe 56)

Experiential Recipe 56.

Beef and Barley Soup

Serves : 30

Ingredients

(1) Beef stock	:	1 ½ gallons
(2) Pearl barley	:	6 cups
(3) Finely chopped vegetables consisting of celery onions, parsnips, carrots, parsley	:	4 cups
(4) Butter	:	½ cup
(5) Flour	:	½ cup.

Method

(1) Prepare all required ingredients.
(2) Bring stock to boil, add barley.
(3) Let simmer for 1 ½ hours.
(4) Saute all the vegetables in butter, add flour, improvise a roux.
(5) Stir into barley stock.
(6) Simmer for ½ hour more or until barley is completely tender.
(7) Season with salt, pepper.
(8) Sprinkle with fresh chopped parsley and serve.

BOSTON CLAM CHOWDER

This delightfull soup is also known as New England Clam Chowder. It is completely different from soups called Manhattan or Coney Island Clam Chowder, which are not chowders by definition. Clam chowder is served with oyster crackers. (Ref. Experimental Recipe 57)

1. Keep soup hot in bainmarie only.
2. Do not exceed a bainmarie temperature of 160°F.

Experimental Recepe 57.

Boston Clam Chowder

Serves : 30

Ingredients

(1)	Diced salt pork	:	1 cup
(2)	Thyme	:	To taste
(3)	Bell peppe, diced	:	1 cup
(4)	Salt	:	To taste
(5)	Celery, diced	:	2 cups
(6)	Pepper	:	very little
(7)	Onions, diced	:	2 cups
(8)	Tarragon	:	very little
(9)	Peeled, dubbed potatoes	:	5 cups
(10)	Butter	:	½ cup
(11)	Milk plus 1 quart whipping cream	:	3 quarts
(12)	Flour	:	½ cup
(13)	Cooked chopped clams and their juice	:	6 cups

Method

(1) Prepare all required ingredients.

(2) Cover potatoes with cold water, bring to boil and simmer for 15 minutes. Add thyme and tarragon.

(3) Saute pork, cubed celery, pepper and onions in butter. Add flour.

(4) Blend the saute, the potatoes, the boiling milk, and the clams in their own juice.

(5) Season with pepper and salt and bring to boiling point again.

(6) Let steep for twenty minutes, at about 185°F.

(7) Transfer to bainmarie and add 1 quart of hot whipping cream.

CANADIAN PEA SOUP

1. In the province of Quebec and Eastern Canada, whole yellow peas are used instead of split ones and the name used is Habitant Soup.
2. Dried green split peas can be used interchangeably.
3. With slight variations, this soup is known under many names. Well known is the French versions, Pottage St. Germane, in which green split peas are used. The soup is served strained or blended with fried bread croutons as a garnish. (Ref. Experimental Recipe 58)

Experimental Recipe 58.

Canadian Pea Soup

Serves : 30

Ingredients

(1)	Dried yellow peas, soaked over night in 3 quarts of stock	: 6 cups
(2)	Thyme	: as required
(3)	Salt	: To taste
(4)	Bacon or salt pork	: ½ pound
(5)	Ham or meat stock (includes 3 quarts used to soak peas)	: 1½ gallons
(6)	Mixed root vegetables (celery, onions carrots)	: 3 cups
(7)	Chopped garlic	: 2 tablespoons
(8)	Bay leaf.	

Method

(1) Prepare all required ingredients

(2) Bring stock to boil, add peas (pre-soaked) and simmer.

(3) Add bay leaf, thyme, and some salt.

(4) Dice bacon or pork fine and saute. Add finely diced vegetables, garlic.

(5) Fry until glassy, then add to soup.

(6) Continue simmering 1-2 hours, until peas are completely tender or mashed up.

CHICKEN OKRA SOUP

This soup is of Creole origin. It has become an favourite and one can find its variations under names like Creole Chicken Soup, Chicken Gumbo, etc. (Ref. Experimental Recipe 59)

To achieve an eye-pleasing soup, vegetables have to be neatly cut and small sizes.

Experimental Recipe 59.

Chicken Okra Soup

Ingredient

(1)	Okra	: 6 cups
(2)	Peeled, deseeded and cubed tomato	: 6 cups
(3)	Onion	: 1 cup
(4)	Rice	: 1½ cups
(5)	Parsnips	: 1 cup
(6)	Chicken fat	: 1 cup
(7)	Celery	: 2 cups
(8)	Cooked, shopped, left-over chicken meat	: 3 cups
(9)	Bell pepper	: 1 cup
(10)	Chicken stock	: 1½ gallons.

Method

(1) Prepare all required ingredients
(2) Cut onion, parsnips, pepper, and celery into ½-inch square slices.
(3) Saute them in chicken fat.
(4) Add hot stock. Bring to boil. Add uncooked rice.
(5) Add tomatoes, with their own juice.
(6) Simmer for ½ hour. Add sliced, cleaned okra (¼-inch wheels).
(7) Continue simmering until tender. Add chicken meat and season to taste.
(8) Serve hot.

CORN CHOWDER

This soup can be considered an American speciality. If these steps are followed, this is a very simple preparation. (Ref. Experimental Recipe 60)

Experim]ental Recipe 60.

Corn Chowder

Serves : 30

Ingredient

(1) Creamed corn	:	6 cups
(2) Finely chopped onions	:	1 cup
(3) Hot milk	:	1 gallon
(4) Finely chopped celery	:	1 cup
(5) Butter	:	¼ lb.
(6) Salt	:	To taste
(7) Flour	:	3 ounces
(8) Pepper	:	As required.

Method

(1) Prepare all required ingredients.
(2) Saute onions in butter until glassy. Add celery
(3) Saute a little longer, then add flour to make into roux.
(4) Pour hot milk on; bring to boil.
(5) Add corn; reheat to boiling point. Season and serve hot.

THOUSAND FLOWERS SOUP

This soup, a true regional specialty is relatively unknown outside of good Italian restaurants. (Ref. Experimental Recipe 61)

Experimental Recipe 61.

Mille Fante (Thousand Flavour Soup)

Serves : 30

Ingredients

(1) Good beef stock	:	1½ gallons
(2) Grated parmesan cheese	:	½ lb.
(3) Sourdough French bread, crust cut off	:	15 slices
(4) Eggs	:	4 whole and 6 egg yolks
(5) Butter	:	½lb.
(6) Whipping cream	:	1 pint

Method

(1) Prepare all required ingredients.
(2) Pan fry the bread slices in butter to a golden brown.
(3) Bring the beef stock to a boil.
(4) Put fried bread into the stock and simmer at least 10 minutes.
(5) Use whisk to whip the bread into small particles.
(6) Continue to simmer 10 more minutes.
(7) Put eggs and yolks into a bowl to mix with the whipping cream.
(8) Whip this mixture over a double boiler to a custard.
(9) Sprinkle the parmesan over the custard and fold in.
(10) Pour the boiling soup-bread mixture into the custard while continuing to whip.
(11) Serve immediately with finely chopped parsley sprinkled on top.

MUSHROOM SOUP

This is a home style soup and also a regional specialty. This soup is easy to make, tasty, and nourishing. Many different combinations with other vegetables can be made. If thickness of soup while in bainmarie is to be kept, soup should never be fully covered. (Ref. Experimental Recipe 62)

Experimental Recipe 62.

Mushroom and Potatoes Soup

Serves : 30

Ingredients

(1) Cubed potatoes	:	12 cups
(2) Roux, made with butter	:	1 cup
(3) Sliced mushrooms	:	8 cups
(4) Fresh butter	:	¼ cup
(5) Beef stock	:	1½ gallons
(6) Chopped parsley	:	½ cup.

Method

(1) Prepare all required ingredients.

(2) Bring stock to a boil, add the potatoes, then simmer for 15 minutes.

(3) Wash and saute mushrooms in ¼ cup of butter.

(4) Add to the simmering potatoes and cook 15 minutes more.

(5) Add warm roux mix in well. Boil fully for 5 minutes.

(6) Add parsley; finish with salt and prepare.

(7) Serve hot.

ITALIAN MINESTRONE

The most popular specialty soup is an Italian vegetable soup called Minestrone. There are a few varieties, but its main flavour consists of fresh vegetables in season, tomatoes, garlic, Italian herbs, and olive oil. For starch content, beans and paste are added. Grated parmesan cheese is sprinkled on top before eating. (Ref. Experimental Recipe 63)

1. For real flavour, the stock must be strong and clear. The soup must simmer only.
2. Garlic must be finely chopped and sauteed golden brown in olive oil.

Experimental Recipe 63.

Italian Ministrone

Serves : 30

Ingredients

(1)	Tomatoes	:	4 cups
(2)	Cabbage	:	1 cup
(3)	Carrots	:	1 cup
(4)	Mushrooms	:	1 cup
(5)	Celery	:	1 cup
(6)	Kidney beans or garbanzos, soaked & precooked	:	2 cups
(7)	Parsnips	:	1 cup
(8)	Cut mecaroni	:	½ lb.
(9)	Leeks	:	1 cup
(10)	Beef stock	:	1½ gallons
(11)	Fresh spinach or chard	:	2 cups
(12)	Olive oil	:	2 ounces
(13)	Zucchini	:	2 cups
(14)	Salt, rosemary, oregano, or basil	:	for finishing
(15)	Peas	:	1 cup
(16)	Grated parmesan cheese	:	for sprinklings
(17)	String beans	:	1 cup
(18)	Finely chopped garlic	:	6 tablespoons.

Method

(1) Prepare all required ingredients.
(2) Wash and clean all vegetables.
(3) Cut all vegetables in uniform 1/3-inch slices or cubes.
(4) Add stock and spices.
(5) Bring to a boil, then simmer for 25 minutes.
(6) Add macaroni and the finely chopped garlic sauteed in olive oil.
(7) Simmer ½ hour more, finish with salt and spice.
(8) Serve with parmesan sprinkled on top or, even better, on the side.

COLD VICKYSSOISE

Despite its French-sounding name, this soup is a new invention by a chef from a leading New York hotel. It has become a favourite all over. (Ref. Experimental Recipe 64)

1. The consistency of this soup could become too thick or too thin, depending on the size of the casserole used. A wide, flat one will evaporate more liquid than a narrow, high one.
2. If the cold soup appears too rich and too thick, it can be diluted with cold, defatted bouillon and milk.

Experiment Recipe 64.

Cold Vickyssoise

Portion : 30

Equipment

Commercial blender or speed cutter.

Ingredients

(1) Beef stock	:	1 gallon
(2) Leeks, cut up	:	3 bunches
(3) Finely chopped chives	:	1 cup
(4) Shallots	:	½ cup
(5) Olive oil	:	1 cup
(6) Raw peeled potatoes, thinly sliced	:	5-6 pounds
(7) Fresh unwhipped cream	:	2 quarts.

Method

(1) Prepare all required ingredients.
(2) Bring beef stock to a boil. And thinly sliced potatoes.
(3) Saute cut-up leeks in olive oil.
(4) Add leeks and potatoes to the simmering stock.
(5) Simmer for about 3/4 hour, then blenderize well. Taste.
(6) Force blended soup through a fine china cap.

(7) Refrigerate until completely cold. Then stir in the cream.
(8) Adjust taste and texture to your liking.
(9) Serve in iced cups with chopped chives as garnish on top.

FRESH VEGETABLE PUREE SOUP

An inexpensive soup from various kinds of fresh vegetables, made in a blender. A mixture of pureed vegetables is called Plottage Carbure. Otherwise it is called Cream of Cauliflower, or Celery Puree Soup, and so on. (Ref. Experimental Recipe 65)

Experimental Recipe 65.

Fresh Vegetable Pure Soup

Portion : 30

Ingredients

(1) Various vegetables such as cauliflower, celery broccoli, peas, asparagus, potatoes, parsnips, leeks : 12 cups
(2) Butter roux : 4-6 ounce
(3) Beet stock : 2 gallons
(4) Whipping cream : 1 pint
(5) Butter : ½ cup.

Method

(1) Prepare all required ingredients.
(2) Wask and clean vegetables.
(3) Cut the clean vegetables to be blended roughly, but reserve 1/3 as furnish.
(4) Cut reserved 1/3 into eye-appealing shape, cover with stock and cook.
(5) Saute the blended vegetables in butter.
(6) Add beef stock and bring to a boil
(7) Simmer until tender, but crunchy.
(8) Add warm roux. Use wire whip to stir smooth.
(9) Boil again, simmer for at least 5 minutes.
(10) Puree in the blender. Reheat.
(11) Add cream and the crunchy cooked 1/3 of the vegetable as garnish. Take off stove.
(12) Finish to taste and serve.

NAVY BEAN SOUP

This is a popular winter soup from the north-eastern region of the United States. Variations of this preparation are well known all over the world. (Ref. Experimental Recipe 66)

Experimental Recipe 66.

Navy Bean Soup

Serves : 30

Ingredients

(1)	Navy beans, soaked in cold stock overnight	:	3 pints
(2)	Pickle and chopped onions	:	2 cups
(3)	Chopped celery	:	2 cups
(4)	Drained, chopped tomato pulp	:	2 cups
(5)	Pickled and finely chopped garlic	:	2 cloves
(6)	Bacon or ham fat	:	4 ounces
(7)	Stock from smoked meat	:	2 gallons
(8)	Chopped ham or bacon	:	2 cups

Method

(1) Prepare all required ingredients.
(2) Wash and clean all vegetables.
(3) Bring the beans in their own soaking stock to a boil.
(4) Add the remainder of the 2 gallons stock, and simmer until beans are nearly tender. This may take 2 - 21/2 hours.
(5) In the meantime, saute onion and celery in ham fat. Add garlic. They should puree easily.
(6) Add this mixture to the tender beans.
(7) Add chopped tomatoes and ham.
(8) Bring to boil again and simmer for at least 5 minutes.
(9) Whip well with wire whisk to break up some of the beans.
(10) Season with salt, pepper.
(11) Serve.

QUESTIONS AND DISCUSSIONS

Fill in the Blanks

Q.1. Read and complete the following statements:

(a) The quantities of fat and flour used for roux must be equal in ....
(b) Lamb bones have a strong flavour and are not used for a general ....
(c) Veloute sauces can be made from meat of ....
(d) True gravy must contain meat ....
(e) Bechamel is the French name for ....
(f) The emulsification of egg yolks and butter is called sauce ....
(g) Brown stock mixed with roux makes ....
(h) Roux is the ingredient which makes a thin liquid ....

(i) Espagnole, one of the mother sauces, has a colour of ....
(j) Blending of roux into a liquid is done best with a ....
(k) Plain white meat stock sauce is called ....
(l) For a roux, the flour is fried to achieve a better ....
(m) The best flavour of meat broth is achieved by adding ....
(n) White stock is made from bones which have not been ....
(o) Tomato sauce can be made from tomato juice or ....

[**Ans.:** (a) weight; (b) stock; (c) fish;
(d) starch and fat; (e) white cream sauce; (f) Hallandaise sauce;
(g) espagnole sauce; (h) thick; (i) brown stock;
(j) rolling boil; (k) broth; (l) consistancy;
(m) garnish; (n) roasted; (o) red vegetable sauce.]

Multiple Choice Type

Q.2. Read each question carefully and select the best answer.

(i) Minestrone, the popular Italian soup, also contains
  (a) Cracked wheat (b) Polenta (corn grits)
  (c) Dumplings (d) Garbanzo beans.

(ii) For the blending of composition sauces, it is best to have a
  (a) Stock pot (b) Soup casserole
  (c) Saute pan (sauteuse) (d) Flip fry pan.

(iii) A cauliflower cream soup is best described as a
  (a) Broth with cauliflower and cream
  (b) Caullflower puree with roux and cream
  (c) Consomme with cauliflower garnish
  (d) Broth with roux and cauliflower.

(iv) Brown stock made from beef bones should simmer
  (a) 3 to 4 hours (b) 4 to 5 hours
  (c) 5 to 6 hours (d) 6 to 7 hours.

(v) To change broth into consomme, it is essential to use
  (a) Sherry wine (b) Egg whites
  (c) Onions (d) Beef extract.

(vi) Mille fante, an Intalian soup, is made of
  (a) Vegetables, cream, cheese, roux, stock
  (b) Chicken puree, cream, roux, parmesan
  (c) Bread, butter, cheese, eggs, cream, stock
  (d) Fish stock, roux, shrimps, onions, cheese.

(vii) Sauce Bearnaise is a derivation of the mother sauce,
  (a) Veloute (b) Bechamel
  (c) Supreme (d) Hollandaise.

(viii) A double consomme is

(a) 2 cups of consomme (b) An extra large cup of consomme

(c) Strong consomme in a cup (d) Tomato consomme.

(ix) To make Hollandaise sauce, it is important that all utensils are of

(a) Nonoxidizing material (b) Copper, lined with tin

(c) Polished aluminum (d) Good heat conduction material.

[**Ans.:** (i) (d); (ii) (c); (iii) (b); (iv) (c); (v) (b);
(vi) (c); (vii) (d); (viii) (c); (ix) (a)]

Matching Type

Q.3. Match the sauce names in Table 'A' with the corresponding igredients in Table 'B'.

Table 'A'	*Table 'B'*
(i) Allemande	(a) Espagnol, mushrooms, red wine, truffles, madeira wine.
(ii) Bigarde	(b) Bechamel, parmesan, cream, egg yolks, white pepper.
(iii) Bordelaise	(c) Veloute, tarragon, butter.
(iv) Champignon	(d) Veloute, horseradish, cream sugar, vinegar.
(v) Estragon	(e) Espagnole, red wine, beef marrow, shallots.
(vi) Chasseur	(f) Veloute, cream, egg yolks, white wine.
(vii) Mornay	(g) Espagnote, orange and lemon peel and juice, red wine sugar.
(viii) Newburg	(h) Espagnole, mushrooms, madeira wine
(ix) Raifort	(i) Bachamel, paprika, cream, sherry.
(x) Perigueux	(j) Espagnole, mushroom, white wine, tomatoes.

[**Ans.:** (i) (f); (ii) (g); (iii) (e); (iv) (h); (v) (d);
(vi) (j); (vii) (b); (viii) (i); (ix) (d) (x) (d)]

Short Answer Type

Q.4. Describes the origin of specialty soups and why do they have emotional appeal to customers.

Q.5. Explain the purpose of sauces used in Culinary Art.

Q.6. Why is it necessary to learn all the foreign names of sauces and other dishes?

Q.7. Define the following:

(a) Gristle (e) Steep

(b) Consistency (f) Mother sauce

(c) Puree (g) Clarify.

(d) Potage

Q.8. Explain the derivatives of the following in one sentence:-

(a) Bechamel sauce (d) Hollandaise sauce

(b) Veloute sauce (e) Tomato sauce

(c) Sauce espagnole (f) Mayonnaise sauce.

[Ans.:

(a) Derivatives of Bechamel Sauce

1. Anchovy
   (a) Bechamel
   (b) 1 tsp anchovy essence,
2. Egg
   (a) Bechamel
   (b) 2 hard-boiled eggs in small dice.
3. Mornay
   (a) Bechamel
   (b) 50gm grated cheese + 1 egg yolk.
4. Onion
   (a) Bechamel
   (b) 100gm chopped or diced onions cooked without colour either by boiling or sweating butter.
5. Soubise
   Same as above but passed through strainer.

(b) Derivatives of Veloute Sauce

1. Caper
   (a) Mutton stock base veloute
   (b) 2 tsp caper. Served with boiled leg of mutton.
2. Supreme
   (a) Chicken stock base veloute
   (b) Well washed mushroom trimmings.
   (c) Served hot with boiled chicken + vol-au-vents.
3. Aurore
   (a) Supreme sauce
   (b) 1 tsp tomato puree.
   (c) Served with boiled chicken, poached eggs chaud froid sauce.
4. Mushroom
   (a) Supreme sauce
   (b) 100gm sliced, well washed, sweated white button mushrooms.
   (c) Simmer for 10 minutes, finish with egg yolk and cream.
   (d) Served with boiled chicken, sweet breads.
5. Ivory
   (a) Sauce supreme
   (b) meat glaze.
   (c) Served with boiled chicken.

(c) Derivatives of Sauce Espagnole

1. Demiglace
   (a) 1/2 brown stock (Estouffade)
   (b) 1/2 brown sauce (Espagnole) reduced to half. Passed through a chinois.
   Correct seasoning.
2. Bordelaise
   (a) Demiglace
   (b) Reduction of chopped shallots

	(c) Red wine
	(d) Mignonette pepper
	(e) Thyme
	(f) Bayleaf.
3. Devilled	(a) Demiglace
	(b) Reduction of shallots
	(c) White wine
	(d) Mignonette pepper
	(e) Cayenne pepper
	(f) Vinegar.
4. Robert	(a) Demiglace
	(b) Browned onions
	(c) Vinegar
5. Charcutiere	(a) Robert sauce
	(b) Juliennes of gherkins.
(d) Derivatives of Hollandaise Sauce	
1. Bearnaise	(a) Hollandaise
	(b) Tarragon in vinegar reduction.
2. Bearnaise Brun	As above, tinned with meat glaze.
3. Choron	(a) Bearnaise
	(b) Tomato puree
4. Foyot/Valoise	(a) Bearnaise
	(b) Meat glaze.
5. Noisette	Hollandaise enriched with beurre noisette.
6. Maltaise	(a) Hollandaise with orange juice
	(b) Grated orange.
7. Mousseline	(a) Hollandaise
	(b) Whipped cream folded in.
8. Mustard	(a) Hollandaise
	(b) Mustard.
9. Paloise	As bearnaise, substituting mint for tarragon.
(e) Derivatives of Tomato Sauce	
1. Americaine	Tomato sauce blended with lobster butter
2. Orientate	(a) American sauce
	(b) Curry
3. Provencale	(a) Tomato puree
	(b) Pieces of garlic made with oil

4. Tartare	(a) Madeira
	(b) Tomato sauce with an infusion of herbs in it
5. Italienne	(a) Tomato sauce
	(b) Demiglace
	(c) Chopped shallots
	(d) Lean ham
	(e) Herbs
6. Portugaise	(a) Tomato puree
	(b) Onions
	(c) Garlic sweated in veal stock.

(f) Derivatives of Mayonnaise Sauce

1. Chantilly	(a) Mayonnaise
	(b) Whipped cream
2. Cambridge	(a) Mayonnaise
	(b) Chopped hard-boiled egg pounded with anchovy fillet.
	(c) Chopped chives, chervil, tarragon
	(d) Finished with chopped parsley
3. Cocktail	(a) Mayonnaise
	(b) Tomato sauce
	(c) Worcestershire sauce
	(d) Tabasco
	(e) Cream
4. Aioli	(a) Mayonnaise
	(b) Finely pounded garlic
5. Andalouse	(a) Mayonnaise
	(b) Tomato puree
	(c) Chopped pimento
6. Abriche	(a) Tartare sauce
	(b) Chopped hard-boiled egg
7. Gloucester	(a) Mayonnaise
	(b) Sour cream
	(c) Fennel
8. Remoulade	(a) Mayonnaise
	(b) Capers
	(c) Gherkins
	(d) Chopped anchovy fillet
	(e) Dijon mustard

9. Tyrolienne	(a) Mayonnaise
	(b) Tomato sauce
10. Thousand Island	(a) Mayonnaise
	(b) Sieved hard-boiled eggs
	(c) Tomato sauce
	(d) Chopped gherkins, pimentos, chives and capers
11. Verte	(a) Mayonnaise
	(b) Cress
	(c) Parsley
	(d) Chervil
	(e) Spinach puree
12. Vincent	(a) Tartare sauce
	(b) Verte sauce

Q.9. Answer the following questions in two-four sentences:-

(a) What is soup ?
(b) Give five examples of consomme ?
(c) What is the thickening agent of Bisque ?
(d) Give three examples of cold soups ?
(e) What is compound butter ?
(f) How will you differentiate between poaching and simmering ?
(g) Explain 'Jus Roti' and 'Jus Lie'.
(h) Give dimensions of "Mecedoine'.
(i) What is Indent ?
(j) What is Rennet (Renin) and where it is used ?

[**Ans.:**

(a) Soup is a nutritive liquid food prepared with meat, poultry, fish and vegetables.

(b) (i) Consomme juliennes (ii) Consomme brunoise
(iii) Consomme celestine (iv) Consomme royale
(v) Consomme dubarry.

(c) Rice along with puree of seafood.

(d) (i) Consomme madrilene
(ii) Gazpacho
(iii) Vichyssoise (potato & leak) etc.

(e) Creamed butter mixed with flavourings - like chopped parsley and lemon juice (beurre maitre d' hotel). Shrimp butter, lobster butter, oyster butter, garlic butter (frozen butter sauce).

(f) Poaching is always done for the delicate meat (white meat or lean meat). In poaching liquor for short time around 80 degrees C. Simmering is a long process below 100 degrees C to cook through joints (stewing) or to extract nutritious substance (stock or curry). Poaching is also called short simmering for lean meat or egg.

(g) Jus Roti is roasted gravy i.e. dripping collected during (after degreasing and deglazing) the roasting is seasoned and served as it is with roasted items. Jus Lie is thickened roasted gravy with arrowroot and flavoured with tomatoes.

(h) Approximate 1/4 inches to 1/4 inches cuber to 3/4 inches to 3/4 inches cubes.

(i) A written requisition made in advance from a department to food stores to procure various commodities.

(j) Rennet is a commercial form (tables) or Renin enzymes (derived from intestine of baby lamb) and it is used to curdle the milk for manufacture of cheese.

Q.10. Answer the following questions in two-four sentences:

(a) What is the ideal temperature for storage of stocks, sauces and soups ?

(b) How will you define sauce ?

(c) Name few roux-based sauces.

(d) Give the name of standard thickened sauce.

(e) Why is sauce or soup not re-boiled after the addition of liaison ?

(f) Explain 'Emulsion' sauces.

(g) How will you correct the consistency, if mayonnaise is too thin?

(h) Name few food items suitable for poaching.

(i) It is said that valuable nutrients are lost during steaming or boiling of vegetables. Suggest an alternative moist method for vegetables.

(j) What is carry over cooking ?

[Ans :

(a) Below 5 degrees C or above 63 degrees C, otherwise bacteria will grow rapidly in the danger zone (5-63 degrees C).

(b) The French word sauce comes from Latin 'Salsus' means salted, reminding that sauces are originally liquid seasoning for food. Now they are also used to complement the flavour, texture and appearance of foods.

(c) (i) Bechamel (ii) Veloute (iii) Espagnole, etc.

(d) Jus Lie - made with gelatinous reduced stock or Jus Roti and thickened by arrowroot.

(e) Because egg yolk present in liaison will get cooked and scrambled (coagulated) causing the same to develop a curdled texture and appearance.

(f) Hollandaise is a hot emulsion sauce of egg yolk and butter. Mayonnaise is a cold emulsion of egg yolk and oil.

(g) Gradually add sauce to fresh egg yolk.

(h) (i) Whole fish (ii) Portioned fish (iii) Chicken (iv) Supreme (v) Eggs (vi) Fresh fruits, etc.

(i) High pressure steaming - the loss is minimized due to little water and air in the cooking chamber and the method is fast.

(j) This is the further cooking which takes place after the joint have been removed from the oven.

Assignments/Activity Type

Q.11. Prepare the followings:

(a) All of the sauces based on roux.

(b) Small quantity of Sauce.

(c) Hollandaise a Potage a la Reins, the de luxe French chicken puree cream soup.

Q.12. Blend some composition sauces as listed on the preceding pages.

Q.13. Clarify two gallons of broth into a strong consomme.

PART - IV

FOOD PRODUCTION

4.1

Frying

CHAPTER OBJECTIVES

After studying this lesson you should be able :

- To identify foods which can be cooked by frying method;
- To demonstrate and practice the deep frying of fish in a batter;
- To demonstrate and practice the pan frying of breaded pork cutlets; and
- To analyze the cooking and produce the southern fried chicken.

The process of deep frying and pan frying are a part of cooking in fat. Let us understand the frying of food in hot fat, whether done in a pan or in a commercial deep fryer. One of the most important difference between frying and sauteing is that fried food must be separated from the cooking fat and be served as dry as possible whereas sauteed food has the small quantities of good fat mixed into the finished dish.

Deep frying and part frying are two important part of cooking in fat. The main characteristic of frying is separation of fat and food after the cooking. Fat is preheated to 325°F. – 375°F. If lower temperatures are used, the food loses its coating, gets greasy, and may not brown properly. Due to the fast browning of the starchy coating in high heat, foods can only be kept in the fryer a short time. As a result, food has to be suitable, small or thin, to become well-done in the same time it takes to brown.

The most popular fried foods are chicken, fish, veal, pork, and vegetables. Sometimes tough vegetables are propelled before they are browned and crisped by frying.

French Fries Cooking in Oil

In general, pan frying and commercial deep frying stay within a heat range of 325°F. to 375°F. Any mild fat, which can be heated to these temperatures without burning, may be used. The degree of temperature needed for frying limits the frying time. A relatively high temperature can only be applied for short cooking times and to small places of food. Frying at 325°F. produced nearly 50% more heat than boiling water at 212°F. It therefore cooks faster. The use of frying temperature lower than 325°. is not practical because of the following reasons :

1. The coating would wash off
2. The fat would penetrate the food, and make it greasy
3. Very little browning would occur.

Cooking without moisture does not help in tendering tough food. Therefore, only tender raw or precooked foods can be fried. The chef must select the correct size and quality of foods he wants for fast frying. Only portion-sized or smaller, tender, moist food pieces can be fried. Either breading or batter coating must be used as shield between food and fat.

Following important guidelines could be used for deep frying :

1. Keep fryer hot only when necessary
2. Keep fat at 375°F.; no hotter
3. Strain or filter fat as often as possible
4. Keep fried foods crisp and greaseless
5. Frying is a fast food process.
6. Food should be fried just before serving.
7. Do not place wet foods in a deep fryer.

Deep fried foods need to be well done. Therefore, frying needs less skill than broiling, and is done by fry cooks who are still on the lowest level of the chef ranks. They must apply all the principles of cooking to frying. Food could be dried out and browned too much. There is no excuse for doing an imperfect job.

All fried foods should be served fresh and dry. In some luxury food and beverage establishments, fried food is served on doily papers (lace) or napkins to be sure of complete greaselessness. Fried foods are served with lemon wedges or sauces. The choice depends on the chef and the customs of the area.

Seafood, in most areas, is saved with tartar or remolded sauces. If no sauce is indicated on the menu, lemon wedges are served. Fresh whole parsley is used to create a more appetizing eye appeal. Warm sauces served with fried foods may be tomato sauce, white cream, or supreme sauces.

Tempura Deep fried shrimp is usually cooked in vegetable oil and is often served with Soy Sauce.

French Fries

The following guidelines can be used for all food items which are fried in batter:

1. The prepared food portions should be salted and dipped in flour.
2. A small bowl with batter should be in the left hand of the fry cook, who is standing close to the fryer.
3. The prepared food be taken with the right hand, put into the batter, then lifted out; extra batter is wiped off on the side wall of the bowl.
4. The cook should dips 3/4 of the food piece into the fat. If the whole piece are dropped into the basket, the soft batter would wrap itself around the wire basket and stick when fried. The food should be hand held for 10 to 15 seconds until the batter develops some crust.
5. The food now is dropped all the way into the basket. The process is repeated with other pieces of food.
6. Most fried foods will float to the top after about 3 to 4 minutes. Doneness depends on the type of fried food. The first order should be checked carefully by breaking it open in the middle. The average frying time can then be set correctly.
7. The cooked food is should be lifted out of the fryer and put on a paper towel to drain. It must be served immediately.

Fish fingers, also known as fishsticks

Fish and Chips

Fish and chips are deep fried in batter, served with french fried potatoes, and some malt vinegar on the side. Any fish fillet can be used, but codfish and haddock are most popular.

Fillet of Sole Only

Fillet of Sole Only is the French version of Fish and Chips. As the name implies, Only fillet of sole can be used. Instead of the vinegar, tomato sauce is served on the side. The french fries may be served. Omitted, or substituted.

Smelts

Fried Breaded Smelts are cleaned smelts, which are salted, breaded and then fried to the order.

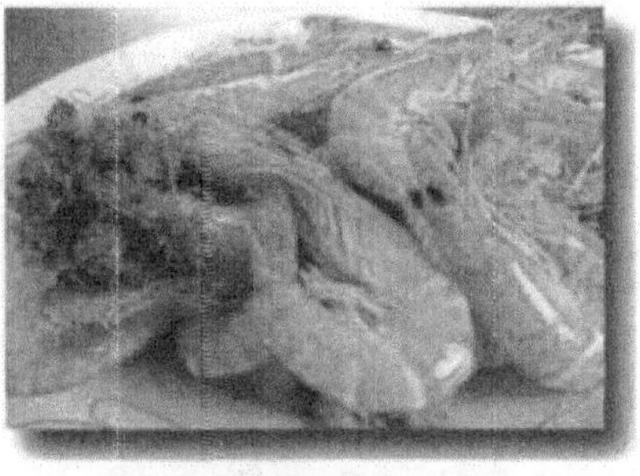

Prawns

Prawns

Fried breaded prawns are raw peeled and deveined prawns, 36/40 or larger, plit open along the vein and *butterfried.* They are salted, breaded and fried like smelts.

Seafood

Fried Oysters, Scallops, Squid, or any other suitable seafood is handled the same way. It may be either breaded or batter fried.

Fried omfret-Fried Pomfret (pla jalamet khao tod)

This is a nice simple dish called Fried Pomfret. In the picture above , you can see the pomfret fish and the tapioca flour.

Southern Fried Chicken

Southern Fried Chicken is made using small Spring Chickens (1-1 1/4lb.), which have been disjointed and salted. A type of batter is chosen and the chickens are fried at 325°F. until done. Often pressure deep fryers, broasters, are used for this preparation. Broasters reduce the cooking time. Southern fried chicken is garnished with honey, corn or banana fritters and french fries. It is often served in a basket.

Viennese Fried Chicken

Vienness Fried Chickens are similar to southern fried chickens, but breading is used instead of the batter. The raw chicken livers and the parboiled gizzards are included with the fried chicken. It is served dry, with lemon and fried parsley.

Breated Pork Cutlet

The cutlets are cut from the pork leg, the boneless loin, or the "Boston" butt. They are pounded and streched with the flat side of a cleaver, salted, breaded, and pan fried to the order.

Winner Schnitzel

Winner Schnitzel is like a pork cutlet but is cut from the leg of dairy veal. The true Winner Schnitzel is served dry garnished with lemons and parsley.

Schnitzel a la Hollstein

Schnitzel a la Hollstein is a Winner Schnitzel garnished with anchovies, capers, and hard boiled chopped egg in addition to the lemon.

Veal Cutlet Parmigiana

Veal cutlet Parmigiana is a breaded veal cutlet, pan fried, topped with a slice of chase and cooked until a brown crust forms. The cheeses used include Mozarella, Swiss, Jack, and Parmesan. A light tomato sauce is served underneath the cutlet or in a side dish.

Chicken Croquettes

About 2 pounds of chopped cooked chicken is mixed with 1 cup of simmering sauce (such as veloute) and brought to a boil. This mixture is seasoned, tightened with 2 or 3 egg yolks, spread on a baking sheet, cooled, and then shaped into cyliners of 1-2½ inches. These rolls are deep-cooled or half frozen, then breaded, and fried to the order.

Croquettes can be made of any mixture of leftover food. Sauce and egg yolks are needed to keep them together. There are seafood, meat, and vegetable croquettes. The combinations and garnishes reflect the taste of the chef.

Fried Food

Fried food should always be golden brown and crisp. Either breaded or in batter, this food should have a light, fluffy appearance. Sauce is never poured over fried food. It is saved underneath or in a side dish (Ref. Experimental Recipe 67 and 68).

Fried Chicken

Chicken Fried Rice

Experimental Recipe 67.

Frying Chicken Pakoda

Ingredients

1. Chicken (cut into small pieces)	:	1 kg, 10-10 gm
2. Garlic paste	:	10 gm
3. Ginger paste	:	1 small cup
4. Corn flour or *Channa* flour	:	2 tbsp
5. Chillie powder	:	2 tbsp
6. *Dhania* powder	:	2 tbsp
7. *Jeera* powder	:	2 tbsp
8. *Garam masala*	:	2 tbsp
9. Oil	:	2 tbsp
10. Salt	:	To taste
11. Oil	:	For frying.

Method

1. Prepare all required ingredients.

2. Cut chicken into small pieces of your own size and wash them thoroughly.
3. Mix the chicken pieces with all the ingredients mentioned and keep them aside fro about 2 to 3 hours.
4. Later, deep-fry the pieces in medium heated oil.
5. At last chop the onion to fine pieces.
6. Garnish the *pakodas* with onion and lemon juice
7. This dish is one of the favourities for East Indians.

Experimental Recipe 68.

Frying & Poaching Gulab Jamun

Ingredients

1. *Mawa*	:	1 kg
2. Cooking soda	:	1 tsp
3. Cardamom Powder	:	30 gm
4. Sugar	:	1/2 kg
5. *Paneer*	:	300 gm
6. *Maida*	:	30 gm
7. Oil	:	To deep fry.

Method

1. Prepare all required ingredients
2. Grate *Khoya* and *paneer* together.
3. Mix with soda, flour, cardamom powder and a little water.
4. Divide into equal portion and make into balls.
5. Heat oil in *kadhai* and deep fry on a slow fire till balls turn into golden in colour.
6. Drain and soak in sugar syrup.

QUESTIONS AND DISCUSSIONS

Fill in the Blanks

Q.1. Road and complete the following statements :—

(a) Breaded fried prawns are made from prawns that are peeled, diveined, and ....

(b) "Viennese Fried Chicken" is always ....

(c) Cooking in fat is sub-divided into sauteing and ....

(d) For the frying process, the size of food must be ....

(e) All fish is tender enough to be ....

(f) A "Veal Cutlet Parmigiana" is a breaded veal cutlet with.............

(g) All fried foods should be served.................

(h) For "Fish and Chips" the fried fish is coated with ....

(i) Croquettes are made of leftover food that has already been ....

[**Ans :** (a) split open along the vein; (b) served dry with lemon and fried parsley; (c) frying; (d) small; (e) fried; (f) cheese; (g) fresh and dry; (h) batter; (i) seasoned]

Multiple Choice Type

Q.2. Read each question carefully and select the best answer :

(i) The best temperature range for frying is :

(a) 225°F. to 275°F (b) 275°F. to 325°F
(c) 325°F. to 375°F (d) 375°F. to 425°F.

(ii) Using a commercial deep-fryer for batter-dipped food is more time consuming than frying breaded foods because :

(a) The batter needs more time to cook
(b) The batter could stick to the wire of the fry banks
(c) Batter-dipped foods cannot be pre-coated and stored
(d) Batter can be fried in lower temperature only.

(iii) A typical Southern Fried Chicken (USA) should be served with

(a) Tartar sauce (b) Honey
(c) Parsley (d) Lemon wedges.

(iv) Chicken croquettes made from leftover cooked chicken meat have a cylindrical shape and are

(a) Dipped in batter (b) Covered with crackermeal
(c) Breaded (d) Dipped in flour and egg.

[**Ans** : (i) (c); (ii) (b); (iii) (b); (iv) (c)]

Short Answer Type

Q.3. Define the following:

(a) Butterfiyed (b) Broaster
(c) Fillet (d) Croquette
(e) Garnish

Q.4. How is a tried product kept crisp ?

Q.5. Are deep frying and pan frying hazard to health?

Q.6. How are frying fats selected ?

Q.7. Explain the term coating. What are the coatings in which foods can be fried?

Assignments/Activity Type

Q.8. Demonstrate the pan frying of breaded pork cutlets.

Q.9. Prepare a "Veal Cutlet a la Parmigiana".

Q.10. Deep fry an order of "Fish and Chips".

Q.11. Bread and fry a serving of "Viennese Fried Chicken".

4.2

Roasting

CHAPTER OBJECTIVES

After studying this lesson you should be able :

- To use to a meat thermometer to establish the doneness of a roast;
- To practice prepare a given piece of meat for roasting;
- To identify bones and unnecessary meat parts to be removed before roasting;
- To select matching pans for roasts;
- To explain the importance of washing and salting of roasts; and
- To establish the approximate roasting time of differently shaped roasts.

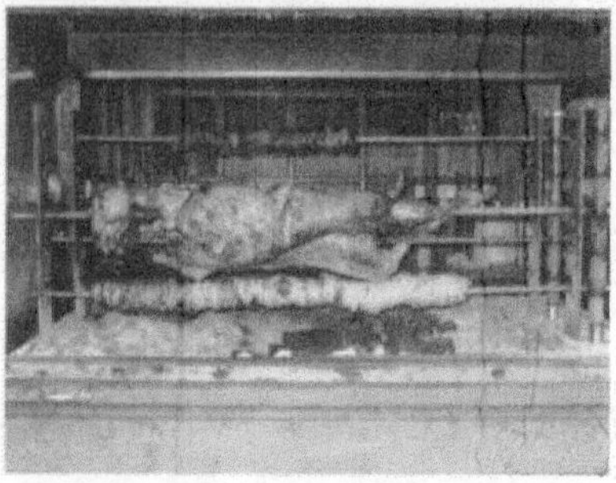

Roasting is dry heat cooking with the intent to evaporate some of the water content that all fresh meats have. To prevent the burning of the roast, time and heat are controlled. When meat (depending on type shape, and desired doneness) is roasted, a ratio is created between time and temperature. Some pieces of meat are cooked better by increasing the heat and reducing the time. Other roasts may need less heat for a longer time. Every roast is different, even if it is the same type, size, and cut of meat as another.

The meat cut selection, boning, trimming, trussing, larding, and salting of the roast are very important preparation steps. All roasting principles and objectives are the same. The trainee cook is advised to use a meat thermometer (his own) until he gains experience.

Pan size must fit meat size. Fat to meat ratio should be the same. If the roast is too fat, some of it is trimmed off. If the roast is too lean, larding, boarding, or oiling must be done. Dark meats are cooked medium or rare. White meats are cooked close to well done. Exceptions to regular roasting principles are ducks and geese. They are tenderized by moist cooking first and then browned.

At all times it must be remembered that roasting alone does not tenderize. Only moist cooking will do that. Meats to be roasted must be tender and young and must be true roasts from prime or choice graded animals. The age of the slaughtered animal in relation to its normal life span is important. Only high quality meat is roasted. For bringing out the flavour of a roast there is no substitute for proper salting.

Brazier with Safety Cover

Roast Chicken

Roasting is cooking of meat in dry heat, with fat only. Roasts do not need added water. The steam which comes from the water content of the roast must evaporate quickly. A low rimmed pan without cover is best for roasting. Meat properly roasted has a brown crust, but it is not dried out. It is juicy and tender, but not overcooked. Roasts are like steaks in many ways. The same meat cut is used, with the same ingredients, and with the same cooking principle. The only differences are the degrees of temperature and the cooking time. A roast is first cooked and then carved. A steak is first cut and then cooked. Any roast, like any steak or chop, is only as tender as the raw meat quality will permit.

Picture-Shish a grill

Roasted Chicken

The time for roasting depends on the kind of meat, its size, its geometric shape, and the heat of the oven. Large roasts need slower heat for a longer time. Smaller roasts need higher heat for a shorter time. Low heat for huge, fat roasts reduces shrinkage. Low heat for lean young roasts increases dryness, causes slow caramelizetion and results in a lower quality. Roasting needs temperatures from 325°F. to 500°F. Ovens need pre-heating. Empty ovens, pre-heated to 400°F., drop in temperature by 20% to 320°F. as soon as the door is opened and the cold roast placed in it. Roasts must be started with a high beginning heat and then reduced after 10 or 15 minutes. Heat must be regulated for a balanced result because the brownness of the roast is important to appearance and taste.

Experienced roast cooks do not use meat thermometers to check the doneness of a roast. Their guidelines are combination of looking at a roast and its drippings, its shape, the oven heat, the cooking time already past, and the application of finger pressure to the meat. For the young cook, it would be wise to use his own quality meat thermometer as a substitute for experience. Thermometers are inserted into the center of the roast. Proper handling of them is the key to satisfactory results.

A MEAT THERMOMETER

A meat thermometer of good quality must be used in the proper way. The sensitive tip of the thermometer is inserted into the center of the roast a short time before the roast is thought to be ready. The degrees of Fahreneit listed reflect the degree of doneness no matter what kind of meat is used.

Carry-over heat and setting time (recirculation of juice) vary with the size of the roast and must be included. Depending on the roast, the retained heat (carry-over heat) during setting time will increase the final reading by about 10-15°F, 140°F for rare or blood rare, 155°F for medium or medium rare and 175°F for well done is generally recommended.

A roast, taken out of the oven at 130°F. + a 10° increase (equalization from the outside to the center) will be rare. But if removed at 140°F. + 10–15°F increase during setting, the roast will be medium or medium rare.

Roast Preparation

The preparation of a piece of meat for roasting depends on the meat itself. The objective or roasting is to provide appetizing, tastey, juicy, hot, easy to eat slices of meat, which are carved to the order. For this result, the extra fat must be cut from the roast. Too much fat cover, which will not be eaten, prevents the lean meat from becoming crusty and brown. The extra fat also does not permit the penetration of the seasoning. This results in a double loss of taste. Too many dripping may fry the lower part of the roast and make the preparation of gravy difficult. Sinews, gristle, and loose pieces of meat, which would only burn must also be removed. Bones stay in, if they will not obstruct the carving. They are good for heat conduction to the center of the boat. But such bones as aitchbones (hipbones), chine bones. (backones), and shoulder blades should be removed without needless cutting of the meat. A roast with too many cuts will not stay as juicy and will fall apart when sliced. Roasts are not tied with strings to fake the appearance of one piece of meat, as is done at the retail counters of the supermarkets. String is used to hold extra fat in place or to improve the shape of the meat or poultry.

The selection of a properly fitting roast pan is very important. The rim should be lower than the meat so that the steam can escape. A heavy material will give better heat conduction and distribution. The pan must be only 2-3 inches larger than the roasts that are in it. If a pan is too large, the drippings will spread and burn before they are made into gravy. A pan with a high rim has more condensation than evaporation of steam and the result is closer to a pot roast.

The Chef must decide if and how fat has to be added to the roast. Roasts that have enough fat of their own can be starred dry at a lower temperature, until enough drippings have collected in the pan. Later the heat is increased. For average trimmed meats, the pan and the surface of the roast have to be oiled lightly. If the meat is truly lean, bacon, salted pork, or plain fat is added.

Larding

In this process strips of bacon or salt pork are put into lean meat with a larding needle. It is a common method for game birds and venison.

Barding

Under this process slices of fat or bacon are tied over lean meat to protect it from drying out. Washing is not needed when the meat is clean. Meat cuts delivered by the supplier can be used as they come. Sometimes soggy paper sticks to the meat and has to be removed.

Larding and Barding

Some cuts lack natural fat, and if they are to be roasted or braised it may be necessary to add fat to keep them tender and succulent. This can be done internally by larding, or externally by barding.

Method

Step 1. Insert a larding needle into the meat following the grain. Thread the needle with chilled pork fat, then pull through.

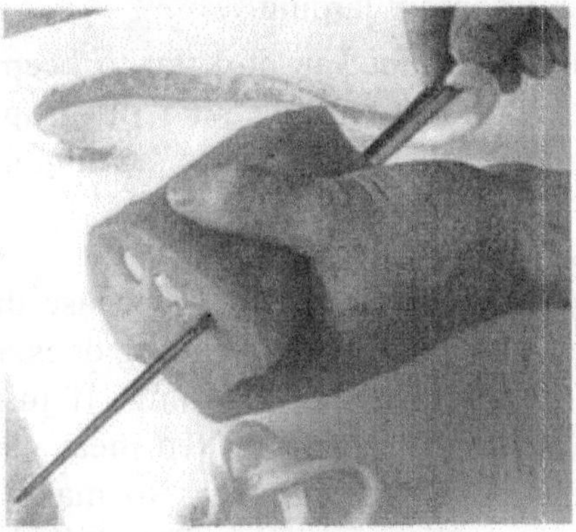

Simple Barding

Step 2. Wrap a thin layer of fat around the outside of the meat and tie in place with string.

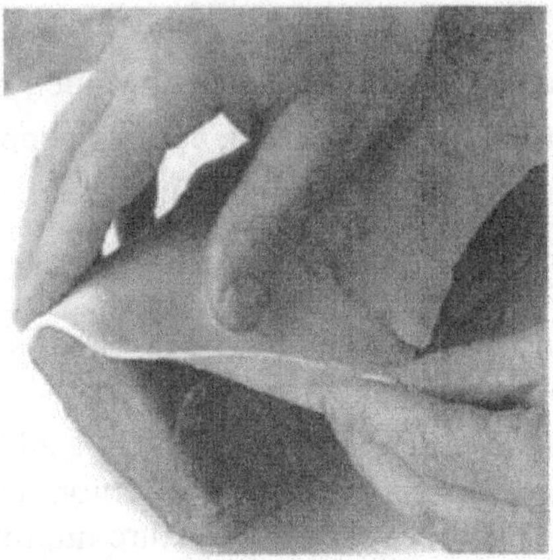

Decorative barding

Step 3. Wrap sides of meat with sheets of fat. Place a zigzag strip of fat along the top, tucking in the ends.

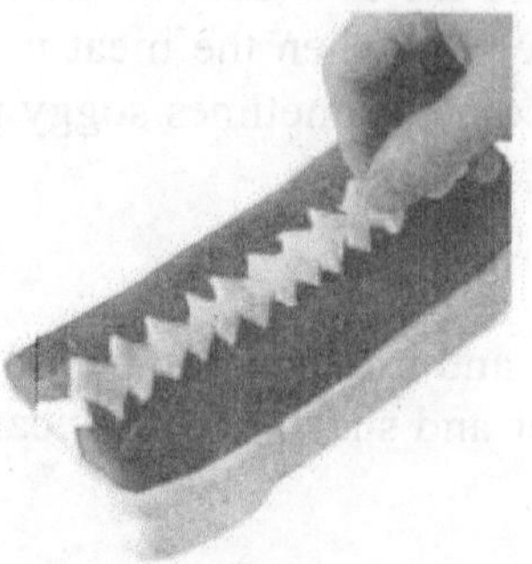

Step 4. This technique is used for moistening lean meat flesh from the inside during cooking. As the lardons of pork fat melt they are absorbed by the flesh, making it more succulent. To add extra flavour, season the fat or marinate it for at least 1 hour before larding.

Step 5. Lean meat can be wrapped in pork fat to keep it moist and help retain the shape of the meat. The barding fat will disappear during cooking; if any remains it should be discarded before serving, unless decoratively applied.

Salting and Seasoning

Some chefs do not salt meat before cooking because they claim the theory that the salt does not pass into the roast, right way of salting does allow the salt to pass into the meat, and that there is no delay in the browning. If juices might be lost, which is doubtful, the taste and flavour of properly salted meat make up for everything which could have been lost. The proof, of course, is to make two identical roasts in two different ways and test them at the same time. The skilled chef knows the right way to salt. A ready roast, wetted and salted on the meat parts (not the fat covers) 30 to 60 minutes before roasting, will be much better than the unsalted one. The wetness dissolves the salt, which osmosis and capillary action sucks into the roast.

Use of Spices and Herbs

Spices and herbs are used as a result of the chefs value judgement:

1. Dark meat, like beef, lamb, and venison, accepts pepper.
2. Pork, which is rather bland, goes well with garlic, lemon zeste, caraway, and some herbs.
3. Lamb can use garlic in addition.
4. Veal (dairy veal) and poultry are often seasoned with herbs such as oregano, theme, basil, sage, and marjoram.

Roasting the continental way uses Mirepoix, which is added at the last quarter (or 25 minutes) of the roasting time. *Mirepoix* consists of onion, carrots, celery, and parsnips, cut into cubes of one inch. This root vegetable mixture improves the flavour of the gravy and also adds some flavour to smaller pieces of meat such as chicken, beef fillet and rack of lamb.

ROASTING OF LAMB

Lamb is a dark meat, which is roasted to medium in the English way. A lamb, even smaller than a calf, has much visible fat. Lamb fat has a peculiar taste, is hard to digest (high melting point because of the high lanolin content), is disliked, and should be trimmed as much as possible. The leg, the racks, and the saddle are popular roasts. Basically, they are roasted like beef, and garlic is used as additional seasoning.

Lamb Chop Crown

Roast of Lamb

Leg of Lamb

Leg of lamb is not too often found on regular dinner house menus. It is used more often in better luncheon rooms, staff cafeterias, and hospitals. Legs weigh from 5 to 8 pounds. They can be boned like a veal leg or roasted "bone in" French style, with only the atchbone removed. Roasting time is 1 1/2 to 2 hours at 350°F. to 375°F. to an in eternal temperature of 150°F. Mirepoix is used for a better gravy.

How to Carve a Leg of Lamb ?

Step 1. Holding the bone, turn the leg so the thickest, meatiest part is uppermost.

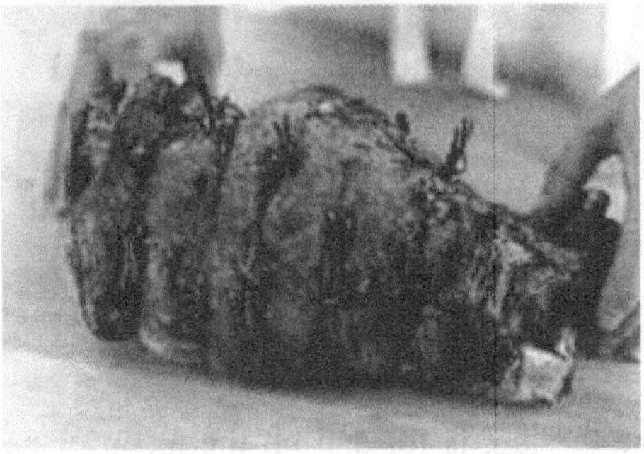

Step 2. Cut a narrow wedge of meat from centre of the joint.

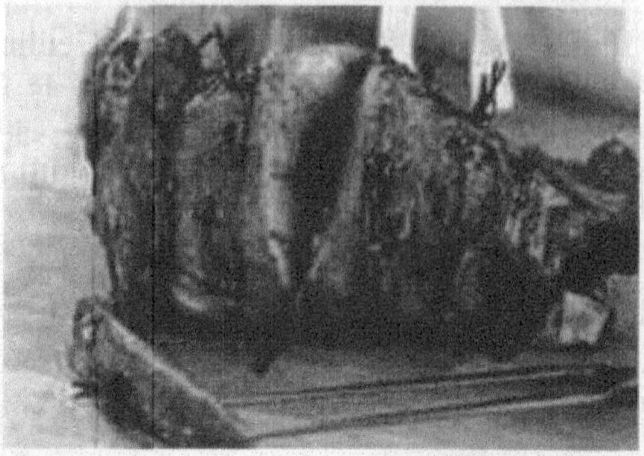

Step 3. Carve slices down to the bone, with the knife angled along the line of wedge. Cut across the base of the slices to free them from the bone.

Step 4. Turn the joint over and carve the remaining meat paralle to the bone.

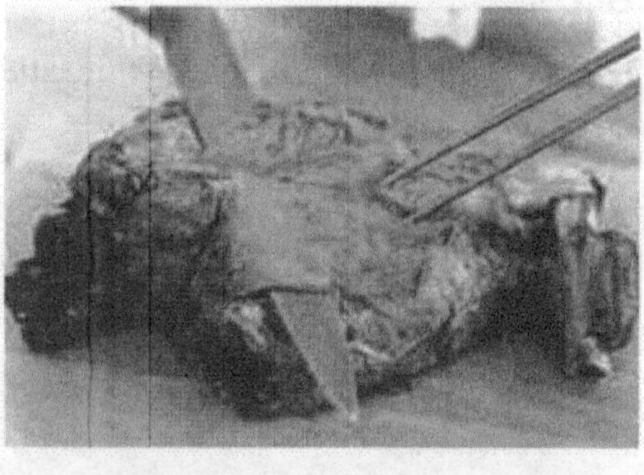

Rack of Lamb

Rack of lamb, unlike the leg, is for and on the menu of nearly every French style restaurant. It is made to the order for two. The racks are center cuts from the loin, with 7 ribs and often frenched. To *french* means that meat from the flank end of the rib is completely removed. During roasting the meat shrinks and the bare bone sticks out. The racks are trimmed, after being frenched. Their trimmed weight is from 1 ½ to 2½ pounds. Racks are roasted to the order, for 18 to 25 minutes to rare, at 475°F. The bare bones are covered with aluminum foil in order to prevent burning. A skillet is used as a roasting pan.

Saddle of Lamb

Saddle of lamb looks like a saddle of veal. It is also a favorites de lux dish for expensive French style restaurants. The steel rod through the spine is used for roasting at 400°F. for 25 to 30 minutes.

ROASTING OF POULTRY AND GAME BIRDS

Poultry and game birds include all kinds of birds from the popular and common turkey to the seldom available wild pheasant. All previously discussed roasting information applies to this group.

Turkey

Turkey has two kinds of meat, white and dark. They are of different appearance, taste, and tenderness. The modern way of roasting this meat is to cook them separately for different lengths of time and temperatures.

Roast Turkey

Boning a roast turkey for machine slicing is needed to get greatest yield. Carving from the carcass is only done in view of the customers. In the back of the house, machine slicing for portion control is the rule. If an electric slicer is not available, and the turkey is hand sliced, pre-boning will increase the yield.

Turkey

Trukey Roast

How to roast poultry ?

How to roast poultry: chicken, duck, goose, quail, guinea fowl, poussin and turkey.

Roasting whole poultry Chicken

Allow 375g per person. Roast for 20 minutes per 450g, plus 20 minutes. Roast at 220°C/gas 7 for the first 20 minutes, then decrease the oven temperature to 190°C/fan 170°C/gas 5 for the remaining time. (Ref. Experimental Recipe 69 and 70)

Experimental Recipe 69.

Boaning of a Roast Turkey

Ingredients

1. Roasted turkey : 1
2. Baker's or kitchen table, wooden top : 1
3. 1-6 inch boning knife : 1.

Method

The legs :

1. Prepare all required ingredients.
2. Separate two drumsticks with the attached hips from the carcass.
3. Loosen ligaments of the drumstick and pull out as carefully as possible.
4. Cut on inside angle of the leg, close to drumstick bone and hip bone. Separate largest piece of dark meat in one whole chunk.
5. Cut remaining meat off hip bone.
6. Slice remaining meat from drumstick.
7. Repeat on second leg.
8. Collect all dark meat and put away for later use.

The breast :

1. Disjoing wing bone from collar bone with a few clean cuts, taking as little meat away as possible.
2. Repeat on other side of breast.
3. Set breast on its hollow opening, with neck part up and keel bone facing toward you.
4. Make one cut along one side of keel bone, from the center of neck opening to the tip of the breast.
5. Make one cut along the wishbone to the center of neck opening. This will connect with first cut.
6. Pull whole breast loose, use left hand for pulling, help with right hand and bonning knife.
7. Repeat on right side.
8. Put two boneless breasts away for later use.
9. Clean the rest of the carcass of meat for hash, salads, soups, etc.

The breast of a large Tom (25-30 lbs.), separated from the legs but still on the carcass, cooks in about 2½ hours at 325-350°F. The breasts are placed in the pan so as to improve the heat circulation. The tip of the breast bone is at the bottom of the pan. The fat and skin-covered throat part sticks up into the air. This new position makes the breast self-basting and prevents it from drying out. The drumsticks and hips are placed in another roasting pan, skin side up,

Roast Turkey with Chestnuts

roasted at the higher temperatures of 350-375°F. for the same time. This results in well done, tender and tasty dark meat, with crisp skin.

Experimental Recipe 70.

Turkey Slicing: Portion Controlled

Equipment

1. Electric Meat Slicer
2. Standard Steam Table Pans
3. Portion Control Scale.

Ingredients

Turkey : One.

Method

1. Prepare all required ingredients.
2. Bone and skin a roast turkey into two breasts, 2 thighs and 2 drumsticks. Wrap in plastic film and chill in refrigerator thoroughly.
3. Slice all dark meat against grain on about No. 12 setting. Move carriage with right hand, catch falling slices with left hand.
4. Divide meat in 1 1/2-ounce heaps and lay them out in a standard steam table pan 3 × 4 rows, 12 orders.
5. Put boneless breast into meat slicer skin side up, bone side resting on slicer carriage, neck end toward slicer blade.
6. Leave control knob on No. 12, move carriage and catch falling slices as in Step 3.
7. Divide sliced white meat into 2 ounce orders. Place on top of previously set up dark meat.
8. When pan is full, cover with wax paper, place in refrigerator until ready to use.
9. When ready to use, pour 1/4 inch of stock over pan, cover, and heat pan slowly on top of range until very hot. Caution – Overheating will toughen meat.
10. Bring out to steam table. Keep meat 140°F., covered.
11. Keep hot gravy separate. Sauce only when ordered.

CHICKEN

Chickens are oven or spit-roasted. Roasting chicken have two basic sizes: 1¾ to 2¼ pound chickens for ½ chicken per order, and 2½ to 3 pound chicken of a ¼ chicken to be served. Chickens are trussed (legs are bound tightly to body) with a large needle and twine. It makes them look more appetizing and they are easier to carve after roasting. All chickens are well salted inside and out, oiled and roasted to light heat A 2-pound chicken is cooked at 475°F. for 50 to 60 minutes and a 3-pond one is cooked at 450°F. for 60 to 70 minutes. Chickens may be larded. Mirepoix is used and gravy is made. For spit-roasting the instructions of the equipment manufacturer should be followed.

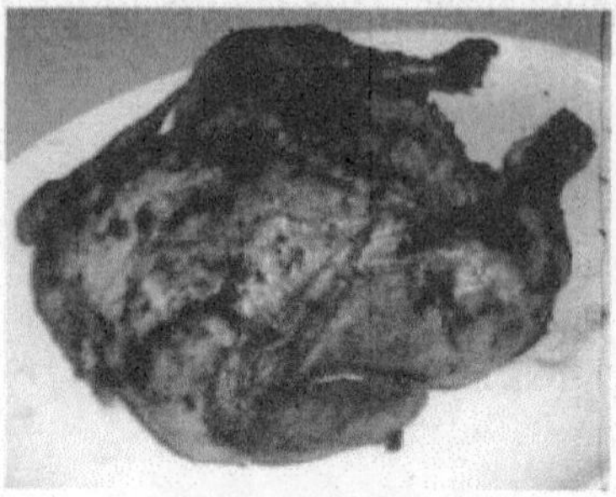

Roast Chicken

Roast Chicken with vegetables

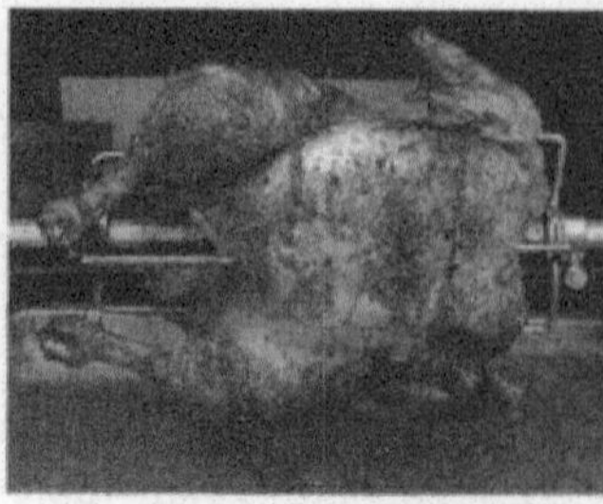

Chicken cooking on a horizontal rotisserie

Cooking Questions: Chicken

Q.1. How do you roast a whole chicken?

Answer Guidance: For best results, set the bird on a roasting rack over a roasting pan. The chicken will cook more evenly and won't be sitting in its own drippings, which will give you crispier skin. For easier cleanup, line the pan with aluminum foil. See our article on roasting chicken for more info:

Q.2. How do you cut a whole chicken into smaller parts?

Answer Guidance: This is a terrific, economical skill to learn! Whole chicken is cheaper than buying pieces, and the leftover parts of a deboned chicken are perfect for soup stocks. Once you've got the hang of it, you can cut up a chicken in no time. To cut up a chicken, follow these simple step-by-step directions:

Q.3. How can you prevent your chicken from being dry?

Answer Guidance: Dry and/or tough chicken is most often caused by overcooking. Recipes often give cooking times, but these are really guidelines.

A few things can affect cooking time. For example, thin pieces of meat will cook more quickly than thick. Heat settings can vary from stove to stove. And even the size and shape of the pan can affect the cooking time. The best way to avoid overcooking is to check your chicken regularly as it cooks.

Q.4. How long can you keep raw or cooked chicken? What are the best storage methods?

Answer Guidance: Raw chicken should be stored in the coldest part of your refrigerator and used within 2 days. Freeze any chicken that won't be used within 2 days.

Frozen chicken can be stored in the freezer for up to one year without sacrificing quality.

A whole cooked chicken can be kept in the refrigerator for 3 days; cut-up cooked chicken can be stored in the refrigerator for 2 days. Cooked chicken should not be left at room temperature for more than 2 hours.

Squab Chickens

Squab chickens are very small and available completely boned, from the inside, for stuffing. They usually weight 3/4 to 1 1/4 pounds and are roasted like chickens for only 20 to 25 minutes in a hotter oven at 500°F.

Pheasants

Pheasants are game birds. They are good only at the times of the year when they have fed on grain. Gourmets roast pheasants for the quality of their breast meat, which must be larded or barded. An herb bouquet of fresh sage, thyme, and basil can be stuffed into the cavity while roasting. They are roasted best in a skillet, with oil, at 500°F. for 15 to 18 minutes. If overcooked, they become tasteless and stringy Farms raised, domesticated pheasants weigh up to 3 pounds, are clean and white, look like chickens, and are roasted like chickens of the same size.

Ducks

Ducks are popular on dinner house menus. Peking duck, used in the USA. must be handled differently than the French Rowen duck, used in Europe. As a result, many of the Fresh cooking methods are not too satisfying. Perhaps the best way to prepare this type of duck is spit-roasting on a charcoal rotisserie for about 3 hours. Under the bird, a drip pan with water will provide moisture and collect fat. A medium fire with the coals on the side, not under the duck, at approximately 325°F. will be enough.

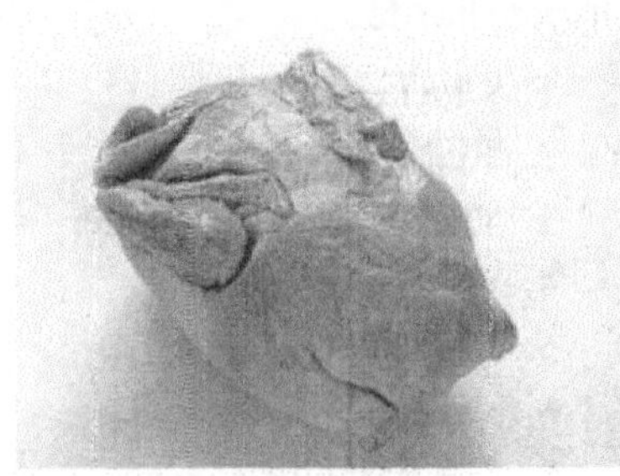

Allow 625g per person. Roast for 15 minutes per 450g. Roast at 230°C/fan 210°C/gas 8 for the first 20 minutes, then decrease the oven temperature to 180°C/fanl 160°C/gas 4 for the remaining cooking time.

Oven roasting will produce a good dish when the following guidelines are observed:

1. Properly defrosted (24 hours under refrigerations) 4 1/2 to 5-pound ducks are well salted at least 2 hours before roasting.
2. The salt should go into the cavity and underneath the skin of the breast. Sage, marjoram, and oregano are among the other seasonings which may be used.
3. Use duck giblets, fat, and mirepoix to prepare a bed for the duck in the roasting pan.
4. Add one inch of chicken stock.
5. Place oiled duck, breast side down, on the bed, cover, and cook in 450°F. (preheated) oven for 30 minutes.
6. Then take off the cover, and continue cooking 30 minutes more. The temperature may need to be reduced to 425°F.
7. After one hour of total cooking time, turn the duck on its back and roast for 30 more minutes. If there are too many fat drippings. Skim off as much as possible. Heat at 450°F. until the duck is browned in the total time of 1 1/2 hours
8. Remove from the oven, cool duck, and make gravy from the drippings as usual.
9. As soon as duck is cool enough to handle quarter it in the same way as a raw chicken would be disjointed, without cutting the carcass in half.
10. Take off the drumsticks with hips and *oyster* (small muscle in part of the pelvis) first. Then make two cuts along the keel bone into the breast, with another at the

neck along the wishbone to the wing bone. Grip breast and wing bone firmly and peel breast meat off the carcass in one piece. The four half-boned quarters are placed, skin side up, in a flat roasting pan, with a little stock at the bottom. Preheat oven to 500°F. Use the highest oven rack and heat duck for 6-7 minutes, until its skin is craps without being burned.

11. Serve with the crisp skin side up, with watercress, and a proper sauce and garnish on the side.

Experimental Recipe 71.

Tandoori Chicken

Ingredients

1.	Chicken (whole)	:	1 (about 1-½ Kg)
2.	Red Chilli Powder	:	1 tsp.
3.	*Garam Masala* Powder	:	1 tsp.
4.	Ginger Paste	:	1 tsp.
5.	Garlic Paste	:	1 tsp.
6.	Green Chilli Paste	:	1 tsp.
7.	Yogurt (Curd)	:	½ cup
8.	Lemon Juice	:	2 tbsp.
9.	Salt	:	To taste
10.	Vegetable Oil	:	For basting.

Method

1. Prepared all required ingredients.
2. Thoroughly clean the chicken.Prick it with knife or fork all over and make slits diagonally.
3. Apply a mixture of red chilli powder, salt and lemon juice all over the body and marinate it for 30-45 minutes.
4. Churn the yogurt and add ginger, garlic and green chilli paste, *garam masala* and mix well.
5. Pour this yogurt mixture over the chicken and toss so that it gets coated well all through, with the paste. Force some mixture in the slits. Marinate it for 6-7 hours.
6. Brush the chicken with little oil. Then put it in a grill and cook for about 20 minutes (almost cooked). Finally bast the chicken with oil and again roast it until fully cooked.

Geese

Geese are seldom found on restaurant menus however they are common in European countries. They are prepared like ducks. Even young geese weigh 8 to 10 pounds, and therefore, must be cooked at a lower temperature for about one hour more. Geese are often stuffed with sour apples or onions during roasting. Seldom are geese served the French way with fruit and wine sauces. They are plain roasted, *au jus*, and served with red cabbage or another hardy vegetable.

Goose

Allow 575g per person. Roast for 15 minutes per 450g. Roast at 220°C/fan 200°C/gas 7 for the first 30 minutes, then decrease the oven to 180°C/fan 160°C/gas 4 for the remaining time.

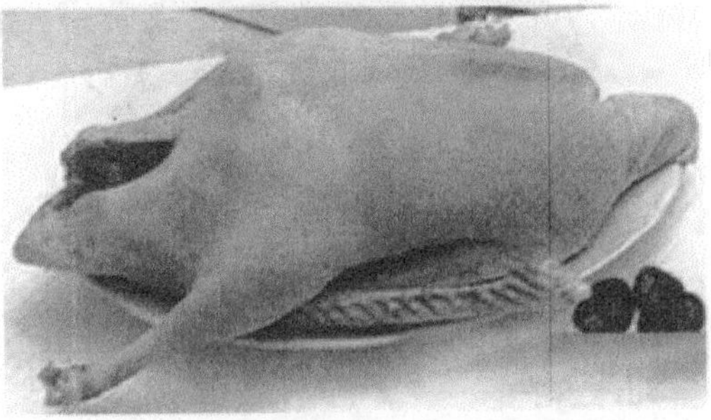

Guinea fowl

Allow a 1.5kg bird for four people. Roast for 15 minutes per 450g, plus 15 minutes. Roast at 200°C/fan 180°C/gas 6 for the calculated tiem.

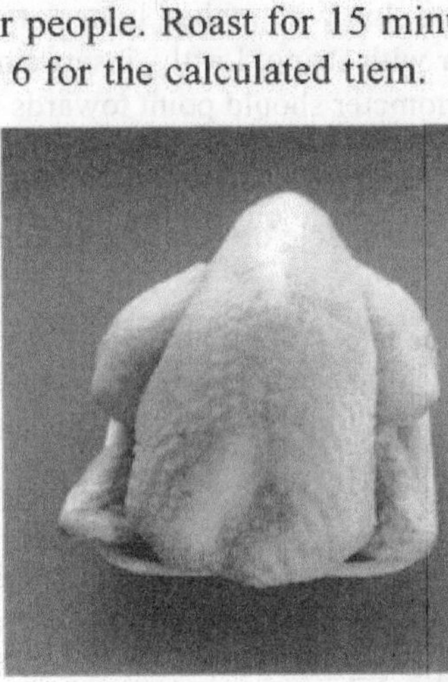

Poussin

A 450g poussin serves one. Roast at 220°C/fan 200°C/gas 7 for 30-35 minutes.

Turkey

Allow 450g per person for a bird under 4.5kg; 275g per person for a bird over 4.5kg. Roast for 18 minutes per 450g, plus 18 minutes. Roast, uncovered, at 220°C/fan200°C/

gas 7 for the first 30 minutes, then, covered, at 190°C/fan 170°C/gas 5 for the remaining time-uncover and increase the oven to 200°C/fan 180°C/gas 6 for the last 30 minutes.

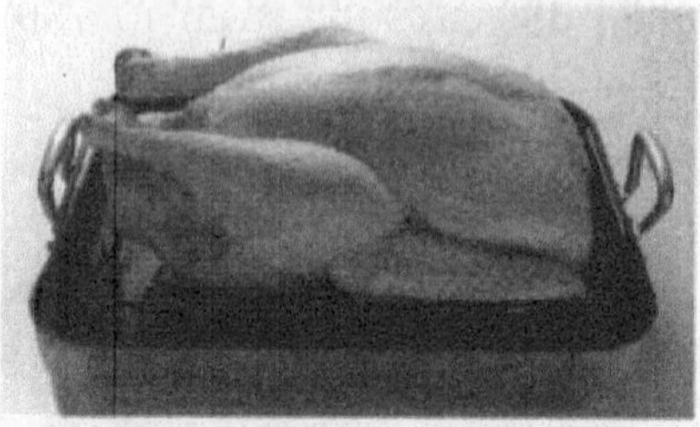

Cooking Questions: Turkey

Q.1. **How do you cook a turkey?**

Answer Guidance: First remove the giblets. Next, rinse the bird inside and out. Pat dry with paper towels. If you are stuffing the bird, stuff loosely, allowing about 1/2 to 3/4 cup per pound of bird. Brush the skin with melted butter or oil. Tuck the drumsticks under the folds of skin or tie together with string. Lastly, insert a meat thermometer into the thickest part of the thigh. The thermometer should point towards the body, and should not touch the bone. Place the bird on a rack in a roasting pan, and into a preheated 350 degree F (175 degrees C) oven. The turkey is ready when the thermometer reads 180 degrees F, about 11-12 minutes per pound. See our article on roasting turkey for more info:

Q.2. **How big should yu turkey be?**

Answer Guidance: Count on 1 to 1 1/2 pounds of turkey (bone-in, whole turkey weight) for each guest, depending whether you want plenty of leftovers or just a few. (If you have lots of guests to feed, consider buying two medium-sized turkeys rather than one giant—the cooking time will be shorter.)

Q. 3. **How do you thaw turkey?**

Answer Guidance: The best way to thaw a turkey is in the refrigerator. Allow one day for every five pounds of turkey. A quicker way is to thaw the turkey in a cold water bath. This will take about 30 minutes per pound. The water should be running, or changed frequently to prevent freezing. You may also use a combination of these methods. Never thaw a turkey at room temperature.

Q.4. **Can you roast turkey the day before Thanksgiving, and reheat it?**

Answer Guidance: No. Partially roasting a turkey the day before to save on cooking time the next day creates the perfect environment for bacterial growth. That said, you can carve the fully cooked bird and layer the meat in a baking dish for re-heating. Seal the baking dish with foil to reduce moisture loss. Since breast meat has a greater tendency to dry out, place it on the bottom of the dish and cover it with gravy if you like, or perhaps a small amount of turkey stock.

Q. 5. **What is the best way to store cooked turkey meat?**

Answer Guidance: As mentioned above, layer the meat in a baking dish and seal it with foil to reduce moisture loss. Since breast meat has a greater tendency to dry out, place it on the bottom of the dish and cover it with gravy if you like, or perhaps a small amount of turkey stock. Cooked turkey will last 3 to 4 days in the refrigerator.

You can also freeze turkey. Sealed in an airtight plastic wrapping or freezer bag, turkey can be frozen for up to four months. Freezing turkey with gravy, will help it retain moisture better.

Thaw frozen turkey overnight in the refrigerator, or use the defrost setting on your microwave. When thawing foods in the microwave, they should be cooked immediately afterwards. When re-heating turkey meat, be sure to heat it to an internal temperature of 165°F (70°C).

Q.6. **How do you deep fry a turkey?**

Answer Guidance: Deep-frying a whole turkey is messy and presents some hazards. So it's always done outdoors. There is some special equipment you need in order to take on this project, and we recommend that you don't attempt this without the right tools. You will need a heavy-duty portable propane burner and a very large stockpot (26 to 40 quart capacity) or a custom-made turkey-frying pot to begin with. For more information, read the in-depth article:

Q.7. **How do you smoke a turkey?**

Answer Guidance: Smoking a turkey is easy provided you have the right equipment. The right equipment, in this case, is a smoker. Smokers allow you to carefully regulate the temperature, which is vital when cooking a large beast over a long period of time. It's possible to smoke a turkey using a charcoal grill, but only if you're prepared to get comfortable next to the barbeque and watch it constantly for the better part of a day.

VENISON

Venison is the generic name for the meat of deer, elk, moose, and other game. Only feed animals are good for roasts. The meat is tougher than beef. Legs, saddles and racks are larded and aged for roasting. The meat must be well trimmed. All fat and skin, like the silver skin of a beef fillet, must be removed to the bare dark flesh. Salt, pepper, paprika, juniper betties, herbs and other spices are used, and the seasoning can be strong. Saddles, double racks, or both together in one piece, are kept straight by a steel rod through the spine. They are roasted to medium at 450°F. from 20 to 35 minutes. Venison from olden animals, not well hung, and therefore tougher, should be prepared in some other way.

A leg of venison, trimmed like a leg of lamb, must be skinned, larded, and well seasoned. It is roasted at 350°F. for 1 1/2 to 2 hours. The meat thermometer can easily be used.

VEAL

Meat known as veal by standards of continental cuisine, comes from calves 10 to 12 weeks old which have been fed only milk and a few added eggs. This type of veal is sold under the name of dairy veal. It is expensive and very hard to get. As soon as calves feed on grass or other vegetable solids, the meat changes. Until the calf has reached the age of at least one year, the meat is neither veal nor beef in quality. Dairy veal is very tender, lean white meat with a pinkish tint. The visible fat is white and firm. Whole legs, shoulders, loins and saddles can be roasted with excellent results.

Leg of Veal

Leg of veal is generally made only for pre-recorded parties in luxury restaurants because it is in short supply, has a high price, and needs much skill for its preparation. Trimming is like that for the pork leg, with the aitchbone and leg bone removed hollow. Veal legs have no fat or skin. The outside of the leg is large or bearded. Oil butter, or pork lard is added, and frequently basting is advisable. Veal weight and quality are irregular. Leg sizes may vary from 7 to 16 pounds. Heavier legs should not be roasted whole. Roasting temperatures are from 325°F. to 350°F. for 55 minutes to 2½ hours. Internal temperature of the roast when removed from the oven is 155°F. mirepoix is added for the last 25 minutes of roasting.

Loin of Veal

Loin of veal is boned like a pork loin except that the center cut and rib end stay in one piece. Larding or braiding is difficult, but the rest of the preparations is the same as for the leg of veal. Cooking time can range from 40 minutes to 1 3/4 hours, depending on its size.

Saddle of Veal

Saddle of veal is the name given to the two trimmed loin ends, not split in half, of a small animal. A saddle of veal (called "Selle de Veau" in French) is a special party dish, carved at the table by the headwaiter, or in the kitchen by the chef and put back on the carcass for serving. It can be served plain, just as the loin or roasted to rare, then finished in one of several fenny ways. Boarding is often advisable for a saddle, which is handled and roasted like a loin. A steel rod is stuck through the spine to prevent curving of the saddle while roasting.

PORK

Fresh pork is more popular all over of the world. Nutritionally, it is better than beef. Pork fat has a lower melting point than beef fat (less stearin), and it is easier to digest. Analysis shows that it is equal to meat in comparative cuts except that it has no stored vitamin A, but more of the other vitamins, such as thiamin. Pork meat is younger than meat has a shorter cooking time, and all cuts can be roasted. For best flavour, proper salting is the first step. Rubbing in a lemon zeste, garlic and caraway seeds also improves the taste.

Cuts of Pork

Pork is the meat of hogs usually butchered before they are one year old. Since hogs are butchered at a young age, their meat is generally very tender with a delicate flavor. It is well suited to a variety of cooking methods.

PRIMAL AND SUBPRIMAL CUTS OF PORK

After a hog is slaughtered, it is generally split down the backbone, dividing the carcass into bilateral halves. Like the beef carcass, each side of the hog carcass is then further broken down into the primal cuts: shoulder, Boston butt, belly, loin and fresh ham.

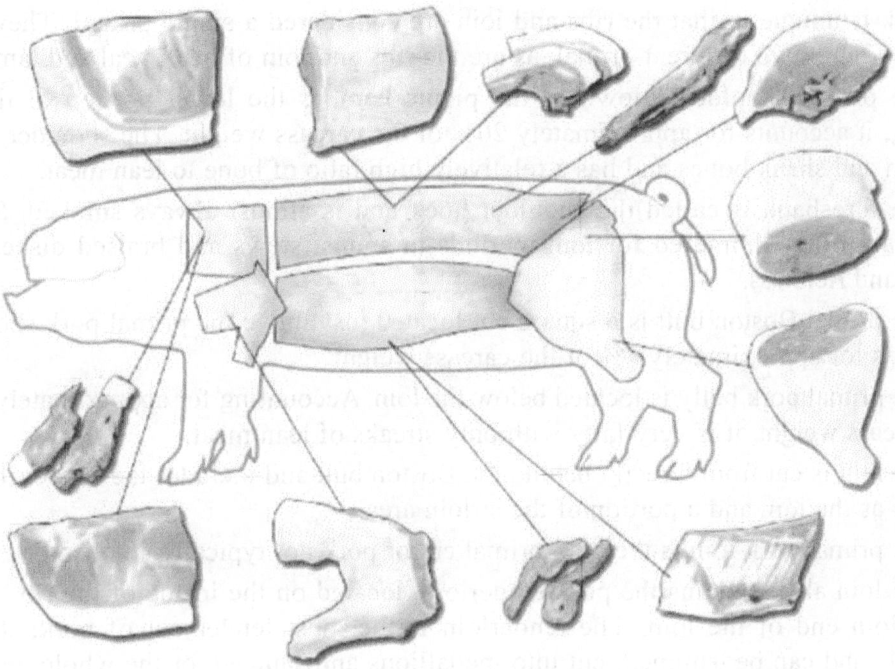

Fig. 4.2A. Cuts of a Pork

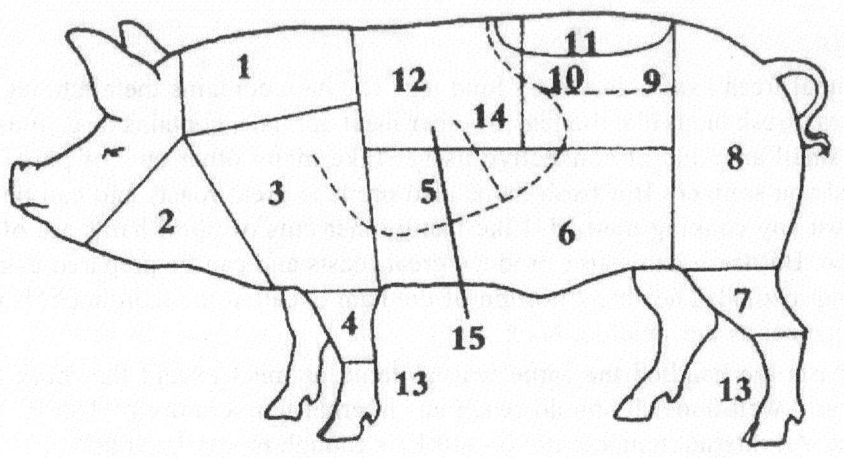

Fig. 4.2B. Cuts of a Pork

Pork is unique in that the ribs and loin are considered a single primal. They are not separated into two different primal, as are the ribs and loin of beef, veal and lamb.

The primal shoulder, known as the picnic ham, is the lower portion of the hog's foreleg; it accounts for approximately 20% of the carcass weight. The shoulder contains the arm and shank bones and has a relatively high ratio of bone to lean meat.

The foreshank is called the shoulder hock and is almost always smoked. Shoulder hocks are often simmered for long periods in soups, stews and braised dishes to add flavor and richness.

The primal Boston butt is a square cut located just above the primal pork shoulder. It accounts for approximately 7% of the carcass weight.

The primal pork belly is located below the loin. Accounting for approximately 16% of the carcass weight, it is very fatty with only streaks of lean meat.

The loin is cut from directly behind the Boston butt and includes the entire rib section as well as the loin and a portion of the sirloin area.

The primal pork loin is the only primal cut of pork not typically smoked or cured.

The loin also contains the pork tenderloin, located on the inside of the rib bones on the sirloin end of the loin. The tenderloin is the most tender cut of pork; it is very versatile and can be trimmed, cut into medallions and sautéed, or the whole, tenderloin can be roasted or braised.

The most popular cut from the loin is the pork chop. Chops can be cut from the entire loin, the choicest being center cut chops from the primal loin after the blade bone and sirloin portions at the front and rear of the loin are removed. The pork loin can be purchased boneless or boned and tied as a roast.

Fresh Ham

The primal fresh ham is the hog's hind leg. The ham contains the aitch, leg and hind shank bones. Fresh ham, like the legs of other meat animals, contains large muscles with relatively small amounts of connective tissue. Like many other cuts of pork, hams are often cured and smoked. But fresh hams also produce great roasts and can be prepared using almost any cooking method. Like many other cuts of pork, hams are often cured and smoked. But fresh hams also produce great roasts and can be prepared using almost any cooking method. The shank portion of the ham is called the ham hock. It is used in the same manner as the shoulder hock.

Pork roasts are handled the same way as lamb or meat except that pork has to be cooked nearly well-done. It should reach an internal temperature of 165°F., but never become dry. An internal temperature of 140°F. is enough to sterilize pork.

A pork roast has enough fat of its own, and can be started dry at low heat until enough of its own drippings are formed. The browning is done by increasing the temperature for the last half of the roasting time. The handling of gravy or jus is like other roasts.

Experimental Recipe 72.

Pork Roast (Roast Pork)

Delicious pork roast with great crackling and the best gravy ever.

Ingredients

1. 200 g of pork per person
2. a small red onion
3. 1 tbsp olive oil
4. 1 teaspoon honey
5. 1 teaspoon white balsamic vinegar
6. one clove of garlic
7. two teaspoons of corn flour

Preparation

Step 1. Pre-heat your oven to 200 degrees centigrade (400 F–gas mark 6).

Nicely dressed roast-a good kilogram for four people. Salt and pepper the roast and place it in a roasting dish. Cut off a small slice of meat for the gravy. Then put the roast into your pre-heated oven 1.5 hours for this 1 kg roast will do nicely.

Step 2. Chop up the red onion . . .

Step 3. . . . and chop the small slice you previously cut off from the roast into thin strips.

Step 4. Pour the olive oil to a small saucepan, heat up the oil and add the meat strips.

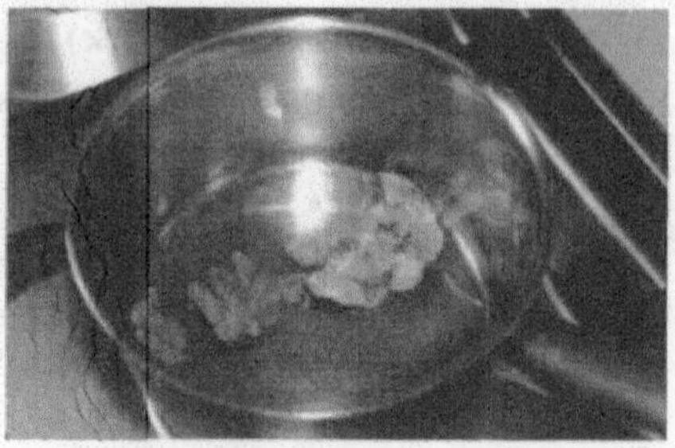

Step 5. Then add the onion and fry together until the meat and onion looks life this - a couple of minutes will do the trick. Then add 300 ml of water (about 1½ glasses).

Step 6. Cut pork cube in half...
Then add 300 ml of water (about 1½ glasses).

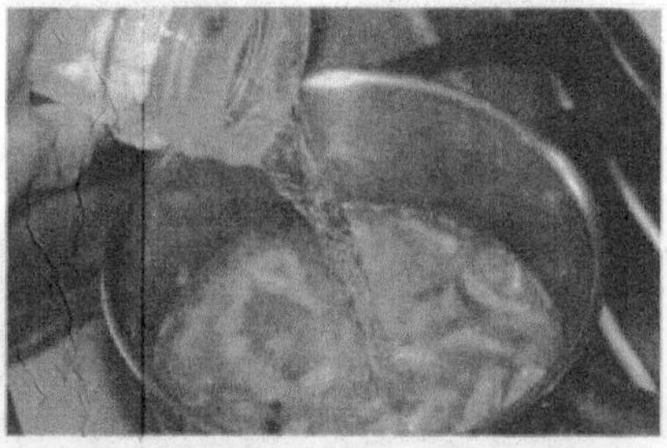

Step 7. Cut your pork stock cube in half...
... and add it to the stock.

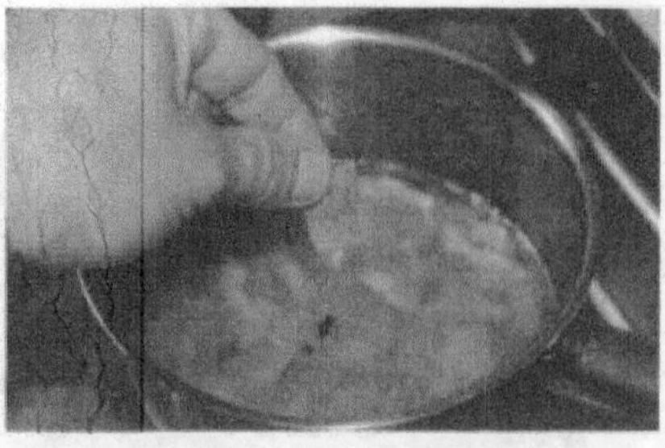

Step 8. We will add a teaspoon of honey as this gives the pork gravy a nice sweet touch as anyone who likes sweet and sour pork will appreciate. Also add the oregano.

Step 9. Talking about sour-now add a teaspoon of white balsamic vinegar.

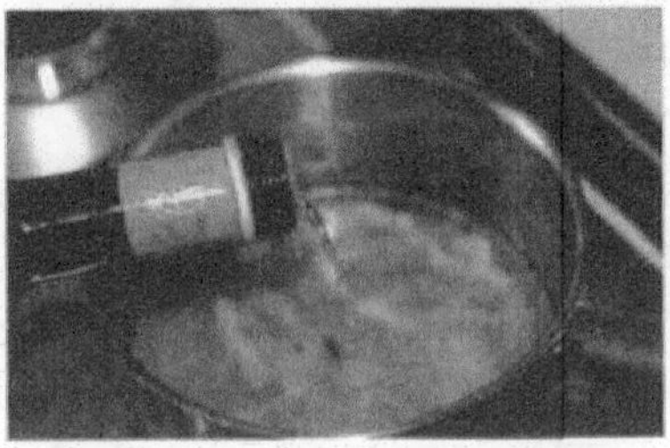

Step 10. And press a clove of garlic into the mixture.

Let the gravy stock simmer on a low flame for a good hour (you can do that whilst the roast is in the oven ...), best with a lid on the saucepan. Replenish the water so you will end up with the 300ml you started off with. After you have started the gravy stock, check your roast. As soon as you have some pork fat collecting in your roasting dish, open the oven every 10 minutes and pour the grease with a spoon over the roast. This will ensure that you get a nice crackling.

Once the roast is done and the crackling looks nice, take the roast out of the oven. Take the roast out of the dish onto your cutting board and put the roasting dish on the hob and light a flame under it. Separate the solid bits (meat and onion) from your gravy stock and throw them away. Pour your gravy stock into the roasting dish and dissolve all the caked-on residue with it. Now separate the fat from the gravy with a gravy separatro or a spoon.

Dissolve two teaspoons of corn flour in 50ml of water and pour about half of this mixture into the roasting dish. Bring to a boil and stir-adjust the thickness of the gravy with the corn flour/water mixture. Add salt and pepper to your taste.

Loin of Pork

Loin of pork is excellent in taste. Salt and some seasonings are necessary because pork is a bland meat.

A whole loin, untrimmed, should weigh from 14 to 16 pounds. It is cut into three parts: the main center cut (more expensive when bought by itself), the butt-end, and the rib-end. The center cut must have the chine bone removed, but the ribs stay as they are. The rib-end is boned completely, or only the chine and the blade tip are removed. The butt-end is best when boned completely. The fillet can be removed and used differently, or it can be tied back into the boned butt-end. Extra fat is removed.

Roasting time depends on the width of each part, not the length of the loin. Center cuts are cooked from 1 hour to 2¼ hours, at 350°F. The butt or rib ends may need 15 minutes longer. The portion yield is about 1 order each 8 ounces of raw trimmed meat.

Roast pork with crackling

Leg of Pork

Leg of pork is also known as a fresh ham. It is roasted with the skin still on only when it comes from young animals. The roasted pork skin, called "crackling", is a delicacy. Average weight of legs is from 14 to 18 pounds, with a portion yield similar to the loin. Salt curing, more than the smoking of a ham, changes a raw pork leg into a tasty ham.

Following procedure could be fellowed to prepare the ham :

1. The alitchbone is removed first.
2. Then the leg bone is cut from the shank bone. The leg bone is removed whole, without cutting the leg open.
3. The lean inside meat is seasoned with salt and the outside skin remains saltfree.
4. The skin must be blanched in water (simmered) to become tender before it is changed into crackling. The done by placing the leg skin side down on a low rack in a high rimmed roasting pan.
5. The pan is half filled with boiling salted water and the skin side of the leg is simmered for half an hour.
6. When done, the blanched skin of the leg is scored with a small sharp knife. The cuts should be parallel and about one fifth of an inch apart. The cuts are across the width of the leg, the same way as the leg is to be carved later.
7. One inch of the blanching liquid is put in a roasting pan. The rest is added to the general stock or is kept for making gravy later.
8. The leg, with the skin side up, is put into the pan of blanching liquid. No salting or basting is done to the scored skin.
9. Initial roasting is at 325°F. for about 3 hours, then the heat is increased.
10. For better browning, another 30 to 60 minutes is added.

    Total cooking time is 3½ to 4 hours at an average temperature of 350°F.

Boston Butt

Boston butt is a squared, trimmed pork shoulder. The blade bone and the shoulder bone are removed. The Boston butt is handled like the rib-end roast and is like it in texture.

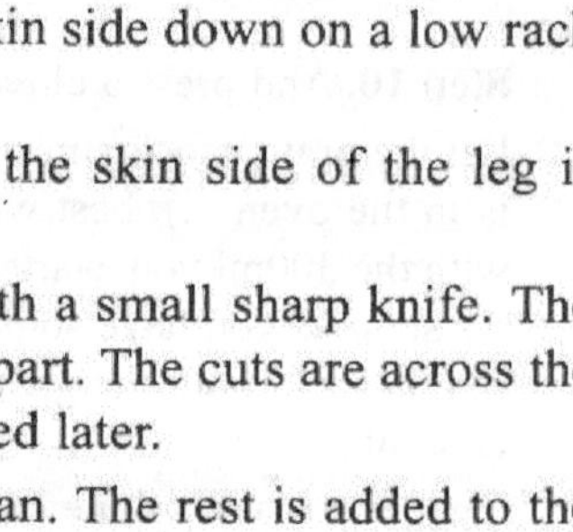

Lamb cutlets

Meat (Beef)

Meat (beef) for a *la carte* or *banquet* use, is roasted medium-rare to rare unless it is specified differently in advance dance. Roasting should be timed so as to reduce the time for warm keeping. This makes a better roast. During setting time, the gravy should be made. If string was used, it is removed now, before the carving starts. General seasoning for beef is salt, pepper and sometimes paprika. Except for the ribs of beef, all beef roasts need a little fat in the roasting pan to cover the bottom and some fat brushed over the lean parts.

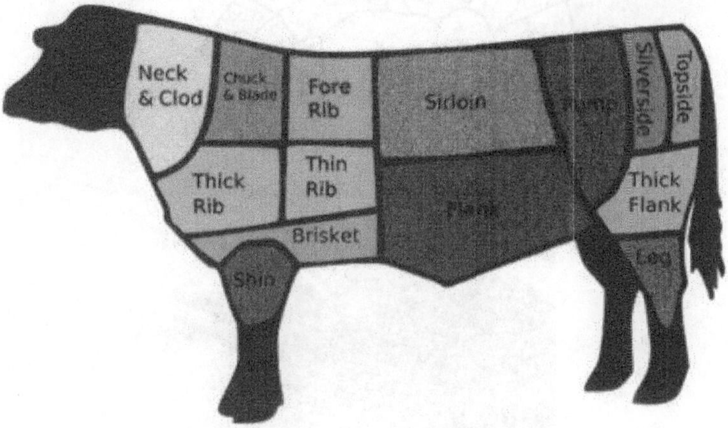

Fig. 4.2A. British Cuts of Beef

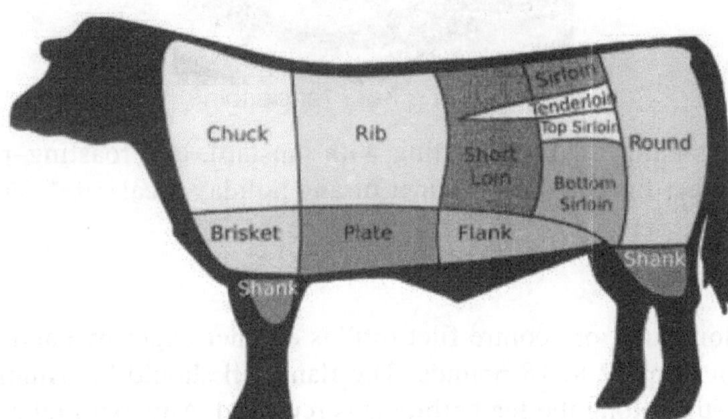

Fig. 4.2B. American Cuts of Beef

Fillet of Meat (Beef) Tenderloin

This portion is the most expensive and most tender of all the meat (beef) roasts. It is served mostly at banquets or pre-recorded parties. The warm-keeping time is limited. The average fillet weighs from 6 to 8 pounds and can be roasted full trimmed or partly trimmed. For elegant presentation, it is trimmed to the silver skin and the lean surface is larded. The trimmed fillet tastes better, and the salt can pass into it easier. The crust is edible. Total roasting time for the trimmed fillet is about 25–30 minutes at 475°F. to 500°F. The untrimmed fillet needs about 45–55 minutes at 450°F. It may serve 12–15 gouts.

Fig. 4.2C. Cuts of Beef

Roasting a Beef Tenderloin

Four steps–seasoning, searing, coating with mustard, and roasting–produce a juicy beef tenerloin perfect for Christmas dinner or any holiday meal. (Ref. Figs. 4.2A, 4.2 B and 4.2C Cuts of Beef)

Strip Loin

The strip, sirloin strip, or "contre filet roti" is another expensive and excellent roast. Strips may weigh from 12 to 18 pounds. The flank tail should be trimmed close to the "eye". The back strap along the featherbrains is removed. Any extra fat cover is trimmed off. Average total roasting time is 50 to 65 minutes at 375ºF. It is best to roast the strip on a bed of bones on a rack. The yield is 18-26 orders.

Top Sirloin

This is not practical for a commercial roast. It is expensive and has an uneven yield because of its structure. It is roasted like the strip loin.

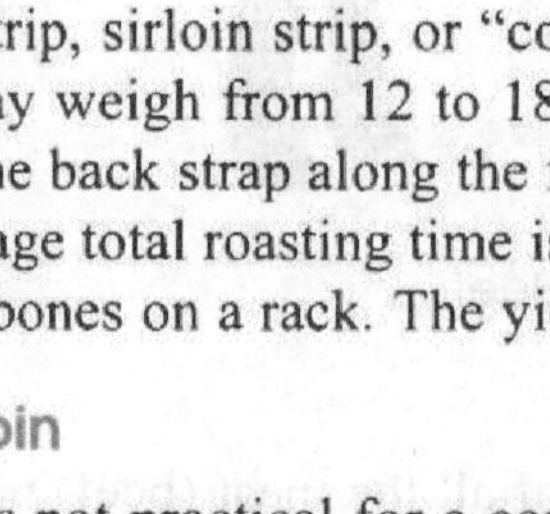

Roast sirloin of beef

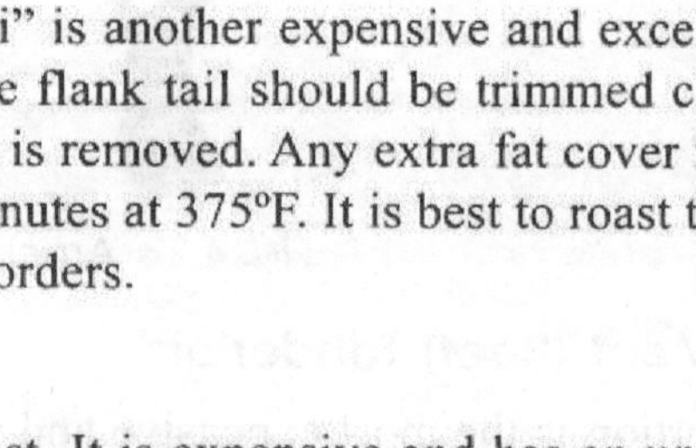

Roast sirloin of beef

Knuckle or Sirloin Tip

This is the least expensive beef roast. It is used for cold cuts, sandwiches, and cold plates. It weighs from 8 to 11 pounds. It has a better yield if trimmed and cut in half, lengthwise. The two halves are started in a skillet like a steak and finished in the oven at 400°F. for 25 to 40 minutes.

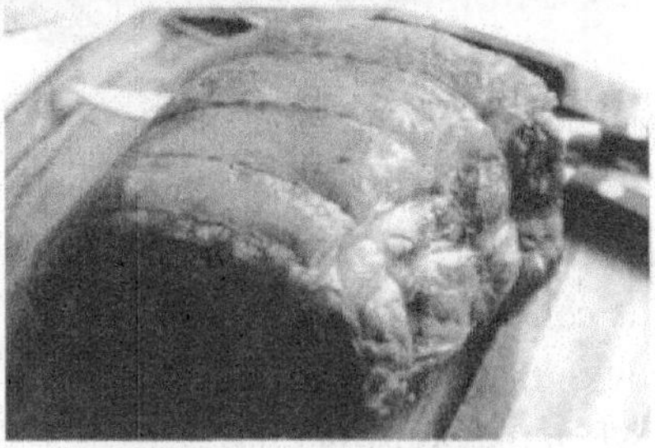

Roast sirloin of beef

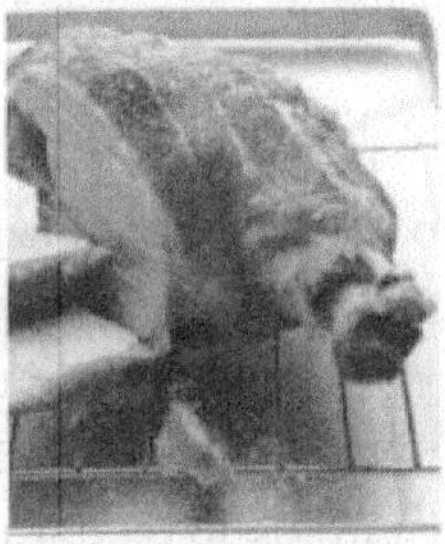

Roast Kanckle

Ribs of Beef

Ribs of meat is an speciality. It is the main fare for many dinner houses or a "House of Prime Ribs". It is fairly expensive, not economic in yield, but the customers are paying the price. Ribs can be bought oven-ready, trimmed (more expensive), or as is. The chef who buys 'as is' and does a little extra work has a better roast and a much better food cost. An electric meat saw is used to cut portion sizes. Ribs of meat may weigh from 24 to 32 pounds, need trimming, and are roasted for 2½ to 3½ hours at 350°F. the roast stands on the rib bones, with the fat cover up. The use of a meat thermometer is advised. For large roasts; more recirculation time has to be allowed, and carry-over heat is significant.

A roast is cooked to an internal temperature of 125°F. to be rare and it is handled as described. "Cotes de Boeuf roti en Sel" is the Parisian way of cooking "Ribs of Beef". It is served from the cart and carved at the table. The trimmed ribs are put into a fitting, high

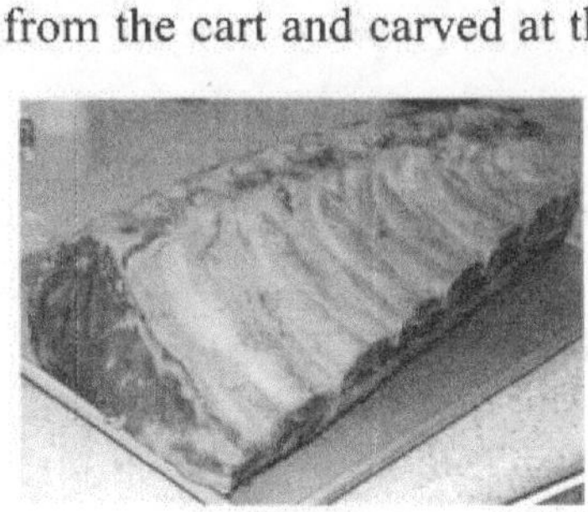

Beef Ribs

Cooking of Beef Ribs

rimmed roasting pan or a deep standard steam table pan. The roast is completely covered with a 2 inch layer of wet salt, which will bake into a hard crust. Coarse or kosher salt is moistened cheerfully first, then filled around and over the roast. The baking is done at 375°F. to 400°F. for about 3½ hours or more. The crust becomes a part of the showy dish and is kept until carving. It acts as an insulation and carry-over heat must be considered. A thermometer is used to check for an internal temperature of 115°F. before removing the roast from the oven. About 50-60 minutes of "setting" must be allowed, which will bring the roast up to 140°F. for rare. This method of roasting is not recommended unless table caring can be done. There are no drippings to make a gravy.

QUESTIONS AND DISCUSSIONS

Fill in the Blanks

Q.1. Read and complete the following statements :

(a) Too much fat cover prevents the edible meat from ....

(b) A New York strip, one of the finest roasts, is called in French ....

(c) When barding, bacon is added to the meat with the help of a ....

(d) Bones of meats to be roasted are removed when they obstruct the.........

(e) One-inch cubed vegetables added to the final stages of roasting are called.............

(f) As a substitute for roasting experience, the trainee cook should use a............

(g) When larding, bacon is added to the meat with the help of a..........

(h) The use of herbs and spices remains the chef's value ....

(i) Preparing the roast for the oven includes the selection of a proper size.......

(j) It is the salt more than the smoking that changes a raw pork leg into a tasty ....

[**Ans.:** (a) becoming crisp and brown; (b) centre filet roti; (c) tied over; (d) carving; (e) mireboix; (f) thermometer; (g) larding needle; (h) judgement; (i) of pan; (j) ham].

Multiple Choice Type

Q.2. Read each question carefully and select the best answer :

(i) A calf, to qualify as dairy veal, is

(a) 2½ to 3 months old and milk-red

(b) 3 to 4 months old and corn-fed

(c) 4 to 5 months old and from a dairy breed

(d) 5 to 6 months old and formula-fed.

(ii) The most popular roast sold in American specialty restaurants is :

(a) Rack of lamb (b) Ribs of beef

(c) Loin of pork (d) Saddle of veal

(iii) Roasts should only be tied with strings for :

(a) Keeping the shape (b) Easier handling

(c) Holding smaller pieces together (d) Making them look larger.

(iv) A young, roasted pork leg, with the skin still on, is :

(a) Salted a day in advance (b) Roasted slowly for 5 hours

(c) Blanched to tenderize the skin (d) Stuffed with "Mirepoix" for flavor.

(v) Roasting has as its first objective :

(a) The use of high heat for fastest browning

(b) The use of low heat to avoid shrinkage

(c) To achieve outside brownness and inside doneness at the same time

(d) To tenderize meat cuts which are too tough to be used as steaks.

(vi) A fitting roasting pan should be :

(a) Of nonoxidizing material (b) Higher than the roast

(c) A little larger than the roast (d) Much largér than the road.

(vii) Of the following beef roasts, the one with the longest cooking time is :

(a) Ribs of Beef roast (b) Sirloin Tip roast

(c) Beef Tenderloin roast (d) Strip Sirloin roast.

(viii) Ten pounds of raw, center-cut pork loin serves 16 orders and roasts for 2 1/4 hours at 375°F. When cut in half, serving only 8 orders, it roasts at 3/5°F. for :

(a) 60 to 75 minutes (b) 80 to 95 minutes

(c) 100 to 115 minutes (d) 120 to 135 minutes.

(ix) Modern cooks realize that turkeys :

(a) Consist of different meat with different cooking times

(b) Have to be preboiled before roasting to be tender

(c) Have to be cooked hotter and longer than before

(d) Have to be cooked very slowly at lowest heat.

(x) The roasting time of a saddle of veal as compared to a veal loin is :

(a) Much less (b) Nearly the same

(c) Half again as long (d) Twice as long.

(xi) Leg of lamb, a dark meat, is an English roast and generally served :

(a) With mint jelly (b) Medium done

(c) Well done (d) Larded or barded.

(xii) Of the following beef roasts, the one with the shortest cooking time is :

(a) "Contre Filet Roti" (b) Roasted New York Strip

(c) Roasted Top Sirloin (d) Larded Fillet of Beef.

(xiii) Trimmed lamb racks for double orders have :

(a) 5 ribs (b) 7 ribs

(c) 9 ribs (d) 11 ribs.

(xiv) Game pheasants are only good when they :

(a) Are roasted slowly (b) Are stuffed with dressing

(c) Have been fed on grain (d) Are roasted like chickens.

(xv) Roast preparations done by chefs do not include :

(a) Larding or boarding (b) Boning and trimming

(c) Aging and tenderizing (d) Washing and salting.

[**Ans.:** (i) (a); (ii) (b); (iii) (a); (iv) (c); (v) (a);
(vi) (d); (vii) (a); (viii) (d); (ix) (a); (x) (b);
(xi) (b); (xii) (d); (xiii) (b); (xiv) (b); (xv) (c)]

Short Answer Type

Q.3. Define the following:

(a) Trussing (b) Larding
(c) Totisserie (d) Disjoint
(e) Keel bone (f) Saddle
(g) Rack (h) Score.

Q.4. Answer the following questions in two-four sentences:-

(a) What is trussing and explain its importance ?
(b) Explain 'Pomme Au Four'.
(c) Explain 'Suet & Lard'.
(d) What is 'Clearmeat' ?
(e) What is 'Panada' ?
(f) Explain 'Ballotine'.

[**Ans.:**

(a) Trussing is to tie leg of meat, poultry, etc. basically to retain its shape during cooking.
(b) Even sized potatoes wrapped in silver foil and baked on salt bed is called 'pomme au four'.
(c) Suet is layer of fat around the kidney and lard is in general pork fat.
(d) Clearmeat is a combination of minced meat, egg white, mire-poix, bay leaf and peppercorns and it is used to clarify stock.
(e) Panada is starch based thick binding agent made out of rice, potatoes, bread and flour.
(f) Ballotine is deboned and stuffed leg of poultry, poached and served hot with veloute.

Q.5. Answer the following questions in two-four sentences:-

(a) Explain 'Barding'.
(b) What is 'Au Gratin' ?
(c) What is the approximate temperature of clay *tandoor* ?
(d) Give names of food items suitable for grilling.
(e) What is the term for roasting when basting is done with butter?
(f) What is the approximate proportion of water; bones; mirepoix for stock ?
(g) Is it possible to make brown fish stock ?
(h) Explain why puff pastry becomes soggy ?
(i) Why does choux paste becomes greasy and heavy ?
(j) Why do cakes crack while baking ?

[**Ans :**

(a) Covering the surface of the tender roast with slices of pork.
(b) This term is generally used in finishing of a dish coated with sauce and grated cheese and put under a salamander to give golden brown colour before service.
(c) Approximate 375 degrees C - 400 degree C.
(d) i. Good quality (tender) cuts of meat
ii. Spring chicken
iii. Sole fish
iv. Lobster

v. Prawns
vi. Mushrooms
vii. Tomatoes
viii. Fillet & steaks of fish, etc.

(e) Poeling.

(f) 10 : 5 : 1

(g) Preferably not, fish bones contain less gelatine and it gets burnt while browning for the same.

(h) Due to under baking or oven is too hot.

(i) Because of basic mixture is over cooked.

(j) If water is too less or baking powder is in excess quantity, the cakes will crack.

Q.6. Answer the following questions in two-four sentences :

(a) What is the marinade for *Tandoori* Chicken ?

(b) How is *Makhani* Gravy prepared ?

(c) How is *Murg Malai Kebab* cooked ?

(d) How is *Gulab Jamun* prepared ?

(e) Name five popular Indian soups or shorbas.

(f) Name five *tandoori* breads.

(g) List five popular Indian chicken curries.

(h) Give a list of five deep-fried Indian breads.

(i) Give the preparation of *Paneer Tikka*.

(j) Name five popular *Tandoori Kebabs* (i.e. Meat, Fish, Poultry).

Ans.:

(a) The chicken is marinated with salt, red chilli powder and lemon juice and then coated with a mixture of thick curd, ginger-garlic paste, *garam masala, degi mirch* and *shahi jeera*.

(b) Cook fresh tomato puree, ginger-garlic paste, *degi mirch*, *garam masala* and white butter till fairly thick then finish with cream.

(c) First boneless pieces of chicken are marinated with salt and lemon juice and then mixed with thick curd, ginger-garlic paste, egg yolk, grated cheese, chopped green chillies and green coriander and cream. Then skewed and cooked in Tandoor.

(d) Mash the mixture of *khoya* and *paneer* (3:1) to a smooth texture, then sprinkle little flour and mix. Shape into small balls and deep fry in medium hot oil till golden in colour. Remove and soak in sugar syrup of less than 'one thread' consistency.

(e) i. Tomato shorba; ii. Madras Soup; iii. Mulligtawny Soup; iv. Dahishorba; v. Sarki.

(f) i. Naan; ii. Parantha; iii. Taftan iv. Bakharkhani; v. Sheermal;

(g) i. Murg Do Piaza; ii. Murg Korma; iii. Methi Murg; iv. Salli Murgi;
v. Murg Badam Pasanda.

(h) i. Poori; ii. Kachori; iii. Luchi; iv. Bhatura v. Dhakai Parauntha.

(i) Big chunks of cottage cheese are marinated in the mixture of thick curd, *besan, ajwain*, red chilli powder, ginger-garlic paste, *garam masala* powder and lemon juice. Then skewed and cooked in *tandoor*.

(j) i. Murg Malai Tikka; ii. Seekh Kebab; iii. Reshmi Kebab; iv. Tangri Kebab v. Fish Tikaa.

Descriptive Answer Type

Q.7. What are the advantages of modern turkey roasting ?

Q.8. Why is pork, with greater nutritional qualities than beef, less popular ?

Q.9. Why is there a need for proper roast preparations ?

Q.10. Why do ready cooked meats have such a high salt level ?

Assignments/Activity Type

Q. 11. Demonstration by instructors and practice by trainees :

(a) Trussing and larding a roasting chicken

(b) Trimming and roasting a beef tenderloin

(c) Preparing and roasting a young pork leg

(d) Frenching and roasting a rack of lamb

(e) Preparing and roasting a goose or duck

(f) Trimming, preparing and trying a Ribs of Beef roast.

4.3

Broiling or Grilling

CHAPTER OBJECTIVES

After studying this lesson you should be able :

- To explain the importance and objectives of broiling;
- To describe the sequence of steps for broiling a steak;
- To demonstrate and practice
  - (a) the broiling of a meat dish and practice;
  - (b) the making of a Brochette;
- To identify the check point for doneness; and
- To list some foods, by their menu names, which can be broiled.

Broiling is known as the oldest from of cookery. Today, it still gives human kind a great emotional and taste satisfaction. Broiling is known in every part of the world. Old-fashioned characoal broialers, even plain wood burning ones, are still used often. Electric or gas broilers are faster and cleaner. Broiling also called grilling, is an important dry heat cooking method. It is an *a la carte* (cooking to the order) process, and the cook incharge is called short order cook or broilerman.

The principles of grilling are the same for all types of broilers. As long as you remember these few basic rules and principles your broiling will become better and better after a short time of practice. Broiling or grilling to the order is an important and popular form of a la cart cookery. Perhaps it is the oldest form of cookery. It has changed very little. Broiling means to cook by dry heat. Burning of charring of meat over the direct fire is not good for health and taste. All rules for roasting also apply to broiling.

Preparations

Although the principles of broiling are the same, there are small differences for some preparations. These differences are the key points of the trade, and learning them will help the beginning cook.

All tender and fat foods broil well. The American public prefers steaks cooked this way. These are tender, portion sizes of meat which can be broiled rare, medium, or well done.

A brochette (French term for spit or skewer) is used to handle small meat or fish pieces for order.

This means that 4, 6, or more pieces of food are held together on one spit. Meat on a skewer is like spit-roasting for one order.

It is most important for the student cook to learn and understand "the checkpoint to doness" Over-cooked broiled meat or fish preparations are not acceptable.

Food cooking on a charcoal grill

Following guidelines would be useful for broiling :

1. Broiling is done by radiation and convected heat, but never by burning food over coals. Charred or burned meat is not the objective of broiling.
2. Fats and liquids must not be allowed to drip on glowing coals or steel, causing flare-ups and scorched foods.
3. Raw meats must be salted and oiled before broiling, but additional seasoning is by choice.
4. Grill marks must show or the eye appeal is lost. Taste, in the case of broiled food, is less important than sight, aroma, and smell.
5. Broiler must be clean at all times. It is done with a wire steel brush and old towels. The grease collection pan is emptied regularly.

The thinner the steak, the hotter the fire, the faster the cooking: The same principles which have explained roasting, recirculation of juices, and the action of carry-over heat must be applied to broiling.

The broiler need to be pre-heated before use. The grill bars must be hot enough to *sear* (scorch) the meat immediately at the first touch. When the bars are hot, they are scraped with a wire brush, then wiped clean with an oiled towel before the first order is made.

A coal shovel and stoker for charbroilers, a carbon dioxide fire extinguisher, a wire brush, towelsm, and the cook's personal tools are used for all broilers

Mis en place (the French name for the work station setup) means that all that is needed for the menu at a given shift is lined up and ready to use. Warm service plates or platters, paper frills for lamb chops, doily papers, and napking are as important as spicies, herbs, salt, and pans of oil, bread crumbs and flour.

All foods must be trimmed, seasoned and oiled slightly before they touch the grill bars. White meats and fish are dipped in bread crumbs before they are oiled. Protein food with low blood content will show grill marks only if dippen in starch Liver is dipped into flour to prevent oxidation. Liver cooked without flour discolours to a greenish tint and does not look appetizing. Vegetables, such as eggplants, zucchini, mushrooms and tomatoes are also dipped into bread crumbs so that some of the moisture is absorbed.

Food on a broiler should be moved or turned only when necessary. Grill marks, seared in by the hot grill bars, will become smeared if the food is moved. The searing is like a rubber stamp pressed on a paper. Food is first put at an angle of about 45° at the grill bar, and broiled for a quarter of the estimated cooking time. Then it is carefully lifted and turned 90°, still on the same side. After half of the total cooking time, the food is turned over, so that the grill marks are easily seen. The food item is then finished to the desired doneness. Constant turning from one side to the other, as some cooks do, adds to the cooking time, dries out the meat, and destroys the grill marks.

The French recognize only steaks which are cooked *saignat* (medium rare or bloody), or *bien cuit* (medium well). French customers realize that steaks should not be charred on the outside and cold inside (*blue or blood rare*). Neither should they be well done and dry. Cooking for the fine distinctions of medium to medium well or between rare and medium rare, is nearly impossible to do. It has happened that a steak ordered rare, but cooked medium well, was returned by the customer with a serious remark that he only wanted a steak rare, not still bloody.

For meat, the best sign of its doneness is to watch for drops of blood-liquid to rise to the grill-marked face of the steak. When this happens the steak is rare inside and if taken off, the recirculation time and warm keeping of several minutes will make it medium rare.

1. To obtain best grill marks for a steak with an estimated cooking time of 6 minutes follow the diagram given in best figure 4.3A.

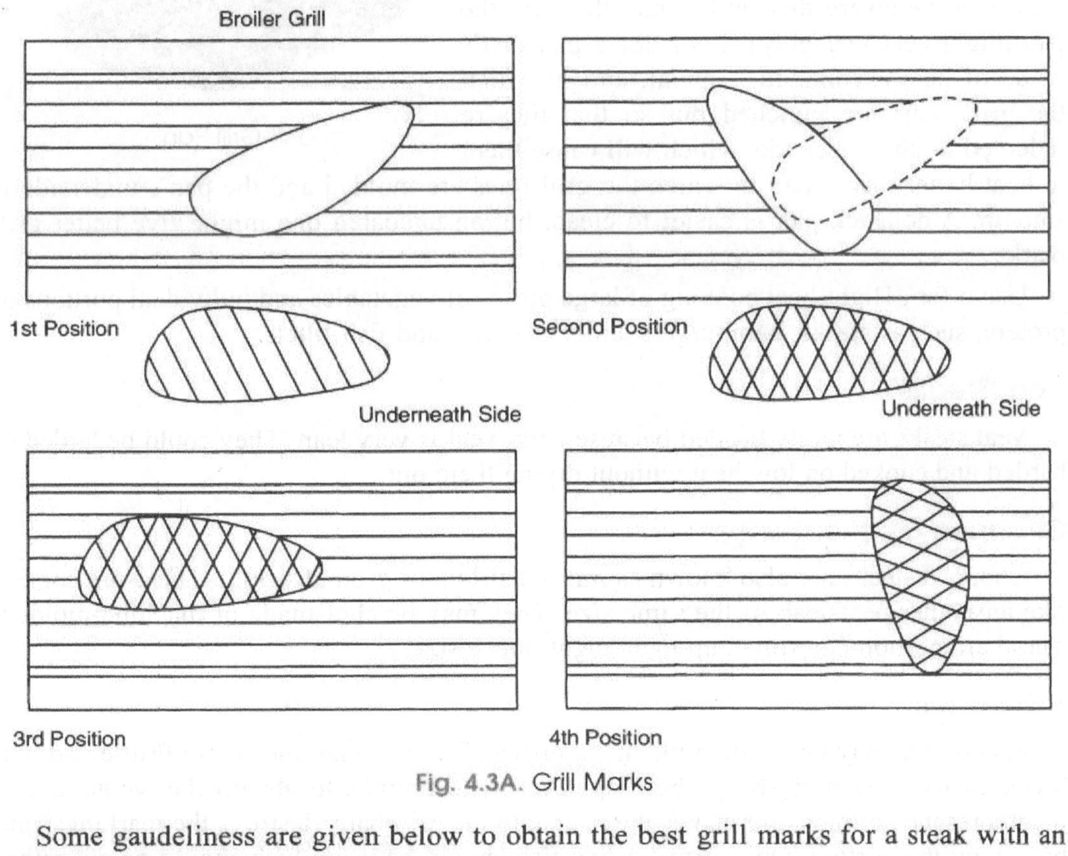

Fig. 4.3A. Grill Marks

Some gaudeliness are given below to obtain the best grill marks for a steak with an estimated cooking time of 6 minutes:

1. 1st position, 1½ minutes

2. 2nd position, + 1½ minutes
3. 3rd position, + 1½ minutes, to 4½ minutes
4. 4th position, + 1½ minutes, to 6 minutes

Chops

Lamb chops (plain or frenched), Lamb Noisette (a boneless loin eye which looks like a filet mignon), English Mutton Chop (cut from a saddle of lamb, with the lamb kidney in the middle), and Pork Chops are all broiled the same way as Tournedos, New York Steaks, or Filet Mignons.

Mixed Grill

Mixed grill is any group of grilled meats. Most popular are lamb chop grillades consisting of lamb chop, lamb, kidney, liver, grilled bacon, pork links, and broiled tomato – served with french fries and watercress.

A grill pan can be round, sequare or rectangular, with the latter shape often big enough to cover two burners to maximize cooking surface (however, be aware that with a pan this big, the pan might heat unevenly). Look for a pan that's made of heavy, conductive metal, and in which the grill lines are punched out so that they're indented on the underside, which will cause them to heat better than a pan in which the grill lines are molded and the pan's underside is smooth. A nonstick pan is easier to clean, but an uncoated one might give better grill marks.

Grill Pan

Use it for : Hight-heat cooking of large pieces of vegetables and individual portions of protein, such as steaks, hamburgers, chicekn breast and fish fillets.

Veal Steaks

Veal steaks are rarely broiled because dairy veal is very lean. They could be larded or barded and cooked on low heat without drying them out.

Chopped Steaks

Chopped steaks are also known as minced sirloin or ground sirloin. These are cooked like any other beefsteak of the same size. They may be chef-made or machine-molded. These are portion-controlled up to an eight-ounce size.

Fish Dishes

Fish dishes may be handled like meat dishes. Fish is sometimes more brittle and will break easily. It should always be dipped in bread crumbs to absorb the wetness. Too much presence of moisture makes them stick to the grill bars, destroys the markings, and breaks up the portion. Only firm-fleshed fish should be used. Fish should be cut rather short and chubby instead of thin and long. This makes it easier to handle. Fish need to be well salted, and then cooked according to its thickness. Some of the most well known fish steaks are cut from halibut, swordfish, salmon, tuna, and seabass.

Broiled Lobster

Broiled lobster is treated as a specialty of New England and Eastern Canada. Live 1½ to 2-pound lobsters are split in half lengthwise. The sack , with its sand, is thrown away. The *coral* (ovary) and other creamy parts are mixed with equal parts of fine french bread crumbs and clarified butter. Clarified butter is made by separating the butterfat from the water and milk solids after the butter has been melted and chilled. The shells of the claws are cracked carefully for easier cooking and eating. The empty shell of the lobster is filled with the coral mixture. The flesh of the tail and claws is lightly salted and brushed with a large amount of butter. The lobster, with the exposed side up, is placed on a baking sheet under a hot *Salamander* (broiler) with over heat for a few minutes. When it has started to brown lightly, it is moved to a 500°F. (or hotter) oven. It is finished in 8-10 minutes more butter is added. The lobster is served with clarified butter on the side, potato chips, and lemon wedges.

Lobster Dinner

Grill-Lobster

Skewered specialty dishes from the Broiler

Prepare pieces of well seasoned meat or fish and put on a *skewer* (spit) with vegetables or fruits. These are broiled and served garnished. The best foods for this specialty are beef fillet ends, lamb, pork, ham, raw turkey, venison (game), beef liver, calves liver, kidney, chicken liver, lobster, scallops, oysters, and prawns. Some of the fillers you can use are bacon, ham, mushrooms, pepper, onion, eggplant, cherry tomatoes, squash, and pineapple. Spices, such as garlic, lemon, soy sauce, saffron, curry, basil, and thyme are used.

Skewers are spits of metal or wood. *Brochette* is their French name. Skewers often are in single-portion size, and are handled like a single steak. Beef and lamb are broiled rare or medium. Other foods are well done. Most of these specialities are still popular under their foreign names.

1. *Shashlick* :It is of Russian origin, has lamb, seasoned with garlic and lemon juice, on the skewer with raw onions and thin pieces of lamb fat for flavour. This is charcoal broiled to medium and then served with coleslaw, dill pickles, pickled beets, and lemon sections.
2. *Shish-kebabs* : These are Armenian-Turkish variation of the Russian Shell-shock with red wine instead on lemon juice. Pilaf or risotto is used as a garnish.
3. *Brochette Caesura* (*Beef tenderloin brochettes*) : This is made of beef fillet ends.

4. Fish-Kebab : It includes oysters, scallops, or other fish and shellfish.
5. *Satays* : These are an Idonesian specialty. Small wooden skewers are lined with curried and spaced raw chicken, pork or shellfish and then broiled.
6. Spiced pork or beef meat balls, wrapped in bacon and broiled on skewers are of Eastern European origin.

There are countless ways of preparing brochettes. The meat, spices, vegetables, garnishes, and sauces may be changed. The taste of this dish is not improved when it is served on a flaming sword. This is strictly a showmanship antic and is not liked by the true connoisseur.

Grilled Chicken

American grilled chicken is a French dish, which uses a very young chicken or squab. After it is split open on the back, the keel bone, ribs and aitchbones are taken out. It is seasoned, dipped in bread crumbs then oiled, pressed in a chicken rack, and broiled slowly for 12 to 15 minutes. Whose squab chickens are best for this preparation. If is served with bacon slices, grilled tomato, and shoestring potatoes.

Grilling

Broiled Chicken with Lemon and Geen Onion Sauce

Chicken with Marmalade and Onions a skillet chicken breast recipe for any occasion

Tandoori chicken tikka rolls Served with a coconut Sauce

Tandoori Chicken

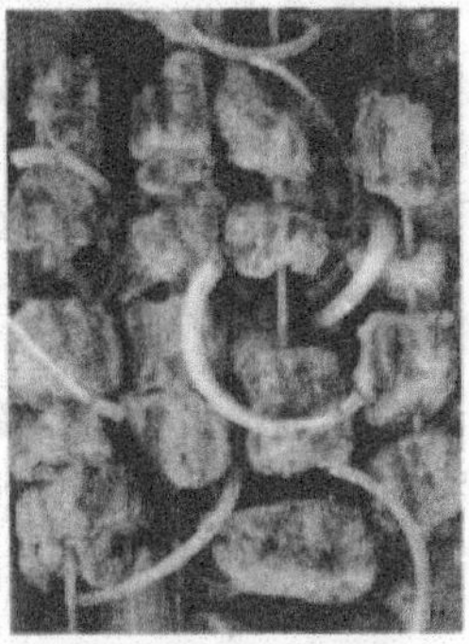

Chicken Tikka

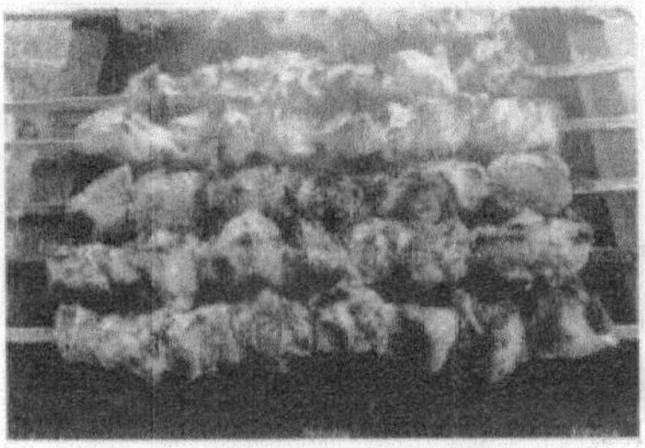

Picture–Shish a grill

Chicken Kebabs

Chateaubriand

Chateaubriand is a fillet steak for two or three, carved at the table by the headwaiter. It is cut from the fillet head, then trimmed slightly and pounded to a 2-in thickness. It is broiled like the filet mignon.

Tournedos

These are also called "Medallions" of Beef. Tournedos are Filet Mignons cut in half. They should be 3/4 to 1¼ inches thick and are cooked accordingly. They are served in pairs, on top of a *creation* (round-cut buttered toast), with a sauce or garnish on the side.

Satay: Satay is a popular food in many South heast Asian countries. It is a dish consisting of diced or sliced chicken, goat, mutton, beef, pork, fish, tofu, or other meats. These are grilled or barbecued over a wood or charcoal fire, then served with various spicy seasonings.

Filet Mignon

Filet Mignon, also called "Coeur de Filet", is 1¼ to 2 inches thick, needs slow cooking and good recirculation time. It could be pounded lightly with a flat side of a cleaver if it is thicker than 2 inches. Cooking and setting time should be 8-10 minutes each.

The rising of the blood-liquid to the surface of the already cooked side is the checkpoint for the cook to take the food off the fire.

New York Steak

New York Steak, also called Boneless Sirloin, Sirloin, Featherbed, New York Steak-Steak and Entrecote must have a thickness of 1 to 1½ inches. It needs a slow fire and 5-8 minutes of recirculation time for a medium-rare steak.

Minute Steak

From the New York Strip, the minute steak is sometimes called a "Lady's Cut Steak". It is ½ inch thick, at most, and it must be cooked very hot and fast, not more than 1½ minutes per side. Only parallel grill marks are needed.

Experimental Recipe 72.

Paneer Tikka

Ingredients

1.	Paneer	:	250 gm
2.	Thick Curd	:	1/2 cup (tied in cloth for 2 hrs)
3.	Ginger	:	1" grated
4.	Garlic	:	1/2 crushed
5.	Red Chilli Powder	:	1 tsp
6.	Tandoori Masala	:	1/2 tsp
7.	Chaat Masala	:	1/2 tsp
8.	Sugar	:	1/2 tsp
9.	Cumin Seeds	:	1/2 tsp (crushed)
10.	Capsicum, Onion, Tomato, Carrot	:	1 tbsp each (long thin strips)
11.	Julilennes	:	1/2 tbsp (finely chopped)
12.	Coriander	:	1 tbsp
13.	Butter	:	1 tsp
14.	Salt	:	To taste.

Method

1. Prepare all required ingredients.
2. Cut paneer into 1/2" horizontal slabs.
3. Mix the red chilli, salt, sugar, cumin *tandoori masala*, half the ginger-garlic and chopped coriander in the curd. Mix well.
4. Crush the slabs of *paneer* liberally with this dip on both sides and edges.
5. Marinate for 30 minutes.
6. For cooking grill the *paneer* over hot charcoal.
7. Add butter and place slices to sizzle till light brown.
8. Flip and repeat for other side. Cut into bite size square and arrange in serving dish.
9. Add remaining butter to pan, heat.
10. Add juliennes vegetables, *chaat masala* and salt to taste.
11. Pour over the tikka paneer. Serve hot with tiny fruit forks and sauce.

Experimental Recipe 73.

Brochettes Preparations

Ingredients

1.	Brochettes (meat wrapped with bacon)	: 10
2.	Trimmed Fillet Ends	: 4lb
3.	Olive oil, to be mixed with garlic	: 1 cup
4.	Thinly sliced bacon, 25 slices	: 1 lb.
5.	Stainless steel skewers,	: 8"– 10 long pieces
6.	Mushroom caps, diameter	: 20 pieces
7.	Salt and fresh ground pepper	: To taste
8.	Sage leaves, fresh and large	: 50
9.	Additional spices	: optional
10.	Garlic, fresh and squashed	: 3 cloves
11.	Vegetables, fruits for addition or change	: optional.

Method

1. Prepare required ingredients
2. Cut meat into 50 chunks of same size.
3. Salt and prepare the meat
4. Mix with half a cup of the garlic-olive oil
5. Steam or branch mushrooms caps for 30 seconds
6. Cut onions into single leaf rectangles of 1/2 to 1 1/2 inches
7. Cut each bacon slice in half and line up in rows on the working table
8. Blanch age leaves in boiling salt water for 2 seconds and place one in the middle of each 1/2 bacon slice
9. Place drained meat chunks in the middle of sage leaf
10. Roll up meat in bacon and sage leaf
11. Divide the 50 meat-bacon rolls into 10 portions of 5 each
12. Place one mushroom on the skewer by peering it carefully from the top and sliding it to the ring end of the skewer
13. Pierce one onion piece and slide it next to the mush room.
14. Center the first meat piece, with the skewer piercing and holding the bacon end
15. Add second onion piece
16. Add second piece of meat, same way as before
17. Continue the lineup, to a total of 5 meat and 6 onion pieces
18. Use mushroom cap as the second end piece, with the top pointing outside
19. Continue until 10 brochetters are made
20. Place them on oiled bake sheet. Pour remaining olive oil over them
21. Keep refrigerated until broiling to the order.

BROCHETTES

Brochettes

This step-by-step process is used for any brochette, shish-kebab or shell-shock. Only the points stressed are important. The combining of meats, vegetables or fruits and their seasoning is a value judgement and reflects the taste of the individual chef. The skill exactness, and speed of preparing this dish reflects the craftsmanship of the cook (Ref. Experimental Recipe 72 and 73). Food on a skewer is cooked for the same time to the same doneness, therefore

1. Food is cut to uniform thickness and size.
2. Food on a skewer resembles a straight, even row.
3. Food on a skewer is centered for balance.
4. Food on a skewer needs a little space between pieces for that circulation.
5. Skewers are oiled before they are stuck through the meat.

Unless ordered otherwise, they should be medium-rare, with good grill marks on the flat sides. They are taken off the sewer by the server in front of the guest. Sauces and garnishes are by choice of the chef.

QUESTIONS AND DISCUSSIONS

Fill in the Blanks

Q.1. Read and compete the following statements:

(a) Before foods can be seared, the broiler must be very...............

(b) In the broiler, fat from meats or seafood must not drip into the..........

(c) The most popular broiler dish in the USA is the ....

(d) The grill bars of the broiler are cleaned best with a ....

(e) Regardless of broiler type used, the principles for broiling are the ....

(f) Food on the broiler is not turned ....

(g) For a thin steak, the temperature of the fire must be very...............

(h) Food from the broiler should not be ....

(i) Grill marks are a very important part of ....

[Ans: (a) hot; (b) glowing coals or steels; (c) New York Steak; (d) wire steal brush and old towels; (e) same; (f) until the grill mark are easily seen; (g) hot and fast; (h) moved or turned only when necessary; (i) an eye appeal]

Multiple Choice Type

Q.2. Read each question carefully select the best answer :

(i) Mixed grill could mean any combination of foods from the grill, but he most popular is a combination of :

(a) lobster, prawns, scallops, oysters
(b) pork chop, bacon, winner, french fries
(c) lamb chop, liver, bacon, pork links
(d) chicken, chicken livers, tomatoes, mushrooms.

(ii) The term "frenched" lamb chops implies :

(a) it has a bacon slice wrapped around
(b) it is a lamb T-Bone
(c) it has the rib bone scraped clear
(d) it is a boneless chop.

(iii) Seafood, to be broiled easier, should have the characteristic of :

(a) tenderness (c) leanness
(b) firmness (d) tastiness.

(iv) When watching a steak being broiled, a "usual checkpoint appears when:

(a) the grill marks become visible
(b) the first juice drops rise to the cooked surface
(c) the fat rim of the steak is getting brown
(d) the steak stops dripping juice.

(v) Cooking a minute steak to rare will need :

(a) 3 minutes (b) 5 minutes
(c) 4 minutes (d) 6 minutes.

(vi) A new England Broiled Lobster is :

(a) shelled raw lobster meat on a skewer, grilled
(b) shelled cooked lobster meat on a skewer, broiled
(c) a cooked half lobster, buttered and browned with grill marks
(d) a live lobster split in half, cooked in salamander and oven.

(vii) A chateaubriand (file mignon for two or three) should be :

(a) ¾ of an inch thick (b) 1¼ inches thick
(c) 2 inches thick (d) 2½ inches thick.

(viii) A 10-ounce Filet Mignon, cooked to rare, will need :

(a) 5 minutes of cooking time (b) 7 minutes of cooking time
(c) 9 minutes of cooking time (d) 11 minutes of cooking time.

(ix) A minute steak should have a thickness of :

(a) ½ inch (b) ¾ inch.
(c) 1 inch (d) 1¼ inches.

(x) Small pieces of beef fillet-ends placed on a skewer and broiler are called:

(a) Brochette Chasseur (b) Shush Kebab
(c) Shashlick (d) Indonesian Stay.

(xi) The English Mutton Chop is a special cut from the :

(a) Top sirloin (b) Saddle

(c) Rack (d) Loin.

(xii) A 10-ounce center cut of fillet, 2 inches thick and broiled is called :

(a) Chateaubriand (b) Coeur de Filed

(c) Tournedo (d) Noisette.

[**Ans.:** (i) (c); (ii) (c); (iii) (c); (iv) (a);
(v) (a); (vi) (d); (vii) (c); (viii) (c);
(ix) (b); (x) (a); (xi) (b); (xii) (a)]

Short Answer Type

Q.3. Is the eye appeal of grill marks really important ?

Q.4. Why are the holding times for some steaks different than for others ?

Q.5. Does a restaurant or a chef have any responsibility for guiding customers to healthier food (in regard to charring) ?

Q.6. Could a meat thermometer be used on broiled steak ?

Q.7. Explain the importance of cooking steaks to the degree requested.

Q.8. Describe the advantages of a la carte cookery.

Q.9. Define the following:

(a) Aitchbone (d) Brochette

(b) Satay (e) Mis-en place

(c) Entrecote (f) Tournedo.

4.4

Sauteing: Griddle Frying

CHAPTER OBJECTIVES

After studying this lesson you should be able :

- To explain the principle and method of sauteing, griddle frying,
- To identify and list suitable saute fats;
- To demonstrate and practice
  - (a) he sauteing of Filet of sole Meuniere.
  - (b) the cooking a chicken saute with musthrooms;
- To describe the procedured of cooking of sauteed, deglazed foods; and
- T7o list the names of different chicken saute preparations.

Sauteing is sometimes called flip frying. It is a form of griddle of pan frying. Food is first (sauted) in small quantiles of good fat which become a part of the finished dish. The general term *frying* should mean that food is cooked while floating in fat and then is separated from it after the frying is done.

Sauteing is one of the most used processes of today's cookery. It is one of the simplest things to do. The principles of tender foods, uniform cutting, use of good fats, high heat without burning or overcooking, and the addition of good pre-made sauces must be applied exactly and with understanding. Note the fact that the good fats which are used become a part of the preparation, controls the amount that can be added. Deglazing adds the finishing touch to dishes, and gives them their specific taste and appearance. All sautes are done in the same way. Today, there are some of the most elegant, tasty and appealing dishes prepared in the "luxury dinner houses". In sauteing, the texture and flavour of fresh fried food is preserved and mixed with the quality of pre-made sauces and garnishes.

Skillet

The term 'sauteing' does not really mean the same as flip frying. Flip frying is the part of sauteing where small-cut ingredients are flipped into the air, then are caught in the pan again. By this process they hopefully mix and turn from one side to the other. For all larger meat and seafood cuts, the regular chef's fork, the pallet knife or a spatula is used to turn the cooked foods. A good working cook never attempts to flip a pan with half a dozen chicken breasts or several orders of fish fillet. Therefore, sauteing must be accepted to mean cooking in only a little fat which then becomes an ingredient of the finished dish.

A cook sautes onions and green peppers in a fry pan

Prawns a la Creole is a flip-fried dish. For practical reasons, it is the same dish as Supreme of halibut Creole. The man difference is that the boneless halibut fillet order can be sauteed, griddle-fried, or "baked". When transferred to the dinner plate, pre-made creole sauce finished with wine and butter could be sauced (spooned) over the fish.

Many more preparations exist. An Entrecote (French name for a New York cut raw Sarloin Steak), could be broiled and served with pre-made Bordelaise in a sauce boat. This would be done to keep the eye-appealing grill marks visible. Or the same steak could be griddle-fried, placed on the dinner plate, and sauced with the Bordelaise Sauce.

In this *true* saute preparation, the sauce will reflect the brandy flavour, the meat drippings, and the aroma of the finely chopped shallots sauteed in browned butter. It is important to note the fact that the ingredients are raw until used and that they could be stored or put in a different preparation. Here where the advantage of sauteing lies. At the same time, this process needs the know-how of a skilled and responsible cook.

The understanding and mastery of basic cooking processes allows the cook to analyze the ingredients of an unknown dish and recreate it without difficulty. By applying the sauteing process, the cook can, as a bartender mixes new drinks, create many new and unusual dishes based on his own ideas of taste and artistry.

Sauteing is the fast browning of tender foods in good fat, with the fat becoming a part of the cooked dish. It is a type of quality cookery and has become very popular. The fast saute method is very good for the tender meats now available as a result of special breeding and feeding. In vegetable cookery, to keep both taste and nutrition, sauteing is best.

Culinary art standards consider these fats tastier and healthier than other: olive oil, refined salad oils, butter, clarified butter, fresh pork fat, and in some cases, chicken or goose fat. The fat is chosen to compliment the food cooked in it. Food which have been eaten by humankind for thousands of years with no ill effects, are probably safer than many of the new, advertised foods which have not been checked or observed for many years.

A saute pan is similar in appearance to a fry pan or skillet, except that instead of the flared, sloping sides, it has straight sides, about 2 to 3 inches high. This design maximizes the cooking surface, helps to contain the food in the pan as it's cooking (especially if you're making tossing motions while sauteeing foods), and it also is the ideal shape for cooking food in which you're going to be adding liquid to make a sauce. Be sure to buy a pan that comes with a tight-fitting lide so you can use it to cook grains or rice. Also known as: Sautoir or Sauteuse (often has slightly sloping sides or two short loop handles). (Ref. Experimental Recipe 74).

Saute Pan

The chef's pan combines design elements of a skillet, saucepan and stir-fry pan for a versatile pan. It has a long handle, is deeper than a skillet, and has a rounded shape and flared sides so that liquid can evaporate easily or suace can be stirred with a whisk. This pan is similar in shape and function to a saucier.

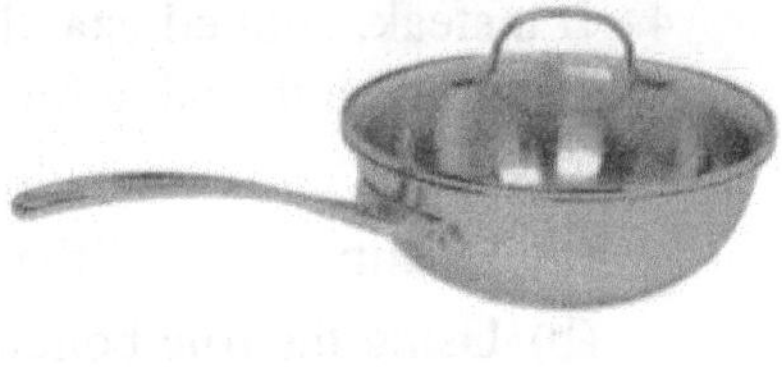

Chef's Pan

Use it for: Braised dishes, risotto, cooking grains and rice, stir-fry, reductions.

Experimental Recipe 74.

Saute Cabbage

Ingredients

1. Cabbage	:	250 grams
2. Oil	:	1 tablespoon
3. Garlic	:	10 cloves
4. Pepper	:	As per taste
5. Salt	:	As per taste.

Method

1. Prepare all required ingredients.
2. Finely shred the cabbage.
3. Heat oil in a deep-bottomed pan, saute the garlic for 4-5 minutes and add the cabbage.
4. Saute on a medium flame for 4-5 minutes. Add salt and pepper as per taste.
5. Cover and cook for 5-7 minutes.

DEGLAZING

Deglazing means to use up the caramelized leftover juices that remain in a skillet after meat has been sauteed in it. It is done by adding a small amount of liquid to cook these juices loose. This can be done only if juices exist. When sauteing potatoes or buttered almonds there can be no deglazing. For fish a la "Meuniere", extra butter is browned in the skillet with the fish and then poured over it for serving. Again, deglazing can not be done. For freshly made meats served in a small amount of sauce, deglazing does take place. Beef a la Stroganoff is the typed example of both sauteing and deglazing. "A Saute is not a Stew". Most deglazing is done with some wine or brandy first (called flaming), and then a suitable sauce is used as a follow-up. The making of sauces in discussed in Chapter 3.11. Sauces are made before the sauteing is done.

Guidelines for Preparing Entrecote Bordelaise

1. Under correct conditions, as detailed below, the cooking time of a medium rare steak of this size is about 6 minutes.
2. Medium rare is the best way to serve and steak for the best flavour, texture, and appearance.
3. These 6 minutes of total heat exposure include the flambe time.
4. If a steak, cooked exactly to medium rare, is covered with the hot sauce and left standing on the table for a additional 5 minutes, it probably will become well done
5. The term "correct conditions" applied to the following:
   (a) Quality grade of the meat itself (prime or choice)
   (b) Using the true boneless sirloin (New York cut)
   (c) The pounding of the steak to a 3/4-inch thickness. This loosens the fibres, that is, tenderizes it and, thus, reduces cooking time.

   (Ref. Experimental Recipe 75)

SAUTEED FOODS WITHOUT DEGLAZING

Sauteing food without deglazing generally mean that the food served without any sauce, or with only the liquid which has been formed as the by-product of the process. An example of this is in the cooking of sliced or whole raw mushrooms. These are washed in slightly acid water, lifted out, and sauteed immediately. Because of the washing, there is more mushroom juice, which you may keep to prevent the mush rooms from drying out during storage. Raw carrots, asparagus, green peas, cabbage and many more vegetables may be sauteed in a covered skillet, in the same way as the mushrooms. In many areas, it is the custom to pre-boil vegetables, store them under refrigeration and saute them, as needed, in butter.

Pasta is the name used for all types and shapes of noodles, is produced in a dehydrated state. Pasta must be boiled in water first. In quality cookery, all pasta and most boiled vegetables are sauteed before serving. On a menu if you find Egg Noodles Sauteed in butter it simply means that butter was used for the sauteing instead of another fat.

If you are sauteing meat without deglaxing in such a preparation food values and taste are wasted. It is of interest to note that many connoissiers prepare sauteed and deglazed steaks instead of broiled steaks.

Experimental Recipe 75.

Entrecote Bordelaise

Ingredients

1. Sirloin steak	:	2 (16 doz each)
2. Chopped shallots (substitude with finely chopped onions and garlic if shallots are not avaliable)	:	3 tablespoon
3. Olive or other good cooking oil	:	1 ounce
4. Butter	:	2 ounce
5. Brandy	:	1 ounce
6. Basic brown sauce (Espagnol)	:	1/3 cup
7. Red Bordeax wine	:	1/3 cup
8. Clean watercress	:	1/6 bunch.

Method

1. Prepare all required ingredients.
2. Clean and wash the meat.
3. Trim excess fat off meat, and pound to the thickness of 3/4 inch. Score if necessary, Salt
4. Leave brandy in original bottle, but have other ingredients measured.
5. Prepare brown sauce.
6. Pour oil into heated skillet.
7. Put steaks in the pan.
8. Saute on high heat (sizzling noise) for 40 to 60 *seconds*.
9. Reduce heat to approximately 375°F. and cook 1 minute more.
10. Turn meat over and continue to cook for 60 more seconds.
11. Add butter in small flocks around steak.
12. Add shallots to steak in the same way.
13. Swish around in pan, or stir, but not longer than another 60 seconds.
14. Pour brandy into the hot pan.
15. Let alcohol burn away. (For safety reasons, always have the cover of the pan at hand. In case fire gets out of control, smother it by covering the pan.)
16. Turn heat down to prevent burning of pan.
17. Remove steaks, to warm dinner plates.
18. Pour red wine into pan, bring to a boil.
19. Use spatula to stir simmering residue and loosen it from pan.
20. Add the brown sauce and whisk until smooth.
21. Ladle sauce over the steaks, not necessarily all of it. (Too much sauce on a plate makes a dish look cheap.)
22. Decorate plate and steak with watercress instead of parsley.

Stuffed orange pepper

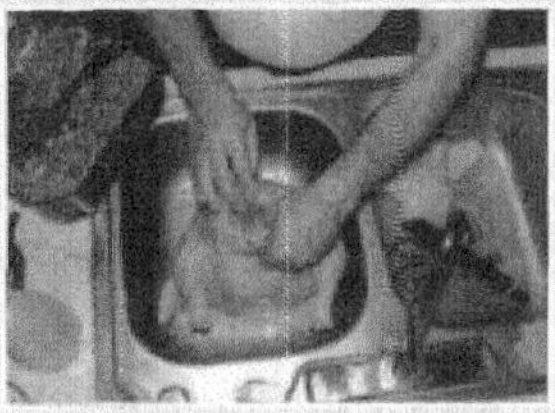

Stuffing a turkey

Fish a la "Meuniere" is one of the most common fish preparations, with slight regional variations. A portion-sized fillet of any fish is salted, dipped in cream, then in flour (a simple way of coating) and sauteed in a small quantity of clear butter. When the fish is about 80% done, add a small piece of fresh butter brown and pour over the fish before serving. Chopped parsley and a few drops of fresh lemon juice are added as a final touch.

SAUTEED DEGLAZED FOODS

Raw, sauteed vegetables can also be deglazed. This process is done by adding a small amount of veloute or bechamel sauce and some cream. These are then called creamed vegetables, for example, creamed spinach, creamed carrots, and creamed peas. Green

Experimental Recipe 76.

Hangarian Pork Chops

Portion Size: 6 single

Ingredients

1. Center cut pork chops with full rib bone, chine bone removed	:	6 single Portion - sized,
2. "Lesco" sauce	:	1½ cups
3. Hungarian paprika	:	1 tablespoon
4. Sour cream with 1 tablespoon of flour stirred in 1 ounce oil	:	1½ cups
5. Fresh butter	:	2 ounces
6. Finely chopped garlic	:	½ teaspoon.

Method

1. Prepare all required ingredients.
2. Pounds the pork chops to a thickness of one-half inch.
3. Salt them well; dip one side into flour.
4. Heat skillet very hot; pour in the oil.
5. Put all the chops in with the floured side down.
6. Saute over medium heat until brown, about 2 minutes.
7. Turn chops over, (once only); continue sauteing for 2-3 minutes.
8. Reduce heat, left pan, and drain off surplus fat.
9. Add butter to pork chops in the pan and brown the butter.
10. Add the garlic, saute until garlic is golden brown.
11. Remove the chops, their first side (floured) up, to service plate.
12. Add paprika to the drippings.
13. Deglaze with the Lesco sauce.
14. Bring to a boil and add all the sour cream.
15. Bring to a full boil again, then simmer quickly into a smooth and velvety sauce.
16. Spoon over the pork chops and serve.

peas can be sauted with bacon, onions, and chopped romaine lettuce and then deglazed with some light veloute sauce. They are called "Petit Pois a la Franachise" or "Peas a la parisienne" Deglazed saute dishes which look like stews, but are not stews. By the same principle as in the examples given, chicken, lamb, or pork could be sauteed and deglazed with a sauce. For instance, Chicken, Lamb, or Pork Curry can be made by using a curry sauce. There exists an endless variety of meat sautees in the form of chops, Noisettes, Scallopini, grenadins, and Entrecotes.

PORK CHOPS

Sauted pork chops are all made in the same manner, with a difference final garnish. This step-by-step description of pork chops Hungarian style can be applied to any sauteed pork-chop preparations. (Ref. Experimental Recipe 76).

1. Pork chops must be cut with the full rib bone still in, then trimmed and pounded, to loosen the fibres for faster cooking.
2. Meat must be salted well, while still raw.
3. Sauteed (or roasted or broiled) meat should not be cooked super well done and thus dried out.

Experimental Recipe 77.

Scallopini with Marsal

Ingredient

1. Veal Scallopini, pounded, salted, and flour dipped	:	18
2. Brown sauce	:	½ cup
3. Olive oil	:	2 ounces
4. Marsala wine	:	3/4 cup
5. Fresh butter	:	4 ounces.

Method

1. Prepare all required ingredients.
2. Heat skillet very how, then pour in the oil.
3. Put meat into the pan quickly while shaking pan with other hand to prevent burning of the scallopini through uneven heat.
4. After sauteing them for one minute, turn them over and saute one minute more.
5. Add the butter and brown quickly on high heat.
6. Turn heat down; remove scallopini to a dinner plate.
7. Deglaze the skillet with Marsala; cook drippings loose.
8. Add the brown sauce and reduced to a desired smooth texture; turn off heat.
9. Return the sauteed scallopini to the skillet, including the freshly accumulated drippings; mix well together.
10. Portion scallopini on platters, overlapping like shingles, and spoon just enough sauce over them to cover.
11. Garnish with whole parsley and serve.

VEAL SCALLOPINI

Raw scallopini are pieces of dairy veal leg, with no sinews, gristle or fat, pounded to a ¼-inch thickness. The weight per scallopini is about 2 ounced 3-4 pieces to the order. Veal scallopini in different sauces are a favourite with all Italian restaurants . Scanning are very simple to prepare. They can be true gourmet dishes. If all ingredients are of prime quality and are cooked right. like other food preparations, garnishes or styles are interchangeable. Only the basic preparation is always the same. In some areas, scallopini are also called "Piccata" (Ref. Experimental Recipe 77).

Key points to remember

1. Avoid a plate over-filled with sauce.
2. Total sauteing time should be not more than 3 minutes.
3. Never reboil a sauteed meat in the sauce.
4. Serve immediately.

Disjointed Chicken Sautee

Chicken, a very neutral tasting m eat, blends well with many sauces, flavours, and garnishes. Thus, many different combinations of chicken sautees can be made. Garnishes may be specially cut or shaped pre-cooked vegetables, herbs spices, meats, seafood, or whatever might be edible and decorative.

Chickens may be sauteed in different sizes. Semi-boneless chicken quarters are used most often. The leg quarter has the pitch and hip bone removed. The drumstick stays in, so as to preserve the chicken shape. (Ref. Experimental Recipe 78).

The breast, with the wing bone still attached, is peeled off carcass. This boning results in semi-boned and disjointed chicken quarters which still look like chicken when cooked. The boning of chickens must be learned by watching a demonstration and having additional practice.

Chicken Saute Preparation and Corresponding Garnish:

For each order approximately 3 ounces of finished sauce is needed.

1. ***Chicken Saute See***

   1 part red wine 2 parts brown sauce.

   No garnish.

2. ***Chicken Saute Aux Marsala (Or Sherry or Port)***

   Deglaze, as for "Sec" but change red wine to Marsala (Sherry or Port).

3. ***Chicken Saute With Mushrooms.***

   Deglaze as for "Sec".

   Garnish: Garnish: sauteed sliced mushrooms.

4. ***Chicken Princess***

   1/8 white wine, 1/8 asparagus water, 1/4 veloute, 1/2 cream.

   Garnish: asparagus tips, green peas.

Experimental Recipe 78.

Sauteing of Disjointed Chickens

Portions: 10

Equipment

2 skillets, each large enough to hold all legs or all breasts.

Ingredients

1.	Chickens disjointed in 10 legs and 10 breast quarters	: 5 small (2 lbs. each)
2.	Fresh butter	: ¼ lb.
3.	Flour	: 1 cup
4.	Garnish and basic sauces as indicated in each recipesalad or other oil	: 1/4 cup
5.	Salt	: To taste.

Method

1. Prepare all required ingredients.
2. Preheat oven to 375°F.
3. Salt chickens; dip skin side into flour.
4. Take first pan, put in 2 ounces of oil, then heat to smoking point.
5. Put all chicken legs, floured side down, into pan, shake pan, and reduced heat while doing this.
6. Increase heat, to saute the floured side, until it is golden brown, *Keep pan moving.*
7. Turn each leg over.
8. Put pan with chickens into a pre-heated 375°F. oven.
9. Use second pan and repeat steps above with the breasts. *Work fast.*
10. After 15 minutes for legs and 10 minutes for breasts, the chickens are ready to be deglazed.
11. Chickens may be kept warm for 1-2 hours and finished when needed.

For deglaxing or Finishing

12. Drain surplus fat from the pan. Chickens stay in the pan.
13. Return pan and chickens to a low fire. Add two ounces of fresh butter.
14. Melt and slightly brown butter.
15. Add clear liquid (wines, brandy, clear stock or cream) from recipe. Increase heat.
16. While doing this, turn each chicken piece once to assure that colour and flavour from liquid are distributed evenly.
17. Reduce heat, remove chicken pieces to serving platter, and keep warm
18. Add the remaining sauces. Use whip to stir into smooth liquid.
19. Simmer, (or boil) for 1 or 2 minutes, depending on existing and desired sauce texture.
20. If sauce is not smooth, but is full of burned residues, strain.
21. When sauce is smooth, add garnish, wait until thoroughly hot.
22. Spoon just enough sauce over chicken for a n elegant presentation.
23. Pour remaining sauce into sauce boat and serve on the side.
24. The finished chicken dish should be decorated with a little whole parsley or watercress, unless a different garnish is indicated.

5. ***Chicken Creole***

   ¼ red wine, ¼ tomato sauce, ½ Spanish sauce.

   No garnish.

6. ***Chicken Meringue***

   1/3 white wine, 1/3 tomato sauce, 1/3 brown mushroom sauce.

   Garnish: crayfish tails or a 1/2-ounce bay shrimp.

7. ***Hungarian Chicken***

   ½ sour cream, ½ paprika sauce.

   Garnish: sauteed bell pepper, onions, and tomato cubes.

8. ***Chicken Jerusalem***

   1/3 white wine, 1/3 veloute, 1/3 heavy cream. Garnish: sliced Jerusalem artichokes (topinambour), chives.

9. ***Chicken raphael Well***

   1/3 white wine, 1/3 veloute, 1/3 heavy cream.

   Garnish: sliced globe artichoke bottoms, sliced mushrooms.

10. ***Chicken Chasseur***

    ½ red wine, ½ brown sauce.

    Garnish: tomato cubes, sliced mushrooms, green onions.

11. ***Chicken Saute Italian***

    ½ red wine, ½ brown sauce.

    Garnish: fried garlic, shallots, scallions, mushrooms, and tomato concuss.

12. ***Coq Au Vin***

    2/3 burgudny wine 1/3 brown sauce, a dash of sherry.

    Garnish: mushroom quarters, pearl onions, bacon lardons.

13. ***Chicken Bombay***

    1/2 curry sauce, 1/2 cream.

    Garnish: diced green apples, papaya, tomato concasse on top of curry sauce, chopped parsley.

Shellfish Sautes

Shellfish sautes can be made of raw of precooked seafood.

Cleaned and frozen prawns, lobsters, and scallops should be sauteed from the raw stage.

If cut properly, their cooking time is only minutes.

Crab legs for sauteing are used, pre-cooked only. Again, the same principles are used as in meat sautees.

Lobster Newburg

Cup-up lobster meat is sauteed in butter.

It is deglazed with 1/2 ounce dry sherry, 1 ounce bechamel sauce, and 2 ounces heavy fresh cream.

Cayenne pepper and salt to taste are added.

Crab legs, "Bordelaise"

Cooked, shelled crab legs are sauteed in butter with some fine chopped shallots.

It is deglazed with ½ ounce brandy and 2 ounces brown-red wine sauce.

Sprinkled with chopped parsley when served.

Scamps Maximilin

Raw, peeled, defined, butterflyed prawns (scampi are prawns from the Adriatic sea) are sauteed in clear butter.

Then they are deglazed with I ounce dry white wine, 1 ounce heavy veloute sauce, 2 ounces of sour cream and ¼ teaspoon of chopped dill weed.

Prawns Creole

Raw, peeled, defined, butterflyed prawns are sauteed in butter.

They are deglazed with 1 ounce dry white wine and 3 ounces of Spanish sauce (creole sauce).

GRIDDLE

A griddle, a large stationary skillet, is used only for short order cooking. The griddle has more disadvantages than advantages, however. The griddle is excellent for the cooking of large quantities of hotcakes. Perhaps this was its original purpose. But when it is used as the instrument for all breakfast cookery, it is both wasteful and less than mediocre in its product. Meats are better cooked on a broiler. Pork links and bacon should be cooked in the skillet. The griddle easily dirties up during rush hours. It also needs constant cleaning. Unlike the skillet, it cannot be brought to the sink and washed, not can it be exchanged for another one.

QUESTIONS AND DISCUSSIONS

Fill in the Blanks

Q.1. Read and complete the following statements :

(a) The immediate deglazing is done with some..................

(b) The Entrecote Bordelaise is a steak which translates as ....

(c) A griddle must be visualized as a large ....

(d) Shellfish sautes can be made from seafood that is either cooked or ....

(e) Saute cooking has the characteristics of luxury ....

(f) Sauteing meat is a waste of taste if it is done without ....

(g) Sauteed potatoes are an example of sauteing without ....

(h) Sauteed fish "Meunier" is dipped first in ....

[**Ans.:**

(a) caramalized left over juices that remain inthe skillet after meat has been sauteed in it; (b) Newyork cut raw sarloin steak; (c) stationary skillet; (d) raw; (e) cuisine; (f) deglazing; (g) glazing; (h) cream]

Multiple Type

Q.2. Read each question carefully and select the *best* answer:

(i) The sauce which makes up the saute preparation Bordelaise is composed of :

(a) While wine and creole sauce
(b) White wine, dill, cream and brown sauce
(c) Red wine, shallots, brandy and brown sauce
(d) Red wine, sherry, cayenne pepper and cream.

(ii) A griddle should be considered a large stationary skillet most efficient for the

(a) Frying of fish (b) Broiling of steaks
(c) Cooking of luxury cuisine (d) Cooking of breakfast hotcakes.

(iii) Entrecote Bordelaise and Crab Legs Bordelaise have the following in common

(a) Both are served in dinner houses
(b) Both are saute dishes
(c) Both are served with the same sauce
(d) Both are served under cooked.

(iv) "Newburg" is a most popular preparation for

(a) Fried fish fillets (b) Sauteed oysters
(c) Veal scalloping (d) Shelled lobster meat.

(v) Sauteing is ideal for vegetable cookery because

(a) It retains more vitamin C
(b) It retains taste and nutritional value
(c) It saves the cutting up of vegetables
(d) It is liked better by customers.

(vi) The saute cooking of luxury cuisine does not consider one of the followings a suitable fat:

(a) Pork fat (b) Shortening
(c) Olive oil (d) Butterfat.

(vii) Saute chickens which are disjointed and semiboned weigh an average each of

(a) ¾ to ¼ lb (b) 1¼ to 1¾ lb
(c) 1¾ to 2¼ lb (d) 2¼ to 2¾ lb.

(viii) Sauteing without deglazing is customary for the following dishes with the exception of

(a) Beef Stronganoff (b) Buttered Egg Noodles
(c) Buttered Almonds (d) Home Fried Potatoes.

(ix) The difference in cooking time for disjointed chicken legs and breasts is

(a) Zero minutes (b) Two and a half minutes
(c) Five minutes (d) Seven and a half minutes.

(x) Sauteing gains wider acceptance slowly but constantly for all these reasons, except

(a) Meat quality is getting better

(b) Costs less to produce it

(c) Retains greater nutritional values

(d) Does away with leftover food.

[**Ans.:** (i) (c); (ii) (d); (iii) (b); (iv) (d); (v) (b); (vi) (b); (vii) (d); (viii) (a); (ix) (c); (x) (c)]

Short Answer Type

Q.3. Differentiate between griddle use and saute cookery.

Q.4. How are a saute cook and sauce cook related ?

Q.5. In cooking, what is the relation of skillet size, heat source, and food quantity.

Q.6. What are suitable skillets for sauteing ?

Q.7. Explain "Chicken Saute" dishes in three/four sentences.

[**Ans.:**

1. **Bercy:** Sautee, swirl with white wine, meat glaze, lemon juice,chopped shallots. Add shredded mushrooms and chipolatas. Pour on the chicken pieces.
2. **Blanc:** Sautee in butter, when nearly done, add chopped onions and cook kidney. Moisten with white wine, reduce. Add cream, simmer for 10 minutes. Dress with slices of truffles and cray fish.
3. **Bonne Fomme:** Sautee, swire with white wine and thickened gravy. Garnish with dices of bacon, small onions, and cocotte potatoes.
4. **Chandon:** Sautee, swirl with champagne. Cream and half glaze, add butter, garnish with cocks comb and kidney and surround with muffled chicken croquettes.
5. **Chaussuer:** Sautee, swirl with white wine, brandy, tomatoes, add sliced mushroom tossed in butter with chopped shallots. Sprinkle with chopped parsley.
6. **Egyptienne:** Sautee in oil, with onion, dices of ham and sliced mushrooms, set with chicken pieces in a cocotte, altering with garnish. Cover with slices of tomatoes when about to serve, add veal stock.
7. **Parmentier:** Sautee, swirl with white wine and thickened gravy. Garnish with parmentier potatoes, sprinkle with chopped parsley.
8. **Paysanne:** Sautee, swirl with white wine. Add paysanne of vegetables and coat with sauce.
9. **Portugaise:** Sautee with butter and oil. When nearly done add chopped onions, white wine, dices of tomatoes, sliced mushrooms, a little garlic, finish cooking, dress surrounded with stuffed tomatoes.
10. **Marengo:** Sautee the seasoned pieces of chicken, deglaze and reduce. Add chopped tomatoes concasse, tomato puree, crushed garlic, button mushrooms and Jus Lie. Serve surrounded with heart shaped crutons, cray fish and French fried eggs.]

Descriptive Answer Type

Q.8. List the names of four different chicken saute preparations.

Q.9. Describe the cooking of sauteed, deglazed foods.

Q.10. List the suitable saute fats.

Q.11. Explain the principle of sauteing.

Assignments/Activity Type

Q.12. Demonstrate the process of chicken disjointing and boning.

Q.13. Define the following :

(a) Griddle,
(b) Deglazing
(c) Newburg
(d) Scampi
(e) Prawn
(f) Pasta.
(g) G. R.A.S.

Q.14. Saute a "Fillet of Sole a la Meuniere"

Q.15. Make a chicken saute with mushrooms.

Q.16. Saute pre-boiled vegetables.

Q.17. Practice chicken disjointing and boning.

4.5

Boiling Meat and Fish

CHAPTER OBJECTIVES

After studying this lesson you should be able :

- To list the reasons for and use of the boiling of protecting food;
- To explain the principles and proceduers of boiling;
- To practice the boilings a corned brisket of beef;
- To practice the boiling turkey breast for sadwich use; and
- To practice and prepare sole a la Bonne Femme.

The cooking of protein foods in clear liquids is known as boiling, simmering, or poaching. Essentially these are the same since only the stage of simmering should be used to reach best results. Poaching is a term applied mostly to fish dishes or to poached eggs. For fish dishes, poaching means simmering in as little liquid as possible, but for the poaching of eggs simmering in a rather large quantity of liquid is essential.

Meat and fish, as a protein food, react to boiling in the same way as to other cooking methods. Moisture prevents caramelization. Over-boiling, unlike overfrying or roasting, will not burn food. Over-boiling does make protein food dry and tasteless and could turn food into pulp.

All plain boiling or poaching uses the same principle. Food is put into boiling liquid; the heat is then reduced to simmering until the food is done. Liquids must have a flavour or their own to prevent needless taste loss of the protein food cooked. Salt is a most important addition to any boiling liquid for fresh protein food. Only those foods which may have been preserved by the curing or salting process may be cooked in plain water. Boiled meat dinners are simple in their presentation. When the boiling liquid is changed into sauces, a large variety of especially poached fish dishes come into existence. Boiling as a meat preparation is applied to large or whole pieces only; but for fish, because of its tenderness and difficult handling, portion cuts are more popular. The logical continuation of boiling is the changing of the broth into sauces.

Boiling.pan

This two-part pan consists of a saucepan that holds around 2 inches of simmering water over the stove burner and a smaller pan that nests over it, in which you can gently heat foods like chocolate or egg-based custard over a steady, moderate heat. Many double boilers come with a lid that will fit both the insert and the bottom pan, which enables the bottom pan to be used on its own. A makeshift double boiler can also be made by nesting an appropriately sized metal bowl into a saucepan, as long as there is enough space for water to simmer below without touching the bottom of the bowl.

Use it for melting chocolate and butter, cooking custard and cream- and egg-based sauces without curdling, cooking polenta, reheating or keeping foods warm.

For food cooked by boiling, the leaching out of nutrients and taste must be prevented. Observe following guidelines to make your task easy:

1. Use only enough liquid (water) to cover the food.
2. Bring cooking liquid to a strong rolling boil first; then slip food into liquid and bring quickly to the boiling point again.
3. Simmer until done.
4. Saturate the liquid with flavour-giving herbs, spices, and salt so as to prevent unnecessary leaching through osmosis.
5. Simmer food until nearly tender, if it is to be served hot.
6. For food to be used cold, carry-over heat (additional tenderization during the cool-off) must be considered.
7. Cooling of boiled protein foods in their own cooking liquid improves their taste.
8. Cooling of fresh cooked foods in cold water results in loss of taste and nutritional values.
9. Simmering of protein food in flavour-saturated stock gives it a better taste than food cooked in water only.

CHARACTERISTICS AND SHRINKAGE

While roasting regulates the heat and time to achieve the desired result; but in boiling the heat degrees are set. Food kept below the simmering point will not tenderize. Food cannot be heated above the rolling boil. Pressure cooking of meat or fish is not advisable since there is no control by inspection, and also broth is not created. Steam cannot be flavour-saturated in the way a liquid can. Pressure steamed meats have less flavour and may be overcooked. Many people believe that steam leaches less than liquid, but this is true in unsaturated water only. It must also be considered that the outside of food exposed to 250°F. moist heat overcooks much more than when it is only heated to 190°F. Over boiling in liquid results in just the same shrinkage and dryness as overcooking by a dry method. When the liquid content of the meat cells is brought to the boiling point, these cells burst open and the natural juices flow into the boiling liquid. Therefore, overcooked protein food, cooked by any method, will be dry and tasteless.

Meat Preparations

All boiled meats are cooked and processed by the same principles. Herbs and spices include salt, peppercorns, cloves, bay leaves, thyme, basil, and parsley. The flavour-giving vegetables are the same as those used in sauce cookery. These are celery, carrots, onions, leeks, parsinps, and sometimes cabbage. The cooking time depends on the kind of meat, its quality, and the size of the piece to be cooked. Boiled meats, when served hot, are often cotton plain, or with mustard and grated horseradish. They may be served in broth or on a plate, covered with sauces of contrasting taste. Boiled meat should be carved to the order, across the grain like a roast. It is kept hot in its own broth.

Chicken

You may boil any size chicken and serve in a pot with vermicelli and vegetables if this is the dish one wants to prepare. Coloured hens or fowl must be boiled as the only practical way to be used. After boiling, the hot chickens are skinned. When cool, they are boned. The meat is used for chicken a la king, creamed chicken, chicken pot pie, chicken salad, sandwiches, and other dishes.

Turkey

Boiled turkey is often used instead of chicken. Turkeys are large, need less handling, and give a better yield. This is especially true when the breast is sliced up for sandwiches. Just as for roast turkey, it is better to separate white and dark meat before cooking. This is for easier handling and better results. Twenty-eight- to thirty-pound turkeys, with legs separated from the breasts but in the same stock pot, simmer approximately 2 1/2-3 hours. When these are cooked, they should be turned so that the breast is down, and covered with aluminum foil while still hot and moist. This prevents needless drying out of the breasts.

Fish

You must boil whole fish of a larger size only if it is to be used for a cold buffet. A fish cooker, for easier handling, must be available. The fish prepared in this way are usually salmon, smaller sturgeons, and large trout. The same principles apply as for the cooking of meat proteins, except, of course, that they have a shorter cooking time. Court Bouillon (stock made from fish bones and soup vegetables) should be used as the boiling liquid. A plain onion and pepper stock, which gives a very sharp taste, can be used for some preparations. Something slightly acid is very often added to fish stock to make it less bland. It should be remembered that vinegars and wines will firm up the flesh of the fish, but lemon juice will tenderize it even more. If a whole salmon is to be cooked for a cold buffet, it is a trick of the trade to add unfavorable gelatine to the liquid after the fish is taken off the fire. The gelatine dissolves in the court bouillon, where the fish has to cool completely. When chilled, it will help to hold the fish in a better shape. (Ref. Experimental Recipe 79)

Experimental Recipe 79.

Fish Bread Roll

Ingredients

1.	Fish	:	500gm
2.	Onion	:	2 medium slice
3.	Ginger garlic paste	:	2 tsp
4.	Turmeric powder	:	1/2 tsp
5.	Red chilli powder	:	1/2 tsp
6.	Garam masala powder	:	1/2 tsp
7.	Grated coriander leaves		
8.	Grated Green chilli		
9.	Salt	:	To taste
10.	Sugar	:	1/4 tsp
11.	Oil	:	To fly
12.	Slice Bread	:	one.

Method

1. Prepare all required ingredients.
2. Clean the fish very well.
3. Boil the fish & make it boneless for making *keema.*
4. Put oil in a pan, add slice onion & saute till colour change.
5. Add boiled fish, ginger-garlic paste, salt, turmeric powder, red chilli powder, *garam masala*, grated green chilli (as per your taste), coriander leaves, sugar— fry it in a low flame till tender. Keep it cool. Now fish *keema* is ready for stuffing.
6. Take a slice bread & soak it in normal water & takeout quickly for giving easy shape.
7. Stuff fish keemma into bread, press the bread in your two hands & give a shape (oval, round)
8. Now heat oil in a *kadahi* and fry the bread-roll till golden brown.
9. Serve hot with chutney and salad.

Poaching

The techniques of poaching is used for portion cut fish pieces. It is very much like boiling, except that less liquid is used. Halt the fish piece is in the poaching liquid, and the upper half cooks in the steam. (Ref. Experimental Recipe 80)

Poaching is done to have a stronger fish stock, which is used to make the sauce which gives the preparation its name. Poached Fillet of sole Bonne Femme, for instance, means that folded fillets of sole are covered with sliced raw mushrooms; then poached in half court bouillon and half white wine and finished with a very light cream sauce.

Expermental Recipe 80.

Poached Egg Curry

Ingredients

1. Eggs	:	2 Nos.
2. Onion cut into very small pieces	:	4 tsp
3. Chilli powder	:	2 tsp
4. Turmeric powder	:	1/4 tsp
5. Coriander powder	:	1/4 tsp
6. Oil	:	1 tsp
7. Water	:	2 glasses
8. Salt	:	To taste
9. Fresh coriander leaves	:	10 gm.

Method

1. Prepare all required ingredients.
2. Heat a pan, and pour oil.
3. Shallows fry the finely chopped onions until brownish in colour. Add chilli powder, turmeric powder and curry and coriander powder. Stir it for another half a minute. Now pour 2 glasses of water to this and boil it. Add salt to it.
4. Once the water is boiled properly, break eggs and put carefully into the water. Let it get cooked for 5-6 minutes. Now carefully turn the eggs to the other side and let it get cooked properly. After 2-3 minutes cut the eggs into two and simmer it for another 1-2 minutes.
5. Poached egg curry is ready.
6. Serve it with rice.

Many fancy named poached fish dishes can be made the same way except the change of the flavour-giving ingredients. If the name and preparations stay the same, the kind of fish is changed. Poaching liquids are made of different wines, stock, water, milk, or beer. Roux, egg yield, or starches change any liquid into sauce. The addition of spices, garnishes, special vegetables, cream, cheeses, and others accounts for the many hundred of varieties which are common.

Following is a list of poached fish preparations made like "Sole Bonne Femme" except with a change of the mushroom garnish to somethings else. The new and different ingredient accounts for the different name; such as

(a) Sole Argenteuil	:	Asparagus tips replace the mushrooms.
(b) Sole duglere	:	Chopped tomatoes and onions replace the mushrooms.
(c) Sole Nantua	:	Crayfish tails replace the mushrooms.
(d) Sole Merguery	:	Olympia Oysters and bay shrimps replace the mushrooms.
(e) Sole Walewska	:	Poached, then covered with a lobster slice and piece of truffle, then glazed with a Mornay (cheese-fish sauce) under the broiler.

FILLET OF SOLE BONNE FEMME

Sole Bonne Femme must be though of as the basic preparation for poached fish dishes. As in most cooking, variations are made by changing some or all of the ingredients and the type of fish used. The principles and techniques remain the same. Poached fish can be made to the order just the same as steak. Fillet always implies skinned and boned fish. A la bonne femme means cooked after the fashion of the homemaker. (Ref. Experimental Recipe 81)

Experimental Recipe 81.

Fillet of Sole Bonne Femme

Equipment

1. A fireproof platter or portion casserole
2. One 8-inch aluminum skillet with cover
3. A whisk,
4. Rubber spatula,
5. Pastry bag, and
6. Star tube.

Ingredients

1. Some Duchess potatoes (optional)
2. Heavy cream
3. Hollandaise sauce, veloute sauce
4. Fresh Fillet of Sole
5. Mushrooms
6. Butter
11. White wine (dry sauterne)
12. Salt.

Method

1. Prepare all required ingredients.
2. Wash and clean the sole fillet.
3. Select 8-10 ounces of sole fillet in 2 or 4 pieces.
4. Score, trim and salt them; portion into 2 uniform packages (paupiettes).
5. Place paupiettes in a buttered skillet, cover fish with about 2 ounces of sliced fresh mushrooms, well washed.
6. Add one bay leaf and a little lemon juice.
7. Pour 3-4 ounces of dry sauterne over fish and cover.
8. Put on low heat; poach for 4-5 minutes.
9. While fish poaches, pipe Duchess potatoes
   (a) onto a fish platter as a border, or.
   (b) into fireproof casserole as a divider.
10. Brown the potato border (divider) under the broiler.

(Cont.)

11. When poached fish is done, transfer it and the mushrooms to the freshly prepared plater and keep warm.
12. Remove the bay leaf; add 2 ounces of veloute sauce and 2 ounces of heavy cream to the fish stock.
13. Simmer well together, reduce a little; taste, and salt if necessary.
14. Take sauce off the heat, cool for a few seconds, then fold in 2-3 tablespoons of Hollandaise sauce.
15. Pour sauce over fish and mushrooms, set platter under broiler for about 30 seconds, until the sauce is golden glazed.
16. It a casserole with the duchess divider was used, fish goes into the larger space. The small space can be filled with butter or parsley parisian potatoes.
17. Serve limmediately either as a fish course or a main course.

Note: (a) The Duchess potato border is not essential to a poached fish preparations and may be omitted.

(b) The sole can be replaced by any fine flaked fish, such as Dover, sole halibut, turbot, or whatever local specialty is available.

Crustaceans

All crustaceans, such as lobster, langustes, prawns, scampi, crabs, and cray fish are boiled by the boiling principles. For fish, slat is of the first importance. A bouquet garni, vegetables, and spices are optional to the region. The cooking time for live lobsters crabs or spiny lobsters of a 1 to ½ pound size, is a total of 10-12 minutes of simmering after the liquid had been brought back to the boiling point. Scampi, langustinos, and prawns, depending on their size, may have a 2-3 minute simmering time after they have been brought back to the boiling point.

Blue Trout

Blue trout is a fresh, unfrozen trout, simmered in fish stock with some white vinegar, parsley, onions, bay left, and salt. The freshly cleaned trout is slipped into the court bouillon which is again brought to the boiling point. Then the trout is taken off the range and steeped. Eight to twelve-ounce portions steep 3-4 minutes. Twelve to sixteen-ounce portions steep 5-6 minutes. Trout for this true gourment preparation should weight 6-8 ounces. They are served with clarified butter, lemon wedge, and parsley potatoes only.

Finnan Haddie

Finnan Haddie is cured, smoked haddock available as fillet or with the bones still in. It is usually blanched in boiling water for a minute or so, drained, then poached in half and half on rich milk. It can be served plain, covered with a light cream sauce, or flaked and mixed with a light cream sauce. Finnan Haddie is most popular in the Eastern USA and Canada.

Boiled leg of Lamb

Boiled leg of lamb is an English dish where a whole leg of lamb, or mutton, is boiled instead of roasted. The procedure is the same as for meat, but with a shorter cooking time. The broth is used for a sauce, (capersauce, mustard sauce, etc.) or finished into a Scotch Broth (Consomme Eccossaise).

Pickled Fresh Pork

Pickled fresh pork is made and handled the same way as corned meat. Since it always comes from younger animals, it has a shorter cooking time than corned beef.

Fresh Boiled Meat

Fresh boiled beef is popular in cold areas. Pieces used are chuck meat, short ribs, brisket, and rump cuts from grades which are lower than good. The cuts should not be too large. The best size is an 8-12 pound average. Boiling a whole bottom round, for instance, is impractical because the heel (shank) and the eye need longer cooking than the sirloin tip (culotte) end. Larger pieces are also hard to handle when cooked. They may break or tear apart when taken out of the broth. Cooking time for short fibs could be 1 ½. hours, for a brisket about 2 hours, and for some heavy chuck or round pieces, as long as 1 ½-3 hours, or more. Lots of soup vegetables, parsley, bouquet garni, peppercorns, a few tomatoes, and a little cabbage should be added to the boiling liquid. The meat should be defatted before serving.

Corned Meat

These are the same meat cuts as those used for fresh boiled meat. They might be of a lower grade, because of the tenderizing characteristic of the curing. Curing means pickling in brine. This is a salt solution, in which Chile Saltpetre (potassium nitrate) has been added. A well-known dish is Corned meat and Cabbage, usually served to the Irish on St. Patrick's Day. Most of the corned beef used in restaurants goes into sandwiches or corned beef meat hash.

Patrami

Pastrami is the same as corned meat except that the cured salted meat is also smoked. Pastrami is beef that has been prepared like ham. Its uses are similar to corned beef, but more is used for sandwiches than anything else.

QUESTIONS AND DISCUSSIONS

Fill in the Blanks

Q.1. Read and complete the following statements:

(a) Saturated liquids prevent taste losses by ....

(b) Pressure steam cooking means taking the risk of ....

(c) The amount of liquid used must be balanced to the amount of ....

(d) Cooling off protein foods in their cooking liquids improves their ....

(e) Steam cooking of meats is wasteful since there is no ....

(f) All boiled meats are cooked by the same ....

(g) All boiled protein foods are started with the liquid brought to a rolling ....

(h) For boiled, just as for roasted food, carry-over heat must be ....

(i) When food is boiled, the leaching out of taste must be ....

(j) Cooling off fresh cooked foods in cold water is a waste of ....

[**Ans.:** (a) osmosis (b) over cooking; (c) food;
(d) taste; (e) control by inspection; (f) principle;
(g) boiled first; (h) considered; (i) prevented;
(j) taste and nutritioned value].

Multiple Choice Type

Q.2. Read each question carefully and select the best answer :—

(i) The correct cooking time for live lobsters or crabs of 1 to ½ pound size is

(a) 6-8 minutes (b) 8-10 minutes
(c) 10-12 minutes (d) 12-14 minutes.

(ii) A common cut of fresh beef for boiling is the :

(a) Rib roast (b) Top sirloin
(c) Knuckle (d) Brisket.

(iii) When boiling large or whole pieces of protein food, it is best that :

(a) The boiling is started with cold liquid
(b) The full boil is maintained for the first 20 minutes
(c) The cooking vessel is well covered
(d) The cooking liquid only simmers.

(iv) Boiled fresh meats will taste better if :

(a) Salt is not added to the liquid at all
(b) Salt is added after the meat is tender
(c) Salt is added to liquid before meat is immersed
(d) Salt is sprinkle on the sliced meat after cooking.

(v) Pastrami, a favourite boiled sandwich meat, is actually a :

(a) Smoked, cured beef brisket (b) Corned beef round
(c) Pickled pork shoulder (d) Smoked lamb leg.

(vi) For the boiling of fish, the most important additions to the boiling liquid is :

(a) Celery (b) Salt
(c) Pepper (d) Bay leaves.

(vii) Poached fish preparations use less boiling liquid for :

(a) A stronger fish and sauce flavour
(b) Less shrinkage
(c) Being served dry
(d) S shorter cooking time.

(viii) To get food boiled properly, the cook adjusts the :

(a) Temperature of the boiling liquid
(b) Time of cooking
(c) Time and temperature
(d) Size of the meat pieces to be cooked.

(ix) Coloured hens or fowl are boiled first, then made into the following preparations except :

(a) Chicken a la King (b) Creamed Chicken

(c) Southern (USA) Fried Chicken (d) Chicken Salad.

(x) Poaching preparations intended for fine fleshed fish, like fillet of sole, should not be made with :

(a) Halibut (b) Smelts

(c) Dover sole (d) Turbot

[**Ans.:** (i) (c); (ii) (d); (iii) (a); (iv) (c); (v) (b); (vi) (d); (vii) (a); (viii) (a); (ix) (c); (x) (b)]

Matching Type

Q.3. Match the garnish of the "Sole" preparations in Table 'A' with the corresponding name in Tables 'B'.

Table 'A'	*Table 'B'*
(i) Lobster slices	(a) Argenteuil
(ii) Oysters	(b) Bonne Femme
(iii) Crayfish tails	(c) Duglere
(iv) Asparagus tipe	(d) Marguery
(v) Mushrooms	(e) Nantua
(vi) Tomatoes	(f) Walewska.

[**Ans :** (i) (f); (ii) (d); (iii) (e); (iv) (a); (v) (b); (vi) (c)]

Short Answer Types

Q.4. Define the following:

(a) Duchess (b) Potatoes (c) Pipe

(d) Court bouillon (e) Pastrami.

Q.5. Make a list of meats and meat cuts best suited for boiling.

Q.6. Can poached fish dishes be made to order?

Q.7. Compare boiling to other cooking methods.

Q.8. How will you select a cooking method which is related to need?

Descriptive Type

Q.9. List the reasons for boiling protein food.

Q.10. Briefly explain the principles of boiling.

Assignments/Activity Type

Q.11. Boil a corned brisket of beef.

Q.12. Compose a formula of boiling liquid to cook a leg of lamb. (Approximate pot size, water quantity, salt and amount of vegetables and seasonings to be added.)

Q.13. Select and boil a chicken for chicken salad. Skin and cool it properly.

Q.14. Prepare Sole Bonne Femme according to the step-by-step outline.

Q.15. Compose as many poached fish variations as possible, based on the step-by-step preparation of "Sole Bonne Femme".

4.6

Pot-Roasting

CHAPTER OBJECTIVES

After studying this lesson you should be able :

- To devise a suitable formula for cooking a plain pot roast;
- To understand the procedure and marinate and cook a basic Sauerbraten; and
- To select a cooking method for a game animal.

The pot-roasting of fresh or marinated meats is commonly named stewing or braising. It is a part of the cooking process called "Caramelizing and tenderizing combined". The word roast stands for a large piece of meat, at least more than three portions in one. Roasted in the pot implies that originally a covered pot was used to retain all moisture, which in turn tenderizes tough meats. Later, when baking ovens became more common, roasting in the oven with the addition of liquid, thereby creating steam, replaced the roasting in the pot. It is better to use the oven for pot-roasting because heat is diffused better and there is less danger of scorching, despite continuing browning of the meat. The small quantity of liquid used at one time guarantees the maximum sauce flavour.

Pinot Noir Pot Roast

Although pot roast is regarded as beef roast, the preparation method is used for all tough meats, regardless of the species of the animal. Therefore, pot-roasting or braising as it is sometimes called, is one of the basic cooking methods in use.

In the past marinades were used as meat preservatives, but there are used today for the distinctive flavour they give to food. Most popular is the German Sauerbraten, a preparation also favoured for game meats. Marinating does not change the basic pot-roasting process. Care has to be taken that the marinade is not too spicy or too sour, since for full flavour of the sauce, the marinating liquid must be used as the braising liquid.

Pot roasts, marinated or fresh, are a basic meat preparation where the flavour of the sauce and the garnish are related to the name of the preparation. All pot roasts can be and should be made in one way only, regardless of their names. The selected preparation method must be fast and simple to fit the production of modern professional cookery. Today, "time is of the essence", both for economic reasons and because overcooking is seen as the destroyer of nutritional food value and quality. Think about the tremendous similarity of pot-roasting as compared to sauteing and sauce making.

A lemon chicken marinade

As implied by its name Pot-roasting, stands for a large piece of meat, (several portions in one), "roasted" in a covered pot such as dutch oven, casserole, brassiere on top of the range. It means cooking with moisture, unlike the true roast where moisture evaporation is the heart of the process. Pot-roasting is a moist cooking process like steaming or boiling, with the difference of browning the meat first. This process changes, or caramelizes, the carbohydrates present and creates a different flavour and appearance. Since as little moisture as possible is used, just as in poaching fish, a maximum sauce flavour is the result. Pot-roasting is a commonly accepted expression however it will be better to call it as Braised Roast.

The process of pot-roasting requires the use of oven or covered casserole. A high-walled roasting pan in the oven and some liquid added at the beginning will give the same results. The term roast always implies a large piece of meat, at least more than three portions in one.

Game

Game can be pot-roasted fresh or in a marinade. Some parts of game animals, when they are young enough, can be prepared as roasts or steaks. Regional cookery of venison or other game prefers to marinate and braise most of the game meats. Game meat in Europe is very well aged, 4 to 8 weeks if the temperature conditions permit it. The meat is also marinated. The marinade, which can be spiced well, takes some of the gamey flavour away. Even if a marinade is not used at all, wine, lemon juice, buttermilk, or sour cream is often a part of the preparation. Since game meat cannot be sold in some regions. The average cook has little chance to prepare these specialities. They are sometimes prepared in private clubs for some of their hunting members. All pot-roasting methods can be applied to prepare wild hare, venison, elk, reindeer, wild ducks, geese, and wild boar.

Pot roast in general is beef meat, but any edible meat that is basically tough can be prepared in the same manner. Meat (beef) cuts that are used come from the round or the chuck. Brisket and flank can also be used. Outside round, sometimes called bottom round, is the best cut. It is free of gristle and ingrown fat. It slices nicely, but is too tough to be used for steak or roast. It is also too lean for ground meat or stew. But there are many chefs who like chuck, knuckles, and even triangle roasts. (Ref. Experimental Recipe 82)

Pot roast, is saved with a plain but concentrated brown sauce. Flavours and names are changed through the addition of wine, cream, garnish, herbs and spices. In short, the same principles of cookery are applied as for saute and sauce cookery.

1. *Jardiniere Pot Roast:*

   A garnish of some separately cooked garden vegetables such as peas, cauliflower, mushrooms, artichokes, carrots, broccoli, asparagus; parsnips, turnips, is added to the brown sauce served over the meat.

2. *Burgundy Pot Roast:*

   Has a garnish of diced mushrooms, fried bacon cubes, and pearl onions added to the brown sauce, which has been finished with a heavy burgundy type red wine.

3. *Western pot Roast:*

   Has garnish of dried prunes and pitted olives added to the brown sauce.

4. *Yankee pot Roast or American Pot Roast:*

   Is a name sometimes used instead of plain pot roast.

5. *Boeuf a la mode:*

   Is the French version, of a larded pot roast. Bacon or salted pork strips are inserted through the middle of the raw piece of meat, which then is cooked in the same way as a plain pot roast, with added red wine.

6. *Braised let of Veal Marengo:*

   Is made from heavy veal legs, not tender enough for scallopine, or even whole or seamed baby beef legs, which can be handled like pot roasts. *A la marengo* (as in chicken Marengo) means that the sauce consists of one part tomato sauce with sliced mushrooms as a garnish. The original classic version also included crayfish tails in addition to the mushroom garnish.

7. *Sauerbraten:*

   Is the German word for a marinated pot roast. There is a mistaken belief that a marinade containing tartatic acids (wine, vinegars) tenderizes meat. If anything, it toughens food while cooking. In the past, marinade was used to preserve meat for a few more days. The tenderizing effect came from the enzyme action during "aging" or storing the meat. Modern food technology believes that from the enzyme action during "aging" or storing the meat. Modern food technology believes that aging is in fact, decaying, While the loosening of the fibres through aging tenderizes, it also changes flavour and possible nutritional values. The acid of a marinade slows the growth of some bacteria in the meat and therefore prolongs its storage life. Very little of the marinade flavour really penetrates the meat. The flavour stays in the sauce which is to be served over the meat. Thus marinating for over 4 to 5 days as it was done in the past is not necessary. It is only important that all the maribade which was poured over the meat, is used to braise and make the sauce.

The cooking of a pot roast, or pot-roasting in general, is one of the important skills of a Chef or Second Cook. It is one of the basic skills of cookery and the processes involved cover a great part of general cooking.

Experimental Recepe 82.

How to make Pot Roast ?

Equipment

1. Heavy casserole with matching cover.

Ingredients

1. Thyme	:	1 teaspoon
2. Bottom round in one piece	:	10 lbs.
3. Salt	:	To Taste
4. Mirepox	:	1 quart
5. Stock	:	2-3 quarts
6. Tomato paste	:	½ cup
7. Stock	:	2-3 quarts
8. Cloves garlic	:	3-4
9. Roux	:	Approximately 3 ounces
10. Bay leaves	:	3-4 cloves
11. Bunches parsley	:	2.

Method

1. Prepare all required ingredients.
2. Wash and season meat.
3. Place into oiled, hot casserole, on cover.
4. Put into 475°F. oven to start browning.
5. After 15-20 minutes, or when meat is browned, add mirepoix and garlic.
6. Roast 10 more minutes.
7. Add tomato paste. Stir well. Roast a few more minutes.
8. Add all remaining ingredients except roux, and only ½ of the stock. Cover.
9. Put back into oven. Reduce heat to 350°F.
10. Leave in oven for about 2 ½ hours or until tender.
11. Add roux. Cook for 5 minutes more.
12. Remove meat from sauce. Cool off, then keep warm.
13. Finish sauce with remaining stock, season to taste, strain and keep sauce in bainmarie. Slice meat to the order, or priceless in the portion control manner.

Experiential Recipe 83.

German Sauerbraten

Equipments

1. A stainless steam table insert, big enough to marinate
2. A braising casserole with a cover.

Ingredients

1.	Thyme	:	1 teaspoon
2.	Whole pepper	:	½ teaspoon
3.	Bottom round, eye of the round or silver side, in one or two pieces	:	10 pounds
4.	Whole pickling spice	:	½ teaspoon
5.	Whole	:	6 cloves
6.	Mixed root vegetables: celery, onions parsnips, carrots, cubed (mirepoix)	:	1 quart
7.	Salt	:	2 teaspoons
8.	Water	:	2 quarts
9.	Garlic, smashed	:	6 cloves
10.	White vinegar	:	2 cups
11.	Juniper berries, crushed	:	20
12.	Sauteing fat	:	3 ounces
13.	Leaves	:	5 bay
14.	Roux	:	2 ounces
15.	Parsley	:	2 bunches
16.	Rich sour cream	:	2 cups.

Method

1. Prepare all required ingredients.
2. Washment clear all vegetables
3. All the spices are put into a cheese cloth bag.
4. Water, vinegar, salt, and all the spices and herbs are brought to a boil, simmered for 2 minutes, then cooled off.
5. The meat is placed in the stainless container with some of the root vegetables, (garlic and parsley), underneath and on the sides.
6. The cooled marinade is poured over the meat with all the meat well covered.
7. Container is covered with plastic wrap and refrigerated from 8 to 72 hours (minimum-maximum)
8. Meat in the container is turned around every 12 hours.
9. Oil is poured into the braising casserole and heated.
10. The drained roast is dipped into flour and browned evenly on all sides.
11. Garlic and the marinated vegetables are added to the sauteing meat.
12. The bay leaves and the spice bag are removed.

(Cont.)

13. The remaining liquid and content are added to the roast, then it is covered and simmered for about 1 ½ hours.
14. The roast is separated from the sauce but continues to cook, covered, over a low fire.
15. A blender is used to satirize the vegetables in the braising liquid.
16. The coarse pulp after sterilization is strained out and the liquid is added to the roast.
17. When sauce starts to simmer, enough roux is added to crate a heavy texture.
18. Cook at leat 10 more minutes, to assure smoothness of sauce, or until the meat seems to be tender. Consider the carry-over heat!
19. When tender, roast is removed from the sauce, the sour cream is added to the sauce, which is to be seasoned and brought again to a full boil.
20. It is best to handle meat and sauce separately in the steam table.

SAUERBRATEN

Sauerbrated, a German word, translates as marinated pot roast. Due to its specific piquant flavour, it has become a popular dish. Its preparations is only slightly different from the making of a regular pot roast. **(Ref. Experimental Recipe 83)**

1. Selection and quality of the meat cut is decisive for the final quality of the preparation.
2. The marinade must not be too sour. It can be diluted with water. No sugar can be added.
3. Cooking time depends entirely on the shape of the meat and its quality. Two hours of total cooking time could be too much.
4. In the USA, German sauerbraten is often served with potato pancakes (Kartoffelpuffer) and red cabbage. In the German speaking countries of Europe, noodles, Spaetzle, dumplings. Gnochi or any pasta is preferred. Red cabbage as a vegetable is not acceptable to this dish either; a sour flavour on the same plate twice is gastronomically wrong.

A sauerbraten is a pot roast, cooked with the addition of acid (wine, vinegar, or lemon juice) and finished in a white brownish sauce, which for better class cookery is finished with sour cream.

QUESTIONS AND DISCUSSIONS

Fill in the Blanks

Q.1. Read and complete the following statements :

(i) In pot-roasting, it is essential that the raw meat is first.............

(ii) Although the term pot-roasting is commonly accepted, a better word would be ....

(iii) Pot-roasting actually means cooking with the retention of.............

(iv) The meat marinade started as a methods of ....

(v) Pot-roasting can be done on top of the range in a pot which is ....

(vi) Marinades are useful to reduce the wild flavour of ....

(vii) The meat used for pot-roasting can be fresh or ....

(viii) Pot--roasting can be done in the oven with the addition of ....

[**Ans.:** (*i*) Bottom round; (*ii*) braised roast;
(*iii*) flavour; (*iv*) meat preservation;
(*v*) covered; (*vi*) the game;
(*vii*) marinated; (*viii*) liquid.

Multiple Choice Type

Q.2. Read each question carefully and select the best answer :

(i) A strongly spiced marinade is good to use on a :—
  (a) Braised leg of venison
  (b) Veal leg "Marengo"
  (c) Roasted sirloin strip
  (d) Braised large turkey.

(ii) The pot-roasting process is mostly applied to :—
  (a) Young and juicy meats
  (c) Tough and lean meats
  (b) Boneless and trimmed meats
  (d) Large chunks of beef meat.

(iii) German Sauerbraten is sometimes served with a side dish which is unacceptable to true gastronomic art. This dish is
  (a) Potato pancakes
  (b) Buttered noodles
  (c) Bread dumplings
  (d) Braised red cabbage.

(iv) A pot roast without a specific name should be served with :
  (a) Tomato sauce and mushrooms
  (b) Cream sauce and vegetables
  (c) Prunes and olives
  (d) Plain strong brown sauce.

(v) In pot-roasting, meat is caramelized and tenderized, which means that the meat is practically :—
  (a) Boiled first then browned
  (b) Browned first then poached
  (c) Roasted first then boiled
  (d) Baked in its own juice.

[**Ans.:** (i) (a); (ii) (c); (iii) (d); (iv) (d); (v) (b)]

Matching Type

Q.3. Match the ingredient listed in Table 'A' with the corresponding preparation is Table 'B'

Table 'A'	*Table 'B'*
(a) White vinegar	1. Burgundy Pot Roast
(b) Red wine	2. Veal leg "Marengo"
(c) Cauliflower, peas	3. Boeuf a la Mode
(d) Tomato sauce	4. Braised Moose Leg
(e) Bacon or salt pork	5. Western Pot Roast
(f) Mirepoix	6. German Sauerbraten
(g) Olives & Prunes	7. Jardiniere pot Roast
(h) Buttermilk	8. American pot Roast.

[**Ans.:** (a) 4, 6; (b) 1, 3, 7; (c) 3; (d) 2, 5;
(e) 3; (f) 8, 1; (g) 2; (h) 6]

Short Answers Type

Q.4. Why is marination is considered a flavour device ?

Q.5. Do different raising methods have different merits ?

Q.6. Explain the types of meats for while pot-roasting is the best cooking methods.

Assignments/Activity Type

Q.7. Define the following:

(a) Marinate (b) Seam

(c) Enzyme. (d) Praise.

Q.8. Pot-roast a beef eye of the round under your supervision.

Q.9. Prepare a Sauerbraten.

Q.10. Demonstrate the preparation of a game animal.

4.7

Braising Portion-Cut Out Meats

CHAPTER OBJECTIVES

After studying this lesson you should be able :

- To explain to differentiate between Swiss steak and Potted steak;
- To give a practical demonstration of the making of veal roulades; and
- To apply a modern working sequence to the braising of steak.

It is expected that by now the students see and understand the very simple structure of cooking and the constant and repeated similarities of work phases. A different approach to working procedures has to be learned now. In the restaurant business, the old adage "Time is Money" is a truism. Cooks could continue to make, for instance, Swiss steaks in the same way as Escoffier and other great culinarians. By taking advantage of the technical progress of our equipment, a modern manner of work sequences can be used, without any loss of quality or flavor. This saves about 25 percent of the time and labour. As a comparison example, two ways in the step-by-step sequence of braising portion-cut meats are given in Table 4.7.

The braising of portion-cut meats explains the similarity of this process to pot-roasting. The only real difference is the size of the meat pieces prepared. Braised steaks, when served in individual casseroles or even braised in them, are called potted steaks. Again, there is no difference in the basic preparation. Swiss steak is the term used to describe a braised steak made like the plain or American pot roast. Steak a la Esterhazy, which is of Hungarian origin, has fancier ingredients, but the preparation method is the same. Roulades are a variety of braised steaks, made from beef or veal, in any desired way. Pork chops and chickens, two basically tender meats, are better tasting and more economical when sauteed only but for special reasons they can be braised. Savory pork chops and Old-Fashioned Chicken in Red Wine are examples.

Braising is a generally used in place of pot-roasting and stewing. The difference is in the size of the piece of meat that cooked. Pot-roasting means the cooking of a large piece of meat only. *Braising* means that portion-cut meat, usually called a steak or chop, is prepared by the 'combination process". It should be seen that a braised Swiss Steak a la jardiniere is made of the very same meat cut and ingredients as a pot roast jardiniere. The Swiss steak is cut to its portion size and then cooked. The pot roast is cooked in one whole piece, then carved for serving. (Ref. Table 4.7A)

Table 4.7A. Procedure of Portion Cut Meat Braising

Conventional	*Modern*
1. Mirepoix is sauteed in a casserole, remaining ingredients and stock are added.	1. Meat is browned, then placed shinglefashion and dry, into flat steam table pan. The pan is covered tightly with aluminum foil. Pan is placed in oven at 350°F. and baked until tender.
2. The meat is browned and added to the sauce in the casserole.	2. Mirepoix and additional sauce ingredients are sauteed in a skillet, covered with a little cold stock, osterized coarsely and simmered for 30 minutes. Roux is added; seasoning checked; sauce simmers 10-15 minutes more before straining.
3. Meat and sauce are simmered together until tender.	3. The drippings from the tender cooked meat are blended with the strained sauce, the garnish is added. A part of the sauce is poured over the meat. The rest is kept separate in the steam table.
4. Meat is separated from the sauce, kept in warmer while sauce is finished with roux, then seasoned and strained.	
5. Strained sauce is combined with the separately cooked garnish and poured over the meat. A part of the sauce is kept separate in the steam table.	

Most important to the trainee cook is the understanding of how to save time and labour. You must use modern equipment to the fullest. By using the Swiss steak procedure as an example, many working processes can be considerably streamlined.

Pork Chops

Savory pork chops are often prepared from chops which are tough and taste fattier than usual. The individual portion-sized chops are pounded lightly for tenderization, salted, dipped in flour, and browned on both sides. They are laid out flat, next to each other, on a rimmed bake sheet. Each pork chop center is covered with 2 tablespoons of spicy, but not starchy, tomato sauce. The sauce is topped with two thin slices of fresh lemon, overlapping, and the lemon slices are topped with one teaspoon of brown sugar. They are baked slowly at 300°F. to 325°F. until done (30 to 45 minutes).

BRAISED SHANKS

Lamb shanks, veal shanks, and pig knuckles must be considered portion-controlled meat cuts, and braising would be one of the best preparations for them. They are handled exactly the same way an any other portion-cut meat, served with bone (Ref. Experimental Recipe 84).

CHICKEN

Coq au Vin a l'Ancienne translates as old-fashioned chicken, trimmed the same as for a chicken saute, is seasoned, dipped in flour, and browened in a skillet. It is then covered with one part strong chicken stock and three parts heavy red wine, seasoned with onions, garlic, a bouquet grainy, allspice, and cloves. After about 25 minutes of braising, the sauce is finished by adding half roux and half cornstarch dissolved in red wine. A garnish of mushrooms, pearls onions, and bacon lardons is added. Chickens today are so tender that sauteing should be preferred to braising. All those chicken saute preparations can be cooked by the braising method if the cook feels that a special degree of "fork" tenderness is needed.

PORK CHOPS

Savory pork chops are prepared from chops which are tough and taste fattier than usual. The individual portion-sized chops are pounded lightly for tenderization, salted, dipped in flour, and browned on both sides. They are laid out flat, next to each other, on a rimmed bake sheet. Each pork chop center is covered with 2 tablespoons of spicy. But not starchy, tomato sauce. The sauce is topped with two thin slices of fresh lemon, overlapping, and the lemon slices are topped with one teaspoon of brown sugar. They are baked slowly at 300°F. to 325°F. until done (30 to 45 minutes).

Braised Meats Preparation : Guidelines

1. Braising meat in the unfinished sauce causes additional time loss when the tender meat is moved from the casserole to the steam table.
2. If starch is added from the beginning, there is danger of scorching, the breakup of meat is easier due to stirring or shaking. If the starch is added to the unfinished sauce after meat has been removed, when tender, at least 10 more minutes of simmering are needed to fully homag enize the sauce.
3. Ostracized vegetables yield more flavour in a shorter time; in many instances even the straining can be omitted when the sauce has been ostracized.
4. The browned meat braises in its own juice without evaporation loss due to the tight cover. The re-condensed drippings (flavor) are blended into the sauce, before it is served.
5. By the new method, meat is handled only once before serving. By the old method it is handled twice with a greater possibility of breaking up the meat orders.

Experimental Recipe 84.

Braised Lamb Shank

Ingredients

1.	Lamb fore shanks	:	6 No.
2.	Coarse salt	:	to taste
3.	Freshly ground black pepper		
4.	Oil	:	3 tapoons + 1/2 cup
5.	Onions roughly chopped	:	2 Nos.
6.	Carrot, roughly chopped	:	1 N0.
7.	Ginger-garlic paste	:	1 tspoon
8.	Tomato paste	:	1/2 cup
9.	Thyme	:	5 sprigs
10.	Bay leaf	:	1 No.
11.	Black peppercorns	:	1 teaspoon
12.	Red wine	:	2 cups
13.	White vinegar	:	1/3 cup
14.	Sugar	:	1 teaspoon
15.	Veal stock or demiglace	:	2 cups or 1 cup.
16.	Chicken stock.		

Method

1. Prepare all required ingredients.
2. Preheat the oven to 325 degrees F.
3. Season the lamb shanks liberally with salt and pepper. With a sharp knife, cut about 1 inch from the bottom (narrow end) of the shank bones down to the bone and all the way around; this will help expose the bone while cooking. Set aside.
4. Heat 3 tablespoons oil in a pot over medium-high heat. Add the celery, carrot, and onion to the pot, and cook until very soft, 8-10 minuts.
5. Add the tomato paste and cook 1-2 minutes.
6. Add the thyme, bay leaf, peppercorns, anchovies, and garlic, and cook another 2-3 minutes.
7. Add the red and white wine, and sugar, raise the heat to high, and bring to a boil.
8. Lower the heat to medium and add the veal and chicken stocks. Leave over medium heat while you brown the shanks.
9. In a saute pan over medium-high heat, brown the shanks well in the remaining 1/2 cup oil on both sides, about I minute for each of 3 sides. Use tongs to flilp the over.
10. Transfer the shanks to a roasting pan and pour the stock mixture on top. Cover with aluminum foil and cook in the pre-heated oven for 1 hour. Remove the foil and cook for another 3 hours, turning the shanks over every half hour until the meat is very soft.
11. Remove the shanks from the braising liquid and strain the liquid. Skim any fat that rises to the surface and use the liqud as a sauce.

Experimental Recipe 85.

Roasted Raan (Kashmiri Style)

Ingredients

1.	Leg of lamb	:	5 lb
2.	Garlic mashed	:	3 cloves
3.	Gresh ginger minced	:	1 piece
4.	Salt	:	1 ts
5.	Turmeric	:	1 ts
6.	Groung cinnamon	:	1/2 ts
7.	Ground cardamom	:	1/2 ts
8.	Cayenne	:	1/2 ts
9.	Ground cloves	:	1/4 ts
10.	Saffron threads	:	1/2 ts
11.	Yoghurt	:	3/4 cup
12.	Blanched almonds	:	2 tb
13.	Blanched pistachios	:	2 tb
14.	Honey	:	1 tb.

Method

1. Prepare all required ingredients.
2. Trim all fat from lamb, and, using a sharp kinfe, make slits all over the leg.
3. Combine the garlic-ginger paste and the salt with the cumin, turmeric, cinnamon, cardamom, cayenne, cloves, and lemon juice to make a paste. If paste seems too thick, add more lemon juice. Spread the paste over the meat, forcing into each slit.
4. Soak the saffron threads in hot water for five minutes.
5. In a blender or food processor put the yoghurt, the blanched nuts and the saffron threads with their water, and puree. Coat the lamb with the puree.
6. Drizzle honey over the meat. It is best to marinate the meat for two days in the refrigearator, or at least overnight. Cover loosely.
7. Pre-heat oven to 450 F and roast lamb in a covered baking dish (use foil wrap if necessary) for 1/2 hour. Reduce heat to 325 F and cook at 25 minutes to the pound, about 1-1/2 hours, until meat is tender.

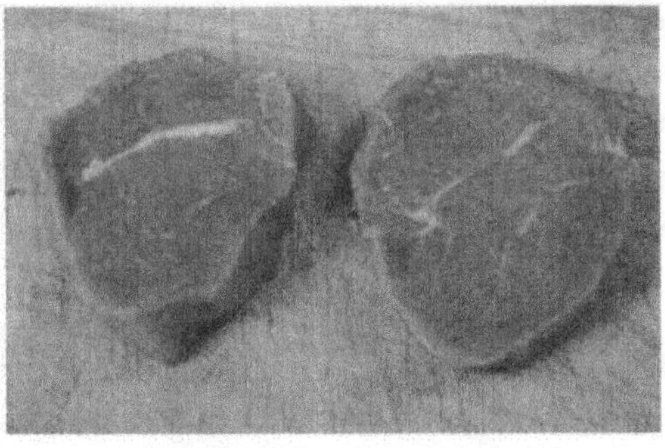

Scotch Beef Braising

Steaks Chuck Eye Steaks

Experiment Recipe 86.

Potted Beef Steak a-la Easterhazy

Equipment

6 bottom round steaks, about 8 ounces each.

Ingredients

1. Flour	:	1 cup
2. Pork fat	:	1/2 cup
3. Onions, celery/carrots, equal parts cut into jelling strips	:	1 pound
4. Garlic, chopped fine	:	1 teaspoon
5. Tomato paste	:	1 tablespoon
6. Beef stock or broth	:	3 cups
7. French mustard	:	2 tablespoons
8. Anchovy paste	:	1 teaspoon
9. Papers chopped	:	1 tablespoons
10. Salt and pepper	:	To taste.

Method

1. Prepare all required ingredients
2. Work and clean all vegetables.
3. Salt and pepper the steaks, drench them in the flour.
4. brown them in a skillet in 1/2 of the fat but keep them rare.
5. Transfer to a suitable casserole, in shingle fashion.
6. Saute the raw vegetable julienne and garlic in the remaining fat to golden brown. Drain surplus fat.
7. Add the tomato paste. Saute for a few more minutes.
8. Add two cups of hot beef stock. Bring to boil.
9. Stir in the mustard, capers and anchovy paste.
10. Pour this sauce over the steaks, then cover the casserole.
11. Braise in 350°F. oven for about 50-60 minutes or until tender. Do not overcook and lose meat texture.
12. If necessary, add some of the remaining cup of stock.
13. When tender, place meat on a serving dish and deep warm.
14. Stir 2 tablespoons of flour into the sour cream.
15. Bring the leftover meat braising liquid to a boil.
16. Stir in the sour cream. Reboil and bring the desired consistency by using all the remaining beef broth.
17. Sprinkle the pickle julienne on top and serve.

BRAISED BEEF STEAKS

Braised beef steaks, often called Swiss steak or potted steak, consist of one piece of beef meat, steak-size per order, prepared like a stew or pot roast. The meat may weigh from 6-12 ounces and could be any cut (but is usually from the round or chuck) suitable for braising. To use a regular steak cut, such as New York, Fillet or even Top Sirloin would be a waste of quality, since these cuts are too tender for stewing. This steak is usually served with noodles or some other form of pasta. (Ref. Experimental Recipe 86).

Beef steaks with boiled vegetables

SWISS STEAKS

The term Swiss steak means that a beef steak from a less tender meat cut than usually used for steaks has been prepared by the combination process. Just as in other preparations, the different names given to these dishes only describe the garnish or a variation of taste ingredients. Otherwise, a Swiss steak is always a braised portion-cut peice of beef meat.

1. Potted Steak a la Esterhazy is a special flavoured Swiss steak, served in an individual fireproof casserole which should have been used to braise the meat in individual portions. Again, new words are used to create the impression that this is not a stew. The procedure given in Experimental Recipe 89 may be followed, but changing some of the ingredients and using a different shape for the cutting of vegetables, many different formulas for Swiss steaks can be created.
2. Beef Roulades are made from raw steak pounded with the flat side of a cleaver to a thickness of about 1/8 inch. The meat is scored (cut in parallel lines) to prevent shrinking, seasoned, and spread with mustard or catsup. A small amount of any filling, plain or combined, is placed close to the long side of the punded steak. These fillings could be anything, such as pork sausage meat, ground beef, fried onions, chopped pickles, sliced or chopped ham, cheese, mushroom, sauerkraut, break dressing, or rice. The meat is rooled, fastended with toothpicks or string, and handlded in the same way as any other Swiss steak prepartion.

This method can be applied to veal, pork, and pultry as well. There are hudereds of regional preparations based on this same principle, and there are just as many different sounding foreign names.

QUESTIONS AND DISCUSSIONS

Fill in the Blanks

Q.1. Read and complete the following statements :

(a) To better understand the making of a Swiss Steak, it should be seen as a miniature ....

(b) A Potted Steak is similar to a braised one except it is served in a ....

(c) Meat roulades, as the name implies, are stuffed meat rolls cooked in the maner of ....

(d) Pork chops or chicken, being very tender nowadays, are rarely ....

(e) To save time and flavour it is advisable to use the available modern ....

[**Ans.:** (a) braised portion-cut piecess of beaf meat;
(b) individual cessorole; (c) other steak preparation;
(d) braised; (e) manner of work sequence]

Multiple Choice Type

Q.2. Read each question carefully and select the best answer :

(i) Savory pork chops, beacause of their slow cooking and sweet-sour flavour, are ideal for the preparation of :
(a) Young shoulder pork chops (b) Regular center cut pork chops
(c) Pounded thinly (d) Fat pork chops from older animals.

(ii) The name Potted Steak is a term used to describe the cooking of a :
(a) Top sirloin steak (b) Swiss steak
(c) Baked chuck steak (d) Fried round steak.

(iii) What all beef roulades have in common is that the meat is
(a) Spiced with mustard (b) Served in brown sauce
(c) Pounded thinly (d) Fastened with toothpicks.

(iv) For the efficient young cook, it is important to familiarize himself with a modern techniques (methods) of making
(a) Coq au vin a l'Ancienne
(b) A filling for beef roulades
(c) Braised steaks or portion-cut meats
(d) A good Swiss steak sauce.

(v) When making Swiss steak the raw meat is cooked on the griddle or in the pan until it is
(a) Charred and medium well (b) Brown and well done
(c) Brown and tender (d) Well browned but rare.

[**Ans.:** (i) (c); (ii) (b); (iii) d; (iv) (a); (v) (c)]

Short Answer Type

Q.3. Does technical advances imply a need for constant re-evaluation of working processes ?

Q.4. Should tender pork or chicken be braised ?

Q.5. Explain the new culinary terminology used for braised meat porton cuts. Why is it important ?

Assignments/Activity Type

Q.6. Prepare plain Swiss steaks in the modern sequence.

Q.7. Demonstrate the preparation of beef or veal roulades.

Q.8. Prepare a potted steak a la "Esterhazy".

Q.9. Define the following:
(a) Roulade
(b) Shingle
(c) Osterize.

4.8

Stewing: Meat Sea Food and Vegetables

CHAPTER OBJECTIVES

After studying this lesson you should be able :

- To practice and cook a burgundy beef stew;
- To practice and cook a veal and mushroom stew;
- To practice and cook a plain beef goulash;
- To prepare and demonstrate the procedure of preparation of a prawn curry; and
- To prepare and demonstrate the procession of lobster stew.

The combination method of caramelizing and tenderizing is known as stewing. The term, *stew*, as a noun, describes cut-up peices of meat and vegetables braised in their own sauce. Stews, much more so than steaks or roasts, can become dishes of poor quality. Cutting food small can tempt cooks to use up all leftovers. There is some concern on the part of customers about ordering stew in a restaurant. Chefs and restaurateurs have liked for new names and terms that avoid the word stew as much as possible. Stews, if properly prepared and cooked, can be some of the best creations of a chef.

You must learn that the difference between meat sauce, meat stew. braised steam, and pottted roast is only in the size of the meat cuts and not in the preparation method. The process called caramlei-zation and tenderization combined includes all, no matter what term is used.

Probably the oldest form of stewing started in one kettle. The Indian curry and the Hungarian Gouslash are still made in this way. In accient preparation the browining of the meat is omitted, but more care is taken to hanndle the sauce, vegetables, and prices. There are other speciality stews like th Italian Osso Buco. The ingredients are a little fancier than in general, but the French-influenced preparation method still remains the same.

Stewing is another term for braising. The noun stew describes meat and vegetables cut into small pieces braised in their own sauce. The public is often concerned about stews in food service establishments because too many partons have been disappointed too often. Restauranteurs know this and trying to avoid the term *stew* on their menus. The only reason for stewing is for its economy. Tough meat cuts, which are not so expensive, can only be boiled, ground or braised. If the basic rules of making a stew are followed, it can become the chef's best creation. The chef must have pieces of meat which are the same in size and quality, free from fat, gristle, and sinews. Overcooking causes mushy meat, which is not a taste delight. When food freshness is combined with knowledge of cooking and careful salting and seasoning, stews may again find greater acceptance.

Stews is a technique to tenderize tough meats. These meats are often not presentable as whole pieces since they are not the same size. They are also not lean nor free of gristle. Thus, the cutting and trimming of the meat to the same size so it will tenderize equally in the same time, is a must. When this cutting and trimming is not done the way it should be done, poor quality stews result. Customers reject poor quality. If stews are made with tender meats only for the purpose of creating a flavour blend, overcooking can be the greatest problem. Fish stews are outdated for modern and even classical cookery, because the saute method of cooking has been developed to a fine point. Customers like their fish and crustaceans as clean and boneless as possible. Fish stews in the shells are not convenient. Fresh sautes are superior to warmed up or even fresh stews. The essentials of a stew are that small-cut food is cooked in its own sauce, with all ingredients blended together, served together, and eaten together. Stewing should only be applied to the use of tough foods. Sauteing replaces stewing for tender foods.

Stew meat is cut from the less tender parts of any food animal. All the meat cubes in one kettle of stew must have the same size and come from the same meat cut to assure uniform tenderizing. The better the meat is trimmed of fat, sinews, (beef) skin, veins, and bones, the better the stew will be. It should be remembered that each cube of beef meat must be thought of as a small pot roast. The same procedure is used for making stew as was used for pot roast and Swiss steak. The reason meat (beef) is used for stew is that a meat carcass has many more not-so-tender meat parts than veal, pork, lamb, or poultry. Stews are made from all the protein foods that are edible. Stew is an economic dish because it uses inexpensive, tougher meat cuts. These small meat pieces can be mixed and extended with vegetables and starches. This stretches the nutritional value.

Curries

Curry is a mixture of spices commonly used in the south east Asian countries. It has a hot, pungent flavour and yellowish-greenish colour. It comes in many different blends and brands, but its taste is always specific curry. From 7 to 50 different spices may be used to blend it. Some of the spices indispensable are : cumin, cayenne, fennel, fenugreek, ginger, gtarlic, nutmeg, turmeric, pepper, cloves, cinnamon. Nearly all dishes spiced with this mixture are called carries. There are Indian, Malayan and Chinese curries. The Chefs of India have created hundereds of different curry varieties. Most Indian curries, are made like stew. Raw cut-up meat, chopped onions, some other vegetables and curry powder or paste are mixed together and cooked over low heat. They are made in same way as the goulash, with curry instead of paprika. Real Far Eastern curries are too hot for Western cuisine. The amount of curry which is used must be

Experimental Recipe 87.

Mutton Dhansak (Meat and Vegetables with Pulses)

Ingredients

1. Lamb	:	500 gms.
2. Toovar daal	:	50 gm
3. Broad field beans	:	25 grams
4. Masoor daal	:	25 grams
5. Yellow moong daal	:	25 grams
6. Feugreek leaves	:	03 gm
7. Brinjal	:	1/4 small
8. White pumpkin	:	50 gm
9. Pumkin	:	50 gm
10. Potato	:	2-Jan
11. Onions	:	4-Jan
12. Tomatoes	:	01 No.
13. Coriander leaves	:	10 Nos.
14. Red chillies	:	02 Nos.
15. Ginger	:	10 gms.
16. Garlic cloves	:	10 gms.
17. Tamarind water	:	1/4 cup
18. Green chillies	:	01 No.
19. Cloves	:	02 Nos.
20. Black peppercorns	:	2-3 Nos.
21. Cardamoms (green)	:	2-3 Nos.
22. Fenugreek seeds	:	1/4 teasppon
23. Mustard seeds	:	1/4 teasppon
24. Turmeric powder	:	1/4 teasppon
25. Garam masala	:	05 gram
26. Salt	:	To taste
27. Ghee	:	20 gm.

Method

1. Prepare all required ingredients.
2. Grind all the ingredients from red chillies to coriander leaves to a fine paste.
3. Grind all the ingredients from cloves to mustard seeds to a fine powder.
4. Wash the daals. Wash and chop the vegetables. Pressure cook the dals along with chopped meat, vegetables, turmeric powder, salt and enough water. Cook till the meat is tender.
5. When done, remove the mutton pieces and keep aside. Grind the remaining dal mixture in an electric mixture or mash with a masher till smooth and then strain.
6. Heat *ghee* in a deep-bottomed pan. Add the onions and fry till thy are crisp and brown. Remove half the fried onions and keep aside.
7. Then add the powdered *masala*, *dhansak masala* and the ground paste into the remaining onions and fry for 5-8 minutes till it emits an aroma. Add water.
8. Add the daals, meat and the fried onions and bring to a boil. Mix gently, check for salt.
9. Serve hot with brown rice and cucumbers.

changed for Western acceptance. Curries are made from al protien foods and vegetables, They are served with plain white cooked rice.

1. *Prawn, Crab, or Lobster Curry* should have the unfinished sauce simmered at least 30-45 minutes. Then the seafood, either shelled or unhselled, is added. This is done because the fish should only stew for 3-5 minutes.
2. *Lamb, Pork, Beef, and Chicken Curry* can be made with the cut-up meats added form the beginning so that sauce and meat will stew together.

Experimental Recipe 88.

Basic Curry Sauce for Meat and Seafood Stew

Ingredients and Method

1. 3 to 4 cups of finely chopped onions and 2 tablespoons of chopped garlic are sauteed lightly in clear butter
2. Depending on the quality of curry powder, 1/4 to 1/2 cup is added and stirred in
3. One cup of tomato puree, 1 quart of white meat or fish stock, 1 pound of peeled, diced, raw potatoes is added.
4. The sauce is then simmered for at least a few minutes before the raw protien food is added.
5. Then it is stewed until done .
6. The curry flavour can be made stronger by adding cumin, all-spice, cloves, and some fresh herbs such as basil, oregano, or marjoram. A curry can be finished by stirring in 2 cups of yogurt or buttermilk, thickened with 2 tablespoons of cornstarch.

LUMB STEW PROVINCALE

Lamb Stew Provincale uses lamb meat which has much indigestible fat. Well-trimmed and defatted lamb leg is the best choice. Again, the basic Burgundy Stew-preparation is used. The garlic should be increased three to five fold, then chopped fine and sauteed separately in olive oil to a golden brown before it is added to the sauce. Wine use is optional. The garnish for the sauce is about three pounds of peeled, de-seeded, cubed tomatoes and one cup of finely chopped fresh parsley.

MEAT SAUCE BOLOGNESE

Meat Sauce Bolognese is a meat sauce dish. Add meat sauces be thought of as meat stews, where the ingredients are chopped small with the help of a meat grinder. In the grinder, a medium to large plate is the best size of meat coarseness. For one weight part of mixed root vegetables, 1 to 2 parts of good quality lean meat (beef) chuck should be used. The preparation of the Burgundy Meat (beef) Stew can be used as a guide. Again the red wine and the garnish are omitted. The onions of the mixed root vegetables should be chopped with a knife for better sauteing. The rest of the mirepoix can be ground. The vegetable juice from the grinding is saved and used later for the sauce. A Bolognese style meat sauce should taste like plain pot roast, strong in garlic flavour and very light on the tomatoes.

Goulash

Beef Goulash is probably the oldest form of stew. The difference between the other stews and goulash is as follows :

(a) The raw meat is not browned separately, but is added to the sauteed onions and spices.

(b) The sauce base for any goulash is made of onions, tomatoes, potatoes and paprika. No other vegetables are used. Marjoram is sometimes added, but garlic and caraway seeds are used generously. Paprika is a spice like chilli powder. It is made from various kinds of dried and ground red peppers (Capsicum annum). This paprika spice gives the goulash its flavour and colour (Ref. Experimental Recipe 89).

Experimental Recipe 89.

Hungarian Beef Goulash

Ingredients

1.	Lean beef chuck,	:	10 pounds cubed about 1 1/2-inch size
2.	Hungarian paprika	:	6 fluid ounces
3.	Chopped onions	:	5 pounds
4.	Pork fat	:	1 pound
5.	Tomato paste	:	6 ounces
6.	Flour	:	1/2 cup
7.	Chopped caraway seeds	:	2 tablespoons
8.	Hot stock	:	About 3 quarts
9.	Lemons, grated	:	Zeste of two
10.	Salt	:	To taste
11.	Fresh chopped garlic	:	2 tablespoons
13.	Marjoram	:	1/2 tablespoon.

Equipment

1. Large sauteuse for onion frying
2. Casserole with lid for stewing.

Method

1. Prepare all required ingredients.
2. Fry the onions in the fat until light golden brown. Drain and keep fat.
3. Add all spices and tomato paste to the onions. Leaves on heat for a minute and stir well.
4. Add two quarts of hot stock. Mix well and let simmer for a few minutes.
5. Add salted raw meat. Mix well.
6. Cover pan tightly. Transfer to pre-heated oven of about 350*F. Stew slowly for about one hour.
7. Check stew for tendernes and taste. Mix flour into accumulated fat on top of stew like a roux.
8. Mix everything very well. Add remaining stock if necessary, and cook meat to finish.
9. Check again. Beware of overcooking. Serve when ready.

Depending on the country which has adoptd it, goulash can be spelled Gulyas, Goulash or Gulakh. Hungarian variations, due to the ingredients used, have more names. A goulash made without tomatoes is called Paprikas. A goulash finished with sour cream in the sauce is called "Poerkoelt". Goulashes are very important to central European cuisine. They are very popular. Many cookbooks are written for goulash only.

1. Any stew loses most of its eye appeal and taste when overcooked. Meat should be chewable. It should have the consistency of a tender New York cut steak.
2. Onions must be chopped and fried uniformy to a golden brown. When the onions are brown, the fat, onions and pan must be separated by draining. Otherwise, the carryover heat will burn the onions.
3. Pork Paprikas — is a basic goulash made with pork meat. The tomatoes are omitted. As a garnish, 3 to 4 pounds of peeled, cubed, raw potatoes are added, just in time to be tender together with the meat. Depending on meat quality and cube size, the braising may take from 35 to 60 minutes.
4. Szekeley Poerkoelt is a basic pork goulash in which a can of drained, chopped sauerkraut is stewed with the meat. The sauce is finished with one quart of rich sour cream, just before serving.

Hungarian Beef Goulashes

Hungarian Beef Goulash is a beef stew, prepared as in Central Europe, especially Hungary, Czechoslovakia and Austria. It can be served with buttered noodles, boiled rice, boiled potatoes, or any other starch. (Ref. Experimental Recipe 89)

LOBSTER A LA AMERICAINE

Americaine is probably the origianal name for this dish and many experts are still arguing which of the spellings should be used. The preparation of *a l'Amoricaine*, for handling live lobsters and other edible crustaccans, is basic. It may be served as a made-to-the-order dish, like other lobster preparations, or the same procedure can be used to make lobster sauce (Sauce Americaine) or lobster soup (Lobster Bisque). The preparation is only effective when live curstacens are used.

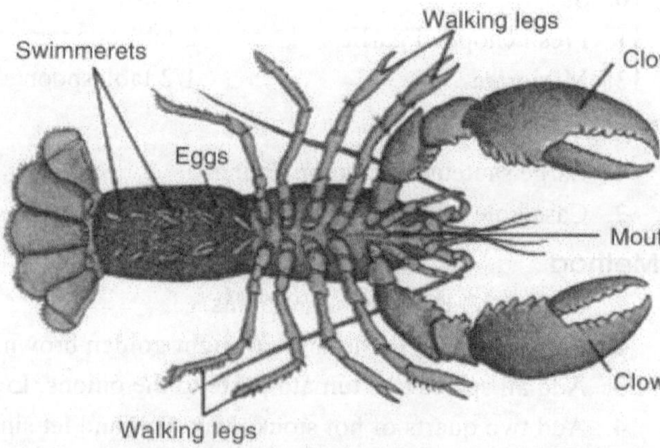

Lobsteres have five pairs of legs, including the large claws

The stewing process extracts from the shells extra flavour and colour.

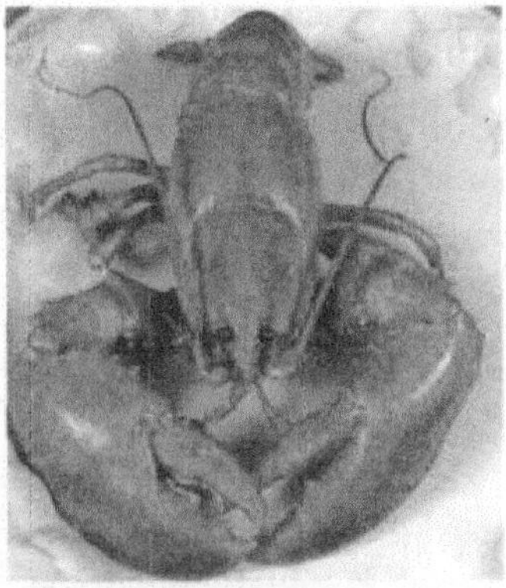

Lobster

Live Lobster

LOBSTER AMERICAINE, AMORICAINE

It is a basic preparation for crustaceans. When made from live lobster, it is called Lobster Stew Americaine. It can be made into basic lobster sauce (sauce Americaine) or Lobster Soup (Bisque). The same procedure is used for the stewing of crabs, prawns, crayfish, and languste. A step-by-step method for this classic preparation is given in Experimental Recipe 90.

Already shelled, edible crustances are tender enought to be sauteed in a few minuts. Long stewing or boiling times. Many people are not aware of the effect overcooking has on protein foods of shelled meat is the cause of poor quality in the final dish. Old fashioned cook book often directed long stewing or protein foods.

1. Whole lobsters for individual orders weigh an average of 1¼ to 1¾ ibs., although larger lobsters can be used.
2. Beware of overcooking. This is an expensive a la carte preparation. A high food cost is combined with skilled handling. These preparations are found only in real luxury restaurants.

Lobstor dish

Experimental Recipe 90.

Loster a L Amoricaine

Ingredients

1.	Live lobster	:	1
2.	Dry white wine	:	1/3 cup
3.	Brandy	:	1¼ ounces
4.	White stock (fish)	:	¼ cup
5.	Shallots, finely chopped	:	2 tablespoons
6.	Tomato sauce, light starch	:	3 tablespoons
7.	Tomatoes, peeled, de-seeded, diced	:	½ cup
8.	Meat glaze (glace de viade)	:	2 tablespoons
9.	Herbs, finely chopped (parsley, coriander, tarragon)	:	½ teaspoon
10.	Fresh butter	:	2 ounces
11.	Clear butter liquid	:	2 ounces
12.	Oil	:	2 ounces.

Method

1. Prepare required ingredients.
2. Wash and clean lobster, shallot, tomoatos parsly, coriander etc.
3. Split live lobster in half, lengthwise.
4. Separate tail and claws, crack claws open.
5. Clean the remaining shell, revserve the coral (lobster roe and liver).
6. Rinse shell. Boil it in salt water to bright red. Reseve for later.
7. Remove the black vein (gut) from the tail.
8. Cut each tail half in two or three pieces.
9. Salt the exposed flesh of tail and claws.
10. Heat oil in a sauteuse to very hot. Add all the lobster meat.
11. Saute, shake pan, and cover for 1-2 minutes. Shell is still red.
12. Drain off the saute oil.
13. Add the fresh butter, garlic, shallots and herbs.
14. Keep on sauteing for one or two minutes.
15. Add the brandy and flame.
16. Deglaze with wine, white stock and tomato sauce. Cover, reduce heat, and simmer 3 to 4 munutes.
17. Remove from heat. Steep with cover for another few minutes. Cool.
18. When cool enough to handle, take meat out of the shell.
19. Reserve the shells for later use (to make lobster butter).
20. Place the meat on a service platter and keep warm.
21. Return saute pan with sauce to heat. Add tomatoes and meat glaze.
22. Bring to a full boil. Then reduce heat and simmer to desired consistency.
23. Mix the coral with the clear butter and stir into the simmering sauce. Taste, season, and bring to a full boil.
24. Pour the sauce over the lobster meat. Use the boiled lobster head as decoration.
25. Serve immediately. If it is a first course, serve with toast. If it is a main course, serve with buttered steamed rice.

Experimental Recipe 91.

Burgundy Beef Stew

Ingredients

1.	Trimmed beef chuck, cut for a stew	:	10 pounds
2.	Tomato paste	:	18 ounces
3.	Onions, chopped	:	3 pounds
4.	Dry, heavey red wine	:	1 quart
5.	Fresh garlic, chopped	:	2 ounces
6.	Pearl or small boiling onions, pre-sauteed	:	2 pounds
7.	Carrots, cubed	:	1 cup
8.	Frozen green peas, defrosted	:	One 2 1/2-Pound Package
9.	Chopped celery	:	3 cups
10.	Mushrooms, cut in quarters, pre-sauteed	:	1½ pounds
11.	Parsnips, cubed	:	1 cup
12.	Oil	:	4 ounces
13.	Chopped parsley	:	1 cup
14.	Roux	:	4 ounces
15.	Bay leaf	:	6 single pieces
16.	Brown stock	:	2-3 quarts
17.	Thyme	:	1-2 teaspoons
18.	Salt	:	To taste.

Equipments

1. Heavy stewing casserole with lid
2. Large skillet or sauteuse
3. Range and banking oven.

Method

1. Prepare all required ingredients.
2. Wash all vegteble and green.
3. Set oven temperature to 500° F. Place empty casserole in it and pre-heat.
4. Mix salt, pepper, and oil into the meat.
5. When casserole is very hot, the oiled meat is put in it, evenly spaced.
6. The meat is cooked, while being stirred often, for 15 to 20 minutes, until well browned.
7. The fat is drained into a skillet or sauteuse and saved for later.
8. The tomato paste, thyme, and bay leaves are stirred into the meat.
9. When the tomato paste has browned, the stew is deglazed with the red wine and simmered for a few mintues. Oven heat is reduced to 350°F.
10. About a quart of the brown stock is added. The casserole is covered and simmered in the oven until nearly tender.
11. When the stew simmers, the onions, garlic, and remaining vegetables are sauteed in the fat to golden brown.

12. These vegetables are deglazed with a quart of stock and then osterized.
13. The osterized sauce is returned to the tip of the range. The stock and the roux are added and simmered for at least 30 minutes.
14. When the meat is about tender, the pre-sauteed mushrooms, onions, and the defrosted raw peas are added to the stew in the oven.
15. The sauce, which is simmering on top of the range, is strained over the stew.
16. The finished stew is brought to a full boil, checked for taste and sauce consistency. It is then transferred to the steam table for holding and serving.

Burgundy Meat (Beef) Stew

Burgundy Meat (Beef) Stew is called Ragout de Boeul Bourguignonne in some luxury restaurants. It is made from the same ingredients as a Burgundy pot roast. As the basic (beef) preparation for all stews, Experimental Recipe 91. shows a step-by-step procedure for Burgundy Meat Stew. Just as for pot roast and Swiss steak., to know how to make one stew is to know how to make all stews. The only changes are the kinds of meat, flavours, garnishes, shapes of the food cut, and the corresponding cooking time.

The Burgundy Beef Stew is an institutional adaptation from the clasic French cuisine. It is a regional creation from the Burgundy area, but other wine-growing areas have had the same ideas. The stew must be made with red wine to deserve this name. (Ref. Experimental Recipe 91)

The quality of any stew depends on meat quality (trim, tenderness, fat). Its eye appeal depends on consistency and colour of the sauce. Taste in itself is disputable. More or less garlic, spices, herbs, or wines do not make the real chef. Amateurs emphasize spice. Professionals try to please many different tastes and have to be careful. Only salt has to be in the dish. The chef who does not salt (except for a salt-free diet), regardless of his reason, is never a real chef.

The colour of the stew should be a rich, reddish brown. The consistency of the sauce should be on the light side. A heavy, thick sauce is neither appetizing nor sophisticated.. The peas should be added shortly before serving in order to keep their nice green colour. The best meat size is large, lean chunks, evenly cut, about 1 - 1½ ounces each, with 5-6 pieces to the order.

Watch total cooking time. For good meat, about 60 minutes could be enough. Consider the time the meat has to be in the steam table. Meat must never be overcooked.

Serving may be best in individual, fireproof casseroles or silver dishes. Be sure that each order gets an equal amount of meat, pearl onions and mushoroom. This is a deluxe preparation of a fine restaurant or a hotel dining room.

Seafood Stews

Seafood, which is almost pure protein, does, not stew well. Fish is too brittle. Shellfish are not practical to stew, and overcook easily so that they become tough and tasteless. Bouillabaise or cioppino are some times called fish stews. They become or coippino are some times called fish stews. They are not. They should be called soups. One shellfish preparation which can be considered as stew is the Lobster a l'Amoricaine.

Experimental Recipe 92.

Osso Buco Mianese

Ingredients

1.	Veal knuckles, sawed 1½ - inches thick	:	4-5 pounds
2.	Finely diced, equal parts of onions, celery and carrots	:	2 cups
3.	Flour	:	about ½ cup
4.	Peeled, de-seeded, cubed tomatoes	:	1½ pounds
5.	Dry wine	:	1 cup
6.	Chopped garlic	:	1 tablespoon
7.	Garni	:	1 bouquet
8.	Zeste and juice	:	from 1-2 oranges and lemons each
9.	Anchovies	:	3-4 fillets
10.	Chopped parsley	:	1/4 cup
11.	Olive oil	:	1/2 cup
12.	Salt	:	To taste.

Procedure

1. Prepare all required ingradients.
2. Wash and clean all vegetable and green.
3. In a casserole with lid, saute the 2 cups of vegetabeles and the garlic, in half of the fat, Set aside.
4. Salt meat, roll in flour, and brown on all sides in remaining fat in another skillet.
5. Transfer meat from the skillet into the casserole with the vegetables on the bottom.
6. deglaze skillet with the wine. Scrape residue loose and pour liquid over the meat.
7. Add the tomatoes, the bouquet garni, and half of the citrus juice to the meat.
8. Cover casserole and stew on low heat in the oven until meat is crunchily tender. This will depend entirely on the meat quality and could be from 3/4 of an hour to 2 hours.
9. In the meantime, chop anchovies and zests together. Add the anchovies, oil, parsley, and 1/4 of the remaining citrus juice.
10. Stir into this mixture about 2-3 tablespoon of flour.
11. When they are tender, remove veal knuckles to warmed platter.
12. Stir the chopped anchovies mixture into the simmering sauce.
13. Check sauce for consistency and taste.
14. Finish as needed with salt, the citrus juice, and stock or bouillon.
15. Depending on the raw material used, size of the casserole, and heat, it could be that the sauce is too watery. In this case, it should be reduced on high heat under constant stirring, untill desired consistency is reached.
16. Remove the bouquet garni. Pour sauce over the meat and serve.
17. To qualify for the name a 'la Milanaise, Risotto Milanaise, is served as a side dish.

OSSO BUCO MIANESE

This popular Italian dish translates roughly as braised veal knuckles. Unlike lamb shanks or ham hocks, which are left whole and used as one peice for one portion, these veal knuckles are sawed into about 1½ - inch round slices with the marrow intact and the meat still around the bones. They are then handled like any other stew, It must never be forgotten that all stews are prepared the same way, no matter how or foreign sounding are their names.

Osso Buco

Osso Buco is a true Italian specialty stew, made of veal knuckle slices with the bones and bone marrow still in. It is a basic stew in the French manner. Since its ingredients are slightly different, the step-by-step procedure of this dish is found in Experimental Recipe 92.

Meat (beef) Stew with Vegetables

Meat Stew with Vegetable is made like a basic Burgundy stew..The red wine is omittted and the garnish is changed to a selection of mixture of carrots, celery, parsnips, onions, turnips, string beans, potatoes or other vegetables as chosen by the chef. The vegetables used must have the same eye-appealing shape. They are added in such fines in the cooking pocess that they are just crunchy-tender at the same time that the meat is ready.

Veal Stew with Mushrooms

Veal Stew with mushrooms uses lean veal shoulder or knuckle meat. Since veal is a white meat, finished Italian dished dish is a light brown colour. Sauce ingredients are finely chopped onions, some parsely, and mushroom trimmings. If the sauce is to be blended or strained, some celery and carrots can be added. A small amount of tomato puree or freshly diced tomatoes and some wine can be used, if desired. The mushrooms garnish are cooked in butter separately. Small ones are cooked whole or halved medium or large mushroom are cubed. A trainee must learn the difference between behaviour meat sauce, meat stew, braised steaks and potted roast is only in the size of the meat cuts and not the preparation method. The process called Caramelization and Tenderization Combined includes all, no matter what term is used.

Probably the oldest form of stewing started in one kettle. The Indian curry and the Hungarian Goulash are still made in this way. In ancient preparation the browing of the meat is omitted, but more care is taken to handle the sauce, vegetables, and spices. There are other speciality stews like the Italian Osso Buco. The ingredients are a little fancier than in general, but the French-influenced preparation method still remains the same.

QUESTIONS AND DISCUSSIONS

Fill in the Blanks

Q.1. Read and complete the following statements :

(a) The noun, stew, stands for braised food in a size that is ....

(b) Beef stews in restaurants are not too ....

(c) When tender foods are stewed, the cook has to prevent ....

(d) Hungarian Goulash and Indian Curry are made by the same ....

(e) Knowing the best suited meat cuts and how to trim them is of the greatest importance in ....

(f) Adding wines or fancy ingredients does not change stewing's basic ....

[**Ans.:** (a) cut put pieces; (b) economical; (c) over cooking; (d) way; (e) stewing; (f) taste].

Multiple Choice Type

Q.2. Read each question carefully and select the best answer :

(i) To call a mixture of small-cut food stew, it must

(a) Have browned meat in it
(b) Be spiced with paprika or curry
(c) Be served with a sauce
(d) Be cooked in its own sauce.

(ii) Osso Buco is an Italian stew with tomatoes and wine, made from

(a) Lamb shanks
(b) Veal knuckles
(c) Beefchuck
(d) Pork shoulder.

(iii) Fish or shellfish are rarely made into stew because they

(a) Are tender foods by nature
(b) Have too many bones
(c) Do not brown well
(d) Do not blend with the vegetables.

(iv) If the cooking time for a stew is short, the additional sauce vegetables have to be

(a) Ground coarse
(b) Adjusted to the cooking time
(c) Cut uniformly large
(d) Osterized.

(v) A Hungarian meat stew finished with sour cream is called a

(a) Gulyas
(b) Paprikas
(c) Poerkoelt
(d) Gulash.

(vi) Curries are a wide field of preparations but what they all have in common is

(a) A rather hot taste
(b) The stewing process
(c) The yellow color
(d) The addition of potatoes.

(vii) Indian stews are food preparations seasoned with a mixture of spice called

(a) Turmeric
(b) Chilli powder
(c) Paprika
(d) Curry.

[**Ans.:** (i) (d); (ii) (b); (iii) (a); (iv) (d); (v) (c); (vi) (a); (vii) (d)]

Short Answer Type

Q.3. Answer the following questions:

(a) Name five popular poached fish preparations.

(b) List few popular fish soups.

(c) Give examples of cold fish preparations.

(d) Name few shallow and deep fried fish preparations.

[**Ans :** (a) (i) filet de sole deglere; (ii) filet de sole mornay;
(iii) filte de stromatee bonne femme; (iv) poisson veronique;
(v) poisson florentine
(b) (i) Fish consomme (Consomme marie - Louise); (ii) Bouillabaisse;
(iii) Potage au crabe; (iv) Bisque de crevettes / homard; (v) Zuppa de pesce;
(c) (i) Cocktail de crevettes / homard; (ii) Tomate monegasques;
(iii) Salad de poisson / fruit de mer; (iv) Saumon fume (smoked salmon);
(v) Caviar;
(d) (i) Poisson meuniere, Poisson meuniere doria, Poisson meuniere amandes;
(ii) Poisson frit a l'orly; (iii) Poisson a l'angaise; (iv) Poisson a la francaise.

Q.4. Name popular sea foods and explain their uses.

[**Ans :** Sea Food

(a) Prawns:

-in salad / hors d'oeuvre	- Prawn cocktail

(b) Lobster:

- in soups	- Bisque
- for grilling	- Grilled prawns / lobster
- for batter frying	- Golden fried prawns
- in various Chinese	- Prawn in garlic sauce preparations
- in cold preparation	- Lobster mayonnaise
- in classical dishes	- Lobster thermidor/ newberg

(c) Mussels:

- in soup	- Bouillabaisse
- in dish	- Moules mariniere

(d) Snails

- starters	- Escargots in la bourgiogon.

4.9

Fricassees, Blanquettes and Casseroles

CHAPTER OBJECTIVES

After studying this lesson you should be able :

- To practice and prepare Chicken Fricassee;
- To practice and make a Blanquette de Veau with Cauliflower;
- To list a variation of "Baked beans" of his own creation; and
- To prepare and demonstrate a beef steak and kidney pie by the second method.

Braised dishes have many different names and flavours but they are still basic stews. This point is stressed often to make the trainee see how simple stews are. Cookery must accept the constant technical and science-nutritional progres of our time. Cooks, in order to provide competitive products, must always look for more economic methods to achieve better, or at least equal, quality creations. The better the young student cook can see through this maze of terms, procedures, and individual side developments, the more effctive a chef he will become.

Fricassees are white stews of poultry. Blanquettes are white stews of white meats. Cesseroles are baked beans, old world style. Casseroles are stews, cooked and served in the same dish. Meat pieces are stews served in a pot pie dish, covered with pie crust or mashed potatoes.

In any restaurant, cuisine can not show greater profit by serving braised foods. The reasons are food waste and the lack of trained cook. For the truly skilled cook who has taste and artistic talents, the process called Caramelizing and tendering combined provides an excellent stage for presenting his skills.

FRICASSEES

A fricassee is a stew. It is made from white poultry meats, such as chicken or turkey. This remains white during preparation. The meat for a fricassee must not be browned. It is handled in the manner of goulash or curry, except that the colourful spices are omitted.

In some dishes the white meat is lightly sauteed. In most cases the meat is poached in a little liquid, which is then changed into sauce by adding a thickener. The thickener could be plain starch, roux, cream, or egg yolks. Vegetables are added. This may be be only chopped parsley in the sauce. It may be a selection or combination of asparagus, artichokes, cauliflower, broccoli, peas, beans, mushrooms, carrots, or others.

Brunswick Chicken Stew

This is a fricassee, with corn and often other vegetables added as a garnish.

BLANQUETTES

Blanquette de Veau

This is a term used for stews of white meats, such as veal, kid, or goat. It is prepared just like a fricassee. Blanquettes, like fricassees, have sauces based on starch, egg yolks or a combination of both. Onions, herb, bouquets and mirepoix are used to season the poaching liquid and are removed before the liquid is changed into sauce.

Preparing Chicken Blanquette

Irish Stew

Irish stew is a white lamb blanquette with onions, lamb meat cubes, sliced raw potatoes and cabbage, seasoned, salted, and arranged in layers in a casserole. The enough boiling liquid is added to cover the meat. The covered casserole is simmered without stirring until the meat is tender. The thinly sliced potatoes completely cook to a pulp and make the thickening for the sauce. At the same time the liquid is reduced. Before serving, the stew is stirred and then sprinkled with chopped parsley.

Baked Beans

Dried navy beans are soaked in cold water overnight, then boiled in their soaking water until very tender. They are drained, if necessary. Many styles are made by using spices, syrup, molasses, sugan, salt, bacon, franks, smoked sausages, or smoked meats. The mixture is placed in a bean pot or any flat casserole and baked for several hours. If it gets too dry, stock water must be added, a small amount at a time.

Baked bean dishes are known all over the world and many varieties exist. They can be made like stews with onions or other vegetables which have been sauteed first. The beans must always be soaked and boiled first.

Cassoulet

A French term for a dish like baked beans is *cassoulet*. It is made with lamb, goose, duck, pork (smoked or fresh) and different seasonings. Cossoulets, like baked beans, are winter dishes served mostly in cold areas or where food poverty demands more economy.

Casseroles

A casserole can be any stew which is cooked and served in the same container. Casseroles may be of single-portion size or larger. They are made of china, ceramic, earthenware, glass, copper and others. Combining food, layer by layer, as in Irish Stew, is a popular way of making them. Casseroles can be made meatless if a starch (pasta or potatoes) replaces the protein.

Praline French Toast Casserole

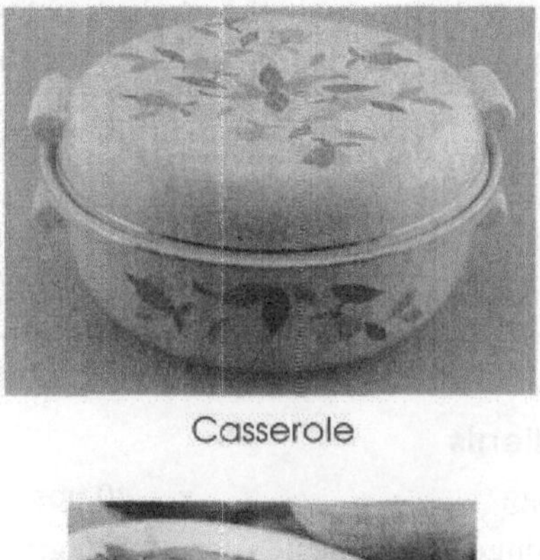

Casserole

Potato casseroles

Apple Chicken Casserole

Beefsteak Pie

Beefsteak pie is a plain beefsteak variation in which the meat is often sliced instead of cubed. This stew is put into a pot pie dish, covered with a pie crust and baked until the crust is done. The second, rather home style, version of this dish is slightly different. The raw seasoned meat mixed with pre–sauteed vegetables is put into the pie dish, covered with a slightly thickened gravy, topped with the pie crust and baked until the meat is tender. The baking time depends on the meat cuts and quality used.

Beefsteak and Kidney Pie

This is made like the beefsteak pie, with sliced pre–sauteed veal or beef kidneys added to the meat. The proportions should be not more than one part kidneys to two parts of meat.

Chicken Pot Pie

A small-cut chicken fricassee, ususally boneless, with vegetables, is handled like the beefsteak pie.

Shepherds Pie

Lamb meat is used instead of beef in the beefsteak pie. The pie crust cover is replaced by a cover of piped potatoes or spread on mashed potatoes (Duchess potato mixture).

The processes of caramelizing and tenderizing combined, have in common that the liquids used to tenderize become a major part of the preparation. Most of them have in common the fact that some or all of the ingredients are browned to obtain the changed flavour. To distinguish the dishes listed in these lessons as completely different from boiled, poached or steamed foods, it must be recalled that in cooking with moisture only (boiling, etc.), the food and liquid are separated as soon as the food is tenderized. In braising, a mixture of proteins, starch and liquid is created. The intent is to serve it exactly this way. (Ref. Experimental Recipe 93)

Experimental Recipe 93.

Dum Ke Ande

Ingredients

1.	Egg	:	40 nos
2.	Ginger-garlic paste	:	100 gm
3.	Watermelon seeds	:	80 gm
4.	Poppy seeds	:	80 gm
5.	Turmeric powder	:	03 tbs
6.	Red chilies pd.	:	03 tbs
7.	Beaten yoghurt	:	03 kg
8.	Oil	:	300 gm
9.	Chopped coriander	:	50 gm
10.	Salt	:	To taste.

Method

1. Prepare all required ingredients.
2. Heat oil and fry the onion till golden brownh. Add ginger garlic paste, ground water melon seeds and poppy seeds. Add turmeric, salt and red chilies powder.
3. Now add yoghurt and stir till it gets mix with spices. Cook till the gravy leaves the fat.
4. Now turn the gravy into the oven-proof dish. Gently break the egg on the surface of gravy. Bake in the pre-heated oven.
5. Serve hot and garnish with green coriander leaves.

The larger number of fancy names comes from the regional origins of the dishes. Some other names were accepted in place of the word stew.

From a nutritional view point, dishes with a long cooking time are not as good for diets as those which cook fast and retain more vitamins. From a customer's view point, long-cooked dishes do not have the same freshness as sauteed, fried or broiled foods. From the restaurateur's viewpoint, long-cooked dishes do not allow for proper portion control. The highly skilled chef who is needed for this type of cooking is not found in the average restaurant.

QUESTIONS AND DISCUSSIONS

Fill in the Blanks

Q.1. Complete the following statements:

(a) Baked bean dishes are , in a technical sense. ....

(b) Meat pies are similar to casseroles or ....

(c) A stew cooked and served in the same container can be called a ....

(d) A fricassee is the name of a stew made from ....

(e) Irish Stew could be classified as a lamb ....

(f) Blanquette is a French name for a white veal ....

(g) Cassoulet is the French name for a form of ....

[**Ans.:** (a) dry navy beans; (b) Stew; (c) Cesserole;
(d) white poultry meat such as chiken or turkey;
(e) blanquette; (f) kid or goat;
(g) dish like baked beans in cassoulet]

Multiple Choice Type

Q.2. Read each question carefully and select the *best* answer:

(i) Cassoulet oulet is the French term for a casserole made with

(a) Beef meat (b) Lamb meat

(c) Fried onions (d) Dried beans.

(ii) A beef stew served with a pie crust is called a

(a) Casserole (b) Beefsteak pie

(c) Shephereds pie (d) Cassoulet.

(iii) A beef goulash served in a pot pei dish with a pie crust has beome a

(a) Beef pie (b) Goulash Casserole

(c) Hungarian Beef pie (d) Beefsteak pie.

(iv) A white stew can be called fricassee when it is made of

(a) goose meat (b) wild duck

(c) boneless chicken (d) domesticated white ducks.

(v) Irish Lamb Stew which contains onions, potatoes and cabbage is made in the method of the

(a) casseole – blanquette
(b) "Lamb a la Provincal"
(c) shepherds pie
(d) cassoulet.

(vi) Blanquettes are unbrowned meat stews from

(a) beef
(b) trukey
(c) venison
(d) veal.

[**Ans.:** (i) (d); (ii) (b); (iii) (d); (iv) (c); (v) (a); (vi) (d)]

Short Answer Type

Q.3. Define:

(a) Fricfassee
(b) Cassoulet
(c) Poultry
(d) Blanquette.

Q.4. Describe some of the important considerations of fricasseeing which would be similar to stewing.

Q.5. Is the confusing terminology of names in cooking necessary?

Assignments/Activity Type

Q.6. Create an original recipe for baked beans.

Q.7. Select and compare various recipes of baked beans.

Q.8. Blanquette de Veau with Cauliflower.

Q.9. Make a Chicken Brunswick Stew.

Appendix A

ESCOFFIER: THE KING OF CHEF'S!

Georges Auguste Escoffier (28 October 1846 – 12 February 1935)

The Father of Modern Cuisine, was a French Chef, restaurateur and culinary writer who refined and organized traditional French cooking techniques. He is a legend among chefs, and the world first true celebrity chef. He was born in the Provence region of France, his culinary journey beginning at the age of 13, his father took him to Nice where he apprenticed at a restaurant owned by his uncle Le Restaurant Français. Escoffier spent 6 decades in the business.

His culinary career was a notable mission, starting at Le Petit Moulin Rouge in Paris. He also worked his way around Paris in some of the finest restaurants and travel quite extensively to hone his craft from France to Monte Carlo, Switzerland, and London. During the Franco-Prussian War (1870) Escoffier served in the French Army as Chef de Cuisine. During his tour of duty he found a great need for tinned foods and spent quite a bit of time developing new methods to can foods. He was the first chef to research and develop techniques for canning and preserving meats and vegetables. Following his tour, Escoffier stepped right back into his career in several restaurants in the Paris area. He steadily moved up the ladder and was well respected and sort after chef.

But it was during his years in Monte Carlo that Escoffier befriended Cesar Ritz. In Monte Carlo Escoffier took control of the kitchen at the Grand Hotel. During the summers he ran the kitchen of the Hotel National in Lucerne, where he met César Ritz. They became immediate friends and business partners (1890). The collaboration of Escoffier and Ritz changed the face of the hotel industry forever. The bar was raised in regards to the development and progress of the standards of hospitality and guest services. Both Ritz and Escoffier ended up at the Savoy Hotel in London where Escoffier served as Head of Restaurant Services. Soon later, Ritz opened a chain of his own hotels, the Hotel Ritz in Paris and the Carlton in London to name a few. Escoffier was the key player in the restaurant end of the establishments. During his time at the Carlton, Escoffier developed a superior reputation for haute cuisine. While at the Savoy, Escoffier developed one of his more famous recipes, Peach Melba, in honor of the popular Austrian singer Nellie Melba who was a frequent guest of the hotel.

Escoffier and Ritz opened the Hôtel Ritz in Paris, in 1898. The Carlton in London followed; this is where Escoffier introduced the à la carte menu. Ritz had a nervous breakdown in 1901, leaving Escoffier alone to run the Carlton until 1919, shortly after Ritz's death.

Escoffier published his first major book in 1902, Le Guide Culinaire; it is almost a bible amongst French culinary enthusiasts' and chefs worldwide. It contains over 5,000 recipes. There is no over estimating the importance of this book in the world of food. His books are greatly respected and used as text books in some of the best culinary schools in the world. His reputation is that of a father, or better expressed a creator of modern culinary techniques.

Auguste Escoffier changed culinary history, furthered the fame of French cuisine all over the world, and touching the undeveloped cooking world with his passion, warmth and artistry. He spoke of menus and recipes as if they were poetry and treated them accordingly. When Escoffier was a boy he wanted to be a sculpture and his father forced him to apprentice in his uncles restaurant. Maybe it's Escoffier's father who is in need of some credit here, if he hadn't forced his son into the restaurant business, we might only have been admiring a grand statue with Escoffier's name on it. You can't eat a statue! I am glad I get to eat his work instead of just look at it.

Escoffier's most notable achievements are revolutionizing and modernizing the menu, cooking techniques and organization of professional kitchens. Escoffier simplified the menus, writing the dishes down in the order in which they would be served (Service à la Russe). He also developed the à la Carte menu.

Most of Escoffier's techniques were based on Antoine Carême's works, however Carême's techniques were over complicated and Escoffier's success was to simplify and modernize Carême's elaborate and styling's. Another of Escoffier's contributions to the world of cooking was to change the aura of the professional chef, and to introduce discipline and consistency where before there had been disorder. Laying out the path that raised the status of cooking from a laborer's task to an artistic undertaking. His kitchens were organized by the brigade system, each section run by a chef de partie. He also replaced the practice of service à la française (serving all dishes at once) with service à la russe (serving each dish in the order printed on the menu). This system is still in place in commercial kitchens worldwide.

He simplified the art of cooking by getting rid of pretentious food displays gaudy and shameless garnishes and by reducing the number of courses served. He also emphasized the use of seasonal foods and sauces that were lighter. Escoffier also simplified professional kitchen organization, integrating it into a single functional unit where it had previously been individual sections that operated independently and often led to overwhelming waste and unnecessary duplication of production and labor.

Throughout his career, Escoffier wrote a number of books, many of which continue to be considered important today. Some of his best-known works include the aforementioned Le Guide Culinaire , as well as Ma Cuisine and Le Livre des Menus.

On top of single handedly changing the face and outlook of the culinary world, Escoffier was quite the philanthroper. He was credited as one of the first people to organize programs to feed the hungry. He also started an organization to financially assist retired chefs. Escoffier received several honors in his lifetime. The French government recognized Escoffier in 1920 appointing him Chevalier of the Legion d' Honneur, and later an Officer in 1928. Escoffier's achievements can be summed as a whole by one quote that was spoken by Germany's Kaiser Wilhelm II when he told Escoffier, "I am the Emperor of Germany, but you are the emperor of chefs."

Appendix B

CULINARY TERMINOLOGY

French term		*Explanation*
		A
A la	:	In the manner of / in the style of
A la carte	:	Single, fresh made food order; not included in dinner
A la mode	:	In a modern way / with ice-cream
Agar-Agar	:	Seaweed gelatin
Albacore	:	White tuna
Allumettes	:	French fries thin as matches; regular matches
Antipasto	:	Appetizer; marinated vegetables in tomatoes, Italian
Aspic	:	Meat jelly, used in buffet work
Au gratin	:	Gratinated, browned under broiler or salamander
a la Creole	:	In the style of Louisiana cookery; with onions, tomatoes, green peppers and sometimes okra.
a la	:	Florentine Foods that have a spinach base such as cream soup with spinach.
a la King	:	A white cream sauce with green peppers, pimento and mushrooms.
Amandine or Almandine	:	With almonds.
au Gratin	:	Topped with bread crumbs and cheese and browned.
au Jus	:	Served in its own juices.
		B
Bain-Marie	:	Wet steam table; steam table
Bar-le-duc	:	Large, seedless currants
Bar-be-cue	:	Meat cooked over open fire
Bayonne Ham	:	French raw ham, like prosciutto, or Westphalian ham
Bellevue	:	Well decorated (beautiful to look at)
Bien Cuit	:	Medium well-done
Bigarad	:	Bitter oranges
Bistro	:	Small bar or tavern
Blanche, to	:	To submerge under boiling water for a short time
Bloater	:	Smoked herring
Boil	:	Cooking of foods in liquids; simmer; steam
Bordure	:	A border of mashed potatoes on a service platter
Braise	:	To cook slowly in fat, with a little added moisture
Brigade	:	Crew of chefs, cooks, bakers, butchers and helpers who work under the executive chef
Broil	:	To cook by the radiation of the open fire

Broth : By-product of foods which have been simmered in liquids

Buffet : Food counter, table with cold foods on display

Buffetier : Buffet Carver Cook

By-product : Something produced in addition to the principal product

Baba : Spongy yeast cake soaked in rum.

Bearnaise : An egg butter sauce in which tarragon, chervil, shallots and meat juices have been added. Sometimes served with tenderloin.

Beaujolais : Region in the southern part of Bourgogne known for its red wine.

Bechamel : White cream sauce made with butter, flour and milk.

Benedict : Poached eggs with hollandaise sauce and ham or bacon served on an English muffin.

Bisque : Creamy soup made with shellfish, usually shrimp and lobster.

Bordeaux : The most important area in France for the production of wine.

Bordelaise : Brown sauce that contains shallots, red wine, tarragon, thyme and sometimes bone marrow.

Bortsch or Borscht : Vegetable soup that contains cabbage and red beets or beef base. Originated in Russia. Bouillabaisse Seafood stew containing crab, mussels, sea bass, onions, tomatoes, saffron, garlic and assorted herbs with white wine and cabbage.

Bouillon : Plain white stock originally. In today's restaurants it is a clear soup made from fish, meat or vegetable.

Bouquet Garni : Assortment of herbs to flavour soups, stew or sauces.

Boursin : Cream cheese flavoured with herbs and garlic. This cheese is factory made.

Brie : French cheese characterized by its white rind and rich, creamy, yellow colour.

Brochette : Foods that are grilled on a skewer for example, beef or chicken with onions, green peppers, tomatoes and mushrooms.

C

Cannelloni : Wide, short, Italian noodles for stuffing

Caramelize : Change colour to brown

Carbohydrates : Compounds of carbon, hydrogen and oxygen (as sugar, starches and cellulose)

Carbonize : Burn

Cassoulet : French term for a dish likebaked beans, but made with lambs, goose or pork

Caviar : Salted sturgeon roe

Cayenne : Very hot red pepper

Cellulose : Fibers of plant food
Chablis : White burgundy wine
Chambertin : Red burgundy wine, expensive
Champignon : Cultured mushroom
Chantille cream : Whipped cream
Char : Burn, carbonize
Chef de cuisine : Master Chef and Administrator
Chef de partie : Master Chef or Skilled Chef
Chef entremetier : Vegetables & Egg Station Cook
Chef garde-manger : Cold Pantry Cook
Chef rotsseur : Roast & Broiler Station Cook
Chemical change : A change in the substance
Chili : Red, green or yellow pepper
Chowder : Soup made with milk, American style
Clarified butter : Clear butter
Clarify : To filter, strain or make clear by use of egg whites
Cocotte : Small, individual casserole
Combination method : Food is exposed to some or all of these: cooking in dry heat air, in liquid or browning. Food is first caramelized by frying or roasting, then tenderized by adding liquid.
Conductor : Carrier of heat
Connoisseur : An exert who is competent to act as a critical judge
Consistency : Degree of firmness; density
Convection : Heat is carried by warm air
Cooking : Heating of food to a certain temperature to make the food edible; preparation of food in general
Coral : Lobster roe liver
Court-bouillon : Fish stock
Cuisine : Styles of cooking
Culotte : Top part of bottom round
Curing : Pickling in brine
Curry : Stew spiced with curry powder
Curry powder : Indian spice combination, pungent, yellow greenish

D

Dejeuner : French for breakfast or brunch
Dehydrated : Dried; the water has been evaporated
Delmonico : Once famous New York restaurant
Deuxieme commis : Skilled cook with 1-5 years of experience
Devilled : Strongly spiced or served with brown butter
Disjointed : Poultry pieces separated at joints; partly boned
Drippings : Roast or saute residues left in the pan
Dust : Sprinkle with flour

Dress	:	Truss, make oven ready for poultry
Dressing	:	Salad sauce, marinade; or a stuffing for a roast
Duchess potatoes	:	Mashed potatoes with egg yolk and butter, through pastry bag
Demi-glace	:	Rich brown sauce that has been reduced.
Demi-tasse	:	Small cup of black coffee.
Drawn Butter	:	Butter that has been seasoned, usually served with fish.
Duchesse Potatoes	:	Mashed potatoes seasoned with nutmeg, butter and egg yolk. Shaped and piped into buttered baking sheet pan.

E

Edible	:	Suitable for eating; eatable
Eggwash	:	Beaten egg with water or milk
Emulsify	:	A liquid mixture suspended in another (usually eggs and oil to prevent separation)
Entree	:	Main course
Entrecote	:	Cut sirloin steak
Escoffier	:	Famous French Chef (1846-1935)
Essence	:	Extract of meat or fish
Eclair	:	Oblong pastry filled with custard for dessert or with creamed food for an entree.
Escalopes	:	Thinly sliced pieces of veal sauteed in fortified butter.
Espagnole	:	Brown sauce.

F

Fillet	:	Boneless slice of meat or fish
Fond	:	Natural juices; or bottom
Frappe	:	Iced
French	:	The meat from the flank end of the rib is completely removed
Fritter	:	Deep-fried, batter coated food
Fines Herbs	:	Assortment of chopped herbs, consisting of parsley, chives, chervil and tarragon.
Fricassee	:	Diced veal or chicken in a white sauce.

G

Gastronomy	:	The art and science of god eating
Gelatinize	:	In the making of roux, this means the starch granules have absorbed liquid to their fullest capacity
Gigot d'Agneau	:	Lamb leg, whole
Gnocchi	:	Italian dumplings
Gratin	:	Gratinated, browned on top
Gratinate	:	To cook with a covering of buttered crumbs or grated cheese until a crust or crisp surface forms

Grill : Broiler

Grillade : Broiled meat

Ground meat : Minced meat

Galantine : Dish of forcemeat, for example, forcemeat of duck.

Goulash : Rich beef stew that contains paprika and onions.

H

Herbs : Aromatic greens for seasoning, dry or fresh

Hofbrau : Beer cellar, with open food buffet

Hofbrau style : Buffet with carver and assembler of sandwiches

Hot slaw : Warm coleslaw

Hollandaise : Sauce containing of egg yolks, butter, lemon juice, white wine and paprika.

Hors d'oeuvre : French word for appetizer.

J

Julienne : Vegetable that is cut in a match-like fashion, like julienne of carrots.

Keel bone : Breast bone

K

Kipper : Smoked, processed herring

Kirsch : Liqueur distilled from fermented cherries. Used in desserts for extra flavour.

L

Lamb Noisette : A boneless loin eye, looked like fillet mignon

Larding : Inserting strips of salt pork into meat to add flavour and prevent drying

Leaching : Extraction of nutrients and flavour from a food through the use of water

Liquefy : To make into a liquid

Liquefiable : Foods which may be made into liquid form

Lyonnaise : Sauteed sliced potatoes with onions.

M

Maraschino : Sour cherry liquor

Marble : Visible fat veins

Marinade : Similar to salad dressing, used also as food preservative and flavouring device

Menu : Bill of fare; sequence of food served at a meal

Mis-en-place : Work station setup

Mock turtle : Turtle soup imitation

Macedoine : Mixture of various fruits or vegetables.

Maitre d'hotel	:	Butter that contains lemon juice, white wine, parsley and Worcestershire sauce.
Marmite	:	Clear broth served in an earthenware pot that usually has beef and vegetables in it.
Mediation or Medallion	:	Small cuts of pork tenderloin or beef.
Milanaise	:	In the style of Milan cookery. A dish that is dipped in egg, bread crumbs, cheese and then fried.
Minestrone	:	Rich Italian vegetables and pasta soup.
Mirepoix	:	Combinations of vegetables, carrots and celery. Used as a basis for sauces.
Mornay	:	White cream sauce where cheese has been added.
Mousseline	:	Hollandaise sauce in which whipped cream is added.

N

Navarin	:	French, generic name for lamb stew
Napoleon	:	Square cut from puff pastry filed with cream.
Newberg	:	Cream sauce where egg yolk and sherry have been added to enrich the taste.
Normande	:	Sauce made from white wine and cream, served with fish.

O

O'brien Potatoes	:	Potatoes that are diced and cooked, then sauted with green peppers, pimentos and bacon.
Osterized	:	Blended to a liquid
Oyster	:	Bi-value mollusk with a rough, irregular shell closed by a single muscle. Also, a small mass of muscle in a concavity of the pelvic bone on each side of the back of a fowl.

P

Parmentier	:	French Health Inspector (1737-1813) who popularized potatoes in France
Pastrami	:	Cured, smoked, beef plate; beef ham
Patissier	:	Pastry Station Cook
Perigord	:	Capital of the French truffle district
Physical change	:	A change only in the appearance, not in the substance
Poach	:	To cook in acidulated water that is simmering
Poissonier	:	Fish Station Cook
Polenta	:	Cornmeal, grits
Polonaise	:	Polish manner or style
Potager	:	Soup Station Chef
Premier Commis	:	Skilled Cook with a minimum of 5 years experience
Prosciutto	:	Italian raw cured and dried ham, eaten raw
(a la) Parisienne	:	Garnish for chicken or fish consisting of mushroom, asparagus, truffle, with a white wine sauce.

Pate	:	Mixture of meat, usually pork, fish or game. Baked in an earthenware dish or in a pastry case, usually served cold.
Petit Four	:	Small cake or pastry.
Provencale	:	Cooking style of southern province of France, consisting of tomato sauce, garlic, herbs and olives.
Pungent	:	Biting or sharp taste or odour

R

Radiation	:	Exposure of food to direct rays from an open flame
Reconstituted	:	Water is added to food in order to return it to its original form
Reduce	:	Boil of extra liquid to make the dish thicker
Rissole	:	Well fried and browned
Roast	:	A cut of meat ready to cook or already cooked; for more than three persons, at least.
Ragout	:	Brown or white stew usually with a-small amount of red sauce.
Ravioli	:	Italian pasta dish filed with meat, vegetables or cheese.
Robert	:	Sauce made with onions, mustard, white wine and vinegar. Often served with roast pork.
Roasting	:	Dry heat cooking with the intent to evaporate some of the water content that all meals have.
Roulade	:	A slice of meat rolled with or without a stuffing and braised or sâuteed.
Roux	:	Mixture of equal part by weight of fat and all-purpose flour. It is used as a thickening agent.
Rump steak	:	Round steak

S

Saffron	:	Orange-yellow coloured pungent spice
Sago	:	Tapioca
Saigant	:	Medium rare or bloody
Salamandar	:	Small broiler for toasting and gratinating
Satay	:	Indonesian skewer specialty
Saute	:	Flip fry; pan fry with little fat
Score	:	To make superficial cuts in parallel lines, to prevent contractions
Sear	:	Score or burn
Seminola	:	Farina; cream of wheat
Shashlick	:	Lamb brochette, Russian
Shallot	:	Member of the onion family.
Shish Kabob or Shish Kebab	:	Beef, lamb, chicken or fish roasted on a skewer served with tomatoes, green peppers, onions and mushrooms.
Smitane	:	Sauce made of white wine and sour cream.

Sole : Delicate tasting fish that is flat. The true sole, English Dover sole is found in Europe only.

Spumoni : Ice cream that is flavoured with fruit, originated in Italy.

Steak Tartare : Tenderloin that has been minced, seasoned and reshaped. It is often served with raw onions, capers and egg yolks. The meat is served raw.

Short : The dish should have only a little sauce to hold the cooked food together

Simmer : Cooking in liquid below the boiling point

Skewer : Spit of metal or wood (brochette in French term)

Sous Chef : Master Chef; Second in command

Spit-roasting : Food is cooked with the heat radiating from an open fire; same as broiling

Steam : Cooking of foods in liquids; simmer, boil

Sterilize : Heating of food to a certain temperature to prevent infections by bacteria

Stew : Cut-up pieces of meat and vegetables braised in their own sauce

Stock : Liquid containing nutritients and flavour that have been extracted from food

T

Tenderize : To make tender by dissolving connective tissues. This causes food to become more digestible.

Tomate : Red vegetable sauce, made from tomato juice

Tournant : Relief (swing shift) Cook

Troisieme Commis : Skilled Cook- first year after apprenticeship

Truss : Tie together for a better shape

Torte : Rich cake layered with cream.

Tournedos : Small round steak from the thicket part of fillet.

Truffe or Truffle : Black fungus that is similar to a mushroom grown underground. It is used as a garnish for the most part because of its high price.

Turbot : Fish that is similar to halibut. It is flat in nature.

V

Vacherin : Dessert that has meringue and whipped cream on pastry.

Veloute : Creamy white sauce made from white stock.

Vermicelli : Thin pasta used in consomme.

Vichyssoise : Soup made consisting of potatoes or leeks, from France.

Vinaigrette : Cold dressing made of oil and vinegar, herbs, spices and lemon juice.

Vol-au-vent : Puff pastry filed with an array of creamed foods.

W

Whitewash : Flour or cornstarch in water; primitive way thickening liquids

Wiener Schnitzel : Veal that has been breaded and sauteed, garnished with anchovy, caper and a lemon slice.

Y

Yorkshire Pudding : Popover pastry usually served with roast beef. Originated in England.

Z

Zeste : Citrus (lemon or orange) peel.

INDEX

A

B

C

D

E

F

G

H

I

J

K

L

M

N

O

P

R

S

T

U

V

W

Z

REFERENCES

All Manners of Food: Eating and Taste in England and France from the Middle Ages to the Present by *Mennell, Stephen*, and Chicago University of Illinois Press.

Art of Cookery Made Easy by *Glasse, Hannah*. London.

Aspect of Chinese Culture by *Zonglin Chang Xukui* Li.

Betty Crocker Cookbook: Everything You Need to Know to Cook Today by *Crocker, Betty*. John Wiley & Sons, Incorporated.

Becoming a Chef by *Andrew Dornenburg and Karen Page*, John Wiley & Sons,

Better Homes and Gardens New Cook Book by *Jan Miller (Editor)*, Blank Book

Bon appétit: *The U.N. Dallas Morning News* Certifies Your Meal, Celebrations, Healing Techniques, Crafts and Culinary Arts added to the Representative List of the Intangible Cultural Heritage

British Food: An Extraordinary Thousand Years of History by *Spencer*, Colin Columbia University Press.

Building a Meal: From *Molecular Gastronomy to Culinary Constructivism*, Columbia University Press

Chemistry and Physics in the Kitchen by *Nicholas Kurti*: Scientific American Magazine

"Coffee in Europe", The *Roast & Post Coffee Company*". Realcoffee.co.uk.

Cooking: The Quintessential Art by *Pierre Gagnaire*, University of California Press

Cooking for Geeks: Real Science by *Great Hacks, and Good Food*, by *Jeff Potter*

Culinaria France by *Dominé, André*, Cologne: Könemann Verlagsgesellschaft mbh.

Culinaria The United States: A Culinary Discovery by *Danforth, Randi, Feierabend, Peter. Chassman, Gary*. New York: Konemann. .

Culinaria Italy by *Piras, Claudia and Medagliani*, Eugenio.. Cologne: Könemann Verlagsgesellschaft mbh

Culinary Art, Gourmet, *Center For Culinary Arts*, Manila, Careers Through Culinary Arts Program, Restaurant Management by Llc Books, Llc Books

"Diet and Romano-*British Society–Archaeozoology*". Archaeozoo.wordpress.com.

Eating in America: a History by *Root, Waverly, De Rochemont, and Richard*. New Jersey: The Ecco Press.

"Eating and Cultural Stereotypes" by *Leung Man-tao*, Eat and Travel Weekly, Hong Kong

Edna's Table (Restaurant) Rydalmere by *Kersh, Jennice. & Kersh*, Raymond. N.S.W. Hodder & Stoughton.

Endurance Exercise and Adipose Tissue by *Nicklas, Barbara* J. CRC Press

Escoffier: The Complete Guide to the Art of Modern Cookery by *Escoffier, Georges Auguste*, John Wiley and Sons.

First Steps to European Cooking by *Lin Ch'ing*. Hong Kong: Wan Li Pub. Co.

"Food Marketing," by *Smith, Andrew (Editor)*. In Oxford Encyclopedia of American Food and Drink, New York: Oxford University Press.

Food and Beverage Cost Controls by *Dopson and Miller*, Wiley

Food Sanitation, ServSafe Essentials, by *Education Institute of the National Restaurant Association*, Wiley & Sons

Fresh from the Vegetarian Slow Cooker: *200 Recipes for Healthy and Hearty One-*Pot Meals That Are Ready When You Are by *Robin Robertson*

Garde Manger: The Art and Craft of the Cold Kitchen by *Culinary Institute of America*, Wiley

Healthy Eating Every Day by *Carpenter, Ruth Ann; Finley, Carrie E. Human Kinetics*

Italian Cuisine: A Cultural History by *Capatti, Alberto and Montanari*, Massimo. New York: Columbia University Press

Indian Cuisine Introduction by *Llc Books*, Books Group, Llc Books

International Public Health: Disease, Programs, Systems, and Policies by *Merson, Michael H. Black, Robert E.; Mills, Anne J. Jones* and Bartlett Publishers.

Kitchen Mysteries: Revealing the Science of Cooking. *Columbia University Press*, New York

Lessons in Excellence by *Paul Clarke*, Ten Speed Press

La cuisine c'est de l'amour, de l'art, de la technique by *Pierre Gagnaire*, Casseroles et éprouvettes

Lawrie's Meat Science by *Lawrie, Stephen; R A Lawrie.* Woodhead Publishing

Microstructural Principles of Food Processing and Engineering by *Aguilera, Jose Miguel* and *David W. Stanley*, Springer

Mr. Sunday's Soups by *Lorraine Wallace, Chris Wallace (Foreword By), Brigit Legere Binns* (Contributions by), Alexandra Grablewski (Photographer)

Molecular Gastronomy: Exploring the Science of Flavor. *Columbia University* Press, New York

Molecular Kitchen and Moleculare Mixology You Can Do What You Imagine by *Dietmar Hoelscher*

Nutrition for Chefs, Techniques of Healthy Cooking by *Claiborn and Ryan*

Origins of Chinese Tea and Wine by *Hong & F. Chunjian*, Asiapac Books Pte Ltd.

"Outback Recipes and Stories from the Campfire" by *Dwyer, Andrew.*

On Food and Cooking: The Science and Lore of the Kitchen by *Harold McGee*, Scribner, New York.

On Food and Cooking: The Science and Lore of the Kitchen by *McGee, Harold Simon* and Schuster

On Cooking by *S.R. Labgensky, A.M. Hause*, Prentice Hall

Paul Prodhomme's Louisiana Kitchen by *Prodhomme, Paul,* New York: William Morrow.

Professional Cooking by *Gisslen*, Wiley

Professional Baking by *Gisslen*

Professional Baking Study Guide by *Gisslen, Wiley & Sons*

Profitable Menu Planning by *John A. Drysdale*, Prentice Hall

Real Australian Food, Australian Bruneteau, by *Jean-Paul*, Tukka

Sauces-Classical & Contemporary Sauce Making by *James Peterson*, John Wiley and Sons

Savoring the Past: The French Kitchen and Table from 1300 to 1789 by *Wheaton*, Barbara Ketcham, First Touchstone

Selected Occidental Cookeries and Delicacies by *Kwan Shuk-yan*, Hong Kong: Food Paradise Pub. Co.

Shelf Life: Supermarkets and the Changing Cultures of Consumption by *Humphery, Kim*. Cambridge University Press

So Easy: Luscious, Healthy Recipes for Every Meal of the Week by *Ellie Krieger, Alexandra Grablewski* (Photographer)

Statement on the 'New Cookery' by *Ferran Adrià, Heston Blumenthal, Thomas Keller and Harold McGee*; The Observer, London.

Study Guide to Accompany Professional Cooking by *Gisslen*

Sustainable Agriculture *by Mason John,* Landlinks Press

Taste of Home Comfort Food Diet Cookbook by *Peggy Woodward* (Editor), Catherine Cassidy (Editor)

The Cambridge Companion to Modern French Culture. by *Hewitt, Nicholas*, The Cambridge University Press.

The Professional Chef by The Culinary Institute of America by *Hoboken*, NJ: John Wiley and Sons.

The Oxford Encyclopedia of Food and Drink in America by *Smith, Andrew* F. Oxford: Oxford University Press.

"The Story of Desi Cuisine: Timeless desi dishes" by *Chandra*, Sanjeev, Smita Chandra. The Toronto Star.

"The History of the Spice Trade in India" by *Louise Marie M. Cornillez.*

Tibetan Marches. André Migot. Translated from the French by *Peter Fleming*. E. P. Dutton & Co. Inc. New York.

Traditional Chinese Food Technology and Cuisine by *Li & Y. Hsieh*. Asia Pacific Journal of Clinical Nutrition.

The Economic Research Service of the USDA. Global Food Markets: Briefing Rooms. *United Kingdom Office of Public Sector Information.* Food Safety Act 1990

The Economics of Food, Farming, Natural Resources, and Rural America. "Briefing Rooms, Food CPI, Prices and Expenditures: Food Expenditure Tables" by *United States Department of Agriculture, USDA Economic Research Service:*

The Concise Gastronomy of Italy by *Del Conte, Anna*. USA: Barnes and Nobles Books.

The Epic History of Italians and Their Food, by *Dickie, John, Delizia*! (New York)

The Curious Cook by *Harold McGee*, North Point Press, Berkeley.

The History Of Food by *Jango-Cohen, Judith*. Twenty-First Century Books

The Making of a Chef: Mastering Heat at The Culinary Institute of America, by *Michael Ruhlman, Holt.* A first-person account of an actual culinary education as it's taught at the most prominent cooking school in the United States

The Meat Buyer's Guide by The *North American Meat Processors Association*

The Oxford Companion to Food *by Davidson, Alan*. Oxford University Press.

The State of Food Insecurity in the World by *Food and Agriculture Organization of the United Nations.*

The Soul of a Chef: The Journey Toward Perfection, by *Michael Ruhlman, Penguin Books*, True stories about the life of the professional chef, via three very different American chefs in three very different cooking environments.

The New Best Recipe by *Cook's Illustrated Magazine, John Burgoyne (Illustrator)*, Carl Tremblay (Photographer), Daniel J. Van Ackere (Photographer)

The Dining Downunder Cookbook by *Cherikoff, Vic and Christie, Benjamin.*

The China Study The Most Comprehensive Study of Nutrition Ever Conducted and the Startling Implications for Diet, Weight Loss and Long-term Health, by *Campbell, T. Colin,* Benbella Books,

Uniquely Australian by *Cherikoff*, Vic

"Vitamin C — Broccoli, Brussels Sprouts", *Your Produce Man*

Wild Fermentation: The Flavor, Nutrition, and Craft of Live-Culture Foods by *Sandor Ellix Katz*

Who's Hungry? And How Do We Know? Food Shortage, Poverty, and Deprivation *by Messer, Ellen; Derose, Laurie Fields and Sara Millman.* United Nations University Press

Whisky: Technology, Production and Marketing, by *Russell*, Academic Press

World Food Italy Evans, by *Matthew; Cossi, Gabriella; D'Onghia, Peter,* CA: Lonely Planet Publications Pty Ltd

WEBSITES

"About Food in Malaysia". http://www.travellersworldwide.com/11-malaysia/11-malaysia-food.

"As Coffee Gets Popular" by M. Soundariya Preetha. The Hindu (Chennai, India). http://www.hindu.com/stories/

"Asia Food Features". Asiafood.org.

"Bread in Antiquity", by Russell, I Bakers' Federation website". Bakersfederation.org.uk.

"British cuisine". uktv.co.uk.

Candie Yoder. "Masala Chai". http://www.culinaryteas.com/Masala_Chai.

"Care for Some Sindhi savouries?" Dnaindia.com.

"Chhattisgarh Cuisine in India". India9.com.

"Chicken Tikka Masala: Spice and easy does it". bbc.co.uk.

"Cooking by Country: England", recipes4us.co.uk, Recipes4us.co.uk.

"Coriander", The Best Possible Taste". Thebestpossibletaste.co.uk.

"Country Profiles" Statistical Yearbook. http://www.fao.org/es/ess/yearbook/

"Curry, Spice & All Things Nice: Dawn of History". Menumagazine.co.uk.

"Cuisines of Andaman & Nicobar". Indfy.com.

"Cuisines of North East India". http://www.north-east-india.com/information/cuisines

"Cuisine of Haryana - Recipes Wiki". Recipes.wikia.com.

"'Curry,' by Lizzie Collingham The New York Times – Book Reviews. http://www.nytimes.com/books/

"Culture of Lakshadweep - India". India.wikia.com.

"Demand for Ethnic & International Foods Reflects a Changing America" by Uralian, Michael National Restaurant Association. http://www.nationalrestaurantassocia tion.com/pressroom/print/index.cfm? ID=1073.

"Diu Island Cuisine". Mapsofindia.com.

"Ethnic Cuisine: Indonesia" by Nancy Freeman. http://www.sallys-place.com/food/cuisines/indonesia.

Ethnic Foods of Hawai'I by Ann Kondo Corum, Bess Press. http: // books.google.com/books?Id = RI9BPVDH8HsC & pg = PA174 & lpg = PA174 & dq = indian + arab + cuisine + influence +- restaurant +- recipes +- earthquake & source = web & ots = tB - g-vxs2A & sig = PdMjRcIkC 1 zqWYda 9 nNVyuAs0FI & hl = en & sa = X & oi = book_result & resnum = 10 & ct = result.

"Foreign Influences in Modern Indian Cooking". Mit.edu.

"Food History Timeline", BBC/Open University". Web.archive.org.

"Food of Haryana, Cuisine of Haryana, Famous Haryana Food, Recipes of Haryana, Haryana Food". Richindianculture.com.

"Food in Mizoram". Mapsofindia.com.

"Food Standards Agency – Curry factfile". http://www.food.gov.uk/news/newsarchive/nov/curryfacts.

"Goa - Daman, Beach, Access, Accommodation/stay, Shopping Options". Travelmasti. com.

"Great British Kitchen". http://www.greatbritishkitchen.co.uk/index.

"Go India: Curry, My Love?" by Viviane Then. http://www.streetdirectory.com/restaurants/singapore/reviews/restaurant-Go_India

"Horseradish", ''Herb & Spice Dictionary" by "Coleman, D. Deancoleman.com. http://www.deancoleman.com/herbs.htm. "Dunlop, F. "Tea", ''BBC Food''". Bbc.co.uk.

"History of Indian Food and Cooking". Inmamaskitchen.com.

"Indian Restaurants in USA". Immihelp.com. http://www.immihelp.com/yellowpages/indian-restaurants-usa.

"Indian Cuisines". YourSingapore.com. http://www.yoursingapore.com/content/traveller/en/browse/dining/cuisines-of-singapore/indian-cuisines.

"Indian Food Gains Popularity During Chinese New Year". http://www.hindustandainik.com.

"Indian food – Indian Cuisine – its history, origins and influences". Indianfoodsco.com.

'Indian Cuisine Is Popular as It's Close to Arabic Food' by K.S. Ram Kumar. Arab News. http://www.arabnews.com.

"Mints" by "Grieve, M. ''botanical.com - A Modern Herbal''". Botanical.com.

"Mizo Cuisine in India". India9.com.

"Meatless Monday: There's No Curry in India". http://www.meatlessmonday.com/site/PageServer? pagename=dyk_curry.

"Nasi, Kari, Biryani & Mee". Veg Voyages.

"Pepper Profile: Cayenne", by "DeWitt, D. ''Fiery-foods.com''". Fiery-foods.com.

"Pondicherry Cuisine". Mapsofindia.com.

"Professor says Indian Eateries are Experiencing a U.S. boom". University of North Texas News Service. http://web3.unt.edu/news/story.cfm?story

"Robin Cook's Chicken Tikka Masala Speech". London: The Guardian. http://www.guardian.co.uk/

"Sindhi Cuisine –". Sindhunagar.com.

"The History of the "Ethnic" Restaurant in Britain", "Menu Magazine", Menumagazine.co.uk.

The History of Ice Cream canalmuseum.org.uk.

"Turkey Club UK". Turkeyclub.org.uk.

"Tikka in No Time" by Monica. Washington Post. http://www.washingtonpost.com/wp-dyn/content/article/AR

Thai Kitchen in East Lansing, Michigan by Nancy Freeman. http://www.restaurantdb.net/restaurants/profile.

"Tandoori Village Restaurant Brisbane". AsiaRooms.com. http://www.asiarooms.com/travel-guide/australia/brisbane/what-where-to-eat/indian-restaurants-in-brisbane/tandoori-village-restaurant-brisbane.

Undernourished Persons by Country, Food security statistics. FAO. http://www.fao.org/faostat/foodsecurity/Files/Number